EDUCATIONAL REGIMES AND
ANGLO-AMERICAN DEMOCRACY

Studies in Comparative Political Economy and Public Policy

Editors: MICHAEL HOWLETT, DAVID LAYCOCK, STEPHEN McBRIDE, Simon Fraser University.

Studies in Comparative Political Economy and Public Policy is designed to showcase innovative approaches to political economy and public policy from a comparative perspective. While originating in Canada, the series will provide attractive offerings to a wide international audience, featuring studies with local, subnational, cross-national, and international empirical bases and theoretical frameworks.

Editorial Advisory Board

For a list of books published in the series, see p. 603

Educational Regimes and Anglo-American Democracy

Ronald Manzer

UNIVERSITY OF TORONTO PRESS
Toronto Buffalo London

© University of Toronto Press Incorporated 2003
Toronto Buffalo London
Printed in Canada

ISBN 0-8020-8780-9

Printed on acid-free paper

National Library of Canada Cataloguing in Publication

Manzer, Ronald A., 1937–
    Educational regimes and Anglo-American democracy /
    Ronald Manzer.

    (Studies in comparative political economy and public policy)
    Includes bibliographical references and index.
    ISBN 0-8020-8780-9

    1. Education and state.   2. Democracy.   3. Politics and education.
    I. Title.   II. Series.

    LC71.M35 2003   379   C2003-900895-9

This book has been published with the help of a grant from the Humanities
and Social Sciences Federation of Canada, using funds provided by the
Social Sciences and Humanities Research Council of Canada.

University of Toronto Press acknowledges the financial assistance to its
publishing program of the Canada Council for the Arts and the Ontario
Arts Council.

University of Toronto Press acknowledges the financial support for its
publishing activities of the Government of Canada through the Book
Publishing Industry Development Program (BPIDP).

Contents

Figures

Tables

Preface

My goal in this comparative political study of the development of educational policies in Australia, Canada, New Zealand, the United Kingdom, and the United States is understanding the political tradition of Anglo-American democracy. Anglo-American democracy is commonly taken to constitute a distinctive political tradition. Similarly, despite their many differences, the politics and public policies of Australia, Canada, New Zealand, the United Kingdom, and the United States are thought to derive from common political ideas, institutions, and practices that set them apart as a subgroup of liberal democracies. Surprisingly little attention, however, has been given to what constitutes the political tradition of Anglo-American democracy; its existence and attributes are largely taken for granted. Here I try to change that situation.

Throughout this project, I have worked on the assumption that essential political principles, values, beliefs, and attitudes are embodied in the formulation, choice, implementation, and evaluation of public policies for primary and secondary education. Through a comparative study of the politics and policies for public education, I have tried to learn what are the common political principles, values, beliefs, and attitudes that constitute Anglo-American democracy, as well as what are the differences contained within this political tradition.

My comparison of Anglo-American educational regimes focuses on five problems of structuring relationships among state, market, and society in the provision of primary and secondary education: the original creation of systems of elementary education in the nineteenth century as publicly provided and publicly governed; the transformation of secondary schools in the early twentieth century to match the emerging structure of occupational classes in capitalist industrial economies; the planning for secondary schools in the development of the welfare state after the Second World War; the accommodation of diversity in public schools from the 1960s to the 1990s in response to increasingly strong assertions of race, ethnicity, language, and religion, not only as criteria for equal treatment, but also as foundations of communal identity; and the educational reforms in the 1980s and 1990s that aimed to adapt public schools to the contemporary challenges of new information technology and burgeoning global capitalism.

In giving an account of the political recognition of these successive and cumulative problems in the political economy of public education, and of the public policies that have been formulated to deal with them, I have relied on the construction of policy narratives for each problem and each country. For each country, I have aimed to describe the development of the main policies for the provision of educational services, focusing especially on curricular design and school organization, and for the arrangements of central and local educational governance. For each case, I have struggled to create a text that was readable, comprehensible, and convincing as an interpretation of complex and thick histories of public education. None the less, given the number of educational jurisdictions being covered, as well as more than 150 years of the history of public education in the Anglo-American democracies, I have had to be selective in my application of this historical perspective. As a way of offering some additional evidence and explanatory commentary on the text, I have resorted to often lengthy notes and extensive references that I hope will help readers appreciate something of the deep below the surface on which I am cruising.

A comparative study of the politics and policies for public education in the Anglo-American democracies is obviously complicated by the varying number of educational regimes – currently, one in New Zealand, four in the United Kingdom, eight in Australia, thirteen in Canada, and fifty in the United States. At one end of this array of educational regimes, sections on the politics and policies for primary and secondary education in New Zealand can be relatively focused and individual. At the other end, sections dealing with public education in the United States necessarily require comparative descriptions and analyses that concentrate on observing general characteristics, specifying regional variations, and merely noting individual particularities. Similarly, because of significant variations in the salience of educational issues across educational regimes, rather than researching and writing about exactly the same policy issues in each case I have developed comparisons that appear to be equivalent in political meaning. The relationship of church and state in nineteenth-century public education, for example, and the effect of information technology and global capitalism on the educational reforms of the late twentieth century are issues that are essentially the same across Anglo-American educational regimes, although eventual policy resolutions may be different. By contrast, problems of racial segregation in the United States, language of instruction in Canada and Wales, Maori education in New Zealand, religious instruction in Great Britain, and multiculturalism in Australia have seemed to me to merit attention because of their political meaning for Anglo-American democracy without necessarily requiring me to create a strictly parallel ethnic, linguistic, racial, or religious policy profile for each of the other Anglo-American democracies.[1]

To my knowledge, no one has previously attempted such a comparison of the development of educational policies in Australia, Canada, New Zealand, the United Kingdom, and the United States. I do hope that the individual policy narratives presented in chapters 1 to 5 will be useful to those who are not familiar with the histories of public education in the various Anglo-American countries. None the less, I do not expect historians who specialize in their research and writing on these countries to find anything particularly surprising or new in my work (with the possible exception of my collection of statistics on the historical development of public education in each of these countries). Rather, my goal in doing the policy narratives is to establish the foundation from which I can make generalizations about what are the main types of Anglo-American educational regimes and how these have changed over time. I then try to use these generic types of educational regimes to interpret the commonalities and differences in their constitutive political principles and values and, at the end, construct an interpretation of the political tradition of Anglo-American democracy.

Given my goal to construct an interpretation of the political tradition of Anglo-American democracy, my priority in comparative policy analysis is to understand the political ideas that are embodied in public policies for educational provision and governance. That includes ideas about what are the proper relationships of state, market, and society in the provision and governance of public education over time – ideas I have identified as responses to a sequence of problems of political economy. Political ideas as causal determinants, along with political institutions, political interests, and political economies, are basic factors that can be used to explain public policies; but my approach in this comparative study gives priority to an alternative conception of political ideas as the constitutive meanings of public policies. Political ideas are the basic elements of political language within and through which people think and talk about their political world and thence articulate their common interests, negotiate modes of political association, and devise courses of collective action. Political ideas provide the medium for people to ask and answer such fundamental questions as which needs can and should be satisfied by public policy, what is the just distribution of public goods among constituent segments of the community, and what arrangements of governmental institutions and practices might optimize democracy and efficiency. Thus, because they advance basic concepts of human need and public good, the ideas at the core of policies give meaning to collective action.[2]

To understand the political ideas that constitute public policies by giving them political meaning requires an interpretive policy analysis. In effect, I propose to read the educational policies of Australia, Canada, New Zealand, the United Kingdom, and the United States as 'text analogues' from which I hope to gain an understanding of what is the political tradition of Anglo-American democracy. This approach requires, first, a typology of relevant political ideologies in order to see the potential range and patterns of political ideas. Next, there must be careful study of key policies for educational provision and governance in order to determine not only what are their core political ideas but also the specific meanings of those political ideas. Then, educational regimes must be studied over time to allow us to observe and interpret key educational policies and their core political ideas.[3] At the end, I conclude that the commonalities of Anglo-American democracy, as well as the differences within it, derive from a historical dialogue of Anglo-American political ideologies that involves conservatism, liberalism, and socialism both opposing each other and divided within themselves. The prospects for Anglo-American democracy, as well as for educational reform, accordingly depend on this ongoing political dialogue that combines established ideological legacies and unpredictable ideological innovations.

The introduction to this manuscript was first presented to a conference of the Transatlantic Program on Public Policy and the Global Economy at the University of Bath in April 1998. For their helpful comments and probing questions I am grateful to Ian Gough, Hugh Lauder, and Graham Room of the University of Bath; Peter Graefe of Université de Montréal; and Joy Fitzgibbon, Lata Narayanaswamy, and

Julie Simmons of the University of Toronto. I owe special thanks to the Canadian project leader for this program. Grace Skogstad, my colleague in the Division of Social Sciences and Department of Political Science at the University of Toronto. Grace consistently asks the hard questions about doing comparative policy studies and, by her encouragement and example to all her students, including me, keeps us working at the answers. Outside my department at the University of Toronto, I have had helpful advice from two colleagues at the Ontario Institute for Studies in Education, Richard Townsend and Stephen Lawton (now at Central Michigan University), and from Jeffrey Reitz in the Department of Sociology. The conclusion was presented to the Department of Political Science Seminar at the University of Toronto in September 2001. I am grateful to Ran Hirschl for asking me to do this seminar and to him and colleagues Edward Andrew, Stephen Clarkson, Janice Gross Stein, David Welch, and Melissa Williams for their questions and comments. They encouraged me to believe that, despite much potential for more research, my immediate project was finally near its end.

Conversations with colleagues about this project have occurred in several other places over many years, including those with Michael Hogan, Helen Nelson, and Ken Turner at the University of Sydney, Michael Pusey at the University of New South Wales, Peter Tannock at the Australian Schools Commission, Don Smart at Murdoch University, Campbell Sharman at the University of Western Australia, and Maurice Kogan at Brunel University. They may well have forgotten by now, but I continue to be grateful for their generous interest in my work and willingness to share their own knowledge and experience as political and/or educational researchers. In writing the final version of the manuscript, I was especially helped by the critical but encouraging comments of an anonymous reader for the University of Toronto Press, another for the Humanities and Social Sciences Federation of Canada, and an anonymous member of the UTP Manuscript Review Committee.

I am also indebted to librarians who keep the collections and help the researchers who use them at the University of Sydney and Australian National University, the state public libraries of Tasmania and Western Australia, the University of Auckland, the University of London Library and Newsam Library of the Institute of Education at the University of London, Queen's University of Belfast, and especially the Government Documents Section of the Robarts Library and the Robert Jackson Library of the Ontario Institute for Studies in Education.

A Leave Fellowship and a Standard Research Grant (410-94-0091) from the Social Sciences and Humanities Research Council of Canada helped to provide financial support for me to meet colleagues and make use of the libraries outside Canada. A research leave from the Division of Social Sciences at the University of Toronto at Scarborough in 2000/ 2001 permitted me to finish the manuscript.

This book is the third on which I have worked through the editorial and publication process with Virgil Duff, executive editor for the University of Toronto Press, and my debt to him for his advice and guidance only continues to grow. Margaret Allen's copy-editing was consistently apt, thoughtful, and elegant. I am especially pleased to have this book published as part of the University of Toronto Press series Studies in Comparative Political Economy and Public Policy, and correspondingly grateful to the series editors, Michael Howlett, David Laycock, and Stephen McBride of Simon Fraser University, for their encouragement.

My greatest debt from my work over the years on this project is owed to my family. While I was starting it during a research leave in Australia, Jennifer and Patricia were going to Greenwich Primary School in North Sydney (and Patricia later that year to North Sydney Girls' High School). Now both are twice university graduates. As parents do, I have learned much about the relationship between educational policy and classroom practice through their school experiences in Australia and Canada. Above all, I cherish their presence in my life and their love. Kathryn also knows my love for her and my dependence on our partnership. Her experience teaching at Witney Secondary Modern School in Oxfordshire many years ago and her more recent volunteer work for the advancement of public education in Canada, including a stint as national president of Canadian Parents for French and her involvement in many educational activities of the University Women's Club of North York and the Canadian Federation of University Women, have been valuable reminders of the professional dedication, civic idealism, and practical politics required to provide good public education. For more than twenty years she has also organized each of my research trips and kept me company, ensuring that I came to know and enjoy the society and culture of the countries on which I have been working, not just the inside of their university libraries. She has waited patiently for this project to be finished while being forthright in her encouragement to get it done. Now it is done, I can finally keep my promise to travel somewhere with her that is not another research destination.

EDUCATIONAL REGIMES AND
ANGLO-AMERICAN DEMOCRACY

Introduction: Educational Regimes and the Comparative Study of Anglo-American Democracy

Anglo-American democracy cannot be understood simply from observing its abstract commitments to the basic political goods of community, equality, and liberty; it must be understood as well through the political institutions and public policies it puts into practice.[1] Because of the close connection between democracy and education, interpreting the institutions and policies of Anglo-American educational regimes is one way of understanding commonality and difference, stability and change, in the ideas and practice of Anglo-American democracy.

Beyond their primary individual and collective activities of teaching and learning, schools have a threefold significance for Anglo-American democracy – instrumental, expressive, and constitutive.[2] First, they are means by which people in a democratic polity collectively strive for civic virtue, economic wealth, social integration, and cultural survival. Second, schools are expressions of the fundamental beliefs, attitudes, values, and principles that underlie Anglo-American democracy. In how they are governed and what they teach, schools express conceptions of human needs, make statements of moral principles, and convey visions of individual and collective development. Third, because they institutionalize ways of thinking and acting in a crucial domain of public and private life, schools are constitutive of Anglo-American democracy. Schools constitute Anglo-American democracy in part by realizing in practice what were the intentions of policy designers; but educational policies also have unanticipated outcomes, thus reshaping or reforming democracy and, over time, giving the political ideas and practices of democracy new meaning.

An 'educational regime' is a stable ordering of political principles and public authority for the governance of education. An educational regime is instituted, first, as a collective response to a primary problem of political economy. Second, its coherence and purpose depend on widespread acceptance of a core of political ideas that may derive from a dominant political ideology but more often will be created from conflict and compromise among the proponents of opposing doctrinal positions.[3] Third, an educational regime implies a distinctive set of public policies covering both the governance and the provision of education. Hence, the concept of educational regime includes the established institutions and procedures for educational governance, allocation of public authority, and style of public decision making as well as the design and implementation of educational programs.

When Anglo-American educational politics and policy are considered in historical perspective, five distinct periods of development can be identified in the creation, adjustment, breakdown, and change of national, provincial, and state educational regimes. Each period is defined by the need to find an answer to a primary problem of political economy, the proper relationship among state, market, and society with particular reference to the provision of education. Each was constructed on the basis of ideologically contested principles, institutions, and procedures. Each incorporated a distinctive understanding of the purposes and problems of public education and worked towards a particular configuration of educational provision and governance.

Interpretations of Educational Regimes

If the purpose of interpreting Anglo-American educational regimes is understanding Anglo-American democracy, there are two prior questions that have to be addressed regarding the attributes of democracy and counter-claims to democracy. First, what is democracy supposed to mean? What are the key elements or primary dimensions of democracy that may be revealed through interpretation of educational regimes? Second, interpretations of Anglo-American educational regimes may disclose not only variations in the meaning of democracy but also limits on its practice. Here the question concerns the potential counter-claims to democracy that are advanced as justifications to limit or constrain the practice of Anglo-American democracy.

Dimensions of Democracy

Democracy is a form of government based on rule by the people. 'People' is understood to encompass all adult citizens within the state; 'rule' refers to the entitlement of each citizen to participate equally in making public decisions. Following Robert Dahl, four conditions must be fulfilled for the process of governmental decision making to be fully democratic:

> Throughout the process of making binding decisions, citizens ought to have an adequate opportunity, and an equal opportunity, for expressing their preferences as to the final outcome. They must have adequate and equal opportunities for placing questions on the agenda and for expressing reasons for endorsing one outcome rather than another ... At the decisive stage of collective decisions, each citizen must be ensured an equal opportunity to express a choice that will be counted as equal in weight to the choice expressed by any other citizen. In determining outcomes at the decisive stage, these choices, and only these choices, must be taken into account ... Each citizen ought to have adequate and equal opportunities for discovering and validating (within the time permitted by the need for a decision) the choice on the matter to be decided that would best serve the citizen's interests ... The demos must have the exclusive opportunity to decide how matters are to be placed on the agenda of matters that are to be decided by means of the democratic process.[4]

Without even putting into question the desirability of democracy as a form of government, each of these four conditions for democratic government is contestable. What constitutes adequate opportunity to participate? What is required for citizens to make informed choices? What is meant by political equality among citizens? Which are the critical decisions that must be made directly by the citizens; which should be left to their representatives? Who qualifies as a citizen for purposes of democratic decision making? Answers to these fundamental questions about the meaning of rule by the people depend in turn on the meaning given to the three essential dimensions of democracy: community, equality, and liberty.

First, who constitute the people? This question focuses on the meaning of community and democratic citizenship. Community refers to the boundaries of citizenship: who is included and who is excluded. In their treatment of citizens as learners, policies for educational provision that are institutionalized in an educational regime may be designed and implemented to deal with learners as undifferentiated individuals. Alternatively, they may divide learners by class or status groups or according to their membership in communal groups based on ethnicity, language, race, or religion. Similarly, in their treatment of citizens as participants in democratic decision making, policies for educational governance may be designed and implemented to deal with all citizens – or perhaps only parents – as individuals. Alternatively, for purposes of educational governance the people may be differentiated according to their class, status, or communal groups.

Community also refers to the grounds on which citizenship is conferred and the rights and obligations that derive from it. The scope, resources, substance, and distribution of educational provision together reveal the shared perception of the individual and collective cognitive capacities that are taken to be essential to a democratic community. Certain knowledge and skills may be assumed to be necessary for all citizens to learn; other knowledge and skills may be learned selectively by some, perhaps even an élite, but not others. Similarly, the functions, levels, size, and representativeness of educational governance show the shared perception of the individual and collective political obligations that are deemed to be essential to a democratic community. As with educational provision, these features also indicate the rights and obligations of citizenship. For example, under the constitution of representative democracy, most policy decisions are made by representatives elected at intervals; the rule of the people is indirect and exercised periodically through accountability of representatives at elections.

Second, whether as individuals or groups, what is the proper relationship among citizens? This question focuses on the meaning of equality and distributive justice. Debates regarding equality of educational provision customarily divide between claims for equal opportunities versus demands for equal standards. What is meant by equal opportunities or standards, however, usually is based on competing ideas of lot, person, rank, or bloc as the bases for justifying equality.[5] Educational provision may be designed and implemented so that each learner is given essentially the same learning experiences, and hence no learner would have any incentive to exchange her or his educational lot for that of any other learner. Educational provision may be shaped to meet the ends or needs of each individual learner, so that each learner has different educational experiences; but again, assuming that each individual's particular educational ends or needs are being met, no one would desire to exchange his or her learning experiences for those of another learner. Equality may be taken to mean equal treatment of learners who have the same academic rank or status, while the existence of inequalities between ranks is explained and justified by manifest differences among students in their ability and achievement. Judgments about equality may also condone differences in educational provision *between* social groups or blocs – for example, boys and girls, Roman Catholics and Protestants, French speakers and English speakers, or black children and white children – but not *within* such groups.

Similarly with respect to educational governance, there may be no important differences in opportunities for citizens as individuals to participate in educational decision making. Alternatively, participation may be differentiated among ranks or statuses (for example, ordinary citizens, citizens who are parents, classroom teachers, head teachers) or equalized between blocs (citizens have the same opportunities to participate, or not, but these opportunities are restricted to educational decision making for particular social groups; for example, voting for Roman Catholic school trustees is restricted to Roman Catholics, and running for the French-language school boards is restricted to French-speaking citizens).

Third, given some form of political equality among citizens, what are the opportunities for citizens collectively to determine their choices and make decisions that, as much as possible, respect each person's needs and wants? This question focuses on the meaning of liberty and political participation. Liberty involves both a private domain of independent action and a public domain of collective action. 'In the first type of situation, freedom is ... a matter of not being personally interfered with by others; in the second, freedom means sharing in the decision-making, which is not being interfered with collectively.'[6]

With regard to educational provision, liberty in the form of freedom from interference entails that meaningful individual choices about the scope, resources, and substance of educational provision do exist, and hence the distribution of educational provision is determined to an important extent by parents and students. By contrast, liberty in the form of freedom of participation implies that important choices about the scope, resources, substance, and distribution of educational provision should be made collectively and that, within the democratically legitimate meanings of community and equality, all citizens have adequate opportunities to participate effectively in making these collective decisions.

With regard to educational governance, at one extreme, liberty in the form of freedom from interference implies the existence of a private market for the supply and distribution of primary and secondary education in which governance is privatized and parents and students as consumers exercise the power of purchase and exit. Alternatively or in addition, a voluntary sector of elementary and secondary schools may be created by parents and students who have shared identities and/or common interests that allow them to work cooperatively in pursuit of their collective educational objectives. At the other extreme, liberty in the form of freedom to participate in educational governance implies the existence of a sector of primary and secondary schools that are publicly governed and, given the scope of legitimate participation – again in part defined by prevailing concepts of community and equality – all citizens have adequate opportunities to participate effectively in determining the functions, level, size, and representativeness of educational governance. Somewhere between a strictly private market and a purely public sector for the supply and distribution of primary and secondary education there may be a public market in which the scope, resources, and governance of elementary and secondary education are matters of public policy, but the substance and distribution of educational provision result from individual choices of parents and students.

Counter-claims to Democracy

Democracy as a principle of government has its limits. Counter-claims to democracy as an attribute of Anglo-American educational regimes can take at least two forms. Taking account of each of these counter-claims adds a further dimension to a comparative interpretation of Anglo-American democracy.

First, democracy as a substantive political end may be displaced by instrumental goals of feasibility, effectiveness, and efficiency. Neither in principle nor in practice does liberal democracy require that all public policies be determined by popular sovereignty. Claims may be advanced that popular election of legislative representatives and/or executive officials does not entail that public policies determining the scope, resources, substance, and distribution of educational provision and the functions, size, levels, and representativeness of educational governance be decided by democratic majorities. Making numerous policy decisions is either not feasible or excessively time-consuming for the citizenry in general; delegation to popularly elected public officials limits democracy but satisfies the criteria for feasibility, effectiveness, and efficiency in educational decision making. Democracy also assumes that all citizens are equally well qualified to make public policies, but many decisions about educational provision and governance may involve issues requiring knowledge and skills that are restricted to an élite group of professional policy makers. Again, delegation to professionally qualified public servants who are directly or (more often) indirectly responsible to the people may be justified in order to determine the set of feasible policies, evaluate their comparative effectiveness and efficiency, and choose the best option. Hence, democracy as a substantive political end is vulnerable to displacement by arguments that feasibility, effectiveness, and efficiency should take priority for immediate decisions but within a framework of democratic accountability.

Second, basic political goods of wealth and security, which are preconditions for democracy, may be cited as justifications for limiting democracy. In less developed countries, persistent conditions of systemic poverty and political violence result in the curtailment of democracy and, often, its displacement by some form of authoritarianism. Poverty, crime, and defence are major political issues in Australia, Canada, New Zealand, the United Kingdom, and the United States, but these countries all have a high average standard of living, relatively safe domestic environments, and well-protected external relations. Even so, whether for the nation in general or for specific social groups, there may be threats to wealth and/or security giving rise to political demands for protective measures that involve putting limits on the practice of democratic principles. With regard to educational policies, perceived threats to national unity may be advanced as a reason to displace academic integrity and individual choice in favour of patriotic rituals and nationalist historicism; international trade and investment imbalances may become the justification for restructuring curricula to reflect national economic priorities rather than individual educational needs; and threats to the survival of minority languages may be the warrant for enforcing the language of instruction in schools. Thus, even in the highly developed Anglo-American countries, the principle of democracy, with its higher political goods of community, equality, and liberty, is vulnerable to curtailment, if not displacement, in political practice by appeals to the need to supply more basic political goods of wealth and security.

Configurations of Educational Policy

With regard to configurations of educational policy, first, there is the question of educational provision. What are the courses of public action (or inaction) that have been chosen by public authorities in order to provide elementary and secondary education? Second, there is the question of educational governance. Who are the public authorities? Who decides what are the policies and how they are implemented and evaluated?

Educational Provision

The provision of elementary and secondary education involves four distinct problems of public policy making: the scope of provision, the commitment of public resources, the substance of teaching and learning, and the distribution of benefits and costs. Each of these public problems raises hard political issues. Only rarely are decisions about the scope, resources, substance, and distribution of educational provision taken on the basis of widespread consensus among policy makers and the public. Usually, there is puzzlement about what are the best courses of action to pursue in providing education, or not, and there are ideological differences of principles, values, beliefs, and attitudes that result in major conflicts of interest and identity.

The scope of educational provision refers to the range of teaching and learning activities that are publicly supported, the choice of policy instruments that determine the boundaries between the public and private educational sectors, and the determination of educational support services. One major issue of scope is the age of learners and the level of teaching at which public support should begin and end. Initially, public provision for education was restricted to five or six years of elementary schooling for children, starting around the ages of six or seven. Over time, the age of learners and the level of teaching have been moved upward to cover young people in secondary schools and downward to cover children in kindergarten and nursery schools. Another important issue of scope is the choice of policy instruments for providing state support to a given range of educational services. Here policy makers confront the choice of building and maintaining public schools, subsidizing and regulating private schools, or striking some balance between public and private educational institutions. A third issue of scope is determining the appropriate range of educational support services – whether delivered by state agencies or supported by state subsidies – such as school libraries, busing, meals, medical and dental health, psychological counselling, and vocational guidance. Each change in the scope of provision – upward or downward in the age of learners and level of teaching, back and forth in the choice between public and private schools, expanding or contracting with regard to the range of support services – has been contested. Nor have the controversies necessarily diminished over time, as some enthusiastically advocate broadening the scope of public provision for education even more while others press to reduce it in favour of private reliance on family and market.

Given the scope of educational provision and conditions of economic efficiency, the supply of resources measures the depth and priority of public commitment to providing for elementary and secondary education. Higher real expenditures on education per pupil over the same number of educational services implies an improvement in the quantity and/or quality of services being delivered to persons in school. Lower ratios of pupils per teacher generally mean that the educational experiences of each learner will be more focused and their progress will be more closely supervised by their teachers. Measures of the resources committed to educational provision also indicate differences in the priority attached to education as a public good compared to production and consumption of private goods and services or other functions of the state, such as national defence, economic development, public health, income security, and social welfare. Of course, care needs to be taken to ensure that comparisons of resources for educational provision distinguish between differences in wealth and differences in effort. Nor can the potential gains be ignored that may result from improving efficiency in the use of the factors of production. None the less, just as increasing the commitment of public resources to educational provision is usually a matter of controversy, so is the reduction of resources, even where the quantity and quality of educational services are said to be assured. Whether there are gains to be made from a more efficient combination of the factors of production is rarely obvious and unambiguous, and a political promise to 'do more with less' will rarely be accepted at face value in educational politics.

The substance of educational provision refers to what should be learned, when, and how. Determining the substance of educational provision requires a theory of learning that will provide understanding of the growth of individual capacities and the contribution specific learning experiences make to educated thought and action, as well as facilitate predictions about the effects of potential governmental interventions, for example, with regard to teacher training, classroom organization, or student testing. Policy decisions about the substance of educational provision include setting general goals regarding what young people should know and what skills they should have, then organizing schools, designing curricula, and hiring teachers in order to achieve these educational goals. Because theories of learning are contested, deciding the substance of educational provision involves resolving political issues rather than simply solving public problems. Disagreements arise over the appropriate divisions for grouping young people in schools – for example, a model that divides elementary (K–8) and secondary (9–12) schools versus one that separates primary (K–6), junior high (7–9), and senior high (10–12) schools or one that divides primary, middle (6–8), and secondary schools. Disagreements also arise over which subjects will be taught and how many hours a week will be devoted to each subject at each level of the curriculum. There are debates about open classrooms and ungraded schools versus formal classrooms and graded schools, and there will be disagreements with regard to whether teaching and learning should be organized by traditional subjects or by interdisciplinary areas. Decisions on teaching methods and curricular materials raise controversial issues that include the selection of textbooks, whether reading should be taught by the phonics or the whole-language method, and how the testing and evaluation of teaching and learning should be designed and implemented. There are also issues of teachers' qualifications in terms of academic and professional education, standards for certification, and expectations for professional development.

Distribution refers to who benefits from the existing (or proposed) scope, resources, and substance of educational provision and who pays for them. Issues of distribution raise questions about what are the major social groups for purposes of describing and assessing who benefits and who pays. These vary among countries and over time in their political and policy relevance. Generally, however, the major social groups for analysing the variations in the distribution of educational provision will include demographic categories based on gender and age; economic classes based on occupation and income; communal groups based on religious affiliation, ethnic identity, racial heritage, and linguistic culture; and regional groups, especially those dividing urban and rural areas.

Educational Governance

As with educational provision, the governance of elementary and secondary education also involves four distinct problems of public policy making: the functions of governance, the levels of public authority, the size of governments, and the representation of major social groups in educational politics, policy, and administration.

Anglo-American theories of the functions of governance have focused on the differentiation of politics, policy, and administration as public activities. Under 'political' or 'patronage' administration, elected politicians not only decided policy but also dominated administration, either directly by performing themselves whatever administrative tasks were required or indirectly by making partisan appointments to the public bureaucracy.[7] Against the partisan appointments and unqualified amateurs of political administration, liberal and conservative reformers advocated a public bureaucracy that would be appointed on the basis of merit and would administer public business without any significant involvement in either politics or policy. In the utilitarian liberal theory of 'ministerial responsibility,' where politics and policy are fused at the top of each department of government in the office of the minister, an elected politician decides policy and is accountable for the work of the department to the legislature and/or electorate. In the liberal-conservative theory of 'civic trusteeship,' policy is decided by an independent trustee or council of prominent citizens who can rise above the particular interests of partisan and sectarian politics and make decisions in the public interest.[8]

Anglo-American theorizing with regard to public accountability of state officials has also acknowledged that, given their technical expertise and professional experience, administrative officials inevitably are, and ought to be, major participants in the function of policy making. In the theory of 'executive leadership,' the function of policy making is envisaged as a joint venture involving political heads and senior officials of government departments, who thus link together the separate domains of partisan politics and bureaucratic expertise.[9] According to the pluralist liberal theory of 'bureaucratic politics,' however, politics inevitably permeates both policy and administration, resulting in a seamless process of political bargaining and exchange, and despite the existence of a merit bureaucracy, the functions of politics, policy, and administration are in practice inseparable. Proponents of 'representative bureaucracy' retort that, even in a situation of unchecked bureaucratic politics, public bureaucracies still command the knowledge and skills to dominate policy. If appointments based on merit also take into account major collective identities such as ethnicity, gender, language, race, religion, and region, then authentic social divisions would be incorporated inside public bureaucracies, thus protecting the merit principle while ensuring responsiveness in bureaucratic policy formulation and implementation.[10]

Theories of political authority differ with regard to the conduct of politics, policy, and administration as public functions; they also differ with regard to the spatial or territorial dimension of politics, policy, and administration. At one end of the spectrum, there are theories of administrative agency and policy tutelage that envisage an essentially national democracy. Here the major issues of educational politics are contested in central state political institutions, and central state educational authorities determine policy goals and set uniform standards. Within this centralized political and policy framework, local authorities may have some discretion to design and manage the details of programs that realize centrally determined objectives.[11] At the other end of the spectrum, there are theories of essentially local democracy. According to the ideology of 'local control,' politics, policy, and administration all exhibit significant territorial variations that must be taken into account in their institutionalization as public functions. Hence, as much as possible, local educational authorities should decide and administer their own policies.[12]

Between opposing ideas of national and local democracy, there are theories of fiscal equivalence and functional interdependence. Fiscal equivalence assumes that central states and local authorities are relatively autonomous but complementary levels of government.[13] The territorial distribution of benefits from different types of educational provision varies from local to national, and jurisdiction over educational decision making should be assigned to local, regional, or national educational authorities according to the territorial impact of each specific type of educational provision. Functional interdependence, by contrast, assumes that educational politics, policy, and administration have national, regional, and local dimensions that are difficult, if not impossible, to divide cleanly among levels of educational governance. Accordingly, central and local educational authorities in general should have concurrent authority and decide jointly.

Arguments about the size of government revolve around the criteria of democracy and efficiency. Educational authorities that are small in territory and population are held to satisfy the conditions for direct or participatory democracy. Such 'small republics' may also be more homogeneous in their political identities and interests, increasing the likelihood of collective consensus on educational policy and administration. Small educational authorities, however, are likely to lack the resources needed to provide the specialized teaching, broader curricula, and range of support services that are feasible in the large elementary and secondary schools maintained by more populous educational authorities. A larger population is likely to be more heterogeneous in its political identities and interests, making the task of finding a collective consensus on educational policy more difficult; but to the extent that greater diversity reduces the risk of a permanent majority, larger public authorities may offer better protection for minorities against the tyranny of the majority. Advocates of small authorities generally insist that the gains from more participatory democracy outweigh the losses in quality of educational provision (if any such losses are even conceded), while advocates of larger authorities counter that the benefits of higher quality and/or lower costs resulting from economies of scale are substantial compared to a negligible, if any, loss of democratic accountability.

On the issue of numbers of public officials, the argument regarding size runs parallel to that with respect to territory and population. On one side, more elected officials facilitate closer ties between the electorate and their representatives, and a larger staff of administrative officials expands the capacity of public authorities to supply multifarious educational services. On the other side, fewer elected officials improve efficiency by reducing the transaction costs of public decision making, and a smaller bureaucracy will be less costly, less bound by red tape, and more immediately subject to democratic accountability.

Theories of educational governance also differ with regard to the representation of collective identities and interests in the public functions of politics, policy, and administration. Liberal and socialist theories of majoritarian democracy hold that citizens elect politicians as their representatives, and hence, depending on the rules of electoral systems, that governments will represent the identity and interests of the majority (or plurality) while respecting the rights of minorities. Alternatively, following a conservative theory of consociational democracy, electorates and public authorities can be segmented on the basis of communal group membership, such as language or religion, and seek reconciliation of their differences through élite accommodation. As for organized interests, they may be excluded entirely from any legitimate part in politics, policy, and administration; they may be restricted to political advocacy as 'pressure groups' or 'political associations,' waging campaigns to influence public opinion and lobbying politicians and bureaucrats but proscribed from direct involvement in policy or administration; or they may be accepted as legitimate partners with government in the design of public policies and even designated as agents of policy implementation.

Problems of Political Economy

The generic problem of political economy is deciding and implementing the relationship of state, market, and society that best provides for the satisfaction of basic human needs.[14] Focusing on the political economy of Anglo-American educational regimes, we can identify five central historical problems regarding the relationship of state, market, and

society in the demand and supply of education. Each problem dominated educational policy making during a particular era, but each also
became integrated as a permanent issue of Anglo-American educational
politics.

Public Instruction

The political economy of public instruction centres on the claim that
elementary and secondary education ought to be provided by the state.
Historically, formal schooling was supplied through leading institutions
of the private, non-market sector, principally religious orders and voluntary associations, as well as small, independent enterprises operating for
profit in the market. By the middle of the nineteenth century, claims for
substantial state involvement in the supply of basic education were conceded as legitimate, but the form and extent of state involvement was
vigorously contested. There were supporters of state aid for schools
operating in the private non-market and (more controversial) market
sectors, proponents of introducing state schools as residual providers of
basic schooling for poor children whose parents could not afford the
costs of private schooling, and advocates of establishing state schools as
the primary, if not exclusive, providers of basic education.

In each of the Anglo-American countries, a regime of public instruction was permanently established during the second half of the nineteenth century, but the governing relationship of state, society, and
market varied substantially, not only across the five countries of Australia, Canada, New Zealand, the United Kingdom, and the United
States, but also within Canada and the United Kingdom.

Industrial Efficiency

The political economy of industrial efficiency centres on the claim that
elementary and especially secondary education should be designed to
serve the needs of the market. The Anglo-American regimes of public
instruction established in the nineteenth century were dominated by the
priorities of state (public order, civic duty) and society (religious faith,
public morality, cultural identity) rather than the demands of either
employers or workers in the market for vocational training and occupational selection. In the late-nineteenth and early-twentieth centuries,
however, there was a remarkable convergence of élite opinion across the
Anglo-American countries that industrial (or 'national') efficiency was

essential to promote national wealth and protect state power, that industrial efficiency had become dependent on a skilled labour force with
technical knowledge and skills, and that formal schooling was an essential instrument to provide future workers not only with a foundation of
general practical knowledge and skills but also with specific technical
knowledge and skills required in the workplace.

Industrial efficiency as a problem of political economy required reorganizing public instruction in the state sector to reflect the priorities of
the market while balancing the non-market interests of state and society.
In each of the Anglo-American countries, from the turn of the century to
the Second World War, general education was reoriented to stress the
goal of preparing and selecting young people for work in an industrial
economy, and vocational training was established alongside academic
education in the organization of schools and the design of curricula.

Welfare State

The political economy of the welfare state centres on the claim that basic
needs of citizens are not necessarily satisfied as a result of their work and
consumption in the market or their membership in societal institutions
of family, neighbourhood, church, and voluntary organizations. State
intervention is required to guarantee individuals and families a minimum income, enable them to meet contingencies such as sickness, old
age, and unemployment, and ensure that all citizens have access to
essential social services without regard to status or class.[15] Advocates of
the welfare state customarily count public education among such essential social services.

Although Anglo-American countries are often classified together as a
distinctive type of liberal welfare state, in practice, commitments to the
welfare state have differed in both breadth and depth across national
and provincial/state governments. At the same time, educational reform
during the grand era of the Anglo-American welfare state from the 1940s
to the 1970s produced very different patterns in the provision and governance of public education as a social service based on the principles of
universality and equality that are the hallmarks of the welfare state.

Pluralist Society

The political economy of pluralist society centres on the claim for recognition and inclusion of ethnic, linguistic, racial, and religious difference

as the foundation of individual identity, social justice, and cultural development. From the 1960s to the 1980s, educational policy in the Anglo-American democracies was primarily fixed on finding a durable relationship of society, state, and market that would meet the difficult standards of legitimacy and justice in a pluralist society.

Where the political economy of the welfare state gave priority to state intervention to remedy market failures, the political economy of pluralist society turned the focus back on the relationship of state and society, while at the same time eroding the functional relationship of state and market fostered under the political economy of industrial efficiency. In the political economy of pluralist society, universality – the master principle of the welfare state – was directly challenged by the principle of diversity. In the provision of elementary and secondary education, claims to incorporate ethnic, linguistic, racial, and religious diversity in Anglo-American educational regimes reopened basic historical issues about the separation of church and state in public schools, state subsidies for private denominational schools, the language of instruction in public schools, the representation of minorities in curricula for history and literature, and the rights of minorities to educational self-government.

Global Capitalism

The political economy of global capitalism centres on the claim that advanced industrial societies are experiencing a revolution in information technology and economic globalization that has transformed the relations of market, state, and society in all their dimensions and, hence, that fundamental restructuring of educational provision and governance has become imperative in order for societies to adjust to, and benefit from, the thrust of global capitalism.[16]

As with the political economy of industrial efficiency at the beginning of the twentieth century, the political economy of global capitalism at the end of the century galvanized an internationalization of elementary and secondary educational policy,[17] from which there emerged a substantial cross-national consensus on strategies of educational reform. The internationalization of educational policy also threatened to subvert historical settlements that were achieved in response to problems in the political economy of the welfare state and pluralist society. Hence, across the Anglo-American democracies, the political rush to adapt public education to the trend of global capitalism met political resistance that aimed to insulate public education from the penetration of global capitalism and the consequent internationalization of educational policies.

Traditions of Political Ideology

The principal problems of political economy in the policy domain of education are not simply puzzles about the best course of collective action; they usually are contests of power. All of the basic questions about whether there is a problem, what are the options for action, and which course of action to choose are contestable. Often there will be disagreement about which of the standards for judging collective action are immediately relevant. Only rarely will there be consensus on the substantive meaning of standards that are applied. Even where there is consensus on the criteria for collective action and what they mean, there almost certainly will remain significant conflicts of individual and group interests. These arguments over puzzles and conflicts of power in turn derive from ideological differences of principles, values, beliefs, and attitudes.

Political thought about the problems of political economy in the Anglo-American democracies historically has been dominated by three grand ideological traditions: conservatism, liberalism, and socialism. Each of these ideological traditions originates from the principle that one sector – society (conservatism), market (liberalism), or state (socialism) – constitutes the core of the ideal political economy and then incorporates the other two sectors into its world-view as subordinate sectors, the institutions and activities of which are instruments for the realization of social purposes embedded in the core sector. Each of these ideological traditions has engaged the others in a dialogical process. Liberalism begat conservatism; out of their antagonism they begat socialism. At the same time, in dealing with changing problems of political economy while engaged in external ideological conflict, each ideological tradition divided within itself.

Communitarian and Liberal Conservatism

For conservatives, the core sector of the ideal political economy is a society that is distinguished by its historical continuity and distinctive culture. As Edmund Burke phrased it, there is a 'partnership not only between those who are living, but between those who are living, those who are dead, and those who are to be born.'[18] Basic institutions and attributes of community in the form of family, clan, church, language, ethnicity, race, class, and nation give meaning to human existence. At the same time, conservatives assume that humans are by nature sinful and warring; civilization is fragile. Hence, the overriding and never-ending problem of political economy is the achievement and preservation of social order. For conservatives, therefore, society ought to be an organic hierarchy in which individuals are unequal in status and are governed by command and obedience based on relationships of legitimate authority, but while accepting their place in the community and doing their duty, are none the less secure in their collective identity.

The integrity and justification of the conservative state derive from its foundation in a historical society. The capacity of the state as an instrument for collective action provides the potential power to protect and develop the community that is its foundation. Consistent with the organic hierarchy of society, political rule belongs by divine right and natural ability to a privileged élite. The members of this governing élite have the responsibility to direct the state and, in conjunction with community élites (notably, clerical authorities), to guide their community in a way of life determined by them to be the good or proper way. At the same time, because the state incorporates the organic hierarchy of society – the legitimating principle of public authority – the state in turn becomes a symbolic expression of social order justifying allegiance and obliging obedience.

Classical conservatism originated in the seventeenth and eighteenth centuries as a reaction against liberal advocacy of individualism in markets and politics. The idealized past was a feudal society in which economic production and distribution were regulated by the norms and conventions of the organic, hierarchical relations of lords and peasants. The penetration of capitalist markets in the nineteenth and twentieth centuries could not be ignored by conservatives, but many of them continued to defend their core principle of social and political hierarchy, first, by asserting the absolute priority of society in its various forms of family, church, language, ethnicity, race, and culture against the penetration of the price system, and second, by willingly using the state as an instrument not only to subsidize key societal institutions but also to regulate the market in defence of societal claims.

Where 'communitarian' conservatives resisted or even proposed to suppress the penetration of capitalist markets at the expense of traditional society, other 'liberal' conservatives became proponents of the market as a key sector in the ideal political economy. Liberal conservatives advocated the virtues of the market as a means of creating economic wealth and power, but their vision of market institutions and operations was quite different from the individualistic competition under a price system that was theorized by classical liberal political economists. Rather than the possessive individualism advocated by classical liberals, liberal conservatives advocated possessive collectivism.[19] Capitalist markets were envisaged as hierarchical oligopolies, divided between, on the one hand, a few giant enterprises that would dominate production and distribution and manage (if not entirely control) prices and, on the other, many small or medium-size firms in which decisions were shaped by industry hegemons. For liberal conservatives, the organic hierarchy of traditional society need not be inconsistent with the organization of capitalist markets, especially where members of traditional élite families assume control of big business. Rather, possessive collectivism in capitalist markets can reinforce the organic hierarchy of traditional society, while at the same time providing a legitimate instrument for the circulation of élites. Hence, the hierarchy of the capitalist market ought to be recognized as a legitimate principle of the conservative political economy, overlapping but not necessarily entirely congruent with the organic hierarchy of traditional society. Similarly, for liberal conservatives the state's functions should be extended to include promoting and protecting the hierarchy of capitalist markets. Here the classic form of collaboration between state and market would take the form of concertation between state officials and big business, whereas communitarian conservatives would be more likely to give priority to concertation between state officials and clerical authorities.

Utilitarian and Ethical Liberalism

For liberals, the core sector of the ideal political economy is the market, which is theorized as institutions and processes for the production and distribution of goods and services by voluntary exchange under a price system. The key assumption is the pursuit of self-interest, as Adam Smith argued in his classic theory of liberal political economy: 'It is not from the benevolence of the butcher, the brewer, or the baker, that we expect our dinner, but from their regard to their own interest. We address ourselves, not to their humanity but to their self-love, and never talk to them of our own necessities but of their advantages.'[20] As producers vie to maximize their profits and consumers strive to maximize their satisfaction, progressive adjustments in the prices at which producers are willing to sell and consumers to buy should result in a balance between supply and demand for each product and service. Subsequent theorists of liberal economics, notably Leon Walras and Alfred Marshall, established that the most efficient allocation of resources was achieved in competitive markets, and a succession of liberal political theorists held that private markets were superior institutions for achieving individual freedom of choice in economic decision making.[21]

The functions of the liberal state are defined by the needs and limits of private markets. In the classical liberal theory of John Locke, the state derives from a political association of men whose purpose is protection of their lives, liberty, and property. Adam Smith prescribed the functions of the state as defence, justice, public instruction, and public works and justified each type of state intervention as necessary because of the limits of action based on individual self-interest and the requirements of law and order for the operation of private markets. Jeremy Bentham and James Mill proposed a theory of protective liberal democracy that preserved the traditional competitive capitalist market society and added a limited democratic franchise as an institution to protect the citizenry from oppression by the state officials.[22] In the twentieth century, 'interest group' and 'public choice' versions of liberal political theory have portrayed the institutions of the state and the processes of politics as constituting a political market in which the allocation of benefits and costs results from (ideally) free exchange among self-interested individuals and groups.

The efficiency of private markets in allocating scarce resources and their effectiveness in protecting individual liberty depend on the existence of free competition, informed decision making by producers and consumers, inclusion of all affected interests in the market, and tolerable distribution of the burden of adjusting to market changes.[23] Where these four conditions are not met, markets fail to maximize efficiency and/or liberty. Modern liberals readily concede that in practice markets rarely satisfy the competitive conditions of liberal theory. Consequently, state intervention may be justified in order to regulate monopoly, reduce consumer ignorance, take account of external benefits and costs, or redistribute income to ensure a basic standard of living. None the less, liberals tend to be divided in their receptiveness to state intervention. On the side of classical liberalism, 'utilitarian' liberals are strongly suspicious of state intervention to correct market failures. They worry that the severity of market failures is inevitably exaggerated for partisan effect in democratic political competition and that, even in cases of real failure, the results of state intervention are more likely to worsen than to improve economic welfare. Against this classical liberal distrust of the state, 'ethical' liberals are essentially optimistic about the institutions and processes of democratic politics and are much more inclined to resort to public regulation of markets and public supply of goods and services to compensate for the failure of private markets and ensure the satisfaction of basic human needs.

The division between utilitarian and ethical liberals in their views about state intervention in private markets can also be found in their respective views of the proper relationship between state and society. Classical utilitarian liberalism advocated not only a substantial restriction on state intervention in the market but also an uncompromising separation of state and society. In early Anglo-American liberalism, this separation of state and society initially concentrated on defending religious freedom against an established church,[24] but subsequently, utilitarian liberals insisted equally on a range of social and moral rights and freedoms that were intended to ensure protection for individuals in the private pursuit of their preferences (thus maximizing their utilities), not only in the market but also in the society. In particular, utilitarian liberals defended the principle of voluntarism in non-market social organization and, thus, protection for individual freedom from interference by the state.

In the writings of John Stuart Mill, T.H Green, Leonard Hobhouse, and John Dewey, there was created a view of individuals who realized their full development as much, if not more, through private activities in their society and public activities in the state as through economic activities in the market. In Mill's theory of an ethical-liberal political economy, for example, 'the good society is one which permits and encourages everyone to act as exerter, developer, and enjoyer of the exertion and development, of his or her own capacities.'[25] A democratic state and a capitalist market facilitate this human advancement better than any other political economy, but equally, since material progress or mere satisfaction of material wants is not an end in itself, state intervention could well be justified by an ethical argument based on the potential contribution of public policies to individual development. These 'ethical' liberals took seriously the potential of state intervention and public policies to support, encourage, and even create the conditions for individual growth and development that in turn cannot easily be separated from cultural communities within which individuals form and reform their goals and ambitions. These thinkers were concerned to protect individual liberty, but they also recognized the importance of cultural identity to the proper functioning of a well-ordered and just society.[26] Hence, they have a different view from utilitarian liberals concerning the legitimacy of state intervention to protect the culture of a society, including minority cultures in pluralist societies.

Democratic Socialism and Social Democracy

For socialists, the core sector of the ideal political economy is the state. The central principle of the socialist state is democracy conceived not only as political and legal equality but also as economic and social equality. True equality is unattainable as long as a relatively small class of owners and managers of the means of economic production can use their private economic power in conjunction with the coercive power of the capitalist state to dominate the masses, who have no comparable power. Socialist theorists are divided between those who see the state in capitalist society as an essentially subservient instrument of the ruling class of owners and managers of the means of production (as Karl Marx and Friedrich Engels pithily described it, 'nothing more than the executive committee of the bourgeoisie') and those who conceive the state as a relatively autonomous apparatus of state officials dedicated to defending and advancing the universal, as opposed to particular, interests of capital. Whichever view of the state in capitalist society is held, however, the socialist state based on the principle of democracy is seen as the instrument to attack and resolve the fatal class divisions of the capitalist political economy and hence realize economic and social justice.

In Anglo-American socialist thought, this transformation of the capitalist political economy is generally advocated as being achieved by parliamentary democracy rather than revolutionary change. First, socialist parties must win control of public authority by successfully competing against bourgeois (liberal and conservative) parties in democratic elections, and then socialist governments can progressively and systematically reform public law, policy, and administration to serve the needs of all citizens equally. During this phase, the goal of the socialist state is redistribution of economic power. This may be accomplished by changing private ownership and control of key private enterprises into public ownership and control that will be responsive to democratic political direction, by extensive regulation of capitalist markets to protect the interests of workers, by redistribution of income and wealth to equalize economic resources and social welfare, and by public supply of essential social services based on the principle of universality.

In the course of constructing a program of state intervention to remedy the failures of capitalist markets, the Anglo-American socialist tradition became divided between democratic socialism and social democracy. Democratic socialists desire to transform capitalist society. In their radical communitarian vision, the ultimate socialist state is an egalitarian order, governed by cooperation and consensus, in which all citizens are full participants. This democratic-socialist ideal is perhaps best expressed by Karl Marx's well-known criterion: From each according to his abilities, to each according to his needs. For democratic socialists, participatory democracy must not only be the master principle of state institutions and operations, it must also determine the institutions and operations of the market. Economic democracy in the form of worker participation in, and ultimately control of, the governance of public and private enterprises is the essential counterpart of political democracy.[27]

By contrast, social democrats aim to reform capitalist society. In their view, socialist states can coexist with capitalist markets. In addition to vigorous state action to satisfy basic needs through income redistribution and social services, social democrats advocate state intervention to create and maintain a balance of economic power between labour and capital. In their strategy, a socialist government in concert with trade unions should aim to negotiate a class compromise with organized business, thus replacing the unfettered market power of capital with multilevel collective bargaining through bipartite or tripartite institutions.

In socialist ideology, capitalist society is crippled by class conflict that originates in capitalist markets. Class divisions determine not only work but also life in the family, neighbourhood, church, region, and nation. For socialists, the organization of the working class as a social movement through such organizations as workers' educational associations, consumers' cooperatives, women's auxiliaries, and sports clubs is an essential extension of their strategy to build class consciousness and countervail capitalist power. Within the socialist tradition, democratic socialists are more likely than social democrats to focus their thinking about the ideal political economy on societal institutions and activities. For democratic socialists, the institutions and practices of participatory democracy are not only the essential features of a good state and a good market, they are also marks of a good community. None the less, for democratic socialists as for social democrats, historically the core of working-class power in striving for the ideal political economy is the political alliance of socialist party and trade unions; it is the key that will reform, if not transform, the capitalist state.

Comparisons of Anglo-American Democracy

Educational regimes are focused on a primary problem of political economy, hold a recognizable core of organizing ideas, and have a distinctive set of public policies for the provision and governance of education. Interpreting the politics and policies of Anglo-American educational regimes is taken here as a useful way to understand Anglo-American democracy. Politicians and policy makers, teachers and learners, parents and citizens in the Anglo-American democracies have confronted recurring problems in the political economy of primary and secondary education: determining the boundaries of public instruction, maximizing the contribution of academic and vocational education to industrial efficiency, deciding the place of education in the postwar welfare state, adapting primary and secondary education to the needs of a pluralist society, and reforming education to meet the challenges of global capitalism.

With regard to these problems, choices have been made – whether individual or collective, planned or unplanned, comprehensive or incremental – about the scope of educational provision, the commitment of public resources, the substance of teaching and learning, and the distribution of the benefits and costs of primary and secondary education. Choices have also been made about the desirable relationship of politics, policy, and administration as functions of educational governance, the size of governments, the levels or orders of public authority, and the representation of major social groups in educational governance.

Given a range of ideological positions derived from the grand traditions of Anglo-American conservatism, liberalism, and socialism, the meaning of these educational policy choices can be interpreted in terms of their 'conventional intentions' – that is, not necessarily in terms of the personal intentions of historical actors but rather in terms of the ordinary meaning of political actions inherent in the use of particular policy instruments.[28]

Comparison of the attributes of Anglo-American educational regimes as they change over time is directed at understanding commonality and difference in the ideas and practices of Anglo-American democracy. Understanding commonality in the ideas and practices of Anglo-

American democracy means focusing first on the common political tradition of Australia, Canada, New Zealand, the United Kingdom, and the United States. Here the argument follows those contemporary comparative political studies that, while conceding important national differences, emphasize the distinctive 'liberal pluralist' political culture and policy configuration of the Anglo-American democracies. According to Neil Nevitte and Roger Gibbins, for example, 'Perhaps no other five countries in the industrialized world are more alike; they share not only roughly comparable economies, social structures, and cultural environments, but also the same political tradition.'[29] The first challenge for this comparative study of educational regimes is understanding what is this common political tradition.

If there is an identifiable common Anglo-American political tradition, there also are major cultural, economic, political, and social differences among the Anglo-American democracies. This theme also has been explored in comparative political studies. In particular, studies of Anglo-American political culture have argued that the grand ideological traditions of conservatism, liberalism, and socialism have had very different manifestations in the five countries: hegemonic liberal individualism in the United States; liberalism in Canada touched by toryism in the nineteenth century and socialism in the twentieth; a counterbalance of socialist and tory democracy in the United Kingdom; and the prominence of a radical ethos or idealistic socialism in Australia and New Zealand.[30] In addition to such differences in political culture, there are important differences in historical legacies and political institutions, especially in the federal constitutions of Australia, Canada, and the United States as compared with the unitary constitutions of New Zealand and the United Kingdom and in the constitutional separation of legislature and executive that distinguishes federal and state government in the United States from parliamentary government in the other four countries. Such differences in ideological traditions and political institutions are reasons to expect major differences not only in configurations of policies for educational provision and governance but also in the attributes of educational regimes. Differences in educational regimes, in turn, may be indicators (or even sources) of differences in the ideas and practice of democracy among Anglo-American countries.

Comparative studies of educational regimes also must take account of differences within the Anglo-American democracies. Each country has its own issues of ethnicity, language, race, and region that create distinctive political divisions in the formulation of educational policies and the

construction of educational regimes. These internal divisions are reinforced by institutional arrangements. Even without taking into account
territorial governments, for example, the three federal constitutions
have potentially six different state educational regimes in Australia, ten
provincial educational regimes in Canada, and fifty state educational
regimes in the United States. In addition, the terms of union in the
United Kingdom have resulted in substantial differences of educational
provision and governance among England and Wales, Northern Ireland,
and Scotland.[31] Again, the question with regard to these differences
concerns their significance for understanding the ideas and practice of
democracy – not only the common Anglo-American political tradition
along with its national idiosyncrasies but also the diversity of democratic
ideas and practices within countries. That, in turn, opens the way to a
more complex understanding of the 'common' Anglo-American political tradition, focusing on ideological affinities among regional educational regimes across national borders.

1 Public Instruction

In 1776 there were two landmark events in the Anglo-American political tradition that, among their many effects, initiated a prolonged public debate over the role of the state in the provision and governance of popular education. One of these events was the publication of *The Wealth of Nations* by Adam Smith. The other was the issuance on 4 July of the Declaration of Independence, of which the principal author was Thomas Jefferson. Adam Smith's persuasive vision of the individual liberty and economic efficiency that resulted from capitalist markets not only served immediately to discredit mercantilist theories of imperial economic expansion under the aegis of state protection and regulation; it also focused attention on the emerging features of capitalist society, especially the dismantling of traditional hierarchies of social class in favour of entrepreneurial initiative, voluntary contracts, and labour mobility, as well as the necessary restructuring of the functions of the capitalist state. Along with defence, justice, and public works, Smith urged, public instruction was an essential function of the capitalist state.[1] The Declaration of Independence – with its compelling opening assertion of political nationality, 'We, the people ...' – advanced a powerful claim for individual rights and popular sovereignty as the foundation for democratic self-government. Among the founders of the American republic no doubt there was widespread acknowledgment that nation building on the basis of political democracy would require generous provision for popular education. None was more insistent, or prescient, on the importance of public education for securing and preserving political democracy than Thomas Jefferson.[2]

Over a half-century later, the ideas advanced by Adam Smith and Thomas Jefferson were reforming the Anglo-American political tradition. The repeal of the Corn Laws in 1846 marked the adoption of the liberal theory of free trade in capitalist markets as the official policy of the British government, thus altering the imperial relationship between Britain and its colonies in British North America, Australia, and New Zealand. Fourteen years earlier, the passage of the first Reform Act had initiated the development of political democracy in Great Britain by extending the suffrage to part of the middle class. A decade later, responsible government – the constitutional convention that the executive council advising the governor should enjoy the confidence of a majority of members elected to the legislative assembly – had been instituted in the British colonies of Nova Scotia, New Brunswick, and the United Province of Canada (1848), Prince Edward Island (1851), New South Wales and Victoria (1855), and New Zealand and Tasmania (1856). At the same time, immigration, especially that resulting from the Irish exodus during the potato famine of the 1840s, was shifting the ethnic and religious composition of American cities and British colonies. Similarly, territorial expansion, especially the westward settlement of the United States, was profoundly affecting the cultural and political identities of the Anglo-American frontier societies.

The problem of public instruction as it developed in the Anglo-American states during the first half of the nineteenth century originated in this interdependent penetration of capitalist markets and political democracy. Political arguments to institute public instruction as a legitimate function of the Anglo-American state focused on the need to impart knowledge, skills, and identities to young people who would be not only citizens of nascent democratic polities but also producers and consumers in emergent capitalist societies. The central problem of the political economy of public instruction was reconstruction of the relationships of state, market, and society to make educational regimes that would supply mass education appropriate to the needs of capitalism and democracy.

The overriding political issue that ultimately determined the form and substance, as well as the coherence and consistency, of the policies for educational provision that were incorporated in each Anglo-American educational regime during the nineteenth century was the relationship between church and state in education. Historically, education was generally regarded as the prerogative and duty of church and family. On the question of the relative authority of church and state, material support from the public treasury for the church's educational endeavours was welcome, even expected, as long as it implied no interference with clerical control of the management and curricula of schools. In the face of pressures for the institution of public instruction, nineteenth-century conservatives defended this historical arrangement of state aid for church schools; nineteenth-century liberals and socialists attacked it. For liberals and socialists, church and state ought to be strictly separated, public schools should be secular in their teaching, and ultimate political authority over them should belong to an elected, representative legislative assembly.

In addition to their disagreement about church and state in education, nineteenth-century conservatives, liberals, and socialists differed about the proper constitution of political authority for purposes of educational governance. Issues regarding the institutional design of political authority focused on arranging and conducting the public functions of politics, policy, and administration in political constitutions that were increasingly depending for their legitimacy on the principles and practices of democratic, representative government. They included the constitution of central educational authorities with particular regard for the proper relationship of policy and administration to democratic partisan politics; the constitution of local educational authorities to take account of territorial variations in politics, policy, and administration; and the division of constitutional jurisdictions over educational governance between central and local educational authorities.

In the educational regimes of the Anglo-American states, none of the various liberal constitutional options, let alone any of the conservative or socialist alternatives, proved to be generally acceptable. Eventually, public educational institutions based on liberal political principles were preserved against the protests of Roman Catholic minorities in the United States and British Columbia. Liberal educational institutions were imposed despite Roman Catholic and Anglican church opposition in Australia, New Zealand, and Manitoba. Liberals and conservatives variously compromised in England and Wales, Scotland, Ontario, Saskatchewan, Alberta, and the Maritimes of Canada. Conservative educational regimes defeated liberalism in Ireland, Newfoundland, and Quebec. Thus, very different institutional arrangements for public instruction were initiated across the Anglo-American states and, because they endured virtually intact until after the Second World War, became a formidable long-term influence on the development of Anglo-American democracy.

Australia: Between Conservative and Utilitarian-Liberal Educational Regimes

In the Australian colonies, the first approaches to dealing with the issue of church and state in education between the beginnings of state educational aid in the 1820s and the granting of responsible government in the 1850s included church establishment, public subsidy of church schools, and non-denominational schools based on the model of the British and Foreign School Society or the Irish national system.[3] By the 1850s, South Australia, Tasmania, and Western Australia restricted the allocation of state grants to non-denominational schools only, but the largest colonies of New South Wales, Queensland, and Victoria had state-aided non-denominational systems in conjunction with state-aided church schools. These dual educational regimes did not survive the upsurge and institutionalization of liberal politics that accompanied the movement for responsible self-government. Between 1872 and 1895 the six Australian colonies all passed public instruction acts that closely followed a utilitarian-liberal theory of educational governance by combining ministerial responsibility at the centre with local boards as administrative agents. With regard to religious instruction and observances, however, the utilitarian-liberal argument for strictly secular schools lost out to the majority preference for non-denominational public instruction.

Dual Regimes of Church and State Schools

The Australian model of a dual regime combining non-denominational state schools with voluntary church schools was invented in New South Wales. In 1844, Robert Lowe persuaded the New South Wales Legislative Council to establish a select committee, with him as its chair, to inquire into the state of education in the colony.[4] Lowe, along with most members of the committee, favoured the Irish national system over the existing policy of state grants for church schools. Denominational schools, they agreed, were unnecessarily competitive, inefficient, and expensive; such a system was totally inappropriate to the needs and conditions of a thinly populated country. The Legislative Council approved their recommendation, but church opposition delayed the introduction of 'national schools' until the arrival of a new governor, Sir Charles Fitzroy, who set up a dual regime of denominational and non-denominational schools in 1848. The National Board of Education would establish, maintain, and control non-denominational schools; the Denominational

Schools Board would distribute state aid to Anglican, Catholic, Methodist, and Presbyterian church schools. Church schools were expected to remain dominant in Sydney and the larger towns; the national schools would be established mainly in rural areas.[5] In the national schools, teachers were required to use only textbooks published by the Commissioners of National Education in Ireland, and local clergy were permitted to enter the schools once a week to give sectarian religious instruction. Following the election of a Liberal government, the national and denominational boards were consolidated in 1866, but the unified board remained independent of the executive council until it was abolished in 1880.[6]

Educational regimes that comprised parallel sectors of church and state schools were retained in both Victoria and Queensland following their constitutional separation from New South Wales. A separate denominational board had been appointed by Lieutenant-Governor C.J. La Trobe for the Port Phillip district in 1848, and a separate national board was appointed for Victoria in 1851.[7] The two boards waged an unrelenting competition for enrolments and grants until 1862, when the Common Schools Act was passed by the new Liberal government led by George Higanbotham. The fifth attempt in ten years at educational legislation, this act established a unified board to distribute state aid to both vested schools (owned by the board) and non-vested schools (owned by one of the churches).[8] In Queensland the Primary Education Act of 1860 provided for the Board of General Education to assist in building vested schools, hire and pay teachers, and distribute grants to both national and church schools. As in New South Wales and Victoria, non-denominational religious instruction was given in all national schools, and denominational religious instruction could be given before or after school or during the midday recess.

In Tasmania and South Australia there were brief periods of public subsidy of church schools before grants were restricted to non-denominational schools. Van Dieman's Land governor Sir John Franklin in 1839 had converted the schools of the Church and School Corporation, which formerly belonged to the Church of England, into schools based on the non-denominational curriculum of the British and Foreign School Society. Aid to church schools was restored from 1847 to 1853, but thereafter state support was again restricted to non-denominational schools, following the Irish national model, in which classroom teachers gave non-denominational religious instruction for one hour at the beginning of each school day and visiting clergy gave denominational instruction during one hour of released time each week. In South Australia, grants to Anglican, Catholic, Presbyterian, and Wesleyan church schools were initiated in 1847 but ended in 1851 with the passage of the first education act following the introduction of responsible government. Under its provisions, a central board of education was empowered to aid schools that gave 'good secular instruction, based on the Christian religion, apart from all theological and controversial differences on discipline and doctrine and no denominational catechism shall be used.'[9] These were schools based on the model of the British and Foreign School Society, in which teachers were required to read a chapter from the Old and New Testaments each day and no provision was made for denominational instruction during released time.

In Western Australia the first state grants for elementary education in 1846 were restricted to non-denominational national schools. The national schools used textbooks issued by the Irish national commissioners and operated under the supervision of the General Board of Education, which was chaired by the colonial secretary and included leaders of the Protestant churches. A separate grant for Catholic schools from 1849 to 1856 was cancelled as a measure of fiscal retrenchment. Roman Catholics continued to press for a restoration of state aid to their schools and eventually found an advocate in a Roman Catholic governor, Sir Frederick Weld, who appealed to the 1870 Elementary Education Act in England and Wales as his precedent. The first education act, passed in 1871 by the newly reconstituted, partially elected Legislative Council, provided for a central board of four lay members appointed by the governor with the colonial secretary as its chair; no two members could be of the same religion. This central board governed the state sector and distributed grants to both national and church schools until the 1890s.

Thus, in each of the Australian colonies, a unified board of education was established as the central authority to govern the early years of state involvement in education. Whether lay or clerical in their membership, these central boards were designed to be interdenominational and independent of the colonial government, although members of the executive or legislative council were often appointed to serve as members.[10] In South Australia and Tasmania the central boards emulated the liberal-conservative ideal type by restricting state grants to non-denominational 'national' schools. The central boards of the other four colonies, however, all incorporated a significant compromise between liberal and communitarian conservatives by distributing state aid to both church and state schools.

Utilitarian Liberalism and Ministerial Responsibility in the
Governance of Colonial Education

The abolition of central boards of education, beginning in 1872 in Victoria, and ending in 1893 in Western Australia, marked the triumph of utilitarian-liberal political principles in the construction of Australian educational regimes. Against the conservative squatters and colonial administrators who continued to dominate the early years of Australian responsible government, the rising parties of utilitarian liberals insisted equally on separation of church and state in public education and direct political accountability for public schools through ministerial responsibility.

In Victoria, liberal governments tried in 1867 and again in 1870 but failed to pass bills that would have established a state system of non-denominational schools and replaced the Board of General Education with a minister of education. As premier of Victoria in 1871-2, Charles Gavin Duffy, a liberal Roman Catholic, became the lightning-rod for rising sectarian hostilities, and the election of June 1872 that followed his defeat in the legislative assembly pitted Protestants against Catholics. The Protestants prevailed, and the education reform bill was passed in December 1872. As he introduced the bill, the attorney general gave a classic utilitarian-liberal defence of its proposed administrative arrangements: 'As to administration, the only way we know of, and which we have adopted, of securing the control by this House over the education of the country and the expenditure for that purpose is to constitute a department, which will be called the Department of Education, and which will be presided over by one of the responsible Ministers of the Crown.'[11]

Similarly in the other colonies, ministerial responsibility for public education resulted from a political trend that favoured Liberal parties and utilitarian-liberal principles of educational governance. In Queensland the Liberals in 1873 finally gained a majority over conservative party factions dominated by squatters that had maintained narrow majorities in the assembly and large majorities in the council through the 1860s. The new government set up a royal commission on the control of public instruction, and its recommendation for a ministerial department was duly enacted the next year.[12] In South Australia, debate on the 1875 education bill had revealed strong support for the principle of ministerial responsibility.[13] Three years later, a short bill that aimed to strengthen the clauses on compulsory education in the 1875 education act blew up into a major attack on the public accountability of the Council of Education. At the end of it the House of Assembly was virtually unanimous in voting an amendment to replace the council with a minister and Department of Public Instruction.[14] A Pastoral Letter denouncing 'secularist education' in the public schools, issued by the archbishop and bishop of New South Wales in 1879, aroused predictable controversy, but this time Henry Parkes, now premier, who had persisted in defending the Council of Education as an effective instrument for separating public schools from political influence, finally relented. The next year the Public Instruction Act provided for a government minister as political head responsible for the Department of Public Instruction.[15]

Central Boards, Ministerial Departments, and Local Agents

For local administration, the central boards of education depended on voluntary initiatives of local patrons. Except in South Australia, the central boards had authority to nominate local committees to found and manage elementary schools, but at least initially, the boards generally preferred to encourage local initiatives rather than force them.[16] Later, when Victoria and New South Wales replaced their separate national and denominational boards with unified central boards, local management of national schools by self-nominated patrons was replaced by local school committees (Victoria) or public school boards (New South Wales) whose members were appointed by the central boards.[17] Prior to the introduction of ministerial responsibility, Western Australia was the only colony to replace local patrons or school committees with elected district school boards. Governor Weld's Elementary Education Act of 1871 provided for district school boards of five members each, to be elected by male suffrage using the electoral roll for the colonial assembly.[18]

In the national schools sector, local patrons were essentially administrative agents of the central board of education. The central board provided one-half to two-thirds of the cost of building and equipping a school and paid a basic annual stipend to its teacher. Local patrons had to raise the remaining balance of capital costs, superintend the construction of the school, levy fees and subscriptions to pay operating costs and supplementary stipends to the teachers, and share responsibility for the conduct of the school. In South Australia, national schools were vested in the district councils, municipal corporations, and local committees that had taken the initiative in founding them, but in other colonies, schools established by the national (or general) board were 'vested' schools, the property of the board not the local patrons. Although consideration might be given to the recommendations of local patrons, central boards also appointed teachers and regulated the organization and curriculum of national schools. The duties of local school committees were restricted to routine local administration: general inspection of their school, setting fees, examining accounts, making requisitions, undertaking minor repairs, investigating local complaints against the school, and reporting to the general board.

The elementary education acts of Victoria (1872), Queensland and South Australia (1875), New South Wales (1880), and Tasmania (1885) all replaced management by local patrons or school committees with local administration by district school boards. In Victoria the local boards of five to seven members were elected for three years by district ratepayers; in the other four colonies they were appointed by the minister of public instruction. Except in New South Wales, where the term 'public school board' continued in use, the local boards were formally designated as 'boards of advice,' reflecting the modest expectations of their legislative designers. As with the local patrons who were their predecessors, members of local boards were expected to be guardians of school property, consider complaints against teachers, ensure that statutory requirements for compulsory attendance were observed, and, subject to ministerial approval, determine the use of the school building outside regular hours. Beyond such minor administrative functions, local boards were restricted to giving advice to the minister. Boards of advice were entitled to visit their local schools for purposes of inspection, but they were specifically prohibited from interfering with teaching. The minister and departmental officials retained full responsibility for education in the schools.

The functions of local school boards were designed to be minimal; implementation of the new education acts in the last quarter of the nineteenth century further eroded their position. In Queensland the district boards were never appointed; instead, the departmental regulations issued in 1876 provided for school committees to be appointed by the minister, on the basis of nominations by the subscribers to the building fund in the case of new schools, or of election by male parents and guardians in the case of established schools. An 1877 report on public education in Victoria found that, five years after the passage of the Common Schools Act, 'the leading principle ... has been to substitute supervision from Melbourne for local co-operation.'[19] In South Australia, where the inspector general, J.A. Hartley, from the beginning created a strongly centralized state educational regime, there was considerable criticism through the 1880s of the exclusion of the boards of advice from any real scope for initiative. In 1891 an amendment provided for half the members to be elected by parents, but there was no improvement in their status.[20] In Western Australia the district boards established under the 1871 act in Perth, Fremantle, and Albany, 'for periods at least attended to their duties seriously and contributed to the advancement of education in their localities,' but elsewhere the district boards of education proved ineffective: 'Too often their performance was characterized by the irregular attendance of members at meetings, changes of personnel and failure to sustain interest. This dilatoriness was itself a reflection of public apathy, and after the initial experience of 1871 elections for district boards of education seldom evoked even passing interest.'[21] District boards were retained in the Western Australia Elementary Education Amendment Act of 1893, but their functions were much reduced; for example, the key function of appointing teachers was transferred to the minister of education. By the end of the First World War the boards were in a state of complete collapse.

Secular versus Non-denominational Schools in Utilitarian-Liberal Educational Regimes

In principle, utilitarian liberalism as expounded by its leading theorists, Jeremy Bentham, James Mill, and John Stuart Mill, was adamant in its adherence to strictly secular public education. In practice, however, the utilitarian-liberal regimes of the Australian colonies wavered between non-denominational and secular public schools, and eventually all states made provision for some form of religious instruction.

The education acts of New South Wales (1885) and Western Australia (1895) explicitly provided for non-denominational religious instruction as part of the 'secular' state school curriculum as well as for sectarian religious instruction by visiting clergy during released time. In New South Wales, section 7 provided that 'In all Schools under the Act the teaching shall be strictly non-sectarian, but the words "secular instruction" shall be held to include general religious teaching as distinct from dogmatical or polemical theology'; and, according to section 17, 'In every Public School four hours during each day shall be devoted to secular instruction exclusively and a portion of each day not more than one hour shall be set apart when the children of any religious persuasion may be instructed by the clergyman or other religious teacher of such persuasion.'[22] In Western Australia, government schools were directed to provide four hours of secular instruction daily, plus one hour devoted to religious lessons in which the Bible could be read 'without note or comment.' An amendment to the Elementary Education Act in 1893 provided that ministers of religion or other authorized persons could instruct children of their religious persuasion for half an hour on any day. Parents were entitled to withdraw their children from religious lessons, but secular instruction was defined to include general scriptural instruction to be imparted by ordinary teachers.

The educational policies of Victoria, Queensland, and Tasmania were initially ambiguous about religion in state schools: officially, state schools were secular; in practice, there was usually a place for both sectarian instruction and non-sectarian religious observances. Under the 1872 act, Victorian state schools were restricted to 'secular instruction' during regular school hours, but local school boards, empowered to determine the use of school buildings outside school hours, were able to authorize religious instruction outside school hours. Changes to the regulations in 1883 and 1904 permitted voluntary religious instruction, first in the last half-hour of the regular school day rather than only outside school hours, and then during the first or the last half-hour on one or two days a week.[23] The Tasmanian education act of 1868 omitted any reference to religious instruction, and in the schools, the arrangements of the 1853 act – daily non-denominational religious instruction by teachers and weekly released time for denominational instruction by visiting clergy – remained in effect until the 1885 act, which ended religious instruction by teachers while preserving released time for denominational instruction.[24] In Queensland, religious instruction was omitted from the revised curriculum in 1875, but the 1876 departmental regulations authorized clergy to visit schools to give denominational instruction either before or after regular school hours. A campaign by the Queensland Bible in Schools League, formed in 1890, led to a referendum in 1910 and an amendment to the Primary Education Act that approved instruction in elementary schools in selected Bible lessons from a specially prepared reading book and authorized ministers of religion to attend for one hour a week during regular school hours to instruct children of their denomination.[25]

South Australia was the last bastion of secular public education. The education act of 1875 left an opening for Bible reading – teachers were allowed to open their schools early so that students could read portions of the Bible in the authorized King James or Douay version – but pressure on teachers by the inspector general effectively nullified this option in practice.[26] Subsequent attempts in 1921, 1924, and 1934 to introduce non-denominational religious instruction into South Australian state schools failed because of opposition from both the Roman Catholic church and the Australian Labor party. An amendment to the education act in 1940 finally permitted clergy to enter state schools for a half-hour each week to instruct students of their denomination, and in 1947 class teachers were authorized to undertake sectarian religious instruction voluntarily with the approval of the church concerned.

Canada and Newfoundland: Denominational Regimes, Separate Schools, and Strict Separation

When the national project of continental federation was launched in 1867, section 93 of the British North America Act, 1867, gave provincial legislatures exclusive jurisdiction to make laws in relation to education, subject to the provision that 'nothing in any such law shall prejudicially affect any Right or Privilege with respect to Denominational Schools which any Class of Persons have by Law in the Province at the Union.'[27] Thus, unique in the original Anglo-American constitutions, section 93 aimed to entrench the basic relationships between church and state in public instruction that had been negotiated during the pre-Confederation foundation of educational regimes.

Both before and after Confederation, the 'school question' was consistently one of the most explosive and deeply divisive issues of Canadian politics, resulting in four distinct regimes of public instruction: a dual confessional regime in Quebec and a multidenominational regime in Newfoundland that left effective control of public instruction in the hands of church authorities; a compromise between communitarian conservatives and conservative liberals in Ontario, Saskatchewan, and Alberta that provided for non-denominational instruction in public schools, with separate schools for the minority confession, usually Roman Catholic but sometimes Protestant; a liberal-conservative regime of non-denominational public schools established by law in Nova Scotia (1864, 1865), New Brunswick (1871), and Prince Edward Island (1877) that subsequently was compromised in practice to provide for reserved Catholic schools in each province; and a liberal-conservative regime that provided for non-denominational but not strictly secular public schools, with no state aid for private denominational schools, that was adopted with little opposition in British Columbia in 1872 and imposed in Manitoba in 1890 despite furious resistance by Roman Catholics.

Church and State in the Educational Regimes of British North America

Colonial governments in British North America followed both British and American models in their early support for education. On the one hand, under framework statutes in New Brunswick (1802), Nova Scotia (1808 and 1811), and Upper Canada (1816), non-denominational common schools that followed the models of the town schools of Massachusetts (the parishes of New Brunswick and Nova Scotia) and the common schools of New York (Upper Canada) were built and supported by local voluntary effort and funds with minimal official aid or direction. On the other hand, district schools in Upper Canada (1807) and grammar schools in Nova Scotia (1811) and New Brunswick (1816) followed a British model to provide a socially exclusive elementary and secondary schooling for the children of the colonial upper class – government officials, military officers, lawyers, doctors, and merchants. These schools, while nominally free of church control, in practice operated under Anglican or, occasionally, Presbyterian church influence with a clergyman or minister usually appointed as headmaster.[28] The British influence was also evident in various schemes of state aid to church and other voluntary schools.[29]

Following the recommendation of Lord Durham's report on his investigation into the 1837 rebellions in Lower Canada and Upper Canada, the Act of Union passed by the British Parliament in 1840 imposed a unified government and legislature on the two colonies. The first education act for the United Province of Canada, passed in 1841, empowered the inhabitants of a parish in Canada East (Quebec) or a township in Canada West (Ontario) to elect a board of school trustees to build and maintain one or more common schools in their district. Those who adhered to a denomination different from the majority were entitled to choose their own board of trustees and to build and maintain one or more separate schools for the dissenting minority. When an education act specifically for Canada East was passed in 1846, the school commissions of Montreal and Quebec city were legally divided by denomination: in each city, twelve commissioners were appointed by the municipal council, six Roman Catholic and six Protestant, who would constitute 'two separate and distinct corporations, the one for the Roman Catholics and the other for the Protestants.'[30] Outside the cities of Montreal and Quebec, common schools continued to be non-denominational in law. None the less, with some exceptions where the majority was Protestant, the common schools of Canada East were Roman Catholic in character and governance just as separate schools were Protestant, and the 1869 education act gave legal status to this dual confessional regime.

The first Newfoundland education act of 1836 not only provided for the distribution of public subsidies to voluntary denominational schools but also authorized the establishment of interdenominational district boards to operate non-denominational elementary schools. The act of 1843, however, directed that Catholic and Protestant boards be established in each of the nine school districts, the entire public grant was divided in each district in proportion to the denominational affiliations of the local population, and all interdenominational schools built under the 1836 act were transferred to the management of a denominational school board. The formation of sectarian Protestant boards then became the main political issue until 1874, when Newfoundland was divided into Roman Catholic, Anglican, and Methodist school districts with twenty-three to twenty-five school boards each throughout the island. The Free Church of Scotland and the Congregational Church were each given two district boards, in St John's and Harbour Grace, and one board covering the whole of Newfoundland was authorized for the Kirk of Scotland.[31]

In contrast with the denominational regime instituted in Canada East, the Act for the Establishment and Maintenance of Common Schools in Upper Canada, which split the educational governance of Canada West from that of Canada East in 1843, insisted on the principle of non-denominational public instruction while providing separate schools for the denominational minority. The act specifically prohibited any child in a common school from being required 'to read or study in, or from, any Religious Book, or to join in any exercise of Devotion or Religion, which shall be objected to by his parents or guardians.'[32] Where the teacher of the district common school was Roman Catholic, Protestant residents might apply to have a separate school with a Protestant teacher; where the teacher was Protestant, Roman Catholic residents were entitled to apply for a separate school with a Roman Catholic teacher. Separate schools were subject to the same inspections and regulations as common schools and were entitled to a share of the legislature's annual appropriation for public instruction based on the number of children in attendance. When a reform liberal government led by Robert Baldwin and Louis-Hippolyte LaFontaine passed an education act in 1849 that strengthened local educational governance, secularized the common schools, and abolished separate schools, Egerton Ryerson, the assistant superintendent, who was a liberal conservative and devout Methodist committed to non-denominational instruction, refused to administer the new act and submitted his resignation. The government retreated. An order-in-council then authorized Ryerson to administer the schools under the 1843 act until 1850, when a new act, framed by Ryerson, affirmed both the non-denominational character of common schools and the minority denominational right to separate schools. In 1853, again on Ryerson's recommendation, separate schools were given an equal share of provincial school grants, according to their average attendance, and their supporters were effectively exempted from taxation for common school purposes and prohibited from voting in elections for common school trustees.[33]

In the North-West Territories, provisions for central educational governance initially were based on the Quebec (and Manitoba) model of a dual confessional regime. Under the 1884 ordinance, the territorial board of education was divided between Roman Catholic and Protestant sections, and provision was made for denominational school districts throughout the territory. Through a series of amendments culminating in a 1901 ordinance – the last education act before Saskatchewan and Alberta were granted provincial status in 1905 – the educational regime of the North-West Territories became virtually identical to the pre-Confederation regime of Canada West. In each school district, one school was designated as the common school, and a separate school was organized only where the denominational minority voted for it. The local board of each common school was authorized to direct that its school be opened with the Lord's Prayer, and the last half-hour each day could be devoted to religious instruction from which children were excused at the request of their parents.

In the Maritime colonies of New Brunswick, Nova Scotia, and Prince Edward Island the regimes of public instruction established prior to Confederation were non-denominational in law, including provisions for teaching religious principles common to Christian believers, ensuring that religious exercises were not compulsory, and prohibiting the use of the Bible as a means of inculcating specific doctrines. None the less, the common schools in predominantly Catholic communities were Roman Catholic in practice, and in urban districts such as Halifax, Charlottetown, Summerside, Saint John, and Fredericton, designated elementary schools were reserved for Catholic children. In Nova Scotia, for example, Archbishop Thomas C. Connolly tried to get statutory recognition of separate schools when the education bills of 1864 and 1865 were under consideration, and again on the eve of Confederation, but the Conservative premier, Charles Tupper, rejected this appeal, asserting that Catholics would always be well represented in cabinet and their interests thus protected. Under an arrangement subsequently negotiated by William Henry, a Protestant who represented the predominantly Catholic constituency of Antigonish in the assembly, all common schools in Nova Scotia remained legally non-denominational, but local agreements designating certain schools as reserved for Catholic children were de facto sanctioned. In New Brunswick, where about 250 schools in predominantly Catholic districts had received grants under the 1858 Parish Schools Act while teaching denominational doctrine and using denominational books and prayers, there were riots in Caraquet over implementation of the requirements of the 1871 Common Schools Act for non-sectarian public schools that resulted in two men being killed.[34] The five Roman Catholic members of the legislative assembly were then able to negotiate concessions by the provincial cabinet that reinstated a local option for Catholic schools.[35]

British Columbia and Manitoba adopted a fourth type of educational regime – non-denominational public instruction with no provision for separate or reserved minority denominational schools and no state aid for private denominational schools. In the case of British Columbia there was relatively little political controversy. British Columbia's first education act, in 1872, followed an 1865 ordinance of the colony of Vancouver Island by making an explicit commitment to non-denominational public instruction: 'All Public Schools under the provisions of this Act shall be conducted upon strictly non-sectarian principles. The highest morality shall be inculcated, but no religious dogma or creed shall be taught.' By contrast, the introduction of non-denominational public instruction in Manitoba caused one of the landmark crises in Canadian politics. As in Quebec, the School Act of 1871 divided the Manitoba provincial education board between Catholic and Protestant sections, each with its own school districts to administer, and split the education grant between them. The basis for this denominational (and in effect linguistic) duality was eroded over the next two decades by an influx of English-speaking Protestant settlers, not to mention the polarization between Protestants and Catholics caused by the Métis Rebellion of 1884 followed by the hanging of its leader, Louis Riel. Sponsored by the

Liberal government of Thomas Greenway, the Public Schools Act of
1890 replaced dual confessional public instruction with a non-denominational regime similar to that of British Columbia. Roman Catholic
school districts were abolished, and religious instruction and observances were prohibited during regular school hours.[36]

Central Educational Authority: Ministerial Responsibility
versus Civic Trusteeship

The 1843 school act for Canada West designated the provincial secretary
as chief superintendent of public instruction with responsibility to apportion the grant, administer the act, and report to the assembly. Appointed as assistant superintendent for Canada West in 1844, Egerton
Ryerson pressed for a clear separation of educational policy and administration from partisan politics by the establishment of a central board of
education to which he would be responsible as superintendent. When a
sympathetic Conservative ministry instituted the General Board of Education in 1846, Liberal reformers immediately attacked the independence of both the board and its superintendent from the ministry and
legislative assembly.[37] Back in power in 1850, they reformed the General
Board as the Council of Public Instruction with functions of making
general regulations, approving textbooks, and classifying teachers. The
council's policies were implemented by the chief superintendent, but in
practice the council appears not to have promulgated any policies other
than those recommended by the chief superintendent, who was directly
accountable to a minister of the crown rather than to the Council of
Public Instruction.[38] This formal separation of politics from policy and
administration by means of dual accountability lasted until Ryerson's
retirement in 1876, when the office of chief superintendent was abolished and the minister of education assumed direct political and policy
functions for public instruction in Ontario.

   In Nova Scotia (1841), New Brunswick (1846), and Prince Edward
Island (1877) the constitution of central educational authorities followed the British approach to governing public instruction but, rather
than a committee of the Privy Council, named the entire executive
council as the board of education or council of public instruction.[39] In
each case, the chief superintendent of public instruction served as a
member as well as secretary of the board or council.[40] This form of
collective ministerial responsibility for public instruction continued on
the Island until 1931, when a minister was given individual responsibility

for the education portfolio, and even longer in New Brunswick (1936) and Nova Scotia (1949).

Independent boards of education were originally established as the central authorities governing public instruction in Manitoba (1871), British Columbia (1872), and the North-West Territories (1884), but these boards were shortly abolished in favour of making the provincial/ territorial executive council the board of education or council of public instruction. In British Columbia, when superintendent John Jessop and the Board of Education resigned in protest against changes to the 1872 act proposed by the government of G.A. Walkem, elected in 1878, the government transferred the board's duties to the cabinet, with the super-intendent as its executive officer. The provincial secretary was the minis-ter in cabinet responsible for education until 1891, when it became customary to appoint a minister of education, but a department of education was not officially established in British Columbia until 1920. The Manitoba Board of Education was transformed into an advisory body in 1890, when the Public Schools Act terminated the dual confes-sional regime, and central control of public instruction – as well as direction of the newly established Department of Education – rested with a committee of five cabinet ministers until 1908, when a minister of education was appointed as political head and a deputy minister as permanent administrative head. The independent dual confessional board of the North-West Territories was replaced in 1892 by a council of public instruction that was essentially a political body comprising the territorial executive committee plus four non-voting members (two Prot-estant and two Roman Catholic) appointed by the territorial executive.[41] The council in turn was reorganized in 1901 as a department of educa-tion with the 'premier' (F.G. Haultain) as commissioner responsible to the territorial assembly and a deputy commissioner (J.P. Calder) as administrative head, and this model of minister of education as political head and deputy minister as administrative head was continued when the provinces of Saskatchewan and Alberta were constituted in 1905.

Two provinces were exceptions to this trend to ministerial (or execu-tive council) responsibility. Quebec (then Canada East) initially followed a pattern of central governance similar to that in Canada West under Ryerson, but sustained pressure by the Roman Catholic bishops for church control of public instruction resulted in separation of the Coun-cil of Public Instruction into Roman Catholic and Protestant committees in 1869. In 1876 the education portfolio was dropped from cabinet, and the Council of Public Instruction was given full independence and authority over provincial education.[42] From then until the reform of 1964, the Quebec Department of Public Instruction operated as a dual hierarchy headed by a common superintendent, with separate Roman Catholic and Protestant secretaries who were responsible respectively to the Roman Catholic and Protestant committees of the Council of Public Instruction. In Newfoundland a Department of Education with its own minister was not established until 1920, and even then the superintendents of Anglican, Roman Catholic, and Methodist schools maintained their former control.[43] Seven years later, the office of minister was dropped, and the functions of central governance were transferred to a denominationally representative 'bureau' of education that included the prime minister, the three superintendents, and the secretary for education as administrative head of the department. Under the British Commission of Government (1934–49) there was another attempt to secularize central educational administration by abolishing the denominational superintendencies and appointing a commissioner of home affairs and education as political head. Two years later, however, separate executive officers were appointed within the department to administer, respectively, the schools of the Church of England, the Roman Catholic Church, the United Church of Canada, and the Salvation Army.[44] When Newfoundland entered Confederation in 1949, the commissioner and the secretary were replaced by a minister and a deputy minister; the organization of the department by denominational sections remained unchanged.

Central and Local Authorities in the Foundation of Canadian Educational Regimes

The original institutions and practices to govern public instruction in Canada involved provincial control of educational policies and local administration of schools. The central board and chief superintendent provided the legal framework and policy direction, but the priority of central educational authority during the pioneering phase of educational establishment was to stimulate local communities to elect trustees, build schools, hire teachers, enrol their children, and vote tax levies. School boards were treated as public institutions of local communities rather than administrative agents of provincial departments of education.

Throughout Ontario, the West, and most of the Maritimes, school districts were independent of other local governments. In the cities, single-school districts were soon amalgamated to form unified school boards that had jurisdiction over all elementary and, eventually, also secondary schools within the municipal boundaries.[45] Outside the cities, the boundaries of school districts, were set by the distance children were expected to walk to school, somewhere between nine and twenty-five square miles. In these small districts, three trustees, elected usually one each year for a three-year term at the annual school meeting of resident property owners, were authorized to build and maintain a school and appoint and dismiss teachers. Operating costs of the school were paid primarily by a levy on local property voted at the annual school meeting. The pupil population was small, often not many more than the ten to fifteen pupils required under provincial law as the minimum for establishing a school district. Most schools had one room and one teacher.

The chief superintendent's influence depended in part on his authority to disburse and withhold provincial grants on the basis of local performance, but it also depended on the willingness of local officials to comply with central directives. Ryerson's role as superintendent has been well described as 'the public instructor' of teachers and trustees.[46] He attached great importance to informing and advising local authorities, explaining their responsibilities, and mediating local disputes. Similarly, chief superintendents in other provinces depended primarily on their powers of persuasion and leadership rather than the imperatives and sanctions of bureaucratic regulation. The regulations of these tutelary superintendents were intended to impose a central vision of educational progress and to discourage anti-educational behaviour by local trustees and teachers; but they also were designed to inform and persuade trustees and teachers, who had limited skills and little knowledge, what needed to be done to maintain their schools and teach their pupils.[47]

In Quebec and Newfoundland, school boards also enjoyed considerable educational, administrative, and financial autonomy. School commissions for each parish in Quebec determined the school tax rate based on the valuation of property within their districts; appointed, paid, and dismissed teachers; and, under the supervision of the Catholic and Protestant denominational committees of the council, regulated courses of study in their schools. Boards under the Roman Catholic committee of the Council of Public Instruction generally accepted the church as 'the ultimate moral and temporal authority in all matters related to Quebec education,'[48] while the Protestant committee operated more as a gathering of representatives from the Quebec Protestant community, pursuing the common interests of the Protestant school commissions and coordinating their few joint enterprises but leaving the commissions with substantial communal autonomy. In Newfoundland, school boards for each denominational district were appointed by the government on the recommendation of denominational superintendents, and legislative grants were simply divided among them on the basis of denominational affiliation as reported in the census of population. The boards were authorized to appoint and dismiss teachers and prescribe courses of study and textbooks, but the Council of Higher Education, established in 1893 and comprising the denominational superintendents and the heads of denominational colleges in St John's, prescribed the syllabus and set external examinations for upper grades in all schools.[49]

New Zealand: Foundation of a Classical Liberal Educational Regime

In New Zealand a brief and controversial policy of colonial grants for church schools from 1847 to 1852 was replaced by a variety of communitarian-conservative and liberal-conservative arrangements for church and state schools during the period of provincial control over education. These included public subsidy of church schools, complementary sectors of state and church schools, and non-denominational public schools. With the dissolution of the provinces, the Education Act of 1877 established a unified educational regime that was founded on three basic principles of nineteenth-century liberalism: a minister of education responsible for national education to the legislative assembly, decentralization of educational governance to district school committees that were elected by local ratepayers and regional education boards that were elected by members of school committees, and a statutory separation of church and state that prohibited religious instruction and observance in public primary schools.

Church Schools, Public Schools, and Provincial Regimes

In October 1847, 'An Ordinance for Promoting the Education of Youth in the Colony of New Zealand' was enacted by Lieutenant-Governor George Grey and the Legislative Council. The ordinance was intended primarily to support the advancement of missionary education among the Maoris, but Grey was well aware of how unpopular the restriction of aid exclusively to Native education would be with the colonists. Accordingly, the ordinance authorized disbursement of grants to the Bishop of

New Zealand, the head of the Roman Catholic church in the colony, the superintendent of the Wesleyan Mission, and the ministers of any other religious denominations that were providing education in the colony.[50] Grey defended the ordinance on the grounds that state aid to church schools was now established practice in Britain and that only the churches had shown any interest in promoting Native education. The ordinance was fiercely attacked, however, and resulted in relatively little aid to colonial schools before education became a provincial responsibility in 1852.

Two prominent liberal critics of Grey's 1847 ordinance were Alfred Domett, colonial secretary for New Munster, and William Fox, agent for the New Zealand Company and disciple of Jeremy Bentham and James Mill.[51] According to Domett, no government was morally justified in compelling parents to send their children to sectarian schools that conflicted with their religious faith, or in imposing school taxes on dissenters in order to finance denominational schools. Since compulsory attendance and local taxation were necessary for efficient schools, in school districts with small populations the only practical policy was a system of state-financed secular schools. Fox, in his report on education for the Wellington provincial council in 1854, similarly emphasized the responsibility of the state, in the absence of denominational consensus, to provide for secular education.

> The State being satisfied that ignorance is the fertile parent of crime and pauperism, both inflicting vital injuries on itself, and that education even of a secular character is a great check to them, it is as much bound to give secular education as to employ a policeman or a poor-law guardian. The fact of the people not being able to agree on any general system of religious instruction, does not absolve the State from providing secular [education], but it does absolve it from the obligation of contributing pecuniary aid to the denominational schools. The State provides schools in which it teaches all that, *as a State*, it is bound to teach – it is not incumbent upon it to aid those schools which undertake to teach something more or something else.[52]

These classic liberal arguments for secular education did not immediately prevail. Among the provincial councils that had jurisdiction over public education after 1852, only Wellington in 1855 required that no religious instruction be given in any assisted school and that no ministers of religion be permitted to teach in, or interfere in the conduct of, a school except as an elected member of the school committee. Two years later, this strict prohibition on religious instruction was amended: teachers were permitted to teach the Bible if written permission was obtained from the school committee, the committee approved the version of the Bible being used, and the teaching was done without notes, comments, or doctrinal interpretations.[53]

In other provinces, there were various provisions for religious instruction and observances in colonial schools, but nowhere was strict secular education the preferred option.[54] In Canterbury, for example, provincial grants under the education ordinance of 1857 were given directly to the heads of the Anglican, Presbyterian, and Wesleyan churches until a provincial board was established in 1863. The board's schools were essentially non-denominational Protestant in their religious instruction, and church schools continued to get grants from the Education Board until 1873, when the dual regime was ended.[55] In Auckland, beginning in 1857, the Board of Education distributed provincial grants to support voluntary schools in which the local patrons or committees of management were free to make provision for religious instruction without interference from the provincial board. This policy of public subsidy lasted until 1869, when the Common Schools Act restricted provincial grants to non-denominational schools. The 1856 Otago education ordinance incorporated the militant evangelical Presbyterian assumptions of the majority Scottish Free church. Reading the Holy Scriptures and instruction in the principles of religious knowledge were held to be 'consonant to the opinions, religious profession, and usage of the great body of the people,'[56] and teachers were expected to be qualified to impart both religious and secular knowledge. An ordinance of 1862 removed the religious qualification for teachers but required that the Bible be read daily and prohibited religious instruction contrary to evangelical Presbyterian doctrines. The education ordinance in Nelson (1856) required that religious instruction in provincial schools be free of sectarian controversy and given at hours convenient for conscientious objectors to withdraw. When Roman Catholics protested against being taxed to support non-denominational schools, the provincial council authorized the Board of Education to transfer revenue from their school taxes to any group of ratepayers establishing a denominational separate school; in practice, only Roman Catholics took advantage of this provision.[57]

Provincial ordinances all provided for strong local control of education. The form of educational governance initially adopted in Wellington, Nelson, and Otago became the model that was eventually adopted in other provinces. The provincial superintendent was authorized to divide the province into districts and make arrangements for the election of a school committee by the householders of each district. School committees appointed teachers, prescribed the general course of instruction, and managed their schools. Each school committee appointed a representative to the provincial education board, which set regulations for the establishment and management of schools, allocated provincial grants to the school committees, exercised general supervisory powers over school committees, and employed inspectors to visit schools, enforce regulations, and report to the board. Arrangements for local finance varied. In Wellington, for example, each school committee had authority to levy a rate on local householders for the support of education. In Nelson, a tax of £1 was levied on each householder plus five shillings for every child of school age (five to fourteen), and the resulting school fund was distributed by the provincial board.

Towards the end of provincial government, the radical liberal approach to local educational governance that characterized the first phase of New Zealand state education broke down in several provinces.[58] None the less, both the liberal principle of local democracy and its institutionalization in school committees and education boards survived the provincial era and were incorporated as basic elements of the national educational regime established by the Education Act of 1877.

Ministerial Responsibility, Education Boards, and School Committees

When he introduced the 1877 education bill, Charles C. Bowen, minister of justice in the Liberal government of Sir George Grey, observed that a central issue of public instruction was 'occasioned by the different opinions men hold as to central and local administration – how far control should be enforced, and how far the system should be locally administered.' Bowen asserted that the Liberal government's bill was a decentralizing one: 'The Bill we intend to submit to this House provides entirely for local administration, subject to the ultimate control in certain particulars, especially in matters of expenditure.'[59] A minister of the government would be responsible to the House of Representatives for national education, and seven-eighths of the cost of education would be paid out of the consolidated fund. There would be a national department of education; however, the department would issue minimal regulations to organize and manage the central administration, determine the method for allocating grants, examine and classify teachers, establish and maintain training colleges, prescribe national standards of education, and ensure financial accountability of education boards, to the department.

The organization of local educational governance under the 1877 act continued to comprise education boards and school committees. School committees were elected by the residents of each local school district to establish and manage one or more schools in their district, subject to the approval and supervision of the education board and its inspectors. The twelve education boards, with jurisdictions roughly corresponding to the former provinces, were elected, at first by the members of local school committees, later by a vote of district householders.[60] The education boards had power to appoint and transfer teachers in schools under their control, but all teachers were required to hold a certificate of competency from the minister of education. Each education board set its own pay scale and classification scheme for teachers and pupil-teachers. Revenues of the education boards came mainly from the national government's grant as well as rents, endowments, fees, and donations. From these revenues, the education boards paid the full costs of education in their districts including teachers' salaries and the costs of the maintenance and education of pupil teachers, the purchase of school sites and buildings, capital repairs and improvements, and grants to school committees for general educational purposes.

Despite Bowen's stated commitment to local democracy, the Liberal government's original bill in 1877 weakened the education boards, in particular by establishing a national inspectorate as part of the Department of Education. As the 1877 act was finally passed, however, only the inspector general was an official of the department. All other inspectors were appointed by, and responsible to, the education boards.[61] The initial complement of the Department of Education comprised just three officials: secretary, inspector general, and clerk; and the secretary and the inspector general were the only professional officers in the department for many years. Under the new national regime, the elected members of the education boards were often the same as before 1877; and especially in Auckland, Canterbury, and Otago, they usually included among their members three or four parliamentary representatives who stoutly defended local democracy in education against centralizing pressures from the department and the teaching profession. Administrative personnel of the education boards also continued largely unchanged. In sum, the constitutional position of education boards was changed by the 1877 act, but in practice, the powers of the boards were initially little if at all diminished.[62]

National Regime, Secular Schools

The diversity of provincial provisions for education from 1852 to 1876 made the place of religion in state schools a critical issue in the formation of a national educational regime. Attempts in 1871–2 by successive prime ministers (William Fox and Julius Vogel), who based their proposals on the Nelson scheme of separate schools, failed to win acceptance. In the 1877 education bill, Bowen took the standard liberal position that denominationalism in state-supported schools was not only expensive and inefficient, it was also contrary to religious conscience. None the less, since the great majority desired the inclusion of Bible reading in school, schools should be opened each day by reading the Bible and reciting the Lord's Prayer; all other instruction would be secular.[63] During consideration of the bill in committee, an amendment to strike the clause requiring the Lord's Prayer and Bible reading and insert the provision 'that teaching shall be entirely of a secular character' was carried by a vote of thirty-nine to nineteen. An amendment to allow Bible reading at the discretion of school committees was similarly defeated. Another amendment to allow aid for separate schools also failed. The Legislative Council in its turn approved an amendment that public schools should open each morning with the Lord's Prayer; that, too, was rejected by the House of Representatives.

Notwithstanding this statutory requirement for secular instruction, 'schools continued to operate after 1877 in a professedly Christian, predominantly Protestant milieu, which saw nothing odd in a certain amount of traffic between secular schooling and revealed religion.'[64] In 1897 a Presbyterian minister and the Anglican bishop persuaded the Nelson Education Board to exercise its discretion under the Education Act to set the opening and closing hours of its schools in order to reduce formal school hours from three to two and one-half for one morning each week. Religious teachers were given the use of school buildings during the released time, and a secular lesson that was voluntary for teachers and pupils was given in another room for conscientious objectors.[65] Similarly, five minutes of released time was provided where schools chose to start their day with religious observances. Policies of released time were not widely adopted elsewhere in New Zealand prior to the

Second World War, in part because the main pressure group for religious education, the Bible-in-Schools League, scorned it as 'slinking in by the back door.'[66] The New Zealand Council for Christian Education, founded in 1949, was more willing to accept the compromise of released time, and the practice gradually spread from about 10 per cent of schools in 1930 to 80 per cent by 1960.[67]

United Kingdom: Communitarian-Conservative versus Liberal-Conservative Principles

State aid to elementary education in England, Scotland, and Wales originated in the 1830s in the classic communitarian-conservative form of public subsidies for church schools. In Ireland a different approach was attempted, with a liberal-conservative regime of non-denominational 'national' schools. When state schools eventually were established in England and Wales (1870) and Scotland (1872), they were also organized on essentially liberal-conservative principles – a central authority held accountable by ministerial responsibility, locally elected school boards that operated as administrative agents for the centre, and public schools that gave non-denominational Christian religious instruction along with their secular curriculum – but at the same time the voluntary sector of church schools continued to receive state grants. Meanwhile, by the middle of the nineteenth century the 'Irish system' had become in practice a denominational regime.

Public Subsidies for Voluntary Schools in England, Scotland, and Wales

In England and Wales the dual regime comprising state-operated non-denominational schools and state-provided voluntary schools originated in the two rival voluntary societies that were formed in the early nineteenth century to provide for the mass schooling of poor children using a monitorial system of teaching. The British and Foreign School Society (1808) and the National Society for Promoting the Education of the Poor in the Principles of the Established Church (1811) took for granted that education should be permeated by religious teaching based on the precepts of Christianity. On the place of denominational doctrine in mass education, however, they were deeply and bitterly divided. The British and Foreign School Society supported non-sectarian Christian instruction and advocated simple Bible teaching as the foundation for a unified Christian education. The National Society stood for exclusive clerical control of education. It was willing to accept state aid for mass education but rejected state control, and it insisted on teaching the doctrines and liturgy of the established Church of England.[68]

In contrast with the absence of legislative design for elementary education in England and Wales, in Scotland in 1696 the Scottish Parliament had enacted the Act for Settling of Schools, which imposed a duty on the heritors (owners and occupiers of land) of each parish to establish a school and maintain a schoolmaster. In practice, the parish schools were 'voluntary schools coordinated by the agency of the general assembly [of the Church of Scotland] in much the same way that the English voluntary schools were coordinated by the various voluntary societies.'[69] In addition, heritors often neglected their duty to support parish education, and school promoters had to rely on voluntarism to mitigate persistent educational deficiencies. As early as 1709 the Society in Scotland for Propagating Christian Knowledge was formed to promote elementary education, especially in highland areas 'where error, idolatry, superstition and ignorance do most abound, by reason of the largeness of parishes and scarcity of schools.' More than a hundred 'sessional schools' were established in towns by the kirk sessions of local congregations, and from 1824 the education committee of the General Assembly of the Church of Scotland also established 'assembly schools,' mainly in the highlands and islands. The Free Church after the Disruption of 1843, the Roman Catholic church, and the Episcopal Church of Scotland also maintained their own schools in the nineteenth century.[70]

Parliamentary grants to assist in building elementary schools in England and Wales were first paid in 1833 to promoters of schools recommended by the National Society and the British and Foreign School Society,[71] and subsidies to schools of the Church of Scotland were initiated the next year. The parliamentary grant for education was distributed directly by the Treasury until 1839, when a committee of the Privy Council comprising the lord president, the lord privy seal, the chancellor of the exchequer, and the home secretary was established to determine needs and priorities in the distribution of state aid.[72] The education committee met about once a month, while the lord president visited the Privy Council Office daily to deal with the business of its departments, including education, and settle more controversial matters. The secretary of the Education Department, which provided administrative support to the education committee and the lord president, handled routine decisions but also exercised considerable influence over policy.[73]

As early as 1841 a few members of Parliament began to express dissatisfaction with the accountability of the education committee and urge that responsibility for education be assigned to one minister. In 1855, when three bills, each proposing a ministerial department for education, were introduced in the House of Commons, Lord John Russell conceded that the time had come formally to recognize the lord president as minister of education and also to provide for representation of the Education Department by a minister sitting in the House of Commons.[74] The next year, by order-in-council, the lord president was given a separate charge over the Education Department, assisted by the vice-president of the Privy Council's committee on education, who would represent the department in the House of Commons. Henceforward, the lord president and the vice-president assumed that they could exercise the policy-making authority of the education committee without having to convene it.[75]

Liberal-Conservative Principles and Communitarian-Conservative Practice in the Irish National System

In 1831, faced with growing Roman Catholic resistance to the educational activities of Protestant societies, such as the Association for the Discountenancing of Vice and Promoting the Knowledge and Practice of the Christian Religion, the London Hibernian Society, and the Kildare Place Society, which were financed by parliamentary grants and the lord lieutenant's school fund, the chief secretary for Ireland (Edward Stanley) appointed the Commissioners of National Education in Ireland to aid and regulate elementary schools that offered 'combined literary and separate religious education.'[76] In these national schools, children of all religious denominations would receive their secular education together. Separate religious instruction for each denomination would be given, on school premises if desired, at any time on at least one day each week set aside for the purpose and on other days before and after the regular school program.

In its first two decades, the (board of) Commissioners of National Education enjoyed its highest prestige and autonomy, serving as an influential model for establishing central boards of education in the colonies of Canada and Australia. The first commissioners operated with considerable freedom from supervision by the Irish government.[77] They were appointed by the lord lieutenant, the crown's representative in Ireland, but he did not interfere in their work and never exercised his power of removal. The board's funds were subject to annual votes in

Parliament, which also received annual reports, but Parliament exercised no serious surveillance over the board's activities. By about mid-century, there began a gradual decline in the board's autonomy, in particular as a result of stricter controls on its operations by the Treasury and the Civil Service Commission,[78] but the board of commissioners was not finally displaced by direct ministerial responsibility until 1922, after the partition of Ireland, when education in the north was restructured along British lines.

The Irish national system was established in law as non-denominational; in practice, it came to operate as a denominational regime. Initially approved by most Roman Catholics, the national system was unacceptable to bishops of the Church of Ireland because it presumed to separate religious and secular instruction, and it was rejected by Ulster Presbyterians because Roman Catholics were represented on the board of commissioners and because certain passages of the Bible offensive to Roman Catholics were excluded from reading in national schools. The Church of Ireland refused to join the national system and continued to operate its own church schools, with the result that in the south of Ireland, only Roman Catholic children were left in national schools.[79] As for the north of Ireland, the board of commissioners soon yielded to pressure from Ulster Presbyterians, relaxed its rules on non-vested schools, and thereby tacitly sanctioned denominational schools.[80] By approximately mid-century, there were still a few non-denominational schools with joint managers and teachers, a mixed student body, and the local Protestant parsons and Catholic priests providing religious instruction to their respective adherents. Throughout most of Ireland, however, Catholic children were taught in schools normally run by a Catholic manager, usually the parish priest, and staffed by Catholic teachers; Protestant children were taught in Protestant schools managed by the local vicar or landlord and staffed by Protestant teachers.[81]

Dual Regimes of Non-denominational Public Schools and Denominational Voluntary Schools in England, Scotland, and Wales

The public debate in England between the National Education League (NEL) and the National Education Union (NEU) over the establishment of a system of state schools simply recast and renewed the sixty-year political conflict between advocates of denominational versus non-denominational Christian education. In 1869 a group of Birmingham liberals led by Joseph Chamberlain formed the National Education League to press for a system of universal elementary education that would be public, compulsory, and maintained by local property taxation.[82] Through its numerous branch committees and close ties with trade unions, the league was able to mobilize a degree of political pressure not seen since the campaign of the Corn Law League (in which many NEL members also had been involved). Alarmed by the league's activity, supporters of church schools responded by founding in Manchester the National Education Union. Where the league anticipated the absorption of voluntary schools into a state-maintained and publicly governed non-denominational system, the union sought to make denominational voluntary schools the core of mass elementary education.[83]

The vice-president of the education committee of the Privy Council, W.E. Forster, rejected the platforms of both the NEL and the NEU.[84] As Forster saw it, the league would 'drive out of the field most of those who care for education and oblige the Government to make use solely of official or municipal agency'; and, unless it were endowed with very generous state subsidies, the union would be unable to provide an adequate system of voluntary schools. Concluding that both schemes taken separately would be too costly to the public purse, Forster presented a bill that proposed to maintain the existing voluntary sector and establish public school boards to fill gaps left by voluntary organizations. Under his bill, voluntary denominational schools would receive larger public subsidies, equal to half their maintenance costs. Where voluntary schools failed to meet local educational needs, school boards would be formed to levy rates and (with direction and assistance from the Education Department) build, maintain, and manage state schools. Forster's original bill gave school boards authority to aid voluntary schools from local rates and to designate board schools as secular, non-denominational, or denominational. Unrelenting opposition forced the Gladstone government to concede amendments that prohibited school boards from making grants to voluntary schools or giving denominational religious instruction in board schools.[85]

The Education (Scotland) Act, 1872, generally followed the model of the Elementary Education Act, but it departed from it in one important respect: rather than create school boards to fill gaps left by voluntary schools, the 1872 act divided Scotland into school districts and required the establishment of a school board in each district. Responsibility for the former parochial and burgh schools was transferred to these school boards. Voluntary schools were given the choice between being transferred by their managers and hence becoming state schools or remaining under voluntary management and continuing to receive central government grants but not aid from local rates. The act gave official recognition to the custom of religious instruction in Scottish schools, where parents desired it, and provided for religious instruction and observances subject to withdrawal of any child for reasons of conscience.[86]

In England and Wales, under the 'Cowper-Temple clause' of the Elementary Education Act, school boards were permitted to choose between non-denominational and secular schools; in practice, they opted for programs of non-denominational instruction.[87] Similarly, almost all of the 931 school boards set up under the Education (Scotland) Act authorized religious instruction in their schools, but in contrast with the diversity of non-denominational programs in England and Wales, the Scottish boards, with a few exceptions, approved programs of religious instruction and observance that subscribed to the tenets of Presbyterianism.[88] Not surprisingly, most managers of voluntary schools affiliated with the Church of Scotland and the Free Church chose to transfer their schools to the public boards. Managers of Episcopal and Roman Catholic church schools, however, refused to transfer their schools until 1918, when stronger guarantees were given concerning the denominational character of schools in the public sector and state aid to voluntary denominational schools was terminated.[89]

Dual Ministerial Responsibility and the Tutelary Relationship between Education Departments and School Boards

Even by British standards, the transition of the central educational authority from collective conciliar governance to individual ministerial responsibility was unusually slow and piecemeal. The 1856 order-in-council in effect gave the lord president and the vice-president dual ministerial responsibility for education, but the day-to-day work was done by the vice-president. As education got more attention in the House of Commons after 1870, the role of the vice-president increased accordingly.[90] The vice-president became de facto minister of education, but on important matters of policy the formal responsibility of the lord president could not be ignored.[91] Liberal critics of the dual ministerial responsibility for education – for example, the Playfair commission on the machinery of government in its 1874 report – were countered by arguments that appealed to the state's dual responsibility for segmented sectors of school boards and church schools under the 1870 education act. Dual ministerial responsibility thus symbolized, and served to legiti-

mize, the dual organization of elementary education that blended
communitarian-conservative and liberal-conservative principles.

When the parliamentary grant for Scottish schools was formally separated from the grant for England and Wales in 1847, Scottish nationalists
began pressing for a separate committee of the Privy Council or national
board of education for Scotland.[92] The establishment of the Scotch
Education Department in 1872 (it became 'Scottish' in 1918) as a separate department under a Privy Council committee for education in
Scotland failed to satisfy the Scottish critics, not surprisingly, perhaps,
given that the Scottish committee had the same president and vice-
president and the same permanent secretary as the committee of council
for England and Wales. During the debate in 1884–5 on the creation of a
minister responsible for Scottish affairs, there was a dispute as to whether
education should be part of the new Scottish minister's responsibilities.
Despite opposition from the Scotch Education Department, patriotic opinion in Scotland prevailed.[93] The post of secretary for Scotland (it became
secretary of state for Scotland in 1926) carried with it the duties of vice-
president of the Scotch Education Department, but the lord president
continued to have a formal responsibility for Scottish education and
occasional influence on policy. Thus, in Scotland as in England and Wales,
dual ministerial responsibility continued to the end of the century.

In contrast with the statutory provision for school boards throughout
Scotland, the creation of school boards in England and Wales depended
on demonstrating a deficiency in voluntary provision. In London, a
school board of forty-nine members (increased to fifty-five in 1882) was
elected by ratepayers in eleven electoral divisions, four to seven members
from each division. Outside London the boroughs and parishes of England and Wales were designated as school districts. A borough council or
parish ratepayers could by a majority vote request the establishment of a
school board, but the Education Department determined whether a
deficiency in the provision of elementary education in the district existed and, hence, whether a school board should be formed. The department also had authority to impose a school board on a district where
school accommodation was shown to be insufficient and no local action
was being taken to supplement it. The slow rate of formation of boards,
the failure to establish boards in more than half the counties of England
and Wales, the number of contested attempts to establish boards, and
the fact that more than two-fifths of the boards were formed compulso-
rily – all attest to widespread and persistent local opposition to school
boards in England and Wales.[94]

Despite differences in their statutory establishment, school boards in England and Wales had constitutions and powers broadly similar to those of Scottish school boards. In both cases, school boards were elected at large by ratepayers in each district for three years and (except for London) varied in size from five to fifteen members, depending on the population of the district. The boards had authority, whether directly or through their appointed official, to manage any school they leased, rented, or built. They fixed the rate of weekly fees, appointed teachers, and enforced attendance. The boards set local rates for school support and ordered borough and county councils to collect the revenue needed to supplement income from pupil fees and annual grants of the central government. For major capital expenditures, boards were able to borrow from the Public Works Loans Commissioners.

The central education departments exercised considerable control over school boards both in England and Wales and in Scotland through the instruments of grant regulations, departmental inspectors, and district auditors. The introduction of compulsory attendance in a school district was subject to approval by the department. The department also approved each board's scale of fees.[95] The department set conditions governing sites, buildings, qualifications of teachers, and content of curriculum, and it could withhold the annual grant or refuse approval of loan applications unless the board conformed. The duties of Her Majesty's Inspectors included annual inspections and reports on individual schools, examination of pupils in the subjects recognized for annual grant, examination of pupil-teachers working for certificates, and evaluation of certificated teachers.[96] Annual grants were based on average attendance and results in annual examinations conducted by the inspectors. Teachers' careers were determined by the evaluations inscribed annually on their certificates by the inspectors and by their success in getting students passed at their examinations, and thus generating grant revenue for their school board.[97] In England and Wales, the accounts of each school board were inspected annually by a district auditor appointed by the Local Government Board.[98] Any item not sanctioned by statute was to be 'disallowed,' and if money for the disallowed item was already expended, whoever had authorized the payment was personally liable for the amount.[99]

Given these extensive regulatory powers over school boards, the Scotch Education Department, despite its location in London from 1885 to 1921, was a more actively controlling and directive office than the Education Department, making Scottish education more uniform and central-

ized than was the case in England and Wales.[100] Indeed, the Education
Department appeared to favour stronger school boards in England and
Wales, albeit operating within a general policy framework determined by
the department. The vice-president (A.J. Mundella), for example, stated
in a Birmingham speech in 1883 that the preferred policy for the department in dealing with the school boards was to 'leave them freer – let
them find out by experiment what was the best method for their locality.'
Similarly, as the secretary of the department, Patrick Cumin, told the
Royal Commission on the Working of the Elementary Education Acts
(the Cross commission, 1886–8), 'At present, the great defect is, that all
the localities look to the central Department to govern them in all sorts
of particulars, whereas they ought to govern themselves.'[101] None the
less, only the largest school boards – London, Birmingham, and Manchester in England; Edinburgh and Glasgow in Scotland – had any
capacity for relative autonomy in policy development. Elsewhere, although school boards were continually tutored and prodded to become
efficient local educational managers, they were essentially administrative
agents of the education departments with regard to all the major areas of
educational policy except for employment of teachers.

United States: Liberalism, Democracy, and Racial Exclusion

Public education was not included in the Constitution of the United
States among the powers of the federal government; it was part of the
residual jurisdiction of state governments. The state educational regimes
that were founded in the nineteenth century varied markedly in their
details of organization and policy, but they rested on four general principles of state organization and public policy. First, the primary agencies of
educational governance were local school boards that usually were elected
by local ratepayers but in some cases were appointed by municipal
councils. Second, state legislation provided for the election or appointment of a state superintendent of schools and/or a state board of
education. These central state authorities had general powers to supervise school boards, allocate state grants, collect statistics, and promote
public education, but their direct control over school boards was relatively weak. Third, public education rested on a constitutional separation of church and state, but for most American liberals of the nineteenth
century this meant non-denominational Christian religious instruction
and observance in public schools, not strictly secular education. Fourth,
the regimes of public education founded in the nineteenth-century

United States were racially segregated. At the end of the century, in its decision on *Plessy* v. *Ferguson*, the U.S. Supreme Court advanced a doctrine of 'separate but equal' that would uphold and legitimate racially segregated schools until 1954.

American Liberalism and Local Democracy

The town school committees and community school districts that developed in Massachusetts during the eighteenth and early nineteenth centuries, as well as community school districts in the state of New York, provided the models for local democracy in educational governance in the United States. In New England, New Jersey, Pennsylvania, and the midwestern states, where the two forms of local educational governance coexisted, town school committees and community school boards waged a half-century war over the control of public schools. In Massachusetts, for example, the state assembly passed legislation empowering town school committees to abolish the school districts in 1853, 1859, and 1869, but on each occasion the legislation was quickly repealed, until the town school district was finally established as the basic unit of local educational governance in 1882.[102] Other states in New England that experienced a similar conflict between town school committees and community school districts subsequently followed the example of Massachusetts and adopted the town school district as their basic unit of local educational governance – New Hampshire in 1885, Maine in 1892, Rhode Island and Vermont in 1893, and Connecticut in 1909. Local school districts were consolidated into township units in Pennsylvania in 1854 and New Jersey in 1894. In the Midwest, Indiana, which had provided for governance by community school districts in its first school law of 1833, adopted the township as its basic unit of educational governance during the constitutional convention of 1851.[103] Township districts were also established in Iowa, Michigan, and Ohio, but in these states the community school district was the dominant agency of local educational governance.[104]

Community school districts were introduced as the basic unit of local educational governance in New York in 1812, and this model of local educational governance was successively adopted in central and western states as state educational regimes were given their first legislative recognition in Ohio (1821), Illinois (1825), Indiana (1833), Michigan (1837), Iowa (1838), and California (1852).[105] At the outset these state laws were usually permissive rather than mandatory, granting residents legal authority to meet and form a school district and to levy a tax on local property to pay for their school. The board of a community school district typically comprised three trustees, elected by local residents for three years and with powers to employ teachers and levy taxes. Among local governmental agencies, the school board was often the only one with major responsibilities for raising and spending public funds.[106]

Outside the South, most community, town, and city school districts were administratively and fiscally independent of other local governments.[107] At the turn of the century, school trustees were popularly elected in twenty-six of the twenty-seven states where the community school district was the basic unit of local educational governance and in ten of the eleven states with town and township school districts. Trustees of community school districts had authority to levy taxes in seventeen states; town and township school committees levied their own taxes in seven states.[108] In big cities, however, city officials commonly had appointive or fiscal authority, or both, over the school board.[109] Among fourteen big cities in 1900 only three – Boston, St Louis, and Pittsburgh – had elected school boards with final authority, subject to state limits on local tax levies, to determine their operating budgets. The school boards of five cities were selected independently of their city's local government – elected in Cleveland, Detroit, Houston, and Los Angeles and appointed by a panel of circuit-court judges in Philadelphia; but the city council or, in Cleveland, city tax commission had final authority to approve operating budgets. In New York, Chicago, Baltimore, and San Francisco the mayor and in Milwaukee the city commission had authority to appoint the members of the school board; and the city council, board of estimates (New York), or board of supervisors (San Francisco) had final authority to approve the school board's operating budget. As for Buffalo, in 1900 it had no school board; its schools were governed directly by city council from 1839 to 1914.

In southern states, in contrast with northeastern, central, and western states, the county was adopted as the principal unit of local educational governance, and school trustees were generally appointed by the governor, state board of education, or county court judges rather than elected. Under the first law for public schools in the southern states, passed in Maryland in 1825, the governor appointed county school boards and the county boards appointed district school boards. The Maryland law was subject to a referendum, which failed to pass, and Maryland remained without any state provision for public instruction until the adoption of the 1864 state constitution and a school law that provided for county boards. State school legislation in North Carolina in 1839 provided for judicial appointment of five to ten county 'superintendents of common schools' to divide their county into school districts, levy school taxes, and allocate state grants; district trustees were elected after 1841.[110] Under Louisiana's first state school law of 1847 the parish, a territorial division equivalent to the county in other states, was chosen as the basic unit of local school governance. Members of county boards were appointed, at first by the governor and later by the state board of education. During the era of Reconstruction, from 1868 to 1877, public instruction in the South was reconstituted on the basis of community or town school districts, long familiar in northeastern and central states and now expanding with the frontier throughout the western territories. During the post-Reconstruction period, however, school districts were subsumed by county unit organization, or by a dual regime of county and city school districts, in South Carolina (1877), Georgia (1887), and Florida (1889), and later in Alabama (1903), Tennessee and Kentucky (1906), Virginia (1927), and West Virginia (1935). District school boards continued to function, but in most cases they were appointed by the county boards and their duties involved minor business carried out under the direction of county officials.[111]

Democratic Principles in the Organization of State Educational Authorities

Four models of political accountability of state superintendents of public education can be found in the nineteenth-century constitutions of northeastern states; none of them made the state superintendent a popularly elected office. First, the governor appointed the state board and the board in turn appointed its 'secretary' in Massachusetts, where the great school promoter Horace Mann was the first secretary (1837–50), and Connecticut, where Henry Barnard introduced 'An Act for the Better Supervision of Common Schools' (passed in 1838) and served as the first state superintendent (1839–43).[112] Second, in the state of New York from 1854 to 1904 the legislature appointed both the Board of Regents and the superintendent of public instruction.[113] Rhode Island's first state school legislation, which was passed in 1845 following an investigation by Henry Barnard, also provided for the state legislative assembly to appoint a state commissioner of education, and Barnard served as the first commissioner (1845–9).[114] Third, after experiments with state boards and superintendents appointed by governors, the legislative assemblies of New Hampshire (1867) and Vermont (1874) settled on nomination of the state superintendent by the governor and election by the state legislature. Fourth, in Maine (1854), Pennsylvania (1857), and New Jersey (1889) the office of state superintendent was established as one appointed by and responsible to the governor.[115]

In central and western states, with the exception of Minnesota, the state superintendent of education was popularly elected.[116] In some cases, notably Indiana (1851) and Illinois (1854), the office was elective from the outset. In other cases, the original constitution of the office followed the eastern models of appointment by the governor or election by the state assembly. For example, under the first Michigan constitution of 1835 the state superintendent of public instruction was appointed by the governor; the constitution of 1850 made the state superintendent an elected official. Ohio elected its first state superintendent in 1837 by a joint resolution of the House and the Senate; in 1840 the duties were reassigned to the secretary of state until a state commissioner of common schools was established as an elective office in 1853. Missouri also started with appointment of the state superintendent by the governor in 1839, switched to having the secretary of state carry out minimal statistical and reporting functions (1841–54), and then returned to appointment by the governor (1854–61) before abolishing the office as an economy measure until the end of the Civil War, when it was restored as elective.

From Iowa in 1846 to Arizona and New Mexico in 1912, twenty states entered the union. Only Kansas among these twenty territories had a territorial superintendent elected by the people on the eve of statehood.[117] Yet, with the exception of Minnesota, the method prescribed in the state constitution in each case was popular election of the state superintendent of education.[118] The common pattern in these states with elected superintendents was an ex officio state board of education comprising the governor, the superintendent, and one or two other officials, such as the secretary of state, treasurer, auditor, or surveyor general, whose functions related to the statistical-reporting, financial-accounting, or land-management activities of local school boards. Later, these ex officio political boards were usually reconstituted as ex officio or appointed professional boards with restricted mandates to advise the superintendent and carry out specific responsibilities.[119]

Only four southern states – Alabama, Kentucky, Louisiana, and North Carolina – made unbroken provision for a separate state superintendent of public instruction before the Civil War; in two of them, Alabama and Kentucky, the superintendent was popularly elected.[120] Under the terms of the Reconstruction Act of 1867, ten states of the former Confederacy had established an office of state superintendent by 1870: directly elected in Alabama, Mississippi, North Carolina, South Carolina, and Texas; elected by the legislature in Arkansas and Virginia; and appointed by the governor in Florida, Georgia, and Louisiana. As conservative Democratic governments returned to power, states that had not already provided for a popularly elected superintendent, with the notable exception of Tennessee, one after the other adopted this model of public accountability.[121]

Whether elected or appointed, the policy-making and administrative authority of state superintendents and state boards of education was restricted in two ways. First, in accordance with nineteenth-century liberal theories of public accountability, the public functions of politics and policy making were assumed to reside in the state legislature; the function of state superintendents and state boards of education was administration. The provisions of state constitutions, not to mention the rivalries and jealousies that resulted from the separation of legislative and executive powers under state constitutions, made it clear that the function of state educational policy making belonged to the legislature. The state superintendent and state board of education were confined to enforcement of laws and implementation of policies that emanated from the state assembly. Second, the authority of state superintendents and state boards of education in the nineteenth century was limited by local democracy. The relative autonomy of local school boards was protected by their financial independence from state authorities and by restrictions on the powers of state authorities. State superintendents and/or state boards of education in most states examined candidates and issued licences to teach. State superintendents and/or boards also had specific powers to prepare and prescribe courses of study, determine textbooks, prescribe rules and regulations for the administration of public schools, and exercise general control and supervision of public schools, but no state officials exercised general powers of administrative control over local school boards.

Neither in political theory nor in administrative practice were local school boards treated as the administrative agents of state educational authorities. Nor were central and local authorities partners in a common enterprise of educational policy making and administration. Rather, they were relatively autonomous authorities, working as public agencies for the most part in separate policy-making and administrative compartments that were defined by state legislative assemblies. State educational authorities and local school boards thus had a relationship of essentially fiscal equivalence, and the greatest challenge for those state authorities who were at all concerned to promote public instruction was persuading local school boards to use their powers to levy taxes, build schools, and hire teachers.

Church and State in American Educational Regimes

The foundations of educational regimes in the United States were consistently and unreservedly liberal in their separation of church and state.[122] None the less, most Americans strongly identified their civic ethos and public institutions as Christian. They rejected the establishment of privileged and exclusive state churches, but they did not intend to disconnect Christianity and public life.

Horace Mann's policy of non-sectarian schools in Massachusetts presented the archetypal rationalization of non-denominational Christianity in American public schools and became a model for the rest of the nation. In 1827, as a member of the Massachusetts state Senate, Mann had voted for a law that prohibited school committees from selecting textbooks favouring any particular religious denomination for use in local public schools. When he became secretary of the Board of Education in 1837, Mann found that this law was being widely disregarded. He immediately implemented a policy of strict enforcement of non-sectarian instruction, insisting that 'The fundamental principles of Christianity may & should be inculcated. This should be done thro' the medium of a proper text-book to prevent abuses. After this, each denomination must be left to its own resources, for inculcating its own faith or creed.'[123] As Norman has observed, 'This was the educational expression of the unofficial "establishment" of national Protestantism in the United States during the nineteenth century.'[124]

The formation of state educational regimes from the 1820s to the 1860s coincided with the arrival of large numbers of Roman Catholic immigrants from Ireland and Germany in the cities of the United States. There they encountered hegemonic Protestant majorities that rejected Roman Catholicism because of its alleged superstitious doctrines and idolatrous worship, subversion of individual rationality and responsibility, and demands for subservience to the spiritual and temporal authority of a foreign sovereign. Doctrinal divisions were accentuated by Protestant fears of job competition and falling wages attributed to an influx of unskilled Irish labourers. Protestant churches that had fought each other bitterly in the early nineteenth century now drew together to oppose what they saw as a common threat to their Protestant and republican America.

Fears that the new Catholic immigrants would receive public funding for their separate denominational schools led Protestant majorities in most states to insert in their state's constitution clauses that prohibited state aid to church schools, either by introducing constitutional amendments, starting with New Jersey in 1844, or by including prohibitions in their first constitutions, as was the case in Michigan (1835) and Wisconsin (1848). As states barred the allocation of public funds to voluntary denominational schools, they also made provision for teaching what Horace Mann had advocated as the 'common core' of Christianity.[125]

Non-denominational Christian religious observance in public schools was thus affirmed as a founding principle of American state educational regimes; it also meant that, however many Roman Catholic children might be forced in practice to attend public schools, Roman Catholics could never accept the founding principles of American public education. The ferocity of anti-Catholic reaction to attempts to open state schools to Catholic teaching turned the Roman Catholic church in the United States towards the task of building an alternative, voluntary Catholic sector, but progress was slow despite increasing pressure from the Vatican.[126] In 1884, at the third plenary council, the hierarchy of the American Catholic church adopted a national educational policy, subsequently approved by Rome, under which a Catholic school would be established in every parish and parents were required to send their children only to these parochial schools. In effect, the third plenary council's edict marked the real beginning of the Catholic school system in the United States.[127] In the early 1840s there were about 200 Catholic elementary schools in the United States and 2,246 in 1880, with an enrolment of 3.9 per cent of all pupils in public and parochial elementary schools. By 1910 there were 5,856 elementary and 1,549 secondary Roman Catholic schools, with 6.4 per cent of total public and private enrolment, and in 1920 there were 6,551 elementary and 1,552 secondary Catholic schools, with 8.3 per cent of total enrolment.

Racial Segregation in the Foundation of American Educational Regimes

Prior to the Civil War, provision for public education in the South was sporadic and impoverished; for African-American children, slave or free, it was non-existent.[128] In the North, African-American children also were regularly excluded from attending the 'common' schools.[129] Smith School was opened in Boston in 1820 as a public primary school for black children, and separate schools for black children were also established in Lowell, Nantucket, New Bedford, Salem, and Worcester as well as Portland (Maine) and Providence. In 1823, acting on a recommendation of the state superintendent of public instruction, the state of New York adopted a policy of organizing separate schools for black children; legislation in 1864 authorized school districts to organize separate schools for black children, provided they were supported in the same manner as schools for white children. Similarly, in Connecticut (1830) and Pennsylvania (1854), local school districts were given authority under state law to establish separate schools for black children. The school laws of Ohio (1829), Indiana (1837), and Illinois (1847) all restricted the common schools to white children and thus relegated African-American children either to separate public schools by state regulation (Ohio) or local option (Illinois) or to non-public charity and mission schools (Indiana). Pressure from abolitionist organizations succeeded in ending separate schools in several towns in New England but not in Providence, or in Boston, where the Boston Primary School Committee's policy of separate schools for black children was upheld in 1849 by the Massachusetts Supreme Judicial Court in *Roberts* v. *City of Boston*. In 1860, 90 per cent of African-American children attending northern schools were segregated in separate schools.[130]

Over the last half of the nineteenth century, *de jure* school segregation was prohibited in northern states. The Massachusetts state legislature abolished separate schools in 1855, and laws banning separate schools were passed in Rhode Island (1866), Connecticut (1868), Illinois (1874), New Jersey and Pennsylvania (1881), and New York (1900). In practice, most African-American children continued to be assigned to segregated schools. The influx of southern black migrants into northern cities, especially after the turn of the century, was accompanied by increasing residential segregation by race. School districts, in turn, reacted to these demographic changes by redrawing attendance areas in order to maximize the separation of black and white children, creating optional attendance zones so that white parents could remove their children from schools with large black populations, and adding upper grades to black primary schools in order to prevent children from these schools being promoted to neighbouring white junior high schools.[131]

As *de jure* segregation of public schools in northern cities became de facto segregation, *de jure* segregation of public schools for black and white students was being established throughout the South. After the Civil War, public schools were racially segregated by law under military government in Florida (1866) and during Reconstruction in Arkansas (1868), North Carolina (1868), and Georgia (1870). In other southern states, as Democrats got control of state governments from Republicans, school laws and state constitutions were altered so as to require black and white children to attend separate schools.[132] Outside the former Confederate states, public schools were segregated by law in Delaware, Kentucky, Maryland, Missouri, West Virginia, and the District of Columbia, and state legislation authorized local authorities to organize separate schools for black and white children in Kansas and Oklahoma.

Beginning from the case of five-year-old Sarah Roberts in 1849, there was a succession of decisions in appellate state courts and federal district courts that cited *Roberts* v. *City of Boston* in upholding segregated schools.[133] State-mandated segregation of schools was upheld by courts in Indiana and Ohio in 1850 and subsequently in California, New York, West Virginia, and Missouri.[134] In making its decision in *Plessy* v. *Ferguson* (1896) to uphold a Louisiana law that mandated 'separate but equal' accommodations in railway trains for black and white passengers, the U.S. Supreme Court explicitly condoned racially segregated public schools.[135] The next year, in *Cumming* v. *School Board of Richmond County, Virginia*, the court allowed a Virginia school, district to close its black high school, and hence left African-American parents with virtually no hope of being able to win a legal claim to equal, even if segregated, public education.[136]

Educational Regimes and the Problem of Public Instruction

Beginning early in the nineteenth century, public instruction as a problem of political economy was focused on the issue of the necessary and proper role of the state in the provision of mass education. Indeed, the very idea of the public sector as it developed in nineteenth-century Anglo-American political thinking was decisively shaped by prevailing opinion about the state's obligations with regard to public instruction.

Generally, there was consensus that public instruction should be restricted in its scope to elementary schooling, cheap in its claim on public (and private) resources, and practical in its content, with a curriculum centred on teaching basic skills of reading, writing, and arithmetic and rudimentary knowledge of national literature, history, and geography. Everywhere, however, there were profound ideological differences and fierce political conflicts over the religious content of public instruction and the distribution of the benefits of public instruction by denominational affiliation. These ideological differences and political conflicts also extended to the relationship of church and state in the governance of public instruction. By the middle of the nineteenth century, three types of educational regimes had been developed that attempted to resolve the issue of church and state in the provision and governance of public instruction. By the 1890s a choice among the three regimes had been made in each of the Anglo-American educational jurisdictions, and in different places each type of regime survived to structure educational provision and governance into the second half of the twentieth century.

One type of educational regime designed to deal with the problem of public instruction with only incremental change was based on public subsidy of elementary schools that were owned and operated by church authorities, religious communities, and voluntary societies such as the British and Foreign School Society, the National Society for Promoting the Education of the Poor in the Principles of the Established Church, and the Society for the Propagation of the Gospel. Public authorities – the Treasury, Education Department, secretary for Scotland, Commissioners of National Education in Ireland, governors of British colonies, central boards of education – allocated grants to support the building and maintaining of voluntary denominational and non-denominational schools. Against the nineteenth-century liberal theory of parliamentary government and ministerial responsibility, communitarian conservatives, who defended the authority of the church in educational governance, advocated an institutional separation of educational policy from partisan politics. In Great Britain, where liberal theory had the strongest impact on early institutional design, central educational governance was assigned to a committee of the Privy Council. In the colonies, the central state agency for governing public instruction typically was an independent board of education, comprising representatives of both church and state, whose prime responsibility was allocating the block grant for public instruction approved annually by the legislature.[137] If common educational policies were needed, these were reached by a process of collective agreement among the major denominations represented on the central board. Communitarian conservatives assumed, however, that for the most part the need for interdenominational policies and the demand for public accountability were minimal. Consequently, the content and organization of instruction, including the crucial choice of religious instruction and observance, were decided by each school's governors or sponsors.

In the first half of the nineteenth century, versions of this type of educational regime were initiated by public grants to church and voluntary schools in England and Wales, Scotland, and the colonies of Australia, British North America, and New Zealand. In addition, although started as a regime of public subsidy for non-denominational schools, by the middle of the nineteenth century the Irish national system in practice had evolved into a regime of public subsidy for church schools. By the end of the nineteenth century, however, denominational educational regimes based exclusively on public subsidy of sectarian schools were surviving only in Ireland, Newfoundland, and Quebec.

The second type of educational regime attempted to resolve the issues of religion in the curricula and governance of public instruction by establishing complementary sectors of church and state schools. Church schools continued to be managed by their communal governors or sponsors and to be free to disseminate their distinctive sectarian doctrines; but in return for state funding, they increasingly yielded the secular elements of their curricula and provisions for school governance to direction from, and accountability to, public educational authorities. Complementing this sector of church schools was a sector of state elementary schools that were non-denominational in their religious instruction and observances and managed by local boards of trustees whose members usually were elected by local ratepayers. Initially governed by central boards comprising civic and clerical notables who were government appointees, in the second half of the nineteenth century these dual regimes of church and state schools generally became governed centrally by departments of education headed by a minister of public instruction who was responsible to the legislature, or by a council of public instruction comprising members of cabinet. In contrast with the communal autonomy that was characteristic of denominational educational regimes, central education departments in dual regimes of church and state schools were more assertive in creating curricular frameworks for public instruction, setting standards for students' attainments and teachers' qualifications, and making regulations for school buildings and maintenance.

Versions of this type of dual educational regime with complementary sectors of church and state schools were operative in several provinces of New Zealand between 1852 and 1877; each of the colonies of Australia variously between 1848 and 1893; in the Maritime provinces (de facto), Ontario, and the North-West Territories in Canada; and in England and Wales and Scotland in the British Isles. Devised as compromises between communitarian conservatives, and liberal conservatives, dual regimes were subjected to increasing attack by utilitarian liberals, who insisted on both direct accountability for the provision of public services to elected representatives of the people and rigorous separation of church and state in public policy. By the end of the nineteenth century, dual regimes had been terminated in Australia and New Zealand, but educational regimes based on providing public instruction through complementary sectors of state and church schools remained the chosen means for the provision and governance of public instruction in England and Wales, Scotland, and six of nine Canadian provinces.

The third type of Anglo-American educational regime was based on the classical liberal principle of strict separation between church and state in the provision and governance of public instruction. In the United States there were no nineteenth-century experiments with public subsidy of church schools or complementary sectors of state and church schools as there were in Australia, Canada, New Zealand, and the United Kingdom. From the outset, educational regimes in the United States were founded on the principle of providing state funding solely to public schools. Subsequently, New Zealand, the six colonies of Australia, and the Canadian provinces of British Columbia and Manitoba also adopted regimes of public instruction that excluded private schools from receiving state aid.

Under these regimes of public instruction that authorized state funding only to public schools, private schools were conceded to be legitimate providers of elementary (and secondary) education; but, because they were not open equally to all children regardless of denomination, insisted on teaching their distinctive denominational doctrines, or refused to teach state-approved curricula, such schools were not entitled to state grants. Public instruction was provided primarily through elementary schools that were owned and operated as public institutions subject to state control and accountability. On the crucial issue of religious instruction in public schools, in order to maximize attendance in public schools and at the same time protect minority rights, utilitarian liberals held that religious education could, and should, be separated from instruction in other subjects and excluded from the curriculum of public schools. Liberal conservatives were equally committed to the inseparability of religion and public life, but they believed that basic religious and moral principles could be articulated and taught independently of denominational doctrines. In the liberal-conservative view, public instruction should be non-denominational, imparting common religious principles and beliefs while excluding the doctrines and liturgies of particular denominations. Denominational instruction would be provided at home or in church, but it also might be given at school outside the official curriculum during released time or in extra classes before or after school. With the notable exception of South Australia, these liberal-conservative ideas on non-denominational religious instruction and observances generally prevailed in the Anglo-American regimes that were based on separation of church and state.

In the ideal model of regimes for public instruction that confined state aid to public schools, educational jurisdictions were divided between central and local educational authorities, both of which were popularly elected. In practice, however, these regimes varied greatly in the relative importance of central versus local educational authorities and in their legal requirements for direct versus indirect electoral responsibility of educational officials. At one extreme, the Australian colonies created regimes of public instruction that were governed from the centre according to the principles of ministerial responsibility and bureaucratic administration, with a restricted, and steadily declining, role for local school trustees. At the other extreme, in the educational regimes of the central and western regions of the United States, both state superintendents and local trustees were popularly elected and educational decision making was dominated by local school boards. Between these polar types, the regimes of the northeastern United States, as well as Minnesota, combined elected local school boards with appointed state superintendents who were responsible either directly to the governor or state legislative assembly or indirectly to the governor through an appointed state board of education. Making allowance for the constitutional differences between parliamentary government and the separation of powers, this is also the type of regime that was operative in New Zealand from 1877 to the First World War. Yet another variant was instituted in the southern states of the United States, sprung from a union of communitarian-conservative tenacity on racial segregation and utilitarian-liberal pressures of American democracy, which combined popularly elected but weak state superintendents with county school boards variously appointed by the governor, state board of education, or county councils.[138]

By the end of the nineteenth century, public instruction had become a major enterprise of Anglo-American governments. Government expenditures on public instruction approximated 1 per cent of gross domestic product (Figure 1; Table 1) and varied from 5 per cent of total government expenditures in Australia to 14 per cent in the United States (Figure 3; Table 3). In the 1890s, full-time teachers constituted 0.6 to 0.9 per cent of the labour force in Australia, New Zealand, and the United Kingdom, and they were an even more important component (1.4 to 1.6 per cent) of the labour force in Canada and the United States (Figure 5; Table 6). Statistics on government employment at the end of the nineteenth century are missing for Canada and New Zealand, but Figure 6 and Table 7 do suggest that there was a clear separation between Canada and the United States, where teachers comprised 36 per cent of total government employment; Great Britain with teachers at 14 to 16 per cent of government employees; and New Zealand and Australia, where 8 per cent of government employees were teachers. The commitment of governments to spending per student on public instruction in comparison with spending per capita on other public functions was still rising at the turn of the century in Canada, the United Kingdom, and the United States, but it had stabilized in Australia and had even begun to fall in New Zealand (Figure 4; Table 4). Even so, government expenditures per student, which were running at 5 to 7 per cent of gross domestic product per capita across the Anglo-American democracies, implied a relatively consistent societal commitment to public instruction relative to national wealth (Figure 2; Table 2).

By the end of the nineteenth century, public instruction was very much the dominant form of elementary and secondary education. Enrolments in private schools in the mid-1890s were 8.4 per cent of total enrolments in elementary and secondary education in the United States, 9.8 per cent in New Zealand, and 18.6 per cent in Australia (Table 10).[139] In public schools, classes were relatively large, bespeaking the general expectation for efficiency in the delivery of public instruction, but the ratio of enrolments to full-time teachers varied markedly in the mid-1890s from 36.2 in the United States and 40 in Canada to 50.3 in New Zealand, 58.8 in the United Kingdom, and 66.9 in Australia (Figure 7; Table 8). Public instruction was also designed and implemented primarily as elementary education. Enrolments in the secondary grades nine to twelve in the United States, for example, were only 1.6 per cent of the total of elementary and secondary enrolments in public schools in 1889–90, rising to 3.5 per cent by the turn of the century. In New Zealand, 1.9 per cent of students in public primary, Maori village, and grant-aided schools were enrolled in secondary schools in 1895, while in England

and Wales 1.8 per cent of total enrolments in state and grant-aided schools in 1904–5 were secondary students, and in Scotland, 2.6 per cent.[140]

What does this pattern of educational regimes reveal about the state of Anglo-American democracy during the era of public instruction, and what were the legacies of these regimes for the development of Anglo-American democracy in the twentieth century? Two opposing visions of mass education contended for control of the design and regulation of public instruction throughout most of the nineteenth century. Both had deeply flawed conceptions of community, justice, and liberty, and hence severely restricted understandings of the meaning and practice of democracy.

On one side, liberals advocated the exclusion of private schools from state funding, in part because they saw common public schooling as the foundation of emerging political democracy (including serving as a defence against the dangers of democracy), in part because concentrating enrolments in public schools promised economies of scale necessary for cheapness and efficiency in the supply of mass education. Yet the liberal principles of religious tolerance and strict separation of church and state in the provision and governance of public instruction – regarded as essential for both freedom of individual conscience and cheapness of public financing – totally in principle and extensively in practice excluded from the benefits of state-supported public instruction the children of those committed to denominational religious instruction and observance, principally Roman Catholics.

On the other side, although there were exceptions, such as the restriction of public grants to Roman Catholic schools in Southern Ireland or to Presbyterian schools in the New Zealand province of Otago, educational regimes based on classical conservative ideas about public subsidy of church schools were generally more inclusive, at least with regard to the major divide between Protestants and Roman Catholics. Under denominational regimes, however, while instruction in elementary schools might be publicly financed, its purpose was not the creation of a national identity or unified public. Children in school were segmented primarily by their denominational communities, not united by their common school. Imparting communal identity, not civic nationalism, was the overriding priority of elementary school in denominational regimes. Hence, denominational educational regimes lacked any fundamental concept of a people as a community with a shared political identity and unifying public interests.

Nor did compromises between liberals and conservatives in the form of educational regimes based on complementary sectors of church and state schools resolve the dilemma. As with the denominational regimes of Ireland, Newfoundland, and Quebec, dual regimes were inclusive, at least with respect to the consequential divide between Protestants and Roman Catholics. In practice, however, the political compromises between conservatives and liberals were so fiercely contested that, in their aftermath, sectors of state and church schools inevitably remained sharply divided and deeply distrustful. In such an emotive political environment, any integrating vision of public instruction for a religiously pluralistic, democratic society was impossible to expect; but, because they were founded on the idea of state schools serving the public interest, with separate or reserved schools to protect the denominational minority, dual regimes appeared to have a certain potential for accommodating democracy and pluralism. Even so, the question remained whether anyone except for liberal conservatives (or conservative liberals) could find such a regime legitimate and just for the long term.

2 Industrial Efficiency

In the late nineteenth and early twentieth centuries, élite opinion in each of the Anglo-American countries became fixated on industrial efficiency. Material prosperity and national security were identified with maximizing economic productivity and surpassing international rivals. The new imperative of national industrial efficiency inspired demands for reforms that would fit public education to the needs and opportunities of an industrial economy. The main purpose of public education was no longer simply the elementary schooling of virtuous citizens and/or believing Christians; it must now include assigning young people to occupational classes and supplying them with appropriate vocational training. The attention of educational policy makers shifted accordingly from elementary to secondary education, which was seen to be more relevant for teaching basic knowledge and skills specific to different occupational classes. By the early twentieth century, public provision for secondary education had become the prime focus of educational policy making in the Anglo-American countries, with the debate concentrated on four major issues of secondary school organization and curricular design.

The first issue concerned the relative size of the private and public sectors and the respective roles of private and public schools. Secondary education in the nineteenth century was provided through an assortment of grammar schools, public and private academies, and higher grades in elementary schools, but the dominant providers were mostly institutions in the private or voluntary sector. Public policy that aimed to expand the provision of secondary education could continue to rely on the private sector by reforming existing legislation that regulated the incorporation of voluntary secondary schools and by increasing public grants to encourage their establishment and maintenance under local trustees or managers. Alternatively, it could shift public regulation and resources to building secondary schools in the public sector, or pursue a strategy of joint public and private provision.

A second issue was the degree of fit between the curricula of secondary schools and the structure of occupational classes in an industrial economy. Secondary education in the nineteenth century varied from the classical tradition of grammar schools through the modern curriculum of academies to the practical subjects of higher elementary schools, but the focus in all institutions was academic education. Setting industrial efficiency as the national priority raised the question of reorganizing secondary schools and redesigning their curricula to correspond to the educational requirements of major occupational classes of an industrial economy. Separate academic, commercial, industrial, agricultural, and domestic science curricula were advocated in order to meet the arguably different educational requirements of professionals and managers, clerical and sales employees, trades and industrial workers, farmers and farm labourers, and housewives. Public debate focused on the appropriate balance between academic and vocational education in public secondary schools and the organizational effectiveness of specialized academic and vocational secondary schools versus multilateral secondary schools that offered parallel academic and vocational programs within the same school.

Third, proposals to expand secondary education in the public sector reopened issues of educational governance concerning the role of central authorities in the design of secondary educational policy and the reorganization of local educational authorities to provide for effective and efficient secondary schools. Central educational authorities acquired a new mandate to pursue the priority of industrial efficiency and the national interest in the organization and design of secondary education. At the same time, relative to elementary education, the quality of secondary education was much more dependent on school size; larger schools could support more extensive course offerings and more specialized teachers. The higher costs of secondary education, especially for vocational training, threatened to exacerbate inequalities between wealthy, populous local educational authorities and small, poor school districts that had been formed to maintain elementary schools. Hence, the shift in priorities to secondary education was accompanied by a vigorous, often rancorous, debate about the need to reorganize elementary school districts to fit the requirements of secondary education, expand financing by central educational authorities to compensate for inequalities of district wealth and population, and strengthen the capacity of central educational authorities to dominate policy and regulate administration. Taken together, these issues of district reorganization, educational finance, and policy mandate fundamentally challenged arrangements for educational governance that had been institutionalized in the foundation of Anglo-American educational regimes.

Fourth, the expansion of secondary education reopened the issue of the relationship between church and state in the provision of public education. The role of central educational authorities in redesigning secondary education to promote industrial efficiency renewed and extended the challenge of state versus church authorities for control of educational policy. At stake were, first, the central purpose of education as the promotion of industrial efficiency versus sectarian indoctrination and, second, the design of the curriculum around occupational selection and vocational training rather than religious instruction and observance. In addition, reorganization into larger school districts seemed certain to result in more heterogeneous school districts and hence threatened to undermine local accommodations on religious instruction and observance in public schools.

Just as the issues of educational regime foundations were given distinctive ideological expression during the nineteenth century, so the problem of industrial efficiency in secondary school organization and curriculum was given competing ideological analysis, critique, and prescription at the turn of the century. Similarly, just as the foundation of educational regimes varied in principle and practice among the Anglo-American countries, so did their policies to reorganize and reform secondary education for the purpose of industrial efficiency. From right to left, the fundamental ideological divisions over industrial efficiency and secondary education focused on the relative importance of public versus private institutions, the subject matter of secondary schooling, the class structure of school organization, and the meaning of equality with regard to the accessibility of secondary education.[1]

On the right, communitarian and liberal conservatives sought to preserve an organization of secondary education that was class specific, class divisive, and for the most part class confirming, but they disagreed with regard to what should be the curricula of class-specific schools in an industrial economy.[2] Communitarian conservatives resisted the incursion of vocational education into the traditional academic curriculum. Liberal conservatives promoted not only the expansion of scientific and technical education but also the establishment of vocational secondary schools as working-class counterparts to academic secondary schools.

In the centre, utilitarian and ethical liberals pressed for secondary education that would be neither class confirming nor class divisive; they disagreed with regard to the need for class-specific secondary education. Utilitarian liberals were more inclined than conservatives to recognize a larger body of academically talented students, to let the preferences of qualified students determine the distribution of places in class-specific secondary programs, and to combine class-specific programs in multilateral schools so as to alleviate the class-divisive effects of class-specific secondary schools. Ethical liberals, by contrast, rejected class-specific secondary education in favour of integrated academic and vocational education in comprehensive secondary schools.

On the left, socialists conceded the existence of class-specific and class-divisive secondary school organization and curricula but disagreed on whether they were also necessarily class confirming. Within an entrenched, class-based educational regime, which they regarded fatalistically as unjust but inescapable in a capitalist economy, both social democrats and democratic socialists pressed for bloc-regarding equality that would rectify the quantitative and qualitative deficiencies of educational provision for the children of working-class parents. Social democrats concentrated their efforts on promoting vocational secondary schools as institutions dedicated to the educational interest of the working class, however, while democratic socialists advanced much more radical plans for equalizing opportunities for talented working-class children to maximize their educational potential and overcome the class divisions of capitalism.

Australia: Liberal-Conservative Regimes with Centralized Bureaucratic Administration

During the first decade of the twentieth century, there was a marked shift in the language used to express the purposes of public education in Australia. Following his visit to Canada and the United States in 1902, Peter Board, the director of education for New South Wales, emphasized the priority of 'education for industrial progress.' The director of education for South Australia, Alfred Williams, while attending the Imperial Conference on Education in 1907, advocated 'education for social efficiency.' Frank Tate stressed the linkage between 'national progress and educational efficiency' in his 1908 report as director of education for Victoria. C.A.P. Andrews, the Western Australian director, spoke at the

1911 Imperial Conference on Education of the need to create 'an articulated system of education,' and J.D. Story in 1914 described the goal of Queensland's public schools as 'education for national efficiency.'[3]

This convergence of educational purpose was the result of similar thinking about the perceived shortcomings of public education in Australia and the requirements for its reform. The regimes of public instruction established in the nineteenth century had aimed to give rudimentary elementary schooling; secondary education remained essentially an exclusive sector, the preserve of private denominational and non-denominational grammar schools.[4] The goals of 'industrial progress,' 'social efficiency,' 'national efficiency,' and 'national progress' required changes to deepen and diversify the civic education of public elementary schools to reflect the more demanding and complex requirements of an industrial economy. Equally if not more important, secondary education could no longer be left to educational institutions outside the public sector. Nor could it be limited to an academic course leading to university and the professions. The public sector had to develop secondary educational courses to prepare young people for entering a diversity of occupations in industry, commerce, and agriculture.

Ideas and Institutions for Public Secondary Education

The Australian designers of public secondary education for industrial efficiency did not aim to supplant the private sector of independent grammar schools. Public secondary schools would provide an alternative route to higher education and professional occupations, but only for a minority of students; their primary function would be vocational education for working-class children. According to the 1901 report of the Victoria Royal Commission on Technical Education, chaired by Theodore Fink, 'The class of students for whom provision would be made by [public] continuation schools would be largely the children of the working classes, who will ultimately have to support themselves by manual work; and the instruction afforded would differ distinctly from secondary education, which has for its main object the training of young men for the professions. As a matter of fact, only a very small proportion of the boys attending the state schools can ever reach the secondary school, or the University.'[5] Frank Tate, the Victoria director of education who was responsible for designing the Victoria Education Act of 1910, admired the academic curriculum of independent grammar schools but thought it was too literary for state schools, which should educate working-class children to serve industrial progress.[6] Peter Board in New South Wales saw education in industrial society as being caught in a dilemma between the technical division of labour, which required a managerial élite to direct the technically skilled mass, and the requirements of modern citizenship, which imposed civic responsibilities on the masses while endowing them with widespread leisure that offered scope for acquiring cultivated tastes.[7] State policies had to give a common education to all young people as citizens, as well as equal opportunities for the discovery of individual interests and tastes. Not all young people were equally potential recruits for commerce, industry, home making, and the professions, however; and pupils should be grouped in secondary education together on the basis of their future occupational classes.

Based on the common assumption that public education was preparatory for either 'intellectual' or 'manual' work and that school organization should correspond to this dichotomy of occupational classes, the development of public secondary education in Australia between the turn of the century and the Second World War varied in particulars among the states but was remarkably uniform in spirit and structure. From the qualifying examinations at the end of elementary school, there were essentially two tracks.[8] The academic track, usually with a commercial option, was laid through state high schools where the curricula of arts, science, and commercial subjects were rigidly constrained by the requirements of public external examinations. Alternatively, intermediate high schools (New South Wales, Tasmania) or higher elementary schools (South Australia, Victoria, Western Australia) offered general and commercial courses leading to the intermediate examination for pupils aged twelve to fifteen, after which they would transfer to a high school or leave school. The vocational track was laid through junior technical schools (Victoria, Tasmania), superior public schools (New South Wales), and central schools (South Australia, Western Australia) that variously offered commercial, industrial, domestic science, and agricultural courses and qualified their successful pupils for entry to technical and trade schools.[9] A partial exception, in structure if not in spirit, was Queensland. There, secondary education continued to be dominated by the scholarship examination taken at the end of elementary school that paid tuition fees for the winners to either state-endowed grammar schools or independent (mainly church) secondary schools. A 1912 act that provided for state high schools offering general, commercial, and domestic science courses resulted in the establishment both of multilateral schools in country towns where there were no grammar schools and of separate general, commercial, industrial, and domestic science high schools in Brisbane.

Passage through public secondary schools was strictly controlled in each state by competitive qualifying examinations conducted by an independent public authority. During the nineteenth century, Australian universities conducted their own examinations for entrance to university, as well as intermediate secondary examinations (Sydney beginning in 1867, Adelaide beginning in 1887), and in the case of Adelaide, even entrance examinations to secondary schools. Promotion within public elementary schools was determined by departmental inspectors, who visited each school annually and formally assessed both pupils and teachers. As secondary schools and courses were developed, external examinations were reorganized. Formal examination of pupils by departmental inspectors was ended in all states between 1902 (Western Australia) and 1913 (South Australia). In each state, external examinations were established at the pre-entry, intermediate, and leaving grades of secondary school, and in all states except for Tasmania, administration of external examinations was transferred from the universities to boards of public examiners that comprised representatives of the state university, the department of education, and registered independent schools.[10] State departments of education conducted examinations and issued certificates for pupils completing post-primary vocational courses that did not lead to an intermediate or leaving examination, but these vocational certificates had little status compared to the intermediate and leaving certificates. In New South Wales, for example, the commercial course in superior public schools was extended from two to three years in 1917 so that pupils could sit for the intermediate certificate. When the domestic science and industrial courses were similarly extended in 1925, the superior school certificate was dropped, and in 1932 superior public schools were officially reclassified as intermediate high schools.[11]

Over the first half of the twentieth century, Australian state high schools were selective at the point of entry, and they remained highly selective throughout their curriculum. Compared to Canada and the United States, where there was a rapid expansion of secondary enrolments from the 1910s to the 1940s towards parity with enrolments in elementary education, in Australia enrolments in public secondary education remained relatively low as a proportion of total enrolments in public schools, and they were overwhelmingly concentrated in the lower secondary years, with only a small minority proceeding past the intermediate to the leaving certificate. Private secondary schools continued to be the predominant institutions for delivering upper secondary education. In the mid-1940s, New South Wales was the only state where the majority of matriculating students came from public secondary schools.[12]

Executive Leadership, Bureaucratic Administration, and Organized Teachers

A key change in the governance of public education in Australia in the late nineteenth and early twentieth centuries was the appointment of professional educators as administrative heads of state departments of education or public instruction. The acts that set up state departments of education in South Australia (1878) and Tasmania (1885) had recognized the office of inspector general as administrative head and, in the case of Tasmania, changed the title of the office to director of education. In Victoria (1872), Queensland (1875), New South Wales (1880), Tasmania (1885), and Western Australia (1893), however, the new departments of education or public instruction were placed under the direction of an undersecretary, who managed the small clerical staff. The chief inspector or inspector general, who was head of the corps of school inspectors, reported to the minister through the undersecretary. When Cyril Jackson was appointed as inspector general in Western Australia in 1897, he demanded direct access to the minister, and the inspector general was made administrative head of the Education Department. The Fink commission strongly criticized the designation of an administrative officer as head of the Victoria department to whom the inspector general was subordinate. Under the 1901 Education Act, the office of inspector general was renamed director of education, recognized as head of the department, and given wide authority to determine the organization and duties of inspectors, office staff, and teachers. Commissioners G.H. Knibbs and J.W. Turner made the same criticism in their report on education in New South Wales, and the inspector general, renamed director of education, was made head of the Department of Public Instruction in 1905. J.D. Story, who dominated education in Queensland as undersecretary (1905–19), was a former chief clerk, but thereafter the office of undersecretary, which was renamed director of education and undersecretary in 1928, was held by men with lengthy experience as teachers and inspectors.[13] Thus, with the exception of Story, who indeed proved the rule by making himself into a professional educational administrator, all of the directors of education who led the reform of Australian education in the early twentieth century were professional educators with impressive careers as teachers, inspectors, and heads of teachers' training colleges prior to their appointment as director of education.

The formal organization of departments of education was modified to reflect the diversification of state educational activities. From the simple functional division between inspectors and clerical staff that character-ized departments in the late nineteenth century, superintendents (chief inspector in Victoria) of technical education were appointed in each state, and the functions of superintendence and inspection were sepa-rated between primary and secondary education. In Victoria, for exam-ple, following the recommendations of the Fink commission, the 1901 reorganization created the offices of chief inspector and assistant chief inspector for primary schools, a chief inspector of technical education was appointed in 1911, and in 1914 Tate appointed Martin Hansen (subsequently director, 1928–31) as the first chief inspector of secondary schools. In New South Wales, based on the recommendations of the Knibbs–Turner commission, G.H. Knibbs was appointed as the first superintendent of technical education in 1905, and when he resigned the next year, J.W. Turner replaced him. An inspector of secondary schools was appointed in the chief inspector's branch in 1911, and in 1920 separate offices of chief inspector were established for primary and secondary schools. Similarly, the 1915 Education Act in South Australia provided for a tripartite reorganization of the department under super-intendents of primary, secondary, and technical education. Superin-tendents of technical education were also appointed in Western Australia (1907), Queensland (1908), and Tasmania (1918), but in these three states separate primary and secondary branches were not organized until the 1940s.[14]

Teachers' salaries and working conditions were determined through a complex process of collective bargaining that involved departmental officials, teachers' unions, public service boards, and industrial arbitra-tion courts. Initially, teachers were employees of the state departments of education. Their recruitment, assignment, classification, promotion, and discipline were determined by the departments of education. Salaries were based on schemes of payment by results under which teachers were paid according to the number of their pupils who passed departmental inspection. Not surprisingly, centralization of policy and administration related to teachers' salaries, career development, and working conditions fostered the formation of state-wide organizations to protect collective interests. Between 1878 (Victorian State School Teachers' Union) and 1905 (Tasmanian Teachers' Federation), teachers' unions were formed in each state.[15] Over the same period, the merit principle was being introduced into state civil services, public service boards or commissioners were emerging as powerful central agencies of administrative and financial control, and industrial arbitration courts were being established as a distinctive Australian instrument for resolving collective bargaining disputes through independent arbitration proceedings that heard and judged the conflicting claims of employees and employers.

The general pattern of teachers' salary determination involved negotiations between senior officers of the department of education and representatives of the state teachers' union. Differences over the salary schedule that were not resolved through bipartite negotiations might then be referred for public hearing and arbitration to an industrial court, but practices varied among the states.[16] In Queensland, for example, the Industrial Arbitration Act was passed in 1916; and the next year the salary agreement reached between the Department of Public Instruction and the Queensland Teachers' Union was registered with the state industrial court. Thereafter, as with the salaries of other state civil servants, the salary schedule of the teaching service was fixed by reference to the industrial court. In Western Australia, by contrast, teachers avoided going to the state arbitration court because of the existence of an appeal board, set up under the Public Service Appeal Board Act (1920), that comprised representatives of the department and the union as members and a judge of the Supreme Court presiding.

Appointments, promotions, and discipline of teachers were similarly governed by quasi-corporatist institutions and procedures. Beginning in 1903, two teachers sat on the appointments advisory committee that dealt with appointments, transfers, and promotions of teachers in New South Wales. In Victoria the Teachers Act of 1905 provided for a classification committee comprising the chief inspector, a head teacher, and an appointee of the public service commissioner to prepare a promotions list and recommend appointments and transfers. In South Australia a teachers' classification board was provided under the 1915 Education Act. When the teaching service was removed from direct authority of the Queensland department in 1922, the public service commissioner assumed authority over appointments, transfers, promotions, and dismissals; but decisions of the public service commissioner (who was J.D. Story until 1939) could be appealed to a board comprising a magistrate, an appointee of the public service commissioner, and a representative of the Queensland Teachers' Union. Similarly, decisions of classification boards could be appealed to the public service board in New South Wales, the public service commissioner in Victoria, or the public service appeal board in Western Australia. Tasmania was an exception to this trend to regulate teachers by state public service boards. The Tasmanian teaching service continued to be employed under the Education Act until 1973; there was a classification committee representing teachers and the department and a disciplinary appeals tribunal, but no promotions appeal tribunal until 1966.

Rationalization of state educational governance as centralized bureaucratic administration left no significant role for local educational authorities. Tasmania was the first state to abolish its boards of advice; in 1907 the functions of the boards were transferred to municipal councils.[17] The Victoria Education Act of 1910 replaced boards of advice with school committees elected for each school by parents, and their activities were restricted to routine administration and maintenance such as interior decoration and the improvement of grounds. Local advisory boards in South Australia were replaced by school committees in 1915, and in Western Australia, where district boards were abolished in 1922, legislative recognition was given to the organization of parents' and citizens' associations to augment amenities for individual schools.[18] Finally, in 1936 an amendment to the Public Instruction Act in New South Wales authorized the formation of a parents' and citizens' association in each state school to promote the interests of the school by bringing parents, citizens, students, and teaching staff into close cooperation; to assist in providing equipment and promoting the recreation and welfare of the pupils of the school; when requested, to advise the minister of public instruction on the material requirements of the school; and to work with the teaching staff in public functions associated with the school. Public school boards, which had long since passed into desuetude, were replaced by district councils, comprising two representatives of each parents' and citizens' association in the area, 'for the purposes only of advancing the common interests of state schools in that area' by assisting teaching staff and departmental officials when required with raising scholarship funds, implementing transportation arrangements, and improving school libraries.

Canada and Newfoundland: The Institutional Ambivalence of Liberal-Conservative Reform

The leading advocate of educational reform for industrial efficiency in Canada was John Seath, superintendent of education for Ontario. Commissioned in 1909 to design a system of technical education, Seath introduced his plan by observing that 'the problem of Education for Industrial Purposes has engaged the attention of almost every country in Europe and almost every state of the Union, as well as of almost every province of our own Dominion.' There were three reasons for the present importance of the problem: rivalry among the nations for commercial supremacy, imperfect provision for training skilled workers, and the need to extend the scope of state education to include vocational as well as cultural training. 'Of the foregoing causes the most potent is the keen rivalry amongst the nations for the control or at best a due share of the markets of the world – a rivalry which is continually being intensified by increasing facilities for communication and transportation.'[19] As the idea of reforming secondary education to promote industrial efficiency gained ground in the early twentieth century, everywhere in Canada, except for Quebec and Newfoundland, two related but distinct approaches to secondary educational reform were advanced.

First, in concert with business interests and organized labour, educational reformers who wanted to reorganize public instruction to fit the needs of occupational selection for an industrial economy campaigned for vocational secondary education as an alternative to academic secondary education. They focused on the organization of secondary education in city school districts, and their preferred model was a partite system in which specialized vocational secondary schools were educational institutions separate from conventional academic high schools.[20]

Second, as enrolments in academic high schools continued to expand, educational reformers who were concerned to adapt the secondary curriculum to fit the needs of mass education pressed their case to develop a general secondary program as an alternative to the traditional academic program. Essentially, these reformers proposed to combine academic and general programs in bilateral secondary schools. These very different types of secondary school organization each claimed to secure educational effectiveness and efficiency; both incorporated a different concept of educational justice from the lot-regarding equality of uniform secondary organization and curriculum.

Ideas and Institutions of Mass Secondary Education for Industrial Efficiency: Uniform Academic Courses versus Vocational and General Courses

The regimes of public instruction established in Canada and Newfoundland from the 1840s to the 1870s soon raised as a matter of public policy the organizational relationship between elementary and secondary schools. In the educational regimes of the Maritimes, Protestant Quebec, Ontario, and the West, elementary and secondary schools were incrementally reorganized as vertically integrated public institutions. In the Maritimes and Ontario, direct state aid for private schools was terminated as all grammar schools and many academies were incorporated into the public educational regime. Similarly, Protestant school boards in Quebec took over existing academies as well as establishing new high schools. In the western provinces, where there was no tradition of grammar schools and academies, secondary schools were founded from the outset as public institutions. The curriculum of these public high schools was overwhelmingly academic. Courses of study were designed to prepare students for entrance to arts, science, law, medicine, and engineering programs at colleges and universities or to teacher training at provincial normal schools. Core subjects invariably included English language, composition, and literature; British, Canadian, and ancient history; Latin, Greek, and French or German; arithmetic, mathematics, algebra, and geometry; and natural sciences. Optional subjects by the turn of the century commonly included bookkeeping, household science, and manual training, but their orientation also was academic rather than practical, giving them little if any vocational value.[21]

In the educational regimes of Roman Catholic Quebec and Newfoundland, by contrast, private denominational colleges with the aid of state grants preserved their hegemony over secondary education. Until the four-year, terminal cours primaire supérieur was introduced in 1929, Roman Catholic school boards in Quebec made no provision for postelementary education. Secondary education was exclusively the realm of classical colleges founded and maintained – initially without state assistance – by Roman Catholic orders. Their independence from state educational authorities in making decisions about their curricula, methods of instruction, and teaching personnel was long and firmly established. Similarly in Newfoundland, the confessional organization of colonial education was based on a split between mass elementary education in school districts organized throughout the province and élite secondary education in denominational academies or colleges located in St John's. Offering both elementary and secondary education, the colleges functioned as day schools for children of the St John's commercial and professional élite and as boarding schools for children of prosperous outport merchants.

Not surprisingly, given John Seath's ideas and leadership, Ontario had by far the most developed system of specialist vocational high schools. Based on Seath's extensive survey of vocational education in the United States and Europe, the Industrial Education Act of 1911 provided for general industrial training for early school-leavers, establishment of technical schools or technical departments in high schools, and provincial grants for both day and evening technical classes. Under the provisions of the 1911 act, there were eleven technical and industrial day schools operating in Ontario by 1918 and sixty-two in 1939.[22] Enrolments in technical secondary courses reached 30 per cent of total secondary enrolments between the wars.[23] Elsewhere in Canada, there were only two separate vocational high schools in the Maritimes, both resulting from New Brunswick's Vocational Education Act of 1918, and none in Quebec; but in the four western provinces there were vocational high schools in the main urban centres – Winnipeg in Manitoba; Regina, Saskatoon, and Moose Jaw in Saskatchewan; Calgary, Edmonton, and Lethbridge in Alberta; and Vancouver, Victoria, New Westminster, and Trail in British Columbia.

In addition to developing specialist vocational schools, Ontario and the West introduced curricula that differentiated among academic, general, and vocational education. In Ontario, for example, the regulations for secondary school programs were revised to recognize seven programs: matriculation, normal school entrance, general, commercial, manual training, household science, and agriculture. Significantly, the most controversial changes were the separation of matriculation from normal school entrance and dropping Latin and a modern language as compulsory for normal school entrance.[24] A major revision of Alberta's curriculum in 1922 provided for six courses: normal school entrance, university matriculation, agricultural, commercial, technical, and general. When British Columbia's curriculum was restructured in 1929–30, the new credit system differentiated between a university program that required provincial departmental examinations and restricted students to 6 to 12 elective credits out of 120 and a general program that had no external examinations, required a sequence of courses in at least one vocational subject, and allowed 74 elective credits.[25] Despite the diversity of secondary programs that were formally recognized in provincial regulations, with the exception of specialist vocational high schools in the cities, most secondary schools in Ontario and the West between the wars offered only academic programs leading to matriculation and normal school entrance. Similarly, in the Maritimes there was a belated move to diversify provincial secondary curricula during the 1930s, but in practice secondary education continued to be almost exclusively academic until after the Second World War.[26]

An important feature of the secondary education that was constructed in Canada in the latter part of the nineteenth century was external examination of pupils at two critical junctures, first, the end of elementary school and entrance to high school, and second, the end of high school and entrance to university. Written examinations for high school entrance administered by departments of education were introduced as secondary education began to expand in the last quarter of the nineteenth century. Universities administered their own entrance examinations until after the First World War, when joint matriculation boards were established representing universities and departments of education. In British Columbia, for example, university and departmental examiners began operating as a single board of examiners in 1918. Prior to 1918, they had met for purposes of liaison, but matriculation examinations were conducted by the University of British Columbia, while all other external examinations at high school entrance and each grade level were set by the board of examiners of the Department of Education. Similarly, universities in Ontario administered their own entrance examinations until 1919, when the matriculation board was reorganized to include representatives of the Department of Education, and henceforward the combined matriculation and departmental examinations were administered by the registrar's branch of the department. Beginning with the province of Ontario in 1904, the curricular and pedagogical impact of high school entrance examinations was moderated by systems of accreditation that permitted pupils from accredited elementary schools to enter high school without taking the provincial examination, and high school entrance examinations were eliminated in all provinces between 1930 (Alberta) and 1950 (Ontario). Departmental matriculation examinations, by contrast, were retained in all provinces until the late 1960s or early 1970s.

Industrial Efficiency and Educational Governance in Canada

From the turn of the century to the Second World War, as provincial departments of education expanded and diversified their activities, the office of the senior administrative official in each province – variously designated as chief superintendent, chief director, deputy minister of education, or some combination of these titles – came to dominate departmental administration and policy. The deputy ministers' wide span of control ensured their domination over the administrative routine of their departments and presented formidable barriers to political interference in administration. Their position as administrative masters also ensured their involvement in educational policy making. Moreover, deputy ministers normally were experienced professional educators who typically had long careers first as teacher and principal, then as inspector, and finally as chief inspector or assistant deputy minister before becoming deputy minister. Having become deputy minister, they generally retained their office for many years.

In the last quarter of the nineteenth century, departments of education varied in size, but, except in Quebec and Newfoundland, their administrative organization was very much the same, being based on a simple division of activities between school inspection and clerical work. In Ontario, which had the largest department, the staff in 1867 consisted of the chief superintendent, a deputy superintendent, a grammar school inspector, three clerks, and a messenger; in the 1890s, the central office still had fewer than twenty employees and only two new offices: inspector of public libraries and registrar. At the turn of the century, the education office in New Brunswick comprised the chief superintendent of education, eight school inspectors, and four clerks. In British Columbia, the superintendent of education was supported by four inspectors of schools and two clerks.

From the late nineteenth century to the Second World War and beyond, the pattern of departmental expansion consisted of adding new branches or divisions to the existing organization. Departments acquired responsibility for curriculum design and school supervision in the areas of secondary and vocational education, and they began to provide new provincial educational services, such as correspondence courses, textbook distribution, and special education.[27] The lines of departmental policy and administration all ran directly into the office of chief superintendent, chief director, or deputy minister of education.[28] By the 1940s, provincial departments of education typically had twelve to fifteen officials who reported directly to the chief superintendent, chief director, or deputy minister of education.[29] These included superintendent or chief inspector of elementary schools, superintendent or chief inspector of secondary schools, director of curriculum, director of technical and vocational training, director of teacher training or principal of the provincial normal school, supervisor of provincial schools or principals of provincial schools for blind and deaf children, director of the correspondence school, registrar of teacher certification and departmental examinations, textbook bureau manager, school attendance officer, director of school administration, librarian, and departmental administrative officer or accountant.

Deputy ministers of education dominated departmental administration and policy, but they were subject to strong political and policy direction from provincial cabinets. The policy function of premiers (when they wanted to exercise it) and ministers of education (when premiers let them exercise it) was unchallenged by deputy ministers, who continued, as professional administrators, to be subject in both theory and practice to the constitutional and political paramountcy of the principle of ministerial responsibility. Hence, the development of provincial educational policy depended on close collaboration of politicians and administrators in their role of executive leadership. On the one hand, ministers of education, if not always unwilling, were simply unable to master the details of policy and administration required to dominate their departments in the way ministers had been able to do in the late nineteenth century.[30] Only three ministers of education in the first half of the twentieth century had extensive experience as professional educators prior to their political careers, and all of them worked with deputy ministers who also were experienced professional educators.[31] On the other hand, provincial government in Canada is usually 'premier's government.'[32] Hence, in describing the relationship between educational politics and policy it is essential to take into account the relationship not only of ministers and deputies but also of premiers and deputy ministers of education. Indeed, from the turn of the century to the 1940s there were several cases where premiers retained the office of minister of education for themselves; however, even where premiers did not directly minister the education portfolio, their political clout by all accounts was an effective countervail to even the most entrenched deputy ministers of education.[33] Thus, provincial educational policy making in the first half of the twentieth century became a form of executive leadership jointly conducted by the premier and minister of education as politicians on one side and the chief superintendent, chief director, or deputy minister of education as the departmental administrative head on the other side.

With regard to local educational governance, early experiments with consolidation of school districts in Canada were initiated after 1903, the year in which the Macdonald Consolidated School Project was launched, but there was no significant impact on the size and number of school districts prior to the Second World War. In Nova Scotia, there were 1,769 school districts operating in 1895 and 1,758 in 1939, of which 83 per cent employed only one teacher. New Brunswick in its 1871 education act replaced parish districts with 1,426 small school districts, approximately the same number that existed in 1944. In Ontario there were 4,400 school districts operating in 1870 and more than 6,000 in the 1930s. In the western provinces, the number of school districts rose rapidly with settlement. In Manitoba, for example, the number of districts was 774 in 1891 and 2,270 in 1936; in Saskatchewan there were 869 districts in 1905 and 5,146 in 1937. Overall, in the mid-1930s the average Canadian school district had about 90 students compared with an average of 200 students in the United States.

Politically powerless to implement effective policies of district reorganization, provincial departments, as an alternative, steadily diminished local discretion by the proliferation of departmental regulations (implemented by cadres of provincial inspectors) that aimed to control all phases of local education. Local property taxation on average provided 80 to 90 per cent of school board revenues from the late nineteenth century until the 1940s, but the size and distribution of local district budgets were substantially determined by provincial policies.[34] Provincial departments of education prescribed standards for school site selection, construction, maintenance, and equipment as well as procedures for annual school meetings, district budget preparation, and grant applications. Provincial normal schools trained teachers and provincial departments of education issued the licences required to teach in public schools. Provincial curricula authorized textbooks and determined courses of study at every level. Provincial inspectors regularly visited schools, observed and questioned pupils and teachers, and reported their findings and recommendations to the provincial superintendent.[35]

Canadian educational policy communities from the turn of the century to the Second World War thus were state directed. There was no educational civil society to challenge the expansion and diversification of provincial departments of education, the institutionalization of executive policy making in the relationship of premiers, ministers, and deputy ministers, and the departments' detailed control over all phases of local educational provision and governance. The rapid organization of teachers' unions in all provinces except Quebec between 1914 and 1920 was a political reaction to the decline in the material position of teachers during the war,[36] and from the outset, these new teachers' unions had both professional and political objectives.[37] The organization of school trustees, in turn, was a reaction to the provincial organization of teachers. In some cases, departments of education actively promoted the provincial organization of school trustees as a counter to the provincial organization of teachers.[38] As yet, however, neither organized teachers nor organized trustees were accepted as participants in provincial educational policy making. In particular, the provincial organization of Canadian teachers between 1914 and 1920 did not immediately result in their recognition by ministers and departmental officials as legitimate advocates of teachers' interests with a right of access to the policy-making inner circle, if not to participate in policy making at least to advise. That recognition remained to be won in the postwar years by a combination of political pressure on the part of teachers' organizations and of changing personnel and outlook on the side of ministers and officials in the departments of education.

New Zealand: A Liberal-Conservative Regime with Divided Local Governance

In the electoral campaign of 1899 the platform of the Liberal party included a promise to bring primary, secondary, technical, and university education within the reach of all young people. R.J. Seddon, who had become prime minister of the Liberal government after the death of John Ballance in 1893, interpreted this as meaning that 'the State should step in to see that the poor children who are endowed by Nature with brains have an equal chance of using them to advantage with the children of the rich.'[39] Earlier that year, when the Reverend W.J. Habens died in office, the Liberal government had appointed George Hogben, former inspector of schools for the North Canterbury Education Board and rector of Timaru Boys' High School, as secretary of education and inspector general of schools. From 1899 until his retirement in 1916, Hogben conceived and implemented a national regime of public primary, secondary, and technical schools based on the principles of competitive selection on the basis of merit, partite organization of secondary education, and centralized control by the Department of Education. His crowning achievement, the Education Act of 1914, consolidated the institutions and regulations of a liberal-conservative educational regime that endured in its essentials until the 1960s.

Ideas and Institutions for State Secondary Education in the Era of Industrial Efficiency

The Education Act of 1877 had been designed primarily to create a national regime of elementary education, but there was also a modest provision for secondary education. Education boards were authorized to establish district high schools, which were primary schools topped by secondary classes, and thirteen such schools were operating by the turn of the century, mainly under the Otago board. In addition, the Education Reserves Act of 1877 provided that one-quarter of the revenue from the education reserves of the provinces should be spent on secondary education. During the 1877–8 session, twelve endowed secondary schools were founded or reconstituted, and by the turn of the century there were twenty-six endowed schools, each incorporated with its own board of governors by a separate act of Parliament.[40] There were also 332 scholarships offered by education boards to assist primary-school pupils to continue their education at a secondary school.

Following the appointment of George Hogben as secretary and inspector general and the re-election of the Seddon government in February 1899, public secondary education was vigorously expanded and diversified. In 1901 the education boards were offered special grants to add secondary departments to rural primary schools in which there were twelve or more secondary students in attendance. The number of district high schools jumped from thirteen in 1900 to fifty-nine in 1905, and enrolments rose from 600 to 2,900.[41] Three weeks after yet another victory at the polls on 25 November 1902, the Seddon government instituted free-place regulations under which endowed schools got a conditional £6 grant for each primary-school graduate admitted without having to pay tuition fees.[42] The next year, the Secondary Schools Act consolidated general regulations governing the establishment of new secondary schools and the provisions for free places. Under the Manual and Technical Instruction Act of 1902, technical day schools were opened by education boards in the four major centres of Wellington (1905), Auckland (1906), and Christchurch and Dunedin (1907), as well as Wanganui (1911) and Invercargill (1912).[43] Technical high schools were formally recognized in the Education Act of 1914, and thereafter, with their own boards of managers and separate teaching service, they were developed as an alternative to academic secondary schools and district high schools.

Enrolments in secondary schools, technical high schools, and district high schools grew slowly from 2.5 per cent of total enrolments in 1900 to 5.3 per cent in 1915, 8.5 per cent in 1925, 12 per cent in 1935, and 15 per cent in 1945. Enrolments were also heavily concentrated in the first two years of secondary school (junior first and second in the 1910s and 1920s, forms three and four in the 1930s), which ended in examinations for the intermediate certificate. In 1915, 50 per cent of 13,036 students in public secondary education were enrolled in secondary schools, 19 per cent in the higher grades of primary schools, 16 per cent in district high schools, and 15 per cent in technical high schools. By 1945, there were 39,107 students enrolled in secondary education, with 45 per cent in secondary schools, 28 per cent in technical high schools, 18 per cent in district high schools, and 8 per cent in combined (technical/academic) schools.

During the 1920s and 1930s there were experiments to increase retention in secondary education, but no substantial improvement was achieved. One problem was the transition from primary to secondary education. In 1922 the first intermediate school was opened, based on the model of the American junior high school, and there were twenty-five in operation by 1945. At first giving a three-year program, intermediate schools were cut back to two years in 1932 and thus essentially reduced to the status of elementary schools. Another problem was the hegemony in both secondary schools and district high schools of the academic course leading to university entrance. During the interwar years, secondary schools began to offer alternative courses to university entrance – commerce, domestic science for girls, and industrial or agricultural courses for boys – but at the beginning of the Second World War, 75 per cent of boys and 60 per cent of girls continued to be enrolled in the matriculation course. Technical high schools moved in the opposite direction. In the large technical high schools of Auckland, Christchurch, and Wellington, 15 to 25 per cent of the students were registered in academic courses in 1939, and in smaller centres, where there was a technical high school but no separate secondary school, 45 per cent of boys and 36 per cent of girls were taking academic courses. In addition, regulations governing the formation of 'combined schools' that offered both academic and technical courses were issued in 1931, and there were seven combined schools in operation before the war.[44]

Secondary education in New Zealand was strongly selective prior to the Second World War. External examinations controlled entry to secondary school, advancement to upper forms, and entrance to university. Between primary school and secondary school, there was the proficiency examination conducted by district inspectors. In 1878 the first inspector general, W.J. Habens, had established a scheme of annual examinations in basic subjects conducted in each elementary school by inspectors. In 1894, George Hogben, then an inspector, persuaded the department to turn the examination of children in standards one and two over to teachers, and after Hogben became inspector general, examinations over the first five standards (grades one to seven) of primary school were transferred to teachers in 1900. Inspectors continued to administer the proficiency examination at the end of standard six on which a free place in secondary school depended, until secondary fees and the proficiency examination were both abolished in 1936 following the election of a Labour government committed to free post-primary education for all.[45] At the end of secondary school was matriculation, administered by the university, which was introduced in 1888 and quickly came to dominate the secondary school curriculum.[46] Between the proficiency examination and matriculation, at the end of form four, there was the intermediate certificate, which could be granted on the basis of either internal examination or teachers' recommendations in accredited schools; prior to the Second World War the majority of students took the intermediate certificate as an external examination that for most of them marked the end of their life in school.

Bureaucratic Administration, Organized Teachers, and Education Boards

The centralization of policy and administration under George Hogben as secretary and inspector general occurred in two key steps. First, in 1901 the Public School Teachers' Salaries Act established uniform salary scales and staffing standards for all schools under the authority of education boards. The boards were allotted grants to cover the national scales and henceforth ceased to be free agents in setting teachers' salaries and determining pupil-teacher ratios in their schools. Second, under the Education Act of 1914, district school inspectors were transferred from the education boards to the Department of Education. The centralization of the inspectorate facilitated the implementation of a national policy on the appointment and grading of primary teachers. More importantly, the inspectors constituted a national corps of education officials whose professional and practical knowledge of teaching and administration made them the dominant influence on educational policy and administration over the next two decades.[47]

The higher priority for secondary education, the introduction of technical education, and the transfer of district inspectors to the department set the stage for a major reorganization of the Department of Education. The first secretary of education was John Hislop, former secretary and inspector for the Otago Education Board, who had been instrumental in the development of the 1877 Education Act, with W.J. Habens as inspector general. When Hislop retired in 1886, first Habens from 1886 to 1899 and then Hogben from 1899 to 1905 assumed the duties of both offices. E.O. Gibbes, who started as clerk in the first year of the Department of Education, was appointed as secretary in 1905, with administrative rank equal to the inspector general, but Hogben kept control of educational policy. When Hogben retired in 1916, the office of inspector general was retitled director of education with the secretary his subordinate as administrative officer in charge of the clerical staff. The office of chief inspector was then divided into three branches, with the appointment of a superintendent of technical education (1919) and separate offices of chief inspector for primary and secondary schools (1920).

Founded in 1883 as a union of public school teachers, from the outset the New Zealand Educational Institute pressed the national government to limit the authority of education boards and establish a national teaching service with uniform salary scales and conditions of work. On the two most important policy changes that decisively undermined the authority of the district education boards – the nationalization of teachers' salaries in 1901 and the transfer of school inspectors to the department in 1914 – the institute was the most prominent and influential advocate for centralization. The institute was also successful in its lobbying to participate in the administration of the teaching service. In 1895 the Public School Teachers' Incorporation and Court of Appeal Act gave statutory recognition to the institute and provided for a tribunal, comprising a magistrate resident in the district and two representatives of, respectively, the district education board and the institute, to hear appeals of a teacher's dismissal, suspension, or compulsory transfer (1911 amendment) or salary reduction (1914 amendment).

Local authority over the appointment of teachers was further constrained by the establishment of a national graded list of all public school teachers. Under the 1877 Education Act, appointments of teachers to primary schools were made by school committees from short lists prepared by their district education board. By the turn of the century, the education boards had established various criteria governing appointments, promotions, and dismissals of teachers, such as educational attainments, length of service, and inspectors' reports.[48] In 1908 the Auckland education board began to make its nominations from graded lists that left no discretion to the school committees, and under pressure from the New Zealand Educational Institute, provision for a national graded list of public school teachers was included in the Education Act of 1914. Following the implementation of the national graded list, the institute was successful in getting an amendment to the Education Act in 1920 that made the list the basis for all general appointments in the primary teaching service. Education boards were authorized to transfer teachers at the same level without advertising the positions, as long as the senior inspector was consulted first, but if a teacher was transferred to a position with a higher salary, the board was required to advertise the position, invite applications, and appoint the applicant who stood highest on the graded list. The grading of teachers was based on inspection in each district, with results collated by the district inspectors' grading board, over which the chief inspector presided. The 1920 amendment also established a grading appeal board made up of representatives of the department and the institute, with an independent chair. All but marginal authority over teachers' appointments was thus nationalized and bureaucratized in the annual assessments of district inspectors, the collective construction of the graded list by the inspectors' grading board, and the decisions of the grading appeal board.

The political position of education boards was also weakened by the shift in priorities from primary to secondary education and the split between the two levels in responsibility for governance. The delivery of secondary education was dominated by secondary schools and technical high schools, over which the education boards had limited influence. After an initial burst of growth from 1901 to 1905, district high schools, which were directly governed by the education boards, languished in terms of schools and enrolments until the 1920s, and even as expansion of district high schools resumed during the 1930s and 1940s, they were eclipsed by the numbers and enrolments of secondary schools and technical high schools. In contrast with secondary schools, which had independent boards of governors, technical high schools were legally organized under the authority of education boards, but each school had its own board of managers. Moreover, the boards of technical high schools tended to establish direct relationships with the technical education branch of the Department of Education, and with the entrenchment of boards of managers in the Education Act of 1914, control over technical education by district education boards became purely formal.[49] The amendments to the Education Act in 1920 established three separate sets of grading systems, salary scales, and methods of appointing teachers, and there were separate schedules of grants for primary, secondary, and technical schools.

During the 1920s there was mounting criticism of the separation of primary education under the education boards from secondary education under the boards of governors of secondary schools and boards of managers of technical high schools. In its 1930 report on educational reorganization in New Zealand, the Parliamentary Recess Committee on Education, which included both the then (Harry Atmore) and future (Peter Fraser) ministers of education as members, recommended that the three types of boards be merged to form unified boards of public education. A bill to establish district education councils with jurisdiction over all types of public primary and secondary education was drafted in 1938 during the first term of the Labour government, but it was allowed to lapse in the face of opposition from secondary school boards and the Labour government's growing preoccupation with the prospect of war.[50] The local governance of secondary schools and technical high schools independent of the education boards meant that no local educational authority had responsibility to develop an integrated system of public education. By the logic of institutional arrangements, that function belonged exclusively to the department.

United Kingdom: Secondary Educational Reform and the Élitist Ideology of National Efficiency

In the late nineteenth and early twentieth centuries, an ideology of 'national efficiency' was conceived in Britain that cut across the established lines of partisan politics, encompassing such prominent political, administrative, and intellectual leaders as the Conservative prime minister Arthur Balfour, the Liberal member of Parliament R.B. Haldane, the civil servant Robert Morant, the Liberal peer and former prime minister Lord Rosebery, and the Fabian socialists George Bernard Shaw, Sidney and Beatrice Webb, and H.G. Wells.[51] These advocates of national efficiency aspired to discredit the ideas, institutions, and practices that were seen to have dangerously disadvantaged Britain in the competition for international economic ascendancy. They envisaged an orderly, planned society led by an élite comprising experts in science, business, and politics. They aimed to integrate science and government, improve the productivity of British workers, and utilize the methods of business to guide the conduct of public policy. With regard to the machinery of government, the proponents of national efficiency were particularly critical of local government. Ad hoc agencies, notably the school boards and the Poor Law guardians, stood in the way of administrative uniformity that would eliminate duplication of effort and wasteful rivalries.[52] Bringing all local governmental activities under the control of county and county borough councils would result in an effective simplification of governmental organization, improved coordination of local services, and proper constitution of public accountability.

The ideology of national efficiency gave high priority to reforming British education, but it proposed to perpetuate the separation of mass education from the education of the élite. Its cult of expertise, combined with perceived limits on public resources, led to recommendations that restricted secondary education to fee-paying children of the middle class plus a small number of working-class children who were successful in competing for one of the limited number of free places or state scholarships. As for governance, public education ought to be consolidated with other functions of local government under the control of county and county borough councils.

In England and Wales, educational reform based on the ideology of national efficiency was largely accomplished in the Education Act of 1902, despite opposition from traditional Conservatives, the Liberal party and Nonconformist allies who saw the act as an affront to religious liberty, and radical liberals and socialists who were more concerned about social justice than national efficiency.[53] The principles of the 1902 act, in turn, shaped the first education act in Northern Ireland following partition; while in Scotland, where classical liberalism was relatively stronger, the ideas of national efficiency were slower to be adopted but ultimately prevailed in the Education (Scotland) Act of 1929.

Academic Secondary Education in Selective Schools

Simultaneously with the creation of public regimes for elementary education in England, Scotland, and Wales, there arose the issue of state involvement in education in grammar schools and burgh schools.[54] There were two main questions. First, should education in grammar and burgh schools be a track separate from education in elementary and parish schools or should it be intermediate education between the education provided in elementary and parish schools and the higher education offered in university colleges? Second, should education in grammar schools be organized independently of the state, with or without the aid of public grants, or should it be provided within the framework of a public educational regime that encompassed both elementary and secondary education?

A predominantly public regime of secondary education was created in Scotland. The Education (Scotland) Act of 1872 transferred control of both burgh and parish schools to school boards, and eleven former burgh schools were recognized under the act as 'higher class schools.' Because higher class schools had to be maintained by endowments, fees, and subscriptions without support from parliamentary grants or local rates, most school boards opted to expand secondary education in upper classes of parish schools rather than open more higher class schools.[55] During the 1880s the independent sector of Scottish secondary education was reorganized by a commission established under the Educational Endowments (Scotland) Act of 1882, which closed seventy-seven endowed schools and transferred forty-seven others to school boards, leaving only thirty-four endowed schools to operate independently under their governing bodies. In 1892, following the recommendations of a committee of the Scotch Education Department (SED) on secondary education and teacher training, the Education and Local Taxation Account (Scotland) Act provided for parliamentary grants to be given to both higher class and parish schools, county secondary education committees with joint representation of local authorities and school boards were created to report on educational deficiencies and distribute local grants to secondary schools, and endowed schools (now 'grant-aided schools') qualified for grants from the Scotch Education Department and county secondary education committees. Parliamentary allocations were increased steadily through a variety of miscellaneous grants that were consolidated under the Education (Scotland) Act of 1908 in a central fund for secondary education. At the same time, school boards were authorized to support secondary schools from local rates.[56] Grant-aided schools steadily lost ground to public secondary schools, however; by the 1930s, only fourteen of the original thirty-four grant-aided schools were still in operation.

Secondary education in Ireland, by contrast, was the preserve of voluntary church schools. These schools were maintained by pupils' fees, royal and private endowments, church foundations, and Roman Catholic teaching orders. The Board of Commissioners of Intermediate Education for Ireland, which was established in 1878, distributed grants to secondary schools based on the results of examinations conducted by the board, and under the Intermediate Education Act of 1914, a teachers' salary grant was distributed to the managers of Catholic and Protestant schools 'for the purpose of promoting the employment upon reasonable terms of an adequate number of duly qualified lay teachers in intermediate schools.'[57] Following the partition of Ireland, the 1923

Education Act authorized managers of intermediate schools in Northern Ireland to transfer their schools to one of the regional or county borough education committees. Few did so. By 1944, only nine of seventy-five secondary schools were managed by an education committee.

In England and Wales there developed an educational regime that combined public and voluntary secondary schools. The first significant state intervention in secondary education occurred during the 1860s, when first the nine leading grammar schools were investigated by the Public Schools Commission (the Clarendon commission, 1861–4),[58] and then the Schools Inquiry Commission (the Taunton commission, 1864–8) looked at the remaining 782 endowed schools. Both commissions defended class-divided and class-confirming education in an exclusive sector of independent grammar schools.[59] As a result of recommendations by the Taunton commission, the Endowed Schools Commission was established in 1869 with authority, which was transferred in 1874 to the Board of Charity Commissioners, to approve the foundation of new grammar schools and revise the terms of foundation of established schools, but it did not make grants to the schools it regulated. Grants for teaching science and art were distributed to endowed secondary and higher-grade elementary schools for pupils who were successful in examinations conducted by the Science and Art Department, and grants for teaching science were also made by local authorities under the Technical Instruction Act of 1889.[60] Most important as a precedent for state involvement in secondary education was the Welsh Intermediate Act, passed in 1889, which instituted joint education committees in each county, comprising three representatives of the county or county borough council and two members appointed by the lord president. These committees were authorized to establish schools intermediate in their curriculum between elementary schools and university colleges, to be financed by pupil fees, rates levied by the council, and matching parliamentary grants. Each school was required to give scholarships to 10 to 20 per cent of its pupils, with one-half of the scholarship pupils receiving free places.[61]

In its 1895 report on secondary education in England and Wales, the royal commission chaired by James (later Lord) Bryce, working from classic principles of liberal-conservative educational thought, proposed to expand provision of secondary education in England and Wales, reform the traditional curriculum by integrating classical and modern subjects, and increase scholarships for meritorious students from elementary schools.[62] The commission's recommendations were generally implemented in the Education Act of 1902, the regulations defining secondary education issued in 1904, and the supplementary regulation of 1907 on free places. The 1902 act established county councils and county borough councils as local education authorities (LEAs) responsible for developing both elementary and 'higher' education in their areas and authorized central and local grants to existing endowed schools as well as the establishment and maintenance of secondary schools by the new local education authorities. In 1904 the Board of Education issued new regulations defining secondary education as a complete, graded course of studies beginning at age eight or nine (or twelve or thirteen for those who went to elementary school) and continuing at least to age sixteen or seventeen and to age eighteen or nineteen for those going to university. The four-year course from ages twelve to sixteen was taken to be the core, with a proper balance maintained between literary-humanist and scientific-technological subjects.[63] The Bryce commission's proposal for a scholarship ladder from elementary to secondary education was implemented in 1907 in the form of a supplementary regulation that all secondary schools charging fees while receiving grants from the Board of Education had to provide free places for 25 per cent of their annual entry to pupils from elementary schools, 'subject to the applicants passing an entrance test of attainments and proficiency.'

Academic, Technical, and Practical Education in Partite Systems of Public Secondary Education

At the turn of the century, there was not much demand for technical secondary education; future engineers and technicians were expected to receive their preparatory education in a grammar school.[64] Skilled manual workers could not be expected to undertake such an academic secondary course, however, and young men did not enter apprenticeships until about age sixteen. Accordingly, as Sir Michael Sadler concluded in his 1904 report on secondary education in Liverpool, there appeared to be a need for 'a new type of school, taking boys from the public elementary schools at about thirteen, and keeping them to fifteen or sixteen with a course of instruction in which manual training would be given an important place.' The next year the Board of Education began to offer grants to support day technical classes, and in 1913 'junior technical schools' were officially recognized as schools providing full-time classes for post-elementary pupils aged thirteen to sixteen who were aiming towards skilled apprenticeships in engineering and other industries.

Between the wars, the expansion of public grammar schools and junior technical schools, as well as of higher classes in elementary schools (sometimes consolidated in 'central schools'), was accompanied by increasingly focused debate about the purpose and organization of post-elementary education.[65] The official declaration of cardinal principles came in 1926 in the report of the Consultative Committee on the Education of the Adolescent chaired by Sir William Henry Hadow. According to the Hadow committee, 'There are diversities of gifts, and for that reason there must be diversity of educational provision.'[66] Noting that on average 8 per cent of children in primary schools continued to secondary schools, the Hadow committee anticipated some expansion of existing grammar schools as well as more places for students aged thirteen plus in junior technical and trade schools. A third type of education that was neither narrowly academic nor strictly vocational should be taught in 'modern schools' and 'senior classes' in which subjects such as history, geography, mathematics, and modern languages would be 'directly and obviously brought into relation with the facts of every day experience' and emphasis placed on practical applications.[67] None the less, the committee insisted on one key condition: 'It is the necessity of ensuring, in the development of other forms of post-primary education, that nothing is done to cripple the development of secondary schools of the existing types.'[68]

Twelve years later, the tripartite organization of secondary education implicit in the Hadow committee's report was made explicit by the Consultative Committee on Secondary Education with Special Reference to Grammar Schools and Technical Schools, chaired by Sir Will Spens. According to the Spens committee, a new code of secondary regulations was needed that would recognize grammar, modern, and technical schools as three types of secondary schools and administer them under common regulations. Nevertheless, the élite academic character of the grammar school was taken for granted.[69] In contrast with the Hadow committee's reticence about the proportion to be selected for grammar school, the Spens committee suggested 15 per cent of the secondary-school age group as an acceptable standard. The committee also gave much stronger support to lowering the age of entry to junior technical schools from thirteen plus to eleven plus and developing them into selective schools that would provide a scientific and technical counterpart to grammar schools.

In contrast with the tripartite system conceived and initiated in England and Wales, in Scotland the public secondary regime was essentially bipartite, divided between academic and general education, with a large proportion of bilateral schools. The Technical Schools (Scotland) Act of 1887 authorized school boards to establish schools for secondary technical instruction, but it was not implemented by the boards. Consequently, the alternative to academic secondary education in higher schools evolved out of the supplementary courses and advanced departments in parish (elementary) schools. A committee of the Scotch Education Department on secondary education and teacher training in 1888 recommended that grants for secondary education be given to both higher class and parish schools and that advanced classes in parish schools be restricted to practical and vocationally biased courses.[70] As a result of the departmental committee's recommendations, a leaving certificate examination to be taken only by students in higher class schools was created in 1888, and four years later, when grants were extended to both higher class and parish schools, a separate merit certificate was introduced for elementary school pupils over age thirteen who satisfied inspectors by doing advanced work in specific subjects. Post-elementary work in parish schools was initially consolidated in 1903 in the form of 'supplementary courses,' which were partly general but predominantly vocational – commercial, industrial, rural, or domestic – and then reorganized in 1923 as 'advanced divisions' in which the curriculum was broader and less vocationally specialized, leading to the award of a day-school certificate after a two-year or three-year course.

Most advanced divisions were still attached to elementary schools, although some were housed in separate central schools, and one-quarter of secondary schools offered both leaving-certificate and advanced-division courses. This diversity of institutional provision did not affect the basic dichotomy of élite and mass in Scottish secondary education. As a senior official explained the position of the Scottish Education Department,

> the school population falls into two parts – the majority of distinctly limited intelligence, and an extremely important minority drawn from all ranks and classes who are capable of responding to a much more severe call. It is vital for the body politic that each of these should have the very best education which it is possible to devise, but the education must be adapted to their capacities and matters will not be helped by ignoring the difference between them.[71]

In Ireland, technical education developed separately from 'national' (elementary) and 'intermediate' (secondary) schools. The Department of Agricultural and Technical Instruction was created in 1899 to allocate grants and make regulations for technical schools that were organized, operated, and partially financed from local rates by urban district and county councils. Trades preparatory schools (later called junior technical schools) operated in conjunction with technical schools for further education to provide technical education and training for boys who had reached the higher standards of the national schools and wanted to prepare for work in a skilled trade. Following partition, elementary and technical schools in Northern Ireland continued to be governed independently in urban areas as urban district councils retained their status as technical education authorities; however, technical schools established by county councils were placed under the control of regional education committees, which also governed elementary schools. In 1925–6, eight junior technical schools had 14.5 per cent of the total enrolments in secondary education; by the end of the Second World War there were twenty junior technical schools with 16.1 per cent of secondary enrolments.

Educational Governance and the Problem of British National Efficiency

For England and Wales the Board of Education Act in 1899 brought together the Education Department, the Department of Science and Art, and the educational functions of the Board of Charity Commissioners in a single department for which the president of the board had individual responsibility as political head of the new department.[72] Robert Morant's commitment to the goal of national efficiency was reflected in his reorganization of the Board of Education when he became its permanent secretary in 1903. The inspectorate was divided into elementary, secondary, and technical branches corresponding to the administrative divisions within the board, and there were nine inspectorial divisions for England plus one for Wales, each divided into districts. Thus, there was a clear chain of command from the permanent secretary through the chief inspector and divisional inspectors to district inspectors, who were the link with the new local education authorities. Morant also insisted that the board's senior staff attain and maintain high professional standards and expert knowledge of educational problems.

Professionalism and organization were thus to be the hallmarks of the Board of Education under Morant's aegis, and accompanying them was the assumption that in the dual partnership between the Board and the LEAs it would be the Board that would be the dominant partner. As revealed in the reform measures initiated in 1903, this assumption represented a marked change from the previous ethos of the Education Department which had preferred, under the legacy of Kay-Shuttleworth, to act in an advisory manner.[73]

In Scotland from 1885 to 1921 the first two secretaries of the Scotch Education Department, Sir Henry Craik and Sir John Struthers, clearly dominated educational policy and administration. 'They bequeathed to their successors powerful tools of control, a widespread habit of obedience among educationists outside, and a secondary-school system that enjoyed a level of development that was both uniform and high by British standards of the time.'[74] Within the Scottish Office, the SED had substantial autonomy until the 1950s. Until 1918, there were more than 900 school boards, almost all too small to affect policy development, and even after 1918 few education authorities had the resources to challenge the SED. The most significant educational interest group was the Educational Institute of Scotland, founded in 1847 as an omnibus organization to promote education and evolving into a pressure group for class teachers; however, its relations with the SED were not close.[75]

For purposes of local educational governance, the Bryce commission had recommended 'Local Authorities for Secondary Education in every county and county borough.' These would be separate from the school boards and would levy rates for the support of existing secondary schools, initiate the establishment of new endowed and public schools, and award secondary scholarships to the top elementary students. In addition to charging county and county borough councils with the provision of secondary and technical education in their areas, however, the Education Act of 1902 abolished the school boards and mandated every county and county borough council, any borough council with a population over 10,000, and any urban district with a population over 20,000 to manage the elementary schools in its area.[76] The debate on the education bill in the House of Commons was heated and the campaign in the country even more intense. Sectarian hostilities over the issue of maintaining voluntary schools from local rates gave the debate its passion, however, not the abolition of the school boards, which disappeared by an amendment during the committee stage of the bill.[77]

In Scotland there was greater resistance to abolishing the school boards as basic units of local educational governance. As head of the Scotch

Education Department, Struthers sympathized with the British government's desire to replace the school boards with county councils, but there was strong opposition from organized labour, branches of the Independent Labour party, and also members of the clergy, who tended to dominate elections to school boards.[78] As a compromise, the 947 school boards were replaced in 1918 by thirty-eight ad hoc education authorities, elected for three-year terms; these were independent of county councils but lacked power to levy their own rates. Organized teachers and officials in the Scottish Education Department persisted in disparaging these ad hoc authorities, and as part of a general reform of Scottish local government in 1929, local educational governance became the function of twenty-nine county and four burgh councils.[79]

Following the partition of Ireland in 1920 the government of Northern Ireland was reconstituted as an elected parliament and seven ministerial departments. Among them was the Ministry of Education, which took over the work of the former commissioners for national and intermediate education. The arrangements for local educational governance in the first education act passed by the Parliament of Northern Ireland in 1923 were adapted from the 1902 act for England and Wales.[80] County and county borough councils were designated as local education authorities formally responsible for approving budgets and levying rates. In the case of Belfast and Londonderry, education committees of the county borough councils were authorized to manage local schools. In the counties, local management was assigned to regional education committees, the members of which were appointed by the minister of education based on nominations by county and district councils.[81] In contrast with the relationship of policy tutelage instituted by Robert Morant between the Board of Education and local education authorities in England and Wales, the Ministry of Education for Northern Ireland generally treated the education committees as its administrative agents. Arrangements for local governance, membership of education committees, annual budgets, school building, administrative procedures, and curriculum development were subject to detailed ministry planning and approval. The large voluntary sector, both Roman Catholic elementary and grammar schools, was somewhat less vulnerable to direct control by the ministry but was none the less governed by ministry regulations and dependent on ministry grants. The principal constraint on the ministry's control over elementary and secondary education in Northern Ireland was the recalcitrance of denominational interests with regard to religious instruction and observances in public schools.

Reorganization of local educational governance reopened the issue of church and state in public education, but in each country the nineteenth-century arrangements between public and voluntary sectors were preserved and extended. In England and Wales, where by 1900 enrolment in state elementary schools matched enrolment in voluntary schools, there was another raucous campaign between Anglicans and Nonconformists over the place of religion in public education.[82] At the end of it, the 1902 Education Act removed the 1870 prohibition on local state aid, creating a sector of 'non-provided' voluntary schools for which local education authorities paid the costs of maintenance but not the costs of buildings or repairs.[83] In Scotland, state aid to denominational voluntary schools was prohibited under the 1918 act, and the new ad hoc education authorities assumed complete control over transferred schools – including control of the appointment and dismissal of teachers – while foundation managers retained a veto over teachers' appointments 'in respect of religious belief and character.' Given this protection of denominational instruction in public schools, combined with the loss of state aid, within two years only thirty-five elementary schools remained outside the public sector.[84] In Northern Ireland, consistent with the Government of Ireland Act that prohibited the Parliament of Northern Ireland from making any law to establish or endow any religion, the Education Act of 1923 restricted denominational religious instruction to released time outside regular school hours. Following an aggressive campaign by the United Education Committee of the Protestant Church, however, the act was amended in 1930 to permit Bible instruction during regular school hours and to ensure Protestant representation on county borough, regional education, and school management committees.[85] Most managers of Protestant schools still remaining in the voluntary sector now transferred their schools to local authority control; no Roman Catholic schools were transferred.[86]

United States: Aspirations for Progressive Reform versus the Hegemony of Utilitarian Liberalism

The Progressive movement, which aimed to reform American politics and public administration in the late nineteenth and early twentieth centuries, was ideologically bisected. On one side were ethical liberals, who remained committed to the Jeffersonian belief in community consensus and direct democracy. For them the cure for corruption of American democracy was more democracy; they advocated the initiative, referendum, recall, direct election of senators, home rule, and proportional representation. On the other side were liberal conservatives, whose hope for the future was a more scientifically planned and administered society. For them the crisis of American democracy was not simply corruption but also inefficiency; the cure required creating a professional bureaucracy strictly separated from partisan politics and applying scientific planning and management by experts to the public functions of policy and administration.[87]

Both ethical-liberal and liberal-conservative branches of the Progressive movement were engaged in the American debate about public education and industrial efficiency from the 1890s to the 1940s. Both sides broadly agreed on the issues of educational reform: expand the provision and improve the quality of secondary schooling, integrate elementary and secondary schools in a comprehensive system of public education, and reorganize the governance of public education to balance its dual purpose of civic and vocational education. They sharply disagreed, however, on the design of school organization and curriculum and the reconstitution of state and local educational governance. Liberal conservatives advocated élitist academic secondary education, partite systems of academic and vocational secondary schools, state and local educational governance based on a model of civic trusteeship, and centralized state authority to plan and implement educational reform. Ethical liberals advocated integrated academic and vocational education, egalitarian provision of mass secondary education, preservation of neighbourhood democracy in local educational governance, and educational collaboration and support rather than centralized planning and regulation by state educational agencies. Despite the importance of these ethical-liberal and liberal-conservative ideas in public debate about education, by the 1920s policy discourse and institutional reform were dominated in practice by a distinctive American ideology of utilitarian liberalism that advocated secondary education for all in multilateral high schools combined with fiscal equivalence as the guiding principle of educational governance.

Academic, Vocational, and Multilateral Public High Schools

Through most of the nineteenth century, only a small proportion of Americans obtained any formal education beyond the common (elementary) school. Latin grammar schools had become virtually extinct.[88] Some students got post-elementary schooling in higher grades of elementary schools or public high schools that state assemblies authorized school districts or federated 'union' districts to organize in conjunction with the development of the common schools.[89] Most of those who got post-elementary schooling attended academies that were independently established by public charter, legal incorporation, or endowed foundation. Financed mainly by tuition fees and patrons' subscriptions, with occasional state aid in the form of land grants, academies were middle-class institutions.[90] In contrast with the narrow curriculum of Latin grammar schools, English, arithmetic, and natural sciences were core subjects in the academies, modern foreign languages, especially French, had an equal place beside classical languages, and a varied assortment of other subjects was offered to satisfy the particular preferences of patrons and parents.[91]

During the quarter-century following the Civil War, there was a spirited debate throughout the United States on the issue of making public high schools an integral part of state educational regimes, including several court cases in which the constitutionality of state spending on secondary education was challenged.[92] Not only the constitutionality but also the legitimacy of the public high school as a state educational institution was thus settled. Sometime during the 1880s, public high schools passed academies in total enrolment, and by the turn of the century they were the dominant providers of secondary education in the United States.[93]

Rather than the diversity of subjects and courses that had characterized the academies, secondary programs offered in public high schools were limited initially to a few parallel courses of study among which the 'classical' and 'English' courses were easily predominant. As enrolments grew after the Civil War, however, there was a proliferation of subjects and courses.[94] In 1887 the national council of the National Education Association (NEA) appointed the Committee of Ten on Secondary School Studies with a mandate to find ways and means of achieving greater uniformity in courses of secondary education and requirements for admission to colleges and university. The committee collected data from forty high schools and sponsored nine curriculum conferences.[95] Its final report, delivered in 1894, recommended that secondary education should be organized in four courses of study – classical, Latin-scientific, modern languages, and English – and that each course should include basic requirements for foreign languages, mathematics, English, science, and history.[96] Observing also that there was 'a very general custom in American high schools and academies to make up separate courses of study for pupils of supposed different destinations,' the committee and the conferences were unanimous in rejecting such differentiation: 'every subject which is taught at all in a secondary school should be taught in the same way and to the same extent to every pupil so long as he pursues it, no matter what the probable destination of the pupil may be, or at what point his education is to cease.'[97] The Committee of Ten evidently saw high school as a narrowly academic institution that admitted an élite group of young people and prepared them for entry to the professional, managerial, scientific, technical, and cultural élites.

Without stating so explicitly, the committee's plan implied that alternative educational institutions would provide vocational training to complement the academic high schools.[98] During the 1890s an alliance was formed between business interests, mainly organized in the National Association of Manufacturers, and liberal-conservative educators who advocated public vocational education as a means to achieve industrial efficiency.[99] Organized business wanted schools to produce efficient and productive skilled workers who could adapt to the requirements of mass production. Vocational educators such as David Snedden, the Massachusetts commissioner of industrial education, and Charles Prosser, executive secretary of the National Society for the Promotion of Industrial Education, took the view that the transition from school to work had broken down in industrial society. Specialization and the mechanization of industrial labour had undermined apprenticeship; informal training on the job was no longer efficient or effective. In their ideal model of partite secondary education, basic education in primary school would be followed by an integrated program of academic and vocational studies in middle school or junior high school. From there, young people would be guided to specialized college-preparatory, commercial, industrial arts, and domestic science high schools for the final years of their secondary education.

An alternative model of comprehensive secondary education was advocated by ethical-liberal educators and a segment of organized labour. By 1910 the Committee on Industrial Education of the American Federation of Labor was voicing its support for industrial training in public schools.[100] Workers were divided, however, between those who saw their children as future workers and hence direct beneficiaries of vocational training in school and those who saw vocational training in a class-divided school system as a barrier to social mobility. At the same time, ethical-liberal educators such as John Dewey, Jane Addams, and Paul Douglas wanted to restore meaning to work and promote democracy in the workplace of industrial society through an integration of vocational and academic education. In 1917, just as the Smith-Hughes Act was being passed in Congress, Dewey spoke out against narrow training in trades, 'which would utilize public schools primarily to turn out more efficient laborers in the present economic regime,' in favour of vocational education that 'would utilize all the resources of public education to equip individuals to control their own future economic careers, and thus help on such a reorganization of industry as will change it from a feudalistic to a democratic order.' Rather than create two kinds of schools, 'one of a trade type for children whom it is assumed are to be employees and one of a liberal type for the children of the well-to-do,' Dewey advocated comprehensive schools that would focus on the development of personal intelligence, give all students a respect for useful work, and 'utilize active and manual pursuits as the means of developing constructive, inventive and creative power of mind.'[101]

Between these liberal-conservative and ethical-liberal ideas for reforming secondary education, the NEA Commission on the Reorganization of Secondary Education in 1918 articulated a set of 'cardinal principles of secondary education' that derived from an essentially utilitarian-liberal educational philosophy.[102] According to the commission, 'The purpose of democracy is so to organize society that each member may develop his personality primarily through activities designed for the well-being of his fellow members and of society as a whole.' To achieve a high level of 'social efficiency,' each individual had the responsibility of choosing 'that vocation and those forms of social service in which his personality may develop and become most effective.' In order to facilitate socially efficient choices by individuals with regard to their education, the commission advocated a vertical differentiation of secondary schooling between senior high schools (grades ten to twelve) and junior high schools (grades seven to nine). Junior high schools would be comprehensive schools providing a transition between primary and senior high schools. In senior high schools, horizontally differentiated programs would be required to provide for individual differences among students and for the varied needs of society. The commission recommended agricultural, business, clerical, industrial, fine arts, and household arts programs, as well as a curriculum for those having 'distinctively academic interests and needs.' English and social studies would constitute the common core of all programs, and there would be social mingling of students in different tracks through unified administration of the school and shared activities such as team sports, social events, and school government.

Thus, for the commission, the multilateral high school was the 'prototype of a democracy in which various groups must have a degree of self-consciousness as groups and yet be federated into a larger whole through the recognition of common interests and ideals.'[103]

The report of the Commission on the Reorganization of Secondary Education articulated an emerging consensus and won the policy debate. Beginning with such schools as the Chicago English High and Manual Training School (1890) and the Boston Mechanic Arts High School (1892), specialized high schools for commercial and technical education had been established in several major cities. The commission's report was severely criticized by advocates of these specialized vocational schools, and their approach was influential in the original design of the Smith-Hughes Act of 1917, which offered federal aid for vocational education.[104] During the passage of the Smith-Hughes Act, however, an amendment was adopted that left the states to choose whether vocational courses at the secondary level were offered in separate vocational schools or general high schools; and only Massachusetts (where Snedden was just finishing his term as commissioner), Connecticut, and Wisconsin opted to restrict federal and state funding under the act to separate vocational schools. After 1918 the trend was to assimilate vocational education as tracks inside multilateral secondary schools. Large cities tended to keep the specialized vocational high schools already in operation but usually turned to multilateral organization in building new schools.[105] A major national survey involving 994 secondary schools in the early 1930s classified 76.5 per cent of them as comprehensive high schools, 10.6 per cent as academic high schools, 8.8 per cent as trade schools, and only 4.2 per cent as agricultural, commercial, or technical high schools.[106] The majority of 'comprehensive' schools, as well as most of the specialized vocational schools, grouped subjects into programs or tracks that had different educational and occupational objectives.[107]

In contrast with other Anglo-American educational regimes, where certificates of secondary education and qualification for university entrance resulted from the same external examinations, in the United States for the most part there were no state external examinations for school leavers and two competing methods of determining admissions to colleges and universities. Admissions under an accreditation system originated in 1869–70, when the University of Michigan began to admit, on the basis of their school records, graduates of high schools that had 'a sufficient number of competent instructors,' as determined by the university's faculty. Similar accreditation systems were implemented by several midwestern and southern state universities, while in Indiana and Minnesota accreditation was managed by the state departments of education. After the turn of the century, voluntary regional associations of colleges, universities, and high schools were organized to develop common standards for school inspections and staff qualifications as the basis for granting accredited status.[108] The alternative system was admission by examinations conducted by the College Entrance Examination Board, which was initiated by several northeastern colleges at Columbia University in 1900. The original 'College Boards' involved essay questions derived from detailed prescriptions of what students should have studied in high school. As the secondary school population grew and colleges tried to enlarge their clienteles accordingly, the prescribed curricula for College Boards were gradually widened.[109] In different ways, both accreditation systems and College Boards did affect the college-preparatory tracks of American high schools, but neither had the determining impact of external public examinations in educational regimes outside the United States.[110]

State Superintendents, State Boards, and Strong Governors

Liberal-conservative Progressive reformers were agreed that educational progress, especially in rural areas, required centralization and the strengthening of state educational governance. State superintendents ought to have outstanding administrative ability, impeccable professional credentials, and extensive professional experience; they should be chosen through a national search, not one restricted to a single state. Such a choice was impossible where popular election continued to be the method of choosing the state superintendent.

As one way of reconstituting state educational governance, professional educators proposed to replace popular election of the state superintendent with an independent state board of education as the general policy-making body for state education. In this model of civic trusteeship, the members of the state board would be appointed by the governor for lengthy, overlapping terms and thus be insulated from direct involvement in partisan politics. The state board would also be separated from the details of administration, which would be assigned to the department of education headed by a state superintendent appointed by and responsible to the state board of education. Specialists in government and public administration, by contrast, tended to prefer a model of executive leadership that concentrated policy-making authority in the office of the governor. As the elected head of the executive branch, the governor would appoint the chief executive officers of all departments of government, including the state superintendent of education. The governor might also appoint a state board of education to serve as an advisory body on state educational policy, but the state superintendent as head of the department of education would be directly responsible to the governor.[111]

At the end of the nineteenth century, the Progressive theory of civic trusteeship, under which the governor appointed the state board of education and the board then appointed the state superintendent, was operative only in Connecticut (since 1865).[112] The Progressive theory of civic trusteeship evidently inspired the restructuring of state educational governance in Vermont (1912), Maryland (1916), Minnesota (1919), New Hampshire (1919), Delaware (1921), and Arkansas (1931). These educational regimes had similar features: they had relatively small state boards of five to nine members, members were appointed for overlapping terms of five or six years by the governor, the boards had general responsibility to determine elementary and secondary school policies, and each board had power to appoint a state superintendent and hold that official responsible as its chief executive officer.[113]

The alternative model of strong executive leadership, which gave the governor power to appoint the state superintendent of education, was already operative in six states at the end of the nineteenth century: Maine, Massachusetts, Minnesota, New Jersey, Pennsylvania, and Tennessee. Power to appoint the Massachusetts commissioner of education was transferred from the governor to the state board of education in 1900 but then reverted to the governor in 1919. Following an investigation of public education that severely criticized the condition of rural education, the method of selecting the superintendent of public instruction in Ohio was changed in 1913 from popular election to appointment by the governor. In Virginia the state superintendent, who had been elected since 1902, became an appointee of the governor in the constitutional revision of 1928, and exclusive authority to appoint the Rhode Island superintendent of state education was given to the governor in 1935.[114]

By 1940 the state board of education was appointed by the governor and in turn appointed the state superintendent in seven states, and in eight states the state superintendent was appointed by the governor. In several states – Oklahoma (1911), California (1913), Idaho (1913), Nevada (1931), and Kentucky (1934) – the membership of state boards had been altered to reduce ex officio and professional representation and give the governor power of appointment. In general, the powers of state boards also had been expanded.[115] None the less, thirty-two states (out of forty-eight) continued to elect their state superintendent of education, a proportion (67 per cent) not very different from the 69 per cent (thirty-one of forty-five states) that had relied on popular election in 1900. Where superintendents were elected officials embedded in state politics, state boards had little chance of becoming the focus of political authority and policy responsibility in state educational governance.

Progressive Reform of Local Educational Governance

Nineteenth-century American city school boards, elected or appointed on a district or ward basis, were based on the ethical-liberal principle of neighbourhood democracy. They also assimilated the practices of patronage politics. Decisions on construction, contracts, textbook selection, teacher appointments, and school budgets were made by the political machines that had come to dominate city government in the United States. In the late nineteenth and early twentieth centuries, under the influence of Progressive principles, educational reformers campaigned to separate patronage politics from educational policy making and to increase the influence of city superintendents as professional chief executive officers responsible to their school boards. The Progressive reform program for local educational governance included abolition of district or ward school boards, centralization of policy-making authority in a single city-wide board, reduction of the size of city boards to five to seven members, and substitution of election or appointment at large for representation by wards or districts.

During the second half of the nineteenth century, there was a trend to appoint city superintendents of schools to whom boards delegated the details of personnel management, selection of texts, and supervision of teachers.[116] From 1892 to 1917, school boards in twelve major cities were reorganized, reducing their average size from twenty-eight to ten members, and in each case ward or district representation was replaced by election at large (Boston, Cleveland, Detroit, Los Angeles, Milwaukee, St Louis), appointment by the mayor (Baltimore, Chicago, New York, San Francisco), or appointment by judges (Philadelphia, Pittsburgh).[117] None the less, in many big cities – notably Boston, Chicago, Los Angeles, and New York – political machines continued to control centralized school boards. Putting their trust in institutional reform, Progressive reformers 'were often blind to the ways in which older forms of political behavior –

both external to the system and internal, among the employees – could creep back into the remodeled structures.'[118]

For Ellwood P. Cubberly, who was the foremost proponent of Progressive principles in educational administration, educational reorganization in city school districts was definitely the model for reconstituting rural educational governance.[119] Independent community school districts had been well suited to the development of public education in a frontier society; now they were a barrier to educational progress.[120] Reorganization on the basis of towns or townships was an improvement over the small school district, but these units were still not large enough. Based on the lessons of city educational governance, 'but also excellent examples in the county-unit school systems of such states as Maryland, Florida, Georgia, Louisiana, and Utah,' the best unit of local educational governance would be the county.[121]

The hopes of Cubberly and other Progressive reformers that the county would become the general unit of local educational governance were disappointed. The variety of types of districts, as much as the total number of districts in the 1930s – 109,000 common school districts, 6,000 town or township units, 2,500 union or consolidated districts, 7,000 independent and city school districts, 1,300 separate high school districts, 845 county districts for both elementary and high school, and 160 county high school districts – testifies to the popular unwillingness to rationalize local educational governance. Notable also is the continuing influence of regional political cultures. At the end of the 1930s the community school district was still the primary unit of local educational governance in twenty-five states – mostly in the central and western regions of the United States; towns or townships constituted the basic unit in eight eastern states as well as one midwestern state; and the county was the basic unit in eleven southern and two southwestern states.[122]

Educational Regimes and the Problem of Industrial Efficiency

By the early twentieth century, educational regimes that had been organized to provide elementary public instruction were being challenged to extend the scope, increase the resources, and reform the content of public educational provision in order to deal with the commonly perceived problem of industrial efficiency. Maximizing productivity in an industrial economy was thought to require better educated professional and managerial workers for whom a modern secondary education in liberal arts and science was an essential intermediate educational stage between elementary school and higher education or professional training. Maximizing productivity in an industrial economy equally required better trained clerical and industrial workers, for whom courses in commercial and technical subjects were an essential educational means to make an efficient transition from school to work. Whether they were organized on the basis of strict separation between public and private sectors or as complementary sectors of church and state schools, most Anglo-American educational jurisdictions in the early twentieth century not only extended the scope of their public schools fully to embrace secondary education but also sought to reform their secondary curricula by modernizing classical academic courses and introducing new options of general and technical programs as integral parts of public regimes. The main exceptions were the three denominational regimes of Newfoundland, Northern Ireland, and Quebec, where traditional academic courses continued to dominate secondary education, denominational schools were the main service providers, and marginalized sectors of vocational education were segregated from the mainstream of elementary and secondary schooling.

Reforming public education for industrial efficiency implied a major expansion in the commitment of public resources in order to finance not only the expansion of academic and general secondary education but also the development of relatively more expensive technical secondary education. Between 1900 and 1945, moreover, government spending on public education was affected by the shocks to public agendas and fiscal priorities of two world wars and an economic depression. Government expenditures on public education did rise in Canada, New Zealand, the United Kingdom, and the United States to 2 to 2.5 per cent of gross domestic product by the mid-1930s (but only 1.4 per cent in Australia) before dipping as a result of the Second World War (Figure 1; Table 1). With regard to the delivery of educational services relative to national income on an individual basis, government expenditures per student varied from 5.6 per cent to 7.3 per cent of gross domestic product per capita in the first decade of the twentieth century but increased in all countries by the mid-1930s to 10.1 to 14.7 per cent before decreasing during the war, most noticeably in Canada and the United States (Figure 2; Table 2).

Prior to the 1940s, spending on public education accounted for only 3 to 6 per cent of total government spending in Australia and New Zealand, 7 to 10 per cent in the United Kingdom, and 10 to 18 per cent in

Canada and the United States (Figure 3; Table 3). As for the relative priority of government spending on education in the public sector, government expenditures per student rose substantially as a percentage of government expenditures per capita in Canada (80.5 per cent) and the United States (86 per cent) in 1925–6 and to a lesser ratio in the United Kingdom (60.6 per cent) in 1912–13 and fell between 51.5 to 56.7 per cent in 1935–6 (Figure 4; Table 4). By contrast, the ratios of government spending on education per student compared with total government spending per capita were much lower in Australia (28.8 per cent) and New Zealand (20.5 per cent). Not surprisingly, given the huge defence expenditures incurred by all countries, government expenditures on public education fell between 2 per cent (Australia) and 3.6 per cent (United States) of total government expenditures at the end of the Second World War, and international differences virtually disappeared in government spending on education per student compared to total government spending per capita.

In contrast with the increases in government spending on education relative to both gross domestic product and total government expenditures, increases in the employment of full-time teachers as a percentage of the total labour force from 1900 to the 1920s and 1930s were scarcely significant and, except for New Zealand, had disappeared by the end of the Second World War (Figure 5; Table 6). Peacetime employment of teachers was 6 to 9 per cent of total government employment in Australia and New Zealand and fell from 15.3 per cent in Great Britain in 1910–11 to 10 per cent in 1937–8 (Figure 6; Table 7). Teachers were a much larger and consistently important component of government employment in Canada (about 38 per cent between the wars), while the employment of teachers in the United States fell from 36.3 per cent of government employment at the turn of the century to 28.3 per cent in 1929–30, then dropped to 16 per cent in the middle of the Depression.

Measures of improvement in the quality of public education during this period are ambiguous. On the one hand, early in the century there were significant differences in the ratios of enrolments to full-time teachers in public schools, ranging from 54.1 in Australia in 1905 to 35.7 in the United States in 1905–6 (Figure 7; Table 8). Over the next four decades, the range of differences narrowed, from 30.1 in Australia in 1945 to 26.1 in the United Kingdom in 1946–7. On the other hand, no simple pattern is evident in another measure of changes in quality, government spending per student (Table 5). Average annual increases in real government expenditures per student were quite positive early in the century in Canada, New Zealand, the United Kingdom, and the United States, but only the United Kingdom sustained a relatively high (4.6 per cent) increase annually from 1925–6 to 1935–6. Average annual increases were initially lower in Australia but jumped to 4.7 per cent annually from 1915 to 1925. From the mid-1930s to the end of the Second World War there were positive rates of growth in Australia, Canada, the United Kingdom, and the United States, while the larger rate of increase in New Zealand (5.1 per cent) no doubt resulted from the strong commitment to improving public education on the part of the Labour government elected in 1935.

Educational reform for industrial efficiency shifted the focus of policy development from elementary to secondary education. As a result there was a clear improvement in retention in the intermediate grades (Tables 9A to 9E). Enrolments in intermediate grades ranged from 6.3 per cent of students in public elementary and secondary schools in Australia in 1915 to 15.9 per cent in the United States in 1915–16, and 20 per cent of students in Great Britain were age twelve to fourteen in 1913–14. By 1945, 21.7 per cent of Australian students were enrolled in intermediate grades ranging up to 25.3 per cent in New Zealand. The improvement in enrolments in senior grades, however, was much more variable. In the United States in 1915–16, 4.3 per cent of students were enrolled in senior grades; by 1945–6, 17.1 per cent of students were attending senior grades, with most of the improvement having taken place by 1935–6. The increase in the percentages of students in upper secondary years was less impressive than in the United States but none the less significant in both Canada (2.9 per cent in 1915–16; 9.2 per cent in 1945–6) and New Zealand (0.9 per cent in 1915; 10 per cent in 1945). In Australia, by contrast, the enrolments in senior years increased only from 0.3 to 2.9 per cent of total enrolments, and in the United Kingdom 1 per cent of students were age fifteen and over in 1913–14 rising to 3.8 per cent in 1945–6.

Beyond the commitment of public resources, the educational problem of industrial efficiency was one of how to reorganize secondary schools: whether to construct a partite secondary system by establishing separate schools for each major type of secondary program; create multilateral secondary schools by designing separate academic and vocational streams, usually with a core of common subjects, to be offered within the same school; or give priority to individual student development and integrate academic and vocational studies in comprehensive high schools. In addition, there were recurring issues of the respective roles to be played by public versus private sectors of secondary schools, the degree of centralization in educational policy and administration compared to local governance, and the ongoing relationship of church and state. Generalizing from the various specific resolutions of these major issues of educational provision and governance, three main types of educational regimes can be identified that were designed to reform secondary academic and vocational education in pursuit of industrial efficiency.

First, the educational regimes of Australia, New Zealand, and Scotland combined partite systems of secondary schools with centralized governance. Secondary schooling for the academic élite in Australia and New Zealand was generally differentiated and segregated in separate schools from both vocational secondary education in commerce, industry, agriculture, and domestic arts and general secondary education that was essentially advanced public instruction. In Scotland, where technical schools were not developed, there was a bipartite system of élite academic education in secondary schools and general education in the higher grades of parish schools. Secondary educational selection was implemented and legitimated by public external examinations that determined entry to secondary education, passage from lower secondary years to upper secondary years, and matriculation at the end of secondary school. Although endowed schools became less important in Scotland, élite academic secondary education continued to be the mission of denominational and non-denominational schools in the private sector. Especially in Australia, despite such notable exceptions as Sydney Boys' High School, Sydney Girls' High School, and Perth Modern School, the public sector was regarded as a residual provider of upper-secondary academic education. State secondary schools were primarily expected to deliver advanced general and vocational education for the masses.

Individual ministerial responsibility had been firmly established in Australia and New Zealand as the central principle of public accountability in their educational regimes to govern public instruction, and it was equally present in Scotland by the end of the nineteenth century. Given the public problem of industrial efficiency in the early twentieth century, educational administration became dominated by directors of education or permanent secretaries who were professional educators, and the function of educational policy was carried out by a conjugation of executive leadership involving ministers of education or secretaries of state as policy-making politicians with directors of education and permanent secretaries as policy-making administrators. In Australia and New Zealand, this centralization of educational policy and administration was reflected in, and reinforced by, the unionization of teachers and agreements on quasi-corporatist procedures to regulate teaching services. In Australia, educational regimes became systems of bureaucratic administration as district school boards were replaced by school councils or committees of parents and citizens that were expected to conduct school-level promotional and improvement activities and refrain from meddling in the business of educational governance. Historical agencies of local educational governance continued to operate in New Zealand. None the less, the bureaucratization of educational policy and administration, in particular the centralization of school inspection and teaching service, combined with the split between education boards responsible for post-primary education in district high schools and boards of governors and managers of academic and technical high schools to ensure that in practice local bodies were administrative agents of the New Zealand Department of Education. As for Scotland, the amalgamation of school boards in 1918 followed by the reorganization of local educational governance as a function of county and burgh councils in 1929 did not noticeably affect the previously established relationship between the Scottish Education Department and the school boards as its administrative agents.

In the case of Canada, the educational regimes that were reformed for industrial efficiency presented a more ambivalent variation on the partite systems of secondary schools and centralized governance found in Australia, New Zealand, and Scotland. Under the pacesetting Industrial Education Act of Ontario, passed in 1911, technical departments were authorized in academic high schools, but the thrust of the legislation – and the clear intention of policy makers – was the establishment of separate academic and vocational secondary schools in cities throughout the province. Separate vocational secondary schools were also instituted in New Brunswick and major cities of the western provinces, but not in Nova Scotia until 1953 or in Prince Edward Island until 1964. At the same time, academic high schools in Canada often included a general program along with the traditional matriculation program, and many of them offered some sort of business or commerce option as well. As with the educational regimes of Australia, New Zealand, and Scotland, entrance to high school depended on passing departmental examinations, although this hurdle was gradually removed between 1930 and 1950, and matriculation was determined by external public examinations administered jointly by provincial departments of education and provincial universities.

The constitutional conventions with regard to political accountability for provincial education in Canada were also ambivalent. In Ontario and the West the individual responsibility of ministers of education was well established, but in the Maritimes the collective responsibility of cabinets acting as provincial councils of public instruction survived until the 1930s and 1940s. None the less, deputy ministers of education in all provinces (except Quebec) were now invariably professional educators with long careers as teachers, inspectors, and administrators prior to starting their normally lengthy tenure as administrative heads of their provincial departments. Educational policy was the product of central executive leadership that combined ministers (and premiers) as politicians with deputy ministers as administrators. At the local level, larger urban districts, which were authorized to appoint their own administrative staffs headed by a city inspector or superintendent and hence exempted from provincial inspection, tended to develop a modest degree of administrative autonomy from their provincial department, but with rare exceptions, policy direction remained firmly under provincial control. Otherwise, attempts to consolidate school districts had little effect prior to the Second World War, and most school districts were still small jurisdictions that were strictly subordinate as administrative agents of provincial departments.

In a second type of approach to dealing with the problem of industrial efficiency, the educational regime of England and Wales combined a partite system of secondary schools with more decentralized educational governance. The educational regime envisaged in the landmark reports of the Bryce and Hadow commissions assumed an inherent distinction between intellectual and manual work in industrial economies and proposed an organization of secondary schools that would correspond to such an occupational class structure. Especially in England, there was an influential private sector for élite academic secondary schooling. Under the regulations designed and implemented starting in 1904, grammar schools in the public sector also provided a traditional academic education in liberal arts and science for an élite group of students, junior technical schools delivered vocational education that focused on industrial training, and general secondary education was available for a minority of ordinary students in the higher grades of elementary schools. Despite being strongly selective, however, the regime did not have a centralized system of public examinations as was the case in Australia, Canada, New Zealand, and Scotland.

The abolition of school boards and the designation of general municipal governments as local education authorities had a decentralizing effect on educational policy making in England and Wales. As the new central authority for education, the Board of Education, now clearly led by its president as political head with individual ministerial responsibility, acquired a more influential role of policy leadership through commissioning policy reports, framing educational regulations, and inspecting local schools; however, the close regulation and strict auditing to which school boards had been subjected since 1870 were substantially lifted. A nascent policy community involving officials of the Board of Education, organized teachers, and associations of education committees and municipal corporations also began to form in the 1920s and 1930s, a development that reinforced this relationship of policy tutelage that focused educational policy at the centre while granting more administrative discretion to local authorities and curricular freedom to school staffs.

As a third type of educational regime for industrial efficiency, the educational regimes of the United States in general combined multilateral public secondary schools and decentralized educational governance. Beginning in the 1890s, separate commercial and technical high schools were established in several big cities for the purpose of delivering vocational secondary education, but the policy recommendations of the NEA Commission on the Reorganization of Secondary Education in 1918 defined the principles for organizing secondary education as several separate streams for college preparation and vocational training within the same school. By that time the United States was already the clear national leader in the provision of secondary schooling, and the rapid expansion of secondary schools, especially of enrolments in the upper secondary years where vocational subjects were more often offered as options to the academic stream, ensured that, well before the Second World War, the model of multilateral secondary schooling dominated educational regimes in the United States.

Under the influence of Progressive educational and political theorizing preoccupied with the need for professionalism and efficiency in public management, there were movements in the United States to strengthen educational policy and administration, first, by amalgamating small school districts into larger township or (even better) county school districts, and second, by creating offices of state superintendents, appointed by the governor, to give strong central policy and administrative direction to state education or, alternatively, state boards of education appointed by the governor to make general educational policy and also appoint the state superintendent to act as their chief administrative officer. These Progressive reform movements had some successes in several northeastern and central states, but the majority of states continued to elect their state superintendents, thus in effect opting for populist democracy over managerial efficiency. Similarly, with the exception of the South, where the county school district was the historical tradition and an instrument of county machine politics rather than civic trusteeship, prior to the Second World War there was no evident trend to abandon the preference for local democracy in educational governance that had been institutionalized as part of the nineteenth-century regimes of public instruction. In contrast with bureaucratic administration in the Australian states, the policy tutelage adopted in England and Wales, or the relationship of administrative agency in eight of nine Canadian provinces, New Zealand, and Scotland, the relations of state and local educational authorities in the United States persisted as institutionalized fiscal equivalence, with state superintendents, state school boards, and state departments of education operating in one political arena and an array of local school boards with various, often overlapping, territorial boundaries in another. State and local educational jurisdictions, if not entirely exclusive domains, were none the less still relatively autonomous in their politics, policy, and administration.

The reform of curricula and the reorganization of schools to deal with the problem of industrial efficiency were overwhelmingly concentrated in urban public secondary schools. Overall, while the size of the private sector continued to vary across educational regimes, the private sector in each country did not change in size relative to the public sector from the turn of the century to the Second World War (Table 10). Nor did redesigning educational regimes for industrial efficiency result in major changes in the various relationships of church and state in public education that had been created during the founding of regimes of public instruction during the nineteenth century. In the surviving denominational regimes of Newfoundland, Northern Ireland, and Quebec, vocational education and training were not only underdeveloped but also outside the structure of public secondary education. Separate or reserved schools for Roman Catholics in Ontario, Saskatchewan, Alberta, and the Maritimes and voluntary schools in England and Wales and Scotland continued to operate with traditional academic curricula that were largely unaffected by the problem of industrial efficiency. Similarly, the programs of Roman Catholic schools in Australia, New Zealand, and the United States emphasized standard academic subjects.

Within the public sector, policy responses to the problem of industrial efficiency envisaged a strong connection between state and market in the political economy of urban education. Partite secondary systems and multilateral high schools were designed for public secondary education in cities and towns. Secondary education in rural areas, whether delivered in small district high schools or as an extension of elementary schooling, continued for the most part to be a conventional academic program. Thus, the efforts to reproduce the occupational class hierarchy of industrial capitalism in public education were concentrated in urban public secondary schools, and this concentration exacerbated three types of inequality: between urban and rural public schools; between urban public schools and mass separate, voluntary, and parochial schools, which were excluded from public funding for secondary vocational education and training; and between urban public schools and élite private schools, which continued to deliver a traditional academic ('professional') course fitted to educating the children of the business, professional, and managerial classes.

Giving priority to the problem of industrial efficiency tended to undermine the local democracy that had been a major feature of regimes of public instruction. In the United States, the aspirations of liberal-conservative Progressive reformers to centralize educational governance were mostly unfulfilled. Outside the United States, however, centralization of educational governance ranged from policy tutelage on the part of the Board of Education in England and Wales through treating school boards as administrative agents of provincial governments in Canada and Scotland to centralized bureaucratic administration in Australia and New Zealand. Maximizing economic productivity for purposes of national wealth and security as an objective of educational policy was also advanced as a reason to replace the judgments of uninformed citizens and partisan politicians with decision making by professional educators with regard to the design and implementation of academic and vocational curricula. In turn, this threatened to restrict the freedom of citizens to participate, if not in educational politics, certainly in educational policy making and administration.

Focusing on the public problem of industrial efficiency tended to shift political conflicts and policy arguments from the meaning of community, with its inherent tension between civic nationalism and communal identities – the primary concern during the founding of regimes based on public instruction – to the meaning of equality, with particular reference to equality of educational opportunity and the relationship between élite and mass education in an industrial economy and democratic polity. Introducing the inequalities of occupational class in industrial society and the issue of state versus market on top of historical divisions over religion, language, and race in public education not only divided conservatives, liberals, and socialists from each other, it also increasingly divided these ideological traditions within themselves. Across the Anglo-American educational jurisdictions, the shape of thought and argument about the organization and content of public education was dominated by liberal-conservative and utilitarian-liberal ideas, while communitarian conservatives were now very much on the defensive. Yet other voices – those of ethical liberalism, social democracy, and democratic socialism – were also now being heard. These had found some expression in the nineteenth-century argument about public instruction, but now began to acquire a new force and coherence.

3 Welfare State

The devastating impact of worldwide depression in the 1930s and the challenging problems of postwar reconstruction in the 1940s together shifted the political agenda and transformed the structures and purposes of government in the Anglo-American democracies. Economic growth remained a high priority. To the array of existing interventions through industrial policy were added stabilization policy instruments to minimize fluctuations in the level of economic production, rates of unemployment and inflation, and balance of trade. Social security was the new priority; the welfare state was the counterpart of the managed economy. Based on the principles of universality and comprehensiveness, state intervention by means of social policy instruments was decisively extended and deepened to include new measures that sought to moderate or supersede free exchange in markets and thus enhance the social welfare of all citizens.

The development of the welfare state differed greatly among the Anglo-American democracies. In the United States, a weak welfare state featured minimal public assistance, unemployment insurance, and old age security. The moderate welfare states of Australia and Canada added family allowances, universal pensions, and, belatedly, health insurance. In New Zealand and the United Kingdom, relatively stronger welfare states extended their activities to cover national health services and public housing. These differences among Anglo-American welfare states in their health, income security, and housing policies extended to include differences about the place and purpose of public education in the welfare state. Here there were four major issues.

The first issue concerned the very definition of the welfare state: should education be included as a major sector among universal social services provided under the aegis of the welfare state or should its role be restricted to specific universal programs such as school milk and school meals and categorical programs targeted for disadvantaged children?[1] Historically, in each of the Anglo-American democracies public education was seen in varying degrees as serving public purposes of forming communal identity, fostering civic socialization, and furthering industrial efficiency. The concept of the welfare state, based on the principles of universality and comprehensiveness, raised the issue of whether public education ought now to be understood as social policy rather than civic or industrial policy. Treating public education as social policy within the welfare state put priority on making secondary and higher education universally accessible, even while the meaning of accessibility, for example, 'secondary education for all,' might continue to be politically contested. It meant dealing with the effects of economic and social disadvantage on learning. Conceiving education as social policy also had implications for understanding the purpose of public education, shifting the focus of school organization and curriculum design from communal identity, civic socialization, and industrial efficiency to meeting basic needs of children and adolescents for knowledge as the condition to live freely and creatively, with respect and self-respect, participating fully in their community.

A second issue was educational governance in the welfare state. As a political project, the welfare state consisted of state intervention in the market economy by means of positive social programs in order to ensure that the basic needs of citizens were met. Deciding the substance of basic needs as well as the requirements for their satisfaction depended on some combination of expert planning and public deliberation. On the one hand, construction of the welfare state involved the organization of large public bureaucracies staffed by qualified health, education, and welfare professionals who possessed the specialized knowledge and organizational capacity to set standards, assess shortfalls, and develop social programs to meet basic needs. On the other hand, the determination of what were basic needs, which ones should have priority for public provision, and how social programs should be designed to meet basic needs were politically contested questions that required public deliberation and consensus. From this perspective, the priority in reforming governance for the welfare state ought to be put on democratization rather than bureaucratization of social policy making.

Third, public education in the welfare state raised the issue of the relationship between the public and private sectors in education. This was an argument about the domain of equality in the welfare state. For some, the welfare state was a residual safety net; for others it was an ethical commitment to the ideals of social equality and collective solidarity. For those who envisaged the welfare state as residual, the survival and even expansion of the private sector at all levels of education, continued to be welcome rather than problematic. For those who envisaged the welfare state as building a community based on fraternity and equality, the existence of a private sector in education blocked the realization of their dream.

Fourth, public education in the welfare state renewed the issue of the relationship between church and state. Here the argument concerned reliance on individualism versus corporatism in planning and implementing social programs under the aegis of the welfare state. The welfare state could be organized to deliver social programs, including public education, directly from state agencies to individual citizens. Alternatively, programs could be designed to take account of the communal identities or occupational affiliations of citizens so that social programs were designed and implemented in partnership with major communal organizations and/or occupational associations. In public education, the dominant form of communal organization continued to be the church. As with debates over public instruction and industrial efficiency, the question of fitting public education into the welfare state put into a new context the enduring controversy as to whether it should be strictly secular, moderately non-denominational, or avowedly sectarian.

The theory and practice of the welfare state were hotly contested during the postwar reconstruction period. On the one hand, there were outright opponents of the welfare state. Liberals and conservatives who were dedicated to the market simply resisted the expansion of the public economy and especially the increased level of social expenditures that invariably accompanied every definition of the welfare state. On the other hand, proponents of the welfare state held very different understandings of its political meaning and policy implications. The social rights of citizenship constituted the core concept of the welfare state, but they were defined differently by conservatives, liberals, and socialists.[2]

In justifying their plans for the design and implementation of educational policies for the welfare state, communitarian and liberal conservatives relied on a concept of segmental equality. Rather than equal opportunity or social redistribution based on the principal of universality, the conservative idea of social citizenship in the welfare state stressed the priorities of public order and collective welfare. Conservatives assessed the welfare needs of individuals not only against the background of their natural communities of family, church, and neighbourhood but also in the context of their functional attributes of economic class and social status. Adequate provision ought to be made to secure the material needs of all citizens, but neither needs nor adequacy could be determined without reference to the indispensable hierarchies of state, community, and market. The preservation of class and status distinctions essential for material wealth, social stability, and collective welfare in modern societies depended in turn on a corresponding hierarchy of differentiated educational programs. Conservatives assumed that traditional class and status distinctions would continue to provide the primary basis for allocating education. Especially among liberal conservatives, however, there was also a recognition that technological change in advanced industrial economies was transforming the structure of occupational classes so as to vitiate any straightforward intergenerational transfer of class and status identities and differentials. The educational regime of the welfare state had become a crucial instrument for perpetuating hierarchy and legitimizing élites under modern conditions of representative democracy and capitalist markets.

For liberals, public education was not relevant or at best only weakly connected to their idea of the welfare state. Both utilitarian and ethical liberals saw the welfare state as residual, a safety net to the market. Public education, by contrast, was justified by its purposes of civic socialization, industrial efficiency, and individual freedom. Liberals raised no objections to the existence of a private sector in the supply of primary and secondary education. None the less, however much utilitarian and ethical liberals might argue among themselves about the appropriate level of state expenditures on public education, they were agreed that public education should be more than residual to the education privately supplied and more than minimal in its standard of provision. Educational resources were powerful means to realize individual preferences, whether in markets or in politics, and hence equality of opportunity in education was an essential component of social justice in democratic market societies. The distribution of educational services would not be identical for each person; but, given variations in preferences and abilities, each person in school ought to derive value from his or her education equal to the value gained by other individuals from their education. This person-regarding equality depended on individual freedom to choose one's education. Utilitarian liberals perceived individual choice in terms of opportunity to compete for upward class and status mobility, and they defended differentiated secondary tracks as a cost-efficient means to offer students educational choices that were consistent with the occupational class structure of a capitalist industrial economy. For ethical liberals, who were advocates of progressive ('child-centred' or 'student-centred') education, secondary education ought to provide an equal opportunity for all students to get an integrated academic, general, and vocational education, based on their established needs for individual development and broadly conceived for a liberal society rather than narrowly defined by the liberal market.

According to the socialist theory of the welfare state, justice in the production and delivery of social policy required person-regarding equality – equal consideration for each person's individual needs rather than equal lots. Social programs should not necessarily treat each person identically or interchangeably with others. In contrast to the liberal idea of means-regarding equality of opportunity, however, at the core of socialist thinking was a commitment to prospects-regarding equality. Social policy was an essential instrument for equalizing life prospects in order to compensate for individual disadvantage. Disadvantage might require compensatory social programs of the welfare state at many times during each person's life, but childhood and adolescence were crucial stages when social programs, whether targeted directly at children and youth or indirectly at alleviating the poverty of their families and neighbourhoods, could have decisive effects on equalizing life prospects for individual development. Hence, for socialists, education became one of the pillars of the welfare state. Social democrats and democratic socialists might differ with regard to the continuance of élite independent schools or their plans for secondary school reorganization, but they were unanimous that the standards of state educational provision had to be raised to provide an education of the highest possible quality to all persons in school. They were committed to increasing the level of public expenditure on state education, a level that in their view was too low not simply in comparison with relative expenditures per person enrolled in élite independent schools but more generally, given the major impact of educational resources on meeting human needs. They were also committed to expanding the boundaries of state educational provision, downward from primary education to cover kindergarten and nursery schools and upward to encompass postsecondary college and university education.

Australia: Liberal-Conservative Legacies versus
Utilitarian-Liberal Possibilities

The idea of the Australian welfare state, which was developed originally in national reconstruction planning during the Second World War and which then trickled down into state politics, focused on full employment and social insurance. Public education did not figure prominently in either national or state wartime planning.[3] In the immediate postwar years, educational planners and administrators concentrated their efforts on providing places for the larger numbers of children coming into primary schools. As the rising tide of enrolments began to reach secondary school, however, the relatively straightforward problem of physical expansion at the primary level was reformulated to focus on the principle of universality and the provision of secondary education for all. Educational policy making shifted to include not only needs for physical expansion at the secondary level but also issues of secondary school reorganization, curricular reform, and the meaning of equality of opportunity in education.

State educational regimes in Australia, as they developed during the era of the welfare state, had four main features. First, there was a general shift from a liberal-conservative model of partite systems to a utilitarian-liberal model of multilateral secondary schools in which educational tracks were open to consumer preferences rather than restricted by means of competitive selection. Second, a strong strain of liberal-conservative thinking continued to be evident in the emphasis on merit selection and ability grouping in the progress of students inside Australian secondary schools. Third, the expansion of the principle of universality from elementary to secondary education had little effect on the institutional arrangements for governing public education, but it did shift the composition of the teaching force and increase the complexity of curricular development, changes that together strengthened the political position of organized teachers and forced state officials in departments of education to put greater reliance on working in concert with teachers in educational policy networks. Fourth, the expansion and restructuring of public education from the 1950s to the 1970s increasingly threatened the historical duality of educational regimes in Australia. Ironically, by the late 1960s and early 1970s, as the welfare state in Australia realized its apotheosis, protecting the position of the private sector, not only to ensure the survival and renewal of Roman Catholic schools but also to perpetuate the standards and prestige of élite private schools, had become a major priority of national educational policy making.

Applying the Principle of Universality: Partite Systems versus Multilateral Schools

The principle of universality was the contested idea at the core of the Australian welfare state. In the educational policy domain, the principle of universality was symbolized by the slogan 'secondary education for all.' According to the emerging consensus among educational policy makers, the selective impact of external examinations had to be alleviated so that students could move unimpeded from primary into secondary schools. Equally important, greater weight needed to be given to the preferences of students and their parents in making choices among secondary schools and programs. Secondary education for all, however, did not mean the same education for all young people. During the 1950s and 1960s, three different approaches were taken to reorganizing public secondary education in Australia, but each showed a common commitment to the utilitarian-liberal ideas of equal opportunity, unequal talents, and unequal outcomes.

In Tasmania, Western Australia, and Queensland, public secondary education was reorganized from partite systems to multilateral schools. In Tasmania, a tripartite system of academic, technical, and 'modern' (general) secondary schools was officially proclaimed in 1946, following the recommendations of the Education Department's Committee of Inquiry into Educational Extension, but this plan was soon compromised. The technical high schools in Hobart (1949) and Launceston (1950) added foreign languages to their offerings and thus created an opportunity for their students to take either a technical or a 'professional' (academic) course. Academic high schools, which already offered commercial courses, now began to offer technical subjects as well, and four bilateral high schools were opened from 1953 to 1955, with their students divided between academic and general ('modern') tracks. Following his visit to Britain and the United States in 1955 the director of education recommended experimentation with a multilateral form of secondary organization.[4] Modern schools were renamed 'secondary schools,' the first official multilateral secondary school (Taroon High School) was opened in 1958, the standardized classification test – which together with school records and headmasters' recommendations had provided the basis for selection in a partite secondary school system – was dropped in 1962, and the term 'technical high school' disappeared from the official lexicon. In Western Australia, a departmental committee on secondary education in 1954 recommended multilateral district high schools as the standard organization for state high schools, and under the Labor government led by Albert Hawke, multilateral three-year and five-year high schools were built throughout the state.[5] Classes in these schools were grouped according to ability, and beyond first year, students enrolled in one of several predetermined programs, including academic, commercial, domestic science, and technical. In Queensland, state high schools built in the 1950s were multilateral and coeducational, but the academic course continued to dominate. The interim report of the departmental Committee of Inquiry into Queensland Education in 1961 recommended raising the school leaving age to fifteen, transfer from primary to secondary school at the end of grade seven, abolition of the scholarship examination as a test for entry to secondary school, and reorganization of public secondary education in multilateral schools.[6] In Brisbane, where there was a partite system of secondary school organization, Brisbane Industrial High School was closed in 1961, followed the next year by Brisbane Domestic Science and Brisbane State Commercial high schools.

In New South Wales, a more extensive reform shifted the organization of public secondary schools from tracks defined by occupational classes to ability grouping by subjects. The Committee to Survey Secondary Education chaired by the director of education, H.S. Wyndham, assumed that 'secondary education is the education not of a select minority, whatever the base of selection, either social or intellectual, but of all adolescents, irrespective of their interests, talents and prospects.'[7] The committee proposed that at around age twelve all students should proceed without examination from primary to secondary education. The high school curriculum would comprise a set of common subjects in all schools, with an increasing proportion of elective subjects in higher grades. At the end of the fourth year, students would be awarded a school certificate based on a set of external examinations. Two further years of study would take students who chose to continue to examinations for the higher school certificate, the level for university matriculation. When the Wyndham plan was introduced in 1962 there were three levels of courses for the purposes of external examinations ('advanced' for the top quartile, 'credit' for the third quartile, and 'ordinary' for the second quartile), as well as 'modified' courses for the bottom quartile of students. The official policy envisaged comprehensive, coeducational, six-year high schools throughout New South Wales, but intense public criticism persuaded the Department of Education to compromise and allow eleven high schools in Sydney, four in Newcastle, and one in Wollongong to continue to operate as selective academic schools. Seven were still operating as selective schools in May 1984 when a new Labor minister (Rod Cavalier) rescinded the official policy and promised to preserve all existing selective high schools.[8]

In South Australia and Victoria, academic and technical high schools widened their range of subjects and diversified their courses during the 1950s and 1960s so that their programs increasingly overlapped, but the two distinct types of secondary schools remained in existence. In South Australia, selective entry was abolished in the early 1950s so that students and their parents were free to choose between types of secondary school. Once enrolled in an academic high school, however, students were classified on the basis of ability tests and school records into three streams, with only the top stream, which took two foreign languages, headed for the public examinations. In technical high schools, three streams also were gradually defined, with a minority of students following a four-year course determined by the Public Examinations Board, the majority taking a three-year internally assessed course, and the remainder taking a two-year 'alternative' course. In Victoria a departmental committee on post-primary education chaired by the director of education, A.H. Ramsay, observed in 1960 that a multilateral form of secondary organization might have been preferred; however, he concluded that, 'For practical purposes it is not possible to rebuild a system which has developed two distinct types of post-primary education, Secondary and Technical.'[9] As in South Australia, the committee proposed that there be no selective tests for entry; the choice between types of secondary schools should be made by students and their parents. Moreover, subjects taken over the first two years of secondary school should be as much as possible the same, and there should be careful assessment of each student's achievements at the end of two years for the purpose of recommending their transfer to a more suitable program.[10]

A key element of Australian reform to achieve secondary education for all was the abolition of all but the final school-leaving (matriculation) examination. First to be dropped were external entrance and intermediate examinations.[11] Then, in the late 1950s and early 1960s, there was a trend to differentiate the penultimate external examinations taken after ten or eleven years of school from the senior, higher, or honours examinations taken at the end of twelve years. The Junior (Queensland, Western Australia), Leaving (South Australia, Victoria), School (New South Wales), and Schools Board (Tasmania) certificate examinations were revised to provide a general examination appropriate for all secondary students, not simply a junior version of matriculation designed for students in an academic course.[12] Subsequently, these examinations were converted to internal school assessments in Tasmania (1969), Western Australia (1971), Queensland (1972), and New South Wales (1975) and were discontinued in Victoria (1972) and South Australia (1974).[13] By contrast, public external examinations at the end of secondary school were retained in all states except Queensland, where a procedure for externally moderated, school-based assessment was introduced in 1972, and these leaving examinations all continued to be heavily dominated by an academic curriculum oriented to postsecondary studies and professional qualification.[14]

Educational Governance in the Australian Welfare State:
State Officials and Organized Teachers in Concert

The bureaucratic organization of educational administration in the Australian states was essentially unchanged by the growth of enrolments and the expansion of services from the 1940s to the 1970s. The Commonwealth Office of Education was established in 1945, initially in the Department of Post-War Reconstruction, though it later moved to the Prime Minister's Department. Federal educational activities were focused on universities, research, and Aboriginal education, however, and had little impact on the development of public primary and secondary schools administered by the six states until the 1960s, when the first federal grants were made for laboratories and libraries in secondary (including non-government) schools.[15] In New South Wales a separate Department of Technical Education was created in 1949 to administer postsecondary technical education; both secondary academic and technical education were administered by a unified division of the Department of Education headed by the director of secondary education. In other states, the basic organization of departments into a division of administrative services and separate divisions for primary, secondary, and technical education, established during the 1910s and 1920s, was unchanged.

Educational policy making and administration continued to be strongly centralized. In New South Wales an experiment to decentralize state educational administration was initiated in 1946 with the formation of a regional administrative area in the Riverina district. Five more regional administrative districts were established in 1952, eventually expanding to eleven districts. A move to decentralize educational administration in Queensland originated during the 1947 electoral campaign, when the incumbent Labor premier promised to decentralize state departments starting with the Department of Education. Following the Labor party's victory, four regional directors of education were appointed, and three more were added during the 1950s. In both Queensland and New South Wales the degree of administrative decentralization that was actually implemented was quite modest, and over the next two decades no other states followed their lead.[16]

A more substantial change in educational governance institutionalized collective bargaining with regard to salaries, appointments, and working conditions in Victoria, South Australia, and Western Australia. Pressures by the Victorian Teachers' Union (VTU) over many years for an independent Teachers' Tribunal were finally successful in 1946, following the election of a Labor government committed to the VTU proposal. Comprising a representative of the VTU, the Education Department, and an independent chair, the tribunal assumed jurisdiction formerly exercised by the Public Service Board to settle disputes about salaries, terms of employment, and working conditions, including determination of pupil–teacher ratios, appeals from decisions of classification committees about appointments and promotions, and adjudication of disciplinary charges brought against teachers under the Education Act.[17] The Teachers' Salary Board in South Australia, established in 1945 as a counterpart to the Classification Board, comprised representatives of the Department of Education and the South Australia Teachers' Association and was authorized to determine salary ranges, increments, allowances, and qualifications for all teaching positions. In Western Australia, the Government School Teachers' Tribunal in 1960 consolidated appeals concerning salaries, promotions, conditions of service, and disciplinary actions that had been the functions of separate boards, including the Public Service Appeal Board (salaries, classification) dating from 1920 and the Government Employees Promotion Appeal Board established in 1945.

In New South Wales, Queensland, and Tasmania, education departments gained more operational autonomy to decide appointments, classification, promotions, discipline, and allocations of teachers, but public service boards continued to be key decision makers with regard to teachers' salaries and working conditions.[18] Salaries were negotiated between the NSW Teachers' Federation and the Public Service Board during the 1940s and 1950s, but as agreements became more difficult to reach during the more inflationary 1960s, final settlements were determined by reference to the Industrial Commission. Similarly, the Queensland Teachers' Union gave notice of its salary claims to the Department of Education, Public Service Board, and Industrial Commission, and if the Public Service Board declined to negotiate, then the settlement was decided by a hearing before the commission.[19] A Teachers' Salary Board, with its chair appointed by the government, a second member appointed by the Department of Education, and a third member elected by teachers, was created in Tasmania in 1952 to replace direct negotiations between the Tasmanian Teachers' Federation and the Department of Education. When the Public Service Tribunal was established in 1959, its mandate included determining teachers' salaries on the basis of claims by the Tasmanian Teachers' Federation.[20] In all three states, committees dealing with appointments, promotions, and discipline included representatives of the teachers' unions, as did the NSW Crown Employees Appeal Board, the Queensland Appeal Board, and the Appeals Committee in Tasmania.[21]

During the 1960s, with the exception of Western Australia, public examinations boards were reorganized to give education departments and teachers in state secondary schools more influence over curricula for lower secondary education, while state universities generally continued to predominate with regard to the prescription and examination of matriculation subjects.[22] The 1961 Education Act in New South Wales replaced the Board of Secondary Schools Studies – which comprised representatives of the university, the department, and independent schools – with two boards to administer examinations for the School Certificate and the Higher School Certificate, respectively. On the Board of Senior Schools Studies, the universities retained a strong presence (seven out of nineteen members) compared with the department (four members) and the New South Wales Teachers' Federation (three members). On the new Secondary Schools Board, which had jurisdiction over studies leading to the School Certificate examinations, the strong representation of the Department of Education (six out of twenty members) and the NSW Teachers' Federation–Secondary Teachers' Association (four members) contrasted with the much diminished role of the universities (three members).[23] A similar differentiation between boards of Junior and Senior Secondary School Studies was made in Queensland's 1964 Education Act. As in New South Wales, representatives of the department and the Queensland Teachers' Union together dominated the junior board, but representatives of the University of Queensland remained the predominant bloc on the senior board.[24] When the two boards were merged into the Board of Secondary School Studies in 1971, however, eight of the twenty-two members were nominees of the director general of education, seven were teachers, and five represented institutions of higher and further education.[25]

Public examinations boards in Victoria, South Australia, and Tasmania were not formally divided, but they were restructured to give greater weight to education departments and secondary schools. In Victoria, examinations for the Intermediate (year ten) and Leaving (year eleven) Certificates had been conducted since 1912 by the Schools Board of the University of Melbourne, which included representatives of the Education Department and independent secondary schools. Examinations for the Matriculation Certificate (year twelve) were administered by the university's Professorial Board. Following the establishment of Monash University, the Victorian Universities and Schools Examinations Board was authorized to prescribe syllabuses and examine subjects for all three examinations. Its thirty-eight members included seven from each of the universities and the Education Department, as well as representatives of private schools and business interests.[26] Similarly, the Public Examinations Board of the University of South Australia was reorganized in 1968 as an independent statutory authority, with its membership equally divided between secondary and tertiary educational interests and jurisdiction to conduct the leaving and matriculation examinations.[27] In Tasmania, the Schools Board, which had shared authority over public examinations with the University of Tasmania, was established as the sole examining body at the secondary level in 1966, and its reconstituted membership was carefully apportioned among representatives of the University of Tasmania, the Education Department, the Tasmanian Teachers' Federation, and heads of private secondary schools.[28]

Canada: From Ideas of British National Efficiency to American Progressive Education

The welfare state as a national political project in Canada made its official debut in two coloured papers published in 1945 by the Government of Canada. In its white paper on employment and income, the federal government 'stated unequivocally its adoption of a high and stable level of employment and income, and thereby higher standards of living, as a major aim of Government policy.'[29] The 'Green Book,' which was prepared for the 1945 Dominion-Provincial Conference on Reconstruction, outlined the federal government's proposals for a new set of state commitments and program instruments with regard to income security and health care.[30] Missing from this reconstruction planning was any thinking, at least outside the educational policy community, that reforming public schools was a necessary condition for creating a welfare state in Canada.

During and immediately following the Second World War, Canadian educational policy makers, though working in relative isolation from the high priorities of national economic and social policy making, were nevertheless influenced by the ideals and ideas of the emerging welfare state. Turning away from specialist vocational schools in a partite system, they embraced multilateral secondary schools that required a common core of compulsory academic subjects, to be taken by all students, while providing them with a choice of academic and vocational programs. Far from alleviating the structural rigidities of a partite system, however, multilateral secondary schools simply brought them inside the school. Moreover, the popular preference for the academic program and the consequent stigmatizing of general and vocational programs were also imported into the multilateral high school. As a result, during the 1960s there was a second round of reorganizing in secondary education with the aim of providing comprehensive secondary education based on individual student programs within the framework of a credit system.

Provincial commitment to multilateral, and subsequently comprehensive, secondary schools required the consolidation of small rural school sections into larger regional or county school divisions and the equalization of financial capacities between poor and wealthy districts. The existence of larger school districts with adequate fiscal capacity in turn created the potential for an adjustment of intergovernmental relations between provincial departments of education and local school boards from administrative agency to policy interdependence. The advancement of a national educational policy community was more problematic, however, as the federal government restricted its role in policy making for public schools to a limited program of grants for vocational secondary education.[31]

Comprehensiveness and Universality in Canadian Secondary Education: Multilateral Schools versus Comprehensive Education

The dual problem of Canadian secondary education, according to wartime and postwar reappraisals, was to organize a diversity of programs in order to meet the needs of different types of students while at the same time securing equality of opportunity for individual students. In order to alleviate inequalities between urban and rural educational opportunities, a national survey of educational needs by the Canada and Newfoundland Education Association in 1943 recommended the establishment of 'composite' high schools as a solution to the problem of providing for curricular diversity in secondary schools located in smaller communities. In addition, the survey committee argued that 'Operating such a composite high school is a further step in the direction of democracy, whereas the separating of pupils in different kinds of school leads to a distinction between classes almost at the threshold of life. Schools of this type should be set up all over the country for the purpose of training truly democratic citizens.'[32]

Two provinces, New Brunswick and Saskatchewan, initiated secondary reorganization policies based on multilateral schools. Building from a 1939 revision of the provincial curriculum into academic, home economics, industrial, and agricultural programs and the introduction of county school finance boards in 1943 to provide a consolidated tax base, New Brunswick had ten urban and twenty-four rural composite high schools in 1950 and opened ten more urban and twelve rural composite high schools during the 1950s.[33] First elected in 1944, the social-democratic Co-operative Commonwealth Federation government in Saskatchewan adopted as its general policy the recommendation of the Canada and Newfoundland Education Association in favour of composite high schools.[34] By the mid-1950s there were thirty-nine high schools, enrolling about 39 per cent of Saskatchewan's secondary school population and offering both academic and vocational courses.

In other provinces the record was less impressive. Ten fully composite high schools in Alberta, for example, enrolled about 25 per cent of secondary students in the province, and the high school program continued to be dominated by matriculation and general courses – 43 per cent of secondary students were enrolled in the matriculation program, 45 per cent in the general course, and only 12 per cent in the technical, commercial, and home-making courses.[35] In Ontario, which had been the province most committed to educational reform for industrial efficiency based on a tripartite system of academic, commercial, and industrial secondary schools, enrolment in composite secondary schools increased only slightly, from 17.3 per cent of total enrolment in secondary programs in 1938–9 to 19.8 per cent in 1950–1 and 20.1 per cent in 1960–1.[36] Thus, despite growing professional and political support for the concept of multilateral secondary schools, during the 1950s the majority of high school students in Canada continued to attend academic high schools in which they were limited to a choice between matriculation and general courses.[37]

In Quebec, where the Roman Catholic sector in particular had been little affected by either the pre-First World War campaign for industrial efficiency or the post-Second World War creation of the welfare state, educational reform was the heart of 'la Révolution tranquille' that transformed the Quebec state, economy, and society during the 1960s.[38] Following its victory in the provincial election of June 1960, the Liberal government of Jean Lesage appointed a royal commission on education, chaired by the Right Reverend Alphonse Marie Parent, whose final report was issued in five volumes from 1963 to 1966. In a democratic society, the commission asserted, education must be equally accessible to all, but curricula ought to be based on diversity, not uniformity.[39] To realize these principles of accessibility and diversity in policy and practice, the Parent commission proposed to reorganize Quebec public education into six years of elementary school, five years of secondary school, and two years of postsecondary 'institute.' Secondary education from years seven to eleven would be comprehensive education. In the seventh and eighth years (first cycle), students would combine basic subjects with a number of technical electives in order to explore the various domains of human knowledge. From the ninth to the eleventh years (second cycle), students aiming at job preparation and those intending further academic or technical studies would concentrate their electives accordingly, but predetermined curricular tracks would disappear. For years twelve and thirteen, however, the new institutes should be composite or multilateral organizations that would prepare some young people for higher education while offering others both general education and technical and vocational instruction leading to various kinds of employment.[40] Thus, general secondary education would lead gradually to specialization, and a flexible system of electives would ensure that students were not forced prematurely or irrevocably into making final choices among educational programs.

In May 1965 the Quebec Ministry of Education issued Regulation 1, which implemented the Parent commission's recommendations for years one to eleven. The second part of the regulation, covering years seven to eleven, specified that secondary education would not be differentiated by program. Students would determine their individual programs from a set of graduated optional subjects and would be promoted by subject.[41] Bill 21, passed by the Quebec National Assembly in January 1967, created the collèges d'enseignement général et professionel (CEGEPs) as public, secular, and tuition-free postsecondary institutions that would offer a two-year general academic program for university preparation and a three-year technical-vocational program leading directly to employment.

During the 1960s, secondary educational policy in Ontario moved first to multilateral then to comprehensive school organization. In August 1961 the minister of education (John Robarts) announced a reorganization of the three existing courses (general, commercial, and technical) into arts and science; business and commerce; and science, technology, and trades.[42] All three branches would be offered in the majority of secondary schools, making multilateral schools the dominant form of secondary educational organization. In practice, the 'Reorganized Plan' proved to be much less flexible than was promised at its inception.[43] Appointed by the Conservative government of (now premier) John Robarts in 1965, a provincial committee on educational aims and objectives, chaired by Mr Justice Emmett Hall and Lloyd Dennis, reported its disturbance at finding 'still some evidence of educational practice in Ontario that reflects a tendency to segregate students for instruction.'[44] Deploring such class-specific and class-defining education, the Hall–Dennis committee advocated 'a learning continuum' without horizontal or vertical divisions such as elementary and secondary or academic and vocational. In the intermediate (eighth to tenth) and senior (eleventh to thirteenth) years, students would choose their individual programs from a range of courses offered in most subjects at three levels (basic, general, and advanced) within the three broad areas of communications, environmental studies, and humanities.[45] Students would have individual timetables and be promoted by subject. The primary purpose of secondary schools would be integration of general, academic, and vocationally oriented education, leaving training for specific trades or occupations to postsecondary institutions.

The recommendations of the Hall–Dennis committee endorsed an agenda for educational reform that was already well advanced in the Ontario Department of Education. At the operational level, the progressive ideas and managerial skills of top officials in the department, especially then deputy minister J.R. McCarthy, were decisive factors in the reconstruction of Ontario public education as an ethical-liberal regime.[46] During 1967–8, even before the Hall–Dennis committee reported, several high schools were authorized to experiment with individual student timetables, promotion by subject, more optional courses, and easier passage between academic and vocational studies. In 1971–2, all public and separate secondary schools were required to adopt the credit system.

Secondary school curricula in the western provinces were similarly reorganized during the 1960s, initially as multilateral programs in senior high schools and subsequently as credit systems. Under the curricular reforms of the late 1960s and early 1970s, senior high school students in each of the Prairie provinces were required to take courses in social studies, mathematics, and science in grade ten (Saskatchewan) or grades ten and eleven (Alberta and Manitoba), and English in all three years. In British Columbia, all students had 'general education constants' in English, social studies, and physical and health education. Optional credits were chosen from a range of courses offered at each grade level in language arts, second languages, social studies, natural sciences, mathematics, fine arts, home economics, and industrial, agricultural, and business education. As for the Atlantic provinces, their high schools generally offered fewer options than were available in the western provinces, but with the exception of required courses in English or français, students were free to construct their individual timetables.[47]

A vital feature of the introduction of credit systems was the elimination, or at least downgrading, of provincial external examinations. From 1967 to 1972, matriculation examinations administered by departments of education were dropped in all provinces except Saskatchewan, Newfoundland, and Quebec. In Saskatchewan, departmental examinations were retained for a small minority of students, usually attending small rural high schools, whose teachers lacked the subject qualifications required for accreditation. In Quebec and Newfoundland, students were still required to write provincial matriculation examinations, but final marks were weighted equally between the results of provincial examinations and school assessments.

Governing Canadian Public Education in the Welfare State: Functional Interdependence among Departments, Teachers, and Trustees

Postwar educational policy and administration continued to be centralized in provincial departments and dominated by deputy ministers.[48] During the 1960s, however, corporate executive policy making based on the theory of rational decision making became the leading doctrine of public administration and political accountability, and the basic functions of provincial ministries were reconceived accordingly as educational planning, program development, and administrative support. In

1968 the Ontario minister of education, William Davis, told the legislative assembly that though a centralized system of education had served the province well historically, it put too much emphasis on regimentation and conformity. The development of local educational authorities capable of assuming many of its administrative functions required the department to put its priorities on developing 'a comprehensive philosophy of public education,' assessing educational needs, providing a framework of legislation and funding, and serving as 'a resource centre for new information and a clearing house for worthwhile ideas emanating from within and outside the province.'[49] Following a similar rationale, departments of education in provinces other than Quebec implemented reorganizations in the early 1970s that created two to four major divisions focused on educational planning, school programs, and finance and administration.[50]

Establishment of a Quebec ministry of education was the main recommendation of the first volume of the Parent commission's report. Under a deputy minister and (Protestant) associate deputy minister, the commission proposed three divisions, each headed by a director general: instruction, administration, and planning. When the Ministry of Education was duly created in 1964, the Parent commission's recommendations were acknowledged with the formation of the Direction générale de la planification; and, given the appointment of two associate deputy ministers, one for Catholic and the other for Protestant education, the royal commission's argument for functional rather than confessional divisions was adopted. Missing from the new ministry's structure was the vertical integration of educational activities proposed by the commission. Instead, in addition to planning, separate directorates were established for elementary and secondary education, college education, teacher training, higher education, continuing education, equipment, finance, and regional offices, as well as a variety of departmental services such as personnel, legal, information, publications, registrar, and library.[51]

Between the late 1930s and the early 1970s the number of school districts in Canada was reduced from about 23,000 to just over a thousand, and the basic unit of local governance changed accordingly, from small districts based on school attendance areas to regional or county school districts.[52] In these larger school districts, elected boards of five to fifteen members had local jurisdiction over several thousand pupils, a hundred or more elementary and secondary schools, and an array of specialized educational services. Supported by their extensive professional and administrative staffs and more highly qualified and organized teachers, regional and county school boards increasingly assumed more discretion for governing local schools. Formerly detailed regulations of departments of education were rewritten as general guidelines, and provincial inspectors became program advisers and curriculum consultants.

District reorganization created school-age populations large enough to sustain functionally specialized educational programs and facilities, but achieving full parity between rural and urban secondary education still required the equalization of fiscal capacities across city, regional, and county school districts. In the nineteenth century, special municipal and provincial funds were used to assist poor districts, but they were exceptional measures of public charity. From the 1940s through the 1960s, equalizing grants became an integral part of provincial educational policies, as a greater share, if not the main burden, of financing elementary and secondary schools was assumed by provincial governments.[53] Current revenues of public school boards from provincial grants as a percentage of combined revenues from provincial grants and local taxation jumped, on average, from 16 per cent in 1940–1 to 35 per cent in 1950–1 and continued to rise over the next two decades to 55 per cent in 1970–1.[54]

The key policy development that affected relationships between organized teachers and school boards in provincial educational policy communities was the trend to collective bargaining. Beginning in the 1940s, three approaches to collective bargaining were taken: inclusion of teachers under provincial labour relations acts in Alberta (1942) and Quebec (1965); protection of teachers' rights to bargain collectively under specific legislation or sections of the provincial education act in Saskatchewan (1949), Manitoba (1956), Nova Scotia (1956), and British Columbia (1958); and voluntary recognition by school boards in Ontario and New Brunswick. Until the mid-1960s, all three approaches to collective bargaining fixed negotiations at the local level between school boards and local affiliates of provincial teachers' unions.[55] Then, as part of the provinces' wider programs of educational reform, the right of teachers to collective bargaining was legally recognized and negotiations were centralized in New Brunswick (1968), Prince Edward Island (1972), and Newfoundland (1973). Similarly, although negotiations were bi-level in Nova Scotia and Quebec, the most important items of teachers' salaries and working conditions were negotiated centrally.[56]

By the mid-1970s, two opposing patterns of governance were operative in Canadian educational regimes. On the one hand, in Ontario and the West, educational finance and collective bargaining were relatively decentralized.[57] In these provinces, educational policy and administration were characterized by complex interdependence among departmental officials, organized teachers, and school trustees interacting across provincial and local levels of government. On the other hand, in Quebec and the Atlantic provinces, educational finance and collective bargaining were relatively centralized. In these provinces, domination of key policy networks by the department of education reduced school boards to the status of administrative agents, or at best a relationship of policy tutelage, and state capacity for educational reform depended on concertation between the department and the teachers' unions, achieved by centralized collective bargaining.

New Zealand: Social-Democratic Equality of Opportunity versus Liberal-Conservative Principles of Merit Selection and Segmented Equality

In his 1939 annual report, Peter Fraser, minister of education (1935–40) and subsequently prime minister (1940–9), set out the educational philosophy of New Zealand's first Labour government.

> The Government's objective, broadly expressed, is that every person, whatever his level of academic ability, whether he be rich or poor, whether he live in town or country, has a right, as a citizen, to a free education of the kind for which is he best fitted, and to the fullest extent of his powers ... Important consequences follow from acceptance of this principle ... Most important of all, perhaps, it means that the system of administrative control must be such that the whole school system is a unit within which there is free movement. It is only against this historical background that the Government's policy in education can be fully understood. It was necessary to convert a school system, constructed originally on the basis of selection and privilege, to a truly democratic form where it can cater for the needs of the whole population over as long a period of their lives as is found possible and desirable.[58]

This ideal of equality of opportunity was the goal of educational policy and administration in New Zealand from the 1940s to the 1960s.[59] It implied removing barriers to the transition of students from primary to secondary education, offering a range of high-quality programs to meet different needs for post-primary education, and ensuring equality of educational provision between urban and rural districts. It also implied reconstituting the historical compartments of primary and secondary education, academic and technical secondary schools, and central and local authorities into a unified regime of educational provision and governance.

Secondary Education for All in the New Zealand Welfare State

In 1942 the Senate of the University of New Zealand announced that, beginning in 1944, students who passed four years at an accredited secondary school would be granted admission to university without taking the matriculation examination. The university's change in its entrance regulations, made in response to pressures from the New Zealand Department of Education, opened the way to design courses for the first three secondary years that would better fit the needs of all types of students.

The director of education immediately appointed a consultative committee on post-primary education, chaired by William Thomas, former rector of Timaru Boys' High School. In its report the following year, the Thomas committee recommended that the first three years of secondary education (forms three to five) should provide a substantially common program for all students, comprising core subjects of English language and literature, social studies, general science, mathematics, music, crafts or fine arts, and physical education. Studies in these core subjects would occupy at least 50 per cent of class time – a minimum of twenty (out of thirty-five) periods weekly in form three, eighteen periods in form four, and fifteen in form five. The School Certificate examinations would be taken at the end of four years, and in order to encourage every student to obtain a general education there should be no external examinations for core subjects.[60]

In 1945 the Department of Education issued revised regulations for post-primary instruction that implemented the recommendations of the Thomas committee. The school-leaving age, which had been raised by law in 1920 but never implemented, was raised from fourteen to fifteen. The set of core subjects, criteria for core studies, and requirements for external examinations proposed by the Thomas committee were adopted. School Certificate examinations were set in a wide range of more than thirty subjects.[61] Candidates were required to sit for the examination in English and not more than four other subjects. The School Certificate was awarded to students who earned a pass in English and three other subjects. In a significant departure from the recommendations of the

Thomas committee, however, the 1945 post-primary regulations stipulated that students could take the School Certificate examinations at the end of three secondary years (fifth form), when their requirements for core studies had been met.[62]

Curricular differences between secondary schools (and district high schools) and technical high schools, which began to be bridged in the 1930s, disappeared in the immediate postwar years. The Commission on Education in New Zealand, chaired by Sir George Currie, reported in 1962 that unification of secondary and technical education in multilateral schools had been largely achieved and generally accepted: 'The preference in this country for the multilateral type of school, whether co-educational or single-sex, is too marked for any educational administration to ignore, and the Commission sees no really strong educational reason to recommend anything other than what the country so evidently wants.'[63] In contrast with the Thomas committee's proposal for a substantially uniform curriculum during the first three years of secondary education, however, virtually without exception secondary schools, district high schools, and technical high schools organized third- and fourth-form classes into 'professional' (academic), general, technical, and commercial courses. The ability of entrants to secondary schools was assessed on the basis of their school records and performance on school-administered tests. More able students were assigned to the professional or academic course, in which they took two foreign languages and mathematics in addition to core subjects, and in schools large enough to stream classes, they were placed in more demanding classes in core subjects in preparation for School Certificate examinations. Less able students were assigned to less challenging classes in core subjects and took pre-vocational subjects as their options.[64]

The Thomas committee had been very conscious of the difficulty of making provision in a single examination for both an intermediate certificate for the academic élite who would in another year qualify for university and a leaving certificate for the great majority of students who would be heading for jobs in commerce, industry, and public service. When they were first introduced in 1934, the School Certificate examinations – in an attempt to offer students in fifth form an alternative goal to the university entrance examinations, then also taken at the end of fifth form – had aimed to examine both traditional academic subjects for university entrance and a broad range of practical and pre-vocational subjects. The School Certificate examinations won little acceptance, however, being widely regarded as an inferior substitute for university entrance. With the change in requirements for university entrance, the School Certificate examinations quickly became accepted as a major public examination, but hopes of reconciling general education with external examination were frustrated. Locating the School Certificate examinations at the end of fifth form inevitably led school authorities to adapt core studies to the examinations curricula, and the department's policy of a fixed percentage of annual passes (approximately 50 per cent) preserved the examinations as competitive and selective, a norm-referenced rather than a criterion-referenced evaluation.[65]

Secondary education for all implied not only reorganizing post-primary education to meet the needs of students with different types of abilities but also restructuring the relationship between primary and secondary education to form interlocking stages of education. In New Zealand, two important initiatives had been taken under the Labour government during the 1930s to establish this linkage. The proficiency examination at the end of form two had been abolished in 1936, and a commitment was made to develop intermediate schools as the bridge from primary to secondary school.[66] Intermediate schools were expanded from five schools and eleven departments that enrolled 9.1 per cent of all pupils in forms one and two in 1935 to fifteen schools and eleven departments with 20.6 per cent of enrolments in forms one and two in 1945, and by 1960 there were fifty-one intermediate schools and eight departments accounting for 36.3 per cent of students in forms one and two. The Currie commission, in its 1962 report, endorsed this structure of six-year primary schools, two-year intermediate schools (forms one and two), and five-year secondary schools (forms three to upper sixth) for cities and towns. For rural areas, the commission proposed that district high schools (which combined primary and secondary grades) should be replaced by 'composite' schools comprising forms one to six, and the Department of Education immediately began to implement this recommendation.[67]

Postwar Governance in New Zealand: Between Concertation and Conflict in the Educational Policy Community

The advent of the welfare state prompted only minor changes in the organization of the New Zealand Department of Education. Most important from the standpoint of its commitment to secondary education for all young people was the merger of the previously separate divisions of secondary and technical education into a single division of post-primary schools in 1947. Under the direction of the chief inspector of post-primary schools, the inspectorates for secondary and technical schools were unified at the head office in Wellington and in each education district. The office of superintendent of technical education retained responsibility for postsecondary technical education. A tentative functional division between educational programs and administrative services was made in 1947, with the appointment of a second assistant director to whom the executive officers for administration, finance, and buildings reported. The department also established regional offices in Auckland (1948), Christchurch (1960), and Wellington (1963), each with a regional superintendent overseeing the work of district senior inspectors and reporting to the assistant director and a regional executive officer reporting to the assistant director (administration).

Postwar expansion of education had quite different effects on relationships within the New Zealand educational policy community between the Department of Education and the associations of primary and secondary teachers. In the case of policy making and administration for primary education, institutionalized concertation between the Department of Education and the New Zealand Educational Institute was preserved and strengthened. As had been the case since 1924, departmental regulations continued to be submitted for consideration to the institute. In each education district, appointments of primary and intermediate teachers were made by a committee comprising representatives of the local education board, the department, and the institute. In the case of policy making and administration for secondary education, the relationship between the department and organized teachers was more contentious, even confrontational. Consistent with the principle of secondary education for all, a uniform salary scale was introduced for secondary and technical teachers in 1945, but the Secondary Schools' Association (SSA) spurned a merger with the Technical School Teachers' Association (TSTA) until 1952, when a unified salary scale for primary and secondary teachers was introduced. Then the New Zealand Educational Institute approached the technical high school teachers to consider combining with primary teachers, and the SSA reacted by proposing to join the TSTA in forming the Post-Primary Teachers' Association (PPTA). Over the next decade, the PPTA pressed the department hard to increase secondary teachers' salaries and improve student–teacher ratios. Only when the pressures of material expansion of secondary education began to lessen in the late 1960s, and at the same time issues of secondary curriculum and organization were reformulated, did the department and the leadership of the PPTA begin to achieve an easier working relationship in secondary educational policy and administration.

Following the war, there was a modest effort to improve joint consultation and planning between central and local authorities; none the less, the education and secondary school boards continued to be essentially administrative agents of the department.[68] In 1949 a simplified system of grants to the boards gave the education and secondary school boards somewhat greater responsibility for local planning and budgeting, but with the exception of small amounts from endowments, financing continued to come from the national government through the Department of Education. Following the recommendations of a joint committee on educational administration, a Standing Committee on Administration was established in 1956, comprising members of the Department of Education and representatives of the New Zealand Education Boards' Association, to provide a forum for consultation on matters of national educational policy, and subsequently a counterpart Standing Committee on Secondary Administration was also established, involving the department and the Secondary School Boards' Association. As with the Parliamentary Recess Committee on Education in 1930, the Commission on Education in New Zealand in 1962 recommended the establishment of district education councils that would be unified local education authorities for primary and secondary education. The education boards and the secondary school boards, through their respective associations, successfully resisted the proposed merger, however, and the only change was the voluntary creation of three regional secondary school councils in Christchurch, Nelson, and Wellington, through which the constituent boards coordinated the management of their schools and maintained a central office to provide common secretarial and accounting services.[69]

As a result of postwar changes in educational governance, the New Zealand educational policy community became both more diverse and more adversarial. Between the wars, educational policy making and administration had been dominated, first, by the alliance of the Department of Education with the New Zealand Educational Institute against the education boards, and second, by the authority of the University of New Zealand over public examinations that determined the curriculum of secondary schools. After the Second World War, the University of New Zealand accepted a reduced role in the conduct of public examinations, organized teachers were divided between the New Zealand Educational

Institute and the new Post-Primary Teachers' Association, local educational governance continued to be divided between education boards, and secondary school boards, and the Department of Education maintained its separate divisions of primary and post-primary schools. In exercising the consultation, negotiation, and authority that were needed to bridge these rivalries, the director of education continued as conductor, with the assistant director as his concert master.

United Kingdom: Reconciling Selectivity and Universality in Public Education for the Welfare State

The doctrine of the welfare state that was developed in the United Kingdom during the Second World War envisaged the deliberate use of public authority to guarantee individuals and families a minimum income, enable them to meet certain contingencies such as sickness, old age, and unemployment, and ensure that all citizens had access to essential social services without regard to social class or status.[70] In the nineteenth-century founding of public educational regimes, the provision of elementary education had been recognized as an essential state service. In planning for the welfare state, the provision of secondary education for all became the new benchmark for public education. Along with health, housing, and welfare, equal accessibility to public elementary and secondary education of high quality became a social right of citizenship in the emerging welfare state.

During the 1940s and 1950s the major issues of educational politics in the United Kingdom concerned the allocation of public resources to elementary and secondary education and the priority of public education in the welfare state. The original design and implementation of secondary education for all varied across the three educational regimes of the United Kingdom and, within regimes, among local education authorities, but the dominant form of secondary educational organization comprised class-divided types of secondary schools and selection of students by competitive tests of ability. During the 1960s, partite secondary education with competitive selection was increasingly challenged by local plans for multilateral or comprehensive school reorganization. As it grew into a major conflict between the national (as well as local) Conservative and Labour parties, secondary school reorganization became the defining issue for both the place of public education and the meaning of educational equality in the British welfare state.

Secondary Education for All: Partite Systems versus Multilateral and Comprehensive Schools

In November 1940 the Committee of Senior Officials on Post-War Educational Reconstruction was created in the Board of Education. A subcommittee of the principal assistant secretaries who headed elementary, secondary, and technical branches of the board soon reached agreement on a plan to reorganize secondary education in England and Wales, proposing to raise the age of compulsory attendance to fifteen; require part-time attendance at continuation schools; abolish fees for all pupils in maintained secondary schools; establish three types of post-primary schools to be known as grammar, modern, and technical schools; implement uniform regulations, staffing provisions, and grant rates across all three types of secondary schools; and retain eleven plus as the age of transfer from primary to grammar or modern schools, with final transfers among types of secondary school at age thirteen.[71] This administrative agreement on secondary reorganization, reached early in the planning for reconstruction, was incorporated essentially unchanged into the Education Act of 1944.

Pre-war regimes were similarly renewed in Scotland and Northern Ireland. Under the Education (Scotland) Act of 1946, three-year general and pre-vocational courses were designated as 'junior' secondary courses, to distinguish them from 'senior' secondary courses that lasted five or six years and led to examinations for the Scottish Leaving Certificate (SLC). In cities and towns, junior and senior secondary courses were usually accommodated in separate schools, thus creating a bipartite system, but unlike in England and Wales, from the outset bilateral schools were more common, especially in rural areas of Scotland, and enjoyed stronger official support.[72] Students attending bilateral schools were selected before entry for either the 'certificate' (senior) or 'non-certificate' (junior) course, however, and there was normally a rigid separation between the two sides of a bilateral school.[73] As for Northern Ireland, the Education Act of 1947 introduced a tripartite regime of grammar schools, 'secondary intermediate' schools, and 'technical intermediate' schools that was distinguished by its continuing reliance on voluntary grammar schools. Rather than building new grammar schools under public control, the 1947 act offered more generous operating and capital grants to voluntary grammar schools as inducements to reserve places for qualified children from public primary schools.[74]

In England, Scotland, and Wales, each local education authority (LEA) was required to submit to the Ministry of Education or Scottish Education Department (SED) a plan for assessing children for promotion to secondary education. These varied in detail but shared the same general features: transfer was administered by a promotion or transfer board usually comprising representatives of the LEA education committee and teachers; assessments were based on a combination of standardized intelligence or verbal reasoning tests, achievement tests in English and arithmetic, and teachers' evaluations; and the preferences of students and parents had little if any weight in the selection process.[75] Decisions of transfer boards were rarely appealed to the ministry or department and, if appealed, were mostly upheld. Selection in Northern Ireland for public grammar schools and reserved places in voluntary grammar schools was centrally administered but similarly based on achievement tests in English and arithmetic, standardized tests, and teachers' assessments.

Partite systems of secondary education were backed by the Conservative party during the wartime debates on educational reconstruction and stoutly defended by postwar Conservative governments. More progressive Conservatives, such as R.A. Butler, who became president of the Board of Education in 1941, did not object to a few experimental multilateral schools but generally held that secondary education in a selective grammar school ought to be the norm for the academic élite. Conservative governments from 1951 to 1964 approved only limited experiments with comprehensive schools, where local education authorities took the initiative and their plans for reorganization did not result in the closing or merging of existing grammar schools.[76] In addition, comprehensive schools were approved by Conservative ministers of education prior to 1964 only on condition that they incorporated some procedure for selection, streaming, and/or setting of their pupils.[77]

In contrast with the unity of Conservative party opinion in defence of selective grammar schools, opinion within the Labour party was divided between defenders of the 1944 Education Act, for whom the primary concern was achieving equality of equipment, staff, and funding among the different types of secondary schools, and critics of partite systems, who advocated multilateral or comprehensive schools.[78] Within the parliamentary party, the former view initially prevailed, and during the Labour government from 1945 to 1951 both Ellen Wilkinson and George Tomlinson, as ministers of education, defended selective grammar schools as the best means to provide occupational and social mobility for working-class children and to counter the economic and social dominance of independent schools.[79] During Labour's years in opposition from 1951 to 1964, opinion in the parliamentary party shifted in favour of multilateral or comprehensive secondary schools at the same time as plans for multilateral secondary reorganization gained increasing support among local education authorities, especially those controlled by the Labour party.[80]

In July 1965 the Labour government's secretary of state for education and science, Anthony Crosland, issued Circular 10/65 asking all local education authorities in England and Wales to submit plans to reorganize secondary education along multilateral lines.[81] Circular 600, issued by the Scottish Education Department in October 1965, made a similar request to Scottish education authorities.[82] Pressure on the Labour government from its backbenchers mounted during the late 1960s because of the perceived slowness of voluntary reform and the outright refusal of several local authorities to respond to Circular 10/65. In 1970 the new secretary of state for education and science (Edward Short) introduced a bill that would have forced recalcitrant local authorities to submit reorganization plans, but this bill was not passed before the Labour party lost the general election of June 1970. When the Labour party regained office following the 1974 national election, circulars were reissued directing local education authorities in Great Britain to submit their plans to reorganize secondary education, and the secretary of state for education and science was given authority to force their compliance.[83]

In spite of the bitter conflicts of partisan politics and corresponding shifts of departmental policy during the 1960s and 1970s, in England, Scotland, and Wales there was a steady trend towards secondary school reorganization. By the late 1970s, public grammar schools still survived in some areas of England and Wales, but modern schools and technical schools had been virtually all replaced by multilateral or comprehensive schools.[84] In Scotland, most public secondary schools became comprehensive schools.[85] These schools provided a common course for an initial orientation period of secondary education, lasting six months to two years depending on local policy. Ability grouping might be implemented for this common course, depending on local policy; beyond the common course, most schools grouped students according to ability in individual subjects. As a result, by the end of their second year, students in Scottish public secondary schools had become separated into three broad groups: those taking courses leading to the Scottish Certificate of Education examinations in almost all of their chosen subjects; those following non-certificate courses in all of their subjects; and those who were doing certificate work in a few subjects and non-certificate work in other subjects. Similarly, in England and Wales, with the introduction of comprehensive schools, external selective procedures at eleven plus were ended, but in practice selection was relocated inside secondary schools at thirteen plus, when pupils were separated into General Certificate of Education O-level, Certificate of Secondary Education, and non-examination groups.[86]

In Northern Ireland, the tripartite secondary regime gradually became bipartite but remained firmly selective. As secondary intermediate schools realized how much their clientele valued technical and commercial courses, they steadily expanded their vocational offerings. Enrolments in technical intermediate schools fell correspondingly. In 1964 a white paper on educational development in Northern Ireland recommended that technical intermediate high schools be discontinued wherever possible, and the last one closed in June 1974. The first serious challenge to selective grammar schools came from a report of the Advisory Council for Education in Northern Ireland in 1973 that recommended moving to comprehensive schools; it was ignored by the Conservative government. In 1977 the minister of state for education in the Northern Ireland Office announced the Labour government's commitment to eliminate selection at eleven plus and directed education and library boards to make plans for comprehensive reorganization, but this order was withdrawn when the Conservative government was elected in May 1979.[87]

During the wartime planning of secondary education for all, the pre-war systems of junior and senior external examinations were generally agreed to be inappropriate as a leaving examination for students in secondary modern and technical schools. A recommendation by a committee of the Secondary Schools Examinations Council (SSEC) to drop external examinations at age sixteen met strong resistance, however, and in its 1947 report the SSEC retreated to external examinations by subject at both the 'ordinary' and 'advanced' levels.[88] The General Certificate of Education (GCE) with O-level and A-level examinations thus came into effect for England and Wales in 1951, followed by a similarly reorganized Northern Ireland General Certificate of Education in 1963.

Setting sixteen as the entry age for candidates at the first level of external examination in England, Wales, and Northern Ireland was intended to exclude pupils in secondary modern schools and intermediate schools, both of which were designed to take pupils from the selective examination at the end of primary school to the end of compulsory schooling at age fifteen, not only to protect the curricula of these schools from the adverse influence of academic external examinations, but also to reserve the GCE examinations for the academic élite. Far from being restricted to pupils in academically selective programs, however, the O-level examinations attracted a steadily rising number of candidates from all types of schools.[89] As a response, an SSEC committee chaired by Robert Beloe recommended the introduction of a new examination below the level of the GCE designed for students of average ability, thus avoiding the proliferation of private examining bodies outside the GCE while retaining the GCE as an examination for above-average students heading for higher education. The SSEC's recommendation for the Certificate of Secondary Education (CSE) was approved by the minister of education in 1961. Schools in Northern Ireland initially presented their students for CSE examinations administered by the North Western Board of England, and separate Northern Ireland CSE examinations were instituted in 1973 when the General Certificate of Education Committee was restructured as the Northern Ireland Schools Examination Council comprising a GCE board and a CSE board.

In Scotland, where the Higher and Lower grade examinations for the Scottish Leaving Certificate were normally taken together at the end of fifth year (about age seventeen), a year later than O-level examinations elsewhere in the United Kingdom, during the 1950s about 36 per cent of each age cohort were starting the certificate course but only one-third of them were finishing it.[90] To improve retention past fifteen, the new senior chief inspector of schools, John Brunton, got the Scottish Education Department to agree to his plan to introduce an examination at the end of the fourth year of secondary school.[91] The decision, taken in 1955, became effective in 1962 when the SLC was renamed the Scottish Certificate of Education (SCE) with the Ordinary-grade examination at the end of fourth year and the Higher-grade examination a year later. The number of candidates for the SCE examinations then increased rapidly, from 18,500 in 1961 to 125,000 in 1974, at which point 70 per cent of the secondary school age group were studying at O-grade level and 30 per cent were in Higher courses.[92]

Amalgamating grammar schools in the public sector into multilateral or comprehensive reorganization did not affect independent grammar schools, including academically selective direct-grant and grant-aided schools, which, on examination results, were among the best schools in the country.[93] In the autumn of 1965, at the same time as local education authorities were being asked to submit plans for secondary school reorganization, the secretary of state for education and science appointed a departmental committee on independent secondary schools.[94] The first report of the Public Schools Commission in April 1968, prepared under Sir John Newsom as chair, dealt only with independent boarding schools. Its main recommendation, that half of the places in independent boarding schools be reserved for children from the state sector in need of boarding education, was ignored by the government. The commission's second report, which was prepared under David Donnison as chair, focused on independent day schools. It recommended an end to government grants to selective schools. Direct-grant and grant-aided grammar schools should be forced to choose between coming into the state system as fully maintained, non-selective schools or remaining in the independent sector as privately maintained, selective schools. No action was taken by the Labour government prior to its defeat in 1970, but following the re-election of the Labour party, independent selective schools were declared to be ineligible for state grants starting in 1975–6. Of the 177 academically selective direct-grant schools in England and Wales, 119 schools chose independence, including the most prestigious schools such as Manchester Grammar School and King Edward's School in Birmingham.[95] Similarly, when the option for grant-aided status was ended in Scotland in 1985, most of the former grant-aided secondary schools registered as independent schools and became eligible to participate in the Assisted Places Scheme.

Restructuring Educational Governance as Tripartite Partnership

The Education Act of 1944 terminated the authority of the Ministry of Education to issue the School Code, which the Board of Education had used to influence curriculum, and specifically endowed local education authorities with jurisdiction to determine their own curricula. The LEAs, in turn, generally delegated this function to the headmasters of their primary and secondary schools. The curriculum of academic secondary schools was largely determined by the external examinations administered by the Secondary Schools Examinations Council, which was reconstituted in 1946 to comprise representatives of the minister of education along with the universities, local education authorities, and teachers.[96] When the Ministry of Education created the Curriculum Study Group (CSG) in 1962 in order to give the ministry an institutional capacity to participate in the development of national curriculum policy, organized teachers, in particular the National Union of Teachers, and the Association of Education Committees attacked the CSG as creating a precedent for interference by the central authority in making curricula. They demanded the establishment of a representative advisory body as 'a normal procedure in English education,' and in May 1963 the minister conceded by announcing the creation of the Schools Council for Curriculum and Examinations, which would make recommendations, not policy, on all aspects of curriculum and examinations in primary and secondary schools, include representatives of teachers (who would constitute a majority of the council) and local education authorities, and have the Curriculum Study Group as its secretariat.[97]

In contrast with the Ministry of Education, the Scottish Education Department after the war continued to issue detailed school regulations in the form of the School Code.[98] The Scottish Advisory Council on Curriculum was reappointed, but where its reports differed from the educational philosophy and policy preferences of the SED – in particular, in the reports on primary and secondary education of the Sixth Advisory Council (1942–6), which advocated progressive approaches and comprehensive secondary schools – the SED simply ignored their recommendations. Similarly, the advisory council's recommendation to institute a representative body to govern public examinations was not implemented; administering the examinations for the Scottish Leaving Certificate remained the responsibility of Her Majesty's Inspectorate (HMI). By the late 1950s, however, the expansion of Scottish education was forcing the SED to look for means to redistribute its growing burden of educational governance,[99] and three bodies with representative memberships and advisory as well as administrative functions were subsequently established: responsibility for examinations was transferred from HMI to the Scottish Certificate of Education Examinations Board, established by legislation in 1963, with its membership appointed from nominees of universities and colleges of education, associations of education authorities, the Association of Directors of Education, and teachers' unions;[100] the General Teaching Council was established in 1965 to register and discipline teachers and set standards of admission to training colleges;[101] and the Consultative Committee on Curriculum was established as a non-statutory representative body 'to keep the school curriculum under continuous review,' thus creating a locus for developing curricular advice and creating policy consensus that would be seen to be independent of the executive functions of the SED.[102]

Teachers' salaries in Great Britain were determined by bilateral collective bargaining between a panel representing teachers' unions and a panel representing local authorities.[103] For the first decade after their reorganization, the Burnham Main Committee and the National Joint Council (NJC) managed to settle teachers' salaries in England and Wales and Scotland, respectively, without major controversy.[104] In the late 1950s and early 1960s, however, discontent grew among teachers as their claims for increases in the basic scale were resisted while differentials widened within the profession between primary and secondary, grammar school and secondary modern, and graduate and non-graduate teachers. At the same time, there was rising pressure within both the Ministry of Education and the Scottish Education Department to become directly involved as a party to negotiations, not only to ensure that total awards were consistent with the government's overall incomes policy, but also to secure even wider salary differentials in order to improve the retention of experienced and specialist teachers. In March 1963 the minister of education for the first time rejected a provisional Burnham agreement, and legislation was passed that gave the minister temporary authority to impose a settlement. The next year, the Teachers' Remuneration Bill provided for representation of the Department of Education and Science (DES) on the management side of the Burnham Main Committee.[105] The secretary of state for Scotland first used his power to reject an NJC agreement and substitute his own award in 1961, and then again in 1963 and 1966. In 1967, the (by then) Scottish Joint Council for Teachers' Salaries was restructured as the Scottish Teachers' Salaries Committee, which included two SED officials as full members on the management side.

Under the educational reforms of 1944 and 1946 the arrangements for central financing of local educational authorities in England, Wales, and Scotland were essentially unchanged. The grants for 'elementary' and 'higher' education that had been established for England and Wales in the 1918 education act were merged, and the level of support was increased to about 60 per cent of total expenditure by local authorities on education. The amount of the annual education grant for Scotland, in turn, was determined by a formula, also continued from 1918, that was based on central government grants to LEAs in England and Wales. In 1958, separate percentage grants for educational services, except for school milk and meals grants, were merged in a general or block grant that covered nearly all local governmental services. Teachers' unions and education committees opposed the block grant, fearing that it would shift power from education committees to the finance committees of local authorities and thus reduce the status of education from a 'national service locally administered' to a local governmental service, but their campaign failed to persuade the Conservative government.[106] Ending the percentage grants did give local authorities greater autonomy over deciding their priorities. Local education departments, now dependent on budget allocations across functions within local authorities, were forced to become much more involved in the process of local policy making and administration, but it also became easier for local education authorities to ignore ministry guidelines on policy priorities.[107] In general, however, the level of spending by local authorities on educational services was not noticeably affected by the introduction of the block grant.[108]

A major issue of governance in planning for educational reconstruction was the future of small local authorities. Secondary education for all was thought to require large local authorities that would be able to integrate primary and secondary education and provide for different types of secondary education, and accordingly the Education Act of 1944 made the sixty-three county councils and eighty-three county boroughs the sole local education authorities in England and Wales responsible for primary, secondary, and further education.[109] Similarly, in Northern Ireland the Education Act of 1947 abolished the eighteen regional education committees created in 1923 and, following Britain, designated the six counties and two county boroughs of Belfast and Londonderry as local education authorities.[110] In Scotland, where educational jurisdictions were already based on counties and burghs, the boundaries of local authorities for education were left essentially unchanged.

By the 1960s there was increasing support among central ministries, including education, to increase the size of local authorities. The London Government Act in 1963 established the Inner London Education Authority as an independent school board comprising one councillor from each of the twelve borough councils for central London plus the Greater London councillors for the area. Based on the recommendations of the Royal Commission on Local Government in England, which was appointed in 1966 under the chairmanship of a former permanent secretary of the Ministry of Education, Lord Redcliffe-Maud, the Local Government Act of 1972 replaced seventy-nine county boroughs and forty-five counties in England outside the greater London area with thirty-nine counties and thirty-six metropolitan districts; in Wales, four county boroughs and thirteen counties were replaced by eight counties. The 1969 report of the Royal Commission on Local Government in Scotland, chaired by Lord Wheatley, similarly recommended that for 'strategic services,' which included education, larger local authorities would be more efficient and allow for better administration.[111] As a result, in 1973 nine regional councils were established to administer the major functions of local government, including primary and secondary education.

In contrast with the postwar educational trend in England, Wales, and Scotland towards tripartite partnership among central departments, local authorities, and organized teachers, the educational regime of Northern Ireland continued to be riven by denominational and political (nationalist versus unionist) divisions. Local educational governance was divided among the education committees of borough and county councils, the managers of Roman Catholic primary schools, and the governing boards of voluntary grammar schools. In the end, the attempt to import the British model of local education authorities was judged a failure, and legislation passed in 1972 established five area education and library boards, fully funded by the Ministry of Education, with their members appointed by the ministry from nominees of district councils, organized teachers, trade unions, local communities, churches, and maintained school trustees. In this context of communal division, the ministry pursued a strategy of administrative interventionism coupled with policy passivity. On the one hand, the ministry exercised tight financial control over primary and secondary education, dominated the process for deciding teachers' salary schedules (which in turn constituted a major component of ministry expenditures), and continued to issue quite detailed regulations with regard to school-level operations. On the other hand, the ministry lacked any grand vision for educational reform in Northern Ireland, content for the most part to follow the lead of the Ministry of Education/DES policy makers in England while stopping short of pushing any form of comprehensive reorganization that would have challenged the entrenched positions of both denominational interests and voluntary grammar schools. Following the suspension of the Northern Ireland Assembly in 1973, the ministry became the Department of Education for Northern Ireland (DENI), located within the Northern Ireland Office. Its direct public accountability was thereby more obscured, but its ambiguous role at the centre of Northern Ireland's educational politics, policy, and administration was essentially unchanged.

United States: Progressive Legacies and Utilitarian Ascendancy from the New Deal to the Great Society

In Australia, Canada, New Zealand, and the United Kingdom, the political ideas of the welfare state that developed during wartime reconstruction planning variously encompassed major programs of social insurance and a wide range of essential social services, but they all had at their core the principle of universality. In the United States, by contrast, no comparable idea of the welfare state won acceptance during the Second World War, and none emerged in postwar politics and policy.[112] The New Deal left no legacy of a welfare state founded on the principle of universality, nor any framework to incorporate public education as a priority of social policy.

Although the United States lacked a fully developed concept of the welfare state in which public education was tied by the principle of universality to social security, it none the less generally recognized the principle of universality in elementary and secondary education as a legitimate principle of educational policy. Progress towards implementation of secondary education for all young people therefore demanded no rethinking of educational philosophy. Instead, postwar educational reformers in the United States were content to renew their pursuit of the unrealized aspirations of Progressive reformers: availability of general and vocational education as options to academic programs in all school districts; extension of the educational opportunities available in large, wealthy, city and suburban school districts to young people living in small, poor, rural school districts; and reform of state and local educational governance to achieve professional planning and efficient management of public education. Not until the mid-1960s, with the advent of President Lyndon Johnson's push to realize the original dreams of the New Deal by constructing 'the Great Society,' did policy makers in the United States finally attempt to make a connection between the social problems of poverty and racial inequality and the remedial potential of public education.

Universality and Equal Opportunity in American Public Education

The welfare state in the United States had its origins in the New Deal of Franklin Roosevelt, who became president in 1933. Its major innovations in social policy were two contributory social insurance programs – federal old age pensions and federal aid to state unemployment insurance, both restricted in their benefits to workers in covered industries.[113] Roosevelt was not a proponent of federal involvement in public education, and the impact of the New Deal on public education was a byproduct of relief programs rather than the result of a coherent theory of the place of public education in welfare reform.[114] The meagre federal aid in 1934–5 to rescue school districts on the brink of bankruptcy was a one-time-only intervention. New Deal programs for school construction and repair, teacher employment, courses in literacy and naturalization, vocational training and rehabilitation, nursery schools, correspondence courses, educational radio, and student aid were scattered among New Deal agencies. These programs served to expose the deficiencies of established institutions of public education and showed a potential role for the federal government in educational policy, but neither the programs of the New Deal nor the problems they revealed succeeded in penetrating the long-term agenda of American educational reform.

During the Second World War, the two major reports on postwar educational priorities articulated a public agenda that focused on elaborating the Progressive goal of industrial efficiency into a broader concept of social efficiency. In 1940 a special committee of the American Youth Commission asserted that 'The change in pupil population is compelling secondary schools to modify their curricula ... The program of instruction which may possibly have been appropriate when the pupils were few and selected does not fit at all the needs of the great majority of those now in secondary schools.'[115] Vocational education was now an accepted part of secondary curricula, but in most high schools it was 'quite as specialized as were the traditional professional courses' and thus failed to provide the integration of general and vocational studies needed by the vast majority of students. The committee urged a 'fundamental reconsideration of the instructional program of secondary schools' that would give priority to reading as a subject of instruction, include work both inside and outside schools as an integral part of the instructional program, teach social studies 'to provide an effective education for citizenship in a democracy,' deal with 'personal problems' related to physical and mental health and family life, and fundamentally revise the content and methods in teaching conventional subjects. In 1944, in *Education for All American Youth*, the Educational Policies Commission of the National Education Association (NEA) similarly advocated a broader curriculum that would be suitable for the heterogeneous clientele expected to enter postwar high schools. In the ideal high school of 'American City,' according to the commission's proposal, one-third of the time each year would be devoted to a common core of subjects that were designed 'to help students grow in competence as citizens of the community and the nation; in understanding of economic processes and of their roles as producers and consumers; in cooperative living in family, school, and community; in appreciation of literature and the arts; and in use of the English language.'[116] Vocational preparation, whether designed for those entering the labour force directly from school or those continuing with postsecondary studies, would have a high priority, increasing from one-sixth of the typical student's program in grade ten to one-third in grades eleven and twelve; and health and physical education and elective subjects ('individual interests') would each occupy one-sixth of the instructional program. The constitutive idea of public schools in American City was simple but compelling: 'They are committed to the principles that all American youth should have access to equal educational opportunities and that each American youth should have access to educational services suited to his particular needs.'[117]

In all states, secondary schools had become an integral stage of public education. At fifteen or sixteen, the minimum age for leaving school in most states was higher than the normal age of students in their last year of elementary education (standard age thirteen) or junior high school (standard age fourteen).[118] Within secondary schools, even in those cities where separate academic, commercial, and technical high schools survived in the formal organization, multilateral curricula were generally adopted. All students in high school were required to enrol in a common set of core subjects; but, usually beginning at grade ten, classes in both core subjects and optional subjects were combined into curriculum groupings or 'tracks' designated as college-preparatory, general, commercial, industrial, agricultural, and domestic science. These curricular groupings were also in practice rough ability groupings. More able students were guided into the college-preparatory track; less able students were encouraged to take one of the terminal pre-vocational programs. In most high schools, however, students and their parents as consumers of public education had the freedom to choose their high school programs. Class teachers, guidance specialists, and principals invariably made their recommendations based on school records and standardized testing, but students and their parents who were prepared to overrule school authorities usually were able to get their way.

Beginning in 1942 the essay examinations administered annually by the College Entrance Examination Board were replaced by the multiple-choice Scholastic Aptitude Test (SAT) as well as multiple-choice Achievement Tests in basic academic subjects.[119] Because the multiple-choice examinations were disconnected from specific curricula, colleges and universities increasingly began to take the school records of students into account along with their results on the College Boards. Conversely, colleges and universities that historically relied on an accreditation system were becoming more concerned about variations among schools in their grading standards. The American College Testing Program, founded in 1957, was targeted initially at admissions to public institutions of higher education in the midwestern states. Each of the rival programs subsequently acquired distinctive regional territories – SAT in the northeastern, central South, and far western states; the American College Test (ACT) in the midwestern, deep South, and southwestern states.[120] Thus, as accreditation systems and College Boards converged on multiple-choice aptitude and achievement tests in combination with school records, American educational regimes became even more distinctive in their method of certification at the end of secondary school and qualification for higher educational studies.

On 4 October 1957 the Soviet Union launched the satellite *Sputnik I* into orbit around the earth. Within days, the ensuing crisis of national security in the United States was being interpreted as the inevitable consequence of 'soft education.'[121] Right-wing critics of progressive curricular reform, such as Arthur Bestor and Admiral Hyman Rickover, pressed their public campaign against an alleged loss of intellectual rigour, decline of academic standards, and discrimination against gifted students in public schools. Advocates of comprehensive secondary education reacted by asserting the merits of multilevel subjects rather than multilateral schools as the best way to reconcile democratic education with academic excellence. The leading proponent of this approach to educational reform was James Bryant Conant, former president of Harvard University and leader of a major investigation of American secondary education in the late 1950s. Conant proposed that high schools had to be large in order to support advanced academic programs; students should have individualized programs with no classification by tracks such as college-preparatory, vocational, and commercial; all students would be required to include the core subjects of English, social studies, mathematics, and science in their programs; and in the required subjects, as well as in elective subjects where there was a wide range of ability, students should be grouped by subject at three levels: those more able in the subject, a large middle group whose ability was average, and a third group for slow readers.[122]

Neither liberal-conservative nor ethical-liberal prescriptions gained general acceptance as plans to reform the curricular organization of American public high schools. Multilateral curricula that differentiated academic, general, and vocational studies continued to be a prominent feature of public high schools. A quarter-century after the launching of *Sputnik*, for example, a national survey of American secondary education found that 77 per cent of public high schools were offering a mix of academic, general, and vocational studies and that, typically, students were distributed among three more or less distinct programs – academic or college-preparatory (36 per cent), general (35 per cent), and vocational (29 per cent).[123] Multilateral school organization was often combined with multilevel instruction, however, particularly in the core subjects of English, history, mathematics, and science. For example, instruction in tenth-grade English was differentiated by ability groups in 63 per cent of all public high schools, including two-thirds of 'comprehensive' public high schools.

The crisis in American public education caused by the launching of *Sputnik* also inspired sustained efforts at curricular reform, beginning in the late 1950s and continuing through the 1960s. Starting with mathematics and physical sciences, the curricula of major academic subjects successively came under review, impelled by a widely perceived need for the United States to compete with the Soviet Union in space and triumph in the Cold War.[124] These new curricula were developed by national study committees that brought together élite groups of subject specialists from universities and secondary schools, funded by grants from the National Science Foundation of the federal government and private foundations, and relying on their powers of persuasion to secure adoption of their curricular proposals in classrooms.[125]

Whatever their merits with regard to educational philosophy and design, the new curricula encountered major problems of implementation. The 'new math' proved to be difficult for ordinary teachers to understand, especially in elementary schools, and impossible for most parents. The new social studies curriculum was especially controversial, partly because of the change in methodology from history to behavioural sciences, partly because of the shift in foundations from teaching civic virtues to cultural relativism and value-free analysis. By the late 1960s, moreover, the focus on academic excellence was being superseded by a greater concern for equality, as Lazerson, McLaughlin, McPherson, and Bailey have remarked with respect to the new mathematics curriculum: 'In part, like many of the curriculum reform efforts of the 1950s and early 1960s, it was a victim of a shift in priorities toward compensatory learning that marked the debates over equality during the second half of the decade. This shift resulted in a de facto turning away from intellectual rigor.'[126]

Educational Governance from the New Deal to the Great Society

In the immediate postwar period, prevailing normative theories of American educational governance continued to advocate the Progressive model of civic trusteeship in which state boards of education made policy and state superintendents and other professional staff in departments of education were responsible for administration. From 1946 to 1964, for example, the Council of Chief State School Officers officially espoused the combination of lay board policy making and professional administration as 'a proper democratic process that has stood the test of time.'[127] In contrast with the minor impact of Progressive ideas on prewar state educational governance, during the quarter-century following the Second World War there was a visible shift in constitutional policy.

Popular election of state superintendents of education, ensconced in two-thirds of the states in 1940, was no longer the majority form of state educational governance and political accountability by 1970.[128] Thirteen states abandoned popular election of their state superintendent between 1945 and 1970, and neither Alaska nor Hawaii, as new states entering the union in 1959, adopted the method of popular election as all new states had done from 1846 to 1912. The Progressive model of a 'strong governor' who appointed both the state board of education and the state superintendent also suffered a decline in representation, from eight states in 1940 to four states in 1970.[129]

During the postwar years, the majority of states settled on the state board of education as the formal hub for educational policy making, with the state superintendent appointed by the board as its chief executive officer, but there were two approaches to selecting members of the state board. One approach to separating state educational policy from both politics and administration descended from the old Progressive theory of public authority and political accountability: give the governor authority to appoint the state board of education and empower the board to appoint the state superintendent as its chief executive officer. In 1940 this model of state educational governance was found in eight states; by 1970 it was operative in fifteen states. It was the predominant pattern among the eastern states and important also among central states.[130] The other approach was new: popular election of the state board of education, which was then empowered to appoint the chief state school officer as its executive officer. This form of central educational authority and political accountability was first introduced in the states of Colorado (1948), Texas (1949), and Utah (1950); during the 1950s and 1960s it was adopted in eight more states.[131] Except for Hawaii and Ohio, the states adopting this constitutional design all had previously elected their state superintendents of education.

Consolidation of school districts into larger units of local educational governance – another high priority of Progressive educational reformers – became a major national trend in the quarter-century following the Second World War. The primary impact of postwar district reorganization occurred in the twenty-six states where hundreds, even thousands, of elected school boards were administratively and often fiscally independent governmental agencies.[132] In all of these states, there were prewar laws promoting voluntary district consolidation, but these had only a marginal effect until states began to offer significant subsidies for school transportation, imposed requirements on districts to provide for secondary schooling (thus forcing thousands of small elementary school districts into mergers), and introduced state foundation programs as the basis for educational finance. In 1931–2 there were 119,188 school districts in these twenty-six states and 94,654 in 1945–6; by 1970–1 there were 13,470 school districts.[133] For six of the nine states that based their local school governance on elected city, town, and township school committees there were only marginal changes in the number of school districts from the 1930s to the 1960s,[134] but there were major consolidations in Indiana (1,131 districts in 1945–6, 319 in 1970–1), Maine (500 districts in 1945–6, 290 in 1970–1), and Pennsylvania (2,543 districts in 1945–6, 597 in 1970–1).[135] Similarly, in the twelve states that historically relied on county or county and city school boards for local educational governance there was little or no change in the number of school districts, with the exception of Kentucky and South Carolina, where county subdistricts were the focus of reorganization;[136] but two more states, Nevada and Alaska, adopted the county unit during their postwar reorganizations.[137] Overall, the total number of school districts in the United States declined from 127,531 in 1931–2 to 101,382 in 1945–6 and 17,995 in 1970–1.[138]

Historically, educational finance in the United States was characterized by large inequalities in expenditures, not only among states, but also among school districts within states. Reliance on local property taxation as a source of revenue for school districts favoured districts with high assessed property valuation. State funding, which on average comprised 24 per cent of public school revenue in 1890 and only 16 per cent in 1925,[139] was delivered in the form of flat grants, which took the number of pupils, classrooms, or teachers as the basis for calculating the state grant; and even though weights were introduced in most states to take some account of variations in local resources, this type of state aid had only a marginal effect on reducing interdistrict inequalities in fiscal capacity. In 1935, based on a report by Paul R. Mort, Ohio became the first state to enact a state foundation program, and after the Second World War the number of states adopting some form of state foundation program as the means of distributing general-purpose funding increased steadily.[140] By 1971–2, thirty-three states were using a foundation program as their principal method for allocating state funding to school districts, and nine states had adopted percentage equalizing grants or guaranteed valuation plans, which were essentially variants of a foundation program. Only seven states still relied primarily on flat grants.[141]

Facilitated by the widespread adoption of foundation programs, state aid as a percentage of public school revenue, which had risen during the Depression to 29 per cent in 1935–6, increased again from 31 per cent in 1940–1 to 39 per cent in 1947–8 before stabilizing at around 40 per cent over the next two decades.[142] The increase in the percentage of state aid and the shift to foundation programs as the preferred funding mechanism had only a modest effect on interdistrict inequalities, however, in part because flat grants usually were retained to ensure a minimal level of state funding to all school districts, in part because the foundation programs defined for state aid were generally minimal programs, with school districts authorized to spend above the minimum – an option that wealthy districts had much greater fiscal capacity to implement than poor districts. In their critical study of educational finance and equality, John E. Coons, William H. Clune, III, and Stephen D. Sugarman found that none of the state aid programs in place at the end of the 1960s eliminated the financial inequities caused by interdistrict differences in taxable wealth. They concluded that 'There exists no more powerful force for rigidity of social class and the frustration of natural potential than the modern public school system with its systematic discrimination against poor districts ... The pressures for full equality of educational opportunity have always been strong; the governments of the states have long been urged to fulfil their commitment to public education. But the

pressure has always been diverted by deft and frustrating political compromise.'[143]

Initially, consistent with the prevailing ideology of local control, collective bargaining for teachers' salaries and working conditions in the
United States was decentralized between school boards and local affiliates of the National Education Association or the American Federation
of Teachers. Teachers' associations were organized in most states during
the nineteenth century, and prior to the 1960s, local affiliates commonly
made representations to school boards about teacher salaries, benefits,
and working conditions. The first state legislation that made collective
bargaining mandatory in public education was not passed until 1959 in
Wisconsin. Its provision for decentralized bilateral negotiations between
school boards and their local teachers then became the model for
similar legislation in twenty-seven states over the next two decades.[144] At
the local level, the critical breakthrough came in 1962, following a strike
that clearly established the teachers' militancy and bargaining power,
when a collective agreement was reached between the New York City
Board of Education and the United Federation of Teachers.[145] During
the 1960s there was a rapid shift from consultation and representation to
bilateral negotiations, and by the mid-1970s, collective agreements between boards and teachers had been negotiated in more than ten thousand school districts.[146]

Postwar educational governance in the United States was marked by
the emergence of the U.S. Office of Education as a major participant.
Created in 1867 (as part of the Department of the Interior) to collect
statistics and promote public education, during the 1930s and 1940s
the Office of Education shuttled between different departments. In the
context of the expanding administrative apparatus of the New Deal, it
was 'an insignificant backwater, largely ignored, frequently chastised,
and usually despised as a third-rate organization.'[147] When the Department of Health, Education, and Welfare (HEW) was formed in 1953,
following a recommendation of the second Hoover Commission on
Government Reorganization, the Office of Education was relocated from
the Department of the Interior, but any expansion of its policy responsibilities based on federal aid for elementary and secondary education
continued to be blocked by three big issues: conflict over giving federal
aid to parochial schools, opposition to federal funding of segregated
public schools, and fears of federal control over state and local educational institutions.

With the launching of *Sputnik*, the historical impasse blocking federal aid to public education was temporarily broken. Members of Congress, lobbyists, educators, and federal bureaucrats who favoured federal aid to education seized the opportunity to press the case for public education as a vital instrument of national security. The National Defense Education Act (NDEA), passed by Congress in 1958, authorized $70 million a year over four years for matching grants to public schools and loans to private schools for the purchase of equipment used in teaching science, mathematics, and foreign languages, plus another $5 million each year to improve supervisory services in these subject areas (Title III).[148] Annual appropriations of $15 million were also authorized for guidance, counselling, and testing in secondary schools to identify able students and encourage them to attend college (Title V).[149]

The Elementary and Secondary Education Act (ESEA), passed by the U.S. Congress in 1965, was advanced by President Lyndon Johnson (a former elementary school teacher) as an integral part of his 'war' against poverty and vision of 'the Great Society.' The primary purpose of the act was to create programs 'designed to meet the special educational needs of educationally deprived children.' In overcoming the standard political barriers to federal aid to public education, the Civil Rights Act passed in 1964 had disposed of one impediment – the issue of federal aid to segregated schools – by prohibiting discrimination in all federally aided programs. Shifting the focus from general federal aid to targeting educational deprivation was decisive in overcoming resistance from the Roman Catholic church, which opposed general federal aid because of its potentially deleterious effect on the competitive position of parochial schools, and claims based on poverty were important in deflecting critics who feared that federal aid would lead to federal control over public education.[150] Title I of the Elementary and Secondary Education Act allocated funds to local school districts on the basis of the number of low-income families living in the school district (initially defined as earning under $2,000 or dependent on public assistance).[151] The amount appropriated in the first year was less than $1 billion; by 1994, when ESEA came up for renewal, more than $10 billion was being spent, subsidizing 70 per cent of public elementary schools and 20 per cent of secondary schools.[152] The formula was structured so that almost all school districts were eligible for some support, and hence ESEA was 'well designed for obtaining maximum political support that every member of the House and Senate can appreciate.' Because ESEA failed to concentrate federal funding on schools located in the most impoverished neighbourhoods, however, its political allure came 'at some considerable cost in program effectiveness.'[153]

Taken together, the National Defense Education Act and especially the Elementary and Secondary Education Act expanded federal spending on public elementary and secondary schools from $486 million in 1957–8, when the federal government was the source of 4 per cent of total revenue for public schools, to $8.6 billion in 1978–9, when the federal government's share reached its peak at 9.8 per cent of the revenues of public schools. NDEA and especially ESEA also increased the political presence of the Office of Education. Formally part of HEW, the office had substantial autonomy over its legislative and administrative operations and maintained separate policy networks with Congress and educational interest groups.[154] In the presidential election of 1976, the Democratic party candidate, Jimmy Carter, promised to create a separate Department of Education, thereby earning the first official endorsement of a presidential candidate by the National Education Association. President Carter signed the act that established a cabinet-level Department of Education in October 1979.

Educational Regimes and the Problem of the Welfare State

The defining principles of the Anglo-American welfare state were the social rights of citizenship. State intervention was justified in order to ensure satisfaction of the basic human needs of all citizens. That included the need for education. The welfare state implied substantial increases in public expenditures, and hence taxes, to finance a major expansion in the quantity and quality of public educational services. The welfare state also implied substantial restructuring of educational provision and governance in order to achieve comprehensiveness in coverage, appropriateness of fit, and responsiveness of decision making to meet the educational needs of all young citizens. How large should be the rise in public spending and how extensive the restructuring of educational provision and governance to realize the ideals of redistributive universality and social citizenship? To these key questions conservatives, liberals, and socialists gave very different answers. The expansion and restructuring of Anglo-American educational regimes accordingly reflected not only the constraints of historical institutions and ideological legacies but also the postwar realignments of public economies and political ideologies.

A distinguishing feature of the welfare state was its expansion in government spending on social goods and services. Certainly this was true for spending on public elementary and secondary education in Australia, Canada, New Zealand, the United Kingdom, and the United

States. At the end of the Second World War, government expenditures on public elementary and secondary education as a percentage of gross domestic product approximated the levels recorded in the middle of the First World War. Over the next decade, government expenditures on public education returned to the higher levels attained between the wars, then continued to rise over the next two decades (Figure 1; Table 1).[155] Government expenditures on public elementary and secondary education also rose steadily as a percentage of total government expenditures, from a rate of 2 per cent in Australia to 3.6 per cent in the United States at the end of the Second World War to a rate of 6.8 per cent in New Zealand to 14.7 per cent in Canada a quarter-century later (Figure 3; Table 3). Similarly, the employment of full-time teachers rose from 1 to 1.5 per cent of the total labour force at the end of the war to a level of 1.7 per cent in Australia and the United Kingdom to 3.2 per cent in Canada (Figure 5; Table 6). As Figure 6 and Table 7 show, the employment of full-time teachers in public schools also increased as a percentage of total government employment in Australia, New Zealand, and the United Kingdom. Because of increased government employment in new endeavours of the welfare state, as well as large defence forces, full-time teachers as a percentage of total government employment in Canada and the United States initially fell below the levels recorded prior to the Second World War but subsequently also increased during the 1960s.

This expansion of educational provision, as measured by government expenditures on public schools as percentages of gross domestic product and total government expenditures, and of employment of teachers as percentages of total labour forces and total government employment, was due in part to rising enrolments in public schools that resulted from the postwar growth of the school-age population; however, there is evidence that increases in government expenditures on public schools were also augmenting the quantity of educational provision for each person in school and hence improving the quality of their educational experiences. The ratio of enrolments in public elementary and secondary schools to teachers, which had been falling prior to the Second World War, continued to fall after the war (Figure 7; Table 8). Average annual increases in real government expenditures per pupil on public elementary and secondary education were generally higher from the end of the Second World War to the mid-1970s than they were during the periods prior to the war and since the mid-1970s (Table 5). Government expenditures per pupil enrolled in public elementary and secondary education as percentages of gross domestic product per capita (Figure 2; Table

2) and total government expenditures per capita (Figure 4; Table 4) also provide comparative measures of the changing quantity of educational provision for each person in school. In the case of government expenditures per pupil in public schools compared to gross domestic product per capita, there were consistently increasing percentages recorded in each of the Anglo-American countries from the end of the Second World War until the mid-1970s. There also were increases in the ratio of expenditures per pupil compared to total government expenditures per capita; these were especially evident in Australia, but also occurred in Canada, the United Kingdom, and the United States. In New Zealand, by contrast, the ratio of government expenditures on education per pupil to total government expenditures per capita fluctuated between 30 and 35 per cent from 1950 to 1980.

These sizable increases in the total supply of public education in Anglo-American educational jurisdictions, as well as in the average quantity of educational provision for each person in school, were accompanied by substantial variations among countries. Government expenditures on public education, beginning in the 1950s as a percentage of total government expenditures and in the 1960s as a percentage of gross domestic product, were higher in Canada and the United States than in Australia, New Zealand, and the United Kingdom. Increases in full-time teachers as a component of the total labour force were much greater in Canada, New Zealand, and the United States from 1945 to 1970 than in Australia and the United Kingdom. From 1945 to 1950, rates of average annual increases in real government expenditures per pupil in public elementary and secondary schools in all countries were moderate (3.2 per cent in Canada) to high (10.3 per cent in Australia, 10.7 per cent in the United States); and again, from 1960 to 1965 and 1970 to 1975, average annual increases ranged from 4.7 per cent in New Zealand (1960–1 to 1965–6) and the United States (1959–60 to 1965–6) to an amazing 17 per cent in Australia (1970–1 to 1975–6). During the three five-year periods from 1950 to 1960 and 1965 to 1970, average annual increases in real spending per pupil continued to be moderate to high in Australia, Canada, and the United States. By contrast, annual increases averaged less than 2 per cent in New Zealand (1950–1 to 1960–1, 1965–6 to 1970–1) and the United Kingdom (1950–1 to 1955–6, 1965–6 to 1970–1).

'Secondary education for all' was a top priority for all Anglo-American educational regimes from the end of the Second World War to the early 1970s. In the United States, that goal was effectively realized by 1975–6, when enrolments in the senior years of secondary school reached 24.9 per cent of total enrolments (Table 9E). Percentages of enrolments in the senior years of secondary school in Canada (22.5 per cent in 1975–6) and in New Zealand (19.6 per cent in 1975) converged on that of the United States, and remaining differences among these three countries disappeared over the following decade (Tables 9B and 9C). Despite substantial increases in provision for public secondary education in Australia and the United Kingdom, however, the percentages of total enrolments in the upper years of secondary schools, which had been markedly lower than in the United States, Canada, and New Zealand at the end of the war, continued to be lower two decades later – 14.4 per cent of all students were enrolled in years ten to twelve in Australia, and 13.7 per cent of total enrolments were ages fifteen and over in the United Kingdom.

In addition to variations in the trends to expand the supply of public education, there were variations in the restructuring of educational regimes, but both the ideological foundations and the partisan alignments of regimes were changing to deal with the problem of the welfare state. The denominational regimes of Quebec, Newfoundland, and Northern Ireland in each case retained their historical legacies of sectarian education that were founded on the ideas of communitarian conservatism, but at the same time their educational regimes were fundamentally reformed to incorporate features common to the other educational regimes operative in Canada and the United Kingdom. Similarly, other Anglo-American educational regimes continued to reflect the liberal-conservative ideas that had shaped their development from the turn of the century to the Second World War, in response to the widely perceived public educational problem of industrial efficiency. At the same time, however, the welfare state as a problem of public education facilitated the influence of ethical liberalism, the 'new liberalism' that advocated child-centred primary education, comprehensive organization of secondary schools, multilevel curricula to fit individual needs, and termination of external examinations that distorted curricular development and undermined teachers' professionalism. Across the Anglo-American jurisdictions, the recurring and various conflicts of liberal-conservative, utilitarian-liberal, ethical-liberal, and social-democratic ideas resulted in three types of educational regimes.

First, the predominant type of educational regime in Australia and New Zealand featured multilateral secondary schools, public external examinations, and corporatist educational governance. In practice, of course, there were particular variations on this general type. The shift away from partite systems to multilateral secondary schools, a change that was generally initiated before the Second World War and proceeded relatively rapidly after the war, was somewhat constrained in Victoria and South Australia by their legacy of partite systems of secondary schools. In the case of New South Wales, based on recommendations of the Wyndham commission, there were experiments with multilevel structuring of subjects as well as multilateral schools. In New Zealand the choice of track within secondary schools was determined by the rule of academic merit as demonstrated in classroom performance and objective testing rather than the choice of students and their parents. Even where choice of program existed in Australian educational regimes, however, it tended to be available only at the outset of secondary school; once initial choices were made, transfers from one track to another were difficult. As a further effort to facilitate secondary education for all, public entrance and intermediate examinations were either terminated or internalized, but external examinations at the end of secondary school were retained as guardians of the passage from school to work and postsecondary education.

With regard to educational governance in the welfare states of Australia and New Zealand, although education boards and governing bodies survived in New Zealand and regional administrative divisions were initiated in Australia, educational politics, policy, and administration continued to be highly centralized. There was a progressive institutionalization of the relationship between departments of education and organized teachers. Both educational policy and administration were increasingly conducted as joint enterprises between departmental officials and teachers' representatives. As for the relationship of church and state in public education, postwar educational reforms in Australia and New Zealand did not touch the original exclusion of church schools from state aid for public instruction. Hence, in the educational regimes of both countries, schools in the private sector continued to be important providers of elementary and secondary education, growing in order to continue to accommodate about 24 per cent of total enrolment in elementary and secondary schools in Australia and 13 per cent in New Zealand from 1945 to 1965, before declining slightly to 22 per cent in Australia and 11.4 per cent in New Zealand in 1970.[156] With the massive expansion of the public sector and the persistent poverty of the private sector – in particular, the inability of Roman Catholic schools to match the rising levels of educational provision in public schools – the nineteenth-century liberal formula of strict separation between church and state schools became increasingly untenable.

The second type of educational regime in the Anglo-American welfare states, found in the United States and Canada, featured multilateral secondary schools evolving towards comprehensive schools with multilevel subjects and credit systems, no public external examinations, local educational governance through amalgamated school districts that had greater fiscal and administrative capacity, and a more even division between central and local responsibility for educational policy making and finance. During the wartime debates about educational reform, the multilateral high school, which was already the dominant form of secondary institution in the United States, was adopted across Canada as being superior to partite systems of secondary schools on grounds of both democracy and efficiency. During the 1960s, educational regimes in both the United States and Canada also began to experiment with the introduction of credit systems in high schools in which subjects were taught, typically, at three or four levels of difficulty in order to accommodate the different needs of individual students. By the early 1970s, provincial departmental examinations for matriculation at the end of senior high school had been effectively eliminated in all the Canadian provinces except Quebec and Newfoundland, and thus another historical difference between educational regimes in Canada and the United States disappeared.

In both Canada and the United States the amalgamation of small school districts strengthened the policy and administrative capacities of local school boards, while the widespread adoption of foundation plans in both countries, if not alleviating interdistrict inequalities of educational finance, certainly expedited the expansion of educational provision. Nor, indeed, was there any strong belief that favoured total equalization of provision. School boards were expected to make different decisions about the relative importance of spending on public education in their districts, and hence interdistrict variations were inevitable consequences of the workings of local democracy.

In the United States the relationship of state and local educational authorities continued to be predominantly one of fiscal equivalence, deriving from the historical ideology of local control.[157] None the less, larger expenditures and expanding provision were extending the role of state educational authorities, and in several states at least, the movement to reconstitute state boards of education as elected state-wide policy-making authorities seemed to be an attempt to create a relationship closer to functional interdependence between state and local authorities. Even more obviously in Ontario and the western provinces of Canada, larger school districts, greatly expanded responsibilities of local administration, and changes in the administrative culture of provincial departments of education created conditions for change in central–local relationships to some form of functional interdependence. In the relatively more centralized regimes of Quebec and the Atlantic provinces, direct dealings between provincial departments and school boards continued to be conducted as a form of administrative agency, or at best policy tutelage, but in these provinces tripartite networks were formed in key policy areas at the centre of educational policy communities that involved provincial departments, teachers' unions, and trustees' associations.

As in Australia and New Zealand, the ideas of the welfare state in Canada and the United States did not initially challenge the nineteenth-century foundation with regard to the place of race, language, and religion in public education. Racial segregation, despite the U.S. Supreme Court's decision in 1954, did not become a dominating issue of American educational politics until the mid-1960s, about the same time that language was renewed as a major issue of Canadian educational politics. Similarly, until the 1960s, historical settlements on the role of church and state in public education determined the relative growth of the private sector of elementary and secondary schools. The gap between Canada and the United States in enrolments in private schools – about 4 per cent of total enrolment in elementary and secondary schools in Canada in the 1920s and 1930s compared to about 9 per cent in the United States – actually widened after the Second World War as total enrolments in private schools in the United States rose from 10.8 per cent of total enrolment in 1945–6 to 13.6 per cent in 1959–60 before falling back to 11.1 per cent in 1969–70. None the less, for two decades after the war, enrolments in private non-Roman Catholic schools continued to be relatively low in both countries – 1 to 2 per cent in the United States and less than 1 per cent in Canada.[158]

As the third approach to the problem of public education in the making of the welfare state, the educational regimes of England and Wales, Scotland, and Northern Ireland were reformed but not fundamentally restructured after the Second World War. In England and Wales and Northern Ireland there were partite systems of secondary schools with selective examinations that determined entry to grammar, technical, and secondary modern (in Northern Ireland, intermediate) schools. In Scotland there was a bipartite system for cities and towns combined with bilateral schools in rural areas, but in both cases, selective examinations determined entry to the senior (academic) or junior (general) course. External leaving examinations were reformed to award certificates on the basis of individual subjects passed rather than a requirement to pass in a predetermined group of subjects, but the two stages of GCE (O-level and A-level) and SCE (Standard Grade and Highers) continued to be critical junctures in the process of academic and occupational selection.

Under the educational reforms of 1944, 1946, and 1947, local educational authorities in England and Wales, Scotland, and Northern Ireland were now consistently established as education committees of county and county borough/burgh councils, each with a chief education officer as administrative head of the local educational bureaucracy. Because of the postwar national fiscal crisis, the government of the United Kingdom initially exerted relatively strong controls over capital expenditure by local governments, including local education authorities, but from the outset, curricular decision making was decentralized. For England and Wales as well as Scotland, the shift from a percentage grant specifically directed to finance local educational services to a block grant that covered all local governmental services, including education, made little practical difference to the levels of local educational budgets; none the less, it marked the disentanglement of national from local fiscal decision making. Similarly, during the 1960s the reconstruction of national collective bargaining and the formation of national curricular councils in order to represent the major interests of the educational policy communities neatly encapsulated the emerging tripartite partnerships involving departments of education, organized teachers, and associations of local education authorities in Great Britain. In Northern Ireland, by contrast, the Ministry of Education continued to dominate educational administration, despite the unrelenting conflicts and pressures of denominational interests and the sizable establishment of voluntary schools, especially the grammar schools, which jealously defended their relative autonomy.

The three educational regimes of the United Kingdom parted fundamentally from other Anglo-American jurisdictions during the 1940s and 1950s by continuing to give priority to partite systems of secondary schools, despite isolated experiments with multilateral secondary schools, usually by Labour-dominated local councils. The political conflict between advocates of partite systems versus multilateral ('comprehensive') secondary schools took place within the Labour party, and initially at least, the majority continued to view access to selective grammar schools as the essential avenue for academically talented children of the working class to offset the advantages of élite private schools. In 1965 the Labour government at last committed itself to dismantling the partite systems, terminating selective examinations, and delivering public secondary education through multilateral schools. This restructuring of secondary schooling eventually was achieved completely in Scotland and Wales, mostly but not entirely in England, and not at all in Northern Ireland. Even so, the duration of policy implementation and the intensity of political conflict, especially in England, were unprecedented among the Anglo-American educational regimes. Ironically, by the time multilateral schools became the predominant institutions for delivering public secondary education in the United Kingdom, the problem of designing and implementing the welfare state had been displaced by the concern to prevent its unravelling under the pressures of global capitalism.

The politics and policies of the welfare state had both a nationalizing and a realigning effect on Anglo-American educational regimes. In the United Kingdom, Northern Ireland continued to operate as a denominational regime, but in contrast with regimes for public instruction and industrial efficiency, the educational regimes of England and Wales, Northern Ireland, and Scotland came much more to resemble one another in their modus operandi, distinguished in their approach to both school organization and educational governance from other Anglo-American educational jurisdictions. Similarly, in Canada the basic features of denominational regimes were preserved in Quebec and Newfoundland, but the huge historical differences in curricula and governance between Quebec and Newfoundland and the other Canadian provinces diminished as a result of major educational reforms during the 1960s. Not only were the educational regimes of Canadian provinces becoming more alike, they were also becoming much more like the educational regimes of the United States in both their trend from multilateral to comprehensive high schools and their decentralization of the working relationship between ministries of education and local school boards from administrative agency to functional interdependence. The educational regimes of Australia and New Zealand, which historically had regime characteristics similar to those of the United States, Canada, and Scotland, were now differentiated from other Anglo-American regimes by their combined development of multilateral secondary schools with internal selection, retention of external leaving examinations, and centralization of educational governance.

Across the Anglo-American democracies there were very different views about what constituted the welfare state and what should be the place of public education in it. None the less, in all the Anglo-American educational regimes there was a general change from treating public education as a branch of economic policy to seeing it as a vital component of social policy. This shifted the focus of educational advocacy and policy reform from reproducing the occupational hierarchy of industrial capitalism in public education to understanding and meeting the basic educational needs of each person in school. Such an orientation facilitated the spread of progressive educational ideas, especially evident in the United States and Canada but also important among professional educators in Australia, New Zealand, and the United Kingdom. Long-standing assumptions about the distribution of ability, design of curricula, and organization of schools were widely challenged, and in a situation of decentralizing educational governance, the uniformity of educational regimes was further eroded.

Under the aegis of the welfare state, the historical gap in funding between élite private schools and mass public schools was reduced as a result of major increases in government funding for public education. Yet the greater diversity of educational programs in public schools tended to redefine rather than diminish the historical divide between public and private sectors. Élite private schools generally continued to teach a rigorously traditional academic program that was increasingly removed from the pursuit of child-centred or student-centred education in the public sector. Mass private schools were doubly disadvantaged, unable because of their rising relative poverty to match either the curricular diversity of *nouveau-riche* public schools or the academic cachet of élite private schools.

The idea of social citizenship that was central to the development of the welfare state was a decisive influence on thinking about the problems of public education from the end of the Second World War to the 1960s. The commitment to meet the educational needs of people in school, however variously it was undertaken across Anglo-American educational regimes, inevitably turned attention to who exactly were the people in school and what were their needs. These questions in turn reopened long-standing issues of inequality in the treatment of ethnic, linguistic, racial, and religious minorities in the constitution and operation of Anglo-American educational regimes. The focus on needs of people also diverted policy making, especially where decision making was devolved to professional educators in schools, or even classrooms, from the practical demands of educating young people for working lives in advanced capitalist societies. Beginning in the 1960s, however, educational regimes constructed for the welfare state were successively challenged, first to accommodate social diversity and the ideal of pluralist society, and then to reform public education for technological society and global capitalism.

4 Pluralist Society

Historically, the Anglo-American countries have been culturally diverse or plural societies, but their public philosophies have lacked a concept of pluralist society as a defining characteristic and collective good of Anglo-American democracy.[1] On the contrary, public institutions and policies have recognized and promoted 'white Australia' and 'British New Zealand,' an ethnic melting pot with racial segregation of African Americans in the United States, British versus French ethnic and linguistic nationalism in Canada, English linguistic and ethnic imperialism in the United Kingdom, and assimilation of Aboriginal peoples in the frontier societies. In the years following the Second World War, however, especially during the 1960s, the idea of the Anglo-American countries as democratic societies committed in political principle and policy practice to multiculturalism began to be more fully formulated and more strongly advanced. Now it ranks as one of the central problems of Anglo-American primary and secondary education.

Across the Anglo-American democracies, the politics of 'recognition' and 'difference' were similarly constituted with regard to the leading issues but clearly distinctive in their national profiles.[2] Ancient ethnic, linguistic, racial, and religious differences that had been variously assimilated, compromised, or suppressed were revived by renewed aspirations for cultural justice, even as new types of claims were being formulated. The basis of individual development within diverse religious traditions was advanced in all countries as an argument to reopen historical settlements with regard to the relationship of church and state in public education. National minorities of French-speaking Canadians, Welsh and Scots, and Mexican Americans asserted collective linguistic rights in the public schooling of their children. Aboriginal peoples as national minorities, especially potent in the case of the Maori in New Zealand, attacked the oppressive policies and practices of their state-sanctioned educational ghettos. African Americans, neither indigenous national minority nor voluntary ethnic immigrants, won belated legal recognition of the injustice of their segregation in public schools, but their struggle for educational equality confronted an even greater challenge of enforcing desegregation. Immigrant ethnic minorities, a growing presence in the politics of Anglo-American democracies, more openly criticized the exclusionary ethnic-majority nationalism that pervaded Anglo-American educational policies, although their impact differed substantially across educational regimes.

First among the general issues that arose from promoting pluralist society as a collective public good was rethinking the meaning of equality in the provision of public education as involving not simply universality but also diversity. The ideology of progressive education, which reinforced the movement for secondary education for all under the aegis of the welfare state, was dedicated to creating capacities for individual development, but individual development was understood to depend in turn on enabling children to grow and learn within, as well as beyond, their familial cultural communities. Just as the meanings of the accessibility and universality of secondary education were politically contested in the years following the Second World War, so also, with their acceptance as a legitimate issue of public education during the 1960s, were the meanings of difference and recognition contested. Just what sort of claim was being made by minority societal interests for public educational policies in order to realize a truly pluralist society? Multicultural curricula could be designed at one level simply to teach students living together in a plural society the meaning of the major ethnic, linguistic, racial, and religious group identities that constituted their society. Commonly, such multicultural curricula could be extended to include promoting toleration of difference, especially with regard to the attitudes of the majority toward minorities. At another level, multicultural curricula might be designed to celebrate cultural differences, facilitating the potential for individual self-development by portraying the diversity of cultural communities within which students might live their lives within a pluralist society. Alternatively, multicultural curricula could be designed primarily to ensure the survival of cultural communities, whether majority or minorities, putting the priority on inculcating particular cultural identities and preserving communal segmentation in a consociational democracy.

Assuming a commitment to some type of multicultural education, a second issue was its purpose and content. The idea of pluralist society not only revived the claims of particular societal interests against both state and market but also shifted the focus of public education as industrial policy or social policy, where the political economies of industrial efficiency and the welfare state had positioned it, back to public education as civic policy. Legitimizing a more inclusive citizenship regime inevitably exposed established subject matter and teaching methods to pressures for the recognition of difference.[3] Given the diversity of Anglo-American democracies, however, there were hard policy decisions to make about which cultural traditions would merit official recognition, either for inclusion in a multicultural curriculum or for institutionalization as protected communal traditions. That conundrum, in turn, motivated an argument for the state's cultural neutrality in the design and delivery of public education that recalled the nineteenth-century liberal advocacy of non-denominational public schools.

A third issue was educational governance for a pluralist society. Commitment to the principle of a pluralist society raised difficult questions with regard to the representativeness of the institutions and processes of educational politics, policy, and administration. From one perspective, the institutions and processes of educational politics, policy, and administration ought to be designed to ensure that major ethnic, linguistic, racial, and religious groups were represented at every important stage of educational policy making. From another perspective, the institutions and processes of educational politics, policy, and administration should be culturally segmented so that, as much as possible, members of major cultural communities could exercise effective powers of educational self-government. Putting the principle of pluralist society into practice might also run into conflict with other hallowed principles of democracy. For example, liberal democrats defended local democracy, even neighbourhood democracy, as a basic instrument of public deliberation and participatory citizenship. Yet neighbourhoods were often culturally homogeneous and even inclined to discriminate in the local management of their schools. Hence, the intervention of central public authority, including the courts, might be needed to counteract the effects of communal segmentation by neighbourhood schools or local districts in order to create and sustain the principle of pluralist society and the practice of social diversity in schools.

A fourth issue of a pluralist society arose from the fundamental rebalancing of the political economies of public education that was implied by the particularistic claims of minority ethnic, linguistic, racial, and religious groups against the interests of both state and market. For the advocates of multicultural education, formal primary and secondary schooling was an essential instrument for both the intracultural and the intercultural teaching and learning of the languages, histories, literatures, and religions of the constituent communities of each Anglo-American democracy. Schools that neglected this primary cultural mission of teaching and learning not only threatened to sever students from their heritage and thus undermine their quest for identity, they also endangered the survival of cultural communities that were vital to human growth and happiness and impeded cross-cultural understanding that was essential to integrate liberal pluralist society. None the less, educational institutions and policies in pursuit of multiculturalism could also generate social fragmentation and communal isolation, even conflict, rather than intercommunal dialogue and harmonious social diversity. In a plural society that is a liberal democracy, the overriding educational priority of the state had to be the political culture of democracy, the set of principles, values, beliefs, and attitudes of democratic citizens that enabled and sustained the practice of a common public life. Similarly, refocusing teaching and learning on cultural transmission and hence giving priority to language, literature, history, and religion was not necessarily consistent with the needs of a capitalist market society to prepare young people for employment through vocational education and training.

These leading issues with regard to the provision and governance of primary and secondary education in a pluralist society were each defined in political practice by major ideological differences among conservatives, liberals, and socialists. One key dimension was their understanding of communal attributes. Ethnicity, language, race, and religion may be regarded as the characteristics of individuals that provide a basis for common interest or shared value. Ethnicity, language, race, and religion may also be regarded as the characteristics of communal traditions that constitute world-views, determining the very categories of thought and experience by which their members perceive and understand the world in which they live. Implicit in each of these concepts of culture is a different ideological understanding of the relationship between individual and community. Conservatives tended to view communal attributes as collective traditions that constitute world-views, liberals saw communal attributes as common interests or shared values of individuals that provide a basis for voluntary association, and socialists endeavoured simultaneously to recognize that human lives are embedded in communal groups while insisting on the rights of individuals to construct their own identities and histories.

Another point of ideological difference was the imagined structure of pluralist society. In a multicultural or multinational society, the relationships among communal groups may be envisaged as highly stratified, with one communal group enjoying a dominant position and others suffering varying degrees of inferiority and subordination. Stratification based on communal group membership usually, but not necessarily, will be expected to coincide with stratification based on economic class and social status. Alternatively, relationships among communal groups may be idealized as relatively equal, characterized by equal respect and equal citizenship. From right to left, conservatives tended to envisage pluralist society as consistently stratified by economic class, social status, and communal group; for liberals, pluralist society was stratified by economic class and social status but not communal group; and the socialist version of pluralist society was consistently egalitarian.

Conservatives, liberals, and socialists also differed over the role of the state in pluralist society. In conservative ideology, the state had a duty to protect the nation that was its cultural (and spiritual) foundation. In the modern context of social diversity that meant perpetuating a communally stratified society that gave predominance to the founding nation. For liberals, the state in pluralist society ideally should be neutral among communal traditions, leaving it to individuals to pursue in their private activities their personal versions of the good life; but some (ethical) liberals also recognized the legitimacy of state intervention in this private sphere in order to assist individuals whose cultural choices might be relatively disadvantaged. Socialists, by contrast, defended extensive state intervention; their goal was an egalitarian pluralist society that ensured equal citizenship by guaranteeing collective rights.

Australia: Restoring Dual Regimes of Government and Non-government Schools

From the turn of the century to the Second World War, there was some non-British migration to Australia, notably from Italy and Greece, but the Commonwealth government's immigration law, regulations, and assistance were overwhelmingly targeted at British immigrants. Hence, the ethnic composition of the Australian population continued to be overwhelmingly British.[4] From the late 1940s to the early 1970s there was a progressive reduction in restrictive regulations and discriminatory practices in Australian immigration policy. During the 1950s, immigration from southern Europe matched that coming from Britain; during the 1960s, European immigration greatly exceeded British immigration. This postwar demographic change had two major consequences for educational policy.

First, primarily because of European immigration to eastern cities, the Catholic population increased from 20.9 per cent of the Australian population in 1947 to 24.9 per cent in 1961 and 27 per cent in 1971. The need to build adequate schools and hire qualified teachers persistently outran the capacity of the privately funded Catholic sector to cope with the resulting growth of the Catholic school population. Overcrowding put tremendous stress on the facilities and staff of Catholic schools, creating the conditions for a mass public campaign for state aid that culminated in a major reversal of Australian educational policy.

Second, until the mid-1960s the ethnic diversification of Australian population due to postwar immigration had no effect on school curricula and very little on instructional practices. The policy uniformly was assimilation; the practice was neglect. As the director general of education for New South Wales, H.S. Wyndham, told the 1963 Australian Citizenship Convention, 'We deliberately refrain from collecting any statistics in regard to school pupils from overseas. Once they are enrolled in school, they are, from our point of view, Australian children.'[5] During the 1960s, however, there was a change towards more child-centred education, and that made it more likely that the education of migrant pupils would be viewed from the perspective of the children as individuals with special needs.[6]

State Aid for Private Schools: Constructing a Dual Regime for a Pluralist Society

The withdrawal of state aid to church schools in the last third of the nineteenth century galvanized a remarkable effort, led by Roman Catholic bishops, to provide a place in a Catholic private school for every Catholic child.[7] That goal was largely achieved by the 1940s. After the Second World War, the proportion of primary and secondary students in Catholic schools continued to increase until 1965; then it dropped in all states and territories. In Australia as a whole, 31.1 per cent of Catholic children were not attending Catholic schools in 1965; by 1970 the proportion had risen to 40.8 per cent. As Praetz has observed, 'The parish-based nature of the system and the lack of surplus resources, decision-making and co-ordinating structures, and administrative personnel rendered coping strategies piecemeal and inadequate.'[8] The rise in employment of lay teachers – from 20 per cent of teachers in primary schools in 1950 to 65 per cent in 1970 – was essential to the expansion of the Catholic school sector, but it increased operating costs. Average class sizes rose during the 1950s, and overcrowding continued through the 1960s. The pupil–teacher ratio in public schools was 23:1 in 1970 and 16:1 in other private schools, but it was 32:1 in Catholic schools.[9]

The mobilizing incident occurred at Goulburn, near Canberra, in July 1962. A Roman Catholic primary school was threatened with losing its certificate of efficiency from the New South Wales Department of Education and consequently being forced to close unless its toilet facilities were improved. Catholic parents met to voice their bitter disappointment at the failure of the federal and state governments to ease the plight of Catholic schools. At the behest of the local bishop, all Catholic schools were closed for a week, and 640 of Goulburn's 2,070 Catholic students enrolled in state schools. After Goulburn, Catholic parents organized a series of mass campaigns through their parents' and friends' associations in each state and through the national Australian Parents' Council, formed in 1962, which lobbied both state and federal governments.[10]

Australian governments reacted with a succession of competitive bids for Catholic support. In September 1963, the Labor government of New South Wales introduced a program of indirect state aid that provided scholarships to all students in their last four years of secondary education at private schools (as well as scholarships to all students living away from home while attending public secondary schools). Next, during a close federal election campaign in November 1963, Prime Minister Robert Menzies promised Commonwealth scholarships for pupils in both public and private secondary schools and capital grants of £5 million annually for science laboratories and equipment. Following its electoral victory, the Menzies government kept its promise with legislation passed in May 1964. Other state and federal governments emulated these leads.[11] In 1969, another election year, the Commonwealth minister for education and science (Malcolm Fraser) took another, decisive step when he announced the introduction of recurrent grants for primary and secondary private schools – $35 per student at the primary level and $50 per student at the secondary level. As the minister recognized, and defended, with the introduction of these per-capita grants the Liberal–Country coalition government had arrived at a policy of supporting public and private sectors in dual educational regimes. His defence of the new policy – that it was more economical to have a dual regime, that a significant number of citizens preferred an alternative school and had a just claim on public funds, and that it was preferable for the state to subsidize a proportion of the population to stay out of the public schools rather than develop policies to attract, or force, them into it – effectively reversed the principles and objectives that underlay the state education acts of the last third of the nineteenth century.[12]

In opposition since 1949, the Australian Labor party (ALP) won power in December 1972 on a platform that included a commitment to increase the role of the Commonwealth government in providing financial support to both public and private schools.[13] The test for federal aid to elementary and secondary education would not be the distinction between public and private schools but that between wealthy and poor schools.[14] One of the first acts of the new Labor government was the appointment of the Interim Committee for the Australian Schools Commission, with Peter Karmel as chair. The Interim Committee's report in May 1973 advanced a vision of Australian society that gave top priority to acknowledging social diversity and realizing equal opportunity. Fulfilling that vision depended in part on diversity of educational provision. A valuable degree of diversity was already present in existing non-government schools, and federal aid should aim to further the 'development of diversity in the organizational form of schools, in school-community relationships and in the timing of educational experience.'[15]

The Interim Committee rejected uniform per-capita grants as a fair and efficient means to raise educational standards. It recommended instead that private schools be classified into eight categories of need, with levels of per-capita funding scaled according to need, and proposed that federal aid to the two wealthiest categories of private schools should be phased out over 1974 and 1975. The Whitlam government initially decided to go even farther and terminate federal aid to the wealthiest private schools at once, but strong opposition from a coalition of the Roman Catholic hierarchy and wealthy private schools persuaded the Labor government that all students in private schools, regardless of wealth, should be entitled to receive the minimum per-capita grant. Harking back to the nineteenth-century central boards of education, the Schools Commission Act of 1973 created a commission of twelve members that included representatives from government, the primary, secondary, and tertiary education sectors, Catholic parent groups, and the Australian Teachers' Federation. The States Grants (Schools) Act authorized the new commission to implement the financial recommenda-tions of the Interim Committee.[16]

In February 1981 the High Court of Australia ruled that federal grants to private church schools did not contravene section 116 of the Austral-ian constitution.[17] Disappointed by the High Court's decision, the New South Wales and Queensland teachers' unions began campaigns to oppose state grants to private schools, and the annual conference of the Australian Teachers' Federation in January 1982 dropped its draft policy that advocated the integration of government and non-government schools, adopting instead a resolution opposing all aid to non-govern-ment schools. ALP policy on federal aid also hardened to include 'only those non-government schools whose total private and public resources do not exceed the resources of comparable government schools.' Under this criterion, the Commonwealth government would determine the level of resources required to deliver a high standard of schooling ('com-munity standard') and cut off grants to schools that were spending above this level.

Following the Labor party's victory in the 1983 national election, the minister for education and youth affairs, Senator Susan Ryan, announced in July that new guidelines for the Schools Commission would reduce recurrent grants to the forty-one wealthiest private schools by 25 per cent. Once again there was vociferous opposition from a coalition of Catholic and non-Catholic private-school supporters, and again the Labor government retreated from the ALP official policy of phasing out aid to the wealthiest schools. In March 1984 the Schools Commission proposed to classify private schools into twelve categories of need, based on a community standard of $2,195 per student for primary schools and $3,240 per student for secondary schools.[18] Against a minority dissent by the representatives of public-school parent and teacher organizations on the commission, the majority report of the Schools Commission pro-posed that all private schools be eligible for a grant. At its biennial conference, the ALP reaffirmed its policy to end state aid to the wealthi-est private schools, but in August 1984 the minister announced what she called a 'historic settlement' of the conflict over state aid to private schools. The Schools Commission's twelve categories of need and the criterion of community standard were both adopted. The wealthiest schools would not benefit from the increases applying to schools in the other categories but were guaranteed that their existing grants would be maintained in real terms.

Commonwealth and state government grants did not simply ensure the survival of low-fee private schools in Australia, but also contributed to a significant expansion of enrolments in the private sector.[19] The Catholic system, which was near collapse in 1973, experienced a 'significant renewal and growth as a result of the massive infusion of federal and state needs-based funding which flowed from the Schools Commission policies and support.'[20] Religious denominations other than Roman Catholic also took advantage of the provisions for state aid to set up low-fee schools and thus widened the option of private schooling to most of the community. Enrolments in private primary and secondary schools rose from 21.3 per cent of total enrolments in 1975 to 29 per cent in 1995, including a rise in enrolments in private, non-Roman Catholic schools from 4.3 per cent of total enrolments in 1975 to 9.4 per cent in 1995. Prospects for an increasing number of small private schools, and hence further expansion of enrolments in the private sector, were enhanced in 1997 by the Liberal government's termination of the New Schools Policy, which had been introduced by the ALP government in 1985 in order to regulate the negative impact of new or expanded private schools on existing public and private schools. At the same time, the Howard government also established a formula, the Enrolment Benchmark Adjustment, under which Commonwealth funding was transferred from public schools as the proportion of students attending private schools rose.[21]

ESL, Multicultural Education, and the National Policy on Languages

The first national effort to deal with the educational problems of migrant children in Australia was the Child Migrant Education Program announced by the Commonwealth government in 1970 and established in law by the Immigration (Education) Act of 1971.[22] Under the program, the Commonwealth government provided grants to reimburse state departments of education for salaries of specialists in teaching English as a second language (ESL) as well as costs of equipment and materials incurred for ESL instruction. The Child Migrant Education Program was originally conceived as a limited commitment, similar to the federal programs of aid for science laboratories and libraries. The expected levelling of demand did not occur, as the program expanded from an expenditure of $1.8 million in 1970-1, involving 408 full-time equivalent teachers and 21,000 children in special classes, to $10.4 million in 1975–6, involving 1,970 full-time equivalent teachers and 90,810 migrant children.

In its 1973 report on the organization and design of Commonwealth aid to education, the Interim Committee subsumed the education of migrant children under the provision of compensatory education for disadvantaged children. In the same year, however, the first official reservations about the strongly assimilative assumptions of child migrant educational policy were being raised by A.J. Grassby, the minister for immigration in the Labor government of Gough Whitlam.[23] In the general election of May 1974, Grassby lost his seat in the House of Representatives, the Department of Immigration was merged with the Department of Labour, and responsibility for the education of migrant children was transferred to the Department of Education. In October 1974, in collaboration with the two state departments of education, the Commonwealth department launched an inquiry into schools in New South Wales and Victoria that had a high density of migrant children, resulting in the creation of the Committee on the Teaching of Migrant Languages in Schools in November 1974. The committee's report found that regular school programs took a monocultural approach with 'no concessions to the particular needs and backgrounds of migrant pupils' and concluded that 'a positive multicultural approach, particularly at the school level' was essential to improve migrant education.[24]

In its report for the triennium 1976–8, the Schools Commission shifted its position from that taken by the Interim Committee, urging a basic change of educational policy and practice from migrant to multicultural education.[25] As a result, the Child Migrant Education Program was transferred to the control of the Schools Commission in January 1976, and the states and private schools began to get a block grant for migrant and multicultural education that included teaching English to migrant children, heritage languages programs, and ethnic and multicultural studies. Three years later, in response to recommendations for more attention to multicultural education from both the Australian Ethnic Affairs Council[26] and the Committee to Review Post-Arrival Programs and Services to Migrants,[27] the Australian Schools Commission, in its report for the 1979-81 triennium, instituted a new Multicultural Education Program (MEP) to promote general studies aimed at improving intercultural understanding as well as particular studies of ethnic groups resident in Australia, community languages, and bilingual education programs. At the state level, committees were created to administer the disbursement of small grants under the program and to advise state departments of education on the allocation of general grants.[28]

As a result of the Multicultural Education Program, several bilingual programs – English-German, English-Italian, and English-Macedonian – were started in Victoria and New South Wales, and funding was increased for programs sponsored by ethnic communities that provided language instruction outside regular school hours. In general, however, competency in English continued to be seen as the major problem and ESL teaching dominated both heritage languages and ethnic and multicultural studies. A review of the program carried out for the Schools Commission in 1984 concluded that as yet the MEP had made no major impact on Australian education. None the less, the MEP had 'facilitated in a major way the development of programs in languages other than English at the primary school,' and activities funded through the program had 'given new dimensions to the multicultural philosophy.'[29] The Schools Commission's recommendation in its report for the triennium 1985–7 that funding for the Multicultural Education Program be increased was initially endorsed by the Labor government. In August 1986, however, the Hawke government, as part of its budget cuts, announced that Commonwealth funding for teaching English as a second language would be cut and the Multicultural Education Program would be terminated.

The Labor government's priority had shifted from multicultural education to the development of a national language policy.[30] In a report prepared for the Labor government, Joseph Lo Bianco urged the need for all Australian children to learn English and another language, with particular emphasis on community languages and languages of economic importance: 'For planning purposes Australia needs to extend the base of general bilingual skills in the schooling system, harmonize its school languages teaching with its external economic needs, and actively seek to benefit from the presence of communities of Australians whose bilingualism and biculturalism are to our national economic advantage.'[31] Following the release of Lo Bianco's report in May 1987, the Hawke government committed $15 million to begin implementation of the National Policy on Languages. At the same time, federal programs for ESL and community languages were transferred from the Schools Commission to the Department of Education. When the departments of Employment and Industrial Relations and Education were merged in the new Department of Employment, Education and Training after the general election in July 1987, the construction of a national language policy was folded into the Labor government's goal of achieving agreement on a national curriculum. The new minister's policy statement, *Strengthening Australia's Schools*, published in May 1988, portrayed schools as the starting point of an integrated structure for education and training and the foundation for a highly skilled, adaptive, and productive workforce and an informed and cohesive society. In this statement, the goal of language education as a basic element in the creation of a pluralist society was not forgotten, but the weight of priorities had shifted strongly towards the economic utility of learning languages rather than its role in the formation of cultural identities.

Canada: Educational Regimes as Bilingual Consociations

Four regimes of religion and language in public education were constructed during the founding of public education in nineteenth-century Canada.[32] They operated with relatively little questioning or disturbance in national and provincial politics and policy until the 1960s. Then the effects of two intersecting socio-political dynamics transformed the issues of language and religion in Canadian educational politics.

First, a rise of French-Quebec nationalism in the 1950s and 1960s was characterized by a reformulation of ethnic identity in which language, province, and state replaced religion, race, and church as central elements of the symbolic order of French Quebec.[33] In turn, the resulting challenge to Canadian national unity revived the issue of minority-language education in all other provinces. Quebec nationalist demands to make French the official language of instruction were strenuously resisted by the anglophone minority, which was determined to prevent any erosion of its 'historical right' to English schools. Francophone minorities outside Quebec pressed for full recognition of their right to have their children educated in elementary and secondary schools where French was the language of instruction.

Second, the transformation of Canadian society by a postwar influx of immigrants with non-British, non-French national origins had a major impact on both language and religion as issues of educational politics. Ethnic minorities whose mother tongue was neither English nor French pressed inside Quebec to preserve the option to send their children to schools where English was the language of instruction, while outside Quebec they began to question both the majority's imposition of English as the language of instruction and the recognition of French as the exclusive minority right. The new immigrants, notably Italians and Portuguese, gave added impetus to demands for Roman Catholic education, especially in the separate schools of Toronto and the English-speaking Catholic schools of Montreal. The religious diversity of the new immigrants also eroded the historical hegemony of the Catholic–Protestant dichotomy, and public schools that had equated religious neutrality with non-denominational Christianity were slowly (and grudgingly) compelled to acquire a more inclusive perspective on religious instruction and observance.

Official Languages and Public Education inside and outside Quebec

Non-English, non-French immigrants settling in Quebec historically enrolled their children in English-language schools. As the immigrant population increased rapidly during the 1950s and 1960s, especially in the Montreal area, English-language schooling in the Protestant and especially the Roman Catholic sectors expanded correspondingly. Fearing for the survival of French language and culture in Quebec's largest urban centre, Quebec nationalists identified the long-term linguistic incorporation of immigrants into French Quebec as being crucial for its survival and development as a modern francophone society in North America.

The issue was joined in 1967, when the public (de facto Roman Catholic) school commission of the Montreal suburb of St-Léonard began a phased closure of its English-language schools, thus forcing English-speaking Catholics who resided in its jurisdiction, mostly Italian immigrants, to enrol their children in French-language schools. The Quebec Superior Court refused to overturn the board's action on the grounds that neither Quebec provincial statutes nor Canadian constitutional law guaranteed instruction in English. Language laws passed by successive Union Nationale and Liberal governments failed to find an acceptable compromise between Quebec nationalists on one side and English and immigrant communities on the other.[34] Following its election in 1976, the Parti Québécois government responded to nationalist criticism by passing the Charte de la langue française (Bill 101) in August 1977. Bill 101 required that the language of instruction in kindergarten, elementary, and secondary classes be French, and that, with limited exceptions, entry to English-language schools was restricted to children whose mother or father had received elementary instruction in English in Quebec. When linguistic minority groups appealed to the courts, the initial judgments upheld the authority of the Quebec government to legislate with respect to the language of instruction in provincial education.

Reacting to the election of the separatist Parti Québécois, Prime Minister Pierre Trudeau revived the national project of including in the Canadian constitution a bill of rights that provided protection for minority-language rights in education. With the proclamation of the Canadian Charter of Rights and Freedoms in April 1982, the Protestant School Board of Montreal, the Quebec Association of Protestant School Boards, and the parents of six children who had been refused permission to attend English schools went back to court, arguing that Bill 101 violated the guarantee of minority-language educational rights in section 23 of the Charter, and this time they won. Canadian citizens whose first language learned and still understood is English or who received their primary school education in Canada in English were entitled to English-language instruction for their children in Quebec public schools.[35]

Provincial governments that historically restricted the use of French as a language of instruction made some provision for French-language elementary and secondary school instruction even before the proclamation of section 23 in the Canadian Charter of Rights and Freedoms. In 1968, Ontario established the right of francophone students, where their numbers warranted, to receive their elementary and secondary school instruction in separate French-language schools or in separate French-language classes within English-language schools. In 1967 an amendment to the Manitoba School Act permitted French to be used as a language of instruction for up to half the school day, and in 1970 Franco-Manitobans gained minority-language school privileges similar to those available to Franco-Ontarians. Alberta removed its former time restrictions on instruction in French in 1968, permitting French at the discretion of local school boards for up to half the school day, and an amendment to Saskatchewan's education act that freed the Department of Education to determine the use of French by regulation resulted in a minority-language program under which the use of French varied from 100 per cent of instructional time in kindergarten to 50 per cent in grades five to twelve. British Columbia became the last province to make provision for minority-language education when the provincial curriculum was changed to permit the use of French as the language of instruction in elementary grades beginning in September 1978.

Despite official support for minority-language education, enrolments in these programs continued to decline, in part because of the drop in anglophone enrolment in Quebec during the 1980s, in part because of the continuing assimilation of francophone minorities outside Quebec.[36] By contrast, facilitated by a shift in federal aid from vocational training to official languages, enrolment in second-official-language programs outside Quebec rose steadily during the 1970s and 1980s. Perhaps the most significant expression of the new public philosophy of official bilingualism was the rapid expansion of French immersion programs. Beginning from the first experimental classes in St-Lambert, Quebec, in 1967, enrolment in immersion programs was 4.5 per cent of enrolment in second-official-language programs outside Quebec in 1980–1, 12.3 per cent in 1990–1, and 14.2 per cent in 1998–9.[37]

With the exception of New Brunswick, after the 1960s governments in English-majority provinces were willing to expand provision for French-language instruction in public schools but not to adopt language as a principle of educational governance.[38] In *Mahé* v. *Alberta* decided in March 1990, the Supreme Court of Canada ruled that section 23 of the Charter conferred a general right to minority-language education. Where the number of minority-language students was sufficiently large, the linguistic minority was entitled not only to a separate school but also to its own school board. In March 1993, while the Conservative government's bill to provide for French school boards was being considered by the Manitoba legislative assembly, the Supreme Court affirmed that its *Mahé* judgment also applied to Manitoba and hence, by extension, to other provinces, notably Ontario, that were remiss in legislating full rights of local school governance to francophone minorities. Because there were only a few local districts with enough francophone students to warrant the formation of separate francophone school boards, most provinces opted to establish provincial school boards to govern their francophone schools.[39] Under legislation passed in Alberta in 1993, six francophone school boards were created, later amalgamated into three; and in Ontario a recommendation of the Task Force on School Board Reductions for four French public and eight French separate school boards was implemented by the Conservative government in its Fewer School Boards Act passed in April 1997.

Quebec and Newfoundland: The Long Farewell to Denominational Regimes

In its landmark report on Quebec education (1963–6), the Parent commission created an agenda for educational reform as an essential component of Quebec's 'Quiet Revolution.' On the critical issue of language and religion in public education, the commission recommended that Roman Catholic and Protestant school boards should be replaced by secular school boards that would operate both French and English denominational and non-denominational ('neutral') schools.[40] At the time, this recommendation was rejected on grounds of language (French nationalists opposed the entrenchment of English schools) as well as religion (Roman Catholics rejected the introduction of neutral schools). In the 1976 provincial election, however, the Parti Québécois included implementation of the Parent commission's recommendation as part of its nationalist platform and, following its re-election in 1981, introduced Bill 3, which would put school boards throughout the province on a linguistic basis while restricting the constitutionally protected denominational boards of Montreal and Quebec city to their 1867 jurisdictions, areas now covering very few schools.

Challenged by the Quebec Association of Protestant School Boards and the Montreal Catholic School Commission, Bill 3 was judged by the Quebec Superior Court to be unconstitutional under section 93 of the Constitution Act, 1867, and the Liberal government, which was elected in 1985, chose not to appeal the decision. Instead, it introduced new legislation (Bill 107) providing that school boards outside Montreal and Quebec city would be either French or English and that school councils would decide whether their schools would have a denominational orientation or not. The Roman Catholic and Protestant school boards of Montreal and Quebec city would continue to operate alongside new secular French and English boards. Referred to the courts following its passage by the Quebec National Assembly in December 1988, Bill 107 was upheld as constitutional by the Quebec Court of Appeal in September 1990 and by the Supreme Court of Canada in June 1993, but it had not been implemented when the Liberal government was defeated in the 1995 provincial election.

The new Parti Québécois government appointed a fifteen-member Commission for Estates General on Education to make a comprehensive review of the state of education in Quebec, including the issue of language versus religion as the basis for organizing school boards. The final report of the commission, released in October 1996, recommended that denominational school boards, including the constitutionally protected school boards of Montreal and Quebec city, be replaced by French and English boards. The Parti Québécois government immediately announced its commitment to implementing the commission's recommendation. In April 1997 the Quebec National Assembly voted unanimously to seek an amendment through the Parliament of Canada that would abolish the constitutional protection for Roman Catholic and Protestant public education in Quebec. The amendment was passed by Parliament in December 1997, and the new school boards based on language rather than religion came into operation with the 1998–9 school year.[41]

In Newfoundland, based on the report of the Royal Commission on Education and Youth in 1967, the Department of Education was reorganized on a functional rather than a denominational basis, but church control of local educational governance remained intact for another quarter-century.[42] In its March 1992 report, a royal commission on the delivery of school programs and services recommended that denominational school boards be replaced by nine elected, non-denominational school boards.[43] Committed to implementing the commission's plan but unable to get agreement from Roman Catholic and Pentecostal Assemblies school authorities, the Liberal government resorted to a constitutional referendum in September 1995. The government's plan for ten regional school boards that would govern non-denominational schools (open to all students) and separate denominational schools (where parents petitioned and numbers warranted) won 54 per cent of the referendum vote; and, despite some questioning and controversy, the resolution to amend Term 17 of the Newfoundland Act was approved by the House of Commons in June 1996 followed by approval of the Senate in November.[44] As the new non-denominational boards proceeded to implement the plan, some schools were left open as Roman Catholic and Pentecostal. With the backing of their denominational education councils, Catholic and Pentecostal parents with children in schools that were being closed or redesignated as non-denominational sought an injunction, which was granted in July 1997. The Liberal government reacted by calling another referendum, this time on the following simple question: 'Do you support a single school system where all children, regardless of their religious affiliation, attend the same schools where opportunities for religious education and observances are provided?'[45] The answer to this question was 'yes' for 73 per cent of those who voted, the Newfoundland Assembly's resolution was approved by Parliament in December (the same week as the resolution on Quebec school boards was passed), and Newfoundland schools became non-denominational with the opening of the 1998–9 school year.

Accommodating Social Diversity: Heritage Languages, Religious Neutrality, and State Aid

In sharp contrast to the historical struggle over Canadian national identity between British and French ethnic groups, the political wars to redefine Canadian identity and restore national unity in the 1960s and 1970s could no longer be waged without reference to the growing presence and earnest voices of non-British, non-French ethnic groups. Led by the Ukrainian community, their vigorous advocacy of multiculturalism in representations to the Royal Commission on Bilingualism and Biculturalism marked a turning point in the formation of Canadian national identity. Acknowledging the case for cultural pluralism and the necessary role of public education in its preservation and development, the commission recommended that there must be in Canada not only 'a systematic approach to teaching the second official language to members of both the major linguistic communities' but also 'opportunities to study many languages within the context of the public system.'[46] As the public philosophy of pluralist society in Canada came to be identified in terms of bilingualism joined with multiculturalism, particularly following the federal government's commitment to an official policy of multiculturalism in October 1971, the preservation and advancement of languages other than the official languages of English and French became a legitimate issue of provincial educational policy.

Three types of provision for heritage language instruction were developed: bilingual programs within the regular public school system involving the use of a heritage language as the medium of instruction for half of each school day; heritage languages taught as core subjects within the regular school curriculum; and heritage languages taught as subjects supplementary to the regular curriculum, in areas where there is demand for them, sometimes during, but very often outside, regular school hours.[47] In 1971, responding to pressure from its Ukrainian community, Alberta became the first province to amend its School Law to permit the use of languages of instruction other than English or French, followed by Saskatchewan in 1978 and Manitoba in 1979.[48] In each case, the first bilingual program was English-Ukrainian, but bilingual programs have also been developed in Arabic, German, Hebrew, Italian, Mandarin, and Polish in Alberta; German, Mandarin, and Russian in Saskatchewan; and German and Hebrew in Manitoba. Several heritage languages are also taught as optional subjects in primary grades and as sequences of two or three courses for credit in junior and senior high school. In British Columbia, curricula have been developed for grades five to twelve in German, Japanese, Mandarin, Punjabi, and Spanish as options to French as a second language, and Nova Scotia recently restored Gaelic as an optional subject for grades three to twelve. In the provinces of Ontario and Quebec, instruction in a wide range of heritage languages is organized as a supplement to the regular school program and has been provincially supported by financial assistance and curriculum development since 1977.[49]

With religion displaced by language as the predominant issue of Canadian educational politics, its place in public education also has been reshaped by the precepts of pluralist society. When the Charter was proclaimed in 1982, Ontario, British Columbia, and Manitoba all required religious exercises at the daily opening and/or closing of public schools, and Ontario, in addition, required two half-hour periods of religious instruction each week. In other provinces, religious observances were optional, depending on the discretion of school boards.[50] With the support of advocacy organizations such as the Canadian Civil Liberties Association, parents who opposed mandatory religious exercises in schools began legal challenges under section 2(a) of the Charter, which guarantees individual freedom of conscience and religion.

In the first of these cases to reach the appeal court, the Ontario Court of Appeal in 1988 found that a provincial regulation mandating religious exercises at the opening and closing of schools was unconstitutional. Peer pressure and classroom norms tended to force members of religious minorities into conformance with majority religious practices, and hence the provincial regulation had the effect of imposing Christian observances on non-Christians and religious observances on non-believers.[51] The following year, the British Columbia Supreme Court, citing the Ontario precedent, similarly decided that a provincial regulation requiring public schools to be opened each day with reading from the Bible and recitation of the Lord's Prayer was unconstitutional. The Manitoba government tried to save its requirement for Christian religious observances by authorizing each school board to decide by an annual vote not to abide by the provincial regulation in its schools, but the Manitoba Court of Queen's Bench in 1992 ruled that the provincial regulation requiring Christian exercises was none the less unconstitutional: 'to prefer one religion over another, as is now being done in the school system of this province, contravenes the provisions of the Charter relating to freedom of conscience and religion.'[52]

In public schools outside the confessional regimes of Quebec and Newfoundland, religious education historically was left to the discretion of local boards. In Ontario, however, a regulation promulgated in 1944 required two half-hour periods of religious instruction in public elementary schools each week to be devoted to the life and teachings of Jesus as well as Old Testament stories. During the 1960s and 1970s the regulation became increasingly controversial,[53] and following the proclamation of the Canadian Charter of Rights and Freedoms, its constitutionality was successfully challenged.[54] Following the unfavourable judgment in the

Ontario Court of Appeal, a new ministry regulation was issued in December 1990 giving local boards discretion to offer up to one hour of religious education a week as long as their courses did not promote any particular faith. Boards were also allowed to provide classrooms for voluntary denominational education before or after school but had to give fair access to all religious groups.

In the Maritimes, district reorganization and school consolidation in the 1960s and 1970s made it hard to preserve the historical practice of reserving separate schools for Roman Catholics. Large regional schools raised controversial questions about denominational religious instruction and observance for multidenominational student bodies, and giving religious instruction outside the regular school program was complicated by the constraints of bus schedules, the availability of alternative extracurricular activities, and shortages of qualified teachers. In New Brunswick, for example, where the number of school districts was cut from 433 to 33 in 1967, within a decade enrolment in Catholic 'rented buildings' had fallen to 4 per cent of total provincial enrolment.[55] In the Halifax area, following the annexation in 1969 of several suburbs where there were no schools reserved for Roman Catholics, the Halifax Board of School Commissioners provided for a weekly one-hour period of religious instruction in the suburban schools for any denomination that wished to organize a class. Over the next few years, as declining enrolments forced school amalgamations and closures, the same policy was extended throughout the city, and the practice of reserved schools came to an end.[56]

Saskatchewan (1966), Alberta (1967), Quebec (1968), British Columbia (1977), and Manitoba (1981) have instituted programs of provincial grants to private schools and thus provide aid mainly to voluntary denominational schools.[57] In the Atlantic provinces, the minuscule proportion of students in private schools and the financial straits of provincial governments have been convincing obstacles to state aid; in Ontario, however, provincial grants for both separate schools and private schools have been major issues of educational politics. As the expanded postwar school population passed through the primary grades and began to reach secondary schools, the financial pressures of capital expansion, teacher shortages, and curriculum diversification renewed demands for full funding of separate secondary schools as state-provided schools.[58] The governing Conservative party firmly resisted Catholic entreaties, however, until June 1984, when William Davis, on the verge of his retirement after thirteen years as premier and party leader, announced that full funding for secondary separate schools would be introduced over a two-year period beginning in September 1985. Explaining his government's decision before a legislative committee, Davis emphasized the need for tolerance and equity in a pluralist society: 'when we look at our multicultural policy, when we want to make people retain some of the things that are dear to them – we recognize the equity and the logic in a matter of conscience that this is the time for this very fundamental change in policy.'[59]

The Conservative government's decision to give full funding to separate schools led, in turn, to renewed demands that provincial grants be extended to private denominational schools. A commission established by the Conservative government reported in favour of provincial grants to private schools,[60] and when successive Liberal (1985–90) and New Democratic Party (1990–5) governments failed to act, advocates for state aid to private denominational schools turned to the courts. When their appeal reached the Supreme Court of Canada in November 1996, the majority held that providing for public funding of Roman Catholic separate schools, as required under section 93 of the Constitution Act, 1867, while failing to fund private religious schools did not constitute discrimination under either the religious freedom or the equal benefit clause of the Charter of Rights and Freedoms.[61] Five years after the Supreme Court's decision, however, the Conservative government abruptly reversed the policy not to aid private schools. In his May 2001 budget speech, the minister of finance announced the phased introduction of a provincial income-tax credit of 50 per cent (maximum $3,500) for tuition paid to private schools.

New Zealand: Integrating Roman Catholic and Maori Schools

Historically, the national identity of New Zealand has been predominantly formed by a heritage of British nationality. Within this assumptively homogeneous political society, however, there were two major religious and ethnic controversies that impinged persistently on the content and governance of public education. One was the dispute over the place of religious instruction in public schools and the provision of state aid for church schools between conservative supporters of separate denominational schools and liberal advocates of common non-denominational education. The other concerned the curriculum and governance of the education of Maori children.[62]

Integration of Church Schools and State System

After the Second World War, public schools in New Zealand became more non-denominational than secular, but that did not make them any more acceptable to the Roman Catholic church, which persevered in the development of its own voluntary system of primary and secondary schools. The issue of state aid had remained virtually dormant from 1877 until Catholic schools in New Zealand began to encounter severe problems of rising enrolments, teacher shortages, and insufficient and inadequate buildings and equipment after the Second World War. Incremental measures of state aid were introduced for private primary schools, including boarding allowances open to all eligible students whether they attended public or private schools, transportation to and from schools and manual training centres, use of facilities at manual training centres, participation in a free textbook scheme, and subsidies for school equipment and teaching aids. By 1960, state grants to private schools had reached £272,954, large enough to cause the Commission on Education in New Zealand to conclude that any further expansion of state aid might have detrimental effects on the efficiency and quality of the state system.[63]

None the less, during the 1960s the overall financial position of private schools continued to decline. Roman Catholics and Protestants joined forces in 1962 to form the Interdenominational Committee of Independent Schools, led by laity rather than clergy, and it proved to be an effective lobby.[64] Following its re-election in 1969 the National government fulfilled a campaign promise to increase state aid to private schools by introducing a grant to cover 20 per cent of teachers' salaries, rising in stages over seven years to 35 per cent. As a counter-proposal, in its 1972 manifesto the Labour party promised that, if elected, it would offer private schools the option of either integrating with the state system or receiving a grant of 50 per cent of teachers' salaries, and that the resulting increase in state aid would not come at the expense of state schools.

Under the Private Schools Conditional Integration Act, which was passed just before the Labour party lost the general election of 1975, all recurrent operating costs of private schools that opted to become integrated schools were financed by the state, while land and buildings, after upgrading to conform with state standards, remained the property of the churches or foundations. Denominational adherents were guaranteed preference for admission to integrated schools, but there was a quota for non-adherents (usually 5 per cent of registration) if space allowed. As part of the state system, integrated schools were no longer allowed to charge fees, but 'attendance dues' were accepted as a way of financing new capital expenditures. In 1975 there were 383 private schools in New Zealand, including 295 Roman Catholic schools. By 31 March 1983, when the minister of education signed the last of the integration agreements with Catholic schools, 249 Roman Catholic and nine non-Catholic schools had become integrated schools. The private sector was now reduced to 101 schools (including one small Roman Catholic primary school), with enrolments down from 11.3 per cent of total primary and secondary enrolment in 1975 to 3.3 per cent in 1985.[65]

Maori Education: Assimilation, Integration, Consociation

The dominant principles, assumptions, and purposes of Maori educational policy evolved through three distinct paradigms from the 1840s to the 1990s. Initially, there was a long period during which official educational policy was based on the assumption that Maori was a dying culture, and the purpose of Maori education was assimilation into the dominant pakeha culture and society.[66] Following the finding by the 1930 departmental survey that a deep cultural divide between Maori communities and Native schools was impeding the education of Maori children, departmental policy officially became 'adaptation' rather than assimilation. Connecting with the movement started in the 1920s by Apirana Ngata to regenerate interest in traditional culture, new guidelines for teachers in Native schools mandated that Maori pupils learn not only the basic knowledge and practical skills required for living and working in modern society but also the arts, crafts, dances, songs, and legends of traditional society. The Maori language continued to be excluded from the curriculum, however, in part because the majority of teachers in Native schools could not speak Maori, in part because officials remained convinced that the introduction of Maori would undermine the main priority of teaching English.[67]

The first evidence of a fundamental change in thinking about Maori education was the opening of the first Native district high schools in 1941–2 as part of the Labour government's bid to fulfil its 1939 commitment to provide secondary education for every child 'of the kind for which he is best fitted and to the fullest extent of his power.' In these schools, Maori boys would learn the skills of carpentry and associated trades to prepare them for work in towns and cities in the building trades; Maori girls would concentrate on home-making skills of cooking, sewing, and cleaning.[68]

After the Second World War, urbanization of the Maori rapidly increased the proportion of Maori children attending primary schools administered by the education boards and forced the issue of dual administration on which the policy of assimilation had been constructed.[69] On one side, critics of dual administration pressed for the transfer of Maori schools to administration by the education boards and development of national policies to deal with the special needs of Maori students that would apply to all schools. On the other side, protectors of Maori village schools advocated that all schools with predominantly Maori enrolments be removed from the education boards to the control of the Maori school service of the Department of Education. From 1955 to 1962, three landmark investigations into Maori education all reached similar conclusions about the serious educational gap between Maori and non-Maori students, the special needs of Maori children that had to be met in order for them to overcome their disadvantage, and the principle of integration of the Maori in New Zealand education and society as the logical alternative to assimilation.

In 1955, several leaders of the Maori community were invited to join representatives of the educational policy community – the New Zealand Educational Institute, the Post-Primary Teachers' Association, the Education Boards' Association, the School Committees' Federation, the Maori teaching service, the Department of Education, and the Department of Maori Affairs – to form the National Committee on Maori Education. This committee, which was subsequently institutionalized as the National Advisory Committee on Maori Education (NACME), unanimously concluded that Maori schools should be transferred gradually to administration by the education boards, that knowledge of Maori history and culture should be given greater emphasis in the primary school curriculum for both Maori and pakeha students, and that teachers' training should include courses on Maori education and culture.

The policy of Maori integration, which was implicit in the NACME recommendations, was made explicit in a 1960 report by the secretary of the Department of Maori Affairs. Donald Hunn argued that 'full integration of the Maori people into the mainstream of New Zealand life' should be the highest priority for public policy. As a process, integration ought 'to combine (not fuse) the Maori and pakeha elements to form one nation wherein Maori culture remains distinct.' Better education was a critical factor in order to achieve successful integration, and with

71 per cent of Maori children now attending them, board schools had become 'the nursery of integration.'[70] Hunn supported a measured transfer of Native schools and recommended appropriate training for public school teachers to deal with the needs of Maori pupils.

In its 1962 report, the Commission on Education in New Zealand likewise asserted that 'Upon the cultural side of race relationships the common school attended by both races is still seen as one of the great integrating forces in the community.'[71] The commission observed that the assumptions underlying Maori educational policy had changed: 'Although there is no retreat from the belief that the Maori child must be equipped to take his place on terms of equality as a New Zealand citizen, there is a belief now that, in addition, the dignity and pride of race which are his heritage must be safeguarded to him.'[72] The curriculum in Maori village schools and Maori district high schools did include elements of Maori culture, but only a minority went to these schools – in 1960, 28.4 per cent of Maori primary students were enrolled in Maori village schools and 8.5 per cent of Maori secondary students attended Maori district high schools. Convinced 'that Maori education must become an area of special need, requiring special measures and, inevitably, increased expenditure,' the Currie commission recommended, first, that all schools containing a substantial proportion of Maori students should be declared 'Maori service schools' and hence eligible for special services and increased grants, and second, that over the next ten years all Maori schools should be transferred to administration by the education boards.

Some Maori leaders and parents worried about the effects of transferring village schools on provision for the special needs of Maori children, as well as negative consequences for the survival of Maori culture. The proportion of Maori children attending Maori schools further declined to 16.4 per cent in 1965, however, and NACME urged that a deadline be set for the transfer of all Maori schools. On 1 February 1969 the remaining ninety-eight village schools came under the control of the education boards.

During the 1970s a third approach to Maori education developed within Maoridom that made teaching the Maori language the core of the curriculum. Under the policy of assimilation Maori, if not banished entirely, was restricted to being a transitional language in primary school. Under the policy of integration, Maori was accepted as an optional subject that was largely confined to secondary schools but not sanctioned as an alternative language of instruction. According to the Currie commission, for example, English was the language of the society at large; hence, the Maori language was inevitably a second language for the vast majority of Maori. Accordingly, it was essential for Maori children to master English in primary school and logical to introduce Maori as an option in forms one and two (years seven and eight), when studies of languages other than English were added to the curriculum. This position was increasingly challenged by Maori critics during the 1970s, and the 1980 NACME report, *He Huarahi*, asserted that te reo Maori was the foundation of Maori culture. Maori underachievement in school historically could be explained by the low self-esteem of Maori pupils caused by their involvement in educational institutions divorced from the basic principles and practices of the Maori traditional way.

The solution advocated by NACME required changes in both the content and the governance of Maori education. With respect to content, the education of Maori children should be bilingual and bicultural, but it should be founded on their immersion in the Maori language and culture in primary school. As for governance, just as pakeha education was controlled by the majority pakeha community, Maori education ought to be controlled by the minority Maori community. During the 1980s the idea of Maori self-government in education took two practical lines of development outside the regime of state schools.

First, there was the movement organized by Maori women for te kohanga reo ('the language nest'). Te kohanga reo is a cooperative preschool centre where Maori children are immersed in their language and cultural practices. The first te kohanga reo opened in April 1982 at Pukeatea, and their expansion was spectacular. By 1990 there were 612 centres with more than 10,000 children, about 15 per cent of Maori children in the pre-school age group.[73] Initially supported by funding through the Department of Maori Affairs rather than the Department of Education, since the reorganization of 1989 te kohanga reo have been funded on the same basis as other early childhood services through partnership agreements with the Ministry of Education.

Second, unwilling to lose the gains of language and culture from early childhood education in te kohanga reo, Maori parents in the mid-1980s began organizing primary schools (kura kaupapa Maori) in which the teachers were Maori, te reo Maori continued to be the language of instruction, and Maori cultural principles and practices pervaded the curriculum. Section 155 of the Education Act 1989 made provision for fully funded state schools that would provide schooling in Maori, and in February 1990 six pilot kura kaupapa Maori were opened as state schools, operating under charters approved by the Ministry of Education. By

1995, which was designated as Maori Language Year, there were twenty-nine kura kaupapa established or approved for establishment and application received for seventeen more, the first kura tuarua (Maori-medium secondary school) had been opened at Hoani Waititi Marae, as well as a bilingual unit within Western Heights High School in Auckland, and protocols for the establishment and management of future kura had been agreed between the Ministry of Education and Te Runanganui o Nga Kura Kaupapa Maori, the Maori association for the development of kura. Overall, almost 14 per cent of Maori students in New Zealand schools were enrolled in some type of Maori-medium program, and a further 24 per cent were studying te reo Maori as a subject in conventional classes.[74]

United Kingdom: Assimilation versus Integration of Racial and Ethnic Minorities in 'British' Schools

In the autumn of 1963, white parents organized protests against the large numbers of non-white immigrant children who were enrolled in two schools in the London borough of Southall. The Conservative government's minister of education, Sir Edward Boyle, visited the community and later told the House of Commons that one school – Beaconsfield Road School, which was 60 per cent non-white – 'must be regarded now as irretrievably an immigrant school. The important thing to do is to prevent this happening elsewhere.'[75] Educational reform in 1944, 1946, and 1947 took for granted the existence of a British society that, despite its minority national variants in Scotland, Northern Ireland, and Wales, was essentially homogeneous in race, language, religion, and culture. The events in Southall demonstrated that this idea of Britain was no longer valid. Britain was becoming a plural society and, as the minister acknowledged, educational policy would have to change to deal with it. Over the next quarter-century, three issues in particular reveal the ways in which attempts were made to meet the new educational challenges of a plural society.

First, there was the impact of Commonwealth immigration with resulting concentrations of racial and ethnic minorities that primarily affected local education authorities (LEAs), even particular schools, located in the eastern boroughs of London and the industrial cities of the Midlands. The initial reactions of educational policy makers aimed at facilitating assimilation. When these efforts largely failed, the turn towards more integrative policies of multicultural education had much wider repercussions.

Second, postwar educational reform in England, Scotland, and Wales was predicated on the legacies of historical conflict and compromise between Protestants and Roman Catholics over the organization of public schools and the content of religious instruction. The growing secularity of postwar British society did cause some doubts about the overwhelmingly Christian orientation and content of religious instruction, but again it was growing awareness of Britain as not only multiracial and multi-ethnic but also multidenominational that animated the idea of teaching religion as universal human experience and hence confronted the Christian monopoly in British schools. At the same time, in sharp contrast with this growing denominational multiculturalism in Great Britain, the stark division between Protestant and Roman Catholic sectors became more legitimately embedded in the educational regime of Northern Ireland.

Third, the idea of pluralist society as a public good invigorated long-standing claims of Scottish and Welsh nationalist movements. The revival of Scottish nationalism during the 1960s did not substantially affect the politics of British education, in part because Scotland had enjoyed some visible autonomy with regard to educational policy making since 1872, in part because Scottish national identity was not centred on issues of language, including the language of instruction in Scottish public schools. By contrast, not only was educational policy making for Wales historically dominated in a unified educational regime by the problems of educational policy making for England, but the Welsh language was the core of Welsh national culture and identity. Consequently, bilingual education was a perennial issue of educational politics in Wales. From the 1960s to the 1990s, under the aegis of the ideal of pluralist society, it became the constitutive idea and distinguishing policy of an emerging Welsh educational regime.

Immigrant Children, Educational Disadvantage,
and Multicultural Education

When he spoke to the House of Commons in November 1963 about the problems resulting from concentrations of racial and ethnic minorities in British schools, Sir Edward Boyle proposed as a remedy that in future local education authorities should restrict immigrant children from rising above 30 per cent of the enrolment in any one school.[76] The next year, the second report of the Commonwealth Immigrants Advisory Committee concluded that effective cultural assimilation of immigrant children required their dispersal among schools. According to the committee, 'if a school has more than a certain percentage of immigrant children among its pupils, the whole character and ethos of the school is altered. Immigrant pupils in such a school would not get as good an introduction to British life as they would get in a normal school, and we think their education in the widest sense must suffer as a result.'[77]

Thus, the growing presence of racial and ethnic minorities in British schools was formulated as one of assimilating immigrant children into 'British life,' especially school, to which the major barriers were inadequate ability in using English as the language of instruction and the culture shock of being transposed from underdeveloped rural communities to an urban industrial society. Otherwise, the educational problems of immigrant children were not different from the problems of educational disadvantage suffered by identifiable groups of children among the white majority. Tellingly, in its report on primary education, the Central Advisory Council for Education (England), chaired by Lady Plowden, proposed to deal with educational disadvantage by designating 'educational priority areas' based on indicators of economic, social, and environmental deprivation such as family size, overcrowded housing, percentage of unemployed workers, households in receipt of social assistance and free school meals, truancy, and incidence of retarded, disturbed, and handicapped children. Included as a general criterion of educational need was the proportion of children unable to speak English.[78]

Dispersal of immigrant children was officially recommended as policy in 1965 with the issuance of Circular 7/65 by the Labour government's secretary of state for education and science, Anthony Crosland;[79] it proved to be a political and policy failure. As policy, Circular 7/65 was ignored by the Inner London Education Authority and the Birmingham Education Committee, the two authorities that had the largest proportions of immigrant children in their schools. Five years after the circular was issued, a survey conducted for the Department of Education and Science by the National Foundation for Educational Research found no dispersal in two-thirds of the sixty-four areas with significant numbers of immigrant children and only marginal efforts at dispersal, such as manipulation of attendance areas, in one-quarter of the impacted areas. Dispersal that involved daily busing of children had been adopted as policy in only eleven areas.[80] As politics, busing was controversial from the outset in ethnic-majority communities that did not want immigrant children in their schools. Leaders of racial-minority and ethnic-minority communities, who initially had supported busing as a way of defusing white hostility of the sort expressed in Southall neighbourhoods in the early 1960s, came to regard dispersal as discriminatory, imposing an excessive burden entirely on non-white children.

Following the return to power of the Conservative government in May 1970, the 1971 policy statement of the Department of Education and Science on the education of immigrant children advised local education authorities to avoid dispersal where it was not strictly necessary but left the decision to their discretion.[81] The official position of the Department of Education and Science also shifted against identification of racial and ethnic minorities as constituting a separate problem of educational policy. Immigrant children might have special difficulties of English proficiency or cultural adaptation, but otherwise their educational disadvantages were substantially the same as those of native children living 'in the ugly, bare, built-up "twilight areas" – badly housed, lacking social, cultural and recreational amenities, attending schools with frequent staff changes, in poor buildings.'[82] The next year, the department announced that it would no longer collect information about 'immigrant children' since most children of racial and ethnic minorities were no longer properly classified as immigrants and therefore the statistics had become useless as a guide to policy. When the Select Committee on Race Relations and Immigration in its July 1973 report on education proposed that a fund be created to provide for the special educational needs of immigrant children and that the Department of Education and Science set up an immigrant education advisory unit, the department replied that in older urban and industrial areas immigrant children 'are likely to share with the indigenous children of those areas the educational disadvantages associated with an impoverished environment. The Government believe that immigrant pupils will accordingly benefit increasingly from special help given to all those suffering from educational disadvantage.'[83] Consistent with this approach, the education of racial and ethnic minorities was assigned to the department's Educational Disadvantage Unit, created in 1974, and also included in the mandate of the Centre for Information and Advice on Educational Disadvantage that opened in Manchester in 1975.[84]

Bereft of leadership from Westminster, the development of multicultural educational policies by local education authorities was geographically concentrated and pedagogically limited. In 1977 the Inner London Education Authority was the first local authority to commit itself to the development of a policy on multi-ethnic education. By 1981, about twenty-five local education authorities had appointed an adviser for

multicultural education, and a few had produced policy documents.[85]
Research funded by the Schools Council found general acceptance among
local administrators and classroom teachers who were responsible for
multi-ethnic education that the presence of ethnic-minority groups had
curricular implications for all schools, regardless of their ethnic composition. In practice, however, special arrangements for children of ethnic-
minority groups were 'often largely limited to meeting the basic language
requirements of English as a second language learners,' curricular development and in-service teacher education were relatively undeveloped,
resources were limited in a situation of many competing priorities, and
in areas with low proportions of ethnic-minority groups there had been
'little systematic consideration of the need to give all children an understanding of the cultural diversity of the wider society.'[86]

In its last months in office prior to the 1979 general election, the
Labour government established the Committee of Inquiry into the Education of Children from Ethnic Minority Groups, chaired first by Anthony
Rampton and later by Lord Swann. [87] In its final report in 1985 the
committee proposed a concept of a pluralist society 'which enables,
expects and encourages members of all ethnic groups, both minority
and majority, to participate fully in shaping the society as a whole within
the framework of commonly accepted values, practices and procedures,
whilst also allowing and, where necessary, assisting the minority ethnic
communities in maintaining their distinct ethnic identities within this
common framework.'[88] In the debate about multicultural education in
Britain there was confusion between two interrelated and complementary issues: 'on the one hand, meeting the educational needs of ethnic
minority pupils, and, on the other, broadening the education offered to
all pupils to reflect the multi-racial nature of British society.'[89] A good
education for all persons in school should be multicultural, reflecting
the diversity of contemporary Britain and the trend towards global
interdependence. Meeting the educational needs of all persons in school
'would include catering for any particular educational needs which an
ethnic minority pupil may have, arising for example from his or her
linguistic or cultural background.' The school should not be held responsible for 'teaching culture' or 'cultural preservation,' however; 'an
education which seeks only to emphasise and enhance the ethnic group
identity of a child, at the expense of developing both a national identity
and indeed an international, global perspective, cannot be regarded as
in any sense multicultural.'[90]

In its initial response to the report of the Swann committee, the

Conservative government conceded that educational achievement among ethnic-minority groups might be relatively more affected by economic and social disadvantage and certainly that 'all pupils need to understand, and acquire a positive attitude towards, the variety of ethnic groups within British society'; but underachievement was also found among pupils from the majority community. 'The Government's policies are designed to reduce under-achievement wherever it occurs ... In the Government's view, curricular policies at the national, local and school level should ensure that what is taught in schools is meaningful to all pupils.'[91] This emphasis on the educational interests of all children, not simply the members of ethnic-minority groups, became the moral imperative driving the development of the national curriculum that applied to all children equally. Except for Welsh in Wales, heritage or 'home' languages were subsumed within the list of nineteen languages eligible to be taught as foreign languages, and references to multicultural education in the national curriculum were minimized.[92]

Religious Instruction versus Religious Education in the Schools of England, Scotland, and Wales

Although religious instruction and daily religious observances were practically universal in the schools of England and Wales before the Second World War, the Education Act of 1944 for the first time required that 'the school day in every county school and in every voluntary school shall begin with collective worship on the part of all pupils in attendance' and 'religious instruction shall be given in every county school and every voluntary school.' A conscience clause permitting parents to withdraw their children from religious instruction or observances was preserved, as was the proviso that collective worship in county schools must be non-denominational. The act directed each local education authority to adopt a non-denominational 'agreed syllabus' for religious instruction that was acceptable to church authorities (other than the Roman Catholic church) and teachers' unions. Controlled voluntary schools were also required to give religious instruction according to an agreed syllabus, but in addition they could give denominational instruction for two periods each week. All religious instruction in 'aided' or 'special agreement' voluntary schools was permitted to be denominational.[93]

During the first two decades following the passage of the 1944 act, agreed syllabuses overwhelmingly assumed that religious instruction was 'mainly Christian learning, and consisted of a study of the Bible, of early

Church history and of certain major Christian doctrines, practices and moral theories.'[94] Parental opinion strongly supported these provisions for religious observance and instruction.[95] During the 1960s, however, the increasing social diversity of British society began to influence the construction of agreed syllabuses in areas most affected by the arrival of immigrant children in their schools. Local education authorities that had relatively high enrolments of immigrant children – West Riding (which includes Bradford) in 1966 and Lancashire and the Inner London Education Authority in 1968 – took the initiative in revising their agreed syllabuses to transform religious instruction based on the Christian tradition into religious education that aimed to teach a sympathetic but critical understanding of 'the place and significance of religion in human life and so to make a distinctive contribution to each pupil's search for a faith by which to live.'[96] In 1977 the subject committee of the Schools Council on religious education in primary schools stated that the aim was not to foster religious faith but rather to promote 'a sympathetic but critical understanding of religions.'[97] Such a phenomenological conception of the religious curriculum was the basis for the revisions of agreed syllabuses of such local education authorities as Birmingham (1975), Avon (1976), Hampshire (1978), and Manchester (1980).[98]

In its 1985 report, the Committee of Inquiry into the Education of Children from Ethnic Minority Groups advocated 'a non denominational and undogmatic approach to religious education as the best and indeed the only means of enabling all pupils, from whatever religious background, to understand the nature of religious belief, the religious dimension of human experience and the plurality of faiths in contemporary Britain.' According to the committee, 'There should be no conflict between the role of schools in providing religious *education* and the role of community institutions in providing religious *instruction*.' The Swann committee recognized that the right of ethnic-minority communities to seek to establish their own voluntary aided schools was established in law but thought that separate schools catering to minority communities 'would fail to tackle many of the underlying concerns of the communities and might exacerbate the very feelings of rejection which they are seeking to overcome.' The committee also found evidence of difficulties resulting from the requirements of the 1944 act for a daily act of collective worship and urged that the provisions of the act should be reconsidered 'to see whether or not alterations are required in a society that is now very different.'[99] In reply, the secretary of state for education and science, Sir Keith Joseph, declared that the Conservative government had no intention of changing the statutory requirements for collective worship and religious instruction in maintained schools.

The 1988 Education Reform Act did not make religious education one of the subjects comprising the national curriculum, but it did reiterate the statutory requirements of the 1944 act with regard to religious instruction and further required that collective worship in county schools 'shall be wholly or mainly of a broadly Christian character' (section 7[1]) and that agreed syllabuses 'shall reflect the fact that the religious traditions in Great Britain are in the main Christian whilst taking account of the teaching and practices of the other principal religions represented in Great Britain' (section 8[3]).[100] Getting local education authorities and schools to implement the new provisions for religious education proved to be difficult. In June 1992 the minister of state for education (Baroness Blatch) complained that two-thirds of LEAs had yet to redraft their agreed syllabuses in accordance with the 1988 act, and the next year, when the National Curriculum Council analysed twenty-seven agreed syllabuses, it concluded that none of them clearly satisfied the new statutory requirements. The 1993 Education Act ordered every LEA that had not drawn up an agreed syllabus since 1988 to do so (and imposed a further requirement for agreed syllabuses to be revised every five years); in January 1994 the Department for Education issued a circular reiterating that in every agreed syllabus the study of Christianity should be predominant; and the new School Curriculum and Assessment Authority published two draft model syllabuses to serve as frames for local curricular conferences. Implementation then improved, but political debate about non-denominational religious education was not assuaged.[101] Christian conservatives, upset that the model syllabuses failed to allot at least 51 per cent of the time for religious education to Christianity, renewed their lobbying for more denominational instruction, and minority religious groups followed suit by asserting claims for their own aided voluntary schools that would provide sectarian education.[102]

In Scotland, as in England and Wales, until the late 1960s the goal of fostering and nurturing a personal faith in Jesus Christ as Saviour and Lord was assumed to be broadly acceptable for religious instruction in both non-denominational and denominational schools.[103] Religious instruction concentrated on biblical knowledge, and little or no provision was made for religious education that was not Christian and not scriptural. In 1968 a committee chaired by Professor W. Malcolm Millar was appointed by the secretary of state for Scotland to review moral and religious education in Scottish schools; its report four years later was profoundly critical of the traditional approach to religious instruction. Rather than advocating specific religious beliefs, let alone making children learn them, teachers should be exposing children to a number of different attitudes and beliefs while taking care not to throw the weight of their authority behind any one of them.[104] In its first bulletin, the Scottish Central Committee on Religious Education (SCCORE), appointed in 1974, affirmed the curricular goals advanced by the Millar committee that students understand the place of religion in human experience, examine the nature and meaning of existence, explore the meaning of commitment to a religious or moral way of life, and become aware of the wider social and cultural impact of religions.[105]

After religious education became subject to central inspection for the first time in 1983, the Millar report and the SCCORE recommendations became the basis for the development and implementation of a national policy. When national guidelines and attainment outcomes for religious and moral education were issued in 1992, other world religions for the first time were given a meaningful place in the five-to-fourteen curriculum, and a focus on general moral and religious principles and problems took the place of fostering Christian belief and personal commitment.[106]

Northern Ireland's Immutable Denominational Regime

The 1947 Education Act in Northern Ireland did not alter, but simply perpetuated, the alignment of a Protestant state sector against a Roman Catholic voluntary sector. Almost all Protestant (formerly Class I) elementary schools were transferred to become 'county' schools, but only eight Roman Catholic primary schools agreed to accept the new designation of 'maintained' schools, with its superior financial arrangements.[107] Based on the recommendations of a 1964 white paper, the Education Act of 1968 created a new category of 'voluntary maintained schools,' for which management committees were divided between church (two-thirds) and state (one-third) and grants were increased to 80 per cent of approved capital expenditures and 100 per cent of maintenance costs. Hard-pressed financially and given reassurance about the protection of denominational instruction, the Roman Catholic hierarchy finally dropped its long-standing opposition to maintained status. By 1980, all voluntary secondary intermediate schools and most (497 out of 507) voluntary primary schools had become maintained voluntary schools.[108] To offset the concessions made in the 1968 act to Catholic schools,

Protestant churches were recognized as having management rights in new county schools being built in areas where previously no church schools had existed and where, therefore, there were no rights of transferrers. Thus the effect of the 1968 amendment was to entrench and legitimate the dual confessional regime.[109]

During the 1970s and 1980s, efforts to end the violent conflict between nationalists and unionists in Northern Ireland did turn attention to the divisive consequences of the dual confessional regime. The Roman Catholic church remained adamant about preserving denominational schools, but the Annual Synod of the Church of Ireland in 1970 and the General Assembly of the Presbyterian church in 1971 passed resolutions expressing guarded support for integrated schools.[110] Public opinion polls showed majority public support for religiously integrated schools. All Children Together (ACT), an interdenominational organization of parents formed in 1974 to press both churches and government for integrated schools, succeeded in 1978 in getting a new category of 'controlled integrated schools.' When the Protestant churches failed to act, ACT opened its own integrated secondary school, Lagan College, in 1981. Another integrated secondary school and twelve integrated primary schools were established by groups of parents during the 1980s, and a section of the Education Reform (Northern Ireland) Order 1989 obliged the government to support and promote integrated education. Even so, a decade later, there were only forty-three integrated schools in Northern Ireland, 3.6 per cent of the total, and integrated schools remained marginalized institutions in the segregated educational regime and resolutely anti-pluralist society of Northern Ireland.[111]

Ethnic Nationalism and the Language of Instruction in Wales

English was the language of instruction in the educational regime instituted for England and Wales in 1870, but Welsh was used unofficially as the language of instruction in schools in Welsh-speaking areas.[112] The first separate elementary school code for Wales, issued in 1907, decreed that 'any of the subjects of the curriculum may be taught in Welsh' and that provision should be made to teach Welsh history, literature, and geography.[113] A committee of the Board of Education in 1927 proposed a bilingual policy for Wales in which Welsh would be designated as the language of instruction in the early school years and continue to be used for teaching some subjects into secondary school, and a memorandum issued by the Board of Education in 1929 recommended the use of

Welsh in Welsh-speaking areas, English in English-speaking areas, and both in mixed areas. The committee's recommendation to open bilingual schools in English-speaking districts was not implemented until 1947, however, when the first Welsh School (Ysgol Cymraeg) was opened, and by 1960 there were still only twenty-eight primary bilingual schools and one secondary.

The Central Advisory Council for Education (Wales), chaired by Professor C.E. Gittens, in its 1967 report on primary education concluded that 'it is the Welsh language which in large measure gives Wales its own peculiar identity and carries an important part of its historical tradition.'[114] Hence, as a basic principle, every child in Wales should have the opportunity to become reasonably bilingual by the end of primary school. To realize this goal, the Gittens committee recommended a mix of primary schools that variously used Welsh as their language of instruction, offered Welsh immersion, and taught Welsh as a second language.[115]

The Gittens committee's recommendations were officially endorsed by the secretary of state for education and science in 1969, but implementation by local education authorities proved to be uneven.[116] By the mid-1980s, 11.7 per cent of children in primary schools had Welsh as their sole or main language of instruction and another 8.2 per cent had Welsh as the medium of instruction for part of the curriculum, 45.6 per cent were being taught Welsh as a second language only, and 34.4 per cent were going to schools where no Welsh was taught. In maintained secondary schools, 10.7 per cent of students were being taught with Welsh as their first language, 41.6 per cent were learning Welsh as a second language, and 47.7 per cent had no instruction in Welsh.

The Education Reform Act in 1988 made statutory provision in the National Curriculum for teaching Welsh as either a foundation subject (first language) or core subject (second language). Attainment targets and programs of study for Welsh were issued by the secretary of state for Wales in May 1990, and the National Curriculum was fully implemented beginning in September 1992.[117] By 1997–8, Welsh was the sole or main medium of instruction for 17.7 per cent of children in primary schools, and the medium for part of the curriculum for a further 2.2 per cent, 76.5 per cent were learning Welsh as a second language, and only 3.6 per cent had no Welsh instruction. In secondary schools, 12.8 per cent of students were being taught with Welsh as their first language, 66.1 per cent took it as a second language, and 21 per cent were not being taught Welsh at all.[118] Official bilingualism in policy and practice had become the constitutive principle of the nascent Welsh educational regime.

United States: Neutralizing Race, Language, and Religion in Public Schools for the Procedural Republic[119]

During the 1960s, elementary and secondary public education in the United States was engulfed by challenges to the hidden assumptions that were historically embedded in the American idea of a liberal educational regime. In principle, the liberal regime was a procedural republic, open, according to the principle of universality, to all American citizens on the same terms; in practice, state educational regimes, virtually without exception, incorporated the cultural assumptions of a white, English-speaking, Protestant majority.

First, the original 1954 ruling of the U.S. Supreme Court against segregated schools, which caused immediate controversy and opposition in Southern states in the late 1950s, was extended to cover de facto segregation caused by school district boundaries and urban residential patterns. Direction by the courts to redraw the boundaries of school districts and to transport students between schools and districts in order to improve the racial balance of schools thus came to affect most, if not all, states rather than simply the jurisdictions of legally 'separate but equal' education in the South.

Second, the issue of segregation of African-American children in public schools focused attention on inequalities of educational opportunity experienced by other minority groups. The key case was the Hispanic minority. Historically subjected to policies and practices of educational discrimination and cultural assimilation, Hispanic minority groups challenged segregation, but more importantly they also challenged the norms of state educational regimes that had tried not only to marginalize Hispanic students but also to 'Americanize' them by mandating their instruction in the majority language and culture and denying the legitimacy of Hispanic language and culture.

Third, creating regimes of public education that would provide equally for the needs and abilities of each person in school required that public schools be open without discrimination to children coming from all religious faiths, thus erasing the historical Protestant bias of state schools; but recognition that individual development had its roots in communal identity also gave new legitimacy to those who asserted the essentiality of religious instruction and observance to education. Moreover, focus on equality of opportunity by race and ethnicity within state educational regimes served to emphasize the inequalities that existed between the state and private Catholic sectors. Hence, there emerged in a new guise a dilemma, suppressed since the nineteenth century, between majority will and minority rights with regard to the inherence of religion in education.

Black and White in the Schools of Pluralist Society

In 1950 a suit filed by Oliver Brown and twelve other parents with backing from the National Association for the Advancement of Colored People asked the courts to overturn a Kansas law that permitted, but did not require, cities with populations over 15,000 to maintain racially segregated schools. Similar suits challenging laws that required or permitted racial segregation in public schools were filed in Delaware, South Carolina, and Virginia. Combining its decisions on these cases in *Brown* v. *Board of Education of Topeka, Kansas* (1954), the U.S. Supreme Court ruled that 'in the field of public education the doctrine of "separate but equal" has no place. Separate educational facilities are inherently unequal.' The next year, the Supreme Court ordered that the lower courts retain jurisdiction to ensure the implementation of *Brown* 'with all deliberate speed.' Local school officials were required to submit plans for school desegregation to the courts; federal district court judges were directed to determine 'whether the action of school authorities constitutes good faith implementation of the governing constitutional principles.'

In the 'border' states of Kentucky, Maryland, Missouri, Oklahoma, and West Virginia, school districts complied with the Supreme Court's order in *Brown* to desegregate their public schools, for the most part voluntarily.[120] In Delaware, only eleven of eighty-six school districts had adopted policies of desegregation prior to a court order in 1961 that got full compliance. Elsewhere in southern states, progress towards school desegregation in the first decade after *Brown* involved at best token compliance and, more commonly, massive resistance.

A new era in racial desegregation of public education in the South began in 1964 with the passage of the Civil Rights Act.[121] Henceforward, federal agencies were required to withhold federal funds from local authorities that engaged in discrimination by race, colour, or national origin, and the attorney general was authorized to initiate lawsuits based on complaints of discrimination. The substantial increase of federal aid for education under the Elementary and Secondary Education Act of 1965 provided a potential lever for the federal government to press local school districts to desegregate. Initially, the Office of Education set relatively lenient requirements and accepted local plans for freedom of choice that produced token desegregation. Similarly, the Civil Rights Division of the Department of Justice lacked the organization and resources to launch a grand assault. In 1967, however, the Office for Civil Rights (OCR) was created in the Department of Health, Education, and Welfare, taking over responsibility for enforcement of the Civil Rights Act from the Office of Education and combining with the Civil Rights Division in the Department of Justice to develop a more effective strategy to use the threat of termination to eliminate desegregation.[122] The shift in enforcement strategy was evident in the lawsuit (*United States* v. *Georgia*) filed in 1969 against the Georgia Department of Education and eighty-one school districts, which, thus threatened with a loss of federal funding, shortly conceded to federal pressures. A similar approach was used to force an end to segregated public schools in other southern states.[123]

With the end of *de jure* segregated schools in the South, the focus of civil rights policy in public education shifted to de facto segregation in major urban centres outside the South. By the late 1960s it was clear that much of it was the result of a history of discriminatory policies and practices of local school districts.[124] From the outset, however, effective remedies proved difficult to enforce.[125] In the final months of Lyndon Johnson's presidency, the Department of Justice had filed the first lawsuits that challenged segregated schools in big cities outside the South. By the time the first of these cases reached the U.S. Supreme Court, the court had been transformed by President Nixon's appointment of four conservative justices, and officials in the Department of Justice were working hard to block reform rather than promote it. In its 1973 decision in *Keyes* v. *School District No. 1, Denver, Colorado*, the court ruled that de facto segregation in itself was not necessarily unconstitutional; the intent of public authorities to segregate had to be established.[126] The *Keyes* decision thus created the potential for seeking court orders to desegregate northern city schools. The next year, however, in *Milliken* v. *Bradley*, the court imposed severe restrictions on the use of integration orders that forced suburban school districts to join with central city districts in order to achieve integrated schools across a metropolitan area.[127] Given the concentration of the African-American (and Hispanic) population in big cities and the fragmented structure of local government in metropolitan areas, the Supreme Court's decision in effect ensured that central city school districts would remain segregated.[128]

During the 1980s, school desegregation policy came full circle.[129] The first desegregation plans had relied on voluntary transfer. When this approach failed, the courts shifted to mandatory reassignment plans involving such tactics as pairing and clustering schools, redrawing attendance zones, and implementing school busing. Political controversy over 'forced busing,' perceived problems of 'white flight,' and judicially imposed restrictions on interdistrict integration undermined the effectiveness of mandatory plans, however, and many public officials and professional educators reverted to advocating voluntary plans, especially 'magnet schools,' which offered a special curriculum (for example, science and mathematics or the arts) or instructional method (for example, immersion or bilingual language programs) in order to attract students to schools they would otherwise not attend.[130] Usually introduced at first as part of a mandatory reassignment plan to provide an option to forced busing, during the 1980s magnet schools became a key component of plans for desegregation by means of voluntary transfers.[131] A study of desegregation methods in the early 1990s found that 22 per cent of school districts had voluntary magnet schools, 27 per cent combined magnet schools with mandatory techniques, and 6 per cent had magnet schools with controlled choice. In very large school districts (more than 27,000 students), magnet schools were especially important: 29 per cent had voluntary magnet plans, 47 per cent combined magnets with mandatory techniques, and 5 per cent operated magnet schools with controlled choice.[132]

Four decades after the landmark decision in *Brown*, the U.S. Supreme Court issued three judgments that set legal standards for dismantling school desegregation plans and thus allowing school districts to reassign children to neighbourhood schools, even if those schools would become segregated.[133] Desegregation decrees were ruled to be temporary measures. School districts having complied in good faith with the decree and having eliminated vestiges of past discrimination to the extent practicable were entitled to be released from the decree, and once released they no longer needed court authorization in making student assignments or conducting other school operations.[134] Furthermore, once the original violation was remedied, school districts had no constitutional responsibility for the recurrence of racial imbalance caused by demographic changes.[135] Reflecting on these decisions, Gary Orfield concluded that they have grave consequences for racial integration in American schools: 'The country is betting that segregated schools will work in a multiracial society with a rapidly declining white majority ... We are, in essence, sleepwalking back to *Plessy*.'[136]

Bilingual Education for Hispanic Minorities

For purposes of enforcing the Civil Rights Act, the Office for Civil Rights at first counted Hispanic students as white.[137] As a result, Hispanic students could remain segregated without attracting attention from federal authorities, and local school districts could demonstrate progress towards desegregation by integrating African-American and Hispanic students while leaving Anglo-white schools unaffected. In May 1970 the OCR reversed this policy; henceforth, discrimination based on national origin/minority language was prohibited. Furthermore, 'Where inability to speak and understand the English language excludes national origin minority group children from effective participation in the educational program offered by a school district, the district must take affirmative steps to rectify the language deficiency in order to open its instructional program to these students.'[138] Legal recognition of Mexican Americans as a separate class was confirmed by the U.S. Supreme Court's decision in 1973 in *Keyes* v. *School District No. 1, Denver, Colorado*. There the court held that Mexican Americans were an identifiable minority group, constitutionally entitled to recognition as such for purposes of school desegregation. School officials could not treat Mexican-American students as white for the purpose of desegregating schools. Subsequent court decisions extended the application of *Keyes* to Puerto Ricans in New York and Boston.

Despite the favourable decision in *Keyes*, from the late 1960s the Hispanic political priority with regard to equal educational opportunity was getting bilingual education rather than dismantling segregated schools. Especially in urban school districts where concentration of Hispanic minorities made desegregation very difficult, if not totally impractical, bilingual education became a plausible and even preferable alternative.[139] The choice of bilingual education as the preferred strategy for dealing with the educational problems of Hispanic minorities was reinforced by the passage of the federal Bilingual Education Act in 1968.[140] The act recognized the 'special educational needs of the large numbers of children of limited English-speaking ability in the United States' and offered 'to provide financial assistance to local educational agencies to develop and carry out new and imaginative elementary and secondary school programs designed to meet these special educational needs.' Hispanic minority groups, in particular Mexican Americans, supported the act not only as a means of dealing with their children's problems with English as the majority language of instruction but also as a way of maintaining their children's mother tongue and strengthening Hispanic culture in their children's education. The purpose of the Bilingual Education Act was not federal support for minority-language maintenance and bicultural education, however; it was assimilation.

Bilingual education in the United States was conceived and developed as primarily compensatory and transitional, intended to facilitate the assimilation of minority-language students whose learning problems and low achievement resulted from their English-language deficiency.[141] Moreover, the U.S. Supreme Court in *Lau* v. *Nichols* (1974) did not establish bilingual education as the only, or even best, remedy for overcoming English-language deficiencies.[142] The 'Lau Remedies,' issued by the U.S. Commissioner of Education in August 1975 as guidelines for school districts to comply with the Supreme Court's ruling, required elementary schools to provide bilingual education for children who spoke little or no English; they were withdrawn in February 1981 by the new Reagan administration.[143] After Lauro F. Cavazos, the first Hispanic cabinet member, replaced William J. Bennett as secretary of education in 1988, and George Bush became president the next year, the federal government's treatment of bilingual education improved, and in 1994, with the Democratic party controlling both Congress and the presidency, when the Bilingual Education Act was reauthorized as Title VII of the Improving America's Schools Act, it included recognition of the value of having children preserve their home languages. None the less, federal spending on bilingual education continued on an uncertain course, despite a growing number of minority children with inadequate proficiency in English.[144]

Although the Supreme Court's decision in *Lau* did not establish an entitlement to bilingual education, a dozen states did mandate bilingual education, and another dozen introduced legislation permitting it where schools had a critical mass of students from the same language groups whose proficiency in English was limited.[145] Even in these states, however, a large percentage of limited-English students received nothing more than remedial English instruction, the minimum standard under *Lau*.[146] For Hispanic minority groups, the most serious defeats in the struggle for bilingual education came at the end of the decade in two of the three states in which Hispanic Americans are the largest minority group. Decisive majorities in referenda in California (1998) and Arizona (2000) voted to end bilingual educational programs in state public schools.[147]

Thus, a quarter-century after the U.S. Supreme Court declared the segregation of Mexican-American children in public schools to be un-constitutional, hopes to achieve equality of educational opportunity through Spanish-English bilingual education had been frustrated by the 'English-only hegemonic values' that permeate American political culture.[148] At the same time, because few, if any, major desegregation efforts had focused on them, Hispanic children had become the most segregated sector of the school population. In 1968–9, 54.8 per cent of Hispanic students were going to public schools that were predominantly (50–100 per cent) minority compared to 76.6 per cent of African-American students; in 1996–7, 74.8 per cent of Hispanic students attended predominantly minority schools compared to 68.8 per cent of African Americans.[149]

Bible Reading and the Lord's Prayer in Public Schools

In general, little change occurred in either the principles or the practices of the non-denominational Protestant establishment in American state schools between the last third of the nineteenth century and the middle of the twentieth century.[150] When Bible reading and reciting prayers in public schools were challenged in state courts, in the majority of cases their validity was sustained.[151] Hence, the 1940 ruling of the U.S. Supreme Court in *Cantwell* v. *Connecticut*, which used the Fourteenth Amendment to constrain state legislatures from enacting laws interfering with religious rights guaranteed by the First Amendment, had particular significance for church–state controversies involving public education. From 1940, plaintiffs did not have to rely on state law or interpretations of state constitutions in order to challenge state and local educational policies and practices that allegedly interfered with their freedom of religion.

The first challenge to state policies on religion and education in public schools involved released-time programs.[152] At issue in *McCollum* v. *Board of Education* was a program in Champaign, Illinois, organized by an interdenominational voluntary association under which children, with the consent of their parents, were given religious instruction for a period each week. Instruction for the majority of pupils, who were Protestants, took place in their home classrooms; pupils released for Catholic or Jewish instruction or who did not participate in the program went to other rooms in their schools. The U.S. Supreme Court held that the use of a public building for religious teaching was a violation of the

First Amendment and hence the released-time program was unconstitutional. In 1952, however, the Supreme Court upheld the program for released time in New York City under which children attended external religious centres during their released time; the court reasoned that the First Amendment was not violated where a school did no more than 'close its doors or suspend its operations as to those who want to repair to their religious sanctuary for worship or instruction.' Most states responded to the decision in *Zorach* v. *Clauson* by enacting statutes that permitted students to be released from public schools for a designated period of time in order to receive religious instruction off school premises.[153]

The constitutionality of Bible reading and school prayers was first tested in the U.S. Supreme Court in *Engel* v. *Vitale* in 1962. By a majority of six to one, the court found that, even though voluntarily observed, a supposedly non-denominational prayer formulated for use in New York state public schools by the Board of Regents none the less contravened the Establishment Clause. The following year, in *School District of Abingdon Township* v. *Schempp*, again by six to one, the Supreme Court held that such religious observances as reading from the Bible and reciting the Lord's Prayer contravened the First Amendment. By its strict interpretation of the Establishment Clause in *Engel* and *Schempp*, the Supreme Court established the principle that not simply the favourable treatment of one church over another but any official expression of religious belief violated the constitutional requirement for religious neutrality in state education.[154]

Political reactions to the Supreme Court's ban on religious observances in public schools varied across the country: school boards in northeastern and far western states generally complied with the decisions; in midwestern states, open defiance was rare but non-compliance was common in small towns and villages; and in the South there was open defiance.[155] Numerous measures to amend the Constitution to permit prayer recitation and Bible reading in public schools were introduced in Congress; none succeeded.[156] At the state level, another reaction to the Supreme Court's ban on school prayer was legislation permitting moments of silence. In the early 1980s, twenty states provided for brief periods (usually a minute) of silent reflection, voluntary prayer, or meditation; a decade later, thirty states had some such statutory provision.[157] As long as their intent was clearly established as providing for a brief period of meditation and not simply a way of reintroducing prayers into public schools, these laws were held to be constitutional.[158]

State Aid for Parochial Schools

From the middle of the nineteenth century, when their demands for state aid to Roman Catholic denominational schools were decisively – even violently – rejected, until the 1930s, little effort was made by American Catholics to obtain public subsidies for their schools.[159] During the Depression, as the financial plight of Catholic schools became desperate, Catholic hopes for state aid to parochial schools were raised by the U.S. Supreme Court's decision in *Cochran* v. *Louisiana State Board of Education* (1930), in which the distribution of free textbooks to Catholic schools was held to benefit the children as individuals rather than their schools as religious institutions and hence was constitutional.

Both Catholic and Protestant groups were successful in getting textbooks, health services, school lunches, and busing using the individual-benefit justification advanced in *Cochran*. By the mid-1960s, thirty-six states had enacted some type of indirect aid to denominational schools, and under continuing pressure from advocates of private schools, state governments began to introduce more direct forms of assistance. Pennsylvania in 1968 and Connecticut and Rhode Island in 1969 passed laws providing public funds to pay part of the salaries of private school teachers in secular subjects (modern languages, mathematics, physical sciences, and physical education), and the New York state legislature in 1971–2 authorized $33 million annually to purchase 'secular education services for pupils in nonpublic schools.'

The Supreme Court struck down all these attempts to provide direct financial aid to denominational schools.[160] In 1977, however, in *Wolman* v. *Walter*, the Supreme Court upheld a section of an Ohio law authorizing state funds to buy the same secular textbooks that were used in public schools for loan to students attending private schools; provide the same standardized tests and scoring services available in public schools; and pay for therapeutic, remedial, and guidance counselling services for children attending private schools where such services were provided off school premises. A majority of the court, however, found that excessive entanglement between church and state would result from aiding private schools by using public funds for instructional materials, audio-visual equipment, and transportation for field trips.[161]

Perhaps the most controversial issue of state aid to sectarian education has been tax relief for parents of children attending non-public schools. In 1973 the Supreme Court struck down a New York state income tax credit for non-public school tuition on the grounds that 85 per cent of

New York's private schools were sectarian and hence the law aided religion by compensating parents for sending their children to church schools. A decade later, however, in its five-to-four decision in *Mueller* v. *Allen*, the Supreme Court upheld a Minnesota law that provided tax deductions to all taxpayers for tuition, textbooks, and transportation regardless of whether their children attended public or private schools. In the majority's reasoning, a program 'that neutrally provides state assistance to a broad spectrum of citizens is not readily subject to challenge under the Establishment Clause.'[162] Based on the precedent of *Mueller*, Iowa (1987), Arizona and Minnesota (1997), and Illinois (1999) adopted tax credits to help individuals offset the educational costs of private and parochial schools, while Florida and Pennsylvania (2001) introduced tax credits for corporate contributions to scholarship programs that assist children in public and non-public schools to attend their school of choice.[163]

During the 1990s the focus of efforts to give financial assistance directly to parents of children in attending private schools merged into a more general political movement to give parents more freedom to choose the education they wanted for their children, including facilitating the option of private religious schools. Educational voucher proposals were introduced in several state legislatures, as well as Congress, and the first plans to be tested in the courts with regard to the constitutionality of including private religious schools in such programs were upheld on appeal. In 1995 the Milwaukee Parental Choice Program was amended to allow parents to redeem their vouchers at private religious schools, and the Cleveland Scholarship and Tutoring Program introduced tuition vouchers of up to $2,250 that enabled low-income parents to transfer their children to private religious schools.[164] Although overturned in the lower courts, in June 1998 the amended Milwaukee program was judged by the Wisconsin Supreme Court not to violate the Establishment Clause, and the U.S. Supreme Court by a vote of eight to one declined to review the case.[165] Four years later, applying the principle of individual benefit, the U.S. Supreme Court, by a vote of five to four, reversed a decision of the Sixth Circuit U.S. Court of Appeals and ruled that the Cleveland voucher plan also was constitutional. Judicial approval does not guarantee public policy. 'Major public campaigns to defeat voucher legislation and voter initiatives have been launched by opponents, most especially the National Education Association and other public school groups, in places as diverse as California, Oregon, Pennsylvania, Connecticut, and New Jersey.'[166] Certainly, the potential for using vouchers as an effective instrument to deliver state aid to private religious schools in the United States was evident from initial studies of who were the major beneficiaries under the Cleveland and Milwaukee voucher programs. Most students in Cleveland went to parochial schools, and enrolments in Milwaukee showed the same pattern.[167]

In recent years, several programs of state and federal aid to private denominational schools have slipped over the wall of strict separation between church and state, but the U.S. Constitution continues to be 'a blurred, indistinct, and variable barrier.'[168] Recent judicial policy making has been marked by a lack of unanimity on the Supreme Court, as well as conflicting decisions by state supreme courts. As with prayer in public schools, the judgments of the courts with regard to state aid to private religious schools reflect an enduring division in American liberal public philosophy. 'The meaning of respect for religious opinions and rights – indeed the fundamental nature of the civic culture of the United States – remains far from clear.'[169]

Educational Regimes and the Problem of Pluralist Society

From the founding of regimes of public instruction in the mid-nineteenth century through the reforms of public education in the 1940s and 1950s that were inspired by the ideals of the welfare state, differences of religion, language, ethnicity, and race customarily were met with policies designed to assimilate minorities. Where assimilation was impossible to achieve because of differences in language and religion, there was grudging compromise on communal consociation, and where assimilation was impossible to imagine because of racial differences, segregation was enforced. By contrast, from the 1960s to the 1980s, policies for educational provision and governance aimed not simply to tolerate social and cultural diversity but rather to respect, accommodate, and even embrace it. The result by the 1990s was a profound change for most Anglo-American educational regimes – in aspirations at least, if not always in practices – that signalled a major realignment of the principles of Anglo-American democracy.

Three types of educational regimes were created during the nineteenth century in order to deal with the paramount issue of the relationship of church and state in public instruction: denominational regimes in Ireland, Newfoundland, and Quebec; complementary sectors of church and state schools in Great Britain, the Maritimes, Ontario, and the North-West Territories; and strict separation of church and state in regimes of non-denominational or secular public schools in Australia, British Columbia, Manitoba, New Zealand, and the United States. From the 1890s to the 1950s, Anglo-American educational regimes were variously reformed by pressures for vocational training and selection resulting from the pursuit of industrial efficiency and by ideas of equal opportunity and universality that were core principles of the welfare state; none the less, the arrangement of regimes based on different relationships of church and state in public education remained essentially unchanged. From the 1960s to the 1980s, however, the historically defining issue of church and state in public schools was joined with previously subordinate issues of language, race, and ethnicity. As a result, problems of social diversity in Anglo-American educational regimes became multidimensional, and realization of the ideal of pluralist society became a legitimate aspiration of educational policy. By the 1990s there were still regimes based on denominational control, complementary sectors of church and state schools, and separation between church and state; but the characteristics and classification of these regimes had been substantially altered by the multidimensionality and legitimization of social diversity.

First, at the end of the twentieth century, Northern Ireland was the only educational regime based exclusively on public ordination and financing of sectarian schools. The funding formula embodied in the 1968 Education Act in effect legitimized the de facto denominational regime that operated from 1923. The initiative to create integrated schools that brought Protestant and Roman Catholic children together showed that Northern Ireland was not immune to the pressures on all Anglo-American educational regimes to devise ways to accommodate social diversity and resolve historical social divisions. Integrated schools had very limited success, however, and at the end of the century, historic political and religious divisions continued to be fiercely contested.

Second, the classical liberal idea of common schools as public institutions that exclude sectarian religious instruction continued to prevail in all the educational regimes of the United States, but the meaning of non-denominational versus secular public education was now hotly contested. Decisions of the U.S. Supreme Court, from *Engel* v. *Vitale* (1962) to *Lee* v. *Weisman* (1992), substantially undermined the non-denominational Protestant ascendancy that historically had characterized public schools throughout the United States. None the less, the hoary issues of Bible reading, school prayers, and state aid for parochial schools persisted. Conservative and liberal politicians remained implacably split over any constitutional amendments that would permit religious observances in public schools, and ingeniously designed public policies to supply state aid to private schools produced only marginal improvements in the long-term disadvantage of private Roman Catholic schools.

The established language of public instruction in the United States historically was unilingual English. Beginning in the 1960s, programs of bilingual education were widely adopted to facilitate the successful transition from home to school of children whose mother tongue was not English. Bilingual programs were also advocated as ways to promote the legitimacy of minority cultural identities that are vital to the self-respect and learning capabilities of minority students. Not only was there stubborn resistance to this expansion of bilingual education from transitional assimilation to cultural reproduction, the very existence of bilingual programs was also subjected to frontal political attack, notably in California and Arizona.

Racial segregation was a constitutive feature of educational regimes in the United States from their founding as public institutions in the nineteenth century to the 1954 decision of the U.S. Supreme Court in *Brown v. Board of Education of Topeka, Kansas.* The doctrine of 'separate but equal' schools by which racial segregation had been justified in law and practice in the public philosophy of American democracy was shattered, a spurious doctrine of equality at last formally rejected as a contradiction of American democratic principles. Defeating racial segregation in law was intensely conflictual but proved easier to accomplish than overcoming racial segregation in practice. By the 1990s, even as they were being dismantled, policies to counter de facto racial segregation appeared to have fallen short of realizing the ideal of racial equality and integration.

Third, regimes that comprised complementary sectors of denominational voluntary schools alongside non-denominational public schools, established at the origins of public instruction in Britain and the colonies of New South Wales, Victoria, and Queensland, were still operative in England and Scotland, and they had been restored in Australia after a century of strict separation between church and state. The provisions for religious instruction and state funding of voluntary schools were incrementally reformed during the passage of the Education Acts of 1944, 1946, and 1988, but the basic structure remained essentially unchanged from the historical settlements of 1870 and 1902 for England and 1872 and 1918 for Scotland. Beginning in the 1960s there were determined efforts to make religious instruction more multidenominational or interdenominational, in order to accommodate the greater diversity of religious beliefs in the maintained schools of England and Scotland. The outcome of the politics of section 6 of the 1988 act showed the limits on how far such accommodation of denominational diversity should be allowed to proceed. In Australia, the restoration of state aid to private schools during the 1960s and 1970s was expedited by progressively larger interventions on the part of Commonwealth governments, both Liberal–Country and Labor, and effectively restored Australian educational regimes from separation of church and state to complementary sectors of non-denominational public schools and denominational private schools that were substantially, albeit unequally, maintained by public subsidies.

Initial Australian and British policies to deal with social diversity in public education, in particular the Child Migrant Education Program in Australia and the dispersal programs of local education authorities in England, were intended to facilitate the assimilation of immigrants who did not fit the racial and ethnic origins of the Australian or English majority. During the 1970s, however, this assimilative approach was reoriented to one of integration that was founded on respect for racial and ethnic differences, incremental revision of the public identity of Australian and British societies from monocultural to multicultural, and curricular commitment to preservation of cultural diversity within a unified civic nationalism. Once again, the limits of multicultural education in England and Australia were revealed in the failure of the recommendations of the Swann committee to be adopted as an integral part of the National Curriculum and the abandonment of the Multicultural Education Program (as well as the Schools Commission that was its advocate) by Australia's Labor government during the fiscal restructuring of 1987.

Fourth, in Wales, New Zealand, and six provinces of Canada there emerged regimes that likewise featured complementary sectors of non-denominational public schools and denominational separate schools, but in addition they were restructured by their adoption of two official languages. As in England, maintained voluntary schools in Wales survived from the historical settlements of 1870 and 1902, but the progressive commitment to Welsh and English as coequal languages of instruction, embedded in the National Curriculum authorized by the 1988 Education Reform Act, clearly differentiated Wales from the classical version of complementary sectors that was still operative in England.[170] In the case of New Zealand, the integration of Roman Catholic schools into the public sector from 1975 to 1983 shifted public education from strict separation of church and state to a dual regime of state and integrated (denominational) schools that closely approximated the reserved schools of Scotland or the separate schools of Canada, and during the 1990s there was a further differentiation as a result of bilingual programs involving English and Maori and, more importantly, the development of Maori-medium schools. Complementary sectors of non-denominational public and denominational (Roman Catholic) separate schools continued to operate under constitutional protection in Ontario, Saskatchewan, and Alberta, and both Saskatchewan (1964) and Ontario (1985) fortified their separate school sectors by removing historical restrictions on funding the upper years of separate secondary schools. The introduction of substantial public subsidies for private schools in British Columbia (1977) and Manitoba (1981) established the basis for complementary sectors of non-denominational public schools and denominational private schools similar to the approach taken in Australia. In all five provinces, there were major bilingual programs involving the official languages for the English-speaking majority, constitutionally protected French-language schools for the minority, and provision for governance of their schools by the francophone community. When Quebec finally replaced its denominational regime in 1998 by a regime divided by language, the protection of the right of each school council to determine the denominational orientation, if any, of its school effectively transformed the Quebec educational regime into an asymmetrical form of denominational and linguistic duality, in which francophone and anglophone social blocs enjoyed the privileges of self-governance at the level of school commissions and self-governance for denominational blocs was restricted to the level of school councils.

Fifth, in the case of the Atlantic provinces, educational regimes were restructured on the basis of separate educational provision and governance for anglophones and francophones, as was the case in other Canadian provinces, but the nineteenth-century relationship between church and state in public instruction was fundamentally altered. De facto reserved schools for Roman Catholics in New Brunswick, Nova Scotia, and Prince Edward Island disappeared without much political fuss in the early 1970s as part of reform packages that started from the growing conviction on the part of parents that denominational instruction was properly the function of church and family, not school; gave priority to improving educational provision by creating larger schools; reorganized educational provision and governance on the basis of language rather than religion; and introduced truly non-denominational curricula in public schools together with provision for denominational instruction where parents wanted it. In the formerly denominational regime of Newfoundland, a proposal to establish secular school boards with powers to designate the denominational orientation of local schools was blocked by a minority of Roman Catholic and Pentecostal opponents who wanted to preserve a pure denominational regime. The Newfoundland government then won its referendum to establish a regime similar to those in other Atlantic provinces that combined secular school boards, non-denominational schools, and non-denominational religious education with denominational instruction available at the request of parents.

Thus, from the 1960s to the 1980s, communitarian-conservative and liberal-conservative doctrines of assimilation, consociation, and segregation were substantially eroded, first by the utilitarian-liberal principle of tolerance, which advocated true public neutrality with regard to religious, linguistic, ethnic, and racial differences, and next by the ethical-liberal principle of integration, which advocated not simply acceptance of social diversity but rather celebration of it as fundamental to protecting and developing the cultural homes necessary for individual identity and development. Policies of state aid to denominational private schools, integration of denominational schools into the public sector, adoption of heritage-language programs, establishment of bilingual schools, initiatives of multicultural education, and racial desegregation of public schools all aimed to make pluralist society a collective public good.

Beyond the dominant ideal of cultural integration there survived remnants of historical consociational arrangements, notably in the dual regimes of French and English educational provision and governance in New Brunswick and Quebec; the public and separate schools of Ontario, Saskatchewan, and Alberta; and the county and voluntary schools of England and Wales. There was also an emerging potential for consociational arrangements in the te kohanga reo and kura kaupapa movements to protect and develop Maori-language education in New Zealand. In contrast with the situation of the nineteenth century, however, where consociation represented the failure of assimilation, consociation in pursuit of the ideal of pluralist society in the late twentieth century was fundamentally generous and harmonious, adopted in the domain of public education as a measure necessary to ensure the success of societal integration by blocking powerful forces of assimilation and stabilizing the preservation and development of constituent cultural communities.

The problem of public education for pluralist society shifted the balance of priorities in the political economy of Anglo-American educational regimes from the relationship of state and market, where it had been lodged for most of the twentieth century in pursuit of industrial efficiency and the welfare state, back to the relationship of state and society in public education. The great difference from the political economy of the nineteenth-century regimes was the shift in understanding of the meaning of society as 'pluralist society.' Although differing in degree and substance across Anglo-American educational jurisdictions, the ideal of pluralist society became an integral part of Anglo-American democracy in the late twentieth century. At the same time, the long-term development of this collective ideal appeared to be alarmingly vulnerable to the homogenizing forces of global capitalism that came to dominate educational politics and policy during the 1980s and 1990s.

5 Global Capitalism

In the late twentieth century there emerged a remarkably broad intellectual consensus that advanced industrial societies are now best understood as post-industrial societies. At the root of their ongoing transformation is a contemporary technological revolution comparable in its global impact and human implications to the 'agricultural revolution' that began in the seventeenth century or the 'industrial revolution' that dominated world economic development from the early nineteenth century past the middle of the twentieth century. Like the agricultural and industrial revolutions, the contemporary revolution in information technology rests on new techniques of information storage, processing, and communication; a fundamental change in the global political economy; new modes of production and consumption; and new forms of economic and political organization.[1] These changes in turn have affected the key issues of educational policy.

The first issue of technological society and global capitalism as a problem of Anglo-American educational politics and policy making concerned the content of curricula and the academic organization of schools. The importance of advanced technology as a determinant of economic wealth, political power, and cultural survival appeared to impel a shift in primary and secondary education to give much more weight than previously to studies in mathematics, science, and technology. The needs for teamwork and adaptability put a premium on learning skills of language and communication. At the same time, fears about the erosion of human values because of the unrelenting materialism of global capitalism revitalized the case to preserve humanities, arts, and social studies as essential subjects. Similarly, the apparent link between international competitiveness and educational excellence put the focus on selecting and training élites in industry, trade, and research and development; but at the same time, national wealth and productivity also appeared to be related to raising and generalizing mass scientific and technical literacy and numeracy. Such diverse considerations create complex, if not contradictory, pressures for adaptation and change in curricular design and school organization.

Another issue was restructuring primary and secondary educational governance to fit the political economy of global capitalism. The rise of global capitalism destabilized the political economy of the welfare state, reasserting the legitimacy of markets as an instrument for collective decision making while at the same time undermining the legitimacy of public bureaucracies. For purposes of educational decision making, there was a resurgence of public support for the private sector of primary and secondary schools, as well as proposals to institute public markets in which parents and students would have more effective choice with regard to their educational consumption.[2] Restructuring of educational policy communities might weaken the opportunities for policy participation on the part of traditional educational associations, notably teachers' unions, while strengthening the influence of organized business. Prevalent ideas in business enterprises about the utility of separating policy and management – giving middle managers flexibility to achieve the targets set by the corporate directors and senior executives – were advanced as models for restructuring the relationship at one level between ministries of education and local school boards and at another level between school boards and community schools. Throughout there was a persistent argument about the balance of national versus local democracy as a feature of Anglo-American educational regimes and the degree to which school districts and school councils were instruments of public management rather than agencies of communal self-government.

A third issue concerned the competing, even contradictory, demands of fitting Anglo-American primary and secondary education for global capitalism while preserving prior commitments to principles of the welfare state and pluralist society that had been diversely embedded in the public philosophies and policies of Anglo-American educational regimes. The ideas of universality and equality that constituted the core commitment to public education as social policy within the welfare state were not easily reconciled with the concentrated focus on academic achievement and structuring of curricula for national productivity that were advanced as desirable features of educational regimes in the era of global capitalism. In particular, the general commitment to individual development in the educational regimes of the welfare state, which rejected competition and ranking and insisted on the ideal of equal value from their educational programs for each individual student based on their needs, was directly challenged by the restoration of a lot-regarding idea of equality under which applying common educational standards rather than meeting individual needs became the criterion for educational justice. Similarly, common and core curricula that were oriented to the homogenizing imperatives of global capitalism appeared to threaten the inclusive recognition of communal identities that was central to the reconstruction of educational regimes for pluralist society; they also raised concerns not only about the capacity of contemporary educational regimes to respond to the countervailing pressures of localism in the era of global capitalism but also about representing and hence expressing the social diversity of a pluralist society in its public schools.

A fourth issue was the funding of public education in the political economy of global capitalism. Neo-conservative and neo-liberal advocates of the freedom and efficiency of the market did not spare public education from their attack on misdirected and wasteful public spending. During the 1980s and 1990s the financial costs of educational programs that were undertaken to realize the one-time ideals of the welfare state and pluralist society were subjected to harsh scrutiny. The challenge of realigning public education with the needs of global capitalism was thus complicated by a relentless squeeze on educational resources. Stagnant or shrinking budgets threatened to turn the reallocation of educational resources into a zero-sum game, hence raising the stakes and intensifying the animosities of the politics of educational change.

Liberal, conservative, and socialist theorists have largely agreed on the basic features of post-industrial, post-Fordist, postmodern society: the imperative of information technology, the penetration of global markets, the decentralization and deconcentration of bureaucratic organizations, the erosion of state capacity, the deconstruction of state legitimacy, and the homogenization of popular culture. Yet they differ profoundly in their assessments of its impact on human welfare. These ideological differences about technological society and global capitalism in turn generate corresponding differences about what should be the basic purposes of education, the organization of schools, the content of curricula, the role of the state, and the structures of educational governance.

Conservatives recognize the potentially liberating effects of technological society in alleviating human 'suffering from hunger, disease, overwork and conflict from scarcity,' but they also fear 'the threat to liberty and plurality posed by technique, the technical control of human nature, the danger of ecological or nuclear disaster, the decline of nurturing traditions, the banality of education, the deprivation of purpose and meaning to an increasing number of modern men and women.'[3] Technology has to be subordinated to human purpose, developed from educated intelligence, and criticized with persistent scepticism. Liberalism and socialism both fail as philosophies of public education in technological society because they are instrumental, not morally substantive. Particularly in communitarian conservative thinking, there is an ancient tradition of 'liberal education' that should be recovered as the foundation for educating young people in technological society. That tradition comprises not only the great texts of Western literature, philosophy, and science but also the national heritage of language, literature, and history of the community in which students live.

Liberal conservatives, utilitarian liberals, and social democrats stress that contemporary educational institutions and policies ought to create the foundation for lifelong learning, productive work, and educated citizenship in technological society. Accordingly, schools must be dedicated to achieving high levels of knowledge and skills in science, mathematics, and technological studies; they must teach basic skills of effective communication; and they must instil the work ethic and the entrepreneurial spirit on which individual and collective prosperity will in future depend. For purposes of making decisions about academic careers and vocational paths, utilitarian liberals favour a shift from state control to educational markets. State educational monopolies, which are bureaucratic, inflexible, and unaccountable, should be supplanted by private and/or public markets in which parents with adequate information and good counsel are enabled to choose educational programs for their children. For liberal conservatives and social democrats, however, the preparation of young people for productive work and their efficient allocation across occupational classes are too important as determinants of state power and national wealth to be left without direction or management by state authorities. Conservative educational ideology assumes the inevitability and desirability of educational hierarchy and academic élitism, and separating young people by their talents and prospects for work in technological society involves streaming students based on their levels of achievement or constructing class-structured programs that lead students to different occupational futures. For social democrats, however, in order to protect workers' interests, secondary educational curricula should blend core and specialized, theoretical and practical studies, and hence provide students with basic training covering a broad range of occupations so that they can transfer among occupations with relative ease and not be stuck for life in a vocational dead end.[4]

Instead of remedies such as state planning and public or private markets, ethical liberals and democratic socialists advocate direct and equalized public provision for neighbourhood or community schools that operate on the basis of local democracy. The key feature of ethical-liberal and social-democratic thinking is the institution of school councils comprising representatives of teachers, parents, and (where appropriate) students, not as the local managers for central authorities but as the basic units of educational governance. Strengthening the institutions of local democracy at the level of schools allows effective participation of parents (and students) in educational decision making to be combined with the professional competence of teachers. Thus a proper balance can be achieved between the private interests of individuals and families and the public interest of state and society. For ethical liberals, 'child-centred' or 'student-centred' schools advance individual development by providing learning experiences that meet the particular needs of each person in school; hence, they resist a prescribed common curriculum because it fails to take account of individual differences. Democratic socialists share this ethical-liberal ideal of universal human development, but in contrast with ethical-liberal silence, or at least ambivalence, with regard to the political economy of global capitalism, democratic socialists urge a critical approach to educating young people with regard to the ways technology can perpetuate or enhance inequalities in the distribution of resources and power and the material interests that underlie the technical division of labour. 'Through such an educative process people will come to discover that education is not instrumental to a prescribed, predetermined technological necessity but rather technology is subject to human critique, human choice and human agency.'[5] As opposed to individual self-development, democratic socialists stress the development and application of 'collective intelligence' as the condition to achieve democracy in the workplace and make progress towards a fully democratic society.[6] Rejecting ethical-liberal tolerance and social-democratic compromising, democratic socialists also find no justification for private schools: 'They are a manifestation of societies where powerful and privileged groups use their privileges to monopolize the best educational resources in order to ensure the success of their children at the expense of others.'[7]

Australia: Policy Convergence on a National Curriculum and Corporate Governance

On 5 May 1983, the Australian Labor party (ALP) won a majority of the seats in the House of Representatives. Given the ALP's electoral platform and campaign promises, a significant shift in Commonwealth educational policy might have been expected to follow the Labor victory in 1983, away from the conservative policies of Malcolm Fraser's Liberal–National party coalition government back towards the progressive policies of the ALP government led by Gough Whitlam from 1972 to 1975.[8] The initial policy direction of the Labor government was consistent with such an expectation.[9] Then, in late 1984 the minister for education appointed the Quality of Education Review Committee (QERC), chaired by Peter Karmel, who had led the Interim Committee of the Australian Schools Commission for the Whitlam government a decade previously, with a mandate 'to develop strategies for the Commonwealth Government in its involvement in primary and secondary education, for raising the standards attained by students in communication, literacy and numeracy and for improving the relationship between secondary schooling and subsequent employment and education.'[10] Thus began a decade of reform in Australian primary and secondary schools, aimed at establishing a national curriculum that would give Australians an educational advantage in the fast-emerging economy of global capitalism. At the end of the 1990s the states and territories, having reasserted their constitutional and political jurisdiction over the educational policy domain, were still working out the details of the new national approach to primary and secondary schooling.

Commonwealth Leadership, State Jurisdiction, and the Discovery of a National Curriculum

In contrast with the report of the Interim Committee, which had focused on equalizing educational opportunity for students in public and private schools, the report of the Quality of Education Review Committee in April 1985 concentrated on identifying and improving educational outcomes. The committee argued that there were five essential general competencies – acquiring information, conveying information, applying logical processes, performing practical tasks as an individual, and performing tasks as a member of a group. Commonwealth funding should be structured so as to ensure that all students acquired these basic competencies. Federal recurrent grants to state departments of education and non-government school authorities should be based on 'negotiated agreements' that specified educational priorities, such as basic skills or disadvantaged schools. State and non-government educational authorities would also be required to provide triennial 'accountability statements' describing the changes in educational indicators that had been assigned as measures of the negotiated priorities. State departments of education, non-government school authorities, and the Commonwealth Schools Commission all criticized this shift from assessing needs for educational resources to negotiating priorities and evaluating outcomes, but in June 1985 the Hawke government decided to adopt the main recommendations of the QERC report.[11]

In July 1987 the ALP government was re-elected, and John Dawkins was appointed minister for the new portfolio of employment, education, and training. From the outset, Dawkins made it clear that he would use the Commonwealth government's grants for schools as leverage to pursue national priorities in the development of a highly educated and skilled labour force.[12] At a meeting of the Australian Education Council (AEC) in May 1988, he insisted that 'the Commonwealth will not ignore the very real responsibility it has to provide national leadership' and urged cooperation by the state governments in developing a national curriculum that would set out the major areas of knowledge and the most appropriate mix of skills and experience for students in all their school years, while at the same time accommodating the varied curricular needs of different parts of Australia.

After initial hostility to this Commonwealth intrusion, especially evident on the part of the new Liberal government in New South Wales, the state governments eventually agreed to consider the feasibility of Dawkins's proposal. Working parties on federal grants, educational goals, student evaluation, national curriculum, and intergovernmental cooperation in delivering educational services were established. In particular, the working group that comprised state directors of curriculum found that there already was a considerable commonality of curricular content across states and even greater similarity in the general objectives of public education. At the AEC meeting in April 1991, eight 'Key Areas of Learning' – mathematics, technology, English, science, studies of society and environment, languages other than English, the arts, and health – were identified as the basis for producing national statements of typical curriculum experiences in each area and developing 'subject profiles' that described expected educational outcomes, and a curriculum and assessment committee (CURASS) was appointed to develop curricular statements and profiles for the eight key learning areas.[13] At the AEC meeting in July 1993, however, the five non-Labor governments (New South Wales, Victoria, Western Australia, Tasmania, and the Northern Territory) combined to block any further implementation of national curriculum statements and subject profiles.

Rather than proceed with trials and implementation organized through CURASS, the AEC referred the national statements and subject profiles to the state and territorial departments for review and decisions about the role of national statements and profiles in their respective processes of curricular development. Within the state and territorial educational policy communities, the national statements and profiles were subjected to partisan political debates, professional and community consultations, working groups of curriculum specialists, and pilot projects in schools. They were variously adjusted, adapted, altered, and modified before they were implemented; nowhere were they abandoned.[14] The overall result across the eight states and territories was not a prescribed national syllabus in each of these eight learning areas but rather a convergence of state policies on curriculum, assessment, and teacher education that derived from general acceptance of the premises and instruments of outcomes-based education, performance testing, and public accountability. As Kathy McLean and Bruce Wilson concluded in the mid-1990s, 'Statements and profiles are now working their way (in various forms) into the heartland of Australian education. The documents have varying content, approaches and appearances in different States and Territories. Nevertheless, a great change is occurring across Australia in the way we see schooling and the language we use to describe its achievements.'[15]

The national statements and subject profiles were primarily intended to apply to the compulsory years of schooling (kindergarten to year ten). For the post-compulsory years of schooling (eleven and twelve), the framework for curricular reforms was based on 'employment-related key competencies.'[16] In 1990 the Australian Education Council appointed a committee to review post-compulsory education and training.[17] Defining key competencies as 'the essential things which all young people need to learn in their preparation for employment,' the review committee recommended that a set of generic vocational competencies be described in order to provide a common framework of standards across all sectors of post-compulsory education and training. Assigned the task of specifying what are key competencies, an AEC advisory committee identified seven, each having three performance levels: collecting, analysing, and organizing information; communicating ideas and information; planning and organizing activities; working with others and in teams; using mathematical ideas and techniques; solving problems; and using technology.[18] Development, testing, and evaluation of the key competencies proceeded over a three-year period, financed by $20 million from the Commonwealth government. The policy platform of the Liberal–National coalition for the March 1996 national election rejected 'a Commonwealth imposed national curriculum' but supported 'a level of consistency in basic skills taught across the nation,'[19] and following the election of the Howard government, the new Liberal minister gave bipartisan endorsement to key competencies as the framework for post-compulsory schooling. In June 1997, Commonwealth, state, and territorial ministers of education and training agreed on a national strategy that established acquisition of the key competencies as the basic purpose of vocational education and training. A major task of the new national policy would be making nationally recognized packages of vocational education and training an integral part of senior secondary studies and developing 'seamless post-compulsory pathways' so that students were 'able to move freely within the vocational education and training sector and between vocational education and training, senior secondary schooling and universities, while ensuring that outcomes from each are recognised and valued.'[20]

In each state and territory, an independent statutory authority continued to have authority to approve senior secondary courses for credit, determine methods for assessing students, and grant certificates of successful completion.[21] By the mid-1980s, however, external examinations in each of the states and territories had been substantially modified by the introduction of internal assessment by schools as a component of school-leaving certification, by expansion and diversification in the number of subjects that could be studied for public examinations, by the introduction of procedures for scaling marks in order to standardize assessments across subjects and schools, and by expansion of the format of external examinations beyond traditional essay questions to include short-answer questions and objective tests.[22] As educational reform motivated by goals of economic productivity and national competitiveness came to preoccupy educational policy makers over the next decade, there was also general consensus that the historical division of studies between academic and vocational was no longer relevant or appropriate.

None the less, there were definite variations across states during the 1990s with regard to external examinations, certificate requirements, and vocational pathways. In Queensland, Victoria, and the Australian Capital Territory there were no external public examinations, although Queensland students seeking admission to university had to sit the Queensland Core Skills Test and in 1994 all Victorian students in year twelve began taking the General Achievement Test. Boards of studies in New South Wales, Northern Territory, South Australia, Tasmania, and Western Australia continued to differentiate between subjects approved for tertiary entrance, which involved a combination of external examination and school assessment, and terminal courses, which were certified by school assessments alone. With no specific requirements for courses, leaving certificates in Queensland and Tasmania were issued on successful completion of any course. Similarly, there were no restrictions on their choice of courses for students in the Australian Capital Territory and Western Australia, except for a requirement to demonstrate English-language competence in Western Australia, but there was a minimum number of courses that had to be completed in order to get the state leaving certificate.[23] In New South Wales, Northern Territory, South Australia, and Victoria, by contrast, the requirements for leaving certificates included completion during years eleven and twelve of core courses in English, mathematics, and science or technology, as well as optional courses in arts, humanities, or social studies.

All states attempted to improve access to vocational education and training during the post-compulsory years (eleven and twelve) in secondary school. The adoption of a single credential to mark the end of year twelve was accompanied by expansion of vocational studies that was intended not only to meet the standards of state training authorities and thus qualify students for vocational training certification but also to count for credit towards the secondary leaving certificate and even contribute to the calculation of tertiary entrance qualifications.[24] Except for New South Wales and Western Australia, boards of studies made no formal distinction between academic and vocational studies, although courses might be identified with regard to their suitability as preparation for higher education, post-school employment, or further vocational training. In New South Wales, there were two officially recognized pathways through senior secondary school to the Higher School Certificate, one that provided general education and another that combined general education with vocational education and training, and in Western Australia, accredited courses were organized into several programs of study or 'pathways,' each providing preparation for entry to university, technical and further education, or employment in a post-school career area.[25]

Corporate Educational Management for Technological Society

The ministry announced by Prime Minister Bob Hawke following the re-
election of the Australian Labor party in July 1987 retained a two-tier
structure of senior ministers in the cabinet and junior ministers outside
it, but the cabinet was redesigned to enhance ministerial control, achieve
a more strategic focus on public policy, and strengthen budgetary discipline.[26] As part of this major restructuring, the Department of Education and Youth Affairs was merged with the Department of Employment
and Training into the Department of Employment, Education and Training (DEET). The government's aim to match the organization of educational governance to the needs of the national economy was clearly
evident in the message of welcome to the members of the new department by the minister, John Dawkins: 'Employment has been placed first
in the title because it represents our ultimate objective – to help people,
particularly the young, get the best job possible. This is not only in their
best interest as individuals, it is also an important national objective if we
are to have a vibrant economy. This means the Department will play a
central role in gearing Australia to meet the new economic challenges of
the late twentieth century.'[27] The new regimen was consolidated by the
abolition of the Commonwealth Schools Commission in the Employment, Education and Training Act (1988). 'This eliminated the main
source of potential opposition in the bureaucracy, freed the Government to reset the policy agenda, and weakened the capacity of education
institutions and interest groups ... to retard government initiatives.'[28]

As in the case of the Commonwealth government, state portfolios for
education were substantially restructured during the 1980s and 1990s,
very often in the context of general reviews of management in the public
sector, and departmental bureaucracies were reorganized according to
principles of corporate management. Corresponding to similar changes
in other policy domains, Australian ministers of education in the 1980s
and 1990s reverted to the classical liberal formula according to which
the minister gives political direction and makes policy choices and the
bureaucrats are employed to execute, enforce, and manage.[29] In sharp
contrast with the approach taken to reforming state educational governance during the era of industrial efficiency in the early twentieth century, the revival of ministerialism featured 'the appointment of generic
managers with no history in education, drawn from elsewhere in the
public or private sectors ... By 1992, not a single education department
was headed by an educator who had come up through the system.'[30]

Historical departmental divisions that corresponded to primary, secondary, and technical schools were restructured around the major functions of curriculum and standards, school operations, and administrative services, and senior officials were reorganized as state 'executive' or 'management' groups.[31]

Corporate management, with its focus on dividing policy goal setting and performance evaluation at the centre from decisions about implementation in schools, required a change in roles for regional offices. Under the principles of bureaucratic administration that determined Australian educational governance through the 1970s, the regional offices were subdivisions of state departments of education. Regional directors and supervisors were professional educators who customarily began their careers as classroom teachers and school principals and whose prospects for promotion were determined by the hierarchy of departmental offices. Regional offices were primarily concerned with supporting the implementation of departmental policies and programs determined by the director general, deputy directors general, and assistant directors general in head office. During the 1980s and 1990s the operations of regional offices in Victoria, New South Wales, and Queensland were substantially enlarged and extended, as positions dealing with such functions as curriculum development, advisory services, personnel administration, and property management were transferred from the centre.[32] Alternatively, regions in Western Australia (1987), Tasmania (1991), and South Australia (1993) were reorganized into districts headed by superintendents or directors who were responsible for approving school plans, guiding operations, monitoring implementation, and reporting on performance with regard to departmental goals and priorities.

Decentralization of educational management to the level of schools was a key feature of the development of corporate management in Australian educational governance. Within a framework of centrally determined and regionally monitored goals, policies, priorities, and standards that described the vision and core values of state educational regimes, school principals and school councils were expected to prepare their development plans, manage daily operations, and allocate resources to meet the educational needs of their students. In all states and territories, school councils representing parents, teachers, and community, including students in secondary schools, were promoted to provide advice to principals on school management and to participate in the development of school plans. Labor governments tended to emphasize the need not only to increase managerial efficiency but also to improve local democracy. Liberal and Liberal–National governments put their priority on devolving management and strengthening accountability. Overall, however, the burden of local management fell overwhelmingly on school principals, and the line of accountability ran clearly from departmental executive group through regional directors or district superintendents to school principals.[33]

The other issue in decentralizing management to the level of schools was the composition of school budgets. Here the goal of decentralized management was the introduction of 'global' or 'one-line' budgets. In order to maximize efficiency in local operations, schools would be given a block allotment based on number of students and adjusted for such factors as types of programs, costs of maintenance, and categories of students, and each school would have flexibility to allocate its budget among personnel, services, equipment, and supplies. When school-based budgets were first proposed by Labor governments in Victoria (1986), Western Australia (1987), and South Australia (1991), they were successfully resisted by teachers' unions and parents' organizations on the grounds that unacceptable differences would result among school communities; in all three states they were subsequently imposed by the succeeding Liberal or Liberal–National governments.[34] In New South Wales, Tasmania, and Queensland, school-based budgeting was implemented in stages in the early 1990s, beginning with trials on a voluntary basis covering expenditures for equipment maintenance, supplies, and services and eventually extending to cover all operating expenses. Perhaps the most notable effect of school-based budgeting was the resulting change in appointment of classroom teachers. Teachers in Australian states and territories continued to be employed by state departments of education, but the former system, under which teachers transferred from school to school on the basis of their seniority on state-wide promotion lists, was replaced by selection on the basis of merit by the principal, subject to approval of the regional director or district superintendent.

Canada: Back to Basics in Education for a Technological Society and Global Capitalism

In the late 1980s and early 1990s a series of reports emanating from provincial commissions, federal agencies, public institutes, and policy consultants presented the attainment of 'educational excellence' as the central problem of public education in contemporary Canada.[35] They interpreted relatively high drop-out rates, widespread functional illiteracy, and mediocre results in international mathematics and science tests as indicators of educational failure. They explained these educational failures as the result of muddled purposes, fragmented curricula, ineffective governance, and inadequate accountability. Against the prevailing public philosophy and policy practices of cultural pluralism and individual development, these reports advocated the externally established curriculum and standards of a uniform education transformed to meet the competitive demands of the new global capitalism, and they urged the reconstruction of educational governance to refocus responsibility for policy leadership on ministries of education, improve the cost-effectiveness of local management of public schools, and open the policy-making process to parental and community participation.

In the public debate about these policies, the need to adapt public education to the imperatives of economic globalization and technological society was largely taken for granted. Across the provinces, curricular reforms and school reorganization were designed and implemented to strengthen the teaching of core academic subjects, institute stricter procedures for evaluating outcomes, and hold teachers and administrators more closely accountable for achieving predetermined results. Ministries of education were restructured to give policy leadership, school districts were amalgamated in order to cut costs and improve efficiency, school councils were promoted to increase parental involvement, and new partnerships were created between schools and their communities. In contrast with other Anglo-American democracies, however, the process of educational reform in Canada remained relatively decentralized in provincial educational politics, certainly influenced by an interprovincial flow of reports and conferences but none the less lacking a strong national, let alone federal, line of policy development.

Restoring Provincial Control of Curricula and Testing

The introduction of credit systems with subject promotion was a defining feature of educational reform in Canadian high schools through the 1960s into the early 1970s, but there were important differences among provinces in their retention of prescribed courses. In the majority of provinces, required subjects varied from 25 per cent of total credits in Nova Scotia to 33.3 per cent in British Columbia, Ontario, Prince Edward Island, and Quebec, and 35 per cent in Alberta.[36] In these six provinces, the greater room for elective subjects resulted from either limiting the range of required subjects – English and social studies in the senior high schools of British Columbia, Nova Scotia, and Quebec; English and mathematics in Prince Edward Island – or, in the case of Alberta and Ontario, imposing lower credit demands across a standard set of prescribed subjects including English, social studies, mathematics, and science.[37] By contrast, a more traditional minority – Manitoba, New Brunswick, Newfoundland, and Saskatchewan – specified that over half the credits required for graduation from high school were to be taken from courses in English (or français in New Brunswick), social studies, mathematics, science, and physical education and health.[38]

During the 1980s, four provinces introduced major curricular changes that imposed much stricter requirements for secondary education. Under the new régime pédagogique for secondary schools approved by the Quebec cabinet in February 1981, over the full program of secondary studies, 158 of 180 credits were compulsory; for Secondary IV and V, requirements for compulsory subjects were increased from one-third to 78 per cent of total credits.[39] The curriculum for the new Ontario Secondary School Diploma, which was introduced for students entering grade nine in 1984–5, made compulsory sixteen of thirty credits required to graduate.[40] For students entering grade ten in September 1985 in Prince Edward Island, requirements for graduation were raised from fifteen to eighteen courses, including four courses in language arts (one of which had to be a grade-twelve course in the student's first official language) and two courses each in mathematics, social studies, and science.[41] Revised graduation requirements in Alberta, which were phased into effect from 1988–9 to 1992–3, increased mandatory core subjects to 62 of 100 credits for the general diploma and 76 of the 100 credits for the advanced diploma.[42]

During the 1990s, British Columbia and Nova Scotia also adopted curricular reforms that featured more prescribed credits, and Ontario, Newfoundland, and Prince Edward Island further tightened their requirements. The new graduation requirements for grades eleven and twelve in British Columbia (September 1995) specified twenty-eight out of fifty-two credits as 'foundation studies' (English, social studies, mathematics, science, fine arts, applied arts, and career and personal planning); and in Nova Scotia, for students entering grade ten in September 1997, thirteen of the eighteen courses required to graduate were taken from English/français, social studies, mathematics, science, technology, physical education and health, fine arts, and career and life management. In addition, Ontario finally dropped grade thirteen and increased its required courses to eighteen out of thirty for students entering grade

nine in September 1999; Newfoundland imposed new distribution requirements that raised the prescribed credits for English, social studies,
mathematics, and science and thus further restricted the room for
electives; the graduation requirements in Prince Edward Island were
raised to twenty credits in 1999, including ten mandatory credits in
English/français, mathematics, science, and social studies; and in New
Brunswick, where the requirements for francophone students were
already among the most prescriptive in Canada (twenty-three of thirty-
two credits over four years of high school), the credit system was
dropped from grade ten for anglophone students in 1996–7, with
students now required to pass seven courses in core subjects in grades
eleven and twelve. Only the province of Quebec, with its new curriculum for secondary schools announced in 1997, moved to increase the
options for students in the fifth cycle (Secondary IV and V) from
sixteen to twenty-four credits out of seventy-two, but that change still
left the Quebec program above the national median for prescribed
core subjects.

During the 1970s, compulsory, curriculum-based provincial examinations survived as the basis for awarding graduation diplomas to students
leaving secondary school in only two provinces: Newfoundland, where
marks for courses taken for the Grade XI Certificate were composed
equally from the results of provincial examinations and school assessments, and Quebec, where students had to pass examinations of the
Ministry of Education administered during Secondary IV and V and
final marks were divided between their performance on the ministry's
examinations and their teachers' evaluations.[43] When an official attempt
to get Alberta students to write provincial examinations on a voluntary
basis yielded only 20 per cent participation, the minister of education
imposed mandatory provincial examinations, beginning in September
1983 for students graduating from grade twelve and covering work over
the three years of senior high school in English, history and social
studies, mathematics, biology, chemistry, and physics. Similarly, in January 1984 the British Columbia Ministry of Education restored compulsory provincial examinations for subjects in grade twelve, beginning with
algebra, literature, English, chemistry, physics, biology, geology, history,
and languages (French, German, Spanish, and Latin) and eventually
encompassing nineteen subjects by the late 1990s. Provincial examinations in major grade-twelve subjects were rotated in Manitoba from 1991
until 1996, when the ministry switched to setting provincial examinations every year in mathematics and language arts.[44] In New Brunswick,

provincial examinations worth 40 per cent of students' final marks were introduced for core subjects in the francophone secondary sector in 1990–1; in the anglophone sector, provincial examinations for mathematics and English began in 1993–4.[45] Nova Scotia became the first province to administer the Atlantic Canada Examinations, which are being jointly developed through the Atlantic Provinces Education Foundation by the constituent departments of education, starting with grade-twelve examinations in English, English/communications, chemistry, and chimie (immersion) in 1999–2000 and adding physics and biology in 2000–1.

In addition to the restoration of provincial leaving examinations in the majority of provinces, systems of external assessment, including the establishment of specialized agencies with mandates to develop and administer provincial tests, were instituted in order to assess the performance of students across the elementary and secondary programs of study. In the province of Alberta, for example, the Student Evaluation Branch was established in November 1980 and two years later began rotating achievement tests in language arts, mathematics, and social studies at the levels of grades three, six, and nine. Then, starting in 1994–5, as part of the Conservative government's commitment to publish more educational performance indicators and thus allow parents to make more informed choices among schools, tests were administered annually to students in grade three in reading, writing, and mathematics, and students in grades six and nine were tested on the four core subjects of language arts, mathematics, science, and social studies.[46] In British Columbia, under the Provincial Learning Assessment Program, which started in 1991 under the aegis of the Evaluation and Accountability Branch of the Ministry of Education, there were rotating tests in language arts, mathematics, and social studies at grades four, seven, and ten. The ministry switched to annual tests in reading and writing in 1998 and added mathematics and problem solving as part of regular performance testing (Foundation Skills Assessment) in 1999. In Ontario, the New Democratic government in February 1995 appointed the Education Quality and Accountability Office to construct and administer mandatory annual tests in reading, writing, and mathematics for all students in grades three, six, nine, and eleven, a regimen subsequently scaled back by the new Conservative government to universal testing at grades three and eleven and sample testing at grades six and nine.[47] Similarly, based on the advice of the Commission on Excellence in Education, provincial achievement tests on reading, writing, mathematics, and science were initiated in New Brunswick in 1994–5 for students in grades three, six, and nine.

In marked contrast with the movements to develop national educational standards in Australia or even the United States, the Canadian approach to developing national standards for public primary and secondary education relied on interprovincial cooperation rather than federal leadership. The venue was the Council of Ministers of Education, Canada (CMEC), which was established in July 1967 'to enable the Ministers to consult on such matters as are of common interest, and to provide a means for the fullest possible co-operation among provincial governments in areas of mutual interest and concern in education' and where the federal government was an observer, not a member. The School Achievement Indicators Project (SAIP) was approved by the CMEC in September 1989. Its objective was an annual report on levels of educational achievement in Canada using indicators such as rates of participation, retention, and graduation and scores from tests of literacy and numeracy.[48] In December 1991, based on guidelines negotiated by a committee of deputy ministers, the CMEC agreed that the content and methods of the national tests would reflect differences in provincial curricula, be free of cultural and gender bias and stereotyping, and take account of variations in provincial demography. With half the cost paid by the federal government, the first round of national testing began with a test of mathematics achievement given to 47,000 students aged thirteen and sixteen in April 1993 and was completed by tests of reading and writing (1994) and science (1996). The second round of national testing in mathematics was held in April 1997 followed by reading and writing (1998) and science (1999).

Restoring Government Steering, Departmental Control,
and Administrative Agency

During the 1980s and 1990s the recurring theme with regard to reforming educational governance was the need for a clear division of the functions of policy and management, respectively, between provincial education departments and local school boards.[49] In practice, provincial ministries of education did indeed take command of educational policy, especially during the 1990s, but they also tightened their control over local educational governance. In the Maritimes and British Columbia, this simply meant that the ministries of education renewed their historically close control over curriculum design, instructional methods, prescribed textbooks, student assessment, and school organization. In New-foundland the Department of Education announced 'a reorganization, with a shift from direct management by the Department to direction-setting and accountability, and a focus on setting standards, curriculum development and monitoring';[50] but the effect of terminating the de-nominational basis of Newfoundland school boards was to centralize control rather than decentralize management. In Ontario the relation-ship of policy interdependence between ministry and boards was threat-ened even before the departure of the New Democratic government, when the Ministry of Education and Training in February 1995 announced its intention to prescribe the common curriculum, set program stand-ards and outcomes, and institute standard report cards; and the new Conservative government promptly restored the close central controls that were characteristic of educational policy and administration in Ontario prior to the 1960s.[51]

The revival of provincial control over curricula was reinforced by moves to exclude or marginalize district school boards with regard to decisions about taxing and spending for public education. Full provin-cial funding had existed in New Brunswick and Prince Edward Island since the 1970s, with no effective option for school boards to impose additional levies;[52] and in Newfoundland the provincial government paid over 90 per cent of educational costs, including the full cost of teachers and 90 per cent of transportation and construction costs, with 5 per cent raised from school fees or local taxes levied by special school tax authorities. Provincial governments also provided over 90 per cent of the revenues of school boards under the foundation programs that came into effect in Quebec in 1980–1 and Nova Scotia in 1982–3, and in both cases, school boards had only limited discretion to raise additional rev-enues.[53] Educational finance acts passed as part of a program of fiscal austerity in British Columbia in 1982 and 1983 authorized the provincial cabinet to determine all tax rates and set expenditure levels (block funding) for each school district's budget, although beginning in 1986–7, boards were permitted to tax residential property to provide optional local programs and services up to a ceiling of 110 per cent of approved provincial expenditures. Conservative governments bent on fiscal re-structuring in Alberta (1994) and Ontario (1997) centralized decision making about educational funding by setting a uniform provincial rate of property taxation for public education and allocating provincial grants to school boards through formulae that incorporated standard demo-graphic and operational variables.[54] Thus, by the late 1990s a foundation program with a substantial contribution to public school revenues from local property taxation determined by school boards, which was the dominant instrument for educational finance from the 1950s to the 1970s, survived only in the provinces of Manitoba and Saskatchewan.

Another feature of the centralization of educational politics and policy from the 1970s to the 1990s was the extension of provincial control over collective bargaining with regard to teachers' salaries and working conditions.[55] By the mid-1970s, collective bargaining was totally centralized in New Brunswick, Newfoundland, and Prince Edward Island, and bi-level bargaining in Nova Scotia and Quebec put the major issues at the provincial table. In British Columbia, province-wide collective bargaining between the British Columbia Public School Employers' Association (representing the provincial government and school boards) and the British Columbia Teachers' Federation was adopted by the New Democratic government in 1994 as part of a restructuring of labour relations in the provincial public sector.[56] In Alberta, Manitoba, and Ontario, collective bargaining continued formally to be decentralized, but provincial governments imposed major restrictions on its scope. In both Manitoba and Ontario, for example, school boards were allowed to include ability to pay as a factor in negotiations. In Ontario the 1997 Education Quality Improvement Act (Bill 160) removed decision making with respect to preparation time, instructional time, and class size from local collective bargaining to provincial ministry regulation.

Amalgamation of school districts, which was a primary instrument for improving the accessibility of public, especially secondary, education from the late 1930s to the early 1970s, dropped from the agenda of educational politics during the 1970s and 1980s; despite incremental reductions in several provinces, the institutional arrangements for local educational governance in the early 1990s were not essentially different from those two decades earlier. During the 1990s, however, amalgamation of school districts was restored as a major priority of provincial governments across the country. This time around, the argument for amalgamation was not advanced in terms of creating larger school districts with student populations and fiscal capacities adequate to support a full array of elementary and secondary educational services. Rather, the primary motive was efficiency. Too much spending on public education was being wasted on duplication by local educational bureaucracies at the expense of classroom services.

When the Liberal government of Frank McKenna reduced the number of school districts in New Brunswick from forty-two to eighteen, twelve anglophone and six francophone boards, and then abolished school boards entirely four years later, the compelling reason was cutting the operating costs of school boards. Similarly, when the Conservative government of Ralph Klein reduced the number of Alberta school boards from 141 to 68 in 1994, it was announced as part of a package of fiscal reforms that was designed to achieve a 12.4 per cent reduction in the budget of the Alberta Department of Education.[57] Similar assurances that amalgamating school boards would cut costs were made by the Conservative government in Prince Edward Island, where five boards were reduced to three in 1994; again, in 1996, by the New Democratic government in British Columbia (75 districts cut to 59), the Conservative government in Manitoba (57 districts cut to 22), and the Liberal government in Nova Scotia (22 districts reduced to 7); and in Ontario in 1997, following the election of the Conservative government led by Mike Harris on an anti-government platform of cutting taxes and spending (122 districts became 72). After the abolition of denominational boards in Newfoundland and Quebec, which in each case included a major reduction in the number of school districts, only the New Democratic government in Saskatchewan had resisted this method of educational restructuring.[58] Overall, from about 1,000 in the early 1970s and 800 in the early 1990s, the number of school districts had been reduced to 427 by the turn of the century.

As the counterpart of amalgamating school districts, school councils were promoted in all provinces, not only to mobilize parental and communal support for local schools but also to give parents and communities a stronger voice with regard to school decision making. Typically, one-half or more of the members of school councils were elected representatives of parents, with the remainder including the principal as a member ex officio, one or more representatives of the teaching staff, a student in secondary schools, and one or more co-opted representatives of the local community.[59] In all provinces except Quebec, school councils were created as advisory bodies. Their functions included helping to develop mission statements and improvement plans, participating in the selection of the school's principal, and giving advice to the principal and district board with regard to school programs, budget priorities, student discipline, support services, and community partnerships. In Quebec the 1997 Education Amendment Act required the governing boards of schools to meet provincial curriculum requirements and standards set by the Ministry of Education; but, based on proposals by the principal and after consultation with the teaching staff, the boards were mandated to introduce courses beyond the basic curriculum, choose teaching methods and evaluation procedures, increase instructional hours for certain subjects, determine support services for students, and conclude partnership agreements with other schools or local municipalities to supply services.[60]

Under progressive (ethical-liberal) theories of educational governance, the norm for policy networks in provincial educational policy communities on such key issues as educational finance, collective bargaining, school organization, and curriculum design envisaged ministry officials, organized teachers, and trustee associations joined together in a process of mutual consultation and bargaining. In practice, partnerships were rarely easy, and trilateralism varied across the provinces from complex pluralist networks in Ontario and quasi-corporatism in Quebec to more department-directed relationships in New Brunswick and Prince Edward Island. During the 1990s, however, even the pretence of educational partnership was dropped. Trustees' associations were disrupted and weakened by the reorganization of school districts and the shift of policy-making authority from school boards to provincial ministries. The governmental rhetoric of educational reform paradoxically emphasized the importance of committed teachers for its successful implementation in schools, while teachers' unions were widely portrayed as 'special interests' threatening to block meaningful change. Indeed, teachers' unions vigorously, often militantly, campaigned against cuts to spending for public education, fought to preserve their rights of collective bargaining, and opposed centrally prescribed curricula and standardized testing.[61] From their aspirations for tripartite partnerships in the educational policy communities of the 1960s, teachers' unions in the 1990s had become the core of anti-government advocacy coalitions.

New Zealand: National Curriculum and Corporate Management

Educational reform in New Zealand originated in the restructuring of government that followed the election in 1984 of the Labour party under the leadership of David Lange. During its first term, the Labour government encouraged planning for a national curriculum for the compulsory years of school, as well as diversification of post-compulsory schooling to fit the needs both of students bound for university and of those heading for other tertiary education or employment; however, curricular reform languished during the second term as the restructuring of educational governance took priority. From 1987 to 1990 the grand design of the fourth Labour government to separate policy strategy and public management, backed (some would argue, conceived and driven) by the Treasury and the State Services Commission, transformed the governance of public education in New Zealand. With the Labour party fatally divided over the pursuit of its program of economic rationalism and public-sector reform, the national election of October 1990 was won easily by the National party led by James Bolger. The National government retained the principal features of Labour's restructuring of educational governance and switched its attention to the content and outcomes of schooling in the form of a national curriculum, the Achievement Initiative, and the National Qualifications Framework.

National Curriculum, Standards, and Qualifications

Responding to criticism that the Universities Entrance Board Examination was blocking adaptation of post-compulsory secondary education to meet the diverse needs of the growing number of students who were staying in school, the Labour party during the 1984 electoral campaign promised to remove the University Entrance examination from sixth form. Following the election of the Labour party, the minister of education established one committee to inquire into curriculum, assessment, and qualifications in forms five to seven and another to review the entire curriculum from early primary classes to form seven. In June 1985 the committee of inquiry on forms five to seven recommended that the University Entrance examination be dropped from form six; the Sixth Form Certificate based on single-subject credits would be the only national award in form six, and a new board of studies would be given a mandate to develop a wider and more general secondary education, not simply one preparatory for university studies. In July 1987 the Board of Studies was established to advise the minister on curriculum, assessment, and awards in secondary schools, and the School Certificate Examinations Board was abolished.[62]

The committee to review the curriculum for schools, which issued a draft report in July 1986 and, following public consultation, a final report in April 1987, recommended a common national curriculum for years one to ten that would be inclusive of all students, enable them to become independent and lifelong learners, recognize New Zealand's bicultural identity, and reflect the multicultural nature of New Zealand society. The national curriculum should establish a continuum of clear learning objectives throughout the compulsory years of schooling, define a range of knowledge and skills that would enable students to take their rightful place in the current and future economy and society, reaffirm the importance of basics and improve classroom assessment practices and national monitoring procedures, and ensure that national academic standards were comparable to those of New Zealand's principal trading partners. Based on this report, the Department of Education began to draft a national curriculum statement, but throughout the second term of the Labour government, curriculum reform was eclipsed by the restructuring of the governance of education, a task that absorbed most of the attention and energy of policy makers.

During the 1990 electoral campaign, the National party focused its criticism of educational policies on the Labour government's failure to achieve a reform of the national curriculum. Once in office, the National government started the Achievement Initiative in April 1991, designed to establish clear achievement standards for all levels of compulsory schooling. A discussion paper circulated by the (reorganized and renamed) Ministry of Education advanced a framework for national curricular objectives in terms of 'Essential Learning Areas' (language, mathematics, science and the environment, technology, the arts, society and culture, and physical and personal development) and 'Essential Generic Skills' (communication, numeracy, information-handling, problem-solving and decision-making, self-management, social, and work/study skills). Schools would be required to demonstrate that their programs gave all their students access to the full range of essential learning areas and generic skills.

National Curriculum statements, which specified achievement objectives for each essential learning area throughout eight progressive levels of achievement, were drafted, circulated, revised, and approved, first in mathematics (1992), science (1993), and English (1994), and subsequently in technology (1995), te reo Maori (1996), social studies (1997), and health and physical education and the arts (1999). Teachers were expected to assess and report on student progress in terms of the achievement objectives as specified in the National Curriculum statements, and boards of trustees and school principals would evaluate the effectiveness of National Curriculum implementation in their schools. In addition, under the new national assessment procedures beginning in September–October 1995, there was a four-year cycle for monitoring the educational achievements of representative samples of students at ages eight and twelve. Assessment of all students at the 'transition points' of entry to form one (year seven) and form three was introduced in 1996–7.

With regard to standards, assessment, and certification for post-compulsory education and training, the New Zealand Qualifications Authority (NZQA) was charged under the Education Amendment Act 1990 with developing a national framework covering secondary schools beyond the level of the School Certificate and continuing through postsecondary education and training. The new authority's discussion document, issued in March 1991, proposed to define all national qualifications in terms of interchangeable units that specified the skills and knowledge to be acquired in each unit and the standards against which performance was to be measured. The School Certificate would be retained at the end of fifth form but changed from a norm-referenced examination, using the performance of the average student as norm, to a standards-based qualification. The University Entrance, Bursaries and Scholarship Examination would continue to be given at the end of seventh form; and, while some units would be particular to the National Certificate and others to the Bursaries, there would be strong links between the Bursaries and the National Certificate through common learning units.[63]

Breaking down the historical split between academic and vocational studies was a major feature of the NZQA plan: 'The National Certificate will offer an alternative route to employment and further study, and will enjoy equal status with Bursaries. The Government does not intend that there will be first and second class qualifications based on the discredited distinction between *academic* and *vocational*.'[64] In practice, however, the School Certificate and the Bursaries continued to be the ruling school examinations and to be used primarily to rank and select students (norm-referenced) rather than to determine whether students were competent in particular learning areas (standards-based). In February 1997 the NZQA renewed its effort to bring qualifications based on national school examinations within the National Qualifications Framework. Under its new proposal, which was officially adopted in a white paper issued in October 1999, conventional subjects within the New Zealand Curriculum Framework (as well as a few additional subjects such as dance, drama, home economics, and social studies) are described in terms of 'achievement standards' comprising four to nine learning outcomes for each subject at three levels corresponding to the last three years of secondary school. Student achievement is assessed both internally and externally, the result for each standard is graded (excellence, merit, credit, no credit), and an overall mark is assigned for each subject. Credits from both achievement standards and unit standards count towards the National Certificate of Educational Achievement, Level 1 of which replaced the School Certificate in 2002, with Levels 2 and 3 replacing the Sixth Form Certificate (2003) and the University Bursaries (2004).[65]

Educational Governance: Restructuring the Department,
Abolishing the Boards

Following the re-election of the Labour government, Prime Minister David Lange took the portfolio of minister of education and, in July 1987, appointed the Taskforce to Review Education Administration, chaired by a prominent Auckland businessman, Brian Picot.[66] Its report concluded that educational governance in New Zealand 'is a creaky, cumbersome affair,' too centralized in its operations, pervaded by poor management practices, and impervious to widespread 'feelings of frustration in the face of a system that too often appeared inflexible and unresponsive to consumer demand.' According to the task force, 'Tinkering with the system will not be sufficient to achieve the improvements now required. In our view the time has come for quite radical change, particularly to reduce the number of decision points between the central provision of policy, funding, and services and the education delivered by the school or institution.'[67]

After a brief period of public consultation, the Labour government proceeded to implement the recommendations of the Picot task force.[68] On 1 October 1989 the Department of Education became the Ministry of Education, the office of director general was replaced by that of chief executive officer, and a formal agreement was struck between the minister and the chief executive officer on specific outputs to be delivered in return for budgetary revenues. The Department of Education, which had been organized since 1914 into primary, secondary, technical and further education, and administrative services divisions, was reorganized into three major groups of policy, operations, and finance and support; a separate Maori Group/Te Wahanga Maori was added in 1992. The chief executive officer and the four group managers, along with the national property manager, the chief internal auditor, and the director of the communications unit, comprised the ministry's 'strategic management group.' The primary functions of the new ministry were advising the minister on the development of national strategies for educational development, formulating national curriculum objectives and guidelines, approving the charters of educational institutions, providing funding to

state and integrated schools, and contracting for services supplied by the
six new crown educational agencies that had inherited the operational
responsibilities of the former Department of Education.

The Taskforce to Review Education Administration proposed that
schools should be the basic unit of educational governance: 'This is
where there will be the strongest direct interest in the educational
outcomes and the best information about local circumstances. People in
the institutions should make as many of the decisions that affect the
institution as possible – only when it would be inappropriate should
decisions be made elsewhere.'[69] The Education Act 1989 abolished the
education boards that had governed elementary schools since the first
provincial legislation for public education in the 1850s.[70] Every primary
and secondary school was governed by a board of trustees comprising
three to five representatives elected by the parents of students in the
school, a representative of the staff, and the school's principal.[71] Working within national guidelines and subject to the approval of the minister
of education, each board of trustees was directed to prepare a charter
that set out the performance objectives of its school.[72] Funding from the
ministry came in the form of a block grant ('bulk funding') to the board
of trustees, using a formula based primarily on the number and types of
students; the board was responsible for deciding the allocation of its
budget among recurrent operating expenditures, excluding school transport, and (unless the school opted to be fully funded) salaries of classroom teachers.[73] Principals and senior teachers were appointed on
contract by boards of trustees, and conditions of employment in each
school were determined by negotiations between the principal and the
board of each school.

According to the recommendations of the Picot task force, 'Local
decision making should be within national objectives, which are an
expression of the national interest as opposed to purely local interests.
National objectives, however, should be broadbased, should be clearly
expressed as objectives rather than prescriptions, and should allow for
the inclusion of local interests, skills and resources where these are not
contrary to the national interest.'[74] Under the Education Act of 1989,
however, school charters and the National Education Guidelines emerged
as extensive and prescriptive directives from the Ministry of Education to
boards of trustees and school principals as school managers who became
the designated agents of the minister of education.[75] Boards of trustees,
and school principals as their chief executive officers, were required by
their charters to achieve, meet, and follow the National Education Guide-

lines, which included the National Education Goals, the National Curriculum statements, and the National Administration Guidelines.[76] The Education Review Office was established as a statutory authority to monitor the performance of each school with regard to fulfilling the terms of its charter. Persistent poor performance could result in dissolution of the board of trustees and appointment of a commissioner by the ministry.[77]

Under the State Sector Act, effective 1 April 1988, responsibility for collective negotiations of salaries and working conditions for employees in the education service was transferred from the director general of the Department of Education to the State Services Commissioner.[78] Rather than a unified national pay scale, five separate agreements that set income bands within each category were then negotiated for early childhood teachers with the Combined Early Childhood Union Aotearoa (CECUA), primary school teachers and principals separately with the New Zealand Educational Institute as their agent, secondary school teachers through the Post-Primary Teachers' Association, and secondary principals through the Secondary Principals' Association. Within the collectively negotiated bands, boards of trustees retained discretion to determine salaries, and they could also substitute spending on other operating costs for spending on teachers' salaries.

Establishing boards of trustees as legal employers of teachers and putting principals and senior teachers under contract with individual boards of trustees weakened the position of organized teachers in the governance of New Zealand education. In its approach to constructing a new educational regime, the fourth Labour government consciously moved away from its historical partnership with teachers as key agents of educational policy making,[79] and the National government was even more determined to realign policy networks inside the New Zealand educational policy community, making teachers more accountable to their local communities while undermining their capacity for national policy participation. Bureaucratic administration and policy networks based on concertation between the Department of Education and organized teachers (especially the New Zealand Educational Institute) were replaced by managerial conceptions of principal and agent and the adversarialism of pressure-group politics.

United Kingdom: Prescribed National Curricula and the End of Tripartite Partnership

In his speech at Ruskin College, Oxford, in October 1976, Prime Minister James Callaghan criticized imbalances in the curriculum that favoured humanities over mathematics, science, and technology, as well as the 'new informal methods of teaching' and the unwillingness of the teaching profession to be held publicly accountable. He proposed a 'basic curriculum' with 'universal standards' as a way of dealing with these problems. This speech was followed by a series of one-day regional conferences, a green paper that stressed the need for a national framework for curriculum and assessment, and a circular in November 1978 asking local authorities to report on the balance and breadth of curriculum in their schools and their procedures for developing and reviewing curriculum. As the Department of Education and Science (DES) interpreted the resulting information, 'Nobody was managing the curriculum.'[80]

Following the election of the Conservative government, local education authorities (LEAs) and governing bodies were told (Circular 6/81) that they should have clear curricular plans for their schools, and LEAs were directed (Circular 8/83) to report on the steps they had taken to construct and implement curricular policies in their primary and secondary schools. A 1985 white paper affirmed the government's aim to achieve national agreement on curricular objectives and content but still conceded that both local authorities and schools would have major responsibilities in that process.[81] By 1986, however, the role of the Department of Education and Science had shifted from building political and educational consensus for a national curriculum to putting the idea into law and policy.[82] In January 1987 the new secretary of state for education and science (Kenneth Baker), speaking to the North of England Conference on Education, announced the government's intention to introduce a statutory national curriculum for pupils aged five to sixteen.[83] Introduced in the House of Commons in November 1987 and receiving royal assent in July 1988, the Education Reform Act not only transformed educational provision and governance in England and Wales, but its scheme of prescribed subjects, bounded choice, school-based management, and government regulation was also reproduced largely intact in Northern Ireland and adapted in its essentials for Scotland.

Nationalizing the Curriculum in England, Wales, and Northern Ireland

Under section 3 of the Education Reform Act, the national curriculum for students aged five to sixteen in maintained schools of England and Wales comprised the 'core subjects' of English, mathematics, and science plus the 'foundation subjects' of art, foreign language, geography, history, music, physical education, and technology. Welsh was part of the core curriculum in primary and secondary schools that had Welsh as their language of instruction; in other schools in Wales it was a foundation subject. The act authorized the secretary of state for education and science and/or the secretary of state for Wales to issue orders specifying attainment targets, programs of study, and assessment arrangements for each core and foundation subject during four 'key stages' ending at ages seven, eleven, fourteen, and sixteen.[84] At each key stage, students in most subjects would be given several standard assessment tasks (SATs) that would result in their being ranked according to ten levels of attainment.

For England and Wales the ministerial orders for English, mathematics, science, modern foreign language, physical education, and technology were common, issued jointly by the secretary of state for education and science and the secretary of state for Wales. In addition to Welsh, separate curricular orders were issued by the Welsh Office for subjects that incorporate distinctive Welsh educational aims and interests: art, geography, history, and music. The Education Reform (Northern Ireland) Order 1989 stipulated the same core and foundation subjects as the national curriculum for England and Wales; but there were differences in structure and content within subjects, Irish was designated as a foundation subject in schools using it as their language of instruction, and the first key stage ended at the age of eight rather than seven.

Implementation of the national curriculum in England and Wales soon encountered resistance from teachers because of the excessive workload that resulted from administering the SATs.[85] Following pilot testing in 1990, standard assessment tasks in English/Welsh, mathematics, and science were administered by teachers in their classrooms for the first time in the spring of 1991 to all children at the end of Key Stage 1 (age seven). After another year of pilot testing, the first national public tests for fourteen-year-olds in English, mathematics, science, and technology were held in the spring of 1993. This round of tests was disrupted by a boycott organized by the National Union of Teachers, the National Association of Schoolmasters Union of Women Teachers, and the Association of Teachers and Lecturers; and the National Union of Teachers again refused to participate in 1994, when national standardized assessments were extended to cover English, mathematics, and science for eleven-year-old students. Public opinion polls showed widespread support among parents for the teachers' boycotts, and in May 1993 the secretary of state for education and science asked the chair of the new School Curriculum and Assessment Authority, Sir Ron Dearing, to review the national curriculum. Based on Dearing's recommendations, the statutory component of the curriculum for Key Stages 1 to 3 was reduced in order to free 20 per cent of teaching time to be used at the discretion of schools for basic literacy and numeracy skills and for deepening knowledge and understanding of national curriculum subjects. During Key Stage 4 (students aged fourteen to sixteen) English, mathematics, science, and physical education plus short courses in a modern foreign language and technology continued to be compulsory; the other foundation subjects of art, geography, history, and music became optional.[86]

The post-compulsory sixth form was not affected by the reforms of 1988–9 in England, Northern Ireland, and Wales. Indeed, on two separate occasions, the Thatcher government summarily rejected proposals to change the traditional A-level curriculum.[87] Sir Ron Dearing's report on a national framework for the sixteen-to-nineteen curriculum and qualifications in March 1996, prepared at the request of the secretaries of state for education and employment, Wales, and Northern Ireland, proposed to retain GCSE and GCE A-level examinations, along with existing vocational courses, but to restructure them as three pathways: academic, through GCSEs to A levels; applied, through General National Vocational Qualification intermediate and advanced levels leading either to higher education or directly to employment; and vocational, through job-specific National Vocational Qualifications in conjunction with employment or youth traineeships.[88] Dearing's recommendations were not implemented prior to the 1997 election, however, and there had been no move to integrate national qualifications when the Labour government's first mandate came to an end in June 2001.[89]

National Guidelines for Curriculum and Testing in Scotland

In Scotland a national curriculum was not put into law, but from 1987 to 1993 national guidelines were developed that have exerted a powerful structuring effect on Scottish curriculum.[90] The incremental assertion of ministerial leadership that occurred in England and Wales beginning in 1976 had no obvious counterpart in Scotland, probably because, historically, both Scottish Education Department (SED) officials and members of Her Majesty's Inspectorate (HMI) were so deeply involved in making the Scottish curriculum.[91] None the less, as the Conservative government initiated educational reform in England and Wales in 1987, the secretary of state for Scotland issued a consultative paper that proposed to remedy alleged weaknesses in the curricular and assessment practices of Scottish primary and early secondary schools. Detailed national guidelines should be provided to describe the aims, objectives, and content for each element of the curriculum from primary year one to secondary year two, and there should be improved assessment practices and a national testing program to give public assurance that results were being achieved. No national legislation was proposed, but 'the Secretary of State would not rule out introducing legislation to ensure the proper implementation of national policy.'[92]

The national guidelines developed in Scotland were less prescriptive than was initially the case with the national curriculum in England and Wales.[93] Rather than core and foundation subjects, attainment outcomes and programs of study in Scotland were described for five areas – language arts, mathematics, environmental studies, expressive arts, and religious education – and schools were given more discretion in ensuring balance among areas of the curriculum and implementing the national guidelines. Another difference from England and Wales was that, in the original scheme for national testing in Scotland, there were two rather than three tests for English and mathematics, to be administered at the end of years four (age eight) and seven (age eleven). Even so, when the first round of national testing was conducted in 1991, Scottish teachers and parents mounted a vigorous protest, with the result that only half the expected number of children sat for the tests. The format for testing was then modified: the national tests in English and mathematics were administered only when the class teacher's own assessment indicated that pupils had reached the target level of attainment and were ready to take the test. Moreover, test results in Scotland were communicated only to individual students and their parents, and hence no comparisons of students' performances, either within or between schools, would (or could) be made.

For the upper years of secondary studies, a committee chaired by John M. Howie recommended differentiating the existing common pathway, which continued to be dominated by the Highers examination, between a Scottish certificate involving one or two years of general and vocational studies and a three-year Scottish baccalaureate that would be the normal route to higher education.[94] This plan for two tracks through post-compulsory schooling was 'overwhelmingly rejected' by the Scottish educational policy community.[95] Instead, the Scottish Office white paper issued in 1994 proposed to retain Highers, introduce a new level of qualification (Advanced Highers) involving more demanding two-year courses, and integrate existing national vocational courses and certificates into a single curriculum and assessment framework.[96] Following a period of consultation and development that was interrupted by the 1997 general election, implementation of the unified qualification system over a five-year period began in 1999. The credibility of the reform was shortly challenged by a major failure by the Scottish Qualifications Authority in issuing the 2000 examination results. Because of the ensuing political crisis, implementation of 'Higher Still' was slowed; the consensus in favour of a unified qualifications system in Scotland was none the less reaffirmed.[97]

Educational Partnership versus State Regulation and School Choice

The Education Reform Act of 1988 aimed at creating a public market for primary and secondary education in England and Wales. Following its election in 1979 the Conservative government had made its first efforts to expand school choice. Reminiscent of the traditional scholarship ladder, a key element of the Education Act of 1980 was the Assisted Places Scheme, which provided for means-tested fee remission to enable academically talented children from low-income families to attend an independent school.[98] The 1980 act also established an entitlement within the public sector for parents to choose their children's school (although each local education authority was allowed to establish planned admission levels [PALs] to ensure an optimal distribution of total enrolment among its schools); mandated the representation of parents on the governing bodies of schools; and required school governors to provide information to parents on admission policies, examination results, curriculum, discipline, and organization. With the Education Reform Act, the national curriculum was intended to specify the public service to be provided, and publication of the results of national testing would provide evidence of the effectiveness of various suppliers. The 1988 act also aimed to improve effectiveness and efficiency in the supply of educational services by markedly reducing the role of local education authorities as public bureaucracies in three ways: authorizing schools to admit students to fill their physical capacity rather than abide by LEA-planned admission levels (open enrolment); delegating decisions about budgeting and staffing to the governing bodies of schools (local management of schools or LMS);[99] and providing for governing bodies to opt out of LEA control and receive their funding directly from the Department of Education and Science or the Welsh Office (grant-maintained schools).[100]

The Education Reform Act established a national curriculum for England and Wales but did not specify how it would be enforced. Her

Majesty's Inspectorate was judged by the Conservative government to be too close to the teaching profession,[101] and the local loyalties of LEA inspectors and advisers eliminated them as an effective link in a national structure of accountability that would connect head teachers and their staffs to the DES. Accordingly, the Education (Schools) Act of 1992 established the Office for Standards in Education (OFSTED) to conduct inspections of all maintained schools over a four-year cycle, using teams that would bid for the work and include at least one non-professional inspector to represent the interests of pupils and parents. The main functions of HMI, which was cut from 480 to 175 inspectors, were accrediting inspection team leaders and monitoring the work of inspection teams. The 1992 act also terminated the authority of LEAs to inspect schools, although local inspection services could bid for OFSTED contracts, and funding in the rate support grant to LEAs to pay for local inspection and advisory services was removed to finance the operations of OFSTED.[102]

The Education Reform (Northern Ireland) Order 1989 further weakened the role of education and library boards (ELBs) in educational governance by its delegation of financial management to the governing bodies of schools and provision for ELB schools to opt for grant-maintained status while preserving tight central financial control over ELB operations. Under the provisions for local school management in the 1989 order, each county school's budget was determined by its education and library board according to a formula, but administrative responsibility was transferred from the ELB to individual schools. ELBs now had 'an advisory and support role in the implementation of the reform proposals rather than an administrative responsibility,'[103] and 'the rigidity of financial control exercised by the Department leaves the Boards with little scope for innovation and renders the second tier of administration largely inert with regard to interpretation of policy.'[104]

The Assisted Places Scheme that was enacted as part of the Education (Scotland) Act of 1981 was 'designed to widen the range of educational opportunity in Scotland and to give parents a greater choice of school.'[105] In contrast with the limited provisions of the 1980 Education Act in England and Wales, the 1981 Scottish act also gave parents a relatively unrestricted right to choose which school their children would attend.[106] The School Boards (Scotland) Act of 1988 directed the establishment of school boards for all Scottish schools, including majority representation for parents. In contrast with England and Wales, however, functions of staffing, curriculum, and discipline were devolved in Scotland to head teachers, and school boards were assigned a largely advisory role with rights to be informed and consulted about their school's educational, disciplinary, and financial policies and achievements, as well as to participate in the selection of senior staff.[107] In 1989 the Self-Governing Schools Etc. (Scotland) Act introduced procedures for Scottish schools to opt out of control by local education authorities and receive their funding directly from the Scottish Office. In marked contrast with the experience in England and Wales, however, only one small primary and one small secondary school had opted to become self-governing in Scotland before the Labour government rescinded the law in 1997.

The active promotion of a public market for education in England and Wales was accompanied by a process of dismantling the key institutions of an educational partnership among central education departments, associations of local authorities, and teachers' unions that had provided the basis for educational governance from the 1940s to the 1980s. In 1984 the Conservative government replaced the Schools Council with two separate non-statutory bodies, the Schools Curriculum Development Council (SCDC), which was funded half by the DES and half by LEAs, and the Secondary Schools Examinations Council (SSEC), which included no representatives of teachers' unions.[108] Then, under the Education Reform Act, the SCDC was replaced by the National Curriculum Council, funded centrally by the DES; the Curriculum Council for Wales was established in law; and the SSEC was replaced by the School Examinations and Assessment Council, appointed jointly by the secretaries of state for education and science and for Wales.[109] In 1986 the local authority employers and the teachers' unions reached an agreement in the Burnham Committee that conceded control of working conditions to management in return for quite sizable increases in pay, but the new secretary of state for education and science, Kenneth Baker, refused to fund their deal. Instead, Baker introduced the Teachers' Pay and Conditions Bill, which abolished the Burnham Committee, suspended teachers' rights of collective bargaining, and gave the secretary of state authority to determine teachers' pay and conditions.[110] By contrast, the vehement pay dispute between Scottish teachers and the Conservative government from 1984 to 1986 was finally resolved by the appointment of an independent pay review body, but the Scottish Joint Negotiating Committee survived as a tripartite forum for negotiating Scottish teachers' salaries during the 1990s.[111]

The election of the Labour party in May 1997 led to major modifications of the public market created by the Conservatives from 1979 to

1997. The Education (Schools) Act of 1997 abolished the Assisted Places Scheme in England and Wales and diverted the funding from that program to reduce the size of infant classes.[112] The following year, the School Standards and Framework Act (1998) put into law the Labour government's scheme, first set out in the party's 1995 policy statement, *Diversity and Excellence*, that designated community (formerly county), voluntary (aided or controlled), and foundation as three categories of maintained schools and put grant-maintained schools back under the control of local education authorities as 'foundation schools.' The party's election manifesto had promised that 'Labour will never force the abolition of good schools whether in the private or state sector,' and in office the Blair government left any change in the admissions standards of the 163 remaining selective grammar schools to the choice of local parents rather than LEAs.[113] Similarly, comprehensive secondary schools that had taken advantage of Conservative policy to select up to 15 per cent of their pupils were permitted to continue any pre-existing arrangements for partial selection by ability, but the percentage of their pupils admitted on the basis of ability could be reduced by an independent arbitrator if at least ten parents of primary school children complained that local children were being excluded from their neighbourhood secondary school. In its 1992 and 1996 white papers, the Conservative government had not only advocated diversity in types of schools but had also encouraged comprehensive schools to specialize in subjects such as technology and languages in order to give students and their parents more choice.[114] The Labour government rejected the Conservative policy of creating choice through 'structure' (grammar schools, grant-maintained schools), but seized on 'specialization' in comprehensive schools, including its implications for selective entry, as part of Labour's plan to reform public education for technological society. Under the School Standards and Framework Act, secondary comprehensive schools that were recognized as offering a specialization in technology, languages, the arts, or sports were permitted to admit up to 10 per cent of their pupils according to their aptitude in the school's area of specialization. No other new arrangements for selection by ability were allowed to determine entry to comprehensive secondary schools, but the Labour party's election manifesto and the Labour government's 1997 white paper both gave explicit approval to internal selection procedures that assigned students to courses and/or classes within schools according to their ability.[115]

If the Labour government substantially modified the functioning of the public educational market following its election in May 1997, the position of local education authorities as agents of central government initiatives and supporters of largely self-managing schools was much less changed. Under the School Standards and Framework Act, LEAs were required to make 'Education Development Plans' for raising their standards that would meet the approval of the secretary of state. As with the Conservatives, the Labour government tended 'to see LEAs as its agent in administering the national agenda and achieving national targets, and it has placed considerable responsibilities on local authorities to promote high standards of education.'[116] The principles of local management of schools were preserved and extended under 'devolved funding,' a blending of LMS and grant-maintained status that gave schools greater managerial freedom with respect to a higher percentage of their budgets while reducing their control over admissions. The LEA continues to have the role of 'banker and enabler, providing those services which schools need to purchase collectively, but being above all a monitor of quality and coordinator of admissions ... What it is not expected to do is to revert to the political interference in the details of school life which brought local government into such disrepute in the 1970s and which fuelled many of the Conservative reforms.'[117] Nor did the Labour government hesitate to use OFSTED's powers to inspect local education authorities as a means to enforce its commitment to raise standards. Several LEAs with failing reports from OFSTED were subjected to ministerial interventions that included dispatching departmental teams or hiring private consultants to improve management, putting inadequate services out for contract, and, in one case, terminating the entire operations of the LEA.

After 1973, when the Northern Ireland Parliament was dissolved, public schools in Northern Ireland, Scotland, and Wales were centrally governed by education departments in three territorial departments of the government of the United Kingdom. The Northern Ireland Office, the Scottish Office, and the Welsh Office were not a form of field administration for Whitehall functional departments; nor were they an application of administrative devolution.[118] None the less, the four education departments of the United Kingdom were part of the same national government and hence subject to the constitutional and political imperatives of the Westminster model of cabinet government. This was evident in the commonality of priorities and policies with regard to the big issues of contemporary public education: raising the school-leaving age, dealing with budget cuts, reorganizing secondary education into comprehensive schools, introducing national curricula, and reforming public examinations. The establishment of the Scottish Executive Education Department responsible to the Scottish Parliament and the Welsh Executive Education Department responsible to the National Assembly for Wales, which came into effect on 1 July 2000, together with the return of responsibility for the Department of Education for Northern Ireland (DENI) to the Northern Ireland Assembly, are not necessarily conditions for growing independence of educational policy making and concomitant political conflicts across educational policy communities; however, at the beginning of the twenty-first century, they certainly impart a new dynamic to the complex history of interdependent educational policy making in the United Kingdom.[119]

United States: Setting Standards for Utilitarian-Liberal Educational Regimes

As with the reports of the Committee of Ten in 1894 and the National Education Association (NEA) Commission on the Reorganization of Secondary Education in 1918, the 1983 report of the National Commission on Excellence in Education articulated a compelling national problem of public education and thereby created a political opportunity for educational reform. The commission's remedies concentrated on stricter regulation of the educational process – for example, specifying that students take four years of English and three years of mathematics for high school graduation – but the goals of educational reform initiated by the commission's report shifted in the late 1980s and early 1990s from regulating educational process to evaluating student performance. In turn, schooling based on outcomes or results involved establishing goals, setting standards of knowledge and skills, ensuring that schools had the capacity to teach their students at the expected levels of performance, creating incentives for systems and students to meet the standards, and restructuring assessment systems to measure their performance.

Although, historically, considerable importance was put on reforming the governance of public education, the process of designing educational reform for global capitalism had little effect on state and local institutions for educational governance. State educational policy makers, especially governors, assumed a stronger role as leaders of educational reform, but the patterns of state educational institutions and decentralized school districts showed little change from the 1970s to the 1990s. Symbolically meaningful changes were initiated at the level of school governance in the form of legislation for charter schools and voucher programs, but at the end of the 1990s neither innovation had made a major impact on the overall structure and process of state and local educational governance. More telling was the expansion of judicial policy making by state courts from the pluralist issues of religion, race, and language in the public schools to issues of educational equity and adequacy focusing on state legislation for educational finance.

Educational Regulations and Standards for a Nation at Risk

In August 1981, Terrel Bell, secretary of education in the new administration of President Ronald Reagan, appointed the National Commission on Excellence in Education, chaired by David P. Gardiner, president of the University of Utah.[120] In its report, issued in April 1983, the commission raised an educational alarm: 'Our Nation is at risk ... We report to the American people that ... the educational foundations of our society are presently being eroded by a rising tide of mediocrity that threatens our very future as a Nation and a people.'[121] The formerly unchallenged pre-eminence of the United States in commerce, industry, science, and technological innovation was threatened by competitors around the world that were matching and surpassing levels of educational attainment in the United States. The commission found that curricula in secondary schools had been 'homogenized, diluted, and diffused to the point that they no longer have a central purpose. In effect, we have a cafeteria-style curriculum in which the appetizers and desserts can easily be mistaken for the main courses.'[122]

To remedy these problems, the commission proposed that four-year secondary programs be constructed on a foundation of five 'New Basics': four years of English; three years of mathematics, science, and social studies; and a half-year of computer science. In addition, students intending to go to college or university should be required to study a foreign language for two years. Much more time should be allocated to these basic subjects, a provision that would require not only more effective use of existing hours but also a longer school day (seven hours compared to the existing six) and a lengthened school year (200 to 220 days compared to the existing 180). Schools, as well as colleges and universities, should adopt more rigorous and measurable standards and higher expectations for academic performance, and the quality of teachers should be improved by instituting higher salaries and better training.

As secretaries of education during the Reagan presidency, Terrel Bell

(1981–4) and William J. Bennett (1985–8) were visible advocates for educational reform, but the president's official response to the report of the National Commission on Excellence in Education put the responsibility for educational reform on state governments. At the state level, the initial response to the alarm raised by the commission was a plethora of regulations affecting teachers, students, and administrators – what types of courses, how much time for each subject, what topics covered, how much homework, how much participation in sports and other extracurricular activities, how often classes could be missed before a course was failed.[123] Perhaps the most symbolically significant of the new regulations were the changes in state requirements for high school graduation. In 1980 the median state requirement for the number of courses needed to graduate from high school was sixteen courses; by 1996 the median number of courses required had risen to twenty-one.[124] With respect to state-mandated requirements in basic subject areas, as recommended by the National Commission on Excellence in Education, thirty-six states and the District of Columbia required all students to complete four courses in English and/or language arts, and twenty-five states and the District of Columbia required at least three courses in social studies.[125] Sixteen states and the District of Columbia required all students to have at least three courses in mathematics to graduate, and only eight states plus the District of Columbia mandated at least three courses in science.[126] Clearly, standards for graduation from high schools had been raised, but overall the reforms fell well short of the recommendations of the commission.

In September 1989 an 'Education Summit' at Charlottesville, Virginia, which was convened by President George Bush and the National Governors' Association, agreed on a set of six 'National Education Goals' to be achieved by the year 2000: all children would start school ready to learn; the high school graduation rate would be raised to at least 90 per cent; students would leave grades four, eight, and twelve having demonstrated competence in challenging subject matter that included English, mathematics, science, history, and geography, and would also leave school prepared for responsible citizenship, further learning, and productive employment; students in the United States would be first in the world in achievement in science and mathematics; every adult would be literate and possess the knowledge and skills necessary to compete in a global economy and to exercise the rights and responsibilities of citizenship; and every school in the United States would be free of drugs, violence, and the unauthorized presence of firearms and alcohol and would offer a disciplined environment conducive to learning.[127]

At the federal level, proposals to establish programs that would work towards these national goals quickly became mired in partisan controversy.[128] Eventually, in the early morning of 31 March 1994, the Senate voted to end Jesse Helms's filibuster (which stemmed from the modification of his school prayer amendment in conference), the Goals 2000: Educate America Act was passed sixty-three to twenty-two, and President Clinton signed it into law later that day. Based largely on the national goals agreed five years previously at Charlottesville, Goals 2000 promoted voluntary development of state standards with regard to content (what students should know) and performance (how well students ought to know the material).[129] State and local educational authorities were then expected to restructure their curricula, teaching methods, assessment, and accountability around the achievement of these goals and standards. As inducements to cooperate, Goals 2000 offered categorical grants as well as limited waivers on certain federal regulations for schools, districts, and states that introduced qualifying programs.

From 1989 to 1994, while presidents and Congress were trying to negotiate a national framework of legislation based on the concept of national educational goals agreed at the Charlottesville summit, the approach to educational reform in the states was shifting from regulation to ensure minimum competence to the development of educational goals, higher standards, and comprehensive assessment systems. In 1989, for example, even before President Bush and the National Governors' Association met in Charlottesville, legislation in South Carolina established goals that gave priority to ensuring children's readiness for school, reducing high school dropout rates, and raising levels of student performance beyond the minimum required by the state's basic skills test. The South Carolina Department of Education developed 'curriculum frameworks' in eight core subjects describing the knowledge and skills to be attained in each subject and the methods of teaching them, and the state's assessment system was restructured.[130] As another example, following the Kentucky Supreme Court's decision that the state education system was unconstitutional, the Kentucky Education Reform Act (1990) mandated a performance-based assessment program under which six general educational goals and seventy-five 'valued outcomes' provided the basis for developing a curriculum framework covering language arts, mathematics, and science by writing teams of professional educators appointed by the Kentucky Department of Education. State testing based on written examinations, performance events, and portfolios for all students in grades four, eight, and twelve provided the mechanism for holding schools accountable for ensuring that their students met state standards.[131] In Michigan, which had a long tradition of local control, the State Board of Education was empowered in 1990 to define 'Model Core Curriculum Student Outcomes.'[132] Three years later, Public Act 335 defined the 'Core Academic Curriculum' as comprising mathematics, science, reading, social studies, and writing and required each school district to adopt it by 1997–8. A state committee was mandated to set academic performance standards, which would be used by school districts to determine student competence and advancement, and new state graduation tests were based on outcomes derived from the core curriculum.

By fall 1998, forty states had adopted standards in four core academic subjects (English/language arts, mathematics, science, and social studies); Idaho and Iowa were the only states with no official standards in any of the four subjects.[133] In the annual evaluation of state educational standards conducted by the American Federation of Teachers, thirty-six states were judged to have mathematics standards that were clear and specific at all three levels of elementary, middle, and high school, and twenty-eight states had clear and specific science standards at all three levels. Only fifteen states received passing evaluations at all three levels for their English/language arts standards, however, and just six got passing evaluations for their social studies standards.[134]

State systems for measuring student performance also varied markedly. At one end of the continuum, West Virginia was administering a combination of norm-referenced and criterion-referenced tests and writing and performance assessments in the four core subjects over grades one to twelve, and Kentucky used a similar combination plus portfolio assessments over grades three to twelve. At the other end, Iowa and Nebraska had no state measures for student assessment. In twenty states, the four core subjects were being tested using assessments aligned to the state's educational standards, but only eight of the twenty states had assessment systems that comprised four types of measures, not only norm-referenced and criterion-referenced tests, but also writing and performance assessments.[135]

Based on national testing of student performance in mathematics, reading, and science conducted by the National Association for Educational Progress, there was little change between 1994 and 1998 in the overall percentage of grade-four students scoring at or above the 'proficient' level in reading, but there were marked improvements in the national average scores for grade-four mathematics, grade-eight mathematics, and grade-eight science from 1996 to 2000. None the less, there were also substantial and persistent differences among states in the percentages of students who scored at least at the proficient level. Among the states that administered all eight tests, only three were consistently above the national average, and eleven states (most from the South) scored below average on all eight tests.[136]

Educational Governance for a Nation at Educational Risk

The impetus for reform of state educational governance that had been an important feature of postwar educational reform in the United States languished during the 1970s but then revived during the 1980s and 1990s.[137] In contrast with the postwar period, when the strong influence of Progressive ideas favoured giving state boards of education authority to make policy and appoint the chief state school official, recent changes in state institutions of educational governance have been more ideologically ambiguous. As a result, while New York continued to be unique, with its state legislature electing the Board of Regents and the board appointing the commissioner of education, in the 1990s the other forty-nine states were more evenly distributed among four basic models of educational governance.[138] First, the state superintendent was still popularly elected in fifteen states. With the exception of Florida, South Carolina, Washington, and Wisconsin, the state boards of education under this model were all appointed by the governor.[139] Second, in eleven states the governor appointed the members of the state board of education, and the board in turn appointed the state superintendent. Two other states approximated this model.[140] Third, the state superintendent was appointed in nine states by a state board of education that was popularly elected and in two states by a board that had a majority of elected members and a minority appointed by the governor.[141] Fourth, in seven states the governor appointed both the state board of education and the chief state school officer, and three other states had a variant of this arrangement.[142]

In contrast with the quarter-century following the Second World War, educational reform in the 1980s and 1990s involved surprisingly little reorganization of local school governance. The number of school districts decreased from 15,912 in 1980–1 to 14,928 in 1999–2000, an annual reduction of 0.3 per cent. With the exception of the states of Georgia and Tennessee, where there was a change from appointed to elected county boards, the structure of local educational governance was also largely unchanged from the early 1970s to the late 1990s.[143] Across forty-nine states (Hawaii has no institutions for local educational governance), in the 1990s there continued to be a complex array of local school boards that varied by type of municipality, provisions for fiscal independence or dependence, and provisions for election of members versus appointment.[144] In twenty-seven states where historically small community school districts had been variously consolidated, the school boards were virtually all fiscally independent and their members were popularly elected.[145] The school boards of the nine states where districts were based on cities, towns, and townships were also elected, but they divided between fiscal independence (Indiana, New Hampshire, New Jersey, Pennsylvania, and Vermont) and fiscal dependence (Connecticut, Maine, Massachusetts, and Rhode Island).[146] Among the fourteen states where school districts were based on either county or county and city boundaries, school boards in Florida, Georgia, Kentucky, Louisiana, Nevada, Utah, and West Virginia were popularly elected and fiscally independent; in Alaska, North Carolina, and Tennessee they were elected but fiscally dependent. School boards in Alabama and South Carolina all had fiscal independence, and the members of sixty-seven county and seventeen city school boards in Alabama were elected. Forty-four city school boards in Alabama were appointed by the city's governing body, however, and county school boards in South Carolina were appointed by the governor. School boards in Maryland and Virginia were all fiscally dependent on their local city or county council; the majority were appointed in Maryland and elected in Virginia.[147]

Decentralization of educational governance ensured that state provisions for educational finance would continue to be a major issue of American educational politics and policy making. As state governments gradually became more generous in their funding for public education, state aid increased as a percentage of total school revenue from 39.1 per cent in 1970–1 to 49.7 per cent in 1986–7 and was holding at 48.7 per cent in 1998–9. The trend also continued for states to rely on foundation programs or their equivalent to allocate state aid for elementary and secondary education. By 1998–9, forty-four states were using a foundation program as the major instrument to fund their basic support for public schools, three states used percentage equalizing or guaranteed valuation grants, and two states (Hawaii and Washington) had full state funding. Only Delaware relied primarily on a flat grant for its basic support program.[148]

Given the refusal of the U.S. Supreme Court to set a national standard for state programs of educational finance, state courts of appeal were free to reach different conclusions about the constitutionality of their state's funding program.[149] In the early 1970s there were three very different types of decisions. First, in a series of cases (*Serrano* v. *Priest*) from 1971 to 1988, the Supreme Court of California held that the heavy dependence of educational finance on local property taxes resulted in wide disparities of revenue and expenditures across school districts, that the state's foundation program failed to ensure sufficient revenues for poor districts to match the educational provision of wealthy districts, and hence, that the state's foundation program violated the equal protection provision of the California Constitution. Second, in another series of cases (*Robinson* v. *Cahill*) from 1973 to 1976, the New Jersey Supreme Court rejected the claim that education was a fundamental right and, in addition, decided that 'statewide uniformity' in educational expenditure was not required by the New Jersey Constitution. None the less, it also found that there was a constitutional requirement for the state legislative assembly to 'provide for the maintenance and support of a thorough and efficient system of free public schools,' and that the existing regime of educational finance failed to meet this constitutional provision.[150] Third, courts of appeal in several states concluded that public education was not a fundamental right protected by the state constitution, that local governance of public education inevitably led to interdistrict inequalities in educational revenues and expenditures, and that any remedy for such inequalities had to come from the state legislature rather than the courts. In sum, during the first round of constitutional litigation over educational finance from 1971 to 1988, plaintiffs won at the level of the high court in ten states and lost in ten states.[151]

Beginning in 1989 there was a second round of constitutional litigation, usually relying on the state's constitutional provisions for public education. In these cases, claims focused on 'adequacy' as well as 'equity,' that is, all students in the state are entitled to 'have equitable access to adequate educational opportunities that are reasonably designed to allow them to achieve expected educational outcomes.'[152] In 1989 the Kentucky Supreme Court decided that not just the state's funding program but the entire state educational system failed to satisfy the constitutional requirement to provide for an 'efficient' system of public schools; the Montana court ruled that the constitutional guarantee of 'equality of

educational opportunity' entailed 'essentially equal' educational spending in each school district; and the Texas Supreme Court found the
state's system of educational finance to be in violation of a constitutional
provision that required the state to provide an 'efficient system of public
schools.'[153] In 1993, state courts of appeal in Alabama, Massachusetts,
and New Hampshire directly followed the Kentucky precedent, and state
courts of appeal in Tennessee (1993), Arizona (1994), New York (1995),
and North Carolina (1997) similarly held that their state constitutions
required public provision of an adequate education for all students.[154]
Notwithstanding the greater success of plaintiffs in some states since
1989, supreme courts in other states continued to reject constitutional
challenges to provisions for educational finance. For example, supreme
courts in Maine, Virginia, and Minnesota ruled against claims based on
arguments of fiscal inequity, while leaving open the possibility of claims
based on standards of educational adequacy; and state courts of appeal
in Illinois, Rhode Island, and Florida rejected attempts to involve the
judiciary in assessing educational adequacy, on the grounds this was a
matter for the state legislative assembly. Overall, from 1989 to 2000,
plaintiffs won their cases at the level of the supreme court in eleven states
and lost in sixteen states.[155]

   A notable effort to reform local educational governance in the 1990s
originated from the charter school movement. The prospective founders
of a school, who may comprise parents, teachers, or other non-profit
associations, negotiate a charter with a designated authority – usually the
local school board, state board of education, or state university – that sets
out the school's educational purposes, provisions for governance and
finance, mandated educational outcomes, and mechanisms of accountability. As independent legal entities, charter schools, like private schools,
are exempted from most state and local educational regulations; but
they are public schools 'in the sense that they receive state funding, are
nonsectarian, and are prohibited from being selective in student admission or charging tuition.'[156] Beginning with Minnesota in 1991, by 2000
thirty-six states had passed legislation authorizing the establishment of
charter schools.[157] These laws, however, varied considerably in their
provisions for creating autonomous schools that could challenge conventional modes of educational governance.[158] Overall, in October 1998
rankings by the Center for Education Reform, charter school laws were
rated strong in twenty-two states and weak in eleven states.[159] Prospects
for the charter school movement to make an impact on public educational reform in the United States were also limited both by the (so far)

relatively small number of charter schools – 1,684 in September 1999 out of 85,000 public schools overall – and by the opposition of well-entrenched political adversaries.[160]

Educational Regimes and the Problem of Global Capitalism

The leading features of global capitalism in the late twentieth century were rapid innovation in information technology and intense competition for international trade and investment. The immediate effect of these conditions on the political economies of liberal democracies was reassertion of the importance of the market as a mechanism for social decision making at the expense of state and society. In the resulting rearrangement of sectoral functions, the role of civil society was marginalized, and the role of the state was modified in two ways. First, the expansion of the state in size and scope that had characterized the political economy of the welfare state, if not exactly reversed, at least stalled during the 1980s and 1990s. Equally significant for long-term policy development, the historical assumption of unending state expansion was displaced by a comprehension of contraction. Second, the functions of the state operating under conditions of global capitalism were redirected to concentrate on creating conditions for national competitiveness, economic productivity, and private wealth, including the negotiation of international agreements to facilitate free trade, the protection of rights of private property in international transactions, the subsidization of research and development as the foundation for technological innovation, and the creation of a schooled, skilled, and mobile workforce.

This repositioning of state and market in the political economy of global capitalism inevitably affected public policies for educational provision and governance. First, as a major social service that benefited from the rise of the welfare state, public education suffered proportionately when its expansion was interrupted. Second, the pressures of increasing international competition and incessant technological innovation spurred educational policy makers to redesign school curricula and restructure educational governance. For the first time in the historical development of Anglo-American educational regimes, however, major reforms were being planned and implemented without any major or sustained commitment of greater public resources to facilitate change.

The welfare state featured a major expansion in government spending on social goods and services, including public elementary and secondary education. During the 1970s this growth of government spending on public schools was interrupted in all the Anglo-American educational jurisdictions; in the 1990s it remained stalled. From 1970–1 to 1975–6, government expenditures on public elementary and secondary education as a percentage of gross domestic product reached historically high levels in each of the Anglo-American countries, then stayed relatively constant over the next two decades in Canada (until the late 1990s), New Zealand, and the United States and declined significantly in Australia and the United Kingdom (Figure 1; Table 1). Government expenditures on public elementary and secondary education fell as a percentage of total government expenditures from the mid-1970s to the end of the century in Australia, Canada, and the United Kingdom (Figure 3; Table 3). In the case of New Zealand and also the United States there was a substantial decline in government expenditures on public education as a percentage of total government expenditures from 1975–6 to 1985–6; but over the last fifteen years the share of education has been rising, reaching a historical high in New Zealand in the 1990s, apparently because the contraction of the rest of the public sector was relatively much greater. Similarly, in contrast with the rise in employment of full-time teachers as a percentage of the labour force after the Second World War, the comparative employment of teachers more or less stagnated in four countries from the mid-1970s to the end of the century, while in the case of Canada there was a major contraction in the employment of teachers from 3.2 per cent of the total labour force in 1970–1 to 2 per cent in 1985–6 (Figure 5; Table 6). The rise in employment of teachers as a percentage of total government employment that occurred in Australia, New Zealand, the United Kingdom, and the United States from 1950 to 1975 levelled off in the late 1970s and early 1980s but then showed signs of recovery in the 1990s in Australia, New Zealand, the United Kingdom, and the United States (Figure 6; Table 7). In Canada, by contrast, the employment of full-time teachers fell from 14.8 per cent of total government employment in 1970–1 to 9.8 per cent in 1990–1 and then recovered to 11.3 per cent in 1999–2000.

The impact of this widespread check on aggregate commitment of public resources to the supply of educational services for each person in school was somewhat alleviated by falling enrolments in public schools. As Figure 7 and Table 8 show, the ratio of enrolments to full-time teachers continued to fall until the mid-1980s in Australia and the United Kingdom, and in Canada, New Zealand, and the United States for another five years after that. None the less, international differences in student–teacher ratios were overall a little greater in the 1990s than they were in the 1970s.[161]

Perhaps the most striking evidence of the recent downturn in the fortunes of public schools is the binary pattern in average annual increases in real government expenditures per student (Table 5). From the mid-1970s to the end of the century, there was one period of high average annual increases in New Zealand from 1985–6 to 1990–1 and another from 1995–6 to 1999–2000, but these were preceded by a decade of contraction in real government expenditures per student and then interrupted by low growth from 1990–1 to 1995–6. In other countries, the pattern was less clear-cut but generally similar. Periods of moderate expansion (2 to 5 per cent annually) in Australia (1980–1 to 1985–6, 1995–6 to 2000–1), Canada (1975–6 to 1985–6), the United Kingdom (1985–6 to 1990–1), and the United States (1980–1 to 1990–1, 1995–6 to 2000–1) were accompanied in each case by just as many, if not more, periods of low growth (0 to 2 per cent annually) in Australia (1975–6 to 1980–1, 1985–6 to 1995–6), Canada (1985–6 to 1999–2000), the United Kingdom (1975–6 to 1985–6, 1990–1 to 1999–2000), and the United States (1975–6 to 1980–1, 1990–1 to 1995–6).

Government expenditures per student as a percentage of gross domestic product per capita did continue to increase in Canada and the United States from 1975–6 to 1990–1, remained constant in Australia, declined slightly in the United Kingdom (which had recorded the highest levels in 1975–6), and jumped to the top of the league table in New Zealand during the 1990s after a slump in the 1980s (Figure 2; Table 2). With regard to government expenditures per student as a percentage of total government expenditures per capita, the statistics in Figure 4 and Table 4 show a modest contraction during the 1970s and early 1980s that appears to coincide with declining enrolments, but thereafter public schools were relatively less affected by the fiscal restraint that hit the public sector during the 1980s and 1990s. By the end of the century, in the case of the United States, government spending per student as a percentage of government expenditures per capita had returned to levels higher than at any time since the 1920s, and in New Zealand the historically unprecedented rate of spending per student on public education in the 1990s was yet another measure of the survival of public education in the context of a shrinking public sector.

Along with the general levelling in government resources allocated to public elementary and secondary education, there were substantial differences among countries. In contrast with the expansion of public education as part of the welfare state, however, there was also a convergence in resource allocation as well as a shift in international rankings. International differences in government expenditures on public schools as a percentage of gross domestic product generally narrowed in the 1970s and 1980s. The United States was actually the lowest of the five countries in 1980–1, but in the 1990s a gap reopened between New Zealand, followed by the United States and Canada, versus the United Kingdom and Australia. Similarly, government expenditures on public education as a percentage of total government expenditures in Australia approximated those of Canada and the United States in 1975–6 and 1980–1 but then fell back from 1985–6 to 1999–2000 to levels comparable to those in the United Kingdom, while New Zealand surged to 12.7 per cent in 1999–2000. Historical differences with regard to the employment of teachers as percentages of total labour force and government employment had virtually disappeared by the 1990s among Canada, Australia, and the United Kingdom; and New Zealand, where the trend for teachers as a percentage of the labour force was more or less parallel to that in the United States after the Second World War, during the 1990s also increasingly resembled the United States in its higher percentage of total government employees who were teachers.

Constrained within a relatively stagnant, if not actually contracting, commitment of public resources, policy makers across the Anglo-American educational regimes converged on a remarkably similar agenda for the reform of educational provision and governance. Core subjects, common curriculum, mastery learning, external assessment, and high standards were the dominant ideas that reshaped elementary and secondary education in the Anglo-American educational regimes of the 1980s and 1990s. As for the content of this common education, language arts, mathematics, and natural sciences were taken to constitute the foundation for all learning and hence were designated to be taught as core subjects and skills at all stages of elementary and secondary education. It was further determined that the progress of young people through school should depend on their demonstrated mastery of the basic knowledge and skills that were prescribed for each stage of schooling, and that at regular intervals in the schooling of each person there should be external evaluations to assess both the individual student's progress towards attaining specific educational targets and the success of the educational system in achieving its goal to give each person in school a relevant, high-quality education. As for educational governance, consistent with prevailing theories of the 'new public management,' the functions of policy and administration should be divided respectively between central and local educational authorities. The policy framework of public education involving decisions about overall resource allocation to public education, content of the common or core curriculum, standards of educational achievement, and mechanisms of accountability would be determined by central educational authorities. The function of local management should be variously devolved to school boards, school councils, and school principals and their teaching staff. Out of this convergence on the agenda for educational reform there emerged three types of educational regimes.

The first type of educational regime for the era of global capitalism was based on a prescribed curriculum that covers what are essential outcomes with regard to learning discrete subjects and basic skills, how teachers and learners should work together to achieve the expected outcomes, and what forms of assessment are required in order to verify that standards have been attained. The task of deciding educational purposes and policies was assumed by central political authorities; the routine of implementation was assigned to principals, teachers, and parents working together in self-managing schools. On the one hand, at the centre, the minister of education with the advice of top officials in the ministry of education was assumed to have the superior knowledge and political legitimacy not only to set educational standards that would apply to all students within their educational jurisdiction (and hence to attempt to ensure commonality of outcomes), but also to be accountable to the entire political community for ensuring the successful design and implementation of educational programs. On the other hand, in the schools, principals and teachers interacting with parents and students were expected to translate and apply the prescribed curriculum effectively and efficiently to fit the diverse individual and collective learning situations of their particular clienteles, and hence they were held accountable as the managers of implementation to both the political centre and the school community.

The regimes of this type in which schools are the 'direct agents' of the central authority vary in their emphasis in the prescribed curriculum on discrete subjects versus basic skills. They also vary in the managerial discretion that is devolved on schools. Liberal-conservative governments tend to emphasize competence in traditional subjects and to define the role of principals as administrative agents for central educational authorities. Social-democratic governments tend to emphasize competence in generic skills and to see the relationship with school communities in terms of policy tutelage that implies a potential for building local democratic participation in educational governance.

This 'direct agent' model was most thoroughly realized in New Zealand as a result of the introduction of the national curriculum, the abolition of education boards that historically governed primary schools, and the drafting of charters for all public schools that specified in each case the duties of the school principal and its board of trustees. The Taskforce to Review Education Administration apparently envisaged the appropriate relationship between ministry and school as one of policy tutelage; in practice, the relationship emerged as a contract in which the principal and board were treated as administrative agents for the minister of education, their accountability focused on the Education Review Office rather than on their local community.

This model of direct administrative agency was also found in each of the states and the Northern Territory of Australia, as well as in Hawaii in the United States.[162] In Australia there was convergence of curricular planning, facilitated by the Commonwealth government from 1987 to 1993, and attempts to deconcentrate historically bureaucratic administration from the head offices of state departments of education through refurbished regional or newly created district offices to principals of schools. ALP governments, notably in Victoria and Western Australia, attempted on occasion to promote local participation and to activate school communities as partners in governance, while Liberal and coalition ministries preferred to devolve management to school communities, principals in particular, as the administrative agents for centrally determined policies. Generally, however, the educational regimes of Australia met the challenge of overcoming a century of bureaucratic state administration by mutating into a version of the new public management that privileged generic managerial skills and direction at each level of educational governance.

The second type of educational regime put into place for the era of global capitalism combined the establishment of a centrally determined curriculum covering at least the compulsory years of elementary and secondary schooling with substantial devolution of managerial tasks to school communities. However, schools continued to be organized in districts with boards that functioned as intermediate administrative agents for the political centre. These intermediate educational authorities, in turn, permitted central authorities to deflect and diffuse political controversy arising from the implementation of educational reform, especially where resources were being restricted or reallocated, although local boards might also become advocates for local educational interests against the central authority.

A model of intermediate administrative agency was put in place in England and Wales by the educational reforms of the Conservative governments from 1979 to 1997, but various policies aimed at creating a public market for elementary and secondary education suggest that their ultimate goal might have been displacement of the local education authorities in favour of a direct relationship between the Department for Education and Training and the maintained schools. The establishment of locally managed schools, grant-maintained schools, and the Funding Authority for Schools, along with severe constraints on intervention by local education authorities all point to direct agency as the Conservative government's ideal model of educational governance. By contrast, the Labour government elected in 1997 quickly affirmed its commitment to preserve local education authorities as legitimate intermediate agents and pronounced its commitment to a long-term relationship of policy tutelage in principle while in practice effectively using local education authorities as its intermediate administrative agents.

In Scotland and Northern Ireland the subgovernments of education department, local authorities, and teachers' unions were less developed than was the case in England and Wales, and the desire to create a public educational market that would break the power of organized educational interests was correspondingly weaker. In Scotland, where there was no national curriculum put into law, the Scottish Education Department was able to renew its historical control over the Scottish curriculum, backed by its authority to achieve local accountability through its inspectors. The main differences from England were the absence of any major opposition from education authorities, which historically were subservient to the SED, and a willingness, despite prolonged and fierce conflict, to compromise with the teachers' unions short of dismantling established structures for collective bargaining. The educational regime of Northern Ireland essentially adopted the national curriculum of England and Wales and retained the education and library boards that operated as the intermediate administrative agents of DENI, but the Northern Ireland educational regime also was distinctive in its preservation of selective grammar schools and its bisection between two blocs of denominational schools.

Versions of intermediate administrative agency were also restored in Canada. Historically, except for Quebec and Newfoundland, educational regimes based on school districts as intermediate administrative agents existed in all the provinces and territories. Elementary and secondary curricula were designed by provincial departments of education and implemented by local school boards, which were closely monitored by provincial school inspectors. Having substantially retreated from the role of policy prescription and administrative regulation during the heyday of the welfare state, Canadian provincial governments, starting with the Parti Québécois government's approval of its régime pédagogique in February 1981, reasserted central control over curriculum and finance and amalgamated school districts into larger areas that were thought to be more cost-efficient and certainly more easily manageable from the provincial capital.

A third type of educational regime designed to meet the challenge of global capitalism emerged in the continental United States. Here the process of setting standards for learning outcomes, creating curricular frameworks that would encompass key learning areas and generic skills, and establishing state-wide systems to assess performance spread from state to state during the 1980s and 1990s. State educational reform was facilitated, first, by the federal Goals 2000: Educate America Act, which called for the development of national standards, tests to measure the students' achievement of those standards, and federal aid to states and school districts to raise their standards, and second, by the Improving America's Schools Act, which amended the Elementary and Secondary Education Act to require states to have high content standards in mathematics and language arts as a condition for receiving federal aid. By the end of 1996, nearly every state had written and was beginning to implement clearer academic standards for public elementary and secondary schools.[163]

Despite the evident convergence of state policies to reform public schools, the educational regimes of the continental United States continued to be very fragmented, with multiple sites for taking policy initiatives and correspondingly weak means to control policy development. Presidents George Bush and Bill Clinton, their secretaries of state for education, and senior officials of the Department of Education promoted national standards and tests while eschewing federal control of public schools. State governors sharing their political experiences of educational reform through the National Governors' Association, including the national education summits of 1989 and 1996, were instrumental in putting the development of state standards and performance testing on their various state governmental agendas and keeping it there. Chief executive officers of large corporations – for example, the forty-nine business leaders who attended the summit in March 1996 – were stalwart proponents of standards and testing. Chief state school officers, state boards of education, top officials of state departments of education, state affiliates of the National Education Association and the American Federation of Teachers, and education committees of state legislative assemblies variously coalesced to formulate and implement educational reform. Much state educational reform was characterized by low enforcement and imprecise policy directives, however,[164] and school districts continued to be engaged in substantive policy making, not simply devolved management. State standards and assessment schemes created frameworks to coordinate educational provision, but school boards, local superintendents, school principals, and classroom teachers working with local parent–teacher associations retained substantial discretion to decide what would be taught and how, and how learning would be assessed. The historical pattern of fiscal equivalence in intergovernmental relations with regard to educational policy making was superseded. Global capitalism as a problem for public education in the United States fostered relationships of functional interdependence involving federal, state, and local educational authorities and, hence, much less prescriptive policies for school organization and curricular content.

The perceived problem of technological society and global capitalism refocused the attention of reformers on the relationship of state and market in public education. Because the meanings of both 'state' and 'market' were now fundamentally altered, however, there were new questions about the long-term implications of this change in the political economy of Anglo-American educational regimes. In policy analysis and political rhetoric, the traditional goal of public education for democratic citizenship continued to be officially endorsed. In practice, educational reformers, responding to the dynamic of technological change and economic globalization, generally gave higher priority to the economic role of individual learners as future workers rather than to their political role as future citizens. Common and core curricula that were oriented to the imperatives of global capitalism appeared to threaten inclusive recognition of communal identities and raised concerns about the capacity of contemporary educational regimes not only to respond to the countervailing pressures of localism in the era of the global economy but also to celebrate the social diversity of a pluralist society in their public schools. Under the aegis of the welfare state, especially in educational regimes outside the United States, local educational governance actually began to acquire some of the vitality envisaged for it in normative theories of liberal democracy. Centralizing policy in the era of global capitalism, especially in relation to curriculum and finance, turned local authorities and school councils into instruments of public management rather than agencies of communal self-government. A restructuring of educational policy communities also weakened the participation of school trustees and teachers' unions in policy making, relegating them to a reduced role as policy advocates or even to outright political opposition, while strengthening the participation of organized business. Taken together, these trends across educational regimes signalled a potentially major turn, or perhaps return, in Anglo-American democracy and raised corresponding questions about the meaning and practice of Anglo-American democracy at the end of the twentieth century.

Conclusion: Educational Regimes and Comparative Ideas of Democracy

Who are the people who constitute the community? In what ways are they equal? What freedom do they have to make both private and public choices that accord with their needs and wants? These questions derive from the three basic dimensions of democracy as a form of government based on rule by the people – community, equality, and liberty. When they are removed from abstract political principle and applied to specific educational regimes, they constitute not only the framework for describing both the likeness and the diversity of Anglo-American democracy but also the criteria for making judgments about its extent and quality.

First, the democratic community may be conceived as a uniform public whose membership, at least in political principle if not always in political practice, is not differentiated according to their social attributes of ethnicity, language, race, or religion. Alternatively, a multiform public may be seen as encompassing distinct social blocs that are recognized as legitimate grounds for differentiating or segmenting membership in the democratic community.[1] Whether based on an idea of the public as uniform or as multiform, the democratic community will be inclusive, not exclusive, in its membership, extending more or less to include all inhabitants of the state rather than denying membership to one or more categories of people who reside within its borders.

Second, democracy requires that members of the community have adequate and equal opportunity to discover their true interests and those of others, express their preferences, and participate in making collective decisions. The issue for a democratic community is not a simple requirement for non-stratification rather than stratification, however; there is much room for differences within democracies with regard to which relationships ought to be non-stratified and what constitutes the right meaning of equality in these pivotal relationships. Differences can also arise with regard to defining the subjects of equality. Are they equal individuals, or are they equal social blocs?

Third, liberty involves both freedom from interference with private decisions and freedom to participate in public decisions, but these conditions are not necessarily compatible. Members of a democratic community can be effectively and substantially free to choose an education that fits their own needs and wants. Alternatively, they may choose to be confined by uniformity of provision and governance through a state educational monopoly. Members of the community can have substantial opportunity to participate in making collective decisions on the provision and governance of public education; they may also choose to defer to decisions taken on their behalf by political and educational élites. In each case, difficult judgments with regard to more or less democracy rest on the informed nature, goodness of reasons, and justice of the decisions that have been taken.

Educational Regimes for Public Instruction: Founding Ideas of Community, Equality, and Liberty and the Contradictions of Anglo-American Democracy

Anglo-American societies in the nineteenth century were variously divided by denomination, language, race, and ethnicity. The foundation of elementary schools as public institutions created the huge problem of how to deal with the implacable oppositions and conflicting claims that resulted from these social divisions. In general, there were two strategies that represented essentially different ideas of democratic community. One assumed a uniform public served by common (or 'national') schools that were non-denominational or secular, with English as the language of instruction and ethnic or racial differences assimilated into the majority culture of the community. Schools for dissenters and minorities might be established as private schools, but they would have no public funding. The other envisaged a multiform public that comprised distinct social blocs. Public schools created by the majority social bloc to serve its children were then complemented by the establishment of separate schools for dissenters and minorities as publicly funded institutions, thus incorporating and isolating the main conflicts of denomination, language, and ethnicity or race inside the public educational regime.

The idea of democratic community as a uniform public was the rationale for common public schools in the United States, where regimes of public instruction were founded following the initial phase of representative (partially) democratic government. The common schools were expected to provide a practical basic education that would be appropriate for all children living in the neighbouring community. Initially, common schools in the United States were relatively flexible about the language of instruction, reflecting in many cases majorities in their local communities who spoke Finnish, French, German, Spanish, or Swedish; but unilingual English instruction soon became the norm, along with assimilation of ethnic minorities to the majority culture. In principle, consistent with their underlying idea of a uniform public – an idea that included the constitutional separation of church and state — the common schools were non-denominational. In practice, they were dominated by an overarching Protestant culture that was unacceptable to the Roman Catholic church and many Roman Catholic parents as an environment for the education of their children. Even more incompatible with the principle of the common school and the idea of democratic community as a uniform public was the general segregation of African-American children by law or practice in separate schools. Thus, the common schools of the United States in the nineteenth century were dominated by a hegemonic liberal-conservative idea of community as white, non-denominational Protestant, and English speaking.

Outside the United States, pre-democratic educational regimes generally began with state subsidies to church and voluntary schools. As institutions of representative and responsible government were tentatively introduced and gradually extended in Great Britain and its colonies, the common or national school with a non-denominational or even secular curriculum was established as the basic institution of all educational regimes outside the United States, except for Newfoundland, where the first non-denominational schools were quickly abolished, and also the cities of Montreal and Quebec in Canada East. In contrast to U.S. practice, however, there were also generally provisions for funding separate schools for denominational minorities that implied a residual idea of democratic community as a multiform public.

In the United Kingdom and most provinces of Canada, state provision for separate denominational schools was contested, often energetically and bitterly; ultimately, except for British Columbia and Manitoba, dual educational regimes were sustained. In England and Wales, for example, non-denominational common schools were initially established to fill the gaps left by voluntary provision. The 'board' schools steadily came to predominate by the end of the nineteenth century, but voluntary schools with affiliations to the Church of England and the Roman Catholic church continued to be an important part of the dual educational regime. In Scotland, Gaelic was severely restricted as the language of instruction in favour of English (as Welsh was restricted in Wales), but by 1918, Roman Catholic schools had been incorporated into the public sector as reserved schools. The national schools of Ireland were controlled by Roman Catholic majorities in the south and Protestant majorities in the north, but in both north and south, voluntary schools continued to be eligible for state aid. Similarly, for the most part, common schools in Quebec were controlled by Roman Catholic majorities, and separate schools for the dissenting minority were Protestant. In New Brunswick, Nova Scotia, and Prince Edward Island, there were de facto reserved schools for Roman Catholics in the cities, and school boards operating in Acadian communities were conceded linguistic and denominational autonomy. In Ontario, Saskatchewan, and Alberta there was constitutional protection of separate schools for Roman Catholic or Protestant minorities, restricted to elementary schools in Ontario and Saskatchewan; however, English was established as the official language of instruction in public schools, with French grudgingly recognized, if at all, as a transitional language of instruction in the first years of elementary school.

In British colonies that lacked a durable communitarian-conservative presence, the realignments of their politics following the achievement of responsible government typically set liberal conservatives against utilitarian liberals; however, whatever their other differences on public policy, both parties were united on the idea of a uniform public that was not only expressed, but also constituted, by non-denominational schools. In the colonies of Australia and New Zealand the original dual regimes, which were installed during the first phase of responsible government, were subsequently displaced by non-denominational regimes based on the idea of a uniform public. In British Columbia, isolated on the west coast of British North America from the religious and linguistic wars of the eastern colonies, liberal-conservative ideas about non-denominational common schools and English as the language of instruction prevailed virtually without contest from the outset. In Manitoba, as in Australia and New Zealand, the original regime of denominational and linguistic consociation based on the model of Quebec was overturned in 1890 by the Protestant, anglophone majority in favour of non-denominational and eventually unilingual common schooling. In contrast with the case of British Columbia, however, in Manitoba the legitimacy and justice of the provincial educational regime were persistently contested, enduring for a century as a symbol of majority betrayal and minority grievance.

Whether based on an idea of a uniform or a multiform public, Anglo-American regimes of public instruction did not give equal treatment to minority blocs of denomination and language. In Australia, New Zealand, the United States, British Columbia, and Manitoba the non-denominational or secular content of curricula and organization of schools discriminated against Roman Catholics, whose idea of public education was inseparable from that of education under the authority of their church. Manitoba, where constitutional provision for a dual confessional regime also gave de facto protection to minority education for francophones, was perhaps an especially blatant abrogation of minority educational rights by the Protestant, English-speaking majority. In the United Kingdom, church schools continued to receive public subsidies alongside the non-denominational schools operated by school boards. The terms of state aid fell well short of equality between state and voluntary sectors, however, and especially in England and Wales, voluntary schools experienced a steadily deepening financial crisis in the last quarter of the nineteenth century. Similarly in Canada, less favourable terms of state funding for separate schools in Ontario, Saskatchewan, and Alberta meant that Roman Catholic schools were consistently underfunded compared to public schools, and funding for separate schools was restricted in Ontario and Saskatchewan to elementary grades. In the Maritimes the practices of reserving schools for Roman Catholics and using French as the language of instruction provided de facto a measure of equity, but the tendency for francophone majorities to reside in poor school districts meant that Acadian education was systematically underfunded.

With regard to race, segregated schools for African-American children in the United States were notoriously underfunded before the Civil War. Despite some major efforts to improve educational provision for African-American children during Reconstruction, from the 1880s to the 1920s there was a growing gap in southern states between schools for white children and those for black children, so that the U.S. Supreme Court's bestowal of legitimacy on 'separate but equal' schools had no practical significance for educational provision, even if it could be construed as having democratic legitimacy. In states outside the South, where segregated schools were the practice rather than the law, schools for African-American children operated in poor communities and hence, given the reliance on local property taxation for school revenues, they were miserably underfunded.[2]

A central issue in the establishment of regimes of public instruction was the availability of choice between public and private schools. In England and Wales, school boards were directed by law to be established in areas that were not previously served by church and voluntary schools. The intention appears to have been the creation of complementary sectors of voluntary and public schools in which the gaps in education would be filled, but in particular communities there would be no choice for parents and students between public versus voluntary schools. In practice, the school boards steadily invaded the jurisdictions of voluntary schools, with the result that, by the end of the nineteenth century, the viability of voluntary schools was seriously threatened. Subsequently, from the Education Act, of 1902 to the 1988 Education Reform Act, preservation of voluntary schools alongside public schools became a basic principle and problem of educational policy making. In Scotland, by contrast, the establishment of school boards throughout the country in 1872 was quickly followed by the absorption of virtually all but Roman Catholic voluntary schools into public control. Choice for Scottish families rapidly diminished to one that was available only for Roman Catholic families between public and voluntary schools and, after 1918, whether to attend a reserved Roman Catholic school or not. Similarly, in Ontario, Saskatchewan, and Alberta, separate schools were open to the dissenting denominational minority, usually Roman Catholic but sometimes Protestant, while common schools were open to all children living in the school district. Hence, there was choice only for families whose children were eligible to enrol in separate schools. In Australia, New Zealand, and the United States, the establishment of regimes of public instruction effectively terminated public support for church schools. Denominational schools continued to operate, the majority under the auspices of the Roman Catholic church, but they did so against the design of public policy, which, as in other Anglo-American educational regimes, neither denied the right of educational provision outside the public sector nor did anything to prevent the domination of state schools.

As with provisions for the organization and curricula of schools, the original constitutions of central educational governance and political accountability for regimes of public instruction outside the United States also were consistent with the assumption of a multiform public. The idea of community as comprising two or more denominational blocs was the principle underlying the establishment and preservation of the Commissioners of National Education for Ireland, which divided grants between national schools and church schools, and the Council of Public Instruction in Quebec, which divided provincial grants between common schools and separate schools. Other pertinent examples from the early arrangements for regimes of public instruction include the colonies of New South Wales (1848–80), Victoria (1848–72), Queensland (1860–78), and Western Australia (1871–93); the provinces of Auckland, Canterbury, and Nelson in New Zealand; and Manitoba (1870–90) and the North-West Territories (1884–1901) in Canada. In each case there was an underlying assumption that a central board comprising eminent clerical and lay representatives of denominational blocs would represent the major components of the multiform denominational public and legitimize the distribution of public subsidies among various church schools or between non-denominational schools and church schools.

The initial assignment of central functions of educational governance for England, Scotland, and Wales to an education committee of the Privy Council appears to have been based on a similar logic that the denominational division of a multiform public necessitated some form of collective decision making in which the interests of major social blocs could be assured of representation. Despite the complaints of utilitarian liberals that committee decision making obscured individual responsibility and thus weakened public accountability, the form of collective decision making and joint (lord president and vice-president) ministerial responsibility survived until 1899. Similarly, in New Brunswick, Nova Scotia, and Prince Edward Island, designation of the executive council as the provincial board of education, with the provincial superintendent as its secretary, appears to have been a way to reassure Roman Catholic and francophone minorities that their interests, represented in provincial cabinet, were being taken into account in provincial educational policy making. In British Columbia (1878–91) and the North-West Territories (1892–1901) the executive council, and in Manitoba a committee of cabinet (1890–1908), also headed the central governance of public education during the interregnum between central boards of education and the appointment of ministers of education.

In the United States the adoption of state constitutions that included popularly elected state superintendents of public instruction, which was the form of central political accountability adopted in the majority of states, implied the existence of a uniform public. The state superintendent was elected by a majority of this public and hence was directly and individually accountable for the conduct of the limited educational business at the state level. A form of state political accountability in which the governor or members of the state legislative assembly, who were elected by the people, appointed the state superintendent also corresponded to the idea of democratic community as a uniform public but implied a separation both between politics and educational administration and between politics and educational policy that was not evident in the directly responsible and more democratic office of a popularly elected superintendent.

As a form of central political accountability, individual ministerial responsibility was less democratic than an elected state superintendent but more democratic than one appointed by a governor or state legislature, since ministers of public instruction, although appointed by the prime minister or premier, were themselves elected members of the state or national assembly. In each of the Australian colonies, the establishment of public schools as exclusive beneficiaries of state treasuries and the consequent termination of state aid to church schools was accompanied by the creation of an office of minister of public instruction who was assigned individual responsibility within the cabinet to answer to the legislative assembly on matters of educational policy. In New Zealand there were no national ministers of education prior to 1877, when the provincial education boards controlled primary education; after provincial government was abolished, ministers of education then became politically accountable within the New Zealand cabinet and to the legislature for primary and secondary education.[3]

The idea of community that was expressed in Anglo-American regimes of public instruction had a strong regional component. Whatever was the historical sequence involving the origins of democratic government and the foundations of public instruction, the jurisdictions of educational regimes nowhere coincided with the Anglo-American national state. First, the foundations of regimes of public instruction in the United States followed by half a century the creation of the national republic with its federal constitution; public education remained among the residual powers exercised by the states. Second, at the time of the first Reform Act of 1832, often cited as the birth of British parliamentary democracy, the government of the United Kingdom created separate educational regimes for Great Britain and Ireland, and following the second Reform Act of 1867 and the elementary education acts of 1870 and 1872, the Scottish educational regime acquired separate legal status and progressively became, if not entirely independent, at least certainly distinctive from that for England and Wales. Similarly in New Zealand, the creation of regimes of public instruction coincided with the beginnings of responsible government in 1852, and while not mentioned specifically in the federal constitution, public instruction was taken without question to belong to provincial jurisdiction. Moreover, when a unitary government was instituted in 1877, the education boards were the only major institutions of provincial government to survive. Third, in the colonies of Canada and Australia the founding of educational regimes preceded the federal constitution by a quarter-century in the case of the Dominion of Canada and a half-century in the case of the Commonwealth of Australia. In both federations, education was specifically placed within the jurisdiction of the provinces and states.

Local government was an important feature of Anglo-American regimes for public instruction, but there was no consistent institution of local democracy. The prevalent institution was the school district, the majority of them governed by boards of trustees elected by local ratepayers and comprising from three trustees in rural one-school districts to fifty-five for the London School Board. A significant minority of school boards were appointed by county governments in the southern United States, by municipal councils in seven large cities of the United States, by municipal councils and provincial cabinets in cities and towns of the Maritimes in Canada, and by church authorities in Newfoundland.

Variability in Anglo-American ideas of local democracy is also reflected in the working relationship between central and local educational authorities. In the United States, for the most part, at least outside the South, the relationship was one of fiscal equivalence in which state officials and school boards operated with substantial independence from each other, each in their defined sphere of public decision making. Similarly, the education boards of New Zealand exercised significant, even predominant, authority over educational policy and administration during the first two decades of the national regime. In England and Wales the need for discretion to make substantive local decisions was conceded, but the Education Department, based on its claim to superior knowledge, determined the framework of policy and thus set the guidelines for local decision making. This relationship of policy tutelage between central and local authorities in England and Wales verged on administrative agency in Scotland, where the Scotch Education Department exercised comparatively detailed direction over the activities of Scottish school boards. Extensive regulation by departments of education in Canadian provinces outside Quebec made local school boards essentially administrative agents in the conduct of provincially determined educational policies, while in Australian educational regimes the local school boards collapsed into state bureaucratic administration. In

Newfoundland and Quebec the effective absence of central public authority created situations of communal autonomy for school boards in which policy and administrative tutelage, to the extent this was effected, came from church rather than public authorities.

In sum, based on the policies and practices of educational regimes, Anglo-American democracy in the nineteenth century, displayed no consistent idea of the democratic public – uniform in the United States, Australia, New Zealand, British Columbia, and Manitoba; multiform in the other seven provinces of Canada, Great Britain and Ireland, and Newfoundland – and nowhere was the dominant idea of the democratic public, whether uniform or multiform, uncontested. Anglo-American regimes of public instruction comprised multiple social blocs that were variously stratified on the basis of denomination, language, and race. Their democratic communities were in effect 'vertical mosaics' in which the majority cultural community at the apex constituted the nation, and minorities were subordinated according to a scale that measured their cultural distance from the majority. Except for England and Wales and the separate or reserved schools for Roman Catholics in Scotland and parts of Canada, the foundation of regimes of public instruction effectively created state monopolies that did not facilitate educational choice, either between the public and private sectors or within the public sector. Democratic institutions for central and local educational authorities also varied across educational jurisdictions. At the end of the nineteenth century, chief state school officials were popularly elected in thirty-one of forty-five states and appointed by popularly elected governors in six states, and ministers of education were individually responsible for the political direction of public instruction in England and Wales, Australia, New Zealand, Ontario, and British Columbia. Local democracy was predominant in most parts of the United States, except for the South, as well as New Zealand, but it was substantially guided by central policy authorities in Great Britain and subordinated to administrative efficiency in Canada and Australia.

Educational Regimes for Industrial Efficiency: Anglo-American Democracy and the Counter-claims of Occupational Class Hierarchy

Anglo-American ideas of democratic community were substantially revised in the early twentieth century as educational policy makers became fixated on reforming public schools to serve industrial efficiency. As the consensus formed that secondary schools ought to be expanded and diversified to include both academic education and vocational training, the central issue was framed in terms of common schools within which there would be separate tracks for academic ('professional'), industrial, commercial, and home-making courses versus separate schools that specialized in preparing their students for distinctive occupational class futures. In the United States the dominant idea of democratic community involved undifferentiated membership in a common public institution but none the less continued to exclude African-American children and further disadvantaged Roman Catholic children committed by their beliefs (or at least those of their parents) to parochial high schools that could not afford to mount a vocational track. Outside the United States, at least in educational jurisdictions where the problem of reforming schools in pursuit of industrial efficiency penetrated the governmental agenda, types of public secondary schools were generally differentiated on the basis of occupational class from the turn of the century to the Second World War.

The original scope of public instruction was relatively restricted in all Anglo-American educational jurisdictions, and fees were commonly charged. The first priority of policy development was upward extension of the grades covered by elementary education and elimination of fees. Inevitably, there were differences in the ways in which teachers interacted with individual students in their classrooms – for example, giving special attention to the few who showed promise of winning a scholarship to secondary or normal school; but, whether policy was set by central or local educational authorities, the subject matter was differentiated between grades but was generally the same for students at the same grade level. Hence, for any given grade, the learning experiences of persons in school were largely interchangeable. Around the turn of the century, this individual, lot-regarding equality of elementary public instruction changed as, first, secondary education was incorporated as an extension of public instruction for those who passed the qualifying examinations and, second, secondary education was differentiated into academic, commercial, industrial, and domestic schools or tracks. Taking advantage of the upward extension of the scope of public instruction was made conditional on the demonstrated academic merit of children in the basic elementary grades, a liberal-conservative concept of inequalities between ranks of students differentiated by their levels of achievement. The horizontal diversification in the content of public education imported inequalities of occupational classes, roughly in the order of academic, commercial, and industrial arts (boys) or domestic arts (girls). Thus, on top of the vertical mosaic of social blocs based on religion, language, and race, there was added a differentiation of educational programs that corresponded to the hierarchy of occupational classes. In partite systems of secondary schools, or multilateral high schools, where entrance to courses was selective, determined by achievement in public examinations, the educational lots of students were no longer interchangeable. Even in the multilateral high schools of the United States, where students and their parents might have some involvement in the choice of educational track, the subsequent learning experiences of students in different courses were substantially unequal, reflecting the occupational class hierarchy of an industrial society.

Inequalities of rank corresponding to the occupational classes of industrial society and hence educational lots that were no longer interchangeable were justified by selection based on either demonstrated merit or individual choice. The unfairness of selection based on demonstrated merit arose in part from the arbitrary limits on places available in the most prized, first academic and next commercial, courses of study; generally, there were more students qualified than there were places. The unfairness of selection based on individual choice arose, in part, from the inadequate supply of information available to students and parents from the working classes to assess the implications of their choices with regard to their occupational futures. In addition, assuming that subsequent changes of school or track were very difficult if not impossible to make, selection by academic merit and by individual choice both suffered from the inappropriate sorting of students whose abilities and interests were still maturing and therefore potentially changing. In short, the occupational class hierarchy of educational regimes for industrial efficiency resulted in inadequate and unequal opportunities for students and their parents to choose the scope and content of their secondary education. The reform of educational regimes for the purpose of industrial efficiency was pursued largely at the expense of distributive justice.

Not only democratic equality and community were negatively affected; so was liberty. The reorganization of secondary education in the form of partite systems or multilateral schools created a potential for choice among academic, vocational, and general programs. Designing courses of study that corresponded to the occupational class futures of students created incentives to remain in school, but in most Anglo-American educational regimes the availability of choice was severely restricted by the existence of competitive selection procedures. In England and Wales,

New Zealand, and Australia, entry to grammar schools and technical schools was not simply a matter of meeting an established qualifying standard for entry. Places were limited, and there were more applicants than there were places. Similarly, in Scotland and Northern Ireland, where technical high schools were generally undeveloped, competitive examinations at the end of elementary school determined who would be eligible for secondary schools, who would have the option to enrol in junior secondary or intermediate schools, and who would be heading for the workforce. In Canada, entry to academic versus commercial or vocational high schools generally was not competitive and selective. Similarly, in multilateral high schools in the United States, students and parents could choose their preferred educational track. In practice, however, standardized tests and teachers' evaluations, as well as elementary school-leaving examinations, were widely used to allocate students to schools or courses; and only if parents objected, usually because their children had been denied entry to the academic high school or college-bound courses, were students reassigned. Thus, the exercise of parental freedom to choose their children's educational program was severely constrained by public policy in the form of standard operating procedures devised by school districts. If one condition for democratic liberty in parental decision making about the scope and content of their children's educational provision was adequate and equal opportunity to discover and validate the choice that would best serve their children's interests, then freedom to participate was strictly limited in both Canada and the United States.

From the turn of the century to the Second World War, Anglo-American democracy was significantly affected by four types of reform with regard to educational governance. None was general in its implications for prevailing ideas of community and equality, which remained more or less unchanged from regimes of public instruction, but each constituted a major challenge to the idea of liberty. In effect, except for the educational regimes of Newfoundland, Northern Ireland, and Quebec, where industrial efficiency was not much of a factor and denominational regimes remained substantially intact, there were counter-claims to democracy as a principle of educational governance that posed the threat of international competition to national wealth and security and hence justified putting restrictions on the democratic institutions and practices inherited from regimes of public instruction. The imperative of industrial efficiency was also advanced as the justification for creating new hierarchies of participation in educational policy making.

First, educational reform for industrial efficiency was seen to require a redefinition of educational policy as a public function that involved both politics and administration but that required the functions of politics and administration to be kept clearly separated. Ministerial responsibility on the part of elected politicians remained a central constitutional convention, but top administrative officials who were appointed on the basis of merit were regarded as possessing professional and technical knowledge and skills that were indispensable for making good public policies. This theory of executive policy making, in which politicians elected by the people were joined in the process of policy making with bureaucrats appointed for their merit, was advocated by Progressive reformers in the United States at the turn of the century; and while the majority of states retained popular election of the state superintendent, the Progressive model was adopted in the form of provisions for governors to appoint state boards of education, which then appointed the state superintendent (seven states from 1900 to 1940) or, alternatively, for governors to appoint both the state board of education and the state superintendent (eight states from 1900 to 1940). In the educational jurisdictions of Australia, Canada (except for Quebec), and New Zealand, ministers of education exercised formal public accountability and ultimate political direction; however, appointed directors and deputy ministers of education and their assistant directors and assistant deputy ministers for primary, secondary, and technical education were essential partners in policy making, and dominated implementation. In the United Kingdom there was a similar merger of politics (president of the Board of Education, secretary of state for Scotland, minister of education for Northern Ireland) and administration (secretaries of the Board, Scottish Education Department, and Northern Ireland Ministry of Education) in educational policy making. The result of joining politicians and administrators in policy making at the centres of educational regimes was probably more effective and efficient educational policy. The greater distance between educational bureaucracies and partisan politics also reduced public accountability, however, and hence diminished popular freedom to participate in central educational decision making.

Second, educational reform in pursuit of industrial efficiency was accompanied by an expansion and rationalization of educational bureaucracies. Except for Quebec and Newfoundland, there was a general trend in the educational regimes of Australia, Canada, New Zealand, and the United Kingdom to enlarge central departments of education, develop specialized divisions of labour with regard to policy and administration, and solidify their dominance as the core of subgovernments in emerging educational policy communities. In the United States, by contrast, the development of educational bureaucracies and the commitment to scientific management were greater in city school districts than in state departments of education, and the persistence of elected state superintendents as well as the constitutional and practical sharing of politics and policy as public functions between governors and state legislators inhibited any clean realignment of public functions, even in those states that adopted some version of Progressive reforms of educational governance.

Third, elected school boards in Canada and New Zealand were settled in the status of administrative agents of central departments of education; in the states of Australia, they were eliminated completely in favour of state bureaucratic administration. In England and Wales, school boards were abolished in the 1902 Education Act and replaced by education committees of municipal authorities, and parallel reforms of local educational governance were instituted in Northern Ireland in 1923 and Scotland in 1929. In Northern Ireland and Scotland, central authorities exercised detailed direction over the activities of local education committees, comparable to the relationships of administrative agency that prevailed in Canada and New Zealand. While there was less detailed direction of policy and administration by central educational authorities in England and Wales, the effect of the 1902 act was similar to the trend to administrative agency and bureaucratic administration in other Anglo-American educational regimes outside the United States: the goal to increase the effectiveness and efficiency of educational provision at the local level was accomplished by reducing the opportunity for direct public participation in local educational policy.

Fourth, as counterparts to the expansion and rationalization of central educational bureaucracies, classroom teachers and school trustees created state, provincial, and national organizations to represent their interests to central educational authorities and stake a claim to participate in central educational policy making. The legitimacy of teachers' unions and trustees' associations as advocates for professional and local interests inside educational policy communities was generally conceded, but – with the important exception of New Zealand – the idea of freedom to participate in educational policy making did not expand to include a place for collective involvement by teachers and trustees, let alone parents.

In sum, the pursuit of industrial efficiency in educational reform from the turn of the century to the Second World War signalled a retreat, or at best stagnation, in the development of Anglo-American democracy. The scope of public education was redefined to include secondary schooling, although the expansion of secondary enrolments and resource alloca- tion was not immediately impressive. The stratification of social blocs on the basis of religion, language, and race that was the major legacy of regimes for public instruction was left unchanged, and another hierar- chy based on occupational class was added. Reform of educational gov- ernance in Australia, Canada, New Zealand, and the United Kingdom in pursuit of industrial efficiency generally strengthened central executive policy making and central educational bureaucracies and weakened or abolished the role of local educational governance. In the educational regimes of the United States, the development of executive policy mak- ing and the bureaucratization of state departments of education was much more variable, and the spread of managerial models of educa- tional decision making at local levels was undermined by the persistent survival of small school districts that offered local participation at the expense of governmental capacity.

In the end, ideas of democratic community were not more consistent or legitimate on the eve of the Second World War than they had been at the beginning of the century. An anti-democratic idea of educational ranks based on inadequate tests of merit, had been substituted for the simple equality of educational lots. The potential for educational choice had been increased with the expansion and diversification of secondary education; in practice, however, choice was severely constrained by the hierarchical structure of educational programs and the inadequate and unequal access of parents to educational information and advice. Free- dom to participate in educational governance had been significantly restricted in Australia, Canada, New Zealand, and the United Kingdom, and to a lesser extent by the implementation of Progressive theories in the United States in several northeastern states and big cities. More generally in the United States, however, the politics of separated powers and fiscal equivalence frustrated the restrictions on democratic partici- pation that occurred in other Anglo-American educational jurisdictions.

Educational Regimes in the Welfare State: Anglo-American Democracy and the Reformed Agenda of Democratic Community and Equality

After the Second World War, as public education was reconstructed in the context of the emerging welfare state, 'secondary education for all' was the slogan that expressed the political commitment to extend the principle of universality from elementary school to secondary school. Secondary education for all did not mean that educational lots in secondary schools were becoming more alike and interchangeable, nor even that they would be equal in value on the basis of different individual needs. Nor did it mean that individual liberty to choose among the educational programs being offered in secondary schools was suddenly extended. Secondary education for all did signify, however, that a new idea of democratic community was invading Anglo-American educational regimes with an effect comparable to that of the revolution in public philosophy that had led to the founding of regimes for public instruction more than a century earlier. No longer merely a condition for economic productivity and international competitiveness, secondary education had been joined with elementary education as a requisite for democratic citizenship.

Commitment to the idea of democratic community as entailing universal secondary education implied a greater commitment of public resources. Government expenditures on public elementary and secondary education grew after the Second World War relative to both gross domestic product and total government expenditures, and government expenditures on public education per student increased as a percentage of both gross domestic product per capita and total government expenditures per capita. Average annual increases in real government expenditures per student were relatively high in the late 1940s (except perhaps for Canada) and again in the early 1960s; otherwise, probably because of cross-national variations in the politics of educational expansion, there was not much consistency and no obvious pattern to expenditure increases.[4] Despite the larger scale of educational provision, the structure of public education was slow to show the effects of universal secondary education until two decades after the war, when a combination of demographic expansion and higher participation hit the upper secondary years and percentages of enrolments in senior secondary schools began significantly to exceed those reached in the mid-1930s.

Multilateral secondary schools were the defining public institution in the educational regimes of the welfare state. This form of secondary education incorporated an idea of democratic community that gave students a common identity as members of the same educational community, joined together in a range of social activities and sharing important learning experiences, while at the same time pursuing their individual occupational futures. Thus, multilateral schools sought to reconcile and legitimize class hierarchy and democratic citizenship. Advocated in 1918 by the National Education Association Commission on the Reorganization of Secondary Education, multilateral high schools with separate academic, commercial, industrial, and general tracks were easily the predominant institutions of secondary education in the United States by the 1930s, and the 'four-track system' was virtually universal in American high schools by the 1950s. During the 1950s, multilateral high schools were also adopted as the preferred form of secondary education in Australia, Canada, and New Zealand. Despite major experiments by key local authorities, notably the London County Council, the idea of democratic community as formed on the basis of a common civic membership was not seriously addressed in British educational policy making until two decades after the war, when the Labour party returned to power. Then multilateral (or bilateral) schools rapidly emerged as the dominant type of public secondary education in Scotland and Wales while more slowly, but none the less steadily, proceeding to conquer the public sector in England. The only exception to the adoption of multilateral secondary education, with its inherent idea of common institutional membership married to separate occupational destinies, was Northern Ireland.

Multilateral secondary schools sought to reconcile class inequalities rather than remove them. Inequalities of educational lots that resulted from students' pursuit of different courses of study in multilateral high schools were justified on the grounds that students and parents, although guided by the advice of teachers, ultimately had the power to choose their vocational track. This was generally the situation faced by students who were attending high schools in the United States. Multilateral high schools in Australia and Canada followed this utilitarian-liberal model in gradually leaving the choice of educational track to individual students and their parents, facilitated in the case of Australia by the relatively high proportion of non-Roman Catholic students who left the public sector at the end of elementary school and pursued an academic secondary education through independent schools. Alternatively, inequalities of educational lots in multilateral high schools were justified on the grounds that students qualified for places in academic or technical as opposed to general courses by demonstrating their merit in external and/or internal assessments. In the transition from partite systems to multilateral secondary schools, this liberal-conservative principle of selection on the basis of merit was retained in New Zealand and Great Britain.

By the 1960s, both the liberal-conservative justification for inequalities among educational lots based on academic merit and the utilitarian-liberal justification for inequalities of educational lots based on free choice among tracks by students and their parents were being displaced by an ethical-liberal idea of person-regarding equality. According to this educational ideology, programs should be designed to meet the individual needs of each person in school. Students were not given a uniform or identical education; hence, their educational lots were not interchangeable. Rather they followed different educational programs depending on their own needs and talents. Hence, in principle, although the educational programs of individual students were not gener ally interchangeable, all students would get equal value from their different educational careers. Multiple tracks had been justified on such grounds in the past as providing courses of study to meet the educational and vocational preferences of students, but three or four categories of educational programs hardly began to do justice to the diversity of individual needs. A more equitable arrangement for school organization and curricular content would be found in truly comprehensive high schools in which students had individual timetables, subjects were offered at two, three, or even four levels of difficulty, and students proceeded to more advanced courses within each subject on the basis of their achievement in that subject rather than having their promotion depend on passing a group of subjects.

The force of this ethical-liberal idea of person-regarding equality in Anglo-American democracy lay behind the adoption of the comprehensive form of secondary schools. As a plan for organizing secondary schools, comprehensive high schools were recommended by James Conant in his major study of the American high school, the report of the committee to survey secondary education in New South Wales chaired by H.S. Wyndham, the report of the Provincial Committee on the Aims and Objectives of Education in Ontario chaired by Mr Justice Emmett Hall and Lloyd Dennis, and the report of the consultative committee on restructuring secondary education in Scotland chaired by James Munn. Policies based on this form of secondary school organization were variously adopted in educational jurisdictions in the United States and Canada as well as Australia and Scotland as an alternative to multilateral secondary schools, with their three or four curricular tracks aimed at different occupational futures.

The creation of comprehensive high schools was intended to create more freedom for students to choose individual educational programs that matched their individual needs or ends. In principle, students were free to choose not only the subjects they would study, restricted only by a few core subjects that might be prescribed as graduation requirements, but also the level of difficulty at which they would work, subject to meeting the prerequisites for advanced courses. In practice, however, whether because of the practical demands of dealing with mixed-ability classes, ideological commitment to academic distinctions based on merit, or parental and political pressures for preserving some form of competitive selection, teaching subjects at different levels of ability generally regressed into an alternative method of academic ranking.

Central educational governance was not generally affected by the postwar development of the welfare state. Departments of education grew larger, but the model of executive policy making, which combined political accountability on the part of an elected minister of education with professional direction on the part of appointed deputy ministers and directors backed by a formidable array of specialized officials, continued to prevail outside the United States. Indeed, the denominational regimes of Newfoundland (1948) and Quebec (1964) completed the adoption of the institutions of executive policy making by appointing ministers of provincial cabinet who were responsible for public education and by restructuring departments of education, changes that strengthened the provincial government's role in educational policy making, refocused political accountability for public education in provincial politics, and put issues of public education directly on the provincial governmental agenda.

One major innovation in central educational governance did occur in the United States, where a new model of political accountability was introduced with the popular election of state boards of education. This model sought to achieve a more democratic solution to the conundrum of separating politics and policy from administration than had the Progressive model, under which state boards of education were appointed by governors. An elected state board of education appeared to meet a major criticism of the Progressive model that for governors education was only one of several policy domains and, hence, that their responsibility was diffuse and ambiguous. An elected state board of education that would appoint the state superintendent also seemed to make better provision for professional administrative leadership and policy advice than was likely to occur under the original utilitarian-liberal model of a popularly elected state superintendent whose office almost inevitably failed to separate properly the political functions of democratic politics and policy from the professional expertise required for effective and efficient policy and administration. By the 1960s, taken together, states following either the Progressive model of appointed state boards and appointed state superintendents or the revisionist model of elected state boards and appointed state superintendents outnumbered states retaining elected state superintendents, the model that had prevailed since the origins of public instruction.

The expansion of social services, including public education, in the welfare state resulted not only in the enlargement of public bureaucracies but also in the amalgamation of municipal governments. Delivery of social services in the welfare state was facilitated by the amalgamation of small local authorities in order to create governmental units with the capacity to exercise appropriate discretion in adapting central policy decisions to local conditions and then implementing them effectively and efficiently. In Great Britain the Education Acts of 1944 and 1946 eliminated minor local education authorities, leaving only LEAs based on counties and county boroughs. In Canada and the United States, amalgamation of school districts from the Second World War to the early 1970s was a major feature of educational reform. In New Zealand, education boards were given more discretion over the conduct of their local responsibilities, and regional offices were established in New South Wales, Queensland, South Australia, and Victoria for the purpose of deconcentrating state bureaucratic administration. The overall effect was a significant strengthening of local educational governments in Anglo-American educational regimes, a consequence that substantially expanded the capacity of local authorities to share policy making with central authorities in relationships of functional interdependence. The creation of larger school districts, which increased local capacity for policy and administration, also increased the distance between citizens and local authorities, but this higher barrier to direct participation by citizens was potentially offset by the effective increase in points of entry for citizen participation in making educational policy. Access to local authorities became more difficult, but once access was gained, the opportunity to make a difference to educational policy was improved.

Under the aegis of the welfare state, teachers' unions and associations of local authorities, which had been generally restricted to making representations to central educational authorities, were gradually incorporated as participants into the process of policy making. Collective bargaining with regard to teacher's salaries and working conditions was widely institutionalized. Channels of policy advice were established from provincial, state, and national organizations of teachers and local authorities to processes of agenda setting and policy formulation. Other organized interests, especially those of parents and churches, also won recognition, but subgovernments of educational policy communities were generally centred on partnerships of departments of education, teachers' unions, and associations of local authorities. The increasing complexity and interdependence of educational policy communities made it more difficult for citizens to attribute political accountability; none the less, the result was diversification of the bases of representation and participation in policy and, hence, overall extension of freedom of participation for organized interests. As educational policy communities solidified, however, the condition for participation increasingly became inseparable from the capacity for political organization.

The impact of the welfare state on the development of Anglo-American democracy has been a major theme of postwar politics. The commitment of educational regimes to the principle of universality in provision of public secondary education was generally accompanied by an expansion of public resources that created sufficient places in schools to accommodate both the larger numbers of students required to stay in school because of raising the age of compulsory schooling and the larger numbers choosing to remain in school voluntarily past the school-leaving age. In contrast with the nineteenth-century commitment to universality with regard to public instruction, however, universality with regard to secondary education in the mid-twentieth century did not mean equalization of educational lots. The partite systems that were preserved after the war in the United Kingdom obviously reproduced the occupational class inequalities of industrial society, but so also did the multilateral high schools that were developed in other Anglo-American educational regimes, even as they strove to create a common civic identity. Compared with the impact of the welfare state on the development of other social services, notably health and welfare, the postwar expansion of public education was relatively modest.

More importantly, the ideas of democracy that were reflected in Anglo-American educational regimes were surprisingly traditional; changes in educational regimes with regard to ideas of democracy were decidedly incremental rather than transformative. In particular, the innovative idea of person-regarding equality had only a limited influence on the curricula of secondary schools, however influential it may have been in the design of child-centred primary schools. Nor did the adoption of a reformed idea of democratic community, in an attempt to reconcile the norms of uniform public with the realities of occupational hierarchy, immediately affect the legacies of historical conflicts over the suppression, integration, or consociation of social blocs in Anglo-American educational regimes. Historical commitments to the ideas of uniform public versus multiform public did not change, and educational reforms inspired by the development of the welfare state replayed the conflicts of the nineteenth-century foundations of public instruction with nearly the same passions and essentially similar results.

Educational Regimes for Pluralist Society: Transforming the Anglo-American Idea of Democratic Community

In contrast with the limited innovation in the ideas of democracy reflected in the educational regimes of the welfare state after the Second World War, the universal concern for the problem of public education in a pluralist society did transform Anglo-American ideas of democratic community. From the 1960s to the 1980s, three essentially different ideas of democratic community in a pluralist society were incorporated in the educational policies of Anglo-American regimes. One was the classic utilitarian-liberal formula that, to preserve untarnished the sacred principle of a uniform public under conditions of social diversity, the state in a democratic community as much as possible ought to be neutral among competing visions of the good life. A second approach conceded that the realities of social diversity made the classic liberal assumption of a uniform public no longer tenable, if historically it ever really had been, and held that the policies and practices of educational regimes should be adapted as much as possible to encompass the social diversity of the democratic community. This approach envisaged the conversion of the traditional common school from a place of cultural uniformity into a multicultural public institution. Third, a communitarian approach based on an idea of a multiform public adopted policies of separate schools and communal self-governance to create educational regimes that would be consociations of denominational, linguistic, or racial and ethnic communities. These approaches were not mutually exclusive. Indeed, the communitarian approach quite explicitly assumed that only certain cultural groups were sufficiently consequential to qualify for a consociational settlement; others would be treated with tolerant neutrality or encompassed by multicultural integration.

In the United States the problem of pluralist society was met with policies that sought culturally to neutralize educational regimes. For liberals who advocated this approach, the primary task of democratic education was finding ways to create and produce a public comprising citizens who shared the common values necessary to sustain their liberal-democratic state while protecting and respecting the autonomy of each individual. The liberal-democratic state could be neutral about teaching its future citizens the political culture of democracy as the foundation for the good society. In a democratic, pluralist society, citizens must embrace values such as tolerance and respect for others that make social diversity and individual autonomy possible. Primacy must be given to individual rights and choice, and no particular communal traditions can be incorporated in public institutions or supported by public policies without infringing on the individual rights of those who belong to other communal traditions. A liberal state ought to be a neutral state, 'that is, a state without cultural or religious projects or, indeed, any sort of collective goals beyond the personal freedom and the physical security, welfare, and safety of its citizens.'[5]

In their nineteenth-century foundations, educational regimes for public instruction had blatantly violated the principles of neutrality and tolerance. They were not only English speaking, but also white and Protestant. From the 1960s to the 1990s, educational regimes of the United States struggled to achieve neutrality and tolerance as the conditions for integration with regard to race, religion, and language. Racial segregation of schools in law and practice historically was the most cruel denial of democratic community, starkly inconsistent with the founding principles of individual rights, equality under the law, and common public schools as the nurseries of democratic citizenship. The decision of the U.S. Supreme Court in *Brown* v. *Board of Education of Topeka, Kansas* initiated an intensely conflictual process of dismantling segregated and unequal schools for African-American children and bringing all children together in racially integrated schools. An idea of democratic community as racially neutral was obviously the motivation for dismantling legally segregated schools as well as such racially discriminatory policies and practices as rigged school attendance zones and site selection, and this was also the idea that inspired forced busing and magnet schools. The creation of neutral schools with regard to Bible reading and school prayers was the issue beginning with *Engel* v. *Vitale* (1962) and *School District of Abingdon Township* v. *Schempp* (1963), and by its strict interpretation of the Establishment Clause, the U.S. Supreme Court established that not simply the favourable treatment of one church over another but any official expression of religious belief violated the constitutional requirement for religious neutrality in state education. Despite the hopes of Hispanic minorities to achieve bilingual education as a means to protect and develop the dual cultural heritage of their children, the Bilingual Education Act (1968) was conceived and developed as primarily compensatory and transitional, intended to facilitate the assimilation of minority-language students whose learning problems and low achievement resulted from their limited proficiency in English.

An approach to dealing with the problem of pluralist society by attempting to reform educational regimes to reflect or represent the realities of social diversity can be seen in Australian policies of state aid to independent schools and child migrant education. The restoration of state aid to private schools by the Commonwealth and state governments in the 1960s was motivated in part by competitive party politics, pressures of rising costs on Roman Catholic schools, and concern to preserve freedom of choice for parents; however, the rationale advanced by the Interim Committee in May 1973 for a quantum leap in the program of state aid was the importance of protecting and developing the social diversity of Australian society through support for the diversity already represented in the existence of non-government schools. The Australian Child Migrant Education Program originated in 1971 in the Department of Immigration as a vehicle for providing transitional instruction in English as a second language; five years later, when control was transferred to the Australian Schools Commission, the program was transformed into a general program of multicultural education in all primary and secondary schools, aimed not simply at migrant children whose language spoken at home was not English but targeted at all Australian children.

A similar plan to turn public schools into multicultural institutions can be seen in British policies of religious education and racial and ethnic integration. In England and Wales, from the 1960s to the 1980s, the same commitment to having school curricula reflect the realities of contemporary social diversity motivated the revamping of religious instruction narrowly conceived in the Christian tradition into sympathetic yet critical education that took into account the plurality of religious beliefs in contemporary Britain. The recommendations of the Millar committee on moral and religious education in Scottish schools in 1972 launched a parallel reform that resulted in world religions being given a meaningful place in the five-to-fourteen curriculum and a shift in focus from fostering Christian belief to engaging students with general moral and religious principles and problems. The initial approaches to dealing

with the problems of racial and ethnic minorities in English schools – the
dispersal of immigrant children under the Labour government and the
classification of immigrant children under programs to deal with educational disadvantage by the Conservative government – appeared to derive from assimilation into the majority culture, but the commitment of
the Inner London Education Authority to multi-ethnic education in
1977, followed by the work of the Committee of Inquiry into the Education of Children from Ethnic Minority Groups, chaired first by Anthony
Rampton and later by Lord Swann, produced a concept of multicultural
education as a public good appropriate to the cultural diversity of contemporary Britain.

In the case of both Australian and British policies, there was an
underlying assumption that a pluralist society is a public good because it
expands individual understanding of potential avenues for human growth
and development. In the context of deliberation by individuals about the
good life for them, the social diversity of a pluralist society is a public
good because it offers exemplars of different ways to live the good life,
engages people living different lives in constructive dialogue with each
other, and ensures that individuals have real options from which to
choose their cultural home. Rather than attempting to neutralize educational regimes, therefore, state intervention may be justified as a means
not only to sustain and foster the social diversity of pluralist society but
also to ensure that public education does represent and legitimate that
social diversity.

Communitarianism, which has both conservative and socialist versions, constitutes a third way of understanding pluralist societies.[6] Given
their majority, even in a pluralistic society, communitarian conservatives
tend to be exclusionary in ascribing the language, ethnicity, race, and
religion of the people who constitute their nation. They identify state
and nation, put priority on assimilating minorities into the national
culture, and employ state schools as socializing agencies. When they are
forced by political necessity to seek reconciliation between majority and
minority in a multinational state, however, communitarian conservatives
may opt to negotiate a confederation or a consociation within which
traditional communal identities can be reproduced and perpetuated.[7]
By contrast, the radical-communitarian or democratic-socialist idea of
pluralist society envisages an egalitarian society comprising multiple
cultural communities that are endowed with collective rights. According
to this ideological perspective, a democratic society can be organized
around a definition of the good life defined in terms of a particular

communal tradition without this being seen as a depreciation of those who do not personally share this definition.[8] On the one hand, a democratic state can have strong collective goals, provided it is also capable of respecting diversity, especially when dealing with those who do not share its common goals and provided it has adequate safeguards for fundamental rights. On the other hand, a democratic state can be organized to protect and promote a selected set of minority communal traditions without this structure being taken as depreciation of those not included. In both cases, democratic socialists argue, the protection of communal groups is grounded on collective right, but collective right, in turn, is the result of public deliberation and democratic determination about the collective good.

Both communitarian-conservative and radical-communitarian ideas are represented in minority-language educational policies of Canada and New Zealand, as well as in provisions for denominational education. Section 23 of the Canadian Charter of Rights and Freedoms established collective rights to minority-language education for both francophones and anglophones, and the Supreme Court of Canada subsequently ruled that this general right to minority-language education under the Charter included, where numbers warrant, the right of minority educational self-governance. All Canadian provinces outside Quebec now provide for schools that have French as their language of instruction and are governed by francophone district or provincial school boards. While language became the crucial dimension of duality in Canadian educational regimes, historical provisions for de facto reserved Roman Catholic schools gradually disappeared in the Maritimes, and in a much more controversial development, the constitutional protection of denominational public education in Newfoundland was ended in favour of non-denominational common schools (with provision for religious education and observances). In the province of Quebec, also by constitutional amendment after three decades of debate, the dual confessional regime established for purposes of public instruction in the 1840s was converted into a linguistic consociation of francophone and anglophone school commissions. In New Zealand, policies first to assimilate and then to integrate Maori children began to be modified during the 1970s, and Maori-medium schools were initiated during the 1980s and expanded rapidly during the 1990s, in order to give Maori children an education that is bilingual and bicultural but founded on immersion in Maori language and culture. The 1975 Private Schools Conditional Integration Act offered generous terms for the incorporation of Roman Catholic primary and secondary schools into the public sector, thus creating a dual educational regime in New Zealand that abandoned the historical idea of a uniform public for that of a multiform public as in the separate school regimes of Ontario, Saskatchewan, and Alberta or the voluntary school sectors of England and Wales.

Changing ideas of democratic community in a pluralist society affected ideas of equality and liberty. The most powerful defence of equality in educational provision was probably advanced in Australia by the Interim Committee's recommendation to classify private schools into categories of need and to scale federal aid according to need. Subsequently, the principle underlying the distribution of aid to private schools became the subject of intense political conflict between the Labor party, committed to improving equality based on measures of need but unwilling politically to abandon basic levels of aid to wealthy schools, and the Liberal-National coalition, committed to facilitating choice for parents by expanding aid across the board to the private sector without being willing to abandon entirely some concessions to differences in need. Similarly, the New Zealand government's grant to private schools for teachers' salaries, initiated by the National government in 1969 and then increased from 35 to 50 per cent by the Labour government in the 1970s, was reduced to zero by the Labour government in 1990 only to be restored to 20 per cent by the National government in 1991. In Canada the programs of provincial aid to private schools in Quebec and the West, as well as the new tax credit for private-school tuition in Ontario, were promoted as ways to increase the freedom of parents to choose a religious education for their children. In the United States, substantial federal aid was distributed to private schools for libraries, textbooks, and instructional materials, based on the individual-benefit principle, and the U.S. Supreme Court applied the same principle in its decisions in *Wolman* (1977) and *Mueller* (1983) to uphold state programs that delivered limited aid to children in parochial schools. In the United States, however, substantial direct federal and state aid to private schools in future appears to depend on the development of voucher programs that rest clearly on the idea of facilitating parental freedom to choose between public and private schools for the education of their children.

As the problem of pluralist society gripped policy makers in Anglo-American educational regimes from the 1960s to the 1980s, ideas of democratic community were substantially reworked in educational policies and practices from those that were embedded in nineteenth-century regimes of public instruction, but still there was no consistent idea of democratic community. Utilitarian-liberal ideas of a neutral state and a uniform public, ethical-liberal ideas of multicultural education to encompass social diversity, and communitarian-conservative and democratic-socialist ideas that institutionalized collective rights of selected communal groups found various expressions in the transformation of educational regimes. Nor were these ideas anywhere uncontested. In the United States, political battles were fought to restore majority Christian religious observances to public schools, rulings by the U.S. Supreme Court set legal standards for allowing school districts to revert to neighbourhood attendance zones even if schools might become segregated as a result, and bilingual education programs were terminated in California and Arizona following state referenda. In Australia the Multicultural Education Program was terminated by the ALP government in 1986 in favour of the National Policy on Languages, which gave priority to the economic utility of languages rather than the formation of cultural identities. In England and Wales the Education Reform Act directed that collective worship in county schools be 'mainly or wholly of a broadly Christian character' and that the syllabus for religious education should reflect the predominance of Christianity in the religious traditions of Great Britain. Similarly, multicultural education as recommended by the Swann committee in 1985 was downgraded in the construction of the national curriculum introduced in 1988. Perhaps most tragically, the idea of democratic community in Northern Ireland remained frustratingly locked into the historical dual confessional regime that coincided with the apparently impervious divide between loyalists and republicans.

Educational Regimes and Global Capitalism: Anglo-American Liberty as Freedom from Interference versus the Counter-claim of Education for National Prosperity

Educational reforms in the late twentieth century were motivated by the belief that individual advancement and collective prosperity were directly dependent on the general achievement of high educational standards. Common curricula for the compulsory years of schooling from kindergarten to year nine or ten were rewritten to establish standards and outcomes with regard to what each person in school would be expected to know and be able to do at the end of compulsory schooling. Official curricular frameworks defined the boundaries of work to be covered at different stages of schooling. Subject profiles gave more or less detailed direction or advice to teachers about how typical learning experiences should be constructed, what curricular materials were relevant, and what methods of internal and external assessment would be employed to determine whether students had attained officially sanctioned outcomes. Of course, the set standards, curricular content, and achieved outcomes varied across educational regimes, depending on the particular alignments of the liberal-conservative, utilitarian-liberal, and social-democratic policy makers who made educational policy during the 1980s and 1990s. For example, liberal conservatives put more weight on conventional subjects and grades in designing their curricula; the national curricula put in place by the Conservative government of Margaret Thatcher in England, Wales, and Northern Ireland under the Education Reform Act of 1988 and the Education Reform (Northern Ireland) Order 1989 were the classic expressions of this governing ideology. Utilitarian liberals and social democrats were more likely to focus on generic skills and integrated subject areas as the basis for curricular design, as represented, for example, in the curricular frameworks widely developed as part of state educational reforms in the United States and also in the approach to creating a common curriculum advocated by the ALP government of Bob Hawke in Australia. For students in the era of global capitalism, the language of instruction might be the majority English or the minority French, Gaelic, Maori, or Welsh, and the religious milieu of their school might be secular, non-denominational, or denominational. Otherwise, their educational lots were intended to be largely interchangeable within educational regimes during their years of compulsory schooling. Progressive educational practices, with their inherent idea of person-regarding equality based on different needs of learners, to the extent they had any lingering effect, were now confined to early childhood education.

For the post-compulsory years of secondary schooling, educational policy making focused on making clear transitions for students from the common curriculum to their postsecondary careers in university, college, or the workforce. As was the case with the partite secondary systems and multilateral high schools that were developed in response to the problem of industrial efficiency, vocational pathways through senior secondary school were now defined by the occupational class structure of global capitalism rather than the specific educational ends or needs of individual students. The idea of person-regarding equality as the basis of legitimacy in the comprehensive schools of the welfare state was in part displaced by an upward extension of lot-regarding equality, realized by increased requirements for graduation, specification of key generic competencies, prescription of core courses, and increased standardized testing in the upper years of secondary school. At the same time, where differentiated educational pathways were retained in the post-compulsory years, whether formally or informally, by offering various combinations of academic and vocational studies, there were strenuous and sustained efforts to eliminate the historical disconnection between academic education and vocational training. Common school-leaving certificates were adopted, unified qualifications frameworks encompassing academic and vocational education and training were negotiated, and educational pathways that varied from highly academic education to primarily vocational training were created to facilitate the transition from school to postsecondary education and work.[9] Thus, with the notable exception of England, Northern Ireland, and Wales, reforms of post-compulsory curricula and school organization in the 1990s tried to avoid reverting to the segmental equality of partite systems and multilateral schools. None the less, there was a fundamental change in the conception of distributive justice in upper secondary education – not only in the form of an upward extension of the criterion of lot-regarding equality but also in the meaning of person-regarding equality as a criterion for making interpersonal comparisons of educational value among students pursuing different pathways – a shift from a focus on meeting the needs of learners to a focus on maximizing their preferences within a set of officially mandated educational options.

During the 1960s and 1970s, public policies that aimed to subsidize private schools or increase grants for separate or voluntary schools were defended primarily on grounds of communal equity; state aid was essential to preserve not élite independent schools but mass parochial, separate, and voluntary schools that needed larger revenues both in order to match the diversity and quality of tax-supported public schools and also in order to keep their fees low and preserve their viability as options for middle-income and working-class families. In the 1980s and 1990s there was a new justification for designing educational policies to fund private schools or diversify public provision – the creation of options for parents in choosing educational programs and school communities for their children, not only between public and private schools but also within the public sector. Freedom for parents to choose, which involves the potential to exit from public to private schools or within the public sector from one school to another, is a quintessentially utilitarian-liberal idea of liberty as individual freedom to choose according to one's personal preferences, but it was also advocated as vital to ensuring the high quality

and public accountability of all schools. Choice was seen to create competition among schools and hence to protect parents and students against
the lazy monopolies that result from state schools with captive enrolments
based on fixed attendance zones. Thus, for the first time in the historical
development of Anglo-American educational regimes, the criterion of
liberty as freedom for parents to choose the schools for their children's
education was being given serious weight, if not priority, over the norms
of community and equality.

The most extensive efforts to create choice among schools in the
1980s and 1990s occurred in England and New Zealand. The Thatcher
government's policies on open enrolments, grant-maintained schools,
and city technology colleges were intended to create choice for parents
within the public sector, while the Assisted Places Scheme was introduced to create an option for families with modest incomes to send their
children to independent schools. Despite the termination of assisted
places and grant-maintained schools by the Labour government in 1997,
the combined effect of school inspections with public reports by the
Office for Standards in Education, league tables of annual results by
school on the GCSE examinations, and school-based budgets determined by enrolments has resulted in a markedly more competitive public sector, particularly with regard to secondary schools. In New Zealand
the creation of a competitive public sector was accomplished by dismantling the education boards, isolating schools as self-managing entities,
making the budget of each school from the Ministry of Education significantly dependent on the size of its enrolment, opening the enrolments
of schools to students who live outside the normal attendance zones, and
publishing the results of School Certificate examinations by school as
information for parents choosing schools for their children's secondary
education.

In other Anglo-American educational regimes, the policies to create
competition among schools have been more incremental and less
transformative, but the underlying theory of simultaneously increasing
parental liberty and provider efficiency is the same. In Australia the
restructuring and expansion of federal aid to independent schools under the Liberal–National coalition government elected in 1996 was motivated primarily by a commitment to facilitate the option of parents to
choose schools in the private sector to educate their children. In the
United States, magnet schools and charter schools have increased the
options for choice within the public sector, and the introduction of
vouchers in Milwaukee, Cleveland, and Florida has facilitated exit from

the public to the private sector. Probably the least experimental educational regimes with regard to choice have been those in Canada, although there is a charter law in Alberta, with several charter schools in operation as a result, and the tax credit for tuition payments to private schools introduced in Ontario in June 2001 was inspired in part by an ideological commitment to competition as a way of improving both freedom of choice and efficiency of provision.[10]

During the 1980s and 1990s, policies to reform educational governance in Anglo-American educational regimes revived earlier theories of central political accountability based on individual ministerial responsibility, undermined popularly elected local education authorities in favour of school councils elected by parents and staff, reinvented theoretical distinctions between policy as a function of central educational authorities and administration ('management') as the task of local school communities, and restructured the partnerships of the welfare state and pluralist society in educational subgovernments to become more state-directed policy communities. Despite noticeable changes in policy discourse and public agendas, the relationships of educational politics and policy have not been much affected in the United States. In the other Anglo-American countries, however, the implementation of changes to educational governance in pursuit of effectiveness and efficiency under conditions of global capitalism has substantially altered, if not significantly impeded, the realization of basic democratic principles.

With the exception of the devolution of parliamentary oversight of Scottish and Welsh education to the Scottish Parliament and the Welsh National Assembly, and the restoration of responsibility for education to the Northern Ireland Assembly, the formal constitutional provisions for central political accountability in Anglo-American educational regimes did not visibly change in the last two decades of the twentieth century. In the United States, changes in the constitution of educational authority in one state were counterbalanced by changes in other states, or even changes back and forth in the same state. There were no major innovations in central educational governance comparable to the introduction of elected state boards of education after the Second World War, and the long-term trend to replace elected superintendents showed definite signs of depletion. Within established constitutional patterns, however, there was much greater activism with regard to educational reform on the part of governors, both individually and collectively through the National Governors' Association. Similarly, outside the United States, ministers of education became much more visible and active participants in educational politics and policy. In principle, there was an observable reassertion of the theory of ministerial responsibility, focused on recovering the political direction of educational policy from professional educators, by differentiating the fusion of political accountability and policy direction in the minister's office from the tasks of policy implementation and program management given to appointed officials. In practice, there was a tendency to retain the model of executive policy making in which the minister continued to focus on the functions of politics and policy, but with the professional expertise of civil servants based on managerial skills and experience rather than educational knowledge.

Anglo-American educational regimes in the era of high technology and global capitalism featured a devolution of local responsibility for educational governance, from regional authorities to school communities. Central authorities across Anglo-American educational regimes promoted policies for 'school-based management' or 'local school management.' Models varied between those that establish the principal as accountable for school governance, with school councils as advisory bodies, and those that establish the school council as responsible for school governance, with the principal as its chief executive officer and professional adviser. None the less, the goal in each case was greater discretion at the level of school communities to implement educational programs and allocate school budgets in order to maximize effectiveness and efficiency in the achievement of centrally planned targets. As part of this reform, local school boards were abolished in New Zealand, substantially circumscribed in their activities in Great Britain and Canada, and left to wither on the vine in Australia. Outside the United States, local school boards now serve primarily as intermediate administrative agents for central authorities. They may also serve as advocates for local interests in the corridors of power at the centre of educational regimes, but this representative function has been eroded in many cases by further school district amalgamations, which are promoted by claims that they achieve greater economies of scale but have the effect of decisively ending any lingering correspondence between the boundaries of local educational jurisdictions and local community identities.

In contemporary educational reform, principals and councils in school communities are very often portrayed ideally as self-governing entities. The theory of public management that came to pervade Anglo-American educational regimes during the era of global capitalism appeared to promise greater local discretion, especially in schools as key sites for educational decision making, and thus seemed to have the potential to extend democracy by improving the freedom of parents to participate in deciding their children's education. In practice, school communities, like district school boards and local education authorities, usually are circumscribed by a plethora of regulations that make them little more than administrative agents for central authorities. Even where school communities do exercise real discretion, school management is not substantive but instrumental, aimed at improving the effectiveness and efficiency of school communities in achieving expected outcomes that have been centrally determined in the form of state, provincial, and national curricula. In particular, parental participation in collective decision making within school communities is primarily focused on ensuring the effectiveness and efficiency of chosen policy instruments rather than actively deciding the content of their children's education. As for citizens who are not parents, and hence not direct 'stakeholders' or 'clients' in the educational regime, their opportunities to participate in local educational governance have been substantially curtailed.

Educational policy communities, under the aegis of the welfare state and the challenge of pluralist society, became more oriented to tripartite working partnerships among departmental bureaucrats, local authorities, and organized teachers and also more open to representation and participation by diverse societal interests emanating from basic divisions of religion, language, race, and ethnicity. During the era of global capitalism – outside the United States, at least – there was a revival of state-directed policy networks, as pluralist (or corporatist) partnerships of educational policy communities were confronted by the reassertion of political and policy direction by ministers and ministries of education. Teachers' unions were especially targeted for political attack as special interests, because of their defence of progressive educational philosophy and practices, their criticism of external standards and testing that challenged the professionalism and control of teachers in their classrooms, and their opposition to restraints on public expenditures for elementary and secondary education, including teachers' salaries. Educational policy communities outside the United States became systematically bifurcated, as organized teachers were driven into anti-government oppositional coalitions.

Educational regimes in the United States, by contrast, were much less affected by the trend to reassert central political direction over educational policy, turn local authorities into administrative agents for the centre, and restructure educational policy communities from pluralist networks to government domination. Nor have teachers' unions been exiled into permanent opposition from the governing coalitions as has generally been the case in Anglo-American educational regimes outside the United States. American governors and state superintendents simply do not have the policy authority of prime ministers or premiers and ministers of education. None the less, state educational authorities have implemented more extensive regulations and stricter curriculum frameworks. As a result, the historical relationship of fiscal equivalence between state and local levels of educational governance has evolved into a form of functional interdependence that now also includes federal authorities, as opposed to the administrative agency commonly observed in Anglo-American educational regimes outside the United States.

Inherent in the educational reforms to deal with the problems of the welfare state and pluralist society were concepts of justice as person-regarding equality based on need as well as bloc-regarding equality between majority and minority social groups and ideas of democratic community that variously embraced cultural neutrality, multicultural diversity, and communal consociation as the key to social harmony. Educational reforms that were designed to respond to the problem of global capitalism switched to a combination of lot-regarding equality, reminiscent of historical approaches to the problem of public instruction, and person-regarding equality based on utility. They also espoused a revisionist idea of liberty as a dimension of democracy in educational regimes by giving priority to the freedom of parents to choose the instruments of their children's education, as opposed to the historical meaning of liberty as the political accountability of central authorities and freedom of citizen participation in local democracy. Paradoxically, the freedom for students and parents to choose their school was accompanied across the Anglo-American educational regimes by substantial centralization of curricular policy making, stipulation of expected outcomes of schooling, imposition of external testing, and specification of required courses that variously restrict both the freedom of teachers working with parents to vary educational experiences in order to meet individual needs of children during the compulsory years of schooling and the freedom of students to determine the content of their educational programs during the post-compulsory years of schooling.

Anglo-American Democracy in Retrospect and Prospect

Comparative study of educational regimes is one way to understand the historical development and contemporary attributes of the political tradition of Anglo-American democracy. The persistent diversity of these educational regimes despite their encounters with a succession of substantially similar and cumulative problems of political economy has been evident at every turn. Anglo-American democracy is no monolith. Indeed, a retrospective view of educational provision and governance in now seventy-six Anglo-American educational regimes bespeaks difference rather than commonality. Yet out of the complex and diverse histories of educational regimes there does emerge a shared political tradition of Anglo-American democracy comprising variable but complementary ideas of democratic community, equality, and liberty.

Anglo-American democracy, as manifested historically in policies for public education, contained two competing ideas of community. From the middle of the nineteenth century, the liberal idea of democratic community as a uniform public whose members are not differentiated by their social attributes of ethnicity, language, race, or religion was contested by the conservative idea of democratic community as a multiform public comprising distinct social blocs that are legitimate grounds for segmenting membership in the democratic community.

The idea of a uniform public legitimated the practice of majoritarian democracy, in which political institutions and public policies were determined by the will of the largest bloc of voters. Simple majorities, in turn, created democratic communities that were English speaking, Protestant, and white. In both theory and practice, the idea of a uniform public was marred by racial segregation in the United States and religious discrimination in Australia, British Columbia, Manitoba, New Zealand, and the United States.

The idea of a multiform public implied the legitimacy of consociational democracy, in which political institutions and public policies were negotiated between social blocs by processes of élite accommodation. The idea of a multiform public in Canada, Newfoundland, and the United Kingdom grudgingly conceded the political reality, if not always the democratic legitimacy, of denominational and linguistic blocs, but component social blocs were moulded into stratified mosaics. Stratified multiform publics, in turn, meant unequal élites, biased bargaining, and unjust settlements. As with simple majoritarian democracy, nascent consociational democracy created democratic communities that were predominantly English speaking, Protestant, and white.

Just as it had two ideas of community, Anglo-American democracy historically had two ideas of equality, but they were complementary rather than competing. Inside public schools, equality meant ensuring as much as possible that the educational lots of children in elementary schools were interchangeable. The range of educational provision was restricted to a few years of basic elementary instruction. Public financing, especially in the United States, did vary markedly with the wealth of local communities, and despite the countervailing influence of particular dedicated teachers, no doubt the quality of instruction generally varied correspondingly. None the less, in contrast with variation in the bifurcated idea of community across educational jurisdictions, the intention of public instruction as delivering equal educational lots was remarkably consistent across Anglo-American educational regimes.

Lot-regarding equality stopped at the border of the public sector. The relationship between public and private sectors was defined by a form of segmental equality. Inside the public sector, educational lots were designed to be more or less interchangeable, but educational lots were not interchangeable between the public sector and the private sector. In the case of mass private schools, mostly Roman Catholic in their foundation, the educational lots of children in public schools usually were substantially superior. This inequality resulted from the discriminatory majorities and stratified consociations of nineteenth-century Anglo-American democracy. In the case of élite private schools, whether denominational or non-denominational, the educational lots of children in public schools were virtually always substantially inferior. This inequality derived from the powerful consensus across Anglo-American political ideologies, except perhaps for democratic socialism, to refrain from interfering with private choices that go beyond prevailing public standards, even though the consequence might be systematic inequality of opportunity between citizens who can afford superior private provision and citizens who must settle for middling or inferior public provision.

Lot-regarding equality in the status of individual citizens with regard to the delivery of public services was challenged in the late nineteenth and early twentieth centuries by the perceived need to reconcile public instruction with industrial efficiency. Extension of the idea of segmental equality across the public–private border into the secondary years of public education, if not over the entire K–12 curriculum, resulted from widespread commitment to reform public instruction in the image of industrial capitalism. Interchangeable lots could not be sustained throughout the curriculum while at the same time young people were educated and trained for work in stratified occupational classes. Equality of opportunity in the form of interchangeable educational lots in public schools was accordingly reformulated to incorporate tests of academic merit as criteria to determine educational selection and occupational futures.

Historically, educational choice for parents and students was severely restricted. There was a choice to found and patronize private schools as an alternative to public schools, but that was a free and effective choice for only a small minority of families. Many parents who might have preferred a private school for their children could not afford the fees. Many more parents who might have preferred to have their children educated in tax-supported public schools were impelled by their religious convictions to send their children to denominational private schools. School attendance was compulsory during the years of basic schooling. Post-compulsory schooling depended not only on family choice but also on merit selection through secondary school entrance examinations. Parents and students also had virtually no individual choice about the content of education. Not only was school attendance compelled by a collective public decision, but curricula were also decided collectively. Nor did the eventual construction of multilateral schools and partite systems improve individual choice, since entry to secondary tracks and schools was substantially controlled by professional rather than family decisions.

Freedom to participate in collective decision making about educational provision was less restrictive than freedom from interference, but popular access to educational policy making varied greatly across educational regimes. Local initiative was an important factor in the early stages of establishing public instruction in each of the Anglo-American educational regimes. After the initial foundation, local self-determination continued to be an important attribute of policy making in the educational regimes of the United States; a continuing factor in educational administration but making little contribution to policy in Canada, New Zealand, and the United Kingdom; and a rapidly disappearing element of both policy and administration in Australian educational regimes. By the end of the nineteenth century, freedom of participation in public decision making for educational policy was effectively restricted to participation in state, provincial, or national politics in Australia, Canada, New Zealand, and the United Kingdom, all based on parliamentary government with ministerial responsibility, in which citizen participation consisted of voting in general elections, making representations to political élites, and engaging in partisan politics. Even in the more populist political environment of the United States there were sustained efforts by liberal-conservative adherents of the Progressive movement to restrict opportunities for popular participation and to strengthen the control of political and professional élites over educational policy making.

The ethical-liberal and socialist idea of the welfare state as a more egalitarian community did not repudiate the bifurcated idea of Anglo-American democratic community as either a uniform or a multiform public. None the less, principles of universality and comprehensiveness were the grounds for legitimizing the social rights of citizenship. The logic of social citizenship, even one that was primarily residual in its guarantees of economic stabilization and social security, was inevitably inclusive. Even a partial commitment to the principles of universality and comprehensiveness as the basis for realizing a more egalitarian and inclusive community made it impossible to continue ignoring or suppressing the reality of social diversity. Hence, the ideal of social citizenship directly challenged both discriminatory majorities and stratified consociations, impelling them to acknowledge and respect the individual and collective rights of minorities. Three very different routes eventually were taken to make state schools more neutral, to facilitate cultural integration, and to construct more egalitarian consociations. Nor were these three routes mutually exclusive. Each became an important part of the political tradition of Anglo-American democracy.

Penetration of the idea of person-regarding equality into Anglo-American democratic practice resulted from the ideal of egalitarian community envisaged as the foundation of the Anglo-American welfare state. Equality of opportunity as interchangeable lots in lower years of schooling combined with merit selection to unequal tracks in upper years was challenged in the first instance by its failure to take into account the unequal starting points of children at the beginning of their years in school and the steadily deepening inequalities that resulted from assumptions of interchangeable lots and merit selection. Educational lots could not be interchangeable where children started school with different social skills and knowledge. This initial inequality between more and less advantaged students was then compounded over their years in school and eventually confirmed at the point of their selection for places in grammar-school and college-preparatory programs.

Once the justice of taking account of individual differences was conceded in order to compensate for disadvantage, the logic of person-regarding equality was let loose as a test for designing public education to fit, as much as possible, the individual needs and talents of each person in school. The logic of person-regarding equality in turn shone a new strong light on such historical inequalities as those between black and white, Catholic and Protestant, French and English, Maori and pakeha, and mass private and public schools (but not, significantly, between public and élite private schools). Ethical-liberal and socialist advocates of person-regarding equality, who had a communitarian bent, enthusiastically welcomed public policies that sought simultaneously to equalize individuals and social blocs, but even liberal conservatives and utilitarian liberals whose idea of equality was narrowly compensatory were drawn to concede the theoretical principle, if not always the political practice, that bloc-regarding equality with regard to the historical divisions of ethnicity, language, race, and religion was now an essential attribute of Anglo-American democracy.

The idea of liberty in Anglo-American democracy expanded along both its dimensions of freedom from interference and freedom of participation in the years following the Second World War. The principle of universality expressed in the slogan 'secondary education for all' impelled the creation of places in secondary school for all students who chose to be there, and more individual choice with regard to the content of secondary education was progressively introduced, especially where secondary curricula became defined by subject promotion, credit systems, and individual timetables. Freedom from interference within public schools was also extended by the racial desegregation of public schools, the extension of instruction through the medium of minority languages, the provision of easier access to denominational education, and the development of multicultural curricula.

Freedom to participate was diminished by amalgamation of school districts to form large units in which citizen participation became more difficult, but larger school districts did have the capacity to make more substantial policy decisions, so that access, once gained, could increase influence. With the notable exception of Australian educational regimes, greater functional interdependence between central and local educational authorities with regard to both policy and administration created more effective local options for citizen participation in representative democracy. Consolidation of tripartite partnerships of departmental officials, local authorities, and teachers' unions at the centre of educational policy communities opened new possibilities for freedom of participation in Anglo-American representative democracy.

More inclusive and egalitarian democratic communities, whether uniform or multiform in their perceived civic identity, now confront the principles of individual autonomy and market freedom that dominate the era of global capitalism. Global capitalism and its corollary, technological society, are not culturally neutral, however; on the contrary, they are oblivious both in theory and in practice to the claims of social diversity. Hence, egalitarian consociations are confronted by a potential dilemma between protecting communal identities versus improving economic productivity. Multicultural integration is limited by the bias in favour of economically current languages and cultures against traditional minority communities. Even the principled neutrality of the procedural liberal state with regard to ways of pursuing the good life is undermined by policy reforms and institutional restructuring that are designed to improve national economic competitiveness in global capitalist markets.

An appeal to the criteria of effectiveness and efficiency in order to meet the challenges and opportunities of global capitalism has revived the idea of lot-regarding equality as the standard for distributive justice in public education during the compulsory years and into the post-compulsory years across the Anglo-American educational regimes. In contrast with the pursuit of industrial efficiency in the early twentieth century, however, recent efforts to reform the post-compulsory years of schooling have resisted the idea of segmental equality as a complementary standard. Instead, policy makers have constructed educational pathways that fit the perceived educational imperatives of global capitalism, and students are then exhorted to maximize their educational and occupational preferences within that framework. Person-regarding equality based on individual ends or needs, once seemingly at the leading edge of democratic development, has been pushed back to the margins of Anglo-American public philosophy.

Given the displacement of person-regarding equality based on individual ends or needs and the restoration of neo-liberal ideas of lot-regarding equality and person-regarding equality based on utility to the core of Anglo-American political principles, the long-term commitment to bloc-regarding equality also comes into question. Widespread recognition of the legitimacy and justice of person-regarding equality based on needs opened the way for bloc-regarding equality as a political principle and pluralist society as a public good. The logic of lot-regarding equality, as well as that of person-regarding equality based on utility, does not necessarily contradict bloc-regarding equality, but neither lot-regarding equality nor person-regarding equality based on utility entails bloc-regarding equality in the way that the logic of person-regarding equality based on needs did.

In the late twentieth century, driven by élite consensus on what were the best structure, relevant content, and effective methods of education for global capitalism and technological society, the idea of liberty in

Anglo-American democracy once more became split between the concepts of freedom from interference versus freedom of participation. On the one hand, reforming public policy and political institutions in response to perceived pressures of global capitalism and technological society changed the meaning of liberty as freedom from interference. Prescribed curricula that were constructed on the principle of interchangeable lots reduced choice for students being educated in public schools, especially during their compulsory years of schooling, but an increased freedom to choose among schools enhanced their freedom from interference. For example, regulations that required children to attend schools in their prescribed attendance zones were relaxed or withdrawn, and public subsidies were designed to facilitate choice between public and private schools. On the other hand, freedom of participation was eroded by the centralization of educational policy. Local schools and districts were correspondingly undermined as autonomous public institutions, becoming agents of central authorities rather than instruments of local democracy. Similarly, formerly effective routes of representative democracy through pluralist policy communities were closed by the dismantling of tripartite educational partnerships.

Yet as the century turned, educational reform based on centralization of policy decision making in the offices of national, provincial, and state political and bureaucratic élites appeared to represent the will of electoral majorities. The historical tension in Anglo-American democracy between local democracy with central coordination versus central democracy with local management clearly had shifted in favour of public authority and accountability focused on national, provincial, or state governments at the expense of local governments. At the same time, however, the federal constitutions of Australia, Canada, and the United States continued to exert a powerful decentralizing influence on the organization of democratic political participation, and the United Kingdom became more definitely a multinational state. Global capitalism appeared to inspire meso-level politics and policy.

In retrospect, the historical construction of Anglo-American democracy emerges as a dialogical process that has focused on common problems of political economy, has mixed rival traditions of political ideology, and has thus produced similar trends of democratic development. As basic problems of political economy, the ideas of public instruction, industrial efficiency, welfare state, pluralist society, and global capitalism are consistent markers in the histories of Anglo-American educational regimes. Policy choices and outcomes may differ across regimes, but the historical structure of policy narratives is essentially the same. Moreover, the language of policy argument is perfectly comprehensible from the politics of one regime to that of the next. This comprehensibility of policy argument, in turn, stems from a sharing of rival ideological traditions. Conservatism, liberalism, and socialism as political world-views have been constructed within Anglo-American political history, and together they have come to constitute its political tradition.

The historical succession of overlapping problems of political economy that are defined and contested between and within the dominant ideologies of the Anglo-American political tradition has, in turn, imparted a common shape to democratic development across Anglo-American regimes. The advent of public instruction, however deeply flawed in its theory and practice, both reflected and constituted a major advance in Anglo-American democracy, while the reconciliation of Anglo-American democracy and industrial capitalism everywhere produced a perceptible retreat. The pursuit of more inclusive and egalitarian public policies during three decades following the Second World War marked another major advance in the meaning of Anglo-American democracy as including communities more accepting of difference, equality that is person regarding and bloc regarding, and enhanced freedom of participation in public life.

At the beginning of the twenty-first century, Anglo-American democracy appears to have become trapped once more in a recurring democratic dilemma. Citizens fear the outcomes for their individual interests of making democratic collective choices in public institutions. Citizens equally fear the outcomes for their collective interests of allowing private individual decisions to determine public goods. In the face of this dual distrust of the current political economy – in effect, a compound crisis of legitimacy, justice, and democracy – the Anglo-American political tradition presents its contemporary adherents with a conflicted teleological legacy of what are political goods and how they may be achieved. The ongoing contest of rival ideological doctrines within that tradition also creates the space for ideological innovation and public deliberation that enables Anglo-American citizens to seek new understandings of their shared political world.

Figures and Tables

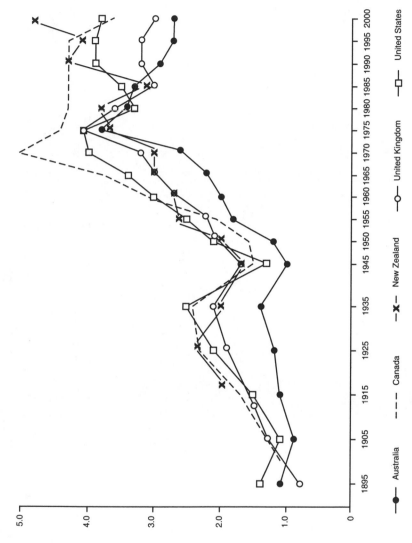

Figure 1. Government expeditures on public elementary and secondary education as a percentage of gross domestic product

Legend:
- Australia
- Canada
- New Zealand
- United Kingdom
- United States

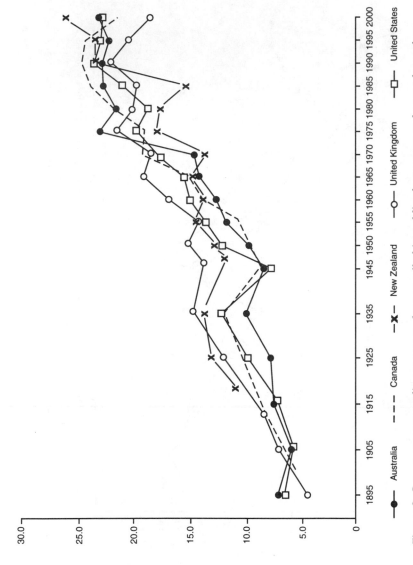

Figure 2. Government expeditures per student enrolled in public elementary and secondary education as a percentage of gross domestic product per capita

Australia ●—— Canada --- New Zealand —✕— United Kingdom —○— United States —□—

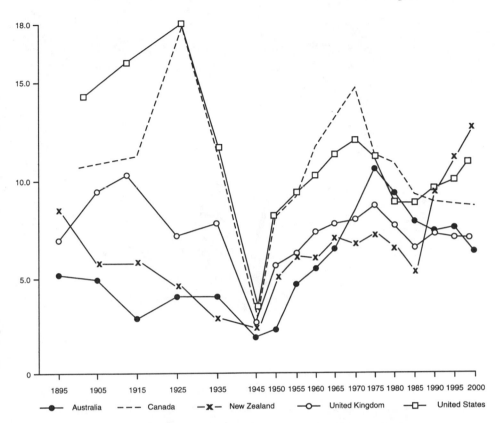

Figure 3. Government expeditures on public elementary and secondary education as a percentage of total government expenditures

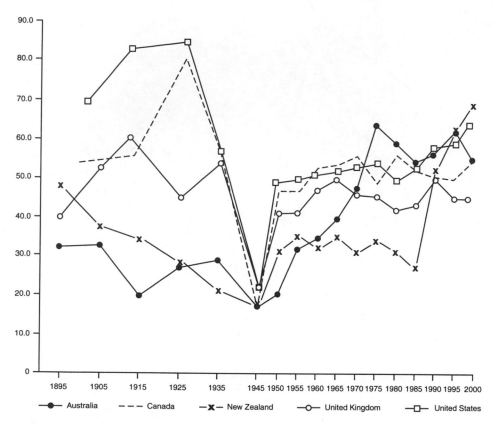

Figure 4. Government expeditures per student enrolled in public elementary and secondary education as a percentage of total government expenditures per capita

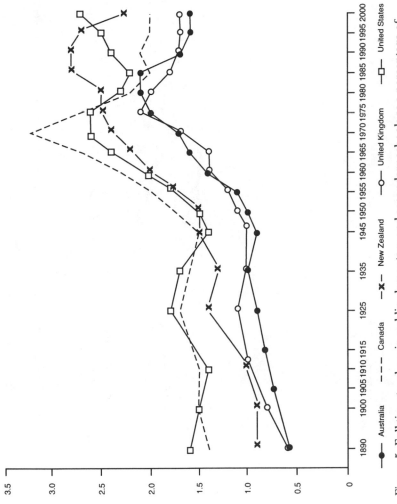

Figure 5. Full-time teachers in public elementary and secondary schools as a percentage of total labour force

Australia   Canada   New Zealand   United Kingdom   United States

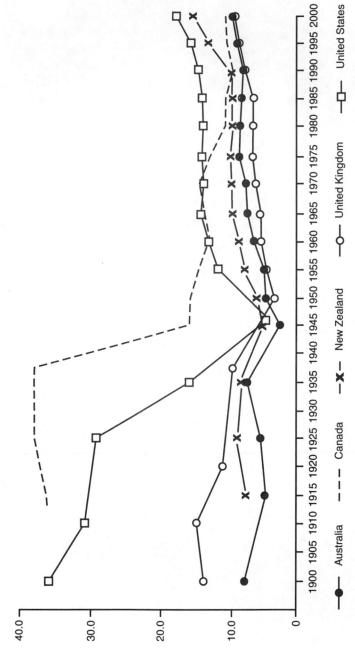

Figure 6. Full-time teachers in public elementary and secondary schools as a percentage of total government employment

Australia ———●———   Canada ——––   New Zealand ——✕——   United Kingdom ——○——   United States ——□——

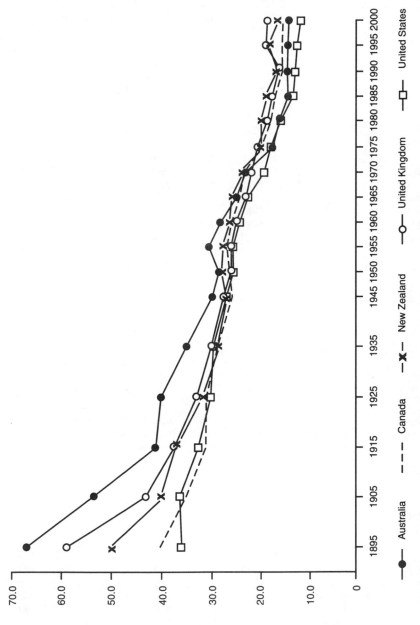

Figure 7. Ratio of enrolments to full-time teachers in public elementary and secondary schools

Australia   ---- Canada   —✕— New Zealand   —○— United Kingdom   —□— United States

Table 1
Government expenditures on public elementary and secondary education as a percentage of gross domestic product

Australia		Canada		New Zealand		United Kingdom		United States	
Year	%	Year	%	Year	%	Year	%	Year	%
1895	1.1					1895–6	0.8	1895–6	1.4
1905	0.9	1900–1	1.1			1905–6	1.3	1905–6	1.1
1915	1.1	1915–16	1.7	1918–19	1.9	1912–13	1.5	1915–16	1.5
1925	1.2	1925–6	2.3	1925–6	2.3	1925–6	1.9	1925–6	2.1
1935	1.4	1935–6	2.4	1935–6	2.0	1935–6	2.1	1935–6	2.5
1945	1.0	1945–6	1.5	1946–7	1.7	1945–6	1.7	1945–6	1.3
1950	1.2	1950–1	1.6	1950–1	2.0	1950–1	2.1	1949–50	2.1
1955	1.8	1955–6	2.1	1955–6	2.6	1955–6	2.2	1955–6	2.5
1960–1	2.0	1960–1	3.2	1960–1	2.7	1960–1	2.7	1959–60	3.0
1965–6	2.3	1965–6	3.8	1965–6	3.0	1965–6	3.0	1965–6	3.4
1970–1	2.6	1970–1	5.0	1970–1	3.0	1970–1	3.2	1969–70	4.0
1975–6	3.8	1975–6	4.4	1975–6	3.7	1975–6	4.1	1975–6	4.1
1980–1	3.4	1980–1	4.3	1980–1	3.8	1980–1	3.6	1980–1	3.3
1985–6	3.3	1985–6	4.3	1985–6	3.1	1985–6	3.0	1985–6	3.5
1990–1	2.9	1990–1	4.3	1990–1	4.3	1990–1	3.2	1990–1	3.9
1995–6	2.7	1995–6	4.3	1995–6	4.1	1995–6	3.2	1995–6	3.9
2000–1	2.7	2000–1	3.6	1999–2000	4.8	1999–2000	3.0	2000–1	3.8

Table 2
Government expenditures per student enrolled in public elementary and secondary education as a percentage of gross domestic product per capita

Australia		Canada		New Zealand		United Kingdom		United States	
Year	%	Year	%	Year	%	Year	%	Year	%
1895	7.1					1895–6	4.6	1895–6	6.6
1905	5.9	1900–1	5.6			1905–6	7.3	1905–6	5.8
1915	7.2	1915–16	8.8	1918–19	11.1	1912–13	8.5	1915–16	7.2
1925	7.9	1925–6	10.5	1925–6	13.2	1925–6	12.2	1925–6	10.0
1935	10.1	1935–6	12.1	1935–6	13.8	1935–6	14.7	1935–6	12.3
1945	8.4	1945–6	8.6	1945–6	11.5	1945–6	13.8	1945–6	7.8
1950	9.9	1950–1	9.4	1950–1	12.9	1950–1	15.2	1949–50	12.3
1955	11.9	1955–6	10.6	1955–6	14.5	1955–6	14.3	1955–6	13.6
1960–1	12.8	1960–1	14.2	1960–1	13.9	1960–1	17.0	1959–60	14.9
1965–6	14.3	1965–6	15.2	1965–6	14.6	1965–6	19.1	1965–6	15.5
1970–1	14.6	1970–1	19.2	1970–1	13.7	1970–1	18.4	1969–70	17.6
1975–6	22.9	1975–6	19.0	1975–6	17.8	1975–6	21.5	1975–6	19.7
1980–1	21.5	1980–1	21.7	1980–1	17.6	1980–1	20.1	1980–1	18.6
1985–6	22.7	1985–6	23.8	1985–6	15.4	1985–6	19.7	1985–6	21.0
1990–1	22.7	1990–1	24.6	1990–1	23.4	1990–1	22.1	1990–1	23.6
1995–6	22.2	1995–6	24.3	1995–6	23.1	1995–6	20.4	1995–6	23.0
2000–1	22.9	1999–2000	22.1	1999–2000	26.0	1999–2000	18.6	2000–1	22.7

Table 3
Government expenditures on public elementary and secondary education as a
percentage of total government expenditures

Australia		Canada		New Zealand		United Kingdom		United States	
Year	%	Year	%	Year	%	Year	%	Year	%
1895	5.2			1895–6	8.6	1895–6	7.0		
1905	5.0	1900–1	10.7	1905–6	5.8	1905–6	9.5	1901–2	14.3
1915	3.0	1913–14	11.2	1915–16	5.9	1912–13	10.3	1912–13	16.2
1925	4.1	1926–7	18.0	1925–6	4.7	1925–6	7.2	1926–7	18.0
1935	4.1	1937–8	10.2	1935–6	3.0	1935–6	7.8	1935–6	11.7
1945	2.0	1945–6	3.0	1945–6	2.5	1945–6	2.7	1945–6	3.6
1950	2.4	1950–1	8.2	1950–1	5.1	1950–1	5.7	1949–50	8.2
1955	4.7	1955–6	9.2	1955–6	6.2	1955–6	6.3	1955–6	9.4
1960–1	5.6	1960–1	11.8	1960–1	6.1	1960–1	7.4	1959–60	10.2
1965–6	6.6	1965–6	13.5	1965–6	7.1	1965–6	7.8	1965–6	11.4
1970–1	8.5	1970–1	14.7	1970–1	6.8	1970–1	8.0	1969–70	12.0
1975–6	10.6	1975–6	11.3	1975–6	7.2	1975–6	8.7	1975–6	11.2
1980–1	9.2	1980–1	10.8	1980–1	6.5	1980–1	7.6	1980–1	8.9
1985–6	7.9	1985–6	9.2	1985–6	5.4	1985–6	6.6	1985–6	8.8
1990–1	7.3	1990–1	8.9	1990–1	9.4	1990–1	7.3	1990–1	9.5
1995–6	7.6	1995–6	8.8	1995–6	11.2	1995–6	7.1	1995–6	10.0
1999–2000	6.4	2000–1	8.8	1999–2000	12.7	1998–9	7.1	1998–9	10.9

Table 4
Government expenditures per student enrolled in public elementary and secondary
education as a percentage of total government expenditures per capita

Australia		Canada		New Zealand		United Kingdom		United States	
Year	%	Year	%	Year	%	Year	%	Year	%
1895	32.3			1895–6	47.7	1895–6	39.5		
1905	32.6	1900–1	53.9	1905–6	36.6	1905–6	53.4	1901–2	70.6
1915	19.6	1913–14	55.5	1915–6	34.3	1912–13	60.6	1912–13	84.0
1925	27.1	1926–7	80.5	1925–6	27.7	1925–6	45.2	1926–7	86.0
1935	28.8	1937–8	51.5	1935–6	20.5	1935–6	53.5	1935–6	56.7
1945	17.2	1945–6	18.3	1945–6	17.2	1945–6	21.8	1945–6	21.9
1950	20.1	1950–1	47.1	1950–1	32.5	1950–1	41.4	1949–50	49.4
1955	31.9	1955–6	46.7	1955–6	34.5	1955–6	40.8	1955–6	50.2
1960–1	34.9	1960–1	52.7	1960–1	31.5	1960–1	46.9	1959–60	50.8
1965–6	40.2	1965–6	53.9	1965–6	34.7	1965–6	49.6	1965–6	52.0
1970–1	48.0	1970–1	56.1	1970–1	31.3	1970–1	45.6	1969–70	53.4
1975–6	63.6	1975–6	48.7	1975–6	34.1	1975–6	45.5	1975–6	54.3
1980–1	59.1	1980–1	55.6	1980–1	31.2	1980–1	42.4	1980–1	49.5
1985–6	53.9	1985–6	52.0	1985–6	26.8	1985–6	43.0	1985–6	53.3
1990–1	57.0	1990–1	50.6	1990–1	51.7	1990–1	50.3	1990–1	57.9
1995–6	62.0	1995–6	50.2	1995–6	62.3	1995–6	45.4	1995–6	58.9
1999–2000	54.8	1999–2000	53.8	1999–2000	69.3	1998–9	45.0	1998–9	63.7

Table 5
Percentage average annual increase during preceding period in real government expenditures per student in public elementary and secondary schools

Australia		Canada		New Zealand		United Kingdom		United States	
Year	%	Year	%	Year	%	Year	%	Year	%
1895				1895–6		1895–6		1895–6	
1905	0.3	1900–1		1905–6	0.4	1905–6	7.0	1905–6	3.5
1915	1.7	1915–16	6.0	1915–16	4.2	1915–16	2.7	1915–16	4.6
1925	4.7	1925–6	2.6	1925–6	3.1	1925–6	4.3	1925–6	5.5
1935	1.5	1935–6	1.6	1935–6	0.1	1935–6	4.6	1935–6	1.6
1945	2.2	1945–6	3.0	1945–6	5.1	1945–6	3.2	1945–6	2.7
1950	10.3	1950–1	3.2	1950–1	6.3	1950–1	4.8	1949–50	10.7
1955	3.9	1955–6	7.2	1955–6	1.7	1955–6	1.4	1955–6	5.5
1960–1	3.2	1960–1	7.8	1960–1	0.6	1960–1	7.3	1959–60	3.2
1965–6	7.9	1965–6	7.1	1965–6	4.7	1965–6	5.5	1965–6	4.7
1970–1	5.2	1970–1	9.4	1970–1	−0.6	1970–1	1.7	1969–70	5.8
1975–6	17.0	1975–6	4.9	1975–6	8.2	1975–6	5.8	1975–6	3.7
1980–1	−0.04	1980–1	5.3	1980–1	−0.6	1980–1	0.3	1980–1	−0.2
1985–6	2.7	1985–6	2.1	1985–6	−1.2	1985–6	1.8	1985–6	4.9
1990–1	0.5	1990–1	1.3	1990–1	11.9	1990–1	4.9	1990–1	3.6
1995–6	1.0	1995–6	0.6	1995–6	1.0	1995–6	−0.02	1995–6	0.4
2000–1	4.4	1999–2000	0.5	1999–2000	5.0	1999–2000	0.9	2000–1	2.4

Table 6
Full-time teachers in public elementary and secondary schools as a percentage of total labour force

Australia		Canada		New Zealand		United Kingdom		United States	
Year	%	Year	%	Year	%	Year	%	Year	%
1891	0.6	1890–1	1.4	1891	0.9	1890–1	0.6	1889–90	1.6
1905	0.7	1900–1	1.5	1901	0.9	1900–1	0.8	1899–1900	1.5
1915	0.8	1910–11	1.5	1911	1.0	1912–13	1.0	1909–10	1.4
1925	0.9	1925–6	1.7	1926	1.4	1925–6	1.1	1925–6	1.8
1935	1.0	1935–6	1.6	1936	1.3	1935–6	1.0	1935–6	1.7
1945	0.9	1945–6	1.5	1945	1.5	1946–7	1.0	1945–6	1.4
1950	1.0	1950–1	1.7	1951	1.5	1950–1	1.1	1949–50	1.5
1955	1.1	1955–6	2.0	1956	1.8	1955–6	1.2	1955–6	1.8
1960	1.4	1960–1	2.3	1961	2.0	1960–1	1.4*	1959–60	2.0
1965	1.6*	1965–6	2.7	1966	2.2	1965–6	1.4*	1965–6	2.4*
1970	1.7*	1970–1	3.2	1971	2.4	1970–1	1.7*	1969–70	2.6*
1975	2.0*	1975–6	2.7	1976	2.5*	1975–6	2.1*	1975–6	2.6*
1980	2.1*	1980–1	2.2	1981	2.5*	1980–1	2.0*	1980–1	2.3*
1985	2.1*	1985–6	2.0*	1986	2.8*	1985–6	1.8*	1985–6	2.2*
1990	1.7*	1990–1	2.1*	1991	2.8*	1990–1	1.7*	1990–1	2.4*
1995	1.6*	1995–6	2.0*	1996	2.7*	1995–6	1.7*	1995–6	2.5*
2000	1.6*	1999–2000	2.0*	2001	2.2*	1999–2000	1.7*	1999–2000	2.7*

* Statistics include full-time equivalent of part-time teachers.

Table 7
Full-time teachers in public elementary and secondary schools as a percentage of total government employment

Australia		Canada		New Zealand		United Kingdom		United States	
Year	%	Year	%	Year	%	Year	%	Year	%
1901	7.8					1900–1	14.1	1899–1900	36.3
1915	4.5	1913–14	35.9	1915	8.4	1910–11	15.3	1909–10	30.9
1925	6.3	1926–7	38.0	1926	9.3	1920–1	10.7	1925–6	28.9
1935	7.6	1937–8	38.0	1936	8.6	1937–8	10.0	1935–6	16.0
1945	2.7	1945–6	15.8	1945	6.3			1945–6	4.6
1950	5.2	1950–1	15.9	1950	6.8	1950–1	4.4	1949–50	12.3
1955	5.1	1955–6	15.3	1955	8.6	1955–6	5.0	1955–6	11.7
1960	6.7	1960–1	13.0	1960	9.3	1960–1	5.9*	1959–60	13.3
1965	7.7*	1965–6	13.8	1965	10.3	1965–6	6.3*	1965–6	14.2*
1970	8.4*	1970–1	14.8	1970	10.2	1970–1	6.7*	1969–70	14.0*
1975	9.0*	1975–6	12.7	1975	11.1*	1975–6	7.5*	1975–6	14.5*
1980	8.8*	1980–1	11.1	1980	10.3*	1980–1	7.3*	1980–1	14.0*
1985	8.5*	1985–6	10.8*	1985	10.7*	1985–6	7.5*	1985–6	14.6*
1990	8.1*	1990–1	9.8*	1990	11.3*	1990–1	8.0*	1990–1	14.9*
1995	9.0*	1995–6	10.7*	1995	13.5*	1995–6	9.2*	1995–6	15.9*
2000	9.9*	1999–2000	11.3*	2001	15.7*	1999–2000	9.7*	1999–2000	17.6*

* Statistics include full-time equivalent of part-time teachers.

Table 8
Ratio of enrolments to full-time teachers in public elementary and secondary schools

Australia		Canada		New Zealand		United Kingdom		United States	
Year	Ratio	Year	Ratio	Year	Ratio	Year	Ratio	Year	Ratio
1895	66.9	1895–6	40.0	1895	50.3	1895–6	58.8	1895–6	36.2
1905	54.1	1905–6	35.0	1905	40.4	1905–6	42.7	1905–6	35.7
1915	42.4	1915–16	30.9	1915	38.3	1912–13	37.0	1915–16	32.7
1925	40.3	1925–6	31.2	1925	32.1	1925–6	32.9	1925–6	29.8
1935	34.6	1935–6	29.2	1935	28.9	1935–6	29.6	1935–6	29.5
1945	30.1	1945–6	26.3	1945	27.5	1946–7	26.1	1945–6	26.9
1950	28.5	1950–1	26.7	1950	28.2	1950–1	26.2	1949–50	26.1
1955	30.5	1955–6	26.9	1955	27.6	1955–6	26.3	1955–6	25.7
1960	28.5	1960–1	26.1	1960	26.5	1960–1	24.2*	1959–60	24.6
1965	24.5*	1965–6	25.0	1965	25.0	1965–6	22.8*	1965–6	22.7*
1970	23.5*	1970–1	21.6	1970	24.2	1970–1	22.2*	1969–70	19.5*
1975	18.6*	1975–6	20.0	1975	21.1*	1975–6	19.8*	1975–6	18.1*
1980	16.4*	1980–1	18.7	1980	19.9*	1980–1	19.0*	1980–1	16.0*
1985	14.8*	1985–6	17.5*	1985	18.9*	1985–6	17.9*	1985–6	14.3*
1990	15.0*	1990–1	16.3*	1990	17.3*	1990–1	17.6*	1990–1	13.5*
1995	15.4*	1995–6	16.4*	1995	18.7*	1995–6	19.4*	1995–6	13.4*
2000	14.9*	1999–2000	16.0*	2000	17.3*	1999–2000	19.3*	1999–2000	12.3*

* Statistics include full-time equivalent of part-time teachers.

360   Tables

Table 9A
Percentage distribution of enrolments in public elementary and secondary schools by grade levels, Australia*

Year	Primary 1–6	Intermediate 7–9	Senior 10–12	Total† %	N
1915	93.5	6.3	0.3	100.0	329,298
1925	88.0	11.2	0.8	100.0	732,047
1935	84.1	14.6	1.3	100.0	797,213
1945	75.4	21.7	2.9	100.0	694,985
1955	76.9	20.1	3.0	100.0	1,208,820
1965	64.6	26.6	8.7	99.9	1,763,809
1975	57.5	28.1	14.4	100.0	2,120.428
1985	52.9	28.9	18.1	99.9	2,076,076
1995	55.0	25.0	19.1	100.0	2,056,382

* Victoria and South Australia are not included for 1915, Tasmania is not included for 1925 and 1935, and Queensland is not included from 1915 to 1945.
† Totals may not add to 100 per cent because of rounding.

Table 9B
Percentage distribution of enrolments in public elementary and secondary schools by grade levels, Canada*

Year	Primary 1–6	Intermediate 7–9	Senior 10–12	Total† %	N
1915–16	82.6	14.5	2.9	100.0	1,536,243
1925–6	75.1	19.0	6.0	100.1	1,884,930
1935–6	71.2	20.6	8.1	99.9	2,032,945
1945–6	68.8	22.0	9.2	100.0	2,048,759
1955–6	68.6	21.8	9.6	100.0	3,078,912
1965–6	59.2	24.6	16.3	100.1	4,621,856
1975–6	50.2	27.3	22.5	100.0	4,939,219
1985–6	50.4	25.4	24.2	100.0	4,140,447
1995–6	49.3	25.4	25.3	100.0	4,815,166

* Statistics for 1915–16 do not include British Columbia and Prince Edward Island; no distribution by grade for secondary grades is available for that year. Statistics for 1995–6 include enrolments by grade in private schools.
† Totals may not add to 100 per cent because of rounding.

Table 9C
Percentage distribution of enrolments in public elementary and secondary schools by
grade levels, New Zealand*

Year	Primary 1–6	Intermediate 7–9	Senior 10–12/13	Total† %	N
1915	88.2	10.9	0.9	100.0	197,876
1925	84.3	13.4	2.2	99.9	240,670
1935	65.7	26.2	8.0	99.9	232,755
1945	64.7	25.3	10.0	100.0	257,175
1955	65.7	23.3	11.1	100.1	392,603
1965	59.1	24.7	16.2	100.0	547,439
1975	54.1	26.4	19.6	100.1	662,528
1985	49.2	26.8	24.0	100.0	660,871
1995	51.5	23.0	25.5	100.0	665,231

* Beginning with 1975, 'Senior' includes Form 7 or Year 13. Enrolments for 1995
include students in non-government schools.
† Totals may not add to 100 per cent because of rounding.

Table 9D
Percentage distribution of enrolments in public elementary and secondary schools by
age levels, United Kingdom*

Year	Age 5–11	Age 12–14	Age 15 and over	Total† %	N
1913–14	79.0	20.0	1.0	100.0	7,066,854
1925–6	71.3	26.3	2.4	100.1	6,854,566
1935–6	70.2	26.5	3.3	100.0	6,778,132
1945–6	72.6	23.7	3.8	100.1	5,848,913
1955–6	71.0	24.8	4.1	99.9	7,740,772
1965–6	65.6	25.6	8.8	100.0	8,187,000
1975–6	60.9	25.4	13.7	100.0	10,017,000
1985–6	56.8	28.5	14.6	99.9	8,080,000
1995–6	62.1	24.7	13.2	100.0	8,124,000

* Statistics for 1913–14 cover Great Britain only; statistics are not available for Ireland.
† Totals may not add to 100 per cent because of rounding.

Table 9E
Percentage distribution of enrolments in public elementary and secondary schools by grade levels, United States

Year	Primary 1–6	Intermediate 7–9	Senior 10–12	Total* %	N
1915–16	79.9	15.9	4.3	100.1	20,351,687
1925–6	70.7	20.0	9.3	100.0	23,580,305
1935–6	61.6	22.0	15.5	100.0	25,760,345
1945–6	59.7	23.2	17.1	100.0	22,477,128
1955–6	60.3	23.8	15.9	100.0	29,585,376
1965–6	54.7	24.7	20.6	100.0	39,884,259
1975–6	47.6	27.6	24.9	100.1	40,416,333
1985–6	49.2	26.4	24.4	100.0	35,416,116
1995–6	52.3	26.3	21.4	100.0	39,920,130

* Totals may not add to 100 per cent because of rounding.

Table 10
Enrolments in non-public schools as a percentage of total enrolments in public and non-public elementary and secondary schools

Australia		Canada		New Zealand		United Kingdom*		United States	
Year	%	Year	%	Year	%	Year	%	Year	%
1895	18.6			1895	9.8			1895–6	8.4
1905	19.0			1905	10.1			1905–6	7.8
1915	18.4	1920–1	4.2	1915	10.6			1915–16	8.2
1925	18.7	1925–6	4.1	1925	10.5	1921–2	5.8	1925–6	9.0
1935	19.1	1935–6	4.0	1935	11.9	1930–1	6.3	1935–6	9.1
1945	24.2	1945–6	5.0	1945	13.2	1946–7	8.9	1945–6	10.8
1950	23.8	1950–1	4.1	1950	13.1	1951–2	7.5	1949–50	11.9
1955	23.9	1955–6	4.4	1955	13.0	1956–7	6.8	1955–6	13.1
1960	24.1	1960–1	4.0	1960	13.2	1960–1	6.8	1959–60	13.6
1965	23.8	1965–6	4.0	1965	13.2	1965–6	7.1	1965–6	13.0
1970	22.0	1970–1	2.4	1970	11.4	1970–1	6.0	1969–70	11.1
1975	21.3	1975–6	3.3	1975	11.3	1975–6	5.5	1975–6	10.2
1980	22.3	1980–1	4.0	1980	10.5	1980–1	6.0	1980–1	11.5
1985	25.8	1985–6	4.8	1985	3.3	1985–6	6.4	1985–6	12.3
1990	28.1	1990–1	4.7	1990	3.8	1990–1	6.7	1990–1	11.3
1995	29.0	1995–6	5.1	1995	3.6	1995–6	6.2	1995–6	11.3
2000	30.8	1998–9	5.5	2000	3.3	2000–1	6.2	2000–1	11.2

* United Kingdom statistics for 1921–2 to 1956–7 cover independent schools in England and Wales; statistics for 1960–1 to 2000–1 are based on non-maintained schools for the United Kingdom.

Notes on Statistics and Statistical Sources

Various statistical series have been constructed to make comparisons among Australia, Canada, New Zealand, the United Kingdom, and the United States with regard to their provision for public education over time. Statistical comparisons have not been attempted for the period prior to the 1890s and 1900s; the difficulties of finding comparable statistics simply became too great to merit pushing the statistical series back beyond the turn of the century. In general, as much as possible, education statistics have been collected for the mid-point of each decade from the turn of the century to the end of the Second World War. From the end of the war to the mid-1990s statistics have been collected at five-year intervals.

B.R. Mitchell, in the introduction to his section on education statistics in *European Historical Statistics 1750–1975* (2nd ed., rev.; London: Macmillan, 1980), page 785, has admirably expressed not only the problems that are encountered in collecting education statistics and the caution that is required in using them but also their potential contribution to policy studies.

Of all the subjects on which statistical material exists, probably none shows less uniformity, both over time and between countries, than education. There is no universal definition of what constitutes a primary school, or a general secondary school ... Then, the statistics of pupils and teachers have not always been collected in a consistent manner, even within the same school system. The date in the school-year to which they relate has been altered on various occasions; the exact meaning of the statistics has changed, sometimes referring to all pupils on the register, sometimes to those in regular attendance, sometimes to those present on a particular day, and sometimes to those present when the inspector visited. Nevertheless, for all the obstacles in the way of precise comparisons, when used with care these statistics do provide useful comparative material, if only of a rough nature.

The following sections describe the nature and sources of the statistical series from the 1890s to the mid-1990s that have been constructed for this study for Australia, New Zealand, the United Kingdom, and the United States with regard to student enrolments, teacher employment, government expenditures on public education, gross domestic product, total labour force, government employment, population, and consumer price indices. Similar notes on statistical sources for Canada are available in Ronald Manzer, *Public Schools and Political Ideas: Canadian Educational Policy in Historical Perspective* (Toronto: University of Toronto Press, 1994), 329–32.

Statistics for the years 1998 to 2001 have been assembled primarily by going to the World Wide Web sites of departments of education and offices of statistics. For Australia the sources are Australian Bureau of Statistics (*http://www.abs.gov.au/ausstats*), New South Wales Department of Education and Training (*http://www.det.nsw.gov.au*), Victoria Department of Education, and Training (*http://www.det.vic.gov.au/det*), Queensland Department of Education (*http://www.education.qld.gov.au*), South Australia Department of Education, Training and Employment (since 1 July 2002, Education and Children's Services) (*http://www.dete.sa.gov.au*), Education Department of Western Australia (*http://www.eddept.wa.edu.au*), Tasmania Department of Education (*http://www.education.tas.gov.au*), Northern Territory Department of Employment, Education and Training (*http://www.deet.nt.gov.au*), and Australian Capital Territory Department of Education, Youth and Family Services (*http://www.decs.act.gov.au*). The sources for Canada are the CANSIM II data base of Statistics Canada (*http://www.statcan.ca*) and Inter-provincial Education Statistics Project, Summary of School Statistics for the Provinces and Territories, *Final Report: Data Covering School Year 1999–2000*, which is available at the Web site of the British Columbia Ministry of Education (*http://www. bced.gov.bc.ca/schools/interprovincial*). Recent statistics for New Zealand have been assembled from Statistics New Zealand (*http://www.stats.govt.nz*) and the Ministry of Education (*http://www.minedu.govt.nz*). The sources for the United Kingdom are Department of Education and Skills (*http:// www.dfes.gov.uk/statistics*), in particular, the 2001 edition of *Education and Training Statistics for the United Kingdom*, and Office of National Statistics (*http://www.statistics.gov.uk*). Statistics for the United States come from the *Digest of Education Statistics 2001*, published by the National Center for Education Statistics (*http://www.nces.ed.gov*), and from the Bureau of the Census (*http://www.census.gov*).

Australia

From 1950 to 1995 statistics for students enrolled and teachers employed in government schools are taken from publications of the Australian Bureau of Statistics: *Official Year Book of the Commonwealth of Australia* (which changed its title to *Year Book Australia* beginning with issue No. 62 for 1977 and 1978 [Australian Bureau of Statistics catalogue number 1301.0]) for 1950 to 1975, *Schools, Australia* (4202.0) for 1980, *National Schools Statistics Collection: Government Schools, Australia* (4215.0) and *National Schools Statistics Collection, Australia* (4221.0) for 1985, and *Schools, Australia* (4221.0) for 1990 and 1995. Statistics for students enrolled and teachers employed from 1895 to 1945 have been collected separately for each state from state government official yearbooks, state statistical registers, and annual reports of state departments of education.

Enrolments

Total enrolments in state primary and secondary schools include enrolments in ordinary schools, special schools, and correspondence classes.

The organization of grades varies among states and over time. In general, primary schools have six grades or classes in New South Wales, Tasmania, Victoria, and Australian Capital Territory and seven in Queensland, South Australia, Western Australia, and Northern Territory. Secondary school involves six forms or years where it follows a six-year primary program and five years following a seven-year program. Enrolments in pre-year one (kindergarten, preparatory, reception, or transition) are included in primary enrolments for New South Wales and Australian Capital Territory from 1945, South Australia and Tasmania from 1955, Northern Territory from 1965, and Victoria from 1975. Queensland and Western Australia do not have pre-year one classes.

The basis of enrolment statistics also varies historically among the states. Before 1960, New South Wales and Western Australia report the December enrolments from 1895 to 1925 and average weekly enrolments from 1935 to 1955. Queensland from 1895 to 1935 and Tasmania from 1895 to 1950 give gross enrolments that count all enrolments including, for students who moved, each time they enrolled in a school. Victoria and South Australia from 1895 to 1955, Queensland from 1945 to 1955, and Tasmania in 1955 give net enrolments that count all students enrolled at any time during the school year but count only once students who moved from one school to another during the year. Beginning in 1960 the enrolments for all states are based on a mid-year census.

Teachers

Statistics for teachers in government schools cover full-time teachers in primary, secondary, and special schools. Beginning in 1965 the full-time equivalents of part-time teachers are also included. Teachers in junior technical schools in Victoria are not included until the 1970s, when it became possible to distinguish secondary from postsecondary technical teachers. Work mistresses, sewing mistresses, monitors, and pupil teachers are not included.

Government Expenditures on Public Education

Statistics are based generally on the sum of net government current and capital expenditures on public primary, secondary, and special education. Expenditures on junior technical schools are not included for Victoria from 1935 to 1955, nor for Tasmania for 1935 and 1945. Statistics are given for school (calendar) years for all states from 1895 to 1950 and for New South Wales, South Australia, Tasmania, and Australian Capital Territory in 1955. Statistics are based on the fiscal year for Victoria, Queensland, Western Australia, and Northern Territory in 1955–6 and for all states beginning in 1960–1. The source of statistics for state expenditures on government schools from 1905 to 1955 is *Official Year Book of the Commonwealth of Australia.* State and territorial statistics for 1895 and 1960–1 to 1995–6 have been compiled from the annual reports of departments of education and state official yearbooks. Direct expenditures on government schools by the Commonwealth government have been added beginning with 1955–6. Where they are not specified, expenditures by the Commonwealth department of education on administration of its programs for schools have been estimated as a share of the costs of general departmental administration based on departmental expenditures on primary and secondary education as a percentage of departmental outlays on all educational programs. The source of information on Commonwealth expenditures on education is Australian Bureau of Statistics, *Expenditure on Education, Australia* (5510.0).

Gross Domestic Product

The source of statistics for gross domestic product from 1894–5 to 1960–1 is B.R. Mitchell, *International Historical Statistics: The Americas and Australasia* (Detroit: Gale Research Company, 1983), 905–7. Where government expenditures on education are reported for school (calendar) years, GDP statistics for two fiscal years have been averaged. For GDP since 1960–1, see Australian Bureau of Statistics, *Australian National Accounts: National Income and Expenditure* (5204.0) as reported in *Year Book Australia.*

Labour Force

Annual estimates of the total workforce from 1900–1 to 1965–6 are given by A. Barnard, N.G. Butlin, and J.J. Pincus, 'Public and Private Sector Employment in Australia, 1901–1974,' *The Australian Economic Review* 37 (1977): 50. Statistics for two fiscal years have been averaged to make comparisons with statistics for the employment of teachers based on school years. The series is continued by adding estimates of the civilian labour force from the Australian Bureau of Statistics surveys of employment and unemployment as reported in *Labour Force, Australia* (6203.0) and statistics on defence forces from *Year Book Australia.*

Government Expenditures

Total government expenditures prior to 1970 are obtained by adding Commonwealth and state consolidated revenue expenditures, Commonwealth and state gross loan expenditures for works and services, and local government expenditures. Transactions of trust funds are excluded. The source for 1895–6 is T.A. Coglan, *A Statistical Account of the Seven Colonies of Australasia 1895–6* (Sydney: Government Printer, 1896), 384, 412. Statistics for 1905–6 to 1965–6 are taken from *Official Year Book of the Commonwealth of Australia.* For 1965–6 and 1970–1 the sources are Australian Bureau of Statistics, *Commonwealth Government Finance* (5502.0), *State and Local Government Finance, Australia* (5504.0), and *Government Finance Statistics, Australia* (5512.0). For total government expenditures from 1975–6 to 1995–6, see International Monetary Fund, *Government Finance Statistics Yearbook.*

Government Employment

Estimates of total government employment from 1900–1 to 1945–6 are taken from Barnard, Butlin, and Pincus, 'Public and Private Sector Employment in Australia, 1901–1974.' After the Second World War, statistics on civilian government employment come from the June or August surveys of the labour force published by the Australian Bureau of Statistics in *Employment and Unemployment* and *Wage and Salary Earners, Australia* (6248.0), which cover administrative employees and other personnel of Commonwealth, state, and local governments, including government business and financial undertakings such as railways, air and road transport, banks, postal and telecommunications, television, and marketing authorities. The source for employment in the armed forces is *Year Book Australia.*

Population

Annual estimates of the population of Australia from 1895 to 1991 are given in B.R. Mitchell, *International Historical Statistics: Africa, Asia and Oceania 1750–1993* (3rd ed.; London: Macmillan 1998), 64–6, and for 1995 and 1996 in *Year Book Australia.* Two calendar years have been averaged for comparisons with fiscal years.

Consumer Price Index

Retail price index numbers for 1895 to 1996 have been taken from Australian Bureau of Statistics, *Year Book Australia 1998* (Canberra: Australian Government Publishing Service, 1998) with 1945 = 100. Indices for two calendar years have been averaged in order to weight expenditures for fiscal years. In order to estimate changes in real expenditures on public education, expenditures in pounds prior to 1965 have been converted at the rate of one pound equals two dollars as prescribed under the Currency Act 1965.

New Zealand

The sources for students enrolled and teachers employed in public primary and secondary schools before 1965 are annual reports of the

Department of Education, which became the Ministry of Education in 1989, the departmental compendium *Education Statistics of New Zealand* from 1965 to 1995, and also *New Zealand Official Yearbook*, published by the New Zealand Department of Statistics (from 1994, Statistics New Zealand).

Enrolments

Total enrolments in public schools include enrolments of full-time students in public primary and secondary schools, Maori schools, and correspondence courses, according to the census taken at the end of December for school years from 1895 to 1925 and on 1 July from 1935 to 1995. For 1925 and earlier years, elementary education comprised a preparatory year and five or six standards, although students could transfer to secondary school after standard five; there were five forms at the secondary level. For 1935 to 1995, primary education involved two preparatory years (primers or juniors), standards one to four, and forms one and two. Secondary education covered forms three to six and (since 1970) seven.

Teachers

Statistics are based historically on the number of full-time principal or head teachers, assistant teachers, and probationary assistant teachers in public primary and secondary schools. Manual training assistants in manual training centres are included; pupil teachers, junior assistant teachers in Maori schools, and sewing mistresses are not included. Because no count of primary school teachers was taken in 1945, the number for 1946 has been used as an estimate for the 1945 statistic. Beginning in 1975 the full-time equivalent of part-time teachers is included.

Government Expenditures on Public Education

The source for statistics from 1895 to 1960–1 is the annual report of the New Zealand Department of Education. For 1965–6 to 1985–6 the source is Department of Education, *Education Statistics of New Zealand*. For 1990–1 and 1995–6, government expenditures on state and state-integrated schools have been calculated from New Zealand Treasury, *Financial Statements of the Government of New Zealand*. Government grants to pre-school kindergartens and play centres are not included.

Gross Domestic Product

Statistics for 1918 to 1938 are taken from B.T. Lineham, 'New Zealand's Gross Domestic Product, 1918/38,' *New Zealand Economic Papers* 2:2 (1968): 16. For 1946–7 to 1960–1 the source is Mitchell, *International Historical Statistics: The Americas and Australasia*, 906, and then *New Zealand Official Yearbook* for 1965–6 to 1995–6.

Labour Force

Statistics for the full-time labour force are based on census returns, beginning in 1891 and ending in 1996, as reported in Statistics New Zealand, *New Zealand Official Yearbook 1998* (Wellington: GP Publications, 1998), 306. The definition of full-time work changed from twenty to thirty hours a week beginning with the 1986 census.

Government Expenditures

For the years 1895–6 to 1975–6, this series was constructed on the basis of financial statistics by adding gross expenditures of the central government and total payments by local authorities minus grants from the central government to local authorities. The source is *New Zealand Official Yearbook*. Beginning with 1980–1 the source of statistics for total government expenditures is International Monetary Fund, *Government Finance Statistics Yearbook*.

Government Employment

Government employment in New Zealand is the sum of employment by state services and local authorities. Historically, state services include the public service, railways, the post office, public education, hospital services, the police, and the armed forces. Local authorities were engaged in the construction and maintenance of roads and streets, the operation and maintenance of public utilities (gas, electricity, water, and transport), and community services. The statistic for 1915, taken from *New Zealand Official Yearbook 1915*, unfortunately does not include the armed forces. Statistics on total government employment for 1926 and 1936 are taken from the census of population. For 1945–6, government employment has been estimated from reports of individual state services, local authorities, and hospital boards as reported in *New Zealand Official Year-*

book. Aggregate statistics of employment for both state services and local authorities are also taken from *New Zealand Official Yearbook* for 1950 to 1985. Statistics on employment in the public sector for 1990 and 1995 are found in Statistics New Zealand, *Labour Market Statistics Tables 1996* (catalogue number 01.029.0096); and government employment in 2001 has been estimated from the census.

Population

Population statistics from 1895 to 1996 are the annual estimates of Statistics New Zealand published in *New Zealand Official Yearbook.* Two calendar years have been averaged to make comparison with fiscal years.

Consumer Price Index

The consumer price index has been constructed from the historical series published in *New Zealand Official Yearbook 1990,* 614, which has the 1988 December quarter as its base, and has been extended to 1995–6 by the series published in *New Zealand Official Yearbook 1998,* 546. Two calendar years have been averaged for weighting fiscal years. In order to estimate changes in real expenditures on public education over time, expenditures recorded in pounds prior to the introduction of decimal currency in July 1967 have been converted at the official rate of one pound equals two dollars.

United Kingdom

Statistics for enrolments and teachers from 1960–1 to 1995–6 and government expenditures on education from 1970–1 to 1995–6 are taken from *Education Statistics for the United Kingdom (Education and Training Statistics for the United Kingdom,* beginning with the 1997 edition), published collectively by the four central education authorities under various designations as Department of Education and Science/Department for Education/Department for Education and Training, Scottish Education Department/Scottish Office Education Department/Scottish Executive Education and Industry Department, Ministry of Education for Northern Ireland/Department of Education for Northern Ireland, and Welsh Office Education Department/Welsh Executive Education and Training Department.

For earlier years, these statistics are compiled separately for England

and Wales, Scotland, and Northern Ireland (before 1920, Ireland) and summed. The sources of statistics for enrolments and teachers for England and Wales are annual reports of the Board of Education, Ministry of Education, and Department of Education and Science. In earlier years, statistics were published separately from the annual report in Board of Education, *Statistics of Public Education in England and Wales*. This practice was also followed in the 1960s and 1970s by the Department of Education and Science in its *Statistics of Education in England and Wales*. Statistics for Scotland are taken from annual reports of the Committee on Education in Scotland before the Second World War and those of the Scottish Education Department after the war. Statistics for Ireland before its partition are taken from annual reports of the Commissioners of National Education in Ireland as well as the Intermediate Education Board for Ireland. After partition, the sources are annual reports of the Ministry of Education for Northern Ireland, supplemented in the 1960s by its publication, *Statistics of Education in Northern Ireland*.

Enrolments

Total enrolments in public schools include students in nursery, primary, secondary, and special schools. Statistics from 1980–1 cover public-sector (state-maintained as opposed to non-maintained) schools. Enrolments prior to 1980–1 include students in state-maintained and state-assisted schools, except for Table 10, where enrolments in non-public schools from 1960–1 to 1995–6 include independent and state-assisted schools. Statistics on enrolments in independent schools in England and Wales from 1921–2 to 1956–7 are taken from Great Britain, Public Schools Commission, *First Report*, vol. 2 (London: Her Majesty's Stationery Office, 1968), Appendix 5, 20–1.

Teachers

In general, teachers for England and Wales, Scotland, and Northern Ireland (before 1920, Ireland) historically include full-time nursery, primary, secondary, and special education teachers in schools maintained by local education authorities or aided by direct grants from the central education authority. Statistics from 1960–1 also include the full-time equivalent of part-time teachers. Student teachers, pupil teachers, and monitors are not included.

In England and Wales, except for a survey in 1896–7, counts of secondary school teachers are not available until 1910–11. From then until the Second World War, the statistics include teachers in maintained and assisted primary and special schools plus teachers in secondary schools on the grant list. Following the Second World War, teachers in England and Wales include teachers in maintained primary and secondary schools, direct-grant grammar schools, and both maintained and direct-grant nursery and special schools.

For Scotland the statistics include full-time teachers in education-authority and grant-aided schools. The statistic for 1946–7 is an estimate based on the report for 1947–8.

For Ireland, only full-time teachers in primary schools are included prior to partition. From 1925–6 to 1965–6, statistics for teachers in Northern Ireland count teachers in elementary schools, voluntary grammar schools (including preparatory departments), and secondary intermediate schools. From 1925–6 to 1960–1, estimates of teachers in junior technical and technical intermediate schools are also included, calculated on the basis of student-teacher ratios in academic secondary schools applied to enrolments in secondary technical schools.

Government Expenditures on Public Education

Aggregate statistics for the United Kingdom for 1970–1 to 1995–6 are taken from *Education Statistics for the United Kingdom* (beginning with the 1997 edition, *Education and Training Statistics for the United Kingdom*) and comprise current and capital expenditures for nursery, primary, secondary, and special education, administration, school health, meals and milk, maintenance grants for pupils over the school leaving age, and transportation of pupils. Before 1970–1, government expenditures on public education for the United Kingdom are the result of separate calculations for England and Wales, Scotland, and Northern Ireland and generally consist of current expenditures from revenue, capital expenditures from revenue, and loan charges.

For England and Wales, expenditures for the Board or (after 1944) Ministry of Education from 1895–6 to 1950–1 are calculated from the Civil Appropriations Accounts. They include central expenditures for administration, inspection, examinations, pension payments to teachers minus pension receipts, and grants to nursery, elementary, and secondary schools other than those maintained by local education authorities. Expenditures by local education authorities during the same period are calculated from statistics published in *Annual Abstract of Statistics*. Expenditures for England and Wales from 1955–6 to 1965–6 are taken from Ministry of Education or (after 1962) Department of Education and Science, *Statistics of Education*.

For Scotland, central government expenditures cover administration, inspection, net payments for teachers' pensions, and grants to voluntary and secondary schools. The sources are *Annual Abstract of Statistics* for 1895–6 to 1915–16 and the Civil Appropriations Accounts for the Scottish Education Department for 1925–6 to 1955–6. Education authority expenditures for 1895–6 to 1945–6 are taken from B.R. Mitchell and Phyllis K. Dean, *Abstract of British Historical Statistics* (Cambridge: Cambridge University Press, 1962) and B.R. Mitchell and H.G. Jones, *Second Abstract of British Historical Statistics* (Cambridge: Cambridge University Press, 1971). Those for 1950–1 to 1960–1 are found in annual reports of the Scottish Education Department, and statistics for both central and local authorities for 1965–6 and 1970–1 are taken from *Scottish Educational Statistics*.

For Ireland, expenditures by the Commissioners of National Education for 1895–6 to 1915–16 are calculated from expenditures on national schools from parliamentary grants published in *Annual Abstract of Statistics* and annual reports of the commissioners. The expenditures covered include salaries and other payments to teachers and monitors in national schools, gratuities to teachers on retirement, salaries and allowances of inspectors, central administrative costs, and maintenance and repair of schools. For this period, payments by the Intermediate Education Board for Ireland are also included. Comparable expenditures by the Ministry of Education for Northern Ireland from 1925–6 to 1965–6 are taken from the ministry's annual reports. Total expenditures on schools in Northern Ireland are obtained by adding receipts of local education authorities from local sources and other government departments to expenditures by the ministry.

Gross Domestic Product

Statistics for gross domestic product at market prices are taken from B.R. Mitchell, *British Historical Statistics* (Cambridge: Cambridge University Press, 1988), 833–5, for 1895 to 1976. For 1980 to 1996 the source is Central Statistical Office (from April 1996, Office of National Statistics), *Annual Abstract of Statistics*. In order to compare expenditures based on school or fiscal years with gross domestic product based on calendar years, GDP statistics for two calendar years have been averaged.

Labour Force

Estimates of the working population of the United Kingdom for 1890 to 1961 are taken from C.H. Feinstein, *Statistical Tables of National Income, Expenditure and Output of the United Kingdom 1855–1965* (Cambridge: Cambridge University Press, 1972), Table 57, T125–7. Feinstein's series includes Southern Ireland to 1920 and excludes it after 1920. The statistics for two calendar years are averaged in order to make comparisons with school years. After 1960–1 the labour force series for the United Kingdom is taken from *Annual Abstract of Statistics*. The statistics are the estimates of total labour force from the June survey at the end of the school year. Again, two years have been averaged to make comparisons with school years.

Government Expenditures

Statistics for government expenditures from 1895–6 to 1945–6 are the sums of gross central government expenditures minus central grants to local governments plus current and capital expenditures of local governments. The source is Mitchell, *British Historical Statistics*, 588–93, 612–16, 619–22, 626–8, 630–3, 638–41. After the Second World War, when capital expenditures of public corporations became increasingly important, statistics for government expenditures are based on national accounts and comprise the sum of current expenditures of central and local authorities and capital expenditures for public corporations, central government, and local authorities. Two calendar years are averaged to make comparisons with school years or fiscal years. The source for 1950–1 to 1970–1 is Feinstein, *Statistical Tables of National Income, Expenditure and Output of the United Kingdom 1855–1965*, Tables 14 and 39, T35–6, T85–7. Statistics for 1975–6 to 1995–6 are taken from International Monetary Fund, *Government Finance Statistics Yearbook* and are the sums of consolidated central government expenditures and local government expenditures minus intergovernmental transfers ('grants from other levels of government').

Government Employment

Historical statistics on government employment in Great Britain are the estimates made by Moses Abramowitz and Vera E. Eliasberg, *The Growth of Public Employment in Great Britain* (Princeton: Princeton University

Press, 1957) for 1891 to 1938, which cover central government departments, the armed forces, and local governments. Official estimates of
employment in the British public sector at mid-June, including public
corporations, are available from the labour-force survey beginning with
1949 and continuing to 1957. After 1957 the labour-force survey reports
employment in the public sector for the United Kingdom. Here the
sources are Great Britain, Department of Employment and Productivity,
British Labour Statistics: Historical Abstract 1886–1968 (London: Her Majesty's Stationery Office, 1982), Tables 152 and 153 for 1950 to 1960, and
the summary of employment in the public sector since 1960 in Office for
National Statistics, *Economic Trends: Annual Supplement 1996/97*, Table
3.4. See also Duncan MacGregor, 'Jobs in the Public and Private Sectors,'
Economic Trends, no. 571 (June 2001): 35–50.

Population

Mitchell, *British Historical Statistics*, 12–14, provides the estimates of mid-
year home populations for 1895 to 1961. For mid-year estimates of
population from 1965, the source is *Annual Abstract of Statistics*. The
estimates for two calendar years are averaged to make comparisons with
school or fiscal years.

Consumer Price Index

The sources are Mitchell, *International Historical Statistics*, Table H1, 847–
50, for 1895 to 1986, and thereafter *Annual Abstract of Statistics*. The base
is 1987 = 100.

United States

The general sources of historical statistics on enrolment of students,
employment of teachers, and government expenditures on public education in the United States are biennial reports of the United States
Office of Education. Statistics on students, teachers, and spending are
included in 'Statistics of State School Systems' published in United
States, Office of Education, *Report of the Commissioner of Education* for the
years 1895–6, 1905–6, and 1915–16 and then as part of *Biennial Survey of
Education in the United States* for the years 1925–6, 1935–6, 1945–6, 1949–
50, and 1955–6. After that, the sources are Office of Education, *Statistics
of State School Systems* and *Digest of Education Statistics* issued annually since

1962 by the National Center for Education Statistics. Data for Alaska and Hawaii are included beginning with the 1959–60 school year.

Enrolments

Total enrolments in public day kindergarten, elementary, and secondary schools from 1870–1 and in private schools from 1889–90 are available in United States, Department of Commerce, Bureau of the Census, *Historical Statistics of the United States, Colonial Times to 1970, Bicentennial Edition* (Washington, D.C.: United States Government Printing Office, 1975), Part 1, series H420 and H426. Total enrolments in Roman Catholic schools as a subset of private-school enrolments are available from 1919–20 to 1969–70 in series H536 and H541.

Teachers

Instructional staff in public day schools includes principals, consultants or supervisors of instruction, classroom teachers, and other non-supervisory instructional personnel such as librarians, guidance counsellors, and psychologists. Teachers in federal schools for Indians and residential schools for exceptional children are not included. Prior to 1965–6, statistics refer to full-time teachers; beginning with 1965–6, they also include the full-time equivalent of part-time teachers.

Government Expenditures on Public Education

Government expenditures on public education in general cover current expenditures for day schools, capital outlays, and interest on school debt. Expenditures for community services, summer schools, adult education, community colleges, and private-school programs when separately reported are excluded. The statistics on school expenditures for 1901–2, 1912–13, and 1926–7 are taken from *Historical Statistics of the United States, Colonial Times to 1970*, Part 2, series Y686.

Gross Domestic Product

Statistics for gross national product for the years 1895 to 1936 are given in *Historical Statistics of the United States, Colonial Times to 1970*, Part 1, series F1. Statistics for gross domestic product from 1945 to 1996 have been taken from United States, Department of Education, National

Center for Education Statistics, *Digest of Education Statistics 2000* (Washington, D.C.: United States Government Printing Office, 2001), 39 (Table 36).

Labour Force

Annual estimates of the total labour force aged fourteen years and over from 1900 to 1947 and sixteen years and over from 1947 to 1970 are given in *Historical Statistics of the United States, Colonial Times to 1970,* Part 1, series D1 and D12, and continued in United States, Bureau of the Census, *Statistical Abstract of the United States.* Statistics for two calendar years have been averaged to make comparisons with data on the employment of teachers that refer to school years.

Government Expenditures

Total federal, state, and local government expenditures on the basis of financial statistics from 1901–2 to 1969–70 are taken from series Y533 in *Historical Statistics of the United States, Colonial Times to 1970,* Part 2, which is continued in *Statistical Abstract of the United States* to 1994–5. Total government expenditures for 1995–6 and 1998–9 have been estimated by adding consolidated federal government expenditures plus total expenditures of state and local governments minus federal grants to state and local governments.

Government Employment

Estimates of total government employment are given for 1900 to 1940 in Solomon Fabricant, *The Trend of Government Activity in the United States since 1900* (New York: National Bureau of Economic Research, 1952), Table B13. Beginning with 1940, aggregate statistics on civilian government employment are taken from *Historical Statistics of the United States, Colonial Times to 1970,* Part 2, series Y272 and Y274, which are continued in *Statistical Abstract of the United States.* Series Y904 provides statistics for military personnel on active duty.

Population

The sources for annual estimates of the population of the United States are *Historical Statistics of the United States, Colonial Times to 1970,* Part 1, series A6 and A7, and *Digest of Education Statistics 2000,* 39 (Table 36). Two calendar years have been averaged to make comparisons with school or fiscal years.

Consumer Price Index

A consumer price index with base 1982–4 = 100 is given for school years 1945–6 to 1995–6 in *Digest of Education Statistics 2000,* 40 (Table 37). For years prior to 1945–6 the source is *Historical Statistics of the United States, Colonial Times to 1970,* Part 1, series E135, and two calendar years have been averaged for comparisons with school years.

Notes

Preface

1 Especially regrettable is the omission, due to limits on my research time
   and opportunities, of a comparative study of aboriginal educational policies
   in Australia, Canada, and the United States; an exploration of the effects of
   gender on educational policies; and the historical development of policies
   with regard to special education and early childhood education. My original research plan included a study of the educational policies of the Republic of Ireland, but reluctantly I decided this had to be a separate project. A
   projected comparison of the Anglo-American educational regimes with the
   educational regimes of Western Europe and Japan also fell by the wayside.
   No doubt inclusion of these comparative studies would have broadened
   and enriched not only my comparison of the Anglo-American educational
   regimes but also my interpretation of the Anglo-American political tradition.
2 See Ronald Manzer, *Public Schools and Political Ideas: Canadian Educational
   Policy in Historical Perspective* (Toronto: University of Toronto Press, 1974),
   4–7. I am following the Hegelian understanding of the relationship between ideas and community as interpreted by Charles Taylor: 'Thus a
   certain view of man and his relation to society is embedded in some of
   the practices and institutions of a society. So that we can think of these as
   expressing certain ideas ... In this sense we can think of the institutions and
   practices of a society as a kind of language in which its fundamental ideas
   are expressed. But what is "said" in this language is not ideas which could
   be in the minds of certain individuals only; they are rather common to a
   society, because embedded in its collective life, in practices and institutions
   which are of the society indivisibly. In these the spirit of the society is in a

sense objectified. They are, to use Hegel's term, "objective spirit."' Charles Taylor, *Hegel and Modern Society* (Cambridge: Cambridge University Press, 1979), 88–9.

3 The literature on interpretive analysis and political science is considerable, but among the important influences on the development of my approach would be J. Donald Moon, 'The Logic of Political Inquiry: A Synthesis of Opposed Perspectives,' in Fred I. Greenstein and Nelson W. Polsby (eds), *Handbook of Political Science*, vol. 1, *Political Science: Scope and Theory* (Reading, Mass.: Addison-Wesley Publishing, 1975), 131–228; David C. Paris and James F. Reynolds, *The Logic of Policy Inquiry* (New York: Longman, 1983), ch. 6; Charles Taylor, *Human Agency and Language: Philosophical Papers*, vol. 1 (Cambridge: Cambridge University Press, 1985); the collection of essays on philosophical hermeneutics and expressive theories of language in Michael T. Gibbons (ed.), *Interpreting Politics* (Oxford: Basil Blackwell, 1987); Terence Ball, 'Deadly Hermeneutics; Or, *Sinn* and the Social Scientist,' in Terence Ball (ed.), *Idioms of Inquiry: Critique and Renewal in Political Science* (Albany: State University of New York, 1987), 95–112; Edward Bryan Portis and Michael B. Levy (eds), *Handbook of Political Theory and Policy Science* (New York: Greenwood Press, 1988), especially the essays by Bruce Jennings, 'Political Theory and Policy Analysis: Bridging the Gap,' ibid., 17–27, and Stephen L. Elkin, 'Political Institutions and Political Practice,' ibid., 111–25; Thomas J. Kaplan, 'Reading Policy Narratives: Beginnings, Middles, and Ends,' in Frank Fischer and John Forester (eds), *The Argumentative Turn in Policy Analysis and Planning* (Durham, N.C.: Duke University Press, 1993), 167–85; Douglas Torgerson, 'Power and Insight in Policy Discourse: Post-Positivism and Problem Definition,' in Laurent Dobuzinskis, Michael Howlett, and David Laycock (eds), *Policy Studies in Canada: The State of the Art* (Toronto: University of Toronto Press, 1996), 266–98; and Patricia O'Reilly, *Health Care Practitioners: An Ontario Case Study in Policy Making* (Toronto: University of Toronto Press, 2000), 6–14.

Introduction: Educational Regimes and the Comparative Study of Anglo-American Democracy

1 This thought is inspired by William Connolly's argument that 'Current liberalism cannot be defined merely through its commitment to freedom, rights, dissent, and justice. It must be understood, as well, through the institutional arrangements it endorses.' William Connolly, 'The Dilemma of Legitimacy,' in William Connolly (ed.), *Legitimacy and the State* (Oxford: Blackwell, 1984), 233.

2 See my introductory comments in Ronald Manzer, *Public Schools and Political Ideas: Canadian Educational Policy in Historical Perspective* (Toronto: University of Toronto Press, 1994), 1.

3 This feature of 'educational regime' corresponds to what I have elsewhere described as 'public philosophy.' Ronald Manzer, *Public Policies and Political Development in Canada* (Toronto: University of Toronto Press, 1985), 13.

4 Robert A. Dahl, *Democracy and Its Critics* (New Haven: Yale University Press, 1989), 108–14. See also David Held, *Models of Democracy* (2nd ed.; Stanford, Calif.: Stanford University Press, 1996), 310–11.

5 By 'person-regarding equality' in public education I refer to educational programs that have been designed to meet the individual ends or needs of each person in school. Students are not given a uniform or identical education; they follow different educational programs, depending on their ends or needs. Hence, the educational programs of individual students are not generally interchangeable, but all students get equal value from their different educational careers. By 'lot-regarding equality' I refer to educational programs that are uniform or identical. Where all students follow essentially the same courses and program, no student would gain or lose value by exchanging his or her educational program for that of any other student. Hence, the educational lots of all students are equal. For a theoretical discussion of the concepts of lot-regarding and person-regarding equality, see Douglas Rae with Douglas Yates, Jennifer Hochschild, Joseph Morone, and Carol Fessler, *Equalities* (Cambridge, Mass.: Harvard University Press, 1981), 85–101. Rae and colleagues observe with respect to person-regarding equality that interpersonal comparisons of value also may be based on utility as an alternative to ends or needs (ibid., 93–5). See also their discussion of 'segmental equality,' where there is a claim of equality for two or more classes of equals, equality being required within each class but not between classes, and 'bloc-regarding equality,' where there is a claim of equality for two or more subject classes, equality being required between these classes (blocs) but not within them (ibid., 29–38). For a delightfully helpful illustration of these different ideas of equality see the discussion of responses from her class on public policy as to how to divide a chocolate cake by Deborah A. Stone, *Policy Paradox and Political Reason* (Glenview, Ill.: Scott, Foresman, 1988), 30–41.

6 Carl J. Friedrich, *Man and His Government* (New York: McGraw-Hill, 1963), 354.

7 Conservatives advocated ascriptive criteria of family and class as the basis for making patronage appointments in order to preserve essential social and political hierarchies. Liberals held that democracy was reinforced and

renewed by the material incentives of public appointments, which grease
the organization of political parties, and by the regular turnover of administrative personnel, which opened public administration to citizen participation. See Donna Robinson Divine, 'A Political Theory of Bureaucracy,'
Public Administration 57 (Summer 1979): 151–2.

8 See Manzer, *Public Schools and Political Ideas*, 20–3. According to the theory
of civic trusteeship the public function of policy making should be separated from both politics and administration, and administration should be
separated from politics. The institutional separation of policy and administration from politics does not mean that there will be no mechanism for
public accountability. Policy-making authorities may be formally appointed
by elected politicians and held answerable for their policies before a popularly elected, representative legislature. What is imperative is securing their
autonomy from partisan politics by the terms and conditions of their
appointment and the norms and practices of their public office.

9 On the history and continuing influence of Anglo-American theories of
'executive leadership,' see Rosamund Thomas, *The British Philosophy of Administration* (London: Longman, 1978), 37–45; Herbert Kaufman, 'Emerging Conflicts in the Doctrines of Public Administration,' *American Political
Science Review* 50 (December 1956): 1063–7; and Joel D. Aberbach, Robert
D. Putnam, and Bert A. Rockman, *Bureaucrats and Politicians in Western
Democracies* (Cambridge, Mass.: Harvard University Press, 1981), 23–6, 241.

10 Given the logical possibilities for separating and/or combining the functions of politics, policy, and administration, there are eight types of public
authority and political accountability. Beyond the mainstream of Anglo-
American theorizing about public authority and political accountability –
which includes political administration, ministerial responsibility, civic
trusteeship, executive leadership, bureaucratic politics, and representative
bureaucracy – there are two essentially anti-democratic models that aim
to isolate the functions of policy and administration from politics. First, in
the theory of 'heroic legislator,' politics and administration are recognized
as impossible to separate; as with politics, the public bureaucracy is penetrated by persistent, traditional societal divisions and political patronage.
Hence, making educational policies that will serve the public interest
requires severing the policy function from both politics and administration.
The theory of heroic legislator depends on the existence of a leader, widely
recognized and admired as having exceptional qualities, who is relatively
autonomous from both politics and administration but none the less able
to exert effective authority over the choice of policy by moral suasion.
Second, under a 'guardian bureaucracy' the functions of policy and admin-

istration are fused, and both are separated from politics. Isolated from policy and administration, politics is an unfocused and irresponsible struggle for partisan position. Isolated from politics, policy making and policy implementation become an undemocratic and non-responsible exercise of executive power.

11 The theories of administrative agency and policy tutelage differ in their view of how much administrative discretion should be accorded to local authorities within the policy framework determined by the central state. According to the theory of administrative agency, the public function of administration has no distinctive spatial or territorial dimension beyond the simple requirement that many public regulations and services must be implemented in different localities. In the theory of policy tutelage, by contrast, administration is perceived to have an important territorial dimension that requires the exercise of considerable discretion on the part of local authorities in order to adapt central policies to local needs. As a variation of policy tutelage, central authorities may determine the goals or outcomes of policy in conjunction with their national (or state/provincial) political function, and local educational authorities are expected to design and implement particular courses of action that will realize the national mandates.

12 To deal with overlapping or joint activities or to realize economies of scale, local communities may institute regional confederations of local communities by sending representatives to regional bodies to which they have delegated authority to design programs and/or manage operations with regard to specific educational activities or services; regional boards, in turn, may send representatives to national boards. For example, local school boards, which have communal autonomy with regard to governing elementary schools in their districts, may be authorized by law to enter into an agreement to constitute a regional school board with its membership comprising representatives from the participating local boards for the purpose of establishing and maintaining a regional secondary school. Representatives of regional school boards, in turn, may constitute a national board with delegated authority to develop national standards for the provision of secondary education.

13 The term 'fiscal equivalence' has been taken from Mancur Olson, 'The Principle of "Fiscal Equivalence,"' *American Economic Review* 59 (May 1969): 483.

14 In this conception of political economy, states and markets are distinguished as structures of institutions and processes by their basic mechanism of collective provision. States make and enforce decisions about production

and distribution of goods and services by the exercise of public authority, which takes the form of a monopoly of the legitimate use of physical force in a specified territory. In markets, decisions about production and distribution of goods and services are effected by the option of private exchange, which takes the form of a voluntary transaction between individuals and/or organizations. In addition to coercion through the state and exchange in the market, in most domains of social policy, including education, there is a third form of collective provision that depends on cooperative and/or voluntary production and distribution. The place of this third sector, appropriately termed 'civil society,' or simply 'society,' in order to differentiate it as a mode of collective decision making from the state and the market, must also be taken into account as a potential sector in dealing with a problem of political economy.

15 Asa Briggs, 'The Welfare State in Historical Perspective,' *Archives Européenes de Sociologies* 2 (1961): 228. See also Ramesh Mishra's description of the modern welfare state as a 'three-pronged attack on want and dependency' comprising a commitment on the part of the state to maintain full employment, deliver universal social programs such as health care and public education, and maintain basic programs of income maintenance for those in need. Ramesh Mishra, *The Welfare State in Capitalist Society* (Toronto: University of Toronto Press, 1990), 18.

16 Susan Strange, for example, has argued 'that the impersonal forces of world markets, integrated over the postwar period more by private enterprise in finance, industry and trade than by the cooperative decisions of governments, are now more powerful than the states to whom ultimate political authority over society and economy is supposed to belong.' Susan Strange, *The Retreat of the State: The Diffusion of Power in the World Economy* (Cambridge: Cambridge University Press, 1996), 4.

17 G. Bruce Doern, Leslie A. Pal, and Brian W. Tomlin have distinguished globalization, which is primarily a technological and economic process, from the internationalization of public policy, 'a process by which various aspects of policy or policy making are influenced by factors outside national territorial boundaries' ('The Internationalization of Canadian Public Policy,' in G. Bruce Doern, Leslie A. Pal, and Brian W. Tomlin [eds], *Border Crossings: The Internationalization of Canadian Public Policy* [Toronto: Oxford University Press, 1996], 4). They argue that policy fields can be internationalized gradually as well as rapidly, internationalization can occur in the absence of globalization, and internationalization is multidimensional, cutting across policy ideas, design, implementation, and participants.

18 Edmund Burke, *Reflections on the French Revolution* (London: J.M. Dent, 1910), 93.

19 On the idea of 'possessive individualism' as the key principle of liberal political economy, see C.B. Macpherson, *The Political Theory of Possessive Individualism: Hobbes to Locke* (London: Oxford University Press, 1962), 263–4.

20 Adam Smith, *An Inquiry into the Nature and Causes of the Wealth of Nations* (New York: Random House, 1937 [1776]), 14.

21 'According to the liberal argument in the tradition of Locke, Smith, the Mills, Spencer, and Dicey, in the market system one responds – for example, takes a particular job – only if the proffered benefits are attractive, hence only if one chooses to do so. In any authority system one is required to work where assigned and obey any other command regardless of benefit. As some people see it, no more needs to be said to prove men freer in markets than in authority systems.' Charles E. Lindblom, *Politics and Markets: The World's Political Economic Systems* (New York: Basic Books, 1977), 45.

22 See C.B. Macpherson, *The Life and Times of Liberal Democracy* (Oxford: Oxford University Press, 1977), 23–40.

23 Manzer, *Public Policies and Political Development in Canada*, 74–5.

24 According to Edward Andrew, 'C.B. Macpherson ignores the religious dimension of British liberalism. Liberalism is not exhausted in the term "possessive individualism" but includes religious freedom. By abstracting from the religious dimension of the English civil war, the Glorious Revolution and the political theories attendant on these events, Macpherson unduly narrows the focus of the founders of liberal doctrine' (Edward Andrew, *Shylock's Rights: A Grammar of Lockian Claims* [Toronto: University of Toronto Press, 1988], 4–5). Andrew's argument aims 'to establish the connection between religious toleration and an individualist market morality' in classical liberal theory.

25 Macpherson, *The Life and Times of Liberal Democracy*, 48.

26 Will Kymlicka, *Liberalism, Community, and Culture* (Oxford: Clarendon Press, 1989), 209.

27 See, for example, the arguments of Carole Pateman, *Participation and Democratic Theory* (Cambridge: Cambridge University Press, 1970), 67–102; and Frank Cunningham, *Democratic Theory and Socialism* (Cambridge: Cambridge University Press, 1987), 128–31.

28 Robert E. Goodin, *Reasons for Welfare: The Political Theory of the Welfare State* (Princeton: Princeton University Press, 1988), 14.

29 Neil Nevitte and Roger Gibbins, *New Elites in Old States: Ideologies in the Anglo-American Democracies* (Toronto: Oxford University Press, 1990), 1.

Nevitte and Gibbins continue, 'Compared with other industrially advanced states, each of the Anglo-American democracies has a long history of open, stable, and liberal democratic style of government. For the most part citizens of the Anglo-American democracies view their systems of government as legitimate, and the transfer of power has rarely taken place in an atmosphere of crisis; it has been routine. Through this century political contests have not been battles about the rules of the game; instead, the battles have been about ideas, policies, leaders, and parties.'

30 The classic analyses are advanced by Louis Hartz, *The Liberal Tradition in America: An Interpretation of American Political Thought since the Revolution* (New York: Harcourt, Brace and World, 1955), 59–64; Gad Horowitz, 'Conservatism, Liberalism, and Socialism in Canada: An Interpretation,' *Canadian Journal of Economics and Political Science* 32 (May 1966): 143–71; Samuel H. Beer, *British Politics in the Collectivist Age* (New York: Alfred A. Knopf, 1965), 69–102; Richard N. Rosecrance, 'The Radical Culture of Australia,' in Louis Hartz et al., *The Founding of New Societies: Studies in the History of the United States, Latin America, South Africa, Canada, and Australia* (New York: Harcourt, Brace and World, 1964), 303–14; and Seymour Martin Lipset, *The First New Nation: The United States in Historical and Comparative Perspective* (New York: Basic Books, 1963), 248–73. In the late twentieth century, political cultures of Anglo-American democracies have been substantially amended by neo-liberal and neo-conservative ideas. See, for example, Barry Cooper, Allan Kornberg, and William Mishler (eds), *The Resurgence of Conservatism in Anglo-American Democracies* (Durham: Duke University Press, 1988).

31 In practice, the main types of educational regimes in the Anglo-American democracies are substantially fewer than the potential number based on constitutional jurisdictions. There are major similarities of educational regime among the states of Australia, the countries of the United Kingdom, and the regions of the United States (for example, New England, the South, the West), and Canada.

1. Public Instruction

1 See the section titled 'Of the Expence of the Institutions for the Education of Youth' in Adam Smith, *An Inquiry into the Nature and Causes of the Wealth of Nations* (New York: Random House, 1937 [1776]), 716–40.

2 For a collection of Thomas Jefferson's writings on the importance of public education, see Gordon C. Lee (ed.), *Crusade against Ignorance: Thomas Jefferson on Education* (New York: Columbia University Teachers College,

1961), especially the third section, 81–103, which includes 'A Bill for the More General Diffusion of Knowledge,' drafted by Jefferson in 1779.

3 In the 1820s, state aid in the first colonies of New South Wales and Van Dieman's Land (Tasmania) was restricted to schools of the Church of England. The Church and School Corporation, founded by Anglican Archbishop T.H. Scott with an endowment of land grants from crown reserves, established a number of church schools, but its objective, which was to gain an Anglican monopoly over elementary education, met increasingly strong resistance from other religious denominations. When Scott left Sydney in 1829, his successor was informed that the corporation's charter would not be renewed. In New South Wales, when the monopoly of the Church and Schools Corporation was formally dissolved in 1833, the governor, Sir Richard Bourke, continued aid to Church of England schools and extended it to include the four Catholic schools in the colony. Bourke objected to aiding church schools, however, and recommended adoption of the system of national schools introduced in Ireland two years earlier. Bourke was able to get official approval for his proposal to introduce the Irish system, but opposition led by the Anglican archbishop, W.G. Broughton, and a Presbyterian clergyman, J.D. Lang, prevented its implementation. Under the aegis of the Church Act (1836), state aid was then given to the Anglican, Catholic, Presbyterian, and Methodist churches, resulting in four systems of state-aided denominational schools until a dual regime was established in 1848.

4 Robert Lowe had arrived in the colony in October 1842 and was immediately nominated to the Legislative Council. He was an adherent of Jeremy Bentham's utilitarianism, concerned to disentangle religion from education and implement a non-sectarian, commerce-oriented curriculum. Alan Barcan, *A Short History of Education in New South Wales* (Sydney: Martindale Press, 1965), 49–50.

5 Ibid., 54.

6 Originally, the 1866 bill provided for the colonial secretary, then Henry Parkes, to serve ex officio as president of the Council of Education. In the debate on second reading, Parkes said, 'The simple idea in this provision is to have a Minister for Education.' See C.C. Linz, *The Establishment of a National System of Education in New South Wales*, Australian Council for Educational Research, ACER Research Series No. 51 (Hawthorn, Victoria: Melbourne University Press, 1938), 51, n28. This provision was deleted in committee, the council was left to elect its own leader, and Parkes eventually came to defend the independent council as a way of protecting public instruction against political influence. See D.C. Griffith, *Documents on the*

Establishment of Education in New South Wales, ACER Research Series No. 70 (Melbourne: Australian Council for Educational Research, 1957), 161.

7 Prior to the separation of Port Phillip as the colony of Victoria, the denominational board in Port Phillip was providing aid to fifty-three church schools compared to only seven schools in the district that belonged to the national board in Sydney.

8 All state-aided 'common' schools, whether vested or non-vested, had to give four consecutive hours of instruction daily in secular subjects. Religious instruction could be given before or after this period. No student could be compelled to receive religious instruction, and no one could be refused admittance to a common school on religious grounds. The board of education created under the Common Schools Act was an independent body of five lay commissioners, no two of whom could belong to the same religious denomination. In appointing the first board, Premier O'Shanassy invited the churches to nominate their representatives: an Anglican squatter and a former member of both the legislative council and the legislative assembly who served as chair, the registrar general who was a Catholic, a Presbyterian businessman and member of the legislative assembly who also had served on the National Board, a Wesleyan businessman, and a Jewish merchant. L.J. Blake, 'The Common Schools Period,' in L.J. Blake (ed.), *Vision and Realization: A Centenary History of State Education in Victoria,* vol. 1 (Melbourne: Education Department of Victoria, 1973), 87.

9 Quoted in A.G. Austin, *Australian Education 1788–1900: Church, State and Public Education in Colonial Australia* (2nd ed.; Melbourne: Isaac Pitman, 1965), 105–6.

10 The first central board of education was established in Van Dieman's Land in 1839 prior to the introduction of responsible government. The board's membership included the colonial secretary, the solicitor general, a member of the Legislative Council, the registrar of the Supreme Court, and a fifth unidentified member. See Clifford Reeves, *A History of Tasmanian Education: State Primary Education,* ACER Research Series No. 40 (Melbourne: Melbourne University Press, 1935), 26. It distributed grants to schools from 1839 to 1848 based on the Nonconformist system of the British and Foreign School Society but resigned when a scheme of denominational grants was introduced. In 1850 a British act of Parliament gave Van Dieman's Land a Legislative Council of twenty-four members, sixteen of them elected. Following a recommendation of the Legislative Council in 1853, the central board was briefly reconstituted, consisting of members of the Executive and Legislative Councils with the colonial secretary as chairman and the inspector of schools as secretary. This board was necessarily

reorganized when responsible government was introduced in 1856 and the Legislative Council disappeared. The next year the central governance of education was divided between northern and southern territorial boards with membership now drawn from the House of Assembly. These were reunited as a single board in 1863 and continued to govern Tasmanian education until the Education Act of 1885 created a ministerial department.

11 Quoted in L.J. Blake, 'Free, Compulsory and Secular,' in Blake (ed.), *Vision and Realization*, vol. 1, 190–1.

12 The royal commission was chaired by the former Liberal party leader, Supreme Court Justice Charles Lilley, who had sponsored a bill for compulsory education, ministerial department, and non-sectarian schools in 1873. The commission also included Samuel Griffith, the new leader of the Liberal party, who subsequently became Queensland's first minister of education. A report to the royal commission by the master of Brisbane Grammar School set out clearly the advantages utilitarian liberals believed would arise from a ministerial department: 'That the presence of a responsible Minister assures the attention in Parliament to educational questions, and keeps alive a popular interest in them; that any maladministration or any abuse may be readily checked; that the administration has passed into the hands of men professionally qualified to deal with educational affairs, and always present on the spot; and that in providing for the education of the people whom they serve, the Minister and his subordinates are free to plant schools wherever they are needed and are not hampered by having to study conflicting claims or opposing interests' (quoted in E.R. Wyeth, *Education in Queensland: A History of Education in Queensland and in the Moreton Bay District of New South Wales*, ACER Research Series No. 67 [Melbourne: Australian Council for Educational Research, 1955], 120–1). This report followed the master's visit to Victoria, where ministerial responsibility had just been introduced.

13 One member of the South Australia assembly argued during debate on the 1875 education bill that 'The Board is in fact nothing but a screen for this person, while they are irresponsible and he is irresponsible, and you can never get to the moving power. The Board screens him. He has all the power of a responsible officer, but none of the responsibility. The responsibility falls on the Board: but you can never get at the Board. (Hear, hear).' Quoted in Colin Thiele, *Grains of Mustard Seed* (Adelaide: South Australia Education Department, 1975), 10.

14 The Council of Education was attacked as a cumbersome and inefficient instrument of administration. The president of the council was the real

force and the council merely a rubber stamp. The president 'was the person, and the only person, who was familiar with the workings of the department. He was the master of the situation, and though not the nominal was the actual head of the department' (ibid., 25–6). Only the creation of a government department with a minister of the crown at its head would achieve the requisite combination of power and responsibility. Following the establishment of the Department of Public Instruction, the former president of the Council of Education, J.A. Hartley, was appointed inspector general, the senior administrative official in the new department, and he continued to be the dominant administrative and policy force in South Australian state education until his retirement in 1896.

15 Other leading Liberals had pressed for direct political accountability; for example, then premier John Robertson introduced a bill in 1876 to establish a minister of education and make teachers public servants. Parkes indicated that he favoured the bill, but it was ruled out of order. In 1878, Parkes and Robertson, formerly political rivals, formed a coalition government with Parkes as premier.

16 The agents of the National Board of Education in New South Wales, for example, were instructed to make every effort to establish new schools but not to interfere where their help was not wanted. During the two years of his agency from 1849 to 1851, for example, G.K. Rusdan undertook five separate tours, riding out of Sydney as far south as Melbourne, north to Moreton Bay, and inland to the New England and Bathurst areas. 'In all these districts his procedure was the same: letters sent ahead some weeks earlier would stimulate local interest and enable him to call a meeting soon after he arrived in a township; before the meeting he would try to visit every person with local influence, secure a suitable chairman and make tentative proposals for patrons; at the meeting he would display the books and regulations of the National Board, speak if requested, and, if the meeting resolved to erect a school, assist the patrons to make their initial application to the Commissioners. If his itinerary permitted he stayed on in the district for a few days (or, the country permitting, doubled back a little later) to ensure that interest did not flag, that promised subscriptions were collected and that a building contract was let.' Austin, *Australian Education 1788–1900*, 54.

17 In Victoria the Common Schools Act of 1862 provided that each school would be under the management of a local committee of at least five members, appointed by the central board with powers to appoint and dismiss teachers, collect fees, and raise half the cost of building and furnishing the schools. See G.S.Browne, 'Victoria,' in G.S. Browne (ed.),

Education in Australia: A Comparative Study of the Educational Systems of the Six Australian States (London: Macmillan, 1927), 83–4. In New South Wales, the Public Schools Act (1866), provided for public school boards comprising at least three members nominated by the central Council of Education rather than appointed locally. These school boards continued until 1875 to be responsible for contributing one-third of the cost of building new schools, and they were expected to visit and inspect the local school and report to the central council. The school boards apparently proved no better than local patrons in attending to their duties, and inspectors' reports continued to be highly critical of local school management.

18 The 1871 education act also required that the electoral roll for district school boards include one parent of each enrolled pupil, so some women had votes as mothers of enrolled pupils. Like the English model on which it was based, Governor Weld's act contained a protection for minorities by means of cumulative and proxy voting. The boards supervised all the schools in their districts that received public grants; they were empowered to introduce compulsory attendance for children between the ages of six and fourteen, and they appointed and dismissed teachers in the government schools. See David Mossensen, *State Education in Western Australia 1829–1960* (Nedlands, W.A.: University of Western Australia Press, 1972), 46.

19 C.H. Pearson, *Report on the State of Public Education in Victoria;* quoted in Austin, *Australian Education 1788–1900,* 253. Pearson, who was headmaster of Presbyterian Ladies College, believed the only safeguard against an autocratic minister or an ambitious inspector general was a balance of authority in local boards, but he found little public interest in school board elections and little inclination on the part of board members to become more active participants in local school government.

20 By the end of 1892, only fifty-eight of ninety-two boards had complete memberships, and that number had dropped to forty-three of ninety-four boards with full memberships by 1896.

21 Mossensen, *State Education in Western Australia 1829–1960,* 57–8. One member of a district board in Western Australia complained in 1874 that the central authority 'has all along been *high-handed* and unyielding. The advice and suggestions, not only of this Board, but of every Board with whose proceedings I have become acquainted, have been set aside, snuffed out, and in many cases treated with covert contempt, and seldom if ever met by argument.' Quoted in Austin, *Australian Education 1788–1900,* 254–5; emphasis in the original.

22 Quoted in Austin, *Australian Education 1788–1900,* 175. In particular,

section 7 appeared to assume that 'non-sectarian' and 'secular' instruction were interchangeable in meaning.

23 In Victoria, the first two decades under the 1872 Act were 'years of stern definition and firm defence of the principle of secularism in the education system' (J.S. Gregory, *Church and State: Changing Government Policies towards Religion in Australia; with Particular Reference to Victoria since Separation* [North Melbourne: Cassell Australia, 1973], 174). Gregory cites as an example the deletion of the lines 'And she thought of Christ, who stilled the waves / On the sea of Galilee' from Longfellow's 'The Wreck of the Hesperus.' See also Austin, *Australian Education 1788–1900*, 240–3. In 1922, about 25 per cent of students were enrolled for voluntary religious instruction, and by 1947, 80 per cent (Gregory, *Church and State: Changing Government Policies towards Religion in Australia*, 192–3). In 1950, the Education (Religious Instruction) Act made it permissible to give religious instruction at any time during the school day.

24 Alan Barcan, *A History of Australian Education* (Melbourne: Oxford University Press, 1980), 101, 146.

25 See Wyeth, *Education in Queensland*, 163–70.

26 J.A. Hartley was a devout Methodist and believed that religion should be strictly the concern of home and chapel, not school.

27 In addition to the standard role of the courts in reviewing the constitutionality of provincial legislation, section 93, (3) and (4), provides an avenue of appeal to the federal government. Where a minority denominational right, whether recognized at Confederation or established subsequently by provincial statute, is infringed by provincial law, there is a right of appeal to the Governor General-in-Council, that is, the federal cabinet. The cabinet then may ask provincial authorities to effect appropriate remedies, and, if provincial authorities refuse, the cabinet may ask the Parliament of Canada, to make laws to enforce the minority's right to denominational education.

28 C.B. Sissons, *Church and State in Canadian Education: An Historical Study* (Toronto: Ryerson, 1959), 13, 223.

29 In Lower Canada, the Royal Institution for the Advancement of Learning was proclaimed in 1802, apparently to promote a school system controlled by an established Church of England. During its twenty active years, beginning in 1818, it set up eighty-four schools, but in spite of offers to divide between Protestant and Roman Catholic committees in 1826 and again in 1829, it failed to gain any support from the majority French-Catholic population of the colony. Bishop John Strachan's bid for establishment of the Anglican church in Upper Canada was unsuccessful, colonial education grants were divided among a number of voluntary societies, including the

National Society for Promoting the Education of the Poor in the Principles of the Established Church, and Bishop Alexander Donnell was allowed by colonial authorities in the 1820s and 1830s to allot part of the colonial appropriation for Roman Catholic priests to teachers in Catholic church schools. The National Society was also active in New Brunswick – eleven National schools were still operating in 1871 – and there were a few schools established by the Society for the Propagation of the Gospel.

30 Quoted in William J. Smith and Helen M. Donahue, *The Historical Roots of Québec Education* (Montreal: Office of Research on Educational Policy, McGill University, 1999), 18. The 1846 act also established a board of examiners in both Montreal and Quebec city, in each case comprising seven Roman Catholics and seven Protestants divided into separate departments, with a mandate to examine candidates for teaching positions and award teaching certificates. Smith and Donahue explain that 'The Québec and Montréal schools were at once confessional and common by law. They were required to admit all children from all parts of the city, regardless of religion.'

31 The Salvation Army was recognized as a separate denomination for educational purposes in 1892, the Seventh Day Adventist Church in 1912, and the Pentecostal Assemblies of Newfoundland in 1954. When Newfoundland entered Confederation in 1949, Term 17 of the Terms of Union provided constitutional protection for denominational rights in education: 'the Legislature will not have any authority to make laws prejudicially affecting any right or privilege with respect to denominational schools, common (amalgamated) schools, or denominational colleges, that any class or classes of persons have by law in Newfoundland at the date of Union' and all public funds for such schools must be distributed 'on a non-discriminatory basis.' In December 1987 an amendment to Term 17 was proclaimed that extended constitutional protection of the right to denominational education to include the Pentecostal Assemblies.

32 See section 54 of 'An Act for the Establishment and Maintenance of Common Schools in Upper Canada,' reprinted in J. George Hodgins (ed.), *Documentary History of Education in Upper Canada from the Passing of the Constitutional Act of 1791 to the Close of the Reverend Doctor Ryerson's Administration of the Education Department in 1876*, vol. 4, 1841–1843 (Toronto: Warwick Bro's and Rutter, 1897), 259.

33 Separate schools in law were elementary schools. Based on an interpretation of the British North America (BNA) Act that only separate schools existing in 1867 were entitled to public funding, the regulations of the Department of Education restricted provincial grants to grades one to

eight. In 1926, the Tiny township separate school board launched a court action seeking to establish a right under the BNA Act to conduct its own secondary schools, gain exemption for separate school supporters from supporting public secondary schools, and receive an equitable share of provincial grants for secondary education. The trial court's judgment, upheld on appeal to the Judicial Committee, recognized that a few separate schools before Confederation were giving instruction beyond the elementary stage in their 'fifth book' classes; but it concluded that no separate secondary schools existed in law prior to 1867, and consequently no right to separate secondary schools could be claimed under section 93. Departmental regulations were revised to recognize grades nine and ten, the equivalent of former 'fifth book' classes, for purposes of provincial grants and local taxation; but extending separate school education to include the senior secondary grades remained a nasty, unresolved issue of educational politics in Ontario until the 1980s.

34 After the passage of the New Brunswick Common Schools Act of 1871 requiring 'that all schools conducted under the provisions of this Act shall be non-sectarian,' the federal government declined to disallow the act. The Judicial Committee of the Privy Council ruled in 1874 that, whatever privileges Catholics might have enjoyed in practice under the 1858 act, they did not have any privileges or rights in law and hence they had no protection under section 93 (1) of the British North America Act. Only five of the forty-one members of the legislative assembly elected in 1875 supported separate Roman Catholic schools.

35 Four concessions were made by the provincial cabinet, but these did not become public until eighteen years later: (1) given the consent of local trustees, children might attend any school in the district; (2) teaching licences would be issued to members of a religious order if they had a certificate from the superior of the order, thus obviating the need to attend the provincial normal school program and take the regular examinations for certification; (3) textbooks would be edited or annotated so as to avoid giving offence to Catholics; and (4) trustees were authorized to approve denominational religious instruction after school hours. When the policy was legally tested in 1896 in *Rogers et al.* v. *The School Trustees of School District No. 2 of Bathurst*, an action by Protestant ratepayers against the school board's policy to rent a convent school from the Sisters of Charity, the trial court held that the non-denominational provision of the Common Schools Act was not violated by the employment of members of a religious order as teachers, permitting them to wear the garb of their order while teaching and to hold Roman Catholic religious exercises before or after school hours. No appeal was lodged.

36 When the constitutionality of the act was tested in the courts, the Supreme
Court of Canada unanimously ruled that the act did prejudicially affect
rights and privileges with respect to denominational schools that Roman
Catholics had enjoyed by practice in 1870, but the Judicial Committee of
the Privy Council reversed the Supreme Court ruling and upheld the act.
In a further action in 1895, the Judicial Committee ruled that Manitoba
Roman Catholics had been affected in their minority rights and privileges
by the 1890 act but that their appeal for redress should be directed to the
federal government rather than to the courts. The Roman Catholic minority then appealed to the federal government to protect its denominational
education rights, an appeal that became a major issue in the election campaign of 1896 won by the Liberal party led by Wilfrid Laurier. Unwilling to
force a federal remedy on the Manitoba government, primarily because of
the implications such an action could pose for provincial rights in Quebec,
the Laurier government settled for only minor concessions: religious
instruction was permitted during the last half-hour where authorized by the
school trustees or requested by parents, and the employment of a Catholic
teacher could be requested for every twenty-five Catholic pupils in a rural
school, or every forty in an urban school.

37 For a decade after 1823 there had been a General Board in Upper Canada
that included Bishop John Strachan as chair, two members of the legislative council, the attorney general, the surveyor general, and the Reverend
Robert Addison. It was abolished as a result of an attack on the policies of
the Tory 'Family Compact' by liberal reformers who feared that the central
board gave the colonial government 'power and bias over the minds of
their children.' R.D. Gidney, 'Centralization and Education: The Origins of
an Ontario Tradition,' *Journal of Canadian Studies* 7 (November 1972): 37.

38 R.D. Gidney and D.A. Lawr, 'The Development of an Administrative System
for the Public Schools: The First Stage, 1841–50,' in Neil McDonald and Alf
Chaiton (eds), *Egerton Ryerson and His Times* (Toronto: Macmillan, 1978),
175.

39 In New Brunswick, when the political membership of the board of education was criticized during debate on the 1871 education bill, the attorney
general pointed out that New Brunswick preferred to follow the examples
of England, where members of the Privy Council comprised the board of
education, and Nova Scotia, rather than those of the non-political boards
of the American states or the colonies of Canada East and Canada West.
Katherine F.C. MacNaughton, *The Development of the Theory and Practice of
Education in New Brunswick 1784–1900* (Fredericton: University of New
Brunswick, 1946), 190.

40 The president of the University of New Brunswick became an ex officio

member of the New Brunswick board under the Common Schools Act of
1871. In Prince Edward Island, the board of education, which had served
as the central governing body since 1852, was reformed under the Public
School Act of 1877 to comprise the executive council, the principal of
Prince of Wales College, and the chief superintendent.

41 The council's quorum consisted of the chairman (F.G. Haultain, who was
'premier' and dominating leader of the territorial executive committee)
and one other member of the executive committee. The Council of Public
Instruction in its entirety met only at the discretion of the territorial executive. Manoly R. Lupul, *The Roman Catholic Church and the North-West School
Question: A Study in Church-State Relations in Western Canada, 1875–1905*
(Toronto: University of Toronto Press, 1974), 81.

42 When Charles-Eugène Boucher de Boucherville, the last minister of public
instruction (and also premier), introduced the bill to replace the ministry
with a superintendent responsible to the Council of Public Instruction, he
made clear his government's intention that the superintendent should be a
distinguished educator able to stand above parties and political considerations. In his words, disbanding the ministry had the purpose of 'protecting
primary education from more or less harmful influences by placing it in an
elevated and serene position where it would not be affected by class distinctions or political pressures.' Quoted by Louis-Philippe Audet, 'Education
in Canada East and Quebec: 1840–1875,' in J. Donald Wilson, Robert M.
Stamp, and Louis-Philippe Audet (eds), *Canadian Education: A History*
(Scarborough, Ont.: Prentice-Hall Canada, 1970), 186.

43 See Mark W. Graesser, 'Church, State, and Public Policy in Newfoundland:
The Question of Denominational Education,' paper presented to the
annual meeting of the Canadian Political Science Association, University of
Victoria, Victoria, British Columbia, 1990, 4; and Phillip McCann, 'Denomi-
national Education in the Twentieth Century in Newfoundland,' in William
A. McKim (ed.), *The Vexed Question: Denominational Education in a Secular Age*
(St John's: Breakwater Books, 1988), 66–7.

44 At the same time, the former bureau of education was reinstated as a
council of education with the commissioner for home affairs and education
as chairman, the secretary for education as vice-chairman and administrative head of the department of education, and the four denominational
executive officers as 'the recognized representatives on educational matters
for their respective religious denominations within the Department.'
Ronald G. Penney, 'The Constitutional Status of Denominational Education in Newfoundland,' in McKim (ed.), *The Vexed Question*, 82–3.

45 In 1847, school sections in the cities of Canada West were amalgamated

under city school boards, with their members at first appointed by municipal councils and then elected after 1850. The Winnipeg school board, originally established in 1871 as Winnipeg Protestant School District Number 10 with three elected trustees, was expanded to twelve elected members in 1876 and given authority to appoint its own school inspector. Trustees on the four city school boards established in 1888 in British Columbia were initially appointed, four by the city council and three by the provincial cabinet; after 1901, they were elected. In the Maritimes, by contrast, the joint appointment of city and town school boards by the municipal council and provincial cabinet continued to be the practice until the reorganization of regional school divisions in New Brunswick (1967), Prince Edward Island (1972), and Nova Scotia (1995).

46 Alison Prentice, 'The Public Instructor: Ryerson and the Role of Public School Administrator,' in McDonald and Chaiton (eds), *Egerton Ryerson and His Times*, 139–41.

47 Provincial policy tutelage was especially important in establishing local property taxation as the basis for financing public instruction. See Ronald Manzer, *Public Schools and Political Ideas: Canadian Educational Policy in Historical Perspective* (Toronto: University of Toronto Press, 1994), 88.

48 Norman Henchey and Donald Burgess, *Between Past and Future: Quebec Education in Transition* (Calgary: Detselig Enterprises, 1987), 192. Every bishop of the Roman Catholic church whose diocese was wholly or partly inside Quebec by right was a member of the Council of Public Instruction and the Roman Catholic committee. Smith and Donahue, *The Historical Roots of Québec Education*, 22.

49 The Council of Higher Education continued operating until 1949, when its function was absorbed by the Department of Education.

50 Assisted schools were required to include religious education in their curriculum. The children of parents dissenting from religious doctrines taught in school were allowed to be excused from these classes. Almost half of Grey's dispatch to the Colonial Office justifying the ordinance was devoted to a defence of the extension of aid to Catholic schools in spite of strong petitions from many colonists against such aid. See John Mackey, *The Making of a State Education System: The Passing of the New Zealand Education Act, 1877* (London: Geoffrey Chapman, 1967), 40.

51 Ibid., 56.

52 William Fox, 'Report on Education,' *Acts and Proceedings of the Wellington Provincial Council, 1853–54*, 10 November 1854, 8; quoted in ibid., 69; emphasis in the original.

53 The amendment failed to induce church schools to institute non-denomi-

national religious instruction and observances in return for provincial aid. Some schools were built and maintained in country districts under the act, but it remained inoperative in towns where private and church schools continued to provide education for virtually the entire provincial period.

54 The 1852 act of the British Parliament that gave New Zealand a form of representative government provided for a quasi-federal constitution. See W.P. Morrell, *The Provincial System in New Zealand 1852–76* (2nd ed.; Christchurch: Whitcombe and Tombs, 1964). The General Assembly of the colony comprised the governor general appointed by the crown, the Legislative Council nominated by the governor general and appointed for life by the crown, and the elected House of Representatives. Responsible government, under which the executive council was formed on the basis of majority support in the House of Representatives, was granted in 1856. Each province was governed by a unicameral elected council with a super-intendent, also popularly elected, as chief executive official. Thirteen areas of jurisdiction, including customs duties, coinage and currency, and marriages, were specified as belonging exclusively to the General Assembly. Education was not assigned to the General Assembly by the constitution act, and following an initial inquiry into the state of colonial education, the General Assembly left education to the provincial councils. Education did come before the General Assembly between 1869 and 1872, but the issue was financial equalization rather than provincial versus national control of education. A national education bill was introduced during the 1871 session but failed to pass (ibid., 226–30).

55 The Education Ordinance of 1871 abolished fees in the Education Board's ('district') schools and ended state aid to church schools in areas consti-tuted as school districts. The denominational conflict that followed reached its peak in April–May 1873, as efforts (eventually successful) were made to establish school districts in central Christchurch. The Education Ordinance of 1874 formally abolished state aid to church schools except where a school was located in a remote area or among an unsettled population. C. Whitehead, 'The Denominational Question in Canterbury Education 1871–74,' *New Zealand Journal of Educational Studies* 7 (May 1972): 76.

56 Mackey, *The Making of a State Education System*, 118.

57 Ibid., 94. The 1856 education ordinance in the province of Nelson pro-vided for religious instruction subject to the conditions that it was free of sectarian controversy and parents who objected to it could withdraw their children from school for that time period of the timetable. Roman Catho-lics strongly protested against the principle of non-denominational schools, and the Board of Education recommended to the provincial council the

adoption of a scheme modelled on Canadian separate schools. When the council approved such an amendment two years later, Roman Catholics were the only ratepayers to take advantage of it and form separate school districts. The province of Westland, established in 1873 just as the provincial system was coming to an end, also adopted clauses from the Nelson ordinance providing for separate schools.

58 When Taranaki was divided in 1874, the new education boards of New Plymouth and Patea wielded wide powers that left school committees as mere advisory or reporting bodies (Ian Cumming and Alan Cumming, *History of State Education in New Zealand 1840–1975* [Wellington: Pitman Publishing New Zealand, 1978], 79). The Canterbury provincial board was abolished in 1875, and central authority was exercised by a secretary of education appointed by the superintendent. In Marlborough, the provincial board and school committees had been replaced by the roads boards, and in Hawkes Bay school committees were dealing directly with the superintendent.

59 Quoted in ibid., 94; see also Mackey, *The Making of a State Education System*, 179.

60 Eight of the twelve education districts corresponded to the former provinces of Auckland, Hawkes Bay, Marlborough, Nelson, Otago, Wellington, Westland, and Southland. Canterbury was divided into North and South Canterbury. The former subdivisions of Taranaki, New Plymouth, and Patea were renamed Taranaki and Wanganui. Education was the only function of government for which former provincial boundaries were retained more or less intact. When the provinces were abolished in 1876, responsibility for general local governmental functions, including roads, was transferred to sixty-three elected county councils.

61 During the first session dealing with the bill in committee, the 'provincialist' interest secured (by a vote of 40 to 17) an amendment that restricted the department to the appointment of a single inspector. A subsequent amendment gave the education boards authority to appoint and remove all other inspectors. This amendment was 'to prove decisive in swinging the balance of power to favour the Boards rather than the Department' (Mackey, *The Making of a State Education System*, 230).

62 New Zealand, Commission on Education in New Zealand, *Report of the Commission on Education in New Zealand* (Wellington: Government Printer, 1962), 70.

63 Charles Bowen had been chair of the Canterbury Board of Education from 1872 to 1874 when, under the education ordinances of 1871 and 1873, first religious instruction and then Bible reading were dropped from the

board's schools. His 1877 proposal for religious observances in national schools was intended to placate Otago members, who had defeated previous attempts at a unified system of schools (Mackey, *The Making of a State Education System,* 182–4, 203). Bowen argued that the inclusion of prayer and Bible reading in schools did not infringe their secular character and referred to American practice to support his case: 'In a number of American states, including Ohio and Indiana, they have absolutely [sic] clauses put into their Constitution Acts to the effect that the Bible shall not be excluded from the schools; and yet, notwithstanding this, the teaching in the schools is purely secular' (quoted in ibid., 228–9).

64 Colin McGeorge, 'Religious Aspects of the Secular System,' in R. Openshaw and J.D.S. McKenzie (eds), *Reinterpreting the Educational Past: Essays in the History of New Zealand Education* (Wellington: New Zealand Council for Educational Research, 1987), 167. The Education Act of 1877 applied only to public schools which were by definition primary schools, including district high schools. Its provisions did not apply to post-primary secondary and technical schools, and as a result these schools operated without legal restrictions on religious instruction and observance.

65 These secular lessons did not appear on the official timetables of the schools, and attendance was not recorded. The minister of education insisted that they be stopped, but they were eventually abandoned because children ceased to attend (Cumming and Cumming, *History of State Education in New Zealand 1840–1975,* 141). An earlier attempt to give religious instruction in Canterbury schools, which similarly took advantage of the education board's discretion to set opening and closing hours of school, 'operated in only a few schools, and did not gain national attention.' C.M. McGeorge, 'The Failure of the "Nelson System" of Religious Education in Canterbury 1878–1897,' *New Zealand Journal of Educational Studies* 9 (May 1974): 67.

66 Ian A. McLaren, *Education in a Small Democracy: New Zealand* (London: Routledge and Kegan Paul, 1974), 50–1.

67 New Zealand, *Report of the Commission on Education in New Zealand,* 680. Under section 32 of the Education Act of 1914, the education boards were authorized to set the opening and closing hours of primary schools, and the boards generally used this power to shorten the usual five hours of instruction by half an hour on one day each week. Section 49(7) of the act then gave each school committee authority to 'grant as it deems fit the use of the school buildings as aforesaid for the purpose of moral and religious instruction' at times other than those fixed for instruction by the education board. Hence, according to the official position of the Department of

Education, the decision to give religious instruction ultimately rested with
each school committee.

68 The National Society's position on clerical control became more extreme
as it fell under the control of the 'Tractarians' in the 1830s. From 1828 to
1832 there were significant changes in the relationship of church and state,
and for a time it seemed possible that the Church of England might be
disestablished and lose its endowments. For example, laws were repealed
that placed restrictions on the civil rights of Roman Catholics and required
municipal office-holders to receive the Eucharist in the Church of England.
Opposed to disestablishment and Protestant tendencies in the church,
members of the 'Oxford movement,' led by John Henry Newman, John
Keble, and Edward Pusey, sought a renewal of 'Catholic' thought and
practice that stressed faithfulness to the teaching of the early and undi-
vided church. Their ideas were published in ninety *Tracts for the Times*
(1833–41), edited by Newman, who wrote twenty-four of them. Within the
Church of England, there were factions of Evangelicals and Broad Church-
men who were willing to cooperate with the state in providing mass education, but for the Tractarians, who controlled the National Society, the
educational authority of the church had to be absolute.

69 Donald H. Akenson, *The Irish Experiment: The National System of Education in
the Nineteenth Century* (Toronto: University of Toronto Press, 1970), 12.

70 S. Leslie Hunter, *The Scottish Educational System* (Oxford: Pergamon Press,
1968), 7–8. The royal commission appointed in 1864 to inquire into the
schools of Scotland counted 1,035 'statutory' schools comprising 917
parochial, 189 side, and 29 parliamentary schools. Side schools were those
established under the Act for Settling of Schools in addition to the parish
school; parliamentary schools were established with the assistance of special
grants from the Treasury. Voluntary denominational schools included 519
Church of Scotland, 202 Society in Scotland for Propagating Christian
Knowledge, 617 Free Church, 74 Episcopalian, 61 Roman Catholic, and 45
schools of smaller Presbyterian denominations. There were also 880 non-
denominational voluntary schools and 900 classed as private venture
schools. See H.M. Knox, *Two Hundred and Fifty Years of Scottish Education
1696–1946* (Edinburgh: Oliver and Boyd, 1953), 56. For an excellent survey
of the supply of schools in Scotland before 1872, see also R.D. Anderson,
Education and the Scottish People 1750–1918 (Oxford: Clarendon Press, 1995),
73–99.

71 The Catholic Poor School Committee was formed in 1847 to distribute a
parliamentary grant for Roman Catholic schools, but the National Society
and the British and Foreign School Society continued to be the largest

recipients of state aid. In 1870, when the state school system was established, 6,382 of the 8,281 voluntary state-aided schools in England and Wales were National Society schools, 1,549 were British and Foreign School Society or Wesleyan, and only 350 were Roman Catholic. Marjorie Cruickshank, *Church and State in English Education: 1870 to the Present Day* (London: Macmillan, 1963), 190.

72 Lord John Russell initially planned to establish an independent board of commissioners similar to the Irish national board, but his sounding of leading Anglicans revealed that an interdenominational authority would be unacceptable. A.S. Bishop, *The Rise of a Central Authority for English Education* (Cambridge: Cambridge University Press, 1971), 19.

73 Keith Fenwick and Peter McBride, *The Government of Education in Britain* (Oxford: Martin Robertson, 1981), 10.

74 Bishop, *The Rise of a Central Authority for English Education*, 42–5.

75 The education committee of the Privy Council continued formally in existence but without making any noticeable contribution to the central governance of English education. The Marquis of Salisbury, for example, informed a select committee of the House of Commons in 1864 that he had convened the committee on three or four occasions but that his actions were ill-received and no one came. W.E. Forster, who served as vice-president from 1868 to 1874, told the 1884 select committee that the committee was 'more a phrase than a reality' and that he had a 'sort of dim recollection that there were one or two formal meetings but they have not fastened themselves upon my memory at all.' In addition to the vice-president, the 1856 order-in-council named the secretary for war and the first lord of the admiralty to the committee of council. However, Lord Granville told a select committee in 1865 that as lord president he chose the members, actual meetings were few, and no records were kept of meetings. Gillian Sutherland, *Policy-Making in Elementary Education 1870–1895* (London: Oxford University Press, 1973), 14–19.

76 In 1828 a select committee of the House of Commons had recommended the appointment of a salaried board to distribute state aid to Irish elementary schools that provided for separate secular and religious instruction. Edward Stanley's plan in 1831 was based on the select committee's report. The first Commissioners of National Education in Ireland were three Anglicans, two Presbyterians, and two Roman Catholics. While additional commissioners were appointed, there was a substantial majority of Protestants on the board until 1860, when a new charter set the number of commissioners at ten Protestants and ten Roman Catholics. The commissioners were eminent members of the clergy, lawyers, landlords, and dons.

All were part-time, unpaid officials except for the resident commissioner, who supervised the routine work and growing administration and who consequently gained considerable influence over the board's operations (Akenson, *The Irish Experiment*, 117–21, 127–30, 140–1).

77 R.B. McDowell, *The Irish Administration 1801–1914* (Toronto: University of Toronto Press, 1964), 245–7; see also Akenson, *The Irish Experiment*, 127, 133.

78 Akenson, *The Irish Experiment*, 331.

79 On the relationship of the Church of Ireland to the Irish national system see ibid., 187–202.

80 Ibid., 161–87. In non-vested schools, local managers were not required to open their school to religious instruction for minority denominations. They were only required to permit children of minority religious denominations to be absent during the periods of religious teaching for the majority.

81 Ibid., 223–4.

82 The National Education League encompassed the usual internal liberal disagreements about the place of religion in state schools. For liberal conservatives such as Sir William Harcourt, state schools should be non-denominational, simply excluding the doctrines and rituals of any particular denomination. Utilitarian liberals such as Sir Charles Dilke and John Stuart Mill advocated secular state schools that excluded all religious teaching or left it to voluntary societies (Cruickshank, *Church and State in English Education*, 16). The league attracted the support of liberal-conservative Anglicans who accepted the principle of non-denominational education – for example, George Dixon who was its first chair – but most of its members came from the main dissenting churches – Baptist, Congregational, Methodist, Presbyterian, Quaker, and Unitarian.

83 Given its objective to expand the existing system of state aid to voluntary schools, the National Education Union (NEU) got its main support from Anglicans and Roman Catholics who were committed to church schools. The NEU was also supported by Methodists who, unlike the British and Foreign School Society, wanted to give denominational instruction in their schools, and by some Congregationalists who had reluctantly abandoned a position of pure *laissez-faire* and accepted state aid while continuing to support the voluntary principle.

84 Ibid., 22. Based on his previous political associations, Forster might have been expected to be somewhat more sympathetic to the National Education League. Forster was a Radical (utilitarian liberal) who had earlier been associated with Richard Cobden and John Bright in the work of the National Public School Association. This association was formed in 1850 to

promote universal, compulsory, free education supported from local rates. Under Cobden's influence it also advocated non-sectarian religious instruction rather than secular schools. See James Murphy, *Church, State, and Schools in Britain 1800–1970* (London: Routledge and Kegan Paul, 1971), 43–4, 49.

85 The author of the private amendment on religious instruction in board schools was William Francis Cowper-Temple, an Anglican and chair of the National Education Union. The 'Cowper-Temple clause' provided that 'no religious catechism or religious formulary which is distinctive of any particular denomination shall be taught in the school' maintained by a school board. Although preferred by Prime Minister William Gladstone and some cabinet members, a strictly secular state sector had no general support in 1870. When an amendment in favour of secular state schools was put to a vote it was overwhelmingly defeated (Cruickshank, *Church and State in English Education*, 28).

86 In contrast with the provisions of the 1870 Elementary Education Act for England and Wales, the Scottish act did not preclude religious instruction from being taught in accordance with a particular denominational content. The preamble of the Education (Scotland) Act, 1872 stated: 'And whereas it has been the custom in the public schools of Scotland to give instruction in religion to children whose parents did not object to the instruction so given, but with liberty to parents, without forfeiting any of the other advantages of the schools, to elect that their children should not receive such instruction, and it is expedient that the managers of public schools shall be at liberty to continue the said custom ...'

87 For example, the London School Board adopted a program of Bible reading accompanied by explanation and instruction in principles of morality, the syllabus in Manchester was warmly praised by Anglican clergy and adopted by other boards sympathetic to a denominational orientation, and after a tense struggle between denominationalists and secularists the Birmingham school board settled on Bible reading without note or comment (ibid., 45).

88 According to one inspector's report in 1878, 'The public schools are to all intents and purposes denominational schools. Public and Presbyterian are practically interchangeable.' Quoted in James J. Robertson, 'The Scottish Solution,' in J.S. Lauwerys and N. Hans (eds), *The Year Book of Education 1951* (London: Evans Brothers, 1951), 330.

89 By 1880 the number of Church of Scotland schools had decreased from 519 to 145, and Free Church schools had fallen from 523 to 39. By contrast, Roman Catholic church schools increased from 22 to 126 and Episcopal church schools from 46 to 73. In 1918, there were only 2 Church of Scot-

land and 1 Free Church voluntary schools still receiving grants compared
to 228 Roman Catholic and 49 Episcopal schools. James Scotland, *The
History of Scottish Education*, vol. 2 (London: University of London Press,
1969), 42–5.

90 In 1870, with the fate of the elementary education bill hanging in the
balance, Prime Minister Gladstone for the first time invited the vice-president to join the cabinet, a recognition of both the incumbent Forster's
abilities and the new importance of education.

91 The lord president continued to have an opportunity to influence educational policy, especially when major changes in legislation or regulations
were being made. Moreover, lord presidents were selected from more
influential, if not more able, patricians of the party, while vice-presidents
were politicians beginning to make their way – the post was one of the first
rungs on the political career ladder (Sutherland, *Policy-Making in Elementary
Education 1870–1895*, 28–9).

92 In 1854 the National Education Association of Scotland began a campaign
to establish a Scottish central authority responsible to Parliament for the
regulation of popularly elected local school boards, a plan that proved unacceptable to English, Welsh, and Irish members of Parliament concerned
to protect religious instruction. When the lord advocate of Scotland, James
Moncrieff, introduced a bill providing for a Scottish board of education
with six members appointed by the crown, four representing the Scottish
universities, and the lord advocate and solicitor general as ex officio members, Scottish members of Parliament voted in favour by a margin of three
to one; but the bill was defeated by a coalition of Conservatives, English
dissenters, and Roman Catholics. See G.W.T. Omond, *The Lord Advocates of
Scotland: Second Series 1834–1880* (London: Andrew Melrose, 1914), 180.
Moncrieff in 1869 again proposed a national system of Scottish education,
this time under a general board of education for Scotland that would be a
committee of the Privy Council with a paid chairman. This bill also failed to
pass. A central advisory board of education was established in Edinburgh to
coordinate the activities of Scottish school boards established under the
1872 act, but it lapsed in 1879.

93 The vice-president, A.J. Mundella, who was English, thought his dignity was
being attacked. The lord president of council, Lord Carlingford, who was
Irish, was concerned to protect the integrity of his department. The senior
officials in the education department – Sir Francis Sandford, Patrick Cumin,
and Henry Craik, who were all Scots – believed that Scottish education
would do better under a non-Scottish minister and preferred a unified
education department to a divided one. See H.J. Hanham, *Scottish Nationalism* (London: Faber and Faber, 1969), 56–9.

94 Sutherland, *Policy-Making in Elementary Education*, 95–6. There were 2,470
school boards formed between 1870 and 1895; 1,065 (43 per cent) were
formed under sections 10 and 40 of the 1870 act by which the Education
Department had to use its powers to compel the establishment of a board
to meet the deficiency of school accommodations, going through the slow
process of public inquiry and final notice (ibid., 352–3).

95 Sutherland, *Policy-Making in Elementary Education*, 85; Eric Eaglesham, *From
School Board to Local Authority* (London: Routledge and Kegan Paul, 1956),
12–14.

96 Sutherland, *Policy-Making in Elementary Education*, 64.

97 Beginning in 1862 for England and Wales and 1873 for Scotland, until
1890 grants to school boards were based on 'payment by results' – central
grants were paid only for those pupils who reached preset standards of
achievement – so that in effect school boards and voluntary schools operated under similar contractual relationships with the Education Department.

98 For an excellent account of the auditors' control over the school boards
in England and Wales, see Eaglesham, *From School Board to Local Authority*,
65–87.

99 In 1885, for example, there were 2,832 disallowances involving 298 local
boards in England and Wales; in 1898, even after the passage of legislation
intended to reduce referrals, there were 2,371 disallowances involving
220 school boards (ibid, 65–6). The person surcharged could appeal the
auditor's decision either to the Local Government Board, which might
reverse the decision or grant relief from repayment, or to the courts. The
Conservative–Liberal Unionist government was able to take advantage of
the court's decision in one such case to abolish the school boards in 1902
and establish county boroughs, county councils, and municipal authorities
as local education authorities. In 1899 the district auditor, acting on a
challenge brought by the Camden School of Art, which was operated by
the Technical Education Board of the London County Council, disallowed
the expenditures of the London School Board for technical education in
schools. The auditor's decision was upheld on appeal to the courts, and
the 'Cockerton judgment' became the government's rationale for the shift
from school boards to local education authorities.

100 Anderson, *Education and the Scottish People 1750–1918*, 165. Anderson
attributes the greater uniformity and centralization of Scottish elementary
education in the nineteenth century in part to the compactness of the
country and the weakness of the voluntary sector. In addition, he observes
that the Scotch Education Department inherited a national tradition in
education that was the legacy of Scottish Presbyterianism.

101 Both A.J. Mundella and Patrick Cumin are quoted in Sutherland, *Policy-Making in Elementary Education*, 92, 95.

102 Two lines of development that were crucial for local governance of education in the United States emerged in Massachusetts in the eighteenth century. First, school committees became differentiated from town government, and second, inside town boundaries school districts were recognized as distinct local jurisdictions. As problems of town government and, in particular, school business increased, selectmen began to appoint separate committees to certify teachers, inspect schools, and report to the town meeting. In 1789 a state law on the certification of teachers and inspection of schools formally recognized the appointment of such special school committees, and in 1826 each town was directed to elect a separate school committee to appoint teachers, supervise instruction, select textbooks, and maintain schools, subject to an annual vote of school support in the town meeting. People who lived in rural areas of a town often established their own schools rather than depend on town facilities, and school districts eventually emerged as subdivisions of towns for providing local school services. The 1789 law granted legal recognition to school districts. Subsequent legislation empowered community school districts to raise revenue by taxation (1801); make contracts, sue, and be sued (1817); and elect district trustees who would choose textbooks and hire teachers (1827). See George H. Martin, *Evolution of the Massachusetts School System* (New York: Appleton, 1894), 83–92.

103 The reorganization legislated under Indiana's 1851 constitution reduced the total number of city, town, and township school districts to 1,033. The school law passed in 1852 provided for township school districts to be governed by three elected trustees, but in 1859 the three elected school trustees were replaced by the township trustee, an elected official in each township, who now added the administration of township schools to such civic functions as social assistance and road maintenance.

104 Outside of Indiana in the Midwest, the township unit was most widely adopted in Iowa, where in 1930 there were 1,015 township districts out of 4,870 school districts. Michigan school law provided the option for township organization in the upper peninsula in 1891 and the rest of the state in 1909, but in 1934, although the upper peninsula was almost completely organized by township, the state as a whole remained predominantly attached to the district system, with 161 township units and 6,710 community school districts. Ohio had a township-based system from 1892 to 1914. See Arthur B. Moehlman, *School Administration: Its Development, Principles, and Future in the United States* (Boston: Houghton Mifflin, 1940), 163.

105 Ellwood P. Cubberly, *Public Education in the United States: A Study and Interpretation of American Educational History* (Boston: Houghton Mifflin, 1919), 162.

106 Samuel Train Dutton and David Snedden, *The Administration of Public Education in the United States* (New York: Macmillan, 1908), 86.

107 Local educational governance in cities usually started with multiple local school districts. As the city's population increased, these local districts were joined into a federation of districts, often based on city wards. Each ward or district had its own board of trustees, which performed basic local administrative functions such as teacher selection and school mainte-nance, and the central city board comprised representatives of each of the wards. These city school districts commonly were recognized in state legislation as distinctive, single-purpose, local agencies, geographically coterminous with city governments but fiscally and administratively inde-pendent.

108 Town school trustees in Alabama were appointed by the county superin-tendent and had no authority to levy taxes. District school trustees in Virginia were appointed by an electoral board, while city and town trustees were appointed by city and town councils; none of the Virginia school boards could levy taxes. In Colorado, first-class districts could levy taxes, but not second-class or third-class districts, and community school boards were restricted in their power to levy taxes in Arkansas, California, Iowa, Mississippi, Missouri, Nevada, Ohio, Tennessee, Texas, and Wyoming. Among states that based local educational governance on town and township school districts, New Hampshire and New Jersey did not author-ize school boards to levy taxes. For a summary of specific provisions at the end of the nineteenth century, see Edwin Grant Dexter, *A History of Education in the United States* (New York: Macmillan, 1904), Appendix F, 610–14.

109 Joseph M. Cronin, *The Control of Urban Schools* (New York: The Free Press, 1973), 24–5. Appointive authority meant that either the mayor or the city council, or one with the consent of the other, had authority to nominate and appoint members of the school board. Fiscal dependence meant that the school board had to obtain approval from a general municipal author-ity – the mayor, city council, board of estimates, or finance committee – for its budget estimates, tax levy on local property, and/or issuing of debentures. For a summary of educational governance in the fourteen big cities at the turn of the century, see ibid., 92–3.

110 Edgar W. Knight, *Public School Education in North Carolina* (New York: Negro Universities Press, 1969 [Boston: Houghton Mifflin, 1916]), 140–7.

After the Democrats regained power, elections for county commissioners were abolished in favour of appointment by local justices of the peace, who were appointed in turn by the state legislature. County commissioners governed public schools until the school act of 1885 restored separately appointed county boards of education and gave expanded powers to county school superintendents. 'Meaningful authority remained largely in the hands of three committeemen selected in each school district by boards of education to oversee the hiring of teachers, the arrangement of the school calendar, and the disbursement of appropriated funds' (James L. Leloudis, *Schooling the New South: Pedagogy, Self, and Society in North Carolina, 1880–1920* [Chapel Hill: University of North Carolina Press, 1966], 7. Leloudis observes that the appointment of school committeemen 'reflected local hierarchies and served as an extension of the political process,' and that school districts were basic units of Democratic party organization. In 1895 a coalition of Republicans and Populists abolished the county boards of education and restored popular election of county commissioners, who appointed local school committees. In 1897, when neighbourhood school districts were replaced by township districts, county boards of school directors, at first appointed by the county commissioners but after 1900 elected, were empowered to appoint the new township school boards (ibid., 120, 127–8, 135–6).

111 United States, Department of the Interior, Office of Education, Walter S. Deffenbaugh and Timon Covert, *School Administrative Units with Special Reference to the County Unit*, Pamphlet No. 34 (Washington, D.C.: United States Government Printing Office, 1933), 10. In South Carolina, following the High School Act of 1907, the districts of counties became increasingly important in the conduct of local educational governance, but district boards continued to be appointed by the county board, which also had the power to levy taxes.

112 From 1849 to 1865 the state board in Connecticut was appointed by the state legislative assembly; thereafter, the governor again appointed the board.

113 From its establishment in 1784, the Board of Regents of the State of New York was elected jointly by the two houses of the New York state legislature. The office of superintendent of public instruction, which was first established under the Common Schools Act of 1812, was appointed by the governor until 1821, when the office was abolished and its duties transferred to the secretary of state. When the superintendent's office was restored in 1854, the legislature retained the power of appointment. The Board of Regents' involvement in managing examinations gave it an

increasing influence over high schools and also brought it into conflict with the superintendent of public instruction. In 1904, the Board of Regents was made the policy-making body for state education and empowered to appoint the superintendent as its chief administrative officer.

114 When the Rhode Island state board of education was established in 1870, comprising the governor, lieutenant-governor, and six members of the General Assembly, authority to appoint the state commissioner of education was transferred from the state legislative assembly to the board.

115 Both Maryland (1864) and Delaware (1875) also provided for the state superintendent to be appointed by the governor. In Maryland the office of superintendent was abolished in the 1867 constitution, and its functions were carried out by the principal of the state teachers' college until 1900, when the office of superintendent was restored with provision for appointment by the governor. Political interests favouring local control secured the abolition of the Delaware superintendent's office in 1887. Three county superintendents who also sat on the state board of education collectively performed the functions of state superintendence until 1913, when the office of state commissioner of education was restored with appointment by the governor.

116 In Minnesota the office of territorial superintendent was first appointed by the governor in 1854. The office continued to be filled by gubernatorial appointment after Minnesota entered the union in 1858, except for the period 1862 to 1867 when, as a Civil War economy measure, the duties of the office were performed (under protest) by the secretary of state. In 1919 the power to appoint the superintendent was assigned to the state board of education.

117 In ten of these cases, the territorial governor had appointed the superintendent of public instruction prior to statehood, no office had existed in four territories, and three territories imposed the duties of superintendent on the territorial secretary of state, auditor, or librarian. The territory of West Virginia was included in the jurisdiction of the state superintendent elected by the Virginia legislature, in Utah the superintendent was appointed by the territorial supreme court, and Oklahoma had a federal superintendent of education.

118 In two cases, the method of popular election of state superintendent was not prescribed in the first state constitution. In Oregon the constitution of 1859 named the governor as ex officio superintendent for five years and empowered the legislature to provide for election thereafter, and this arrangement was retained until 1870, when, first, the legislature itself elected the superintendent and then, two years later, adopted the method

of popular election. In Nebraska there had been an elective superintendent from 1858 to 1861, but when Nebraska entered the Union in 1867, the
territorial auditor was serving ex officio as both territorial librarian and
commissioner of education. In 1869 the offices of auditor and commissioner were separated, the commissioner was made an elective office, and
the 1875 state constitution formally recognized the superintendent of
public instruction as an elective office. In Iowa the office of superintendent of public instruction was established as an elective office in the 1846
constitution, changed to an office appointed by the state board of education in the constitutional convention of 1857, which was dominated by
Republican reformers, and then restored as an elective office in 1864.

119 As one example, the California state board was established in 1852 with
powers to create school districts and apportion state school funds; it
comprised the governor, superintendent of public instruction, and surveyor general. In 1864 the surveyor general was dropped in favour of
the superintendents of schools for San Francisco, Sacramento, and San
Joaquin counties; and in 1866 the board was enlarged to nine members by
adding the principals of the state normal schools and two teachers nominated by the state superintendent. Delegates to the state constitutional
convention of 1879, worried about the danger of graft and corruption in
the exercise of the board's powers to select textbooks, transferred that
power to county boards and reduced the board's membership to the
governor, superintendent, and principals of the normal schools, later
adding the president of the University of California and a professor of
education. Indiana presents another typical case. Legislation in 1852
created a state board of education, including the superintendent, auditor,
treasurer, secretary of state, and governor. In 1865 the membership was
altered to comprise the superintendent, the governor, the presidents of
the state university and the state normal school, and the superintendents
of the three largest cities.

120 'Unbroken provision' for the office of state superintendent of education
here refers to an office independently constituted rather than filled ex
officio by another official of the state government. Louisiana provided for
a state superintendent appointed by the governor in 1847, North Carolina
adopted the method of election by the state assembly in 1852, and Alabama opted for election by the voters for its state superintendent in 1854.
From 1838 to 1850, state superintendents in Kentucky were appointed by
the governor. During a conflict between the governor and the superintendent over state taxation to finance public instruction, the Constitutional Convention of 1849 supported the superintendent, and the office

of superintendent of public instruction was made an elective one in the 1850 state constitution.

121 The office of state superintendent was made popularly elected in Arkansas, 1875; Louisiana, 1877; Florida, 1885; Georgia, 1894; and Virginia, 1902. The Texas constitution of 1869 also provided for an elected state superintendent; the office was abolished in 1876 and then restored in 1884. The exception to the adoption of elected superintendents in the southern states was Tennessee. Tennessee was the first southern state in 1836 to establish an office of superintendent of public instruction elected by the General Assembly. The office was abolished in 1844 in the wake of charges of corruption and spoils arising primarily from textbook scandals, and its duties were transferred to the office of state treasurer. With a Republican government already in place, Tennessee was excluded from the provisions of the Reconstruction Acts. The legislative assembly in 1867 established a popularly elected superintendent, but this office was abolished and its duties returned to the state treasurer in 1870 after a conservative Democratic government had regained power. Beginning with the school act of 1873, the state superintendent was appointed by the governor.

122 The First Amendment of the U.S. Constitution began with a guarantee of separation between church and state: 'Congress shall make no law respecting an establishment of religion, or prohibiting the free exercise thereof ...' The First Amendment did not restrict state governments. At the time of its adoption, however, all the states guaranteed substantial religious liberty. Connecticut, Maryland, Massachusetts, and New Hampshire did retain state assessment to support religion, while permitting taxpayers to choose the religious denomination that would receive their taxes, but the four New England states soon abolished these anachronistic provisions for state endowment of religion, the last being Massachusetts in 1833. Beyond the original thirteen, every state that entered the union after 1787 incorporated in its constitution or basic law prohibitions against any state restriction of freedom of religion or tax levy to support any religion.

123 This comes from an entry in Horace Mann's journal on 20 January 1839, quoted in Raymond B. Culver, *Horace Mann and Religion in the Massachusetts Public Schools* (New Haven: Yale University Press, 1929), 109–10. In his final (1848) report as secretary, Mann vigorously defended his policy of prohibiting sectarian books or instruction in state schools while denying that he had ever attempted to exclude religious instruction or the Bible: 'That our public schools are not theological seminaries, is admitted. That they are debarred by law from inculcating the peculiar and distinctive doctrines of any one religious denomination amongst us, is claimed; and

that they are also prohibited from ever teaching that what they do teach is
the whole of religion, or all that is essential to religion or to salvation, is
equally certain. But our system earnestly inculcates all Christian morals; it
founds its morals on the basis of religion; it welcomes the religion of the
Bible; and, in receiving the Bible, it allows it to do what it is allowed to do
in no other system, – *to speak for itself.* But here it stops, not because it
claims to have compassed all truth, but because it disclaims to act as an
umpire between hostile religious opinions ... Again: it seems almost too
clear for exposition, that our system, *in one of its most essential features,* is not
only not an irreligious one, but that it is more strictly religious than any
other which has ever yet been adopted.' Horace Mann, 'Religious Education,' in Joseph L. Blau (ed.), *Cornerstones of Religious Freedom in America*
(rev. ed.; New York: Harper and Row, 1964), 183–5; emphasis in the
original.
124 E.R. Norman, *The Conscience of the State in North America* (Cambridge: Cambridge University Press, 1968), 139.
125 Events in the cities of New York and Philadelphia in the early 1840s
illustrate the intensity of the conflict. In New York city there was no public
school system in 1840. The only free elementary schooling was provided
by the New York Public School Society, a philanthropic association that
was supported by public subsidies. Bishop John Hughes began a campaign
against the use of the King James version for daily Bible reading and the
blatantly Protestant curriculum taught in the schools of the society and
demanded that city council direct a share of its elementary school subsidies to support Roman Catholic schools. When these demands were rejected, Catholics turned for help to the governor (William H. Seward, who
was sympathetic to their cause) and the state legislature, and much of the
November 1841 state electoral campaign in New York city focused on the
issue of school aid. The outcome appeared to be a victory for Bishop
Hughes. Under the education act passed in April 1842, subsidies to the
Public School Society were ended, a city public school board and a system
of ward schools were established following provisions for local educational
governance elsewhere in the state, and public schools were prohibited
from sectarian religious instruction. In practice, however, the result was
a disappointment for Roman Catholics. Former trustees of the Public
School Society formed a Union party that won control of the new school
board, and under the new state superintendent of common schools, who
was a prominent nativist, Bible reading continued to be an integral part
of the school day. Bishop Hughes thereafter concentrated on building
parochial schools for the education of Roman Catholic children. See Ray

Allen Billington, *The Protestant Crusade 1800–1860: A Study of the Origins of American Nativism* (Gloucester, Mass.: Peter Smith, 1963 [1938]), 143–55; and also Diane Ravitch, *The Great School Wars: New York City, 1805–1973: A History of the Public Schools as Battlefield of Social Change* (New York: Basic Books, 1974), 33–76. In Philadelphia, Bishop Francis Kenrick in November 1842 petitioned the school board against the use of the Protestant Bible and prayers in city schools, seeking that Roman Catholic children be allowed to use the Douay version. The school board's response was initially favourable, but it was immediately attacked by anti-Catholic nativists as an attempt to eject the Bible from the public schools of Philadelphia. After several months of controversy, violence erupted. Roman Catholic churches were attacked, and two were burned to the ground and a convent destroyed before Bishop Kenrick ordered Catholic worship suspended and all Catholic churches closed. Many houses in the Irish section of the city were destroyed by fire, and during three days of rioting, thirteen people were killed and fifty wounded. At the end of it, the school board voted to ban the Douay version from city schools and restored non-denominational Protestant religious observances. See Billington, *The Protestant Crusade 1800–1860*, 220–31; and also Leo Pfeffer, *Church, State and Freedom* (rev. ed.; Boston: Beacon Press, 1967), 436–7.

126 In an instruction to the bishops of the United States in 1875, Pope Pius IX referred to his 1864 papal letter to the Archbishop of Fribourg in which he had attacked secularism in education: 'In all places, in every country where this pernicious plan to deprive the Church of her authority over schools is formulated and, worse still, put into effect, and where youth will consequently be exposed to the danger of losing their faith, it is the serious duty of the Church to make every effort not only to obtain for youth the essential instruction and Christian training, but even more so to warn the faithful and to make it clear to them that they cannot frequent such schools as are set up against the Catholic Church' (Aldo Rebeschini [trans.], *Papal Teachings: Education* [Boston: St Paul Editions, 1960], 52). The 1875 instruction concluded 'It is, therefore, absolutely necessary that all bishops should make every effort to see to it that the flock entrusted to them may avoid every contact with the public schools. To obtain this desired end, what is generally considered most necessary is that, in all places, Catholics should have their own schools and that these should not be inferior to the public ones. Every effort must, therefore, be made to set up Catholic schools where they do not yet exist and to increase the number of and improve the organization of those that already exist so that

instruction and training, on the same level as that of the public schools may be ensured' (ibid., 67–8).

127 Pfeffer, *Church, State and Freedom*, 513.

128 Educating slaves was legally prohibited in all states except Kentucky, Maryland, and Tennessee. Several states also prohibited the education of free black children; in other states they were permitted to attend independent charity schools, where these were available, but not public schools. Some slaves did learn to read and write on plantations where the law was ignored in practice or through the educational work of religious missions, but throughout the South, law and public opinion severely restricted even the most elementary education for black children, whether slave or free.

129 The following portrait of education for African-American children living in the North is based primarily on C.G. Woodson, *The Education of the Negro Prior to 1861* (New York: Arno Press and the New York Times, 1968 [1919]), 307–35.

130 Meyer Weinberg, *A Chance to Learn: A History of Race and Education in the United States* (Cambridge: Cambridge University Press, 1977), 26.

131 Ibid., 78.

132 During the Civil War, Congress in 1862 approved racially segregated schools in the District of Columbia by providing that taxes collected from black residents be used to support schools for black children, and West Virginia, having refused to secede from the Union, provided for racial segregation of public schools in its constitution of 1863. The precedent of the District of Columbia was followed in Florida in 1866, when school taxes were levied on black residents for the support of separate schools. Laws requiring racially segregated public schools were passed in Tennessee and Texas in 1873, South Carolina and Louisiana in 1877, Mississippi in 1878, and Virginia in 1882. Constitutional provision for racially segregated schools was enacted in six states: Alabama, North Carolina, and Texas in 1876, Mississippi in 1890, South Carolina in 1895, and Louisiana in 1898. See John Hope Franklin, 'Jim Crow Goes to School: The Genesis of Legal Segregation in Southern Schools,' *South Atlantic Quarterly* 58 (Spring 1958): 229–34; reprinted in Paul Finkelman (ed.), *Race, Law, and American History 1700–1990: The African-American Experience*, vol. 7, pt 1, *The Struggle for Equal Education* (New York: Garland Publishing, 1992), 405–10.

133 Leonard W. Levy, *The Law of the Commonwealth and Chief Justice Shaw* (Cambridge, Mass.: Harvard University Press, 1957), 109–17. For a good, brief account of the challenge to the legality of the Boston Primary School Committee's policy to enforce segregation in its schools – a challenge

brought on behalf of Sarah C. Roberts by her father, Benjamin Roberts, and pleaded by Charles Sumner, subsequently an antislavery leader in the United States Senate – see Leon F. Witwack, *North of Slavery: The Negro in the Free States, 1790–1860* (Chicago: University of Chicago Press, 1961), 143–50. See also Carl F. Kaestle, *Pillars of the Republic: Common Schools and American Society, 1780–1860* (New York: Hill and Wang, 1983), 176–9. In 1855, Massachusetts passed an act that prohibited racial or religious distinctions in the admission of students to any public school.

134 Truman M. Pierce, James B. Kincheloe, R. Edgar Moore, Galen N. Drewery, and Bennie E. Carmichael, *White and Negro Schools in the South: An Analysis of Biracial Education* (Englewood Cliffs, N.J.: Prentice-Hall, 1955), 35.

135 According to the court, laws permitting or requiring racial segregation had been long recognized as within the competence of state legislatures: 'The most common instance of this is connected with the establishment of separate schools for white and colored children, which have been held to be a valid exercise of the legislative power even by courts of states where the political rights of the colored race have been longest and most earnestly enforced.'

136 In the *Cumming* decision, the court reasoned that the school board was prepared to close its high school for whites rather than maintain the black high school. Hence a court decision to enforce equal protection would simply hurt white students without helping black students. To sustain a claim of equal protection under *Plessy*, the court concluded, the plaintiff had to show that race and race only had motivated the school board's action. In this instance, no such case was deemed to have been established. See James D. Anderson, *The Education of Blacks in the South, 1860–1935* (Chapel Hill: University of North Carolina Press, 1988), 188, 192–3.

137 Alternatively, as in the case of Newfoundland, the legislative grant for public instruction was allocated according to the percentage distribution of denominational populations, thus obviating the need for a central board of education.

138 Two more variants of the American model for governing public instruction can be identified, one in the cities of New York, Chicago, Baltimore, San Francisco, and Milwaukee, where the mayor or city commissioners appointed the school board, and the other in Buffalo, where the city council governed public schools directly.

139 The earliest statistic available for Canada is 1920–1, when 4.2 per cent of students in elementary and secondary schooling were enrolled in private schools. In England and Wales there were 5.8 per cent of elementary and secondary students enrolled in private schools in 1921–2. Not surprisingly,

private schools were more important in educational regimes that provided state aid only to public non-denominational (or secular) schools and hence forced Roman Catholics to turn to private schools for elementary and secondary education. In the United States, for example, enrolments in non-Roman Catholic private schools were only 3.1 per cent of total elementary and secondary enrolments in 1899–1900, and they comprised 5.5 per cent of Australian enrolments in 1905. In New Zealand, 7 per cent of the students in primary and secondary education were enrolled in private Roman Catholic primary schools.

140 B.R. Mitchell, *European Historical Statistics 1750–1975* (2nd ed., rev.; London: Macmillan, 1981), 759.

2. Industrial Efficiency

1 The discussion of types of secondary school organization in this section is based on Ronald Manzer, *Public Schools and Political Ideas: Canadian Educational Policy in Historical Perspective* (Toronto: University of Toronto Press, 1994), 40–3.

2 According to Harold Entwistle, 'Education may be conceived as *classless* or as *class specific, class confirming* even *class divisive*' (Harold Entwistle, *Class, Culture and Education* [London: Methuen, 1978], 64; emphasis in the original). Here I assume that these terms refer to different features of class-based education. 'Class-specific' education involves the provision of separate programs or tracks that lead to jobs in different occupational classes. 'Class-divisive' education refers to class-specific education in which contact between students in different educational tracks is minimized. Students in different educational tracks are socially isolated from one another and probably also physically isolated from one another by reason of attending different schools. 'Class-confirming' education refers to class-specific and (usually) class-divisive education that selects and educates students according to the occupational class membership of their families. As a result, there will be little or no circulation between classes from generation to generation.

3 See John Lawry, 'Understanding Australian Education 1901–14,' in J. Cleverley and J. Lawry (eds), *Australian Education in the Twentieth Century: Studies in the Development of State Education* (Camberwell, Victoria: Longman Australia, 1972), 17.

4 In the nineteenth-century educational regimes there were three types of residual state intervention to supply secondary education. First, a few grammar schools owed their establishment to state initiatives: Sydney

Grammar School (1854), which was founded to provide an education 'not only superior to any that could be obtained in the primary schools of the State but one which should at once fit its pupils for the intelligent discharge of the duties of a commercial and professional life, or fit them for a more advanced course of academic instruction in the halls of the University' (quoted in R.J. Burns and C. Turney, 'A.B. Weigall's Headmastership of Sydney Grammar School,' in C. Turney [ed.], *Pioneers of Australian Education: A Study of the Development of Education in New South Wales in the Nineteenth Century* [Sydney: Sydney University Press, 1969], 115); the Adelaide Advanced School for Girls, where state intervention was justified by the absence of voluntary grammar schools for young women; and the Perth High School (1878), which operated under its own board of governors with direct grants from the state. The most generous state endowment policy was pursued in Queensland, where ten grammar schools were established under the Grammar Schools Act of 1860 with grants of up to £2,000 for each school in capital funding and £500 annually for operating expenses. Second, all states offered scholarships to grammar school based on the results of public examinations at the end of elementary education, and students in state elementary schools were eligible to compete for these. Queensland scholarship examinations, which entitled winners to £50 a year to attend grammar schools, began in 1873, for example, and became a fixed part of the Queensland educational regime until after the Second World War. In Victoria there were 200 scholarships at £10 each a year for three years at grammar schools from 1873 until 1893 when they were dropped as an economy measure. Third, higher classes were available in many state elementary schools, and in New South Wales the 1880 education act provided for 'superior public schools' that offered pupils advanced courses leading to junior and senior public examinations.

5 Victoria, Royal Commission on Education, *Final Report* (1901), excerpt reprinted in A.G. Austin and R.J.W. Selleck (eds), *The Australian Government School 1800–1914: Select Documents with Commentary* (Carlton, Victoria: Pitman Publishing, 1975), section 48, 'Commissioners Make Recommendations on Secondary and Technical Education,' 186; see also A.M. Badcock, 'The Vocational Fallacy in State Secondary Education in Victoria, 1900–1925,' in E.L. French (ed.), *Melbourne Studies in Education 1965* (Carlton, Victoria: Melbourne University Press, 1966), 187–221.

6 Rivkah Mathews, 'Secondary Education in Victoria: The Liberal Dilemma,' in Stephen Murray-Smith (ed.), *Melbourne Studies in Education 1976* (Carlton, Victoria: Melbourne University Press, 1976), 241–4.

7 A.R. Crane and W.G. Walker, *Peter Board: His Contribution to the Development*

of Education in New South Wales, ACER Research Series No. 71 (Melbourne: Australian Council for Educational Research, 1957), 50; J.O. Auchen, *Frank Tate and His Work for Education,* ACER Research Series No. 69 (Melbourne: Australian Council for Educational Research, 1956), 140–1.

8 In his notes on the Victoria Education Act of 1910, Frank Tate observed, 'It aims at creating a co-ordinated system of public education, leading through elementary schools and higher elementary schools and evening continuation classes to trade and technical schools on the one hand, or through elementary schools and high schools to the University or to higher technical schools on the other.' Frank Tate, 'The Education Act 1910: Notes by the Director,' *Victoria: Education Gazette and Teachers' Aid* (30 June 1911): 206; reprinted in Austin and Selleck (eds), *The Australian Government School 1800–1914: Select Documents with Commentary,* 328.

9 In Victoria in the mid-1920s there were 23 junior technical schools, which were attached to technical schools and provided a preparatory course comprising general and industrial subjects, compared to 34 high schools and 46 higher elementary schools. In New South Wales there were 29 high schools; 33 intermediate high schools, 7 of which provided commercial courses; 14 district schools, resulting from a 1905 act under which elementary schools with higher classes attached gave a two-year, primarily vocational course to the intermediate certificate; and 110 superior public schools including 26 technical, 15 commercial, 51 domestic science, and 18 rural schools. In Perth, central schools were separate from primary schools and one central school specialized as a 'junior technical school' in the industrial course; elsewhere in Western Australia, central schools were attached to large primary schools. Beginning in 1915, central schools in Western Australia also offered a general arts and science course for pupils who were unable to gain entry to a high school, and those who were successful in the competitive selection were able to proceed to the leaving certificate at Perth Modern School. In South Australia, Adelaide High School was formed as the first free public secondary school in 1908 by amalgamating the Advanced School for Girls, the pupil-teacher training school, and the Adelaide boys' continuation school; in addition, 7 primary schools with continuation classes in larger country towns were designated as district high schools. In 1921, higher elementary schools were distinguished as schools offering general and commercial courses that took pupils to the intermediate certificate, and in 1925, central schools were recognized as primary schools that had two-year domestic arts, junior technical, and commercial courses leading to the junior technical certificate and potentially beyond that to Thebarton Technical High School.

10 External examinations conducted by boards of public examiners were introduced in New South Wales and Queensland in 1911, Western Australia in 1914, Victoria in 1917, and South Australia in 1923. In Tasmania the department conducted the high school entrance or scholarship examination from 1907 until it was replaced in 1938 by recommendation of the headmaster. In the same year, the University of Tasmania dropped its administration of the intermediate examination, and from 1938 to 1946 the department and the association of independent schools conducted separate intermediate examinations.

11 The uncontested domination of intermediate and leaving certificates resulted in part from their official recognition as standards for entry to the clerical and executive divisions of state and federal public services. Entrants to the executive division also became eligible for a 'studentship' to attend college or university. This became a common route to higher educational credentials for the most able state and federal civil servants until the expansion of enrolments in colleges and universities directly from secondary schools in the 1960s.

12 R.T. Fitzgerald, *Through a Rear Vision Mirror: Change and Education – A Perspective on the Seventies from the Forties,* ACER Research Series No. 97 (Hawthorn, Victoria: Australian Council for Educational Research, 1975), 30.

13 J.D. Story left the Department of Public Instruction to take up the post of public service commissioner, which he held until his retirement in 1939. See Colin Hughes, *The Government of Queensland* (St Lucia: University of Queensland Press, 1980), 200.

14 Departmental reorganizations that split central superintendence of primary and secondary education into separate branches occurred in Queensland in 1944 and Western Australia in 1948.

15 Strictly speaking, the first teachers' union was the South Australia Public Teachers' Association, founded in 1875, but the organization had become inactive by the 1880s. New curriculum regulations in 1885 resulted in the formation of the South Australia Teachers' Association as well as various rural teachers' associations for purposes of professional development, and in 1896 the South Australia Public Teachers' Union was organized as a combined professional and protective association. The Queensland Teachers' Union was founded in 1889 and the State School Teachers' Union of Western Australia in 1898. In New South Wales and Victoria, where secondary and technical teachers had formed separate associations from primary teachers, there was a further stage of amalgamation with the merger of primary, secondary, and technical associations to form the New South

Wales Teachers' Federation (1918) and the Victorian Teachers' Union (1926).

16 The potential for appealing disputes over teachers' salary schedules to the state industrial court was established by law in Queensland (1917), New South Wales (1919), and South Australia (1924). In Victoria, the High Court ruled in 1929 that teaching was not an 'industry,' and hence teachers were not eligible to appeal to the Arbitration Court. Teachers' salaries were set first by changes to a schedule of the Public Service Act and then, beginning in 1940, by recommendations of the Public Service Board to the cabinet, until the Teachers' Tribunal was created in 1946. See O.S. Green and C.J. White, 'A Complex of Organisations,' in L.J. Blake (ed.), *Vision and Realization: A Centenary History of State Education in Victoria*, vol. 1 (Melbourne: Education Department of Victoria, 1973), 1143–4.

17 In Queensland the local boards of advice for which the 1875 act provided were never appointed, and school councils continued to operate under the Department of Public Instruction following the model of local patrons under the former Board of Education.

18 David Mossenson, *State Education in Western Australia 1829–1960* (Nedlands, W.A.: University of Western Australia Press, 1972), 133.

19 See Ontario, Department of Education, *Education for Industrial Purposes: A Report by John Seath* (Toronto: King's Printer, 1911), 1. In its 1913 report, Canada's Royal Commission on Industrial Training and Technical Education strongly recommended expansion of industrial training and technical education in Canadian high schools. In large part, its argument also rested on the imperative of industrial efficiency. With apprenticeship disappearing and major industrial nations such as Britain, Germany, and the United States rapidly improving their technical schools and colleges, the growth of Canada's industrial economy depended on transforming Canadian secondary education from its heavily academic orientation to a balance of academic and technical education, each having its own distinctive occupational orientation. The royal commission also argued that the needs of individuals for knowledge and skills in their future vocations or occupations should be taken into account in determining courses of study. An academic curriculum prepared students for entry to 'the learned professions, other professional occupations, or the leisure class,' but secondary vocational education also should be provided for 'those persons who are to follow manual industrial occupations, producing occupations such as agriculture, conserving occupations such as housekeeping, and commercial and business occupations' (Canada, Royal Commission on Industrial Training and Technical Education, *Report*, vol. 1 [Ottawa: King's Printer, 1913], 136). For

the royal commission's summary of the relationship of technical education and national economic problems, see ibid., 159–66.

20 In his report on industrial education for Ontario, John Seath proposed two types of vocational programs in addition to the academic secondary program. First, 'general industrial schools' would provide a two-year basic course in wood and metal shop work, English, practical mathematics, and science, followed by 'special industrial school,' which would offer specialized courses in trades and industrial occupations. Second, 'technical high schools' (or technical departments) would prepare students for jobs requiring specialized technical knowledge and involving responsibilities greater than skilled mechanics. Their curricula would comprise two years of common technical education followed by two years of specialized courses. Seath was adamant that industrial education be strictly segregated from academic programs: 'The mathematics, science, English, and work-shop courses must be wholly separate from the corresponding classes in the academic High Schools, and must be taught by teachers who have been specially prepared for the work ... The future of the industrial school should not be imperilled by intimate associations, with schools whose main object hitherto has been the preparation for the professions and the universities' (ibid., 340).

21 High schools separate from elementary schools were limited to cities and larger towns. In rural areas, secondary education was provided through secondary departments of elementary schools that were formally recognized as 'continuation schools' in the late nineteenth and early twentieth centuries. See Manzer, *Public Schools and Political Ideas*, 72–3.

22 J.M. McCutcheon, *Public Education in Ontario* (Toronto: T.H. Best Printing Company, 1941), 187–8.

23 Ontario, Royal Commission on Education in Ontario, *Report of the Royal Commission on Education in Ontario 1950* (Toronto: King's Printer, 1950), 20.

24 Robert M. Stamp, *The Schools of Ontario, 1876–1976* (Toronto: University of Toronto Press, 1982), 80.

25 In British Columbia, in addition to the general program, a vocational program was recognized at the level of senior high school where a school board was willing to provide the necessary specialized occupational training and equipment. The objective of this vocational program was 'to train selected pupils in the skills, technical knowledge, attitudes, and habits necessary for successful employment and advancement in skilled occupations.'

26 The 1933 revision of the curriculum in Nova Scotia did add a number of electives to what had been an extremely rigid, academically oriented

program. Industrial arts, home economics, commercial subjects, and agriculture were among the new options, but these subjects were regarded as part of the student's general education until 1942, when a specifically vocational commercial program was introduced. Revision of the New Brunswick curriculum in 1939 established three options to the academic program – home economics, agriculture, and industrial arts – but the new programs remained primarily academic in focus, restricted in their vocational options, and limited in their availability to urban centres until after the Second World War. In Prince Edward Island, students who wished to continue into secondary education after ten years of elementary school enrolled in a three-year academic program at Prince of Wales College.

27 In Ontario, for example, the Department of Education created seven new divisional heads in the first two decades of the twentieth century: inspector of manual training and household science (1901); chief public and separate school inspector (1909); director of industrial and technical education (1912); inspector of elementary agricultural education (1911); and director of professional (teacher) training, inspector of auxiliary classes, and provincial attendance officer (1919). See Robin S. Harris, *Quiet Evolution: A Study of the Educational System of Ontario* (Toronto: University of Toronto Press, 1967), 110. In British Columbia, the Department of Education appointed an inspector of manual training (1907), a supervisor of the summer school of education (1914), a supervisor of industrial and technical education (1914), and a director of elementary agricultural instruction (1915); and the department also established a textbook branch (1908) and took over operation of the school for the blind from the Vancouver school board. See F. Henry Johnson, *A History of Public Education in British Columbia* (Vancouver: University of British Columbia Press, 1964), 92.

28 In Ontario under Conservative governments (1905–19, 1923–34, 1943–56) there was an attempt to divide responsibility for educational policy and administration between a superintendent (1905–19) or chief director and a deputy minister who had responsibility to manage the department of education. During the era of John Seath as superintendent (1905–19) and of Francis W. Merchant (1923–30) and J.G. Althouse (1944–56) as chief director, however, there was no doubt about who was the senior administrative official. Under the government of the United Farmers of Ontario (1919–23) no chief director was appointed, and under Liberal governments (1934–43) the two offices were combined. An attempt to divide educational policy and administration between a superintendent and a deputy minister was also made in Saskatchewan from 1912 to 1932. In this

case, the former deputy minister assumed the office of provincial superintendent, so again there was no doubt about the seniority of the superintendent.

29 One exception was the Alberta Department of Education, where only nine officials reported directly to the deputy minister. This narrower span of control resulted primarily from the appointment in 1939 of a chief superintendent of schools, who was given charge of curriculum, provincial supervisors of instruction, and the office of the registrar. In addition, teacher training was under the jurisdiction of the University of Alberta rather than a provincial normal school. Another exception in the 1940s was Prince Edward Island, where eight or nine officials reported to the deputy minister and director; however, by 1967–8, just prior to reorganization, the deputy minister had fifteen departmental officials reporting to him as well as seven elementary school superintendents and one high school superintendent.

30 The only exception seems to have occurred in Manitoba when Robert Fletcher retired in 1939. Fletcher had been appointed first as secretary of the provincial educational advisory board in 1903; he then became deputy minister of education when the office was established in 1908. The minister (Ivan Schultz), apparently frustrated by his inability to control the department under Fletcher, opted not to replace his deputy minister and instead had the chief inspector and chief administrative officer report directly to him. This arrangement lasted until 1945, when a new minister found himself overwhelmed by the work, a deputy minister (R.O. MacFarlane) was again appointed, and the department was reorganized.

31 J.T.M. Anderson, who was premier as well as minister of education in Saskatchewan from 1929 to 1934, was a former teacher, inspector of schools from 1911 to 1918, and director of education for new Canadians in Saskatchewan from 1918 to 1924. His doctoral dissertation at the University of Toronto was published as *The Education of the New-Canadian: A Treatise on Canada's Greatest Educational Problem* (Toronto: J.M. Dent, 1918). George Weir, minister of education in British Columbia from 1933 to 1941 and again from 1945 to 1947, had been principal of Saskatoon normal school, director of teacher training at University of British Columbia, and joint author with J.H. Putman of the seminal survey of British Columbia education in 1925. Woodrow Lloyd, who was Saskatchewan minister of education in CCF governments from 1944 to 1960, was a former teacher, vice-president and president of the Saskatchewan Teachers' Federation from 1939 to 1944, and member of the executive of the Canadian Teachers' Federation.

As premier and minister of education, J.T.M. Anderson worked first with A.H. Ball, who was deputy minister from 1912 to 1931, and then with J.S. Huff, former chief superintendent of education and principal of the normal school. During George Weir's first term as minister, his deputy minister was S.J. Willis, superintendent from 1919 to 1946; and for his second term, F.T. Fairey, who was formerly provincial director of technical and vocational education (1938–46) and deputy minister and superintendent from 1945 to 1953. When Woodrow Lloyd became minister of education in 1944, J.H. McKechnie retired after ten years as deputy minister because of ill health. The new deputy minister, A.B. Ross, had been a superintendent of schools, director of correspondence instruction, and director of curricula. When Ross reached retirement age in 1947, he was replaced by the superintendent of high schools, Allan McCallum, who continued as deputy minister until 1960.

32 Walter D. Young and J. Terence Morley, 'The Premier and the Cabinet,' in J. Terence Morley, Norman D. Ruff, Neil A. Swainson, R. Jeremy Wilson, and Walter D. Young, *The Reins of Power: Governing British Columbia* (Vancouver: Douglas and McIntyre, 1983), 54.

33 The premiers who also served as minister of education were A.C. Rutherford (1905–10) and William Aberhart (1935–43) in Alberta; Walter Scott (1912–16), W.M. Martin (1916–21), and J.T.M. Anderson (1929–34) in Saskatchewan; John Bracken in Manitoba (1922–3); and in Ontario, G. Howard Ferguson (1923–30), George S. Henry (1930–4), and George A. Drew (1943–8).

34 Manzer, *Public Schools and Political Ideas*, 124. In 1900–1, provincial grants comprised 19 per cent of the total current revenues of school boards from property taxation and provincial grants combined, but there was considerable variation among the provinces, from 10 per cent in Ontario and 14 per cent in Quebec to 77 per cent in Prince Edward Island and 78 per cent in British Columbia. By 1920–1, the national average for provincial grants had fallen to 12 per cent of the current revenues of school boards, then increased to 16 per cent in 1940–1. Provincial grants as a percentage of local revenues in 1940–1 continued to be relatively high in Prince Edward Island (60 per cent) and varied in the rest of the country from 10 per cent in Quebec and 14 per cent in Ontario to 28 per cent in Saskatchewan and Alberta. Provincial grant policies were also calculated to expand local financial support for projects favoured by the provincial department. Provincial departments of education employed an extensive array of percentage grants to stimulate local expenditures in support of favoured

school improvements, especially libraries and laboratories, pupil convey-
ance, more highly qualified teachers, and more specialized curriculum
developments such as manual training and domestic science.

35 Larger urban school districts operated somewhat differently from small
rural districts. Given a sizable population and an adequate tax base, civic
leadership concerned to promote local educational expansion, and multiple schools covering both elementary and secondary education, city districts were authorized to establish their own administrative staff, headed by
a city inspector or superintendent, and consequently were exempted from
provincial inspection. City school boards certainly did not escape the rig-
ours of provincial departmental regulation in the early twentieth century,
but they were allowed a margin of local discretion to govern their schools.

36 The provincial organization of Canadian teachers in the nineteenth century took the form of teachers' institutes and omnibus general educational
associations (Ronald Manzer, 'Selective Inducements and the Development
of Pressure Groups: The Case of Canadian Teachers' Associations,' *Canadian Journal of Political Science* 2 [March 1969]: 105–6). These organizations
aimed at educational, especially professional, improvement and gave
teachers little opportunity to discuss, let alone influence, the policies most
affecting their professional careers: salaries, tenure, and pensions. As
teachers' salaries failed to match increases in the cost of living caused by
wartime inflation, the nine associations newly established from 1914 to
1920 were the Saskatchewan Union of Teachers, later the Saskatchewan
Teachers' Alliance (1914); the British Columbia Teachers' Federation
(1916); the Alberta Teachers' Alliance (1917); the Manitoba Teachers'
Society, the New Brunswick Teachers' Association, and the Federation of
Women Teachers' Associations of Ontario (1918); the Ontario Secondary
School Teachers' Association (1919); and the Ontario Public School Men
Teachers' Federation and the Nova Scotia Teachers' Union (1920). In
addition, the Provincial Association of Protestant Teachers (1916) and the
Prince Edward Island Teachers' Federation (1920) were reorganized to
assert more strongly the collective interests of their teacher members. In
Newfoundland, a provincial teachers' association was first formed in 1890
but had little success until it was reconstituted in 1924.

37 The Saskatchewan Teachers' Alliance, for example, originated from a
rejection by the minister of education of teachers' tenure and salary griev-
ances. The constitution of the Ontario Secondary School Teachers' Federation included professional objectives to discuss and promote the cause of
education in secondary schools, raise the status of the Ontario teaching
profession, and promote a high standard of professional etiquette; but it

also referred to more political objectives to secure material conditions essential to professional service and a larger voice for teachers in educational policy and administration. In its 1921 policy statement, the Alberta Teachers' Alliance set out demands for material benefits such as tenure protection, sick leave, and a pension scheme, and also political objectives such as larger administrative units, collective bargaining, and teachers' representation on committees controlling conditions of work.

38 The Alberta School Trustees' Association (ASTA), for example, was an unassuming organization until its 1919 convention, at which the minister of education joined with ASTA in a vigorous attack on the Alberta Teachers' Alliance (ATA). See John W. Chalmers, *Schools of the Foothills Province: The Story of Public Education in Alberta* (Toronto: University of Toronto Press, 1967), 379–82, 441. The United Farmers' government, elected in 1921, was much more sympathetic to ATA but continued to attempt to preserve a balance between ATA and ASTA. In Ontario the organization of the Urban School Trustees' Association (1920) and the Ontario School Trustees' and Ratepayers' Association (OSTRA) (1921) both followed closely on the organization of three public school teachers' associations, and OSTRA at least was established with the active support of the Department of Education. The Associated High School Boards of Ontario was organized in 1932 to cut the costs of secondary education and counter the power of the Ontario Secondary School Teachers' Federation (Stamp, *The Schools of Ontario, 1876–1976*, 145).

39 I.A. McLaren, 'Education and Politics: Background to the Secondary Schools Act, 1903. Part II: Secondary Education for the Deserving,' *New Zealand Journal of Educational Studies* 6 (May 1971): 3.

40 In 1875 there were four endowed secondary schools operating in New Zealand.

41 G.T. Bloomfield, *New Zealand: A Handbook of Historical Statistics* (Boston: G.K. Hall, 1984), Tables III.13, III.14.

42 The condition required secondary schools receiving capitation grants for free-place pupils to give one additional free place for each £50 of the school's net annual income from its endowments. This condition was revised in the Secondary Schools Act of 1903 so that secondary schools had a choice between receiving the capitation grant for scholarship pupils or providing one scholarship for each £50 of its endowment income. Five schools initially refused to offer free places in return for grants, but financial pressures and competition from city district high schools persuaded the governors of all but one to accept free-place pupils. The exception was Wanganui Girls' College, which refused to accept free-place pupils until the

Education Act of 1914 required all schools to comply (McLaren, 'Education and Politics: Background to the Secondary Schools Act, 1903,' 11–21).

43 There were also small technical day schools started at Napier (1908), Westport (1909), and Nelson (1910). See John Nicol, *The Technical Schools of New Zealand: An Historical Survey*, New Zealand Council for Educational Research, Educational Research Series No. 12 (Christchurch: Whitcombe and Tombs, 1940), 69–118. Under the 1902 act, primary and secondary schools were also offered subsidies to introduce subjects involving manual and technical instruction. Primary schools generally took advantage of these capitation grants to add woodwork, cooking, and agriculture to their curriculum, but there was much less receptiveness on the part of secondary schools, which left the field open to the new technical day schools. In 1914, enrolments at technical day schools were Christchurch 474, Auckland 397, Dunedin 288, Wellington 285, Wanganui 185, Invercargill 177, Napier 79, and Westport 14 (ibid., 115).

44 In 1939, five of the seven technical high schools in smaller centres with no separate secondary schools offered a two-language academic course, and six offered a one-language course. See J.H. Murdoch, *The High School in New Zealand: A Critical Survey*, New Zealand Council for Educational Research, Educational Research Series No. 19 (Christchurch: Whitcombe and Tombs, 1943), 317–21. Academic work in the three city technical high schools was measured by enrolments in foreign languages as a percentage of total enrolment, which were Auckland 14.9 per cent, Christchurch 20.8 per cent, and Wellington 24.6 per cent (Nicol, *The Technical Schools of New Zealand*, 199–201). On the founding of combined schools see ibid., 159–66; and also Murdoch, *The High School in New Zealand*, 327–33.

45 Being awarded the Proficiency Certificate at the end of standard six qualified pupils to enter a high school, a 'competency pass' in the proficiency examination was the qualification to enter a technical high school, and a complete failure meant pupils were inadmissible to secondary education (Murdoch, *The High School in New Zealand*, 43). Beginning in 1937, any pupil who gained a Primary School Certificate or was over fourteen years of age was entitled to a free place in any type of public post-primary school.

46 Prior to 1945 the majority of students took the university entrance examinations at the end of form five, but a small group of students remained another year to take the university scholarship examinations at the end of form six.

47 Leicester Webb, *The Control of Education in New Zealand*, New Zealand Council for Educational Research, Educational Research Series No. 4 (Auckland: Whitcombe and Tombs, 1937), 97.

48 For a summary of the criteria used by various education boards to appoint, promote, and dismiss teachers, see Ian Cumming and Alan Cumming, *History of State Education in New Zealand 1840–1975* (Wellington: Pitman Publishing New Zealand, 1978), 172; and also Webb, *The Control of Education in New Zealand*, 70.

49 Webb, *The Control of Education in New Zealand*, 91. The constitution of governing bodies of existing schools was not altered by the Education Act of 1914, except to require the inclusion of representatives of parents and the district education board where this was not already provided. For secondary schools established in future under the act, the boards of governors would have nine members, comprised of three members of the district education board, three members elected by parents of pupils, two appointed by the government, and one appointed by the local council. Boards of managers of technical high schools after 1914 were similar in their membership: two members elected by the parents of pupils, at least one-third of the total members appointed by the district education board, and other members appointed by the local authorities and associations contributing to the support of the school.

50 New Zealand, Commission on Education in New Zealand, *Report of the Commission on Education in New Zealand* (Wellington: Government Printer, 1962), 82. On the other side of the debate over the future of the education boards – reflecting the belief of the director, T.B. Strong, in the virtues of centralization – in 1927 the Department of Education had advanced proposals to abolish the education boards, Strong also presented the 1930 Parliamentary Recess Committee on Education with a similar scheme for centralization, and a commission on public expenditure in 1932 recommended abolition of the education boards as an economy measure.

51 My summary of 'national efficiency' as an ideology is based on G.R. Searle, *The Quest for National Efficiency: A Study in British Politics and Political Thought, 1899–1914* (Oxford: Basil Blackwell, 1971), 54–106.

52 See, for example, George Bernard Shaw's letter to Graham Wallas in 1899 in which Shaw attempted (unsuccessfully) to dissuade Wallas from supporting 'that foolish democratic mistake, the adhocious School Board' (quoted in ibid., 68).

53 For an account of the influence of the 'efficiency group' on the Education Act of 1902 and the varieties of ideological opposition to national efficiency, see ibid., 101–6, 207–16. The leading exponents of radical liberalism, or 'the new liberalism,' were John Hobson and Leonard Hobhouse. In their version of 'ethical liberalism,' liberty and welfare are together acknowledged as prior political goods, there is an awareness of community as

the basis for development of individuality, and the state as the collective agent of a community must be concerned to provide for each citizen's basic needs. See Michael Freedan, *The New Liberalism: An Ideology of Social Reform* (Oxford: Clarendon Press, 1978), 253.

54 Historically, the grammar schools of England and Wales and the burgh schools of Scotland were independent schools that offered a narrowly academic curriculum based on Latin and Greek grammar and literature. These schools were managed by voluntary boards of governors and maintained by a combination of students' fees, endowment income, and local subsidies. Their classical curriculum was broadened during the nineteenth century to include English grammar, geography, history, mathematics, modern foreign languages, and natural sciences, but the orientation of the grammar and burgh schools to élite academic education and upper occupational classes remained constant.

55 The number of higher class schools under school boards was only seventeen by 1879 and twenty in 1888.

56 Under the 1908 act, higher class schools and grant-aided schools were officially recognized as 'secondary schools.'

57 Initially the Board of Commissioners of Intermediate Education was assigned the annual income from property worth £1 million formerly belonging to the Church of Ireland, which was disestablished by the Irish Church Act of 1869. Income from the former Church of Ireland property was supplemented after 1890 by a budgetary allocation from customs and excise revenues.

58 By the early nineteenth century, several schools were generally recognized as the leading endowed schools: 'What they all had in common was some measure of public esteem. They had all succeeded in being large and outstanding enough to print their names on the public memory' (Vivian Ogilvie, *The English Public School* [New York: Macmillan, 1957], 123). Winchester (1382) and Eton (1440) were two old collegiate foundations that were purely boarding schools. Westminster (1560) shared a similar legal status and high prestige, but included a proportion of day boys. Two former charitable institutions, Christ's Hospital and Charterhouse, had pupils of higher social standing. Harrow, Rugby, and Shrewsbury were former local grammar schools that had expanded their boarding side and attained a special esteem. St Paul's and Merchant Taylors were large London day schools. According to the Clarendon commission, these schools were 'the acknowledged types' on which public school education was being patterned in 'younger institutions of a like character.' The Public Schools Act of 1868 applied to the seven boarding schools; the two London day schools were excluded from its regulation.

59 In setting out what it believed to be the preferences of parents, the Schools
Inquiry Commission identified three grades of education differentiated by
number of years in school and observed, 'It is obvious that these distinctions correspond roughly, but by no means exactly, to the gradations of
society' (Great Britain, Schools Inquiry Commission, *Report of the Commissioners*, vol. 1 [London: Her Majesty's Stationery Office, 1868], 16). One
class comprised rentiers, wealthy businessmen, and professional men,
especially the clergy, medicine, and law, who wanted their sons to continue
school to age eighteen or longer; they had no desire to displace classics
from the curriculum, but many wanted to see mathematics, modern languages, and natural science added to it. An education stopping at age
sixteen would be preferred by larger shopkeepers, rising men of business,
and large tenant farmers, and they would also would want their sons to
follow a modern curriculum, giving no place to Greek and consenting to
Latin only if it were not at the expense of the subjects considered to be
practical for business – English, arithmetic, the rudiments of mathematics
beyond arithmetic, and perhaps natural science and a modern language.
The class comprising smaller tenant farmers, small tradesmen, and superior artisans would prefer an education that stopped at age fourteen, and it
should be 'a clerk's education; namely, a thorough knowledge of arithmetic, and ability to write a good letter' (ibid., 21). According to the Schools
Inquiry Commission, 'Three different kinds of work require three different
kinds of school. Each kind of school should have its proper aim set before
it, and should be put under such rules as will compel it to keep to that aim'
(ibid., 578). As for the daughters of men in these classes, grammar school
education was practically non-existent. The Schools Inquiry Commission
found only fourteen endowed schools for girls, twelve in England and two
in Wales. The commission conceded that the bias of educational endowments towards boys was unjust, but it made no recommendations to encourage the establishment of more girls' schools (ibid., 565).

60 Enrolment in endowed schools was 30,000 in 1895, but only a small proportion entered by means of scholarships from elementary schools – about
2,500 in 1894 and 5,000 in 1900. Most of these scholarships were offered by
local government authorities using their authority under the Technical
Instruction Act of 1889 and the Local Taxation Act of 1890. See S.J. Curtis,
History of Education in Great Britain (6th ed.; London: University Tutorial
Press, 1965), 322.

61 Gareth Elwyn Jones, *Controls and Conflicts in Welsh Secondary Education 1889–
1944* (Cardiff: University of Wales Press, 1982), 8. By the turn of the century, intermediate education was available throughout Wales, and the 1902
act simply ensured that gaps were filled.

62 With regard to the liberal-conservative principles of the Bryce commission, see, for example, its support for the integration of classical and modern subjects in the secondary school curriculum accompanied by its worries that literary and humanist education was being superseded by scientific and technological subjects. 'In every phase of secondary teaching, the first aim should be to educate the mind, and not merely to convey information. It is a fundamental fault, which pervades many parts of the secondary teaching now given in England, that the subject (literary, scientific, or technical) is too often taught in such a manner that it has little or no educational value' (Great Britain, Royal Commission on Secondary Education, *Report of the Commissioners*, vol. 1 [London: Her Majesty's Stationery Office, 1895], 80). See also the commission's proposal for a system of scholarships for children in elementary school that would permit a minority to climb the educational ladder without altering the upper-class ethos of the grammar schools. Indeed, the commission reiterated the recommendations of the Schools Inquiry Commission to differentiate secondary education in grammar schools intended for the children of business and professional men as well as a small élite of working-class scholarship winners from elementary schools.

63 In the 1904 regulations, secondary schools were defined 'to include any Day or Boarding school which offers to each of its scholars, up to and beyond the age of 16, a general education, physical, mental and moral, given through a complete graded course of instruction of wider scope and more advanced degree than that in Elementary Schools.' The traditional academic orientation was evident in the minimum requirements for a four-year course in three groups of subjects: English, including English language and literature, geography, and history; ancient and modern languages other than English; and mathematics and science. See 'Regulations for Secondary Schools 1904,' in J. Stuart Maclure (ed.), *Educational Documents: England and Wales 1816 to the Present* (4th ed.; London: Methuen, 1979), 156–9.

64 Olive Banks, *Parity and Prestige in English Secondary Education* (London: Routledge and Kegan Paul, 1955), 104.

65 On one side there were conservatives who defended the Bryce commission's recommendations for an academic curriculum and a relatively narrow scholarship ladder that would restrict secondary education to exceptional students from elementary schools. Typical of this position was Sir John Gorst's argument in 1903: 'While primary instruction should be provided for, and even enforced upon all, advanced instruction is for the few. It is the interest of the commonwealth at large that every boy and girl

showing capacities above the average should be caught and given the best opportunities for developing these capacities. It is not its interest to scatter broadcast a huge system of higher instruction for anyone who chooses to take advantage of it, however unfit to receive it.' Similarly, Stanley Baldwin in a 1923 election speech 'did not think it wise, as some suggest, to give everybody a secondary education. It is no good forcing every kind of ability into one form of education if the result is going to be to lower the standard which it is the interest of the country to maintain' (quoted in ibid., 119). On the other side were liberals and socialists who advocated accessibility for all young people to secondary education that would range according to their needs from academic to practical studies. J.A. Hobson, for example, advocated not a narrow ladder but 'a broad easy stair' from primary to secondary schooling and a curriculum based on teaching general not élite culture, and R.H. Tawney edited an influential report of a Labour party committee on secondary education that advocated the adoption of a system of free and universal secondary education as official party policy.

66 The Hadow committee recognized that this argument required a segmental concept of equality: 'Equality, in short, is not identity, and the larger the number of children receiving post-primary education, the more essential is it that education should not attempt to press different types of character and intelligence into a single mould, however excellent in itself it may be, but should provide a range of educational opportunity sufficiently wide to appeal to varying interests and cultivate powers which differ widely, both in kind and in degree' (Great Britain, Board of Education, *Report of the Consultative Committee on the Education of the Adolescent* [London: His Majesty's Stationery Office, 1926], 78–9). The phrase 'different types of character and intelligence' implies that the committee was here defending segmental equality rather than person-regarding equality.

67 Ibid., 88. The report of the Hadow committee rejected proposals by technical teachers that junior technical schools admit pupils at age eleven and include a modern language in their curriculum. A foreign language was unnecessary because the junior technical schools 'were expressly planned for the definite object of fitting boys and girls to enter industrial employment immediately on leaving.' If a local authority wanted secondary schools with a wider aim and curriculum it could organize them as secondary schools with a commercial or industrial bias under existing regulations (ibid., 66–7). The Board of Education eventually yielded to the pressures to permit the teaching of a foreign language in junior technical schools, but it held firm on reducing the age of entry (Banks, *Parity and Prestige in English Secondary Education*, 111).

68 Board of Education, *Report of the Consultative Committee on the Education of the Adolescent*, 80.

69 For example, '*The Sixth Form is indeed the most characteristic and most valuable feature in a Grammar School in the training of character and a sense of responsibility, and on its existence depends all that is best in the grammar school tradition.*' Great Britain, Board of Education, *Report of the Consultative Committee on Secondary Education with Special Reference to Grammar Schools and Technical High Schools* (London: His Majesty's Stationery Office, 1938), 166; italics in the original.

70 H.M. Knox, *Two Hundred and Fifty Years of Scottish Education 1696–1946* (Edinburgh: Oliver and Boyd, 1953), 128–9.

71 The senior official was George Macdonald, deputy and later head of the Scottish Education Department; quoted in H.M. Paterson, 'Incubus and Ideology: The Development of Secondary Schooling in Scotland, 1900–1939,' in Walter M. Humes and Hamish M. Paterson (eds), *Scottish Culture and Scottish Education 1800–1980* (Edinburgh: John Donald, 1983), 208–9. Macdonald was responding to recommendations of the Scottish Advisory Council on Education that seemed to threaten the selectivity of higher class schools.

72 In law the Board of Education comprised the president of the Board of Education, the lord president of the council, the secretaries of state, the first lord of the treasury, and the chancellor of the exchequer; but following a pattern previously set by the Board of Trade, the Local Government Board, and the Board of Agriculture, the Board of Education never met. The last recorded meeting of the education committee of the Privy Council occurred in 1890, apparently because the lord president considered a proposal to abandon the grants policy based on payment by results as such a revolution in established policy that it required a meeting of the education committee. The meeting was a perfunctory farce (Gillian Sutherland, *Policy-Making in Elementary Education 1870–1895* [Oxford: Oxford University Press, 1973], 124). Similarly, in Scotland the occasional influence of the lord president came to an end, the Privy Council committee for Scottish education became an empty formality like the Board of Education, and ministerial responsibility for Scottish education was assumed exclusively by the secretary for Scotland. With the appointment of Sir John Struthers as secretary of the Scotch Education Department in 1904, even the formality of issuing education edicts in the name of 'My Lords' ceased.

73 Neil Daglish, *Education Policy-Making in England and Wales: The Crucible Years, 1895–1911* (London: Woburn Press, 1996), 202, 209.

74 Andrew McPherson and Charles D. Raab, *Governing Education: A Sociology of Policy since 1945* (Edinburgh: Edinburgh University Press, 1988), 29.

75 R.D. Anderson, *Education and the Scottish People 1750–1918* (Oxford: Clarendon Press, 1995), 179. Anderson elaborates as follows on the position of the Educational Institute of Scotland (EIS): 'Since there were no national salary scales, it had no negotiating role, and the political system did not encourage officials like Craik to deal directly with pressure groups. Parliament was still the centre of decision-making, and the commonest form of political action was constituency pressure on MPs. By the 1890s the EIS had learnt to play this game, and was active at general elections in seeking pledges from candidates on issues like tenure and pensions. The most formal type of action, much used by school boards, was the deputation to London, which was introduced to the Secretary for Scotland by sympathetic MPs, and submitted its case in speeches backed up by written memoranda. This largely superseded the mass petitions and public meetings favoured before 1872' (ibid.). National minimum salary scales were introduced in 1919 and maintained until 1945, but these were imposed by the SED with minimal consultation and no negotiations with the EIS.

76 Abolition of the school boards had been promoted for several years in both the Education Department and the Conservative party. Sir Francis Sandford, former secretary of the Education Department, while serving as a member of the Cross inquiry into elementary education in 1888, presented the commission with a memorandum showing how the new county councils could take over the work of the school boards and assume responsibility for aiding the voluntary schools (Sutherland, *Policy-Making in Elementary Education*, 204, 222, 233). The commission in its majority report found Sandford's scheme 'worthy of consideration' but premature pending full implementation of the reforms to county government made under the Local Government Act of 1888. In 1896, Sir John Gorst, the vice-president of council for education in the Conservative-Unionist government, introduced a bill, obviously based on Sandford's memorandum, that provided for each county council to appoint a committee to act on its behalf as local education authority. This authority would have as its main functions the distribution of a special grant to aid voluntary schools and the supply of secondary and technical education, but school boards also would be subordinate to the local education authority (Eric Eaglesham, *From School Board to Local Authority* [London: Routledge and Kegan Paul, 1956], 105). The bill passed second reading but was dropped by the government when it encountered opposition from Nonconformist denominational groups

during the committee stage. Gorst's views favouring county councils over school boards were echoed and elaborated in a 1901 memorandum by Robert Morant. If local educational governance were divided between school boards and county councils, there would inevitably be inefficiencies from divided administration and competition between the two types of public authorities. P.H.J.H Gosden, *The Development of Educational Administration in England and Wales* (Oxford: Basil Blackwell, 1966), 175–6.

77 The government's original bill gave county councils the option of retaining school boards to administer elementary education, but this clause was dropped in committee by a vote of 271 to 102. The optional clause had been a concession to the Liberal Unionists, in particular to their leader, Joseph Chamberlain, who was a known supporter of the school boards. Chamberlain missed attending the committee debate because he was hospitalized following a hansom-cab accident.

78 John Stacks, 'Scotland's *Ad Hoc* Authorities, 1919–1930,' in History of Education Society, *Studies in the Government and Control of Education since 1860* (London: Methuen, 1970), 76–8.

79 The boundaries of the ad hoc education authorities corresponded to the thirty-three counties of Scotland and the five burghs of Glasgow, Edinburgh, Aberdeen, Dundee, and Leith. Under the 1929 act, the territorial jurisdictions of the local education authorities were essentially the same as those set for the ad hoc authorities in 1918 except for the creation of two joint county councils (Moray and Nairn, Perth and Kinross) and the amalgamation of Edinburgh and Leith (which had occurred in 1920). Each council was required to establish an education committee, with the majority of members being councillors but at least two members nominated by local churches or denominational organizations. As in England and Wales, the Scottish education committees were financially dependent; they could not raise revenues or incur expenditures without council approval.

80 Donald H. Akenson, *Education and Enmity: The Control of Schooling in Northern Ireland 1920–50* (Newton Abbot: David and Charles, 1973), 49–51. The first minister of education for Northern Ireland was Charles Stewart Henry Vane-Tempest-Stewart, seventh Marquis of Londonderry, whose father had been president of the Board of Education from 1902 to 1905.

81 Eighteen regional education committees were established in the six counties of Northern Ireland: Antrim and Tyrone each had five regional committees; Londonderry had three; and the counties of Armagh, Down, and Fermanagh each had one regional committee. As with the county boroughs, there were education committees for the county councils, but they were advisory bodies rather than administrative agents.

82 Over the last three decades of the nineteenth century, enrolment in volun-
    tary schools increased from 1,152,389 in 1870 to 1,981,664 in 1880 and
    2,486,597 in 1900; attendance at board schools was 769,252 by 1880 and
    2,201,049 in 1900 (Marjorie Cruickshank, *Church and State in English Educa-
    tion: 1870 to the Present Day* [London: Macmillan, 1963], 190). At the same
    time the financial position of voluntary schools steadily deteriorated, and
    by the 1890s church schools were closing at the rate of sixty each year.
    During the 1902 debate, the consensus was that the bill would pass easily
    if it were not for the issues of maintaining voluntary schools and giving
    religious instruction in public schools: '"I would ask anyone whether, if the
    educational objections to the Bill had been the only objections present,
    there would have been a division on the Second Reading," said Mr A.J.
    Balfour at the close of the fifth day of debate, and Mr Dillon for the Irish
    Nationalists was equally emphatic. "If you could eliminate the religious
    difficulty, your Education Bill would pass the Second Reading in a single
    night and the "Committee stage would not take a week."' G.A.N. Lowndes,
    *The Silent Social Revolution: An Account of the Expansion of Public Education in
    England and Wales 1895–1965* (2nd ed.; London: Oxford University Press,
    1969), 65.
83 In the Conservative-Unionist government both A.J. Balfour and Joseph
    Chamberlain initially were opposed to maintaining voluntary schools from
    local rates. Robert Morant, like W.E. Forster in 1870, held that the cost of
    replacing all voluntary schools with public schools would be prohibitive,
    and in the end the secretary's view prevailed. Despite pressure from the
    voluntary sector, the Cowper-Temple clause that permitted non-denomina-
    tional but not denominational religious instruction and observances in
    'board' schools was retained in the 1902 act to apply to the new 'council'
    schools. Under the 1902 act, managers of 'non-provided' schools, which
    usually included one-third appointed by the local authority, appointed their
    teachers subject to approval by the local education authority, and they
    controlled religious instruction in their schools. Secular instruction in non-
    provided schools was controlled by the local educational authorities. In
    1906 a Liberal government bill to extend the control of local education
    authorities over voluntary schools and restrict denominational instruction
    to a minority of Roman Catholic, Jewish, and Anglican schools passed the
    House of Commons by a margin of more than two to one but was exten-
    sively amended by the Conservative majority in the House of Lords so
    that the voluntary sector was left undisturbed and the existing restriction
    on denominational instruction in council schools was relaxed. Rather
    than force an election over the bill, the Liberals dropped it. Two more

efforts by the Liberal government to overcome the deadlock in 1908 also failed.

84 An assessment three decades after the passage of the 1918 act concluded that hostilities over religion in Scottish education had dwindled 'to the few who sincerely believe that the right attitude towards a minority belonging to an authoritarian Church is one of consistent opposition and refusal of concessions, and to those others who would banish all forms of religious education alike from our schools.' James J. Robertson, 'The Scottish Solution,' in J.A. Lauwerys and N. Hans (eds), *The Yearbook of Education 1951* (London: Evans Brothers, 1951), 335.

85 The 1923 Education Act established three classes of elementary schools: Class I primary schools were entirely controlled by local education authorities and included 'provided' schools built by a local authority and 'transferred' schools that had come from voluntary management; Class II schools, which had a special management committee comprising four members named by the former managers or trustees and two members appointed by the local education authority, received full payment of teachers' salaries, one-half of their operating costs, and grants for capital expenditures from the Northern Ireland Ministry of Education; and Class III schools, which had no state representatives in their management, received only full payment of teachers' salaries from the department and usually got one-half of their costs for heating, lighting, and cleaning from local rates. Under the 1930 Education Act, the composition of regional and county borough education committees was altered to require that one-quarter of the members be appointed by the minister of education from among representatives of the denominations transferring their schools, that half the school managers of provided or transferred schools had to be appointed from former managers or representatives of denominations transferring their schools, that school management committees were empowered to establish short lists of applicants for teaching positions in their schools from which the regional or county borough education committee would make a final choice, and that Bible instruction was required if the parents of ten children demanded it.

86 Very few Catholic schools were even reorganized into Class II schools, though doing so would have made them eligible for building and renovation grants from the local rates in addition to the 50 per cent grant from the Ministry of Education. Akenson argues that Catholic schools could have been transferred without endangering Catholic control of their schools 'if the clergy had been willing to transcend their medieval determination to

control the schools singlehandedly and had been willing to enter into partnership with the Catholic laity in controlling the schools through the newly-restructured school management committees' (Akenson, *Education and Enmity*, 115–16).

87 Dwight Waldo, *The Administrative State: A Study of the Political Theory of American Public Administration* (2nd ed.; New York: Holmes and Meier, 1984), 17–19. A merit bureaucracy with its neutral competence and impersonal operation would be the means to renew the separation of governmental institutions, reduce partisan control, protect individual and minority rights against majoritarian tyranny, and revive for an industrial society the spirit of American democracy (William Nelson, *The Roots of American Bureaucracy, 1830–1900* [Cambridge, Mass.: Harvard University Press, 1982], 125). For a classic (and critical) analysis of the impact of scientific management on public education in the United States, see Raymond A. Callahan, *Education and the Cult of Efficiency: A Study of the Social Forces That Have Shaped the Administration of the Public Schools* (Chicago: University of Chicago Press, 1962).

88 Herbert G. Espy, *The Public Secondary School: A Critical Analysis of Secondary Education in the United States* (Boston: Houghton Mifflin, 1939), 30–1. Prior to their decline during the eighteenth century, there were about forty grammar schools in New England and a few in the southern colonies. The first grammar school in the American colonies, Boston Latin School, founded in 1635, was among those still operating at the beginning of the nineteenth century. Outside New England, the most notable grammar school was the William Penn Charter School founded in 1689 in Pennsylvania. See William Marshall French, *American Secondary Education* (2nd ed.; New York: Odyssey Press, 1967), 42–3.

89 Established in 1821 as a post-elementary school option for parents who wished to give their child an education 'that shall fit him for active life, and shall serve as a foundation for eminence in his profession, whether Mercantile or Mechanical,' Boston English High School was the first public high school in the United States. The success of this school led in 1827 to a state law that required every town of more than five hundred families to establish a public high school, and by 1840 there were twenty-six town high schools in operation. The Massachusetts model of public high schools was soon adopted in other New England states, and subsequently, in other states, school districts or 'union' districts were authorized to establish higher grades in common schools or separate public high schools, for example, Iowa (1849), California (1851), New York and Ohio (1853), Penn-

sylvania (1854), Illinois (1855), Michigan (1859), and Indiana (1867). See
I.L. Kandel, *History of Secondary Education: A Study of the Development of Liberal
Education* (Boston: Houghton Mifflin, 1930), 425–44.

90 Elmer Ellsworth Brown, *The Making of Our Middle Schools: An Account of the
Development of Secondary Education in the United States* (New York: Longmans,
Green, 1902), 179. Theodore Sizer has argued that, before the Civil War,
academies were not socially exclusive; but since most were boarding
schools, only reasonably wealthy families could afford to enrol their chil-
dren. Theodore R. Sizer, 'The Academies: An Interpretation,' in Theodore
R. Sizer (ed.), *The Age of the Academies* (New York: Columbia University
Teachers' College, 1964), 36–7.

91 Espy, *The Public Secondary School,* 34

92 B. Jeannette Burrell and R.H. Eckelberry, 'The High School Controversy in
the Post-Civil-War Period: Times, Places, and Participants,' *The School Review*
42 (May 1934): 334.

93 Sizer, 'The Academies: An Interpretation,' 40. By the middle of the nineteenth century, Henry Barnard was able to list 6,185 academies, enrolling
263,096 pupils and covering every state of the union, but following the Civil
War the academies went into a decline. Some were converted into public
high schools, a few became state normal schools for training teachers, some
survived as upper-class private schools, and many simply closed because of
falling enrolments and inadequate finances.

94 One study of high school curricula in the north-central states counted
seven courses in 1860–65, twelve in 1880–5, and thirty-six in 1896–1900.
J.E. Stout, *The Development of High School Curricula in the North Central States
from 1860 to 1918* (Chicago: University of Chicago Press, 1921); cited in
Kandel, *History of Secondary Education,* 458.

95 The NEA Committee of Ten on Secondary School Studies was chaired by
Charles W. Eliot, president of Harvard University. The other members were
four other college or university presidents, a professor of Oberlin College,
the U.S. commissioner of education, the principal of Boston Girls' High
and Latin School, the principal of Albany High School, and the headmaster
of Lawrenceville School (Edward A. Krug, *The Shaping of the American High
School,* [New York: Harper and Row, 1964], 37–8). In its survey of high
schools, the Committee of Ten found that nearly forty subjects were being
taught, many for only short periods (as had been common in the academies) and that, even for traditional subjects such as Latin or algebra, time
allotments varied greatly among schools. The conventional subject orientation of the committee is evident in the breakdown of the nine conferences:
Latin; Greek; English; other modern languages; mathematics; physics,

astronomy, and chemistry; natural history (biology, including botany, zoology, and physiology); history, civil government, and political economy; and geography (physical geography, geology, and meteorology). For the reports of these conferences see National Education Association, *Report of the Committee of Ten on Secondary School Studies with the Reports of the Conferences Arranged by the Committee* (New York: American Book Company, 1894), 60–249.

96 The Committee of Ten considered it expedient to include the courses in modern languages and English, but held that these 'must in practice be distinctly inferior to the other two' (ibid., 48). Industrial and commercial subjects did not appear in any of the four courses, but, 'if it were desired to provide more amply for subjects thought to have practical importance in trade or the useful arts, it would be easy to provide options in such subjects for some of the science contained in the third and fourth years of the "English" programme' (ibid., 50).

97 Ibid., 17.

98 Charles Eliot's commitment to a selective, élitist, academic high school was part of his vision of differentiated education in a class-divided society. According to Eliot there were four classes or 'layers in civilized society which are indispensable, and, so far as we can see, eternal': 'the managing leading, guiding class – the intellectual discoverers, the inventors, the organizers, and the managers and their chief assistants'; skilled workers, who were increasing in numbers and importance with the application of technology to production; 'the commercial class, the layer which is employed in buying, selling, and distributing'; and the 'thick fundamental layer engaged in household work, agriculture, mining, quarrying, and forest work.' In a democratic society, schools should discover talented children in the lower layers and foster their upward mobility. None the less, each class had 'distinct characteristics and distinct educational needs,' 'and our school systems must be so reorganized that they shall serve all four of the social layers or sets of workers, and serve them with intelligence, and with keen appreciation of the several ends in view' (Charles W. Eliot, 'Educational Reform and the Social Order,' *The School Review* 17 [April 1909]: 217–19). In a 1908 address to the National Society for the Promotion of Industrial Education, Eliot advocated trade schools as part-time or full-time continuation schools for children 'obliged to leave the regular public school system by the time they are fourteen, or even earlier.' Teachers in elementary schools would have to sort their pupils 'by their evident or probable destinies' for attendance at academic high schools, technical secondary schools, and trade schools. With each child 'put at that work

which the teacher believes the child can do best,' each child would be ensured 'the happiness of achievement' and the outcome would be consistent with 'the best definition of democracy' (quoted in Krug, *The Shaping of the American High School*, 226).

99 Harvey Kantor, 'Vocationalism in American Education: The Economic and Political Context, 1880–1930,' in Harvey Kantor and David B. Tyack (eds), *Work, Youth, and Schooling: Historical Perspectives on Vocationalism in American Education* (Stanford: Stanford University Press, 1982), 27–30.

100 Ibid., 27–8.

101 John Dewey, 'Learning to Earn: The Place of Vocational Education in a Comprehensive Scheme of Public Education,' *School and Society* 5 (24 March 1917): 332, 334–5. According to Dewey, one approach to vocational education advocated creating 'a dual or divided system of administration,' designing vocational education as training for specific trades, neglecting as useless 'the topics in history and civics which make future workers aware of their rightful claims as citizens in a democracy,' emphasizing routine and drill at the expense of 'an enlarged education,' and conceiving 'guidance as a method of placement – a method of finding jobs.' 'The other idea of industrial education aims at preparing every individual to render service of a useful sort to the community, while at the same time it equips him to secure by his own initiative whatever place his natural capacities fit him for. It will proceed in an opposite way in every respect ... So far as method is concerned, such a conception of industrial education will prize freedom more than docility; initiative more than automatic skill; insight and understanding more than capacity to recite lessons or to execute tasks under the direction of others' (ibid., 333–4).

102 National Education Association, Commission on the Reorganization of Secondary Education, *Cardinal Principles of Secondary Education*, United States Bureau of Education Bulletin No. 35 (Washington, D.C.: United States Government Printing Office, 1918). The seven principles that constituted the objectives of democratic education were health, command of fundamental processes, worthy home membership, vocation, citizenship, worthy use of leisure, and ethical character (ibid., 10–11).

103 Ibid., 24–6.

104 According to Joseph F. Kett ('The Adolescence of Vocational Education,' in Kantor and Tyack [eds], *Work, Youth, and Schooling*, 53), the ideas that shaped the Smith-Hughes Act were those of David Snedden, Charles Prosser, and the National Society for the Promotion of Industrial Education. Snedden vigorously attacked the report of the Commission of Reorganization of Secondary Education, asserting that 'the entire philosophy

of the review committee seems hopelessly academic in the unfavorable
sense.' Snedden was convinced that meaningful vocational education
could only be given in specialized vocational schools that were removed
from the control of state and local authorities for elementary and secondary public education. 'The members of the committee are chiefly preoccupied with the liberal education of youth of secondary school age ... In
spite of its seeming insistence to the contrary it is hard to believe that the
committee is genuinely interested in any vocational education that can
meet the economic tests of our time.' See David Snedden, 'Cardinal
Principles of Secondary Education,' *School and Society* 9 (3 May 1919): 522,
526–7.
105 Edward A. Krug, *The Shaping of the American High School, Volume 2, 1920–
1941* (Madison: University of Wisconsin Press, 1972), 53. The main exceptions were Los Angeles, New York, and Cleveland, all of which built new
specialized vocational high schools between the wars.
106 United States, Department of the Interior, Office of Education, Grayson
N. Kefauver, Victor H. Noll, and C. Elwood Drake, *The Horizontal Organization of Secondary Education*, Bulletin, 1932, no. 17, monograph no. 2 (Washington, D.C.: United States Government Printing Office, 1934), 15–16.
For the most part, schools were classified according to the reports of the
respondents. The uncertainties about such a classification were readily
conceded, and the results probably understate the prevalence of comprehensive high schools. As the authors observed, 'The secondary schools of
the United States do not fall into clearly defined categories. One finds
almost every variation in scope of offering. Trade schools exist separately
and in combination with technical schools. Technical high schools, so-
called, are frequently comprehensive schools. Academic schools usually
have commercial work and they usually have a meager offering in home
economics. They may even have a course or two in practical arts of a very
elementary type' (ibid., 17). Comprehensive high schools varied from
61 per cent of schools surveyed in the northeastern and middle Atlantic
states to 75.5 per cent in the South, 82.5 per cent in the Midwest, and
91.5 per cent in the West. Academic high schools were more prevalent in
the middle Atlantic states (16.6 per cent), the South (15 per cent), and
the Midwest (9.8 per cent) than in the western (6.6 per cent) and the northeastern (2.2 per cent) states. The highest occurrence of trade schools was
in the northeastern states (23.3 per cent) and the middle Atlantic region
(16.1 per cent). The Northeast was also the region with the highest occurrence of commercial (5.6 per cent) and technical (6.7 per cent) high
schools (ibid., 16).

107 Kefauver, Noll, and Drake use the term 'multiple curricula' to refer to the grouping of subjects into programs or tracks within secondary schools and distinguish this form of curricular organization from 'constants with variables,' in which certain subjects are required of all pupils and the remainder are electives. In their survey of 994 schools, they found 44.5 per cent of the comprehensive schools had multiple curricula with electives, 12.4 per cent multiple curricula without electives, and 41.3 per cent constants with variables. Among academic high schools, 51.9 per cent were organized in terms of constants with variables, 35.4 per cent as multiple curricula with electives, and 11.4 per cent as multiple curricula without electives. Multiple curricula, with or without electives, were reported as the form of organization in 75 per cent of technical high schools, 80 per cent of commercial high schools, and 94 per cent of trade schools (ibid., 27).

108 On the history of accreditation, see Krug, *The Shaping of the American High School*, 146–63; and also Krug, *The Shaping of the American High School, Volume 2: 1920–1941*, 63–6. The New England Association of Colleges and Secondary Schools, was founded in 1885, followed by the Middle States Association of Colleges and Secondary Schools on the eastern seaboard (1887), the North Central Association of Colleges and Secondary Schools, involving nineteen states from Montana to West Virginia, and the Southern Association of Colleges and Schools, covering the area from Virginia to Texas (1895), the Northwest Association of Secondary and Higher Schools for Oregon, Idaho, and Washington (1917), and the Western Association of Colleges and Schools in California (1924). The first regional association to establish a formal accreditation program was the North Central Association in 1904, followed by the Southern Association in 1913.

109 In June 1926 a multiple-choice examination that tested general ability and knowledge without being tied to specific curricula was administered for the first time on a trial basis, but essay examinations remained the official method of testing by the College Entrance Examination Board (CEEB) until the Second World War. On the history of the College Entrance Examination Board, see George H. Hanford, *Life with the SAT: Assessing Our Young People and Our Times* (New York: College Entrance Examination Board, 1991), 7–21; and John A. Valentine, *The College Board and the School Curriculum: A History of the College Board's Influence on the Substance and Standards of American Education, 1900–1980* (New York: College Entrance Examination Board, 1987), 3–77.

110 Under the accreditation system, teachers and students were freed from

the pressures of preparing for external examinations, but their schools, at least in the college-preparatory tracks, were required to conform to defined standards of external accreditation commissions, in particular with regard to the qualifications of their teachers. Under the examination system, students were not dependent on accreditation of their schools, but admission depended on their success on the College Boards and hence conformity of their schools with the curricula prescribed by the CEEB for basic academic subjects (Krug, *The Shaping of the American High School*, 155).

111 The 'short ballot' proposed to give the governor power to appoint subordinate officials, but according to the advocates of civic trusteeship there were strong reasons against extending this model of executive leadership to include the governance of public education. In states where a tradition of expert administration was not established, it would be unwise for the governor to have authority to appoint the superintendent; partisan politics inevitably would intrude. In any case, governors had neither time nor qualifications to oversee educational policy making. Similar arguments disqualified state legislative assemblies. Hence, by elimination, the power to appoint the state superintendent should be assigned to a state board of education. Members of the state board in turn would be appointed by the governor for lengthy overlapping terms, say seven years, in order to reduce the incentive for governors to abuse their power of appointment and ensure that no governor would appoint a majority. See Thomas H. Reed, 'A Constitutional State Board of Education,' in Ellwood P. Cubberly and Edward C. Elliott, *State and County School Administration, Vol. II: Source Book* (New York: Macmillan, 1915), 291, 300.

112 In the state of New York, the Board of Regents was given power to appoint the state commissioner of education in 1904, but, contrary to the norms of Progressive theory, the board continued to be appointed by the state legislative assembly.

113 In Connecticut, the oldest adherent of this model, the governor appointed one member from each county and one at large for six-year terms, resulting in a large board of nine members. In Arkansas, the superintendent, previously elected, became an appointment of the state board of education in 1931; a decade later the ex officio board was reorganized so that the governor appointed nine members for nine-year terms, subject to confirmation by the state Senate. The state boards with eight members, in New Hampshire and Arkansas, each had one member, the governor, who was a member ex officio. In Delaware, the six members of the reorganized board were appointed by the governor for relatively short three-year terms.

114 In Rhode Island from 1870 the state commissioner of education had been appointed by a state board of education that comprised the governor, lieutenant-governor, and six members of the General Assembly. The commissioner, not the board, was responsible for determination of educational policy, distribution of state funds, and state administration of elementary and secondary education.

115 In 1940, nine states – Illinois, Iowa, Maine, Nebraska, North Dakota, Ohio, Rhode Island, South Dakota, and Wisconsin – did not have some kind of state board of education. In six states – Colorado, Kansas, Michigan, Mississippi, Oregon, and Texas – the state boards continued to have restricted, specific responsibilities for elementary and secondary schooling rather than general responsibility.

116 From Buffalo in 1837 to Milwaukee in 1859, only 24 cities appointed superintendents of schools. A decade after the end of the Civil War, 142 out of 175 cities having populations of 8,000 or more had appointed city superintendents, and in 1914–15 there were 1,551 superintendents in cities and towns of more than 4,000 population. See Ellwood P. Cubberly, *Public School Administration: A Statement of the Fundamental Principles Underlying the Organization and Administration of Public Education* (Boston: Houghton Mifflin, 1916), 58–9.

117 In the twelve cities, the reduction in the number of school board members when the boards were reorganized was as follows: Cleveland (1892), 26 to 7; Milwaukee (1897, 1907), 42 to 15; St Louis (1897), 21 to 12; Baltimore (1898), 28 to 9; San Francisco (1898), 12 to 4; Los Angeles (1903), 9 to 7; Boston (1905), 24 to 5; Philadelphia (1905, 1911), 43 to 15; Pittsburgh (1911), 47 to 15; Detroit (1916), 17 to 7; Chicago (1917), 21 to 11; New York (1917), 46 to 7. See Joseph M. Cronin, *The Control of Urban Schools* (New York: The Free Press, 1973), 44–50, 70–8, 91–100, 125–30. In San Francisco the four members were appointed by the mayor, but the city superintendent continued to be elected until 1920, when voters in a referendum approved a reorganization to seven members appointed by the mayor and the superintendent appointed by the board (David B. Tyack, *The One Best System: A History of American Urban Education* [Cambridge, Mass.: Harvard University Press, 1974], 160–7). In Chicago the reorganization was politically and legally contested between the mayor and the council for two years before the council finally approved the mayor's nominees (ibid., 171–2).

118 Ibid., 168.

119 According to Cubberly, perhaps the most distinctive feature of city school districts was unity of work. Instead of being divided into hundreds of small

districts with no unity of effort or purpose, city schools were governed
by a small board of representative citizens and a city superintendent who
divided policy and administration based on the model of a modern business corporation with its board of directors and chief executive officer. 'In
a rapidly increasing number of our cities the best principles of corporation control have been worked out and are being put into practice in the
educational organization. In such the board of education for the city acts
much as the board of directors for a business corporation, listening to
reports as to the progress of the business, approving proposals as to
extensions or changes in the nature of the business, deciding lines of
policy to be followed, approving the budget for annual maintenance, and
serving as a means of communication between the stockholders and the
executive officers. The executive officers are employed to discharge
executive functions, and to these executive officers are given power and
authority commensurate with the responsibilities of the positions they
hold. The board of education hears reports, examines proposals, and
legislates, while the executive officers execute the decrees of the board
and supervise the details of the work of their administrative departments'
(Cubberly, *Public School Administration*, 435).

120 Cubberly's indictment of small school districts was harsh. He observed
that 'The large number of district-school trustees required – an army of
thirty to thirty-five thousand in an average well-settled State – in itself
almost precludes the possibility of securing any large proportion of competent and efficient men' and concluded that 'As a system for school
administration the district system is expensive, inefficient, inconsistent,
short-sighted, unprogressive, and penurious; it leads to a great and an
unnecessary multiplication of small and inefficient schools; the trustees
frequently assume authority over matters which they are not competent to
handle; it leads to marked inequalities in schools, terms, and educational
advantages; and it stands to-day as the most serious obstacle in the way
of the consolidation of rural schools. Most of the progress that has been
made in rural education within the past two decades has been made without the support and often against the opposition of the district-school
trustees and the people they represent' (ibid., 52).

121 Ibid., 449.

122 The town or township was the basic unit for local educational governance
in Connecticut, Indiana, Maine, Massachusetts, New Hampshire, New
Jersey, Pennsylvania, Rhode Island, and Vermont. The eleven southern
states with county educational governance were Alabama, Florida, Georgia, Kentucky, Louisiana, Maryland, North Carolina, South Carolina,

Tennessee, Virginia, and West Virginia, along with New Mexico and Utah in the Southwest. This classification of types of local educational governance does not include Delaware, which had a highly centralized state educational organization, although the city school districts of Wilmington and Dover and thirteen special districts were more like county units in average area (131 square miles) and average number of teaching positions (95) than towns. The remaining twenty-five states had the community school district as their form of local educational governance. See Arthur B. Moehlman, *School Administration: Its Development, Principles, and Future in the United States* (Boston: Houghton Mifflin, 1940), 163–4, and also ibid., Appendix F, 610–14. In states where local organization was based on school districts, the average size of districts in 1931–2 was 18 square miles, ranging from 5 square miles in Illinois and New York to 244 in Wyoming and 413 in Nevada. The average number of teaching positions in each school district, including city districts, was five; if cities were excluded, the average was between one and two. In states organized by town or township, the average size was larger, 28 square miles and twenty-seven teachers, ranging from 14 square miles in New Jersey to 97 square miles in Vermont and from twelve teaching positions per town in Maine to seventy-four in Massachusetts. In states having county school districts, in 1931–2 the average district was 377 square miles in area and had ninety-three teaching positions. See United States, Department of the Interior, Office of Education, Walter S. Deffenbaugh and Timon Covert, *School Administrative Units with Special Reference to the County Unit*, Pamphlet No. 34 (Washington, D.C.: United States Government Printing Office, 1933), 4–5.

3. Welfare State

1 The issue of what programs should be included in the definition of the welfare state is raised by Robert E. Goodin, *Reasons for Welfare: The Political Theory of the Welfare State* (Princeton: Princeton University Press, 1988), 4–6.
2 The classic distinction of social rights in the twentieth century from civil and political rights was made by T.H. Marshall, *Citizenship and Social Class and Other Essays* (Cambridge: Cambridge University Press, 1950), 46–74.
3 Tasmania was the only state in which there was a major effort at educational planning by the Department of Education during the Second World War. There the departmental Committee of Inquiry into Educational Extension recommended a tripartite organization that was evidently inspired in its structure and rationale by plans for educational reconstruction in England and Wales. Five modern schools were opened in former

primary schools in 1946, a modern-course curriculum was issued in 1947, and a new modern-course certificate was created in 1948. Similarly in Victoria, a committee on post-primary education that comprised departmental inspectors and representatives of the Victorian Teachers' Union recommended three types of schools for three types of students – academic high schools to provide a liberal education and training for those going to university or teachers' college, junior technical schools, and modern schools to give a three-year non-academic post-primary course. Multilateral schools would be restricted to country districts where the population was not large enough to support separate post-primary schools. In South Australia, a committee on education chaired by E.L. Bean was appointed by the state legislative council in 1942, despite reservations on the part of the Department of Education. Over the next seven years, the committee issued seven reports, none of which had much impact on public education in South Australia. On secondary organization, the Bean committee recommended only modest reforms – multilateral secondary organization in country districts; in cities retention of separate high and technical high schools with a common core curriculum for the first three post-primary grades – but even this was more than the department was prepared to implement (Pavla Miller, *Long Division: State Schooling in South Australian Society* [Netley, South Australia: Wakefield Press, 1986], 219–21). In New South Wales, a conference on educational reform sponsored by the NSW Teachers' Federation expressed support for a four-year general education in comprehensive secondary schools to be followed by two-year specialized courses, and the Board of Secondary School Studies put forward a similar proposal in 1946. This plan for reorganization was deemed by the Labor government to be unacceptable because of the cost of extending secondary schooling from five to six years. Alan Barcan, *Two Centuries of Education in New South Wales* (Kensington, NSW: New South Wales University Press, 1988), 229.

4 See Derek Phillips, *Making More Adequate Provision: State Education in Tasmania, 1839–1985* (Hobart: Tasmanian Government Printer, 1985), 309–10.
5 The last vestige of selective public secondary schools in Western Australia disappeared with the conversion of Perth Modern School to a community high school for the western suburbs in 1959.
6 This report was produced following the re-election of the Country–Liberal party coalition, in 1960. At the time of its election in 1957 the coalition, led by the Country party leader, Frank Nicklin, was the first non-Labor government in Queensland since 1932.
7 New South Wales, Department of Education, *Report of the Committee Ap-*

pointed to Survey Secondary Education in New South Wales (Sydney: Government Printer, 1957), 63.

8 See Barcan, *Two Centuries of Education in New South Wales*, 245, 271, 309. Subsequently, the Liberal government elected in March 1988 established eight additional selective high schools in 1989 and two more in 1990.

9 Victoria, *Report of the Committee on State Education in Victoria* (Melbourne: Government Printer, 1960), 151.

10 As a result, high schools in Victoria steadily increased their proportion of the total enrolment of post-primary pupils, from 40.7 per cent in 1945, to 68.3 per cent in 1965, but separate technical secondary schools survived as an important alternative to academic high schools. In 1945, 10,789 students were enrolled in 28 junior technical schools, 22.5 per cent of total post-primary enrolment; twenty years later there were 78 technical schools (the term 'junior' having been dropped in 1962), which enrolled 44,626 students, 25.4 per cent of the total. A declining minority of students was enrolled in consolidated, central, higher elementary, and girls' secondary schools.

11 By the mid-1960s the only external entrance examinations in Australian public secondary schools were the standardized tests used in New South Wales to determine entry to sixteen selective secondary schools in Sydney, Newcastle, and Wollongong. Abolition of external examinations for the intermediate certificate tended to follow the raising of the statutory minimum age for leaving school from fourteen to fifteen or sixteen. In Tasmania, for example, when the age of compulsory schooling was raised to sixteen in 1946, the old intermediate certificate examination was replaced by the Schools Board Certificate, taken after a four-year course in a high school or junior technical school and increasingly granted by internal assessment in accredited schools rather than by external examination. The matriculation examination administered by the University of Tasmania continued to be the external examination for upper secondary students. A separate modern school certificate, introduced in 1948, was awarded on the basis of internal assessment after a three-year course in an area or modern school. When the modern school certificate was abolished in 1961, the Schools Board Certificate became the common educational goal of all lower secondary students. In New South Wales, where fifteen was implemented as the school-leaving age during the school years 1941 to 1943, examinations for the intermediate certificate became partly internal in 1944, wholly based on internal examinations in 1949, and eventually abolished altogether in 1966. Fifteen as the minimum age for leaving school was finally implemented in South Australia in 1963 and in Victoria

in 1964, and external examinations for the intermediate certificate were subsequently ended in Victoria in 1967 and in South Australia in 1968. In Victoria and South Australia, corresponding to the distinction between academic and technical high schools, there were parallel intermediate and intermediate-technical certificates based on internal examinations.

12 In New South Wales, for example, the School Certificate Examination was designed as a broadly based general examination by subjects, not predetermined programs or groups of subjects. When first given in 1965 the School Certificate Examination was externally set and internally assessed, but it was gradually changed over the next decade into a certificate granted wholly on the basis of school assessments. In Queensland, administration of the Junior Certificate Examination was transferred from the Public Examinations Board of the University of Queensland first to the Department of Education in 1957 and subsequently, by the Education Act of 1964, to the Board of Junior Secondary School Studies, which was established to advise the minister on the first three years of secondary education, 'regard being had to the requirements of a sound general education and to the desirability of providing a variety of courses adequate to meet the aptitudes and abilities of students concerned.'

13 Note, however, that following the recommendations of Barry McGaw (*Shaping Their Future: Recommendations for the Reform of the Higher School Certificate* [Sydney: Department of Training and Education Co-ordination, 1997]), the Reform Further Amendment Act (1999) reinstated statewide external tests at the end of Year 10 for students in New South Wales. School Certificate Reference Tests, which had determined the quota of grades A (excellent) to E (elementary) awarded by the Board of Studies to each school but not reported as individual results for each student, were replaced by four mandatory School Certificate Tests starting in 1998 with English literacy and mathematics and subsequently including science (1999) and Australian history, geography, and civics and citizenship (2002).

14 An independent evaluation in 1976 found that school-based assessment had not affected the dominating presence of testing in Queensland secondary schools. According to the report, 'The predominant pattern which emerges is thus one in which tests and examinations are the imperatives of school life, and the curriculum and tests of information gained are closely co-ordinated, with the moderation procedure acting as a mechanism for the co-ordination.' In their classrooms, teachers continued to rely heavily on testing their students, and 'students are seen very frequently as regarding marks or ratings as the most important outcome of schooling.' W.J. Campbell et al., *Some Consequences of the Radford Scheme for Schools, Teachers*

and Students in Queensland (Canberra: Australian Advisory Committee on Research and Development in Education, 1976), 246–7; quoted in W.F. Connell, *Reshaping Australian Education 1960–1985* (Hawthorn, Victoria: Australian Council for Educational Research, 1993), 304.

15 For an overview of the Commonwealth government's postwar educational activities, see Connell, *Reshaping Australian Education 1960–1985*, 235–43. With regard to public primary and secondary schools, the Commonwealth government paid the recurrent and capital costs of education in the Australian Capital Territory and also the costs of education for non-Aboriginal children in the Northern Territory, but the departments of education for New South Wales and South Australia were responsible, respectively, for educational administration in the two federal territories. Beginning in 1950, the Commonwealth government provided schools and pre-school centres for Aboriginal children in the Northern Territory, and it gave financial assistance to the states for the education of Aborigines.

16 In 1969, the South Australia and Western Australia departments each opened two regional offices, and three were organized in Victoria in 1972. By the late 1970s there were eleven regional offices in both New South Wales and Victoria, nine in Queensland, ten in South Australia, and three in Tasmania.

17 The withdrawal of secondary and technical teachers from the Victorian Teachers' Union led to an amendment to the Teaching Service Act in 1968. Two teachers were added to represent secondary and technical teachers. The tribunal then operated as separate divisions for primary, secondary, and technical teachers on matters of salaries, qualifications, allowances, and classification, but the former composition of the tribunal was retained for dealing with general issues affecting the whole profession such as employment conditions and discipline.

18 An amendment to the NSW Public Service Act in 1955 added a fourth member to the Public Service Board, designated as an appointee from the teaching profession or educational administration. This amendment formalized the previous practice of appointing one of the three members of the Public Service Board from the education profession. See R.S. Parker, *The Government of New South Wales* (St Lucia, Queensland: University of Queensland Press, 1978), 304.

19 The Industrial Conciliation and Arbitration Commission replaced the Industrial Court in 1961. The Public Service Board (PSB) replaced the Public Service Commissioner in 1968. In contrast with New South Wales there was no practice of ensuring that one of the three members of the Queensland PSB came from the education profession. The first board did include the

state director of primary education as a member, but when he became director general of education in 1971, education was no longer represented on the board. Colin A. Hughes, *The Government of Queensland* (St Lucia, Queensland: University of Queensland Press, 1980), 209.

20 The Public Service Tribunal and the Tasmanian Teachers' Federation did not engage in collective bargaining. The teachers' salary claims had to be justified on social and economic grounds and by comparisons with other occupational groups (Michael Pusey, *Dynamics of Bureaucracy: A Case Analysis in Education* [Sydney: John Wiley, 1976], 61). The functions of the Public Service Tribunal were merged with those of the Public Service Commissioner when the Public Service Board was established in 1973. W.A. Townsley, *The Government of Tasmania* (St Lucia, Queensland: University of Queensland Press, 1976), 141.

21 In Tasmania the Appeals Committee, which heard appeals against decisions of the Promotions Committee, comprised the director general and two representatives of the Tasmanian Teachers' Federation (TTF) for cases involving primary teachers, and the director general, the president of the TTF, and a secondary teacher for cases involving secondary teachers (Pusey, *Dynamics of Bureaucracy*, 62, 92, 110, 153). The Appeal Board, which dealt with appeals of decisions by the Public Service Board (or Commissioner) in Queensland, comprised a magistrate and one nominee each of the board and the Queensland Teachers' Union. The NSW Crown Employees Appeal Board, which heard appeals on promotions, classification, discipline, dismissals, and individual salary increases relating to seniority and rank, consisted of the chair, a representative of the employer, and a representative of the NSW Teachers' Federation. Prior to the Teaching Service Act of 1970, the 'employer' was the Public Service Board; thereafter it was the director general of education.

22 In Western Australia a committee on secondary education, chaired by the director general of education (H.W. Dettman), recommended that both the Junior and the Leaving examinations should be replaced by certificates based on school assessments. A new Board of Secondary Education would exercise general oversight with regard to secondary curricula, ensure comparability of school assessments, and award certificates of secondary education (Western Australia, Committee on Secondary Education, *Secondary Education in Western Australia* [Perth: Education Department of Western Australia, 1969], 104–9). The Board of Secondary Studies was established by an amendment to the Education Act in 1969, and the Junior examination was discontinued in 1970. The Public Examinations Board continued to conduct the Leaving examination, however, in part because of misgivings

on the part of private schools and the state university about relying on school assessments for matriculation. In 1972 a Joint Tertiary Admissions Examination Committee was established to plan and conduct a replacement for the matriculation examination that came into effect in 1975. M.A. White, 'Sixty Years of Public Examinations and Matriculation Policy in Western Australia,' *Australian Journal of Education* 19 (March 1975): 73.

23 Barcan, *Two Centuries of Education in New South Wales*, 245. The Board of Senior Schools Studies included one representative of independent (registered) non-Catholic secondary schools and one representative of Roman Catholic secondary schools. The Secondary Schools Board included two representatives of non-Catholic secondary schools and two representatives of Catholic secondary schools. The state director of technical education was a member of both committees.

24 The University of Queensland Act gave the university's senate authority to conduct public examinations. In 1912 the university established the Public Examinations Board, on which the university held fourteen of twenty seats, to conduct junior and senior public examinations. In 1941 the Public Examinations Board was replaced by the Board of Post-Primary Studies and Examinations, a statutory body rather than a university board, on which there were four members from the Department of Public Instruction, seven from the university, seven representing approved secondary schools, and one member representing technical institutes. The university continued to provide chief examiners, and its control over public examinations remained complete until 1957, when administration of the junior examination was transferred to the Department of Education. Rupert Goodman, *Secondary Education in Queensland, 1860–1960* (Canberra: Australian National University Press, 1968), 254, 264–7.

25 Teachers on the Board of Secondary School Studies included four employed in non-government secondary schools, two nominees of the Queensland Teachers' Union, and one from the Queensland Association of Teachers in Independent Schools. From institutions of higher and further education there were two nominees of the University of Queensland, one from James Cook University of Northern Queensland, one representative of the College of Advanced Education, and one representative of the Teachers' College. The membership also included a chair and the executive officer of the board ex officio.

26 The Victorian Universities and Schools Examinations Board (VUSEB) was established by identical statutes passed by the universities of Melbourne and Monash under the authority of their acts. La Trobe University joined the VUSEB in 1966. On the history of the establishment of the board, see

P.W. Musgrave, *Whose Knowledge? A Case Study of the Victorian Universities Schools Examination Board, 1964–1979* (London: Falmer Press, 1988), 39–60. About two-thirds of the candidates for the Intermediate Certificate and one-half of those for the Leaving Certificate came from accredited schools. The VUSEB discontinued the Intermediate Certificate in 1967 and the Leaving Certificate in 1972. The Matriculation Certificate, which was re-named the Victorian Higher School Certificate in 1970 in order to recognize its broader function as a leaving examination, continued to be an external examination (Connell, *Reshaping Australian Education 1960–1985*, 310).

27 Under the 1968 act, the thirty-two members of the Public Examinations Board of South Australia were appointed by the minister of education on the basis of nominations from specific constituencies: ten members of the teaching or administrative staff of the Education Department nominated by the director general of education; six teachers or administrators in non-government schools, two of them nominated by the director of Catholic education, two by the Independent Schools Head Masters Association, and two by the Independent Schools Head Mistresses Association; two members of the academic or administrative staff of the South Australian Institute of Technology nominated by the institute's council; seven members from the academic or administrative staff of the University of Adelaide nominated by the Council of the University; and, similarly, seven members from Flinders University.

28 The Tasmanian Schools Board was created by the Education Act of 1942, comprising four representatives from the Department of Education, four from the university, and four principals of registered secondary schools, and had responsibility for testing general education and awarding the Schools Board Certificate at the end of year ten. Until 1966 the University of Tasmania administered the matriculation examination. As reconstituted by the Education Act, 1966, the twenty members of the Schools Board comprised six members nominated by the Council of the University of Tasmania, four nominated by the director of education, two by the Tasmanian Teachers' Federation, four by the Association of Headmasters and Headmistresses of the Public Schools of Tasmania, and one by the Board of Technical Education, as well as the director of Catholic education or his or her nominee, a representative of parents, and a member associated with the work of a women's organization.

29 Canada, Department of Reconstruction, *Employment and Income with Special Reference to the Initial Period of Reconstruction, 1945* (Ottawa: King's Printer, 1946), 23. Economic stabilization and growth would be achieved within the

framework of a capitalist economy by manipulating trends in private investment and aggregate demand by means of counterbalancing changes in
interest rates, government spending, and tax policy.

30 Canada, Dominion-Provincial Conference on Reconstruction, *Proposals of
the Government of Canada* (Ottawa: King's Printer, 1945), 27–46. The Green
Book proposals owed much to a report prepared by Leonard Marsh for the
federal government's Advisory Committee on Reconstruction (*Report on
Social Security for Canada* [Ottawa: King's Printer, 1943]), and Marsh's report
in turn had been strongly influenced by William Beveridge's report on
social insurance in the United Kingdom.

31 The development of the welfare state in Canada involved major interventions by the federal government to establish national programs for unemployment insurance (which required a constitutional amendment), family
allowances, and old age pensions, and to dispense matching grants to
provincial social assistance and health insurance programs. By contrast,
federal governmental involvement in the financing of public education was
decidedly modest. Under the 1960 Technical and Vocational Training
Assistance (TVTA) Act, which was by far the largest federal intervention,
$950 million in conditional federal aid was transferred to provincial govern-
ments to add vocational departments to existing academic high schools and
build new multilateral high schools to accommodate the expanding secondary school enrolments of the 1960s. TVTA was terminated in 1967,
however, and its successor, the Adult Occupational Training Act, contained
no provision for federal aid to vocational education in secondary schools.

32 Canada and Newfoundland Education Association, *Report of the Survey
Committee Appointed to Ascertain the Chief Educational Needs in the Dominion
of Canada* (Toronto: Canada and Newfoundland Education Association,
1943), 46. For a discussion of various official policy studies, undertaken as
part of postwar planning for Canadian education, that condemned the
segregation of academic and vocational education, see Ronald Manzer,
*Public Schools and Political Ideas: Canadian Educational Policy in Historical
Perspective* (Toronto: University of Toronto Press, 1994), 105–8.

33 The deputy minister in New Brunswick was Fletcher Peacock, a former
director of vocational education in Saint John. In his 1941–2 annual report,
Peacock set out a detailed plan to improve rural education based on fifty
composite high schools, each with at least three departments: college-
preparatory, home making, and agricultural or fishing and navigation. See
New Brunswick, *Annual Report of the Department of Education of the Province of
New Brunswick for the School Year Ended June 30th, 1942* (Fredericton: King's
Printer, 1942), 5–40. Note also that Peacock was a member of the Canada

and Newfoundland Education Association survey committee, which in 1943 recommended adoption of the composite school model.

34 H. Janzen, 'Saskatchewan,' in John H.M. Andrews and Alan F. Brown (eds), *Composite High Schools in Canada*, University of Alberta Monographs in Education 1 (Edmonton: University of Alberta Committee on Educational Research, 1956), 56.

35 Alberta, *Report of the Royal Commission on Education in Alberta, 1959* (Edmonton: Queen's Printer, 1959), 95.

36 The increase in the number of Ontario's multilateral high schools occurred during the 1950s. There were twenty-two fully composite high schools and eighteen vocational high schools in 1938–9, nineteen composite and nineteen vocational high schools in 1950–1, and forty composite and fifteen vocational high schools in 1960–1. Overall enrolment in vocational programs declined from 30 per cent of secondary enrolments before the war to 23 to 24 per cent in the 1950s.

37 Multilateral high schools were even less developed in other provinces of Canada. A decade after the first composite high school was opened at Dauphin, twenty-eight high schools in Manitoba offered the commercial course, three offered home economics, and three the industrial course (J.M. Brown, 'Manitoba,' in Andrews and Brown [eds], *Composite High Schools in Canada*, 49). Of the twenty-eight schools, seventeen were located in Winnipeg and its suburbs. Similarly in British Columbia, the Royal Commission on Education, which reported in 1960, found that outside Vancouver most British Columbia high schools offered only an academic course and a general course. On the choice between the matriculation and the general programs, the royal commission estimated that 60 to 70 per cent of students in most high schools were electing to follow the university program and concluded that the policy of separating secondary students into two streams of junior matriculation and general course had failed (British Columbia, *Report of the Royal Commission on Education* [Victoria: Queen's Printer, 1960], 244). Under Nova Scotia's Vocational Education Act of 1953, academic high schools operated by local school boards continued to offer matriculation and general programs, and vocational programs were restricted to regional vocational high schools, which operated under separate boards appointed jointly by the province and supporting municipalities. In Newfoundland, Prince Edward Island, and Quebec, public secondary schools offered only academic programs; vocational training was given in provincial trade schools.

38 The reorganization of the Roman Catholic secondary curriculum in 1956 resulted in the introduction of vocational programs in secondary schools,

but these programs were not substantially different from the general course and did not attract many students. Arthur Tremblay, 'Quebec Catholic School System,' in Andrews and Brown (eds), *Composite High Schools in Canada*, 21.

39 'Obviously secondary education cannot be the same for everyone. All will participate but not all will start out with the same talents, the same preparation, the same interests, the same needs ... The responsibility of secondary education is to receive the many thousands of students coming to it from the elementary schools, accepting them all, and making certain that each receives the preparation for life best suited to his tastes and abilities.' Quebec, Royal Commission of Inquiry on Education in the Province of Quebec, *Report of the Royal Commission of Inquiry on Education in the Province of Quebec*, vol. 4 (Quebec: Government Printer, 1966), 126.

40 The Parent commission argued that multilateral institutes were essential to the realization of a democratic system of state education: 'It is not enough to make the top-level administration of the system more democratic through a Department of Education inviting participation by the public. It is far more important to eliminate from the system that aristocratic bias which still permeates it in large measure. Of course the most gifted students must be given opportunity fully to develop their talents. Yet it would be profoundly unjust to build the entire system for their benefit as is almost everywhere the case. What must be avoided is favouring, by the very nature of the system, a small group of children and dispensing only second-rate instruction to the remaining mass. It is our firm belief that composite education will allow the best pupils to make better and quicker progress than does the present rigid system. At the same time it will place at the disposal of all a varied, broad, elastic education, able to arouse and maintain the widest range of interests and to prepare for all fields of activity or production' (ibid., 5).

41 Following the recommendations of the Parent committee, provision was also made for a short vocational program to be completed in Secondary IV as well as a long vocational program, completed in Secondary V but occasionally extending into Secondary VI depending on the area of vocational specialization. In practice, as Regulation 1 came into effect in schools, three-quarters of secondary students opted for the general program, one-fifth enrolled in the long vocational program, and only 5 per cent opted for the short vocational program.

42 The delay of more than a decade between the Hope commission's recommendation in favour of multilateral schools in its 1950 report and the announcement of the Ontario government's policy commitment is no

doubt explained by the opposition of the minister of education in the 1950s. John Dunlop was an advocate of traditional academic education and aimed at getting the curriculum 'back to fundamental education, getting it back to stress the subjects that are really essential, in order to equip young people for the work they have to do' (Ontario, Legislative Assembly, *Debates*, 12 March 1958, 777). Fleming reports that 'a departmental official with a responsible position at the end of the 1960s recalls that the 1950s were a grim time for vocational education. In his opinion Dunlop saw no educational value in the program.' W.G. Fleming, *Ontario's Educative Society, Volume 3: Schools, Pupils and Teachers* (Toronto: University of Toronto Press, 1971), 141.

43 Students tended to be streamed into a branch and program by the end of grade nine (or even sometimes grade eight) and found themselves unable to transfer later. Streaming was based primarily on academic achievement rather than the occupational goals of students. The four-year arts and science program, it was hoped, would provide a basic general education for students not continuing to university, but because of its perceived inferior status, very few students chose to take it. See Robert M. Stamp, *The Schools of Ontario, 1876–1976* (Toronto: University of Toronto Press, 1982), 206.

44 'Separate classes for the intellectually superior, separate schools for vocational and academic students, and separate curriculum categories all tend to keep alive the idea that the academically endowed are in some way superior to their vocationally-oriented peers. The practice is sufficiently prevalent to cause the Committee to deplore such survival of class distinctions, and to advocate schools that will accommodate students without invidious distinctions.' Ontario, Provincial Committee on Aims and Objectives of Education in Ontario, *Living and Learning* (Toronto: Newton Publishing, 1968), 67.

45 Ibid., 82.

46 On the crucial role of J.R. McCarthy and other senior departmental officials in developing and implementing educational reform in Ontario during the 1960s, see Eric W. Ricker, 'Teachers, Trustees and Policy: The Politics of Education in Ontario, 1945–1975,' doctoral thesis, University of Toronto, 1981, 302–5, 612–13; and also R.D. Gidney, *From Hope to Harris: The Reshaping of Ontario's Schools* (Toronto: University of Toronto Press, 1999), 75–83.

47 In Nova Scotia and Prince Edward Island, distinctions between academic and vocational students thus disappeared within senior high schools, but both provinces continued to operate separate regional vocational schools. In New Brunswick, although ministry guidelines encouraged provision for

'cross-setting' of courses, the majority of pupils continued to progress through senior high school in one of the three available programs: college preparatory, general educational and occupational, or practical (Council of Ministers of Education, Canada, *Review of Educational Policies in Canada: Atlantic Region*, Submission of the Ministers of Education for New Brunswick, Newfoundland, Nova Scotia, and Prince Edward Island to the OECD Review of Educational Politics in Canada [Toronto: Council of Ministers of Education, Canada, 1975], 25). A credit system was introduced in Newfoundland with the introduction of a three-year program for students entering grade ten in September 1981.

48 From the 1940s to the 1960s there were no attempts to reorganize departments in the Maritime provinces, and organizational changes in Ontario and the West were marginal. They aimed to reduce, if only slightly, the deputy minister's span of control by reorganizing departments into seven to ten directorates, thus decreasing the number of officials reporting directly to the deputy minister, and by appointing associate or assistant deputy ministers. Such changes were consistent with the recommendations of the royal commissions in Ontario (1950), Alberta (1959), and British Columbia (1960), which focused their concerns about departmental organization on reducing the deputy ministers' span of control in order to free them from administrative routine and allow more time for their policy function.

49 Ontario, Legislative Assembly, *Debates*, 4 June 1968, 3881–2; quoted in David M. Cameron, *Schools for Ontario: Policy-Making, Administration, and Finance in the 1960s* (Toronto: University of Toronto Press, 1972), 224–5. Only three years earlier, the Ontario Department of Education had been reorganized into three functional divisions, each headed by an assistant deputy minister: instruction (which encompassed elementary, secondary, and teacher education), provincial schools and further education, and departmental and school administration.

50 When the New Brunswick Department of Education was reorganized as a ministry in 1973, separate divisions of English and French educational services were also established, each having its own assistant deputy minister, and a division of finance and administration, headed by a third assistant deputy minister as well as a director of planning and development, was established to serve both English and French sectors.

51 The Quebec ministry's organization remained essentially unchanged until 1985. Then college and university education was transferred to the Ministry of Higher Education, Science, and Technology, and the Ministry of Education was reorganized into four divisions, each headed by an assistant deputy

minister: planning and educational development, administration, educational network services, and labour relations.

52 See Manzer, *Public Schools and Political Ideas*, 114–16.

53 The common instrument for attempting to equalize fiscal capacity among local school districts was the foundation program, or fixed unit equalizing grant, which established both the unit cost of an educational program to be provided equally in every school district and a mandatory local property tax rate to be applied to the equalized assessed valuation in every school district. The provincial grant paid to each district would be the difference between its expenditure for the foundation program and its revenue from levying the mandatory tax rate. Nova Scotia (1942) and British Columbia (1945) were the first provinces in Canada to use a fixed unit equalizing grant. Fixed unit equalizing grants were subsequently introduced to allocate provincial funding to school districts in Alberta (1961), Quebec (1965), Manitoba (1967), and finally Saskatchewan (in 1970 to replace the variable percentage 'general formula grant' that had been used since 1957). As an alternative to the foundation program, a percentage equalizing grant defined a 'key district,' usually set up as a district with assessed valuation per pupil equal to the provincial average. The percentage of expenditures paid in other districts was adjusted according to the ratio of their assessed valuations per pupil to the assessed valuation per pupil in the key district. Ontario relied on schedules that approximated a percentage equalizing grant from 1944 to 1964, experimented briefly with a foundation program, and then implemented a standard version of the percentage equalizing grant in 1968.

54 This national average for provincial grants as a percentage of total school board revenues encompassed a significant variation in funding policies across the provinces. In 1970–1, provincial grants as a percentage of total combined revenues of school boards from provincial grants and local taxation were 100 per cent in New Brunswick, 92 per cent in Newfoundland, and 74 per cent in Nova Scotia, and ranged in the other provinces from 45 per cent in Saskatchewan to 57 per cent in Quebec and British Columbia.

55 Provincial organization of teachers and trustees and local collective bargaining were both facilitated by departments of education, but the departments remained formally insulated from the details of collective bargaining. The one exception was Saskatchewan, where the Saskatchewan Teachers' Federation (STF) had a close relationship with the CCF government, and Department of Education officials met annually with representatives of the STF and the Saskatchewan School Trustees' Association to settle provincial guidelines for collective bargaining (ibid., 145).

56 Under the 1974 Teachers' Collective Bargaining Act in Nova Scotia, the
minister of education was empowered to bargain 'with respect to salaries
and allowances and terms and conditions of employment that affect teachers generally throughout the province,' and school boards negotiated 'with
respect to matters of only local incidence.' Collective bargaining for Quebec teachers initially was decentralized to the level of school commissions
in 1964, then provincially centralized in 1967, and finally established as
bilevel negotiations in 1974.

57 Ontario's voluntary regime did finally break down under a wave of strikes
in the early 1970s. Compulsory collective bargaining with mediation and
conciliation by the provincial Educational Relations Commission was
introduced in 1975, but this did not change the essentially decentralized
structure of collective bargaining.

58 Quoted in H.G.R. Mason (Minister of Education), *Education Today and
Tomorrow* (Wellington: Department of Education, 1945), 8; see also C.E.
Beeby, *The Biography of an Idea: Beeby on Education* (Wellington: New Zealand
Council for Educational Research, 1992), 124–5. This statement of the
Labour government's policy on education was actually written for the minister by C.E. Beeby, then assistant director and director designate, who was
director from 1 April 1940 (the day Peter Fraser became prime minister)
until his retirement in 1960. According to Beeby, 'In 1939 my own belief in
Fraser's statement as a basis for educational policy was complete, and it lay
behind practically every new project that I was to propose over the next
twenty years' (ibid., 126).

59 In its 1962 report, the Commission on Education in New Zealand, chaired
by Sir George Currie, referred to Peter Fraser's statement as an expression
of social aspiration that the Currie commission had adopted as 'a reasonable working premise': 'Nothing that has been said or written in evidence
before the Commission has given any grounds for believing that there is in
the community any large body of sentiment opposed to the ideas expressed
by Mr Fraser, nor in the 22 years that have passed since he made it has
there been any movement – social or political – which would suggest any
retreat from this viewpoint. Rather it might be claimed that the influence
of the second World War and its aftermath have strengthened this sentiment as one of the dominant democratic ideas of the New Zealand community.' New Zealand, Commission on Education in New Zealand, *Report of the
Commission on Education in New Zealand* (Wellington: Government Printer,
1962), 11–12.

60 The Thomas committee thus described its objectives: 'We have set out to
ensure, as far as possible, that all post-primary pupils, irrespective of their

varying abilities and their varying occupational ambitions, receive a generous and well-balanced education. Such an education would aim, firstly, at the full development of the adolescent as a person; and, secondly, at preparing him for an active place in our New Zealand society as worker, neighbour, homemaker and citizen' (*The Post-Primary School Curriculum*, Report of the Committee Appointed by the Minister of Education in November, 1942; quoted in J. Shallcross, 'Secondary Schools,' in Richard J. Bates [ed.], *Prospects in New Zealand Education* [Auckland: Hodder and Stoughton, 1970], 123). On the work of the Thomas committee see also C. Whitehead, 'The Thomas Report – A Study in Educational Reform,' *New Zealand Journal of Educational Studies* 9 (May 1974): 52–64.

61 For a list of the thirty-four subjects for which School Certificate examinations were set in 1946 and the thirty-one in 1961, see New Zealand, *Report of the Commission on Education in New Zealand*, Appendix G, 788–9.

62 University entrance requirements were now redefined as a pass in the School Certificate examinations and one additional year of study in recognized subjects at an accredited secondary school. Matriculation examinations continued to be set for students who attended non-accredited schools – in the state system, primarily district and technical high schools. At the end of upper sixth (later seventh) form, the University Entrance Scholarship Examination was also retained, but this was a highly competitive examination for an academic élite. The Currie commission, for example, reported that in 1960 there were 8,059 students in sixth-form classes seeking qualification for university entrance and 2,034 already qualified. Of those who had qualified, only 693 were candidates for the University Entrance Scholarship Examination. The commission noted that the majority of secondary schools offered candidates for the scholarship examination but often not more than one or two (ibid., 344).

63 In reviewing the claims and counter-claims of selective versus multilateral secondary organization, the Currie commission thought that in New Zealand the choice of multilateral organization was more the result of social factors than of educational theory. In its view, selective schools would segregate gifted pupils from experiences shared in common with others of lesser capabilities, and this loss might handicap and hinder full exercise of their talents (ibid., 220, 278).

64 Ian A. McLaren, *Education in a Small Democracy: New Zealand* (London: Routledge and Kegan Paul, 1974), 131–2. McLaren observes that cross-setting was also growing in popularity, bringing pupils together from different courses and organizing them in groups according to their ability in particular subjects.

65 Ibid., 129. In 1961 the Department of Education did introduce the Certificate of Education awarded to candidates who passed one or more subjects but failed to obtain the full group pass in English and three subjects required for the School Certificate, and in 1967 the requirement for a group pass was dropped in favour of awarding the School Certificate on the basis of (up to six) single subject passes.

66 In 1936 the Labour government's minister of education (Peter Fraser) invited the New Zealand Council for Educational Research to undertake a study of intermediate schools. The council's report by C.E. Beeby concluded that intermediate schools should '*provide a socially integrative period of schooling for all children passing through the public school system at a point before they diverge along specialized lines.*' C.E. Beeby, *The Intermediate Schools of New Zealand: A Survey*, New Zealand Council for Educational Research, Educational Research Series No. 6 (Auckland: Whitcombe and Tombs, 1938), 210; italics in the original.

67 The pattern of school organization proposed by the Currie commission is summarized in New Zealand, *Report of the Commission on Education in New Zealand*, 196–8.

68 Reviewing the relationship of department and boards in 1970, John L. Ewing concluded that while important educational issues were resolved centrally, there was an increasing level of negotiations and consultations that had resulted in 'a workable and generally acceptable balance of power between the Department of Education and local educational organizations and interests.' 'The Control of Education in New Zealand: Centrality with Minimal Recourse to Party Politics,' *Journal of Educational Administration* 8 (May 1970): 51.

69 See McLaren, *Education in a Small Democracy: New Zealand*, 13; and also J.C. Dakin, *Education in New Zealand* (Newton Abbot, Devon: David and Charles, 1973), 64.

70 Asa Briggs, 'The Welfare State in Historical Perspective,' *Archives Européenes de Sociologies*, 2 (1961): 228.

71 The plan to reorganize secondary education in England and Wales followed closely the recommendations for a tripartite system put forward in 1938 by the Consultative Committee on Secondary Education with Special Reference to Grammar Schools and Technical Schools, chaired by Will Spens. For an analysis of positions taken by senior officials representing primary, grammar, and technical schools, see P.H.J.H. Gosden, *Education in the Second World War: A Study in Policy and Administration* (London: Methuen, 1976), 244, 249, 255, 257.

72 In its 1947 report on secondary education, for example, the Advisory

Council on Education in Scotland advocated bilateral secondary schools as 'the natural way for a democracy to order the post-primary schooling of a given area' (Great Britain, Scottish Education Department, *Secondary Education: A Report of the Advisory Council on Education in Scotland* [Edinburgh: His Majesty's Stationery Office, 1947], 36). Secondary education in Scotland also differed from that in England and Wales and Northern Ireland in the higher percentage of each age group that was admitted to senior secondary schools – 35 per cent as compared with 20 per cent on average to grammar schools in England and Wales. Within England and Wales the percentage of each cohort admitted to grammar schools varied widely among local authorities, from 12 per cent to 25 per cent.

73 S. Leslie Hunter, *The Scottish Educational System* (2nd ed.; Oxford: Pergamon Press, 1971), 100.

74 Ten of the existing grammar schools were controlled by local education authorities, and sixty-seven were voluntary schools that charged fees. Under the 1947 act, 'Group A' voluntary schools agreed to reserve 80 per cent of their places for students whose annual fees would be paid by the local education authority at a rate negotiated and agreed with the Ministry of Education; these schools would receive state grants equal to 65 per cent of their operating and capital costs. 'Group B' schools, with no restrictions on fees or places, received only the grant for operating costs. Only a small minority of voluntary grammar schools opted for the greater independence of Group B status. Given this arrangement, which left 20 per cent of places open in Group A grammar schools for children not successful in the eleven-plus selection, parents who were able to pay the fees might still find a grammar school willing to take their children as non-qualified pupils. Moreover, there was a review procedure by which non-qualified pupils doing satisfactory work in grammar schools could be reclassified as 'qualified' and hence eligible to have their fees paid by the local education authority. See Margaret Sutherland, 'Progress and Problems in Education in Northern Ireland, 1952–1982,' *British Journal of Educational Studies* 30 (February 1982): 138–9.

75 The white paper on educational reconstruction in England and Wales had recommended that at age eleven children be classified 'not on the results of a competitive test, but on an assessment of their individual aptitudes largely by such means as school record, supplemented, if necessary, by intelligence tests, due regard being had to their parents' wishes and the careers they have in mind' (Great Britain, Board of Education, *Educational Reconstruction* [London: His Majesty's Stationery Office, 1943], paragraph 27). In Scotland, the 1946 act explicitly denied parents the right to choose

a course of secondary education from which, in the opinion of the local education authority, their child showed no reasonable promise of profiting.

76 As one Conservative minister of education (Sir David Eccles) put his government's position, 'one must choose between justice and equality, for it is impossible to apply both principles at once. Those who support comprehensive schools prefer equality. Her Majesty's present government prefer justice. My colleagues and I will never agree to the assassination of the grammar schools.' *The Schoolmaster*, 7 January 1955; quoted by David Rubinstein and Brian Simon, *The Evolution of the Comprehensive School 1926–1966* (London: Routledge and Kegan Paul, 1969), 70–1.

77 Christopher Knight, *The Making of Tory Education Policy in Post-War Britain 1950–1986* (London: Falmer Press, 1999), 63.

78 Rodney Barker, *Education and Politics 1900–1951* (Oxford: Clarendon Press, 1972), 79.

79 As Rodney Barker has pointed out, Ellen Wilkinson shared with an earlier generation of Labour members of Parliament an acceptance of the legitimacy of competitive selection that resulted from personal experience of overcoming hardship and deprivation. Describing her own educational experience she said, 'I was born into a working-class home and I had to fight my own way through to the University.' Similarly, George Tomlinson saw his personal experience as an argument for pressing for a fairer chance for able children: 'I was glad of the opportunity of carrying a step further a vow I made as a youth deprived of the opportunity of a secondary education through poverty that no handicap of a similar kind should be allowed to stand in the way of any young person if any action of mine could prevent it.' Ibid., 89–90; see also Michael Parkinson, *The Labour Party and the Organization of Secondary Education 1918–65* (London: Routledge and Kegan Paul, 1970), 38–47.

80 A national survey in 1964 found that one-quarter of local education authorities had made major changes to their selection procedures since 1960 and 71 per cent had formed some type of multilateral secondary school, or intended to do so (Rubinstein and Simon, *The Evolution of the Comprehensive School 1926–1966*, 88).

81 Circular 10/65 outlined six schemes that were more or less acceptable to the department. See Caroline Benn and Brian Simon, *Halfway There: Report on the British Comprehensive School Reform* (2nd ed.; Harmondsworth: Penguin Books, 1970), 56–62, 161–74; and also Alan Kerckhoff, Ken Fogelman, David Crook, and David Reeder, *Going Comprehensive in England and Wales: A Study of Uneven Change* (London: Woburn Press, 1996), 262–4. Kerckhoff and colleagues observe that the minister recognized the unique local

knowledge of the LEAs and their superiority to his ministry in developing and implementing plans for secondary reorganization. Insistence on a single model was likely to thwart or delay indefinitely comprehensive reorganization (ibid., 28). On the functional interdependence between the department and the local education authorities, see also Peter Ribbins, 'Comprehensive Secondary Reorganization: A Case of Local Authority Policy-Making?' in Meredydd Hughes, Peter Ribbins, and Hywel Thomas (eds), *Managing Education: The System and the Institution* (London: Cassell, 1987), 148–76.

82 As in England and Wales, the secretary of state for Scotland expressed a clear preference for all-through schools; a two-tier arrangement of junior and senior schools would be accepted only in areas where geographical considerations were compelling. In response to Circular 600, Scottish local authorities opted strongly for all-through schools, in some cases associated with four-year (age twelve to sixteen) schools intended either as full secondary schools eventually or as feeders for a central six-year school. Ian R. Findlay, *Education in Scotland* (Newton Abbot: David and Charles, 1973), 64.

83 As a result of the Local Government Act of 1972 there were now 105 local education authorities. Sixty-seven of them, including all the Scottish authorities, replied that reorganization would be completed by the end of the decade, 31 were committed to reorganization in principle subject to the availability of resources, and 7 refused outright to reorganize their schools voluntarily. The Education Act of 1976 then required all local education authorities in England and Wales to adopt the comprehensive principle and empowered the secretary of state for education and science to order the submission of local reorganization plans.

84 In England, 9.9 per cent of pupils in public secondary education were attending comprehensive schools in 1965–6 and 89.5 per cent in 1980–1, including 7 per cent in 'middle deemed secondary' schools. In Wales, 28.3 per cent of pupils were attending comprehensive schools in 1965–6 and 96.6 per cent in 1980–1. In 1970–1, 58.5 per cent of Scottish students were attending comprehensive schools; a decade later, 96 per cent.

85 See Hunter, *The Scottish Educational System*, 102–3.

86 David Hargreaves, *The Challenge for the Comprehensive School: Culture, Curriculum and Community* (London: Routledge and Kegan Paul, 1982), 67. In 1979, the secretary of state for Scotland, Bruce Millan, rejected a proposal for three levels of assessment for SCE O-grade courses and examinations because 'with the three types of courses, and the three grades of certificates, you really can have a three-tier school, in fact. I mean, if all went wrong, that is what you would finish up with.' Quoted in Andrew

McPherson and Charles D. Raab, *Governing Education: A Sociology of Policy since 1945* (Edinburgh: Edinburgh University Press, 1988), 309.

87 As part of the 1977 decision to reorganize secondary education in Northern Ireland, an interim selection procedure was introduced based on teachers' evaluations of their pupils and also taking parental preferences into account. This selection procedure was dropped in 1980, however, and a centrally administered test of ability was restored to determine the separation of pupils between grammar and secondary intermediate schools. See Sutherland, 'Progress and Problems in Education in Northern Ireland, 1952–1982,' 139; and also J.A. Wilson, 'Selection for Secondary Education,' in R.D. Osborne, R.J. Cormack, and R.L. Miller (eds), *Education and Policy in Northern Ireland* (Belfast: Policy Research Institute, Queen's University of Belfast and University of Ulster, 1987), 30–3.

88 The SSEC committee, chaired by Cyril Norwood, in its 1943 report, proposed to conduct external examinations and issue certificates on the basis of subjects passed rather than requiring passes in a group of subjects. The first set of examinations, taken at age sixteen, would be conducted internally by teachers in grammar schools and followed by an external examination at age eighteen.

89 In its 1960 report, a committee of the SSEC, chaired by Robert Beloe, found that one-third of GCE candidates came from outside the grammar schools (Great Britain, Secondary Schools Examinations Council, *Secondary School Examinations Other Than the G.C.E.* [London: Her Majesty's Stationery Office, 1960], 9). At the same time, entries to externally assessed examinations other than the GCE were rising. In five to ten years, the committee predicted, almost all schools would be entering pupils for external examinations, primarily the GCE, and this would, in turn, 'exercise great and perhaps decisive influence on the development of the schools.' The Crowther Committee had also reported that the GCE at Ordinary-level was being used as a means of selection for many forms of employment and training that had not required the pre-war School Certificate Examination (Central Advisory Council, *Fifteen to Eighteen*, vol. 1 [London: Her Majesty's Stationery Office, 1959], 48). A point was reached where parents in England and Wales reportedly were expressing preference for one secondary modern school rather than another because it ran a course leading to the O-level GCE examination (K. Watkins, 'The Politics of Examinations,' *Political Quarterly* 36 [January–March 1965]: 60). For an analysis of the creation of the Certificate of Secondary Education, see Ronald A. Manzer, *Teachers and Politics in England and Wales: The Role of the National Union of Teachers in the*

Making of National Educational Policy since 1944 (Toronto: University of Toronto Press, 1970), 84–90.

90 James Scotland, 'Scottish Education, 1952–1982,' *British Journal of Educational Studies* 30 (February 1982): 132. The Sixth Advisory Council's recommendation in 1947 to follow the GCE model and introduce an examination at the end of fourth year was rejected by the Scottish Education Department, but the replacement of group examinations by examination in individual subjects was approved starting in 1951.

91 As John Brunton explained his position to Andrew McPherson and Charles Raab, 'Great numbers of very able youngsters were leaving at the age of fifteen, whenever they could, and I came to the conclusion that they were doing it in the first place because of the Leaving Certificate examination and its form, and secondly, because their courses weren't very appropriate; they weren't catching their interest or inspiring them to continue their education ... Traditionally, both the Lower grade and the Higher grade of the Certificate were taken in the fifth year, and they were quite rigid examinations with a very rigid structure. We came to the conclusion that it would be of great assistance if the first examination could be moved a year forward, so as to hold out a carrot to those who were leaving at the age of fifteen and get them to stay on.' Quoted in McPherson and Raab, *Governing Education: A Sociology of Policy since 1945*, 87–8.

92 Rather than introduce an examination for average students similar to the CSE, the Scottish Certificate of Education Examination Board in 1972 recommended a subdivision ('banding') of the O-grade examination. Political and professional opinion proved to be too deeply divided to implement this recommendation.

93 Regulations for direct-grant and grant-aided schools in 1965 required schools that received the grant to make 25 per cent of their places available to pupils from state primary schools with their fees paid by the local education authority. The authority could, if it wanted, take more than 25 per cent of the places. In 1968, LEAs were taking more than 50 per cent of places at 93 of the 178 direct-grant schools. Those pupils not sponsored by a local authority could have their fees remitted on the basis of a means test approved by the Department of Education and Science. In addition, the department paid a capitation grant for all pupils. In return, the direct-grant schools had to accept that one-third of school governors were appointed by the local authority, and the secretary of state for education and science had the authority to approve new buildings and changes in fees.

94 Anthony Crosland, the secretary of state for education and science, initially

proposed the appointment of a royal commission following the model of the Clarendon and Taunton commissions in the 1860s, but the Labour cabinet refused to give the problem such a status.

95 There were 178 direct-grant schools in 1975; one of them was not academically selective.

96 The Secondary Schools Examinations Council was formed in 1917 to coordinate the work of eight separate university examining bodies that had been variously established since the first school examinations administered by Oxford and Cambridge in 1858. Initially, the council had eighteen members, half of them appointed by the examining bodies and the rest by the local education authorities and teachers. In 1936, the council was reorganized with ten members each to represent the examining bodies, associations of local education authorities, and teachers' organizations and the chair appointed by the president of the Board of Education. In the 1946 reconstitution of the SSEC, direct representation of the examining bodies was replaced by members nominated by their parent universities.

97 For an analysis of the creation of the Curriculum Study Group and the Schools Council for Curriculum and Examinations, see Manzer, *Teachers and Politics in England and Wales*, 90–7.

98 According to a description in the 1960s, the Code 'prescribes the subjects to be taught in all primary schools and requires that, for each primary and secondary school, the education authority shall prepare a scheme of work, in consultation with the head teacher, showing the scope of work in each subject, and submit it for the approval of the district inspector of schools. The district inspector may not alter the scheme but has the power to call upon the authority to produce another. The head teacher is then required by the Code to draw up detailed programmes and timetables based on the approved scheme of work (though he does have power to authorize occasional departures from them.' G.S. Osborne, *Scottish and English Schools: A Comparative Survey of the Past Fifty Years* (London: Longmans Green, 1966), 59.

99 The historical control of the SED in the Scottish educational policy community was destabilized by a succession of events: the decision taken in 1955 to introduce an intermediate O-grade examination to be taken at the end of the fourth year of secondary school; the strike of Glasgow teachers in 1961 over proposals to dilute the profession by lowering standards required for admission to teacher training, an event that severely shook the confidence of the SED in its ability to get teachers to go along; the election of the Labour government in 1964, with its commitment to comprehensive secondary schools; and the raising of the school leaving age (McPherson and Raab, *Governing Education: A Sociology of Policy since 1945*, 247–65).

100 On the role of John Brunton in reforming Her Majesty's Inspectorate, introducing the new O-grade examination, and establishing the Scottish Certificate of Education Examination Board (SCEEB), see ibid., 86–93. Members of the SCEEB were appointed in 1964 and assumed control over the examinations for the Scottish Certificate of Education in 1965.

101 The membership of the General Teaching Council comprised twenty-five elected representatives of teachers in primary and secondary schools, further-education centres, and colleges of education; seventeen members appointed by the secretary of state from nominees by universities (4), central institutions (2), associations of education authorities (4), the Association of Directors of Education in Scotland (3), the Education Committee of the General Assembly of the Church of Scotland (1), and the Scottish Hierarchy of the Roman Catholic Church (1); and four members representing the secretary of state (4).

102 Ibid., 324–6. Four inspectors, two SED officials, nine teachers, eight members from further and higher education, one director of education, and one representative from industry and commerce were appointed as individuals for fixed terms of three years, and the secretary of SED took the chair. In 1987, the committee was renamed the Scottish Consultative Council on the Curriculum.

103 In England and Wales the two pre-war Burnham Committees for elementary and secondary teachers' salaries were reconstituted in 1944 as a unified 'Burnham Main Committee' comprising a teachers' panel and an authorities' panel. The minister of education appointed the chair of the Burnham Main Committee, and ministry officials attended meetings of the committee as observers but did not participate directly in negotiations between the panels. Under the 1944 act, the minister had authority to refuse approval of any agreement but not to alter the terms of an award. Representatives on the authorities' panel were informed of the views of the Ministry of Education (and the Treasury), in particular on the acceptable size of the total award, and the minister was often involved informally in negotiations to overcome deadlock and facilitate agreement between the panels. In Scotland, as a result of representations from the Educational Institute of Scotland (EIS) and the Association of Directors of Education, the National Joint Council (NJC) was established in 1939 to negotiate teachers' salaries. Restructured during the Second World War – a change that included putting conditions of service within its jurisdiction – the NJC had an independent chair presiding over twelve teacher representatives, all members of the EIS until 1964, and twelve representatives of the employers (eight from the Association of County Councils in

Scotland and four from the Scottish Counties of Cities Association) along
with three directors of education, three local-authority officials, and an
SED official as assessors.

104 For an analysis of the settlement of teachers' salaries in England and Wales
from 1944 to 1964, see Manzer, *Teachers and Politics in England and Wales*,
108–43. On the negotiation of teachers' salaries and conditions of work
in Scotland, see McPherson and Raab, *Governing Education: A Sociology of
Policy since 1945*, 207–18.

105 Because of the victory of the Labour party in the general election of
15 October 1964, it fell to a former National Union of Teachers MP,
Michael Stewart, who was now secretary of state for education and science,
to introduce the bill.

106 The campaign against the block grant in England and Wales is described
in Manzer, *Teachers and Politics in England and Wales*, 73–81.

107 Derek Slater observes that the mechanism for calculating and distributing
the block grant was changed in 1966 with the introduction of the 'rate
support grant,' but that 'the principle underlying the general grant remained: the centre could no longer earmark particular parts of the RSG
for particular services such as education.' Derek Slater, 'The Education
Sub-Government: Structure and Context,' in Hughes, Ribbins, and
Thomas (eds), *Managing Education*, 50.

108 Central governmental control over capital spending for school building
was more substantial and more detailed than in the case of current expenditures. Under the education acts of 1944 and 1946 the central education
departments were required to set minimum standards for school buildings, and maximum costs per place were operative for all school building
projects from 1950 to 1974. In England and Wales, capital expenditures
for the four school building programs for nursery, primary, secondary,
and special education, as well as those for further education and teacher
training, were negotiated annually between the Treasury and the Ministry of Education/DES. The agreed total was then allocated among local
education authorities by the ministry/DES (and the Welsh Office for LEAs
in Wales after 1970), not as an allocation of funds with which to pay loan
charges (which were financed through the block grant) but as permission
to borrow and spend a specified amount on a list of projects that took
account of LEA priorities but often might override them in favour of
national priorities (D.E. Regan, *Local Government and Education* [London:
George Allen and Unwin, 1977], 125). Beginning in 1974, however, central
governmental approval for school building was changed to lump-sum
authorizations to each LEA. Similarly, the total amount available annually

for school building in Scotland was negotiated by the Treasury, the Scottish Office, and the SED, and the SED then allocated permission to borrow for school-building projects among local authorities. On the process of decision making with regard to school-building projects in Scotland, see McPherson and Raab, *Governing Education: A Sociology of Policy since 1945*, 186–94.

109 The non-county borough and urban district councils that had been constituted as independent local education authorities for elementary education under Part III of the 1902 act were not entirely eliminated from postwar educational governance. As a compromise, two types of delegated authority were provided in the 1944 act: first, divisional executives comprised a number of county districts grouped together to carry out delegated responsibilities under a scheme drawn up by the county and controlled by an executive containing representatives of the constituent districts and co-opted members; second, non-county boroughs and urban districts might seek to exercise delegated responsibilities as excepted districts. These provisions for delegated responsibilities remained a minor feature of postwar local educational administration, and with the reorganization of local government when the Local Government Act of 1972 was implemented in April 1974, all divisional executives and excepted districts were dissolved.

110 Each county or county borough council appointed three-quarters of the members of the education committee from among its own membership, nominees selected by urban and rural district councils, or other persons interested in education. One-quarter of the members were appointed by the Northern Ireland minister of education as representatives of the denominations that had transferred their schools to the local authority.

111 In particular, the SED complained to the royal commission that the lack of adequate educational staffs in the departments of small local authorities forced it to spend a large portion of its time giving advice and guidance on matters that could have been decided locally and thus restricted the SED's capacity to 'think about the future.' See Edward Page, 'Local Government in Scotland,' in Margaret Bowman and William Hampton (eds), *Local Democracies: A Study in Comparative Local Government* (Melbourne: Longman Cheshire, 1983), 43–4.

112 In the United States, the counterpart of Britain's Beveridge report (William Beveridge, *Social Insurance and Allied Services* [London: His Majesty's Stationery Office, 1942]) was the report of the National Resources Planning Board Committee on Long-Range Work and Relief Policies, *Security, Work, and Relief Policies* (Washington, D.C.: United States

Government Printing Office, 1942). According to Edwin Amenta and Theda Skocpol, 'In contrast to the Beveridge Report, the NRPB's *Security, Work, and Relief Policies* had neither public enthusiasm nor bureaucratic backing' ('Redefining the New Deal: World War II and the Development of Social Provision in the United States,' in Margaret Weir, Ann Shola Orloff, and Theda Skocpol [eds], *The Politics of Social Policy in the United States* [Princeton: Princeton University Press, 1988], 108). They conclude, 'In the United States, World War II and its aftermath did not bring con-solidation of the New Deal, but rather its failure and redefinition. Various liberal plans for completing New Deal socioeconomic reforms were thwarted; health insurance failed; and public assistance was not national-ized. The federal government quit the business of administering public employment programs; even the less ambitious Keynesian public works projects of the NRPB failed to become institutionalized ... Despite the dreams of New Deal and early wartime planners for a distinctively Ameri-can full-employment welfare state, nearly all possibilities for nationalized social policy had been eliminated from the agenda of mainstream politics by the beginning of the 1950s' (ibid., 119–20), 121.

113 Provision for a federal program of old age pensions and federal aid to state programs of unemployment insurance was made in the Social Secu-rity Act of 1935. For an excellent interpretation of the background and development of the act see Ann Shola Orloff, 'The Political Origins of America's Belated Welfare State,' in Weir, Orloff, and Skocpol (eds), *The Politics of Social Policy in the United States*, 37–80.

114 Paula S. Fass, *Outside In: Minorities and the Transformation of American Edu-cation* (New York: Oxford University Press, 1989), 121–3.

115 American Youth Commission, Special Committee on the Secondary School Curriculum, *What the High Schools Ought to Teach* (Washington, D.C.: American Council on Education, 1940), 7. According to the commit-tee, 'The secondary schools emphasize today, as they always have, prepara-tion for occupations of the professional and clerical type – the so-called "white-collar" jobs. The great majority of pupils in secondary schools are led by the studies which they pursue to hope for careers in "white-collar" jobs. Any examination of the opportunities that are really open makes it clear that the hopes fostered by the present educational system are sure to be disappointed for most of those now registered in secondary schools' (ibid., 10).

116 National Education Association, Educational Policies Commission, *Educa-tion for All American Youth* (Washington, D.C.: National Education Associa-tion, 1944), 244. The chair of the Educational Policies Commission was

Alexander J. Stoddard, who had also been a member of the American Youth Commission's special committee. George D. Strayer, professor of educational administration at Columbia University Teachers' College, was also a member of both the 1940 special committee and the 1944 commission. Note, in addition, that Charles A. Prosser, long-time advocate for vocational education, was a member of the special committee of the American Youth Commission, and James Bryant Conant, who became one of the leading advocates for educational reform in the postwar years, was a member of the Educational Policy Commission.

117 Ibid., 308. As the counterpart to secondary education in American City, which was assumed to have a population of 150,000, the Educational Policies Commission also proposed an ideal instructional program for 'Farmville Secondary School,' which was located in a rural area with a village at the centre. The program for the rural high school would cover essentially the same learning areas as the American City high school – occupational preparation, civic competence, personal development, and elective studies. With regard to occupational preparation, however, because of the smaller size of Farmville Secondary School, students preparing for college would combine learning in regular classes with appropriately individualized programs, and vocational education for students intending to go directly into the labour force would focus on agricultural, mechanical, commercial, and domestic knowledge and skills that had importance in rural areas.

118 The junior high school was steadily adopted in more school districts, and during the 1950s the six-three-three organization of primary, junior high, and senior high schools displaced the traditional eight-four organization of elementary and high schools as the majority form of school organization.

119 More academically selective colleges generally required their applicants to take both SATs and ATs, while less selective colleges relied on the SATs alone. In 1948, administration of these tests, as well as those of the American Council on Education and the Carnegie Foundation for the Advancement of Teaching National Teacher Examinations, was transferred to the non-profit Educational Testing Service, which continued to be accountable to the College Entrance Examination Board for the SATs and ATs.

120 George H. Hanford, *Life with the SAT: Assessing Our Young People and Our Times* (New York: College Entrance Examination Board, 1991), 17–18.

121 Herbert M. Kliebard, *The Struggle for the American Curriculum 1893–1958* (Boston: Routledge and Kegan Paul, 1986), 264; and Barbara Barksdale Clowse, *Brainpower for the Cold War: The Sputnik Crisis and the National Defense Act of 1958* (Westport, Conn.: Greenwood Press, 1981), 3–4.

122 James Bryant Conant, *The American High School Today: A First Report to Interested Citizens* (New York: McGraw-Hill, 1959), 46–50. Conant envisaged that all students would be required to take four years of English, three or four years of social studies, one year of mathematics in the ninth grade, and one year of science in the ninth or tenth grade. The 'academically talented' students, who constituted the top 15 to 20 per cent, should be guided by counsellors to take four years of mathematics and three years of foreign language studies. For the highly gifted 3 per cent of the student population, there should be some type of special arrangements such as tutors or advanced placement programs (ibid., 57, 62–3). Note that Conant's positive answer to his basic question ('Can a school at one and the same time provide a good general education for *all* the pupils as future citizens in a democracy, provide elective programs for the majority to develop useful skills, and educate adequately those with a talent for handling advanced academic subjects – particularly foreign languages and advanced mathematics?' [ibid., 15; emphasis in the original]) was made conditional on inplementation of his model of comprehensive secondary education, in particular large schools and ability grouping by subjects.

123 James S. Coleman, Thomas Hoffer, and Sally Kilgore, *High School Achievement: Public, Catholic, and Private Schools Compared* (New York: Basic Books, 1982), 41–5. The survey involved 893 public, 84 Catholic, 27 other private, and 11 'high performance' private high schools. The percentages of students enrolled in curricular programs were based on student self-reporting; the type of high school was determined from administrators' reports on school programs. The student enrolments reported for vocational programs in public high schools were distributed as follows: agricultural, 3.3 per cent; business or office, 10.9 per cent; trade or industrial, 7.2 per cent; distributive education, 2.2 per cent; health, 1.3 per cent; home economics, 1.8 per cent; and technical, 2.6 per cent. Among the 23.4 per cent of public high schools that were classified as 'specialized,' defined as those having 90 per cent or more students in one program, the distribution was 3.3 per cent academic, 9.7 per cent vocational, 9.9 per cent general, and 0.5 per cent other. Comparing public high schools with private schools, the survey found that 71–2 per cent of students in Catholic and other private high schools were enrolled in academic programs, 18–19 per cent in general, and 10 per cent in vocational. In the 'high performance' private schools (eleven schools with high ratios of semifinalists in the competition for National Merit Scholarships), 97.5 per cent of students were enrolled in the academic program.

124 Marvin Lazerson, Judith Block McLaughlin, Bruce McPherson, and

Stephen K. Bailey, *An Education of Value: The Purposes and Practices of Schools* (Cambridge: Cambridge University Press, 1985), 23–4. My references below to the cases of the School Mathematics Study Group and Man: A Course of Study are based primarily on the accounts provided by Lazerson, McLaughlin, McPherson, and Bailey (ibid., 25–42).

125 The 'new math,' for example, was developed by the School Mathematics Study Group, a committee of the American Mathematical Society, which sponsored a series of summer programs comprising professors and teachers of mathematics from 1958 to 1961. Mathematics curricula were rewritten for all levels of school, textbooks and other instructional materials were produced, and in-service training programs were developed for teachers. Similarly, the new social studies curriculum (Man: A Course of Study) was created by Educational Services, Incorporated (later the Educational Development Center), a non-profit organization created by the developers of the Physical Science Study Committee, which secured a grant from the Ford Foundation in 1962 to begin work on revising social studies and humanities curricula.

126 Lazerson, McLaughlin, McPherson, and Bailey, *An Education of Value*, 32; see also ibid., 41–2, 45–6, and Mary Campbell Gallagher, 'Lessons from the Sputnik-Era Curriculum Reform Movement: The Institutions We Need for Educational Reform,' in Sandra Stotsky (ed.), *What's at Stake in the K–12 Standards Wars: A Primer for Educational Policy Makers* (New York: Peter Lang, 2000), 281–312.

127 Quoted in United States, Department of Health, Education, and Welfare, Office of Education, Sam P. Harris, *State Departments of Education, State Boards of Education, and Chief State School Officers* (Washington, D.C.: United States Government Printing Office, 1973), 54; see also United States, Department of Health, Education, and Welfare, Office of Education, Robert F. Will, *State Education: Structure and Organization* (Washington, D.C.: United States Government Printing Office, 1964), 12–18, 34.

128 The nineteen states in which the chief state school officer continued to be popularly elected were Arizona, California, Florida, Georgia, Idaho, Illinois, Kentucky, Louisiana, Mississippi, Montana, North Carolina, North Dakota, Oklahoma, Oregon, South Carolina, South Dakota, Washington, Wisconsin, and Wyoming. The 1961 Oregon constitution established the office of superintendent as elected by the state board of education, but the Oregon Supreme Court in 1965 restored popular election on the grounds that 'elect' and 'election' in the Oregon constitution referred to the people not the state board.

129 The four states that retained appointment of both the state superintend-

ent and the state board of education by the governor in 1970 were New
Jersey, Pennsylvania, Tennessee, and Virginia. The state of New York
continued its unique approach to separating educational policy from
politics and administration with the Board of Regents appointed by the
state legislative assembly and the state commissioner of education
appointed by the board.

130 The seven states that had adopted this form of political accountability
prior to 1940 were Arkansas, Connecticut, Delaware, Maryland, Minnesota, New Hampshire, and Vermont. Among the additional eight states
that adopted this model by 1970, Missouri (1945), Iowa (1953), West
Virginia (1958), and Indiana (1970) had previously elected their state
superintendents. In Massachusetts (1947), Maine (1949), Rhode Island
(1951), and Alaska (1959), the governor had appointed both the state
superintendent and the state board of education. Note, however, that the
state superintendent had been appointed by the state board of education
in Rhode Island prior to 1935 and in Massachusetts prior to 1919.

131 The other eight states that adopted the model of a popularly elected
board with the chief state school officer appointed by the state board were
Nebraska (1952), Ohio (1955), Nevada (1956), New Mexico (1958),
Michigan (1963), Hawaii (1966), Kansas (1966), and Alabama (1969).

132 Here, I am adopting the criteria of administrative and fiscal dependence
and independence of local governments employed by the Bureau of the
Census in its census of governments. United States, Bureau of the Census,
1992 Census of Governments, vol. 1, *Governmental Organization* (Washington,
D.C.: United States Government Printing Office, 1994), x.

133 The average annual rate of reduction in the number of school districts for
these twenty-six states was 1.5 per cent from 1931–2 to 1945–6, 4.5 per
cent from 1945–6 to 1959–60, and 5.6 per cent during the 1960s. Delaware
is not included among the twenty-six states counted as having community
school districts. In Delaware there were 178 school districts in 1965–6, but
only 15 'special school districts' created by the state board of education
and governed by boards of trustees enjoyed administrative and fiscal
independence. The Wilmington City School District was legally independent but in practice ceded power to the city council to approve appropriations supplemental to state financing, and the remaining 'state board unit
districts' were financed directly by state appropriations, their budgets
subject to approval by the state board of education. Following district
reorganization in 1969, the number of school boards in Delaware was cut
to twenty-six, all but one of them fiscally independent and popularly
elected.

134 The number of school districts decreased in New Hampshire between
1931–2 and 1970–1 from 244 to 168 but increased in Connecticut (161 to
169), Massachusetts (355 to 431), New Jersey (552 to 599), Rhode Island
(39 to 40), and Vermont (268 to 277).

135 Another important postwar development in local educational governance
in these states, especially Maine and Massachusetts, was the creation of
fiscally independent regional school districts alongside the original city,
town, and township school committees that remained fiscally dependent
on municipal governments. The Massachusetts law providing for the formation of regional school districts was passed in 1948; that in Maine in
1957. By 1967 there were eighty-one regional school districts in Massachusetts and sixty-five in Maine. In other states relying on elected school boards
that were fiscally dependent on city, town, and township governments,
there were nine fiscally independent regional school districts in Connecticut in 1967 and three in Rhode Island. In Pennsylvania, all school boards
were fiscally independent. New Jersey school boards were all fiscally independent, with the exception of those in some larger cities and a few
townships operating under Chapter VI of the School Code. Similarly, in
New Hampshire all school districts were fiscally independent except for
the school committees in the nine cities of Berlin, Dover, Franklin, Laconia,
Manchester, Nashua, Portsmouth, Rochester, and Somersworth. School
committees of city and town governments in Vermont were dependent
agencies prior to 1967, but subsequently all school districts gained fiscal
independence.

136 In Kentucky the 1934 School Code restricted local governance to county
and 'independent' (city) school districts, thus abolishing county subdistricts, and as a result the number of districts fell from 384 in 1931–2 to
256 in 1945–6 and 192 in 1970–1. In South Carolina, where county subdistricts were the basic unit of local governance before the war, there were
1,792 districts in 1931–2 and 1,703 in 1945–6. In 1951, the newly elected
governor (James Francis Byrnes), realizing that preserving desegregation
would necessitate the provision of adequate schools for black children,
persuaded the legislature to create the State Educational Finance Commission, which brought about a reduction of school districts to 107 by 1955–6.
There was no change in the number of county school districts in Florida,
Louisiana, Maryland, Utah, and West Virginia, and there were relatively
minor changes in Alabama, Georgia, North Carolina, Tennessee, and
Virginia. The number of districts decreased in Georgia from 272 in
1931–2 to 208 in 1945–6 and 190 in 1970–1, in North Carolina from 200
in 1931–2 to 171 in 1945–6 and 152 in 1970–1, and in Tennessee from 194

in 1931–2 to 152 in 1945–6 and 147 in 1970–1. Over the same period, the
number of school districts increased in Alabama from 112 to 124 and in
Virginia from 125 to 134.

137 In Nevada, which had 266 school districts in 1931–2 and 237 in 1945–6, a
survey team from George Peabody College for Teachers urged the governor's State School Committee to adopt county-wide districts, along with a
state foundation program, and as a result the number of school districts
dropped from 176 in 1953–4 to 17 in 1955–6. Alaska historically had a
dual regime comprising territorial schools governed by popularly elected,
fiscally independent city and fiscally dependent borough (county) boards
and Aboriginal schools administered by the federal Bureau of Indian
Affairs (BIA). After the Second World War there was gradual unification
of state and federal schools, and eventually, agreement on transfer of BIA
schools to state management was reached in 1962. Under the provisions
of the Borough Act of 1961, Alaskan school districts were reorganized into
9 borough and 18 city districts.

138 The average annual reduction in school districts was approximately 1 per
cent during the 1930s, 3 per cent during the 1940s, and 5 per cent in both
the 1950s and the 1960s, reaching 9.2 per cent from 1965–6 to 1967–8.
The average annual rate of reduction in school districts then fell to 1.1 per
cent during the 1970s.

139 Paul R. Mort, *State Support for Public Education*, National Survey of School
Finance (Washington, D.C.: American Council on Education, 1933), 26.
These averages hide substantial variation across the states. In 1925 the
highest level of state aid was provided in Delaware (81.5 per cent). Texas
and Utah (37.8 per cent), Arkansas (35.5 per cent), Wyoming (34.1 per
cent), Alabama (33.2 per cent), and Georgia (32.7 per cent) comprised
the next highest level of state support. By contrast, state aid in Connecticut, Florida, Idaho, Illinois, Massachusetts, Missouri, Montana, North
Carolina, Rhode Island, South Dakota, and West Virginia was less than
10 per cent of public school revenue, and in Colorado, Iowa, Kansas,
Nebraska, and Ohio, state aid was less than 5 per cent. Note that these
percentages include an element of federal aid, but during this period that
was not more than 0.3 per cent.

140 Under this type of grant, the state established the unit cost of an educational program to be provided equally in every school district and a mandatory local property tax rate to be levied on the assessed valuation in every
school district. The state grant paid to each district would be the difference between local expenditure for the foundation program and local
revenue from the mandatory tax rate. The 'foundation program' was

conceived during the 1920s by George D. Strayer and Robert M. Haig. See George D. Strayer and Robert Murray Haig, *The Financing of Education in the State of New York*, Report of the Educational Finance Inquiry Commission, vol. 1 (New York: Macmillan, 1923). Working under Strayer's supervision on his doctoral dissertation, 'The Measurement of Educational Need' (1924), Paul R. Mort developed the concept of 'key district,' which adopted average educational provision as the basis for determining the state foundation program.

141 In 1971–2, Arizona and Connecticut used uniform flat grants as their main method for allocating state aid to school districts, and Arkansas, Delaware, New Mexico, North Carolina, and South Carolina used variable flat grants. California and Oregon employed uniform flat grants and Nebraska a variable flat grant in conjunction with their foundation programs. Percentage equalizing grants were being used in Iowa, Massachusetts, New York, Rhode Island, and Vermont, and guaranteed valuation plans were found in New Jersey, Utah, and Wisconsin. See United States, Department of Health, Education and Welfare, Office of Education, Thomas L. Johns, *Public School Finance Programs, 1971–72* (Washington, D.C.: United States Government Printing Office, 1972), 5. The percentage equalizing grant was conceived by Harlan Updegraff (*Rural School Survey of New York State: Financial Support* [Ithaca, N.Y.: 1922]). States using a percentage equalizing grant usually put an upper limit on state aid per student, with the result that it is not much different in performance from a foundation program or fixed unit equalizing grant. As for guaranteed valuation plans, their general formula is algebraically equivalent to the formula for foundation programs. Elchanan Cohn, *Economics of State Aid to Education* (Lexington, Mass.: Lexington Books, 1974), 55.

142 As in the 1920s, interstate variations in state support continued to be substantial. Ten states provided more than half of public school revenue in 1965–6. Delaware still provided the highest percentage of state support (77.3 per cent). Arizona, Louisiana, New Mexico, and North Carolina provided between 61.8 and 66.2 per cent of public school revenue, and Georgia, Kentucky, Mississippi, Nevada, South Carolina, and Washington provided 50.2 to 59.8 per cent. Ten states provided less than 25 per cent of public school revenue, with the lowest levels of state support found in Nebraska (5.2 per cent), New Hampshire (11.6 per cent), South Dakota (12.4 per cent), and Iowa (13.5 per cent).

143 John E. Coons, William H. Clune, III, and Stephen D. Sugarman, *Private Wealth and Public Education* (Cambridge, Mass.: Belknap Press, 1970), xix, 197.

144 By the late 1990s, thirty-three states had enacted laws that compelled
    school boards to negotiate collective agreements with the local teachers'
    union, seven states (Alabama, Arkansas, Colorado, Kentucky, Louisiana,
    Missouri, and West Virginia) allowed collective bargaining as an option of
    the school boards, and nine states (Arizona, Georgia, Mississippi, North
    Carolina, South Carolina, Texas, Utah, Virginia, and Wyoming) prohibited
    collective bargaining in public education. Myron Lieberman, *The Teacher
    Unions* (New York: Free Press, 1997), 48.
145 See Stephen Cole, *The Unionization of Teachers: A Case Study of the UFT* (New
    York: Praeger, 1969), 11–21. The first collective agreement in the United
    States was negotiated in 1944 between the local affiliate of the American
    Federation of Teachers and the Board of Education of Cicero, Illinois.
    Anthony M. Cresswell, Michael J. Murphy, and Charles T. Kerchner,
    Teachers, Unions, and Collective Bargaining in Public Education (Berkeley,
    Calif.: McCutchan Publishing, 1980), 20–1.
146 Cresswell, Murphy, and Kerchner, *Teachers, Unions, and Collective Bargaining
    in Public Education*, 53–4. A 1964–5 survey of collective bargaining in pub-
    lic education identified only nineteen substantive agreements between
    school boards and teachers' unions. Two years later there were 400 agree-
    ments, and by the mid-1970s, 76 per cent of school districts surveyed were
    settling teachers' contracts through collective bargaining (ibid., 24–33).
147 Fass, *Outside In*, 121. The federal government's involvement in public
    education during the New Deal came through several relief agencies that
    worked outside regular school classrooms – Public Works Administration,
    Works Progress Administration, Federal Emergency Relief Administration,
    Civilian Conservation Corps, and National Youth Administration – but
    these experiments with federal educational programs ended one by one
    between 1939 and 1943 as the New Deal agencies organized to combat the
    Depression were either disbanded or shifted to basic training for war
    industries and armed forces.
148 The rationale of the National Defense Education Act (NDEA) was stated
    in its first title: 'The Congress hereby finds and declares that the security
    of the nation requires the fullest development of the mental resources and
    technical skills of its young men and women. The present emergency
    demands that additional and more adequate opportunities be made
    available.' NDEA also established a loan program for students enrolled in
    the sciences, mathematics, engineering, and modern languages at institu-
    tions of higher education (Title II) and national defence fellowships for
    graduate students (Title IV).
149 In keeping with the conception of education as an instrument of national

defence, Title X of the National Defense Education Act provided that no individual could receive funds without filing an affidavit 'that he does not believe in, and is not a member of and does not support any organization that believes in or teaches, the overthrow of the United States Government by force or violence or by any illegal or unconstitutional methods' (quoted in Clowse, *Brainpower for the Cold War*, 167). All recipients of grants under NDEA were further required to swear an oath of allegiance to the United States of America.

150 Harold Silver and Pamela Silver, *An Educational War on Poverty: American and British Policy-Making 1960–1980* (Cambridge: Cambridge University Press, 1991), 96. The President's Task Force on Education, chaired by John W. Gardner, had favoured general federal aid to public education in its 1964 report; if that proved to be politically infeasible, the task force recommended that federal aid to public education be promoted as a means to combat poverty.

151 Other titles of the act authorized federal grants for library material, textbooks, and other printed material (Title II); grants to encourage innovative educational programs, including specialized equipment, new courses, and counselling and social services (Title III); aid for construction of educational research facilities (Title IV); and grants to state educational agencies to improve state educational planning, data collection, and personnel training (Title V). Over the next two years, the act was expanded to provide federal funds to state educational authorities for the education of mentally and physically disadvantaged children and children for whom English was their second language and to help local schools to establish programs to prevent school drop-outs.

152 John F. Jennings, *Why National Standards and Tests? Politics and the Quest for Better Schools* (Thousand Oaks, Calif.: Sage Publications, 1998), 111.

153 Paul E. Peterson, Barry G. Rabe, and Kenneth K. Wong, 'The Evolution of the Compensatory Education Program,' in Denis P. Doyle and Bruce S. Cooper (eds), *Federal Aid to the Disadvantaged: What Future for Chapter 1?* (London: Falmer Press, 1988), 55, 57.

154 Beryl A. Radin and Willis D. Hawley, *The Politics of Federal Reorganization: Creating the U.S. Department of Education* (New York: Pergamon Press, 1988), 14. They add: 'The formal organization chart, from the late 1960s on, showed a Commissioner of Education reporting to an Assistant Secretary for Education who, in turn, reported to the Secretary of HEW. In reality, however, Congress frequently ignored the organization chart and gave direct authority to the Commissioner of Education, delegating specific responsibilities not to the Secretary of HEW but to the Commissioner of

Education.' Rufus E. Miles, Jr (*The Department of Health, Education, and Welfare* [New York: Praeger, 1974], 160) observed that all assistant secretaries in the Department of Health, Education and Welfare were located in the same building on the same floor as the secretary, except for the assistant secretary for education, who was located in a separate building surrounded by the staff of the Office of Education. These physical arrangements, Miles opines, were perhaps symbolic of their ambitions for full cabinet status.

155 Note, however, the exception of Canada, where government expenditure on public elementary and secondary education reached its highest point of 5 per cent of gross domestic product in 1970–1 and declined to 4.4 per cent in 1975–6.

156 Enrolments in private non-Roman Catholic schools in Australia decreased from 5.4 per cent of total enrolments in elementary and secondary education in 1945 to 4.1 per cent in 1970. During the same period, enrolments in private non-Roman Catholic schools in New Zealand fluctuated as follows: 3.1 per cent in 1945, 2.9 per cent in 1950, 2.5 per cent in 1955 and 1960, 3 per cent in 1965, and 2.6 per cent in 1970.

157 An exception to this generalization about the development of functional interdependence between state and local educational authorities was the centralized regime of Hawaii in the United States. At the time of annexation in 1898, Hawaii had a highly centralized government that reflected the legacy of the single monarchy established by Kamehameha in the early nineteenth centuries. This centralization was perpetuated following annexation by the United States. In the case of public education, the territorial governor appointed a board of education that exercised direct administrative control over school operations through the Department of Education. Following statehood, the governor, now elected, continued to appoint the state board, which then appointed the state superintendent as head of the Department of Education. The state superintendent, who is a member of the governor's cabinet, in turn appoints the district superintendents, who administer the seven school districts. District school councils are also appointed by the governor to advise the state board and the district superintendents about community concerns. See Thomas W. Bean and Jan Zulich, 'Education in Hawai'i: Balancing Equity and Progress,' in Zachary A. Smith and Richard C. Pratt (eds), *Politics and Public Policy in Hawai'i* (Albany: State University of New York Press, 1992), 217.

158 In the United States, enrolments in private non-Roman Catholic elementary and secondary schools were 0.8 per cent of total enrolments in 1945–6, 1.1 per cent in 1950–1, 1.2 per cent in 1955–6, and 1 per cent in

1959–60, but then rose to 1.7 per cent in 1965–6, 2.6 per cent in 1969–70, and 3.3 per cent in 1975–6. In Canada, enrolments in private non-Roman Catholic schools accounted for 0.7 per cent of total elementary and secondary school enrolments in 1945–6, 0.5 per cent in 1950–1, 0.6 per cent in 1955–6, 0.5 per cent in 1960–1, 0.8 per cent in 1965–6 and 1970–1, and 1 per cent in 1975–6.

4. Pluralist Society

1 A 'plural' society is culturally diverse; a 'pluralist' society adopts its cultural diversity as a fundamental defining characteristic and collective good. The political issues of a plural society result from conflicting visions of the good society as either culturally heterogeneous or culturally homogeneous. The political issues of a pluralist society result from conflicting prescriptions about the official recognition and support of multiculturalism in public institutions and policies. Graham Haydon makes this distinction with regard to Britain. As a 'plural' society, Britain has a plurality of cultures, ethnic groups, and religions, but that does not mean it is a 'pluralist' society, which must 'involve some approximation to an equality of standing between different cultural, ethnic and religious groups.' Graham Haydon, 'Preface,' in Graham Haydon (ed.), *Education for a Pluralist Society: Philosophical Perspectives on the Swann Report,* Bedford Way Papers 30 (London: University of London Institute of Education, 1987), 9–10.

2 The terms 'politics of recognition' and 'politics of difference, are taken respectively from Charles Taylor, 'The Politics of Recognition,' in Amy Gutmann (ed.), *Multiculturalism and 'The Politics of Recognition': An Essay by Charles Taylor* (Princeton: Princeton University Press, 1992), 25–73, and Iris Marion Young, *Justice and the Politics of Difference* (Princeton: Princeton University Press, 1990). In distinguishing indigenous national minorities, immigrant ethnic minorities, and the special case of African Americans I am following Will Kymlicka, *Multicultural Citizenship: A Liberal Theory of Minority Rights* (Oxford: Clarendon Press, 1995), 11–26; and see also Will Kymlicka and Wayne Norman, 'Citizenship in Culturally Diverse Societies: Issues, Contexts, Concepts,' in Will Kymlicka and Wayne Norman (eds), *Citizenship in Diverse Societies* (Oxford: Oxford University Press, 2000), 18–24

3 On the concept of citizenship regime applied to the case of Canada, see Jane Jenson, 'Recognizing Difference: Distinct Societies, Citizenship Regimes and Partnership,' in Roger Gibbins and Guy Laforest (eds), *Beyond the Impasse: Toward Reconciliation* (Montreal: Institute for Research on Public Policy, 1998), 215–39, and also Jane Jenson, 'Fated to Live in

Interesting Times: Canada's Changing Citizenship Regime,' *Canadian Political Science Review* 30 (December 1997): 627–44.

4 Immigration accounted for 23.6 per cent of Australia's population increase over the first three decades of the century before falling to 4.1 per cent during the Great Depression and the Second World War. The Australian population was 90 per cent British and Irish in 1947, 7 per cent northwestern European, 1 per cent southern European, 1 per cent other whites, and 1 per cent non-white, mainly Aborigines (Lois Foster and David Stockley, *Multiculturalism: The Changing Australian Paradigm* [Clevedon, Avon: Multilingual Matters, 1984], 26). The Labor government's postwar immigration policy aimed at increasing Australia's population by about 1 per cent annually, for reasons of both national security and economic growth, but its preference to admit 90 per cent British immigrants proved to be impossible to realize.

5 Australia, Department of Immigration, *Digest: Report of the Australian Citizenship Convention* (Canberra: Australian Government Publishing Service, 1963), 21; quoted in Brian M. Bullivant, *Pluralism: Cultural Maintenance and Evolution* (Clevedon, Avon: Multilingual Matters, 1984), 54.

6 Jean I. Martin, *The Migrant Presence: Australian Responses 1947–1977*, Research Report for the National Population Inquiry (Sydney: George Allen and Unwin, 1978), 99.

7 One historical exception should be noted. In 1900 Queensland departmental regulations were amended to allow scholarship holders to attend not just one of the state grammar schools but any approved secondary school. According to E.R. Wyeth, 'In this simple way the doors were thrown open wide to private and denominational schools to enjoy the government's bounty, and a principle which earlier had been hardly won was set aside. In a word, the Colony agreed to support denominational secondary schools.' E.R. Wyeth, *Education in Queensland: A History of Education in Queensland and in the Moreton Bay District of New South Wales*, ACER Research Series No. 67 (Melbourne: Australian Council for Educational Research, 1955), 165.

8 Helen Praetz, *Public Policies and Catholic Schools*, Australian Education Review, no. 17 (Hawthorn, Victoria: Australian Council for Educational Research, 1982), 10.

9 As Praetz observes, 'Within Roman Catholic schools, the struggle for survival took its toll. Crowded classrooms lacked even the most basic facilities and equipment. Commonly, Catholic primary and secondary schools were without libraries, special purpose rooms, audio-visual, sporting or playground equipment, and hygienic toilet facilities. Buildings and furniture were often dilapidated and outmoded. The experiential and child-centred

methods, widely employed in other primary schools, could not be used in the huge classes. Little or no in-service training was available and, as many teachers were elderly or untrained, they concentrated on a thorough grounding in literacy, numeracy, and religious instruction' (ibid., 12).

10 B. Bessant and A.D. Spaull, *Politics of Schooling* (Carlton, Victoria: Pitman Publishing, 1976), 122, 127, 186–7.

11 During the February 1965 election in Western Australia, the Liberal party promised direct grants to private schools. The next month the Labor party, out of office, promised free textbooks to children in both public and private schools. In May 1965, a Liberal–Country party coalition won power in New South Wales and legislated more student bursaries for private schools as well as subsidies for their interest payments on capital development. In its 1964 electoral platform, the Liberal government in Victoria announced subsidies for private secondary schools on their interest payments on new buildings. In 1967, in order to fulfil electoral promises after another victory for the Liberals, the budget for these subsidies was doubled, and capitation grants of $10 for each primary student and $20 for each secondary student were introduced. In May 1967 Tasmania also introduced a capitation grant for private schools. In Queensland the scholarship examination for entrance to secondary school was abolished in 1963, but the scholarship allowance was continued to pupils attending private schools, and from January 1967 allowances for each student enrolled were paid directly to each approved private school. In 1969 the South Australian state government made its first direct grants in support of students in private schools – $10 and $20 per student at the primary and secondary school levels, respectively. Following the Menzies example, Prime Minister Henry Holt promised Commonwealth grants for secondary school libraries in his 1967 Senate election campaign speech, and these were enacted in 1968.

12 The minister of education and science in 1969 strongly defended a national policy of two sectors. 'The government favours a continuation of a dual system on both educational and economic grounds. We categorically reject the argument that because a significant number of citizens choose to seek a form of education for their children which they prefer to the State system and are prepared to make financial sacrifices, those citizens cannot expect any help from the State, even though they are easing its financial and physical burdens ... It is our policy to seek out ways of assisting independent schools so that, relying on their own efforts and supported by government, they will be able in the future to provide for that proportion of the school population which in the past has sought education in independent schools' (quoted in J.S. Gregory, *Church and State: Changing Government Policies*

towards Religion in Australia; with Particular Reference to Victoria since Separation
[North Melbourne: Cassell Australia, 1973], 237). According to Don Smart,
'This move was significant in two respects. Firstly, it was a precedent establishing a degree of Commonwealth responsibility for providing non-specific
(i.e. general) recurrent financial assistance to independent schools. Such
a precedent inevitably left the federal government vulnerable to future
pressures for the provision of increasingly extensive general purpose school
funding. Secondly, the relatively placid public acceptance of this exclusively
"State aid" scheme reflected the sea-change of public opinion that had
occurred since the early 1960s, when such a proposal would almost certainly have foundered on community opposition.' Don Smart, 'The Accel-
erating Commonwealth Participation, 1964–1975,' in I.K.F. Birch and D.
Smart (eds), *The Commonwealth Government and Education, 1964–1976:
Political Initiatives and Development* (Richmond, Victoria: Drummond, 1977),
33–4.

13 In 1957, following the split in the ALP and the formation of the Democratic Labor party, the ALP had restricted its previously open platform of
'aid to all forms of education' to aid to government schools only. In 1966,
largely through the efforts of Gough Whitlam, the party's federal conference decided to drop this prohibition on state aid to private schools, and
in 1969, with Whitlam now leader, the conference endorsed a program
of educational reforms that aimed to achieve equality of opportunity by
allocating state aid on the basis of need.

14 In his policy speech on education for the 1972 election, Gough Whitlam
emphasized his party's goal to put an end to inequalities in education: 'The
Labor Party believes that the Commonwealth should give most assistance to
those schools, primary and secondary, whose pupils need most assistance.'
Quoted in J.K. Matthews and R.T. Fitzgerald, *Educational Policy and Political
Platform: The Australian Labor Government*, Australian Education Review, vol.
7, no. 4 (Hawthorn, Victoria: Australian Educational Research Council,
1975), 8.

15 Australia, Interim Committee for the Australian Schools Commission,
*Schools in Australia: Report of the Interim Committee for the Australian Schools
Commission* (Canberra: Australian Government Publishing Service, 1973),
35.

16 Under the 1973 act, the Schools Commission was required 'to recommend
to the Minister of Education after consulting with interested parties, what
Commonwealth government funds should be made available to schools
and school systems throughout the country in order to ensure acceptable
standards' and 'to enquire into and report on any aspect of primary or

secondary schooling.' When making its recommendations, the commission was expected to take into account the need to improve the quality of existing school provision, promote 'increased and equal educational opportunities,' recognize the prior right of parents to choose government or non-government schooling for their children, assess the needs of disadvantaged schools and students, and encourage diversity and innovation in schools.

17 According to section 116, 'The Commonwealth shall not make any law for establishing any religion, or for imposing any religious observance, or for prohibiting the free exercise of any religion, and no religious test shall be required as a qualification for any office or public trust under the Commonwealth.'

18 Following its election in December 1975, the Liberal–National Country coalition government had altered the financial arrangements so as to vary subsidies as a fixed percentage of standard costs in the public sector from 11 per cent for primary schools and 12 per cent for secondary schools in the wealthiest category of private schools to 32 per cent for primary schools and 31 per cent for secondary schools in the poorest category. Among its pre-election promises in 1980, the Liberal–National Country coalition proposed to simplify Commonwealth grants into three categories of need with support of 20, 30, and 40 per cent of the standard costs of a public school and with minimum requirements for contributions from private sources set at 51 and 31 per cent, respectively, for the first two categories and no minimum level of private financing for the poorest schools.

19 The model of state aid to private schools designed by the Interim Committee and developed by the Schools Commission was adopted by the state and territorial governments. A decade after the establishment of the Schools Commission, across the states and territories there were slight differences in the amounts provided and, in the case of South Australia, in the way in which grants were assessed. 'But it is now broadly true to say that each State provides, for each registered non-government school, an amount per pupil which is approximately equal to 20 per cent of the cost of providing for a pupil in a comparable school in the Australian state systems.' R. Selby Smith, *Australian Independent Schools Yesterday, Today, and Tomorrow*, Australian Education Review, no. 19 (Hawthorn, Victoria: Australian Council for Educational Research, 1983), 29.

20 Don Smart and Janice Dudley, 'Australia: Private Schools and Public Policy,' in Geoffrey Walford (ed.), *Private Schools in Ten Countries: Policy and Practice* (London: Routledge, 1989), 112–13.

21 Peter Meadmore, '"Free, Compulsory, and Secular"? The Re-invention of

Australian Public Education,' *Journal of Education Policy* 16 (March–April 2001): 123.

22 This program was the result of an initiative taken by B.M. Snedden, who was appointed Commonwealth minister for immigration in December 1966 and pressed his department to become more involved in child migrant education. A consultant's report prepared for the 1968 Australian Citizenship Convention provided a compelling analysis of the educational problems of migrant children who did not speak English, the inadequate measures taken by state departments of education, and the necessity for 'a special educational policy for migrant children.' Jerzy Zubrzycki, 'The Questing Years,' in Australian Citizenship Convention, *Digest* (Canberra: Department of Immigration, 1968), 24; cited in Martin, *The Migrant Presence*, 107.

23 A.J. Grassby has been described as 'a flamboyant figure with considerable oratorical powers and, probably more than any other individual, has played a major role in shaping thinking about migrants and migrant education in Australia' (Bullivant, *Pluralism: Cultural Maintenance and Evolution*, 58). According to Bullivant, Grassby's thinking about multiculturalism in Australia was greatly influenced by the work of the Royal Commission on Bilingualism and Biculturalism in Canada (Brian M. Bullivant, *The Pluralist Dilemma in Education: Six Case Studies* [Sydney: George Allen and Unwin, 1981], 85). On Grassby's role in the Whitlam government see also Foster and Stockley, *Multiculturalism: The Changing Australian Paradigm*, 54–67.

24 Australia, Department of Education, *Report of the Inquiry into Schools of High Migrant Density* (Canberra: Department of Education, 1975), 6.

25 See Interim Committee for the Australian Schools Commission, *Schools in Australia*, 107; and Australia, Schools Commission, *Report for the Triennium 1976–78* (Canberra: Australian Government Publishing Service, 1975). The Schools Commission's report included a separate chapter on the education of migrant children that began with the assertion 'Australia is a multicultural society.' The commission concluded that 'The multicultural reality of Australia needs to be reflected in school curricula – languages, social studies, history, literature, the arts and crafts – in staffing and in school organization. While these changes are particularly important to undergird the self-esteem of migrant children they also have application for all Australian children growing up in a society which could be greatly enriched through a wider sharing in the variety of cultural heritages now present in it' (ibid., 130). The commission recommended that the Child Migrant Education Program be discontinued and funds for child migrant education be provided to the states through the Schools Commission's general recurrent grants program.

26 The Australian Ethnic Affairs Council, which was created in January 1977 as
an advisory body to the minister for immigration and ethnic affairs, in its
first major report focused its proposals for education on teaching English
as a second language, bilingual education, and heritage ('community')
languages, but it also recommended that 'Schools should be given incentives to develop ethnic-studies programs and to infuse the curriculum in
general with the reality of the pluralist nature of Australian society, with the
object of both enhancing the self-esteem of students of ethnic origin and
giving *all* children a more authentic view of the nature of society.' Australia,
Australian Ethnic Affairs Council, *Australia as a Multicultural Society* (Canberra: Australian Government Publishing Service, 1977), 12; emphasis in
the original.

27 The Committee to Review Post-Arrival Programs and Services to Migrants,
chaired by Frank Galbally, emphasized the need to improve the teaching of
English as a second language and recommended an additional $10 million
for the 1979–81 triennium. The Galbally report also urged that 'schools
and school systems should be encouraged to develop more rapidly various
initiatives aimed at improving the understanding of different histories,
cultures, languages and attitudes of those who make up our society' and
proposed the creation of a special grant of $5 million for multicultural
education (Australia, Department of Immigration and Ethnic Affairs,
*Migrant Services and Programs: Report of the Review of Post-Arrival Programs and
Services for Migrants* [Canberra: Australian Government Publishing Service,
1978], 12, 106). Galbally was a friend of Prime Minister Malcolm Fraser,
and the committee's recommendations were well timed to coincide with
the prime minister's interest in making an appeal to ethnic-minority voters
in the 1979 general election,

28 Millicent E. Poole and Judyth M. Sachs, in their comparison of multicultural education policies in Australia and Britain, conclude that in Australia 'the initiatives came from the federal arena and then were taken up
by state education authorities without contextualizing them. That is, a
similar version of multicultural education advocated by the Commonwealth
government in Australia was to be found in state multicultural policies'
('Education for All: Social Reconstruction or Status Quo?' in Gajendra K.
Verma [ed.], *Education for All: A Landmark in Pluralism* [London: Falmer
Press, 1989], 460). Poole and Sachs provide brief reviews of multicultural
education policies in New South Wales, Queensland, South Australia, and
the Australian Capital Territory and show that in each case the development of policy was a response to the recommendations of the Schools
Commission.

29 D. Cahill (Chief Researcher), *Review of the Commonwealth Multicultural Education Program* (Canberra: Schools Commission, 1984), xii; quoted in L.E. Foster, *Diversity and Multicultural Education: A Sociological Perspective* (Sydney: Allen and Unwin, 1988), 152.

30 The National Policy on Languages had its origins in a project initiated jointly by the Language Teaching Branch and the Education Planning Group of the Department of Education that subsequently received strong backing from the Senate Standing Committee on Education and the Arts in its report tabled in Parliament in February 1985. The objective was to form 'against the broad background of the multicultural nature of Australian society, and Australia's language needs in international relations, commerce, defence and tourism' a comprehensive and coherent national policy that would encompass teaching community languages, Aboriginal languages, Asian languages, English as a second language, and bilingual education (Australia, Department of Education, *Report for 1981* [Canberra: Australian Government Publishing Service, 1982], 16). An inquiry by the Senate Standing Committee on Education and the Arts resulted in a report tabled in Parliament in February 1985 that strongly endorsed the development of a national language policy. As a response to the Senate committee's report, the Labor government then commissioned a report by Joseph Lo Bianco. See Australia, Department of Education, Joseph Lo Bianco, *National Policy on Languages* (Canberra: Australian Government Publishing Service, 1987).

31 Lo Bianco, *National Policy on Languages*, 54. Heading the list of languages of economic importance for Australians were Mandarin Chinese, Indonesian/ Malay, and Japanese (ibid., 125).

32 English was the exclusive language of instruction in the non-denominational common schools of British Columbia and Manitoba. English was the language of instruction with French permitted in elementary schools as a transitional language of instruction in Alberta, Ontario, and Saskatchewan, which had dual regimes of public non-denominational and separate denominational (mostly Roman Catholic) schools. In the Maritimes, where there were de facto reserved schools for Roman Catholics, English was the majority language, with French as a limited minority right in Acadian districts. The state-supported denominational regime of Quebec was a communal consociation of French Catholics, English Catholics, and English Protestants. See Ronald Manzer, *Public Schools and Political Ideas: Canadian Educational Policy in Historical Perspective* (Toronto: University of Toronto Press, 1994), 61–7.

33 See Eric Waddell, 'State, Language and Society: The Vicissitudes of French

in Quebec and Canada,' in Alan C. Cairns and Cynthia Williams (eds), *The Politics of Gender, Ethnicity and Language*, Research Studies for the Royal Commission on Economic Union and Development Prospects for Canada, vol. 34 (Toronto: University of Toronto Press for Minister of Supply and Services Canada, 1986), 86.

34 See Manzer, *Public Schools and Political Ideas*, 183–4.

35 The Quebec government was unable to persuade the courts, under section 1 of the Charter, that the restrictions placed on English-language education were 'reasonable limits prescribed by law as can be demonstrably justified in a free and democratic society.' Section 23 of the Canadian Charter of Rights and Freedoms also provides for a third type of claimant. Where one child has received or is receiving primary or secondary school instruction in French or English, the child's parents have the right to have all their children educated in the same language. Claims for English minority-language rights in Quebec or French minority-language rights outside Quebec apply wherever the number of children of citizens having such a right is sufficient to warrant the provision of instruction in the minority language.

36 In Quebec, enrolment in minority-language (English) education programs as a percentage of total enrolment fell from 15.7 per cent in 1970–1 and 14 per cent in 1980–1 to 9.7 per cent in 1990–1, then rose slightly to 10 per cent in 1998–9. Enrolments in minority-language (French) education programs were 4.8 per cent of total enrolment outside Quebec in 1970–1 and 4.9 per cent in 1980–1 but declined to 4.1 per cent in 1990–1 and 3.8 per cent in 1998–9.

37 Enrolment in second-official-language programs outside Quebec rose from 36.4 per cent of total enrolment in 1970–1 to 44.1 per cent in 1980–1 and 53.3 per cent in 1990–1, then declined to 49.6 per cent in 1998–9. Enrolment in French as a second language in Quebec was 53.8 per cent of total enrolment in 1970–1 and 54 per cent in 1980–1, rising to 57.3 per cent in 1990–1, and holding at 56.7 per cent in 1998–9. Enrolment in French immersion programs was 8.6 per cent of total Quebec anglophone enrolment in 1977–8 and 37.3 per cent in 1998–9. Statistics for second-official-language programs outside Quebec refer primarily to anglophone students learning French, but they also include francophone students in New Brunswick who are learning English. The statistics for 1970–1 do not include Yukon and the Northwest Territories; those for 1980–1 do not include Alberta.

38 The reorganization of New Brunswick school districts in 1967 resulted in amalgamation of English and French communities that previously had

operated as separate school districts. Especially in linguistically balanced towns such as Bathurst, Dalhousie, and Grand Falls, there were prolonged struggles over control of the school board and designation of the language of instruction in secondary schools. In 1978 the Bathurst and Dalhousie school districts were replaced by separate French and English districts, and by 1981 all school districts had been reorganized into parallel systems of English-language and French-language school districts. Prior to the Supreme Court's decision in *Mahé* in 1990 there were only four officially recognized French-language school boards outside New Brunswick: one in Prince Edward Island, one in Nova Scotia, and two in Ontario, organized in Ottawa and Toronto, respectively, in 1988.

39 To satisfy the terms of *Mahé*, provincial school boards were given mandates to govern francophone schools in Prince Edward Island (1991), Manitoba (1993), Nova Scotia (1995), Newfoundland (1997), British Columbia (1997), and Saskatchewan (1998). Legislation providing for the establishment of francophone district school boards was passed in Nova Scotia in 1992 and in Saskatchewan and Alberta in 1993, but Nova Scotia had only two francophone school boards and Saskatchewan nine prior to the establishment of their provincial francophone school boards.

40 See Quebec, Royal Commission of Inquiry on Education, *Report of the Royal Commission of Inquiry on Education in the Province of Quebec*, vol. 4 (Quebec: Government Printer, 1966), chs 5, 6.

41 The procedure for amendment of section 93 followed section 43 of the Constitution Act, 1982, under which constitutional amendments affecting only one province can be made by resolutions of that province's legislative assembly and the Parliament of Canada. In this case the Parti Québécois government took pains to explain that its request to Parliament for a resolution approving the amendment of section 93 should not be interpreted as a change in its opposition to the Constitution Act, 1982. For its part, the federal Liberal government was eager to facilitate the amendment as a demonstration that Canadian federalism could be flexible and reformable with regard to the interests of Quebec.

42 Given the agreement of the Anglican, Salvation Army, and United Church educational authorities to integrate their schools, 270 school boards were reduced in July 1969 to 20 Integrated and 15 Roman Catholic school boards, as well as 1 school board each to govern Pentecostal Assemblies and Seventh Day Adventist schools throughout the province. In September 1969 the Presbyterian Church joined the Integrated Education Council, as did the Moravian Church in 1977.

43 Under the royal commission's plan, a denominational policy commission

would be responsible for advising both the provincial government and the new school councils with regard to educational policies that affected the rights of denominations, overseeing the development of religious education and family life programs, and facilitating pastoral care. See Newfoundland and Labrador, Royal Commission of Inquiry into the Delivery of Programs and Services in Primary, Elementary, Secondary Education, *Our Children, Our Future* (St John's: Queen's Printer, 1992), 217–50.

44 The vote in the House of Commons was 170 to 46 in favour of the resolution. Opponents worried about the size of the majority (54 per cent in favour with a turnout of 52 per cent of those eligible to vote) in the referendum as the basis for amending the constitutional protection of minority rights. They also expressed concern that the results of the Newfoundland referendum might be a dangerous precedent for a referendum on Quebec independence or an attack on religious or minority-language educational rights in other provinces.

45 Under the amendment to Term 17, the Newfoundland legislative assembly 'shall have exclusive authority to make laws in relation to education, but shall provide for courses in religion that are not specific to a religious denomination,' and 'Religious observances shall be permitted in a school where requested by parents.'

46 Canada, Royal Commission on Bilingualism and Biculturalism, *Report of the Royal Commission on Bilingualism and Biculturalism Book IV: The Cultural Contribution of the Other Ethnic Groups* (Ottawa: Queen's Printer, 1969), 138.

47 A fourth type of instruction in heritage languages, not considered here, is provided through part-time programs operated outside regular school hours by voluntary ethnocultural organizations that are financially supported by the federal and provincial governments.

48 Jim Cummins and Marcel Danesi, *Heritage Languages: The Development and Denial of Canada's Linguistic Resources* (Toronto: Our Schools/Our Selves Education Foundation and Garamond Press, 1990), 44. During the founding of regimes of public instruction in the mid-nineteenth century, there was considerable permissiveness about language of instruction, which was generally left to be determined by local school boards. Ethnic-minority groups that were concentrated in a small school district could opt to educate their children in their own language, and in linguistically mixed school districts, where the total population was large enough to support more than one school, schools might be reserved in practice for attendance by children of different mother tongues. During the late nineteenth and early twentieth centuries, however, the issue of language of instruction outside Quebec became defined by a confrontation between English and

French as the languages of instruction, and in the process, other languages were abandoned or rescinded. See Manzer, *Public Schools and Political Ideas*, 61–5.

49 In Ontario, instruction in heritage languages is restricted to 2.5 hours a week, carries no academic credit, and must be given outside regular school hours or by lengthening the school day. Similarly, the Quebec Ministry of Education supports one half-hour of daily instruction in heritage languages, beginning in first grade, and instruction is usually but not always given outside the regular school day.

50 See Judith C. Anderson, 'Students and the Law: Curriculum Implications,' *Education Canada* 30 (Spring 1990): 26–8.

51 In its judgment, the court referred approvingly to the policy of the Toronto Board of Education in order to show that religious exercises could appropriately reflect a multicultural, multidenominational society, and hence be constitutional under section 2(a). School opening exercises in Toronto consisted of singing the national anthem; reading one or more selections from a book of readings and prayers drawn from a number of sources, including Bahaism, Buddhism, Christianity, Confucianism, Hinduism, Islam, Jainism, Judaism, Native peoples, secular humanism, Sikhism, and Zoroastrianism; and a moment of silent meditation.

52 See Manzer, *Public Schools and Political Ideas*, 73.

53 In 1969 a provincial commission chaired by Keiller Mackay recommended elimination of the regulation in favour of informal moral or ethical education that would permeate the entire curriculum and encourage students to make their own value judgments and moral decisions. Mackay argued that the presentation of Bible stories and Christian morals 'does not provide for the objective examination of evidence, nor stimulate the inquiring mind; it does not teach children to think for themselves.' Hence, it had no place in the curriculum. See Robert M. Stamp, *The Schools of Ontario 1876–1976* (Toronto: University of Toronto Press, 1982), 223.

54 In *Corporation of the Canadian Civil Liberties Association et al.* v. *Minister of Education and Elgin County Board of Education*, the trial court held that while the provincial requirement for religious education did not necessarily violate the Charter, the Elgin County board's exclusively Christian course of studies certainly did. Subsequently, the board revised its program to focus on world religious beliefs and practices, but a unanimous decision of the Ontario Court of Appeal in January 1990 found that the Elgin County board's curriculum was not broad enough and that the provincial regulation was inconsistent with constitutional guarantees of freedom of conscience and religion. The decision was not appealed.

55 See Genevieve Hennessy, 'New Brunswick,' in Carl J. Matthews (ed.), *Catholic Schools in Canada* (Toronto: Canadian Catholic School Trustees Association, 1977), 12; and also Elizabeth Dunn, 'Prince Edward Island,' and Haidee Patricia MacLellan, 'Nova Scotia,' in ibid., 5–6 and 15–16.

56 Eric W. Ricker, 'Representation on School Boards in Nova Scotia: Past and Present,' in Edward H. Humphreys, Stephen B. Lawton, Richard B. Townsend, Victoria W. Grabb, and Daina M. Watson, *Alternative Approaches to Determining Distribution of School Boards Trustee Representation*, vol. 1, *Trustee Representation: Theory and Practice in Canada* (Toronto: Queen's Printer for Ontario, 1986), 263; see also David M. Cameron and Peter Aucoin, 'Halifax,' in Warren Magnusson and Andrew Sancton (eds), *City Politics in Canada* (Toronto: University of Toronto Press, 1983), 170–1.

57 John J. Bergen, 'Canada: Private Schools,' in Walford (ed.), *Private Schools in Ten Countries*, 98; and Norman Henchey and Donald Burgess, *Between Past and Future: Quebec Education in Transition* (Calgary: Detselig Enterprises, 1987), 69. In British Columbia, private schools that offer programs consistent with the provincial curriculum, employ certified teachers, and maintain adequate educational facilities are eligible for grants per student equal to 50 per cent of the cost per student in the public school district in which they are located (the grant is cut to 35 per cent where costs per student for the private school exceed those of their local public school district). Similarly, the grant per student for qualified independent schools is 50 per cent of net operating costs per student in public schools in Manitoba and 60 per cent of the grant for basic instruction in public schools in Alberta. Private schools in Quebec are eligible for a base allocation per student (in 2002–3 equal to $2,421 at the primary level and $3,331 at the secondary level) as well as grants for maintenance ($88 per primary student and $131 per secondary student in 2002–3), supplementary allocations for specific programs, and various non-recurring adjustment grants. In Saskatchewan, eight private schools are classified as 'historical high schools,' four of which are fully funded while the other four get 40 per cent of the provincial grant. In addition, four denominational independent schools have negotiated the status of 'associate school' with a public school division, which results in full funding, and three independent schools for students with special needs also are funded by the province. Overall, 17.9 per cent of the revenues of private elementary and secondary schools came from governments in 1971–2, 30.8 per cent in 1981–2, and 27.2 per cent in 1991–2. Claudio Pagliarello, 'Private Elementary and Secondary Schools,' *Education Quarterly Review* 1 (Spring 1994): 46.

58 In sharp contrast to Ontario, in Saskatchewan the demand for full funding

of separate secondary schools encountered little resistance. In 1964, following a brief campaign by a coalition of Catholic school supporters (and with a provincial election on the horizon), an NDP government bill to recognize separate secondary schools as eligible for full provincial funding was approved unanimously by the legislative assembly.

59 Ontario, Legislative Assembly, Standing Committee on Social Development, *Hansard: Official Report of the Debates*, 20 September 1985, S1351–2.

60 Ontario, Commission on Private Schools in Ontario, *Report of the Commission on Private Schools in Ontario* (Toronto: Queen's Printer, 1985).

61 This case resulted from a legal action launched in May 1992 by five Jewish families and four Christian families, with support from the Canadian Jewish Congress, the Ontario Alliance for Christian Schools, and the Ontario Federation of Independent Schools, claiming state aid for private denominational schools. The trial court agreed that the plaintiffs' Charter rights to freedom of worship and equal protection of the law were being infringed, but their claim for funding private denominational schools was dismissed on the grounds that existing legislation fell within the 'reasonable limits' acceptable in a democratic society, as provided under section 1 of the Charter. In July 1994 the Ontario Court of Appeal not only unanimously dismissed the appeal but also ruled that the Ontario government's policy did not constitute an infringement of the appellants' Charter rights. When the appeal was also dismissed by the Supreme Court of Canada in November 1996, the majority decision, written by Mr Justice Frank Iacobucci, concluded that Ontario's funding of Roman Catholic separate schools, as required under section 93 of the BNA Act, did not impose a constitutional obligation to fund other religious schools as well. Constitutional rights to public funding of religious education were limited to those specified at the time of Confederation in section 93. In her dissent, Madam Justice Claire L'Heureux-Dubé argued that 'Denial of any funding to the appellants constitutes not only a financial prejudice, but also a complete non-recognition of their children's educational needs and the children's and their parents' fundamental interest in the continuation of their faith.' She cited section 27 of the Charter on the preservation and enhancement of a multicultural heritage as supporting 'a finding that the interests at stake, the preservation and continuation of the communities in question, form interests fundamental to the purposes of the Charter' (*Globe and Mail*, 22 November 1996).

62 With regard to languages of racial and ethnic minorities other than Maori, in their 1983 report on education in New Zealand the OECD examiners pointed out that adequate provision for them would require 'a major

political initiative and commitment' (Organization for Economic Cooperation and Development, *Reviews of National Policies for Education: New Zealand* [Paris: OECD, 1983], 88). With the exception of Maori, however, the languages of linguistic minorities received no formal recognition as 'heritage' or 'community' languages prior to the development of a national languages policy, which was initiated in 1988 and culminated in the announcement of the New Zealand Curriculum Framework in 1993. *Aoteareo: Speaking for Ourselves*, a commissioned report on the issues of a national language policy that was released for discussion in June 1992, was criticized as being excessively utilitarian, 'focusing almost exclusively on economic needs' while underplaying 'the significance of the study of literature and the learning and appreciation of classical languages' and hence ignoring 'the cultural and literary dimensions of language' (Roger Peddie, 'So Why Are We Waiting? Language Policy Development in New Zealand,' in William Eggington and Helen Wren [eds], *Language Policy: Dominant English, Pluralist Challenges* [Canberra: Language Australia, 1997], 136). The section on language in the 1993 New Zealand Curriculum Framework was assessed much more favourably by Richard Benton as showing 'an openness to linguistic diversity which even a decade earlier would have been quite astonishing. Not only did it affirm the intellectual, social and cultural advantages of language study, and state that "all students benefit from learning another language from the earliest practicable age," it made provision for languages other than English and Maori, and especially for Island Languages and Polynesian languages, to be used as media of instruction.' Richard A. Benton, 'Language Policy in New Zealand: Defining the Ineffable,' in Michael Herriman and Barbara Burnaby (eds), *Language Policies in English-Dominant Countries* (Clevedon, Avon: Multilingual Matters, 1996), 75–6.

63 Accordingly, the commission recommended 'that no change be made in the present public policy relating to the granting of aid to private schools' (New Zealand, Commission on Education in New Zealand, *Report of the Commission on Education in New Zealand* [Wellington: Government Printer, 1962], 716). At the time, the largest amounts of state aid to private schools were being provided for boarding allowances (£58,992), transport of school children (£97,505), and free textbooks (£71,630).

64 Colin McGeorge, 'Private and Integrated Schools in New Zealand: Subsidizing the Illusion of Choice,' *Journal of Education Policy* 10 (May–June 1995): 260.

65 Back in office following the 1984 general election, the Labour government proceeded to reduce the salary grant to private schools from 50 per cent in

1985 to zero in 1990. As a result, after a lull from 1983 to 1988, applications of private schools for status as integrated schools again began to increase. The National government partially restored the salary grant in 1991 to 20 per cent of teachers' salaries, declining to go higher because of fiscal pressures, but this proved insufficient to stop schools from applying for integration (ibid., 267). From 249 in 1989, the number of integrated schools rose to 267 in 1993 and 319 in 1999.

66 Assimilation was the purpose of state provision for Maori education in Lieutenant-Governor George Grey's ordinance of 1847, the Native Schools acts passed in 1858 and 1867, and the provisions for Maori schools in the Native Schools Code of 1880. See, for example, Roger Openshaw, Greg Lee, and Howard Lee, *Challenging the Myths: Rethinking New Zealand's Educational History* (Palmerston North: Dunmore Press, 1993), 39, 41, 45, 47. The Native Schools Code of 1880 provided for the instruction of Maori children in reading, writing, and speaking the English language and in arithmetic, geography, and 'such culture as may fit them to become good citizens.' In drafting and implementing this code, the first inspector of Native schools, James Pope, stressed English as the most important subject of instruction, but he also conceded the use of te reo Maori as a transitional language of instruction in junior classes (J.M. Barrington, 'A Historical Review of Policies and Provisions,' in John L. Ewing and Jack Shallcrass [eds], *An Introduction to Maori Education: Selected Readings* [Wellington: New Zealand University Press, 1970], 32). Pope's successors were less conciliatory, commending teachers who ceased to use the Maori language in their classes and condoning those who punished their pupils for not speaking English in the playground.

67 This emphasis by departmental officials on the importance of teaching English in Native schools was supported by some influential Maoris. For example, Takamoana, who was one of the four Maori members elected to the new Parliament in 1877, asked the government to legislate that Maori children be taught in English only (Barrington, 'Historical Review of Policies and Provisions,' 30). Sir Apirana Ngata, who was the greatest Maori leader in the first half of the twentieth century, condoned the dominance of English in Native schools at a conference on Maori education in 1936, but three years later he reversed this stance on the grounds that English-medium Native schools were subverting Maori culture by producing Maori students who were unable to speak their own language. Ranginui J. Walker, 'Cultural Domination of Taha Maori: The Potential for Radical Transformation,' in John Codd, Richard Harker, and Roy Nash (eds), *Political Issues in New Zealand Education* (Palmerston North: Dunmore Press, 1985), 73–4.

68 Ian A. McLaren, *Education in a Small Democracy: New Zealand* (London: Routledge and Kegan Paul, 1974), 75.

69 In 1945 there were 11,000 Maori children enrolled in Native schools and 15,000 in primary schools administered by the education boards; by 1965 there were 9,000 Maori in Native schools and 46,000 in board schools (Openshaw, Lee, and Lee, *Challenging the Myths*, 69).

70 New Zealand, Department of Maori Affairs, *Report of the Department of Maori Affairs* (Wellington: Government Printer, 1960), 15, 23–4, 78.

71 Commission on Education in New Zealand, *Report*, 402.

72 Ibid., 415.

73 On the success of te kohanga reo, Kathie Irwin, who was one of the government reviewers in 1988, concluded, 'Young children are leaving kohanga speaking Maori and feeling positive about their language and culture. The Te Kohanga Reo movement has also stimulated parents and grandparents to learn, to relearn, and to speak Te Reo Maori again and to utilise Nga Tikanga Maori in daily life and work routines. It has reaffirmed the language and cultural practices of native speakers of Maori.' Kathie Irwin, 'The Politics of Kohanga Reo,' in Sue Middleton, John Codd, and Alison Jones (eds), *New Zealand Education Policy Today: Critical Perspectives* (Wellington: Allen and Unwin, 1990), 118.

74 At the 1 July 1999 school census, there were 4,855 Maori students plus 6 non-Maori students enrolled in 56 kura kaupapa Maori and 21,997 Maori students plus 3,935 non-Maori students enrolled in 396 other Maori-medium schools. Among 144,738 Maori students, 18.6 per cent were enrolled in some type of Maori-medium program as follows: immersion schools, 4,796; bilingual schools, 7,181; immersion classes, 4,251; and bilingual classes, 10,624. As for students learning languages at the secondary level (year 9 and over), there were 20,189 enrolled in te reo Maori compared to 23,705 enrolled in French, 22,155 in Japanese, 7,762 in German, 3,318 in Spanish, 2,276 in Latin, and 1,021 in Chinese.

75 Great Britain, House of Commons, *Parliamentary Debates (Hansard)*, fifth series, vol. 685, col. 442 (27 November 1963).

76 Throughout this section on racial and ethnic minorities in British education, I rely substantially on Robert Jeffcoate, *Ethnic Minorities and Education* (London: Harper and Row, 1984); David L. Kirp, *Doing Good by Doing Little: Race and Schooling in Britain* (Berkeley: University of California Press, 1979); Sally Tomlinson, *Ethnic Minorities in British Schools: A Review of the Literature, 1960–82* (London: Heinemann Educational Books, 1983); and Gajendra K. Verma (ed.), *Education for All: A Landmark in Pluralism* (London: Falmer Press, 1989).

77 Great Britain, Home Office, *Second Report by the Commonwealth Immigrants Advisory Committee* (London: Her Majesty's Stationery Office, 1964), 10.

78 For the Central Advisory Council's recommendations for educational priority areas (EPAs) see Great Britain, Department of Education and Science, *Children and Their Primary Schools: A Report of the Central Advisory Council for Education (England)*, vol. 1 (London: Her Majesty's Stationery Office, 1967), 50–68; on the education of immigrant children, see ibid., 69–74. For a description and assessment of the EPA initiative, see George Smith, 'Whatever Happened to Educational Policy Areas?' *Oxford Review of Education* 13, no. 1 (1987): 23–38; and also Harold Silver and Pamela Silver, *An Educational War on Poverty: American and British Policy-Making 1960–1980* (Cambridge: Cambridge University Press, 1991), 287–317.

79 In a section titled 'Spreading the Children,' local education authorities were given guidelines for dispersal: 'Experience suggests ... that, apart from unusual difficulties (such as a high proportion of non-English-speakers), up to a fifth of immigrant children in any group fit in with reasonable ease, but that, if the proportion goes over about one third either in the school as a whole or in any one class, serious strains arise. It is therefore desirable that the catchment areas of schools should, wherever possible, be arranged to avoid undue concentrations of immigrant children. Where this proves impracticable simply because the school serves an area which is occupied largely by immigrants, every effort should be made to disperse the immigrant children round a greater number of schools and to meet such problems of transport as may arise.' Great Britain, Department of Education and Science, *The Education of Immigrants*, Circular 7/65 (London: Her Majesty's Stationery Office, 1965), 4–5.

80 Great Britain, Department of Education and Science, *The Education of Immigrants*, Education Survey 13 (London: Her Majesty's Stationery Office, 1971), 18.

81 In its 1971 statement, the Department of Education and Science concluded that the increase of immigrant children in school since 1965 had made dispersal less feasible. Where immigrant children were well over 20 per cent of total enrolment, and a number of schools had much higher percentages, it was impractical for local education authorities to think in terms of dispersing children so that there were not more than one-third in any school. There were serious disadvantages to dispersal, including potential infringement of the Race Relations Act and the high costs of busing. Dispersal did deliberately aim to avoid situations in which immigrant children were educated very largely in an environment of fellow immigrants, however, and the unanswered question was whether dispersal would have a better

influence on future community relations. Observing that 'comments in these paragraphs modify significantly the Department's views on dispersal in Circular 7/65,' the department then left it 'for each local education authority to decide what its policy for the education of immigrant children should be' (ibid., 19). When the Select Committee on Race Relations and Immigration recommended in 1973 that dispersal be phased out, the Department of Education and Science replied that this was a matter for the LEAs to decide but that no doubt they would take the Select Committee's views into account. See Great Britain, House of Commons, Select Committee on Race Relations and Immigration, *Education: Volume 1, Report* (London: Her Majesty's Stationery Office, 1973) and Great Britain, Department of Education and Science, *Educational Disadvantage and the Educational Needs of Immigrants: Observations on the Report on Education of the Select Committee on Race Relations and Immigration* (London: Her Majesty's Stationery Office, 1974). Although no longer officially recommended by the Department of Education and Science, dispersal continued to be used as an official policy instrument in a few local educational authorities, notably Bradford and Ealing. Despite praise from independent investigators for their educational programs for immigrant children, the local educational authorities of Bradford and Ealing encountered increasing political controversy over their school busing policies. In 1976 the Race Relations Board filed a lawsuit against Ealing, but the issue was settled out of court by a Conservative council, elected in 1978, which undertook a building program in Southall neighbourhoods to make busing unnecessary (Kirp, *Doing Good by Doing Little*, 85–99).

82 Department of Education and Science, *The Education of Immigrants*, 4–5.
83 Department of Education and Science, *Educational Disadvantage and the Educational Needs of Immigrants*, 2.
84 In 1980 the Conservative government closed the Centre for Information and Advice on Educational Disadvantage as part of a round of program cuts. In making the announcement, the secretary of state for education and science (Mark Carlisle) explained that the centre had 'not wholly fulfilled the expectations raised at its foundation and continued grant aid would not provide value for money in meeting the needs of the educationally disadvantaged.' Great Britain, House of Commons, *Parliamentary Debates (Hansard)*, fifth series, vol. 973, col. 729 (15 November 1979).
85 Tomlinson, *Ethnic Minorities in British Schools*, 23.
86 Alan Little and Richard Willey, *Multi-ethnic Education: The Way Forward*, Schools Council Pamphlet 18 (London: Schools Council, 1981), 28.
87 The Rampton committee was specifically directed to give priority to the

education of West Indian children, and its interim report issued in June 1981 concluded that as a group they were underachieving in relation to their peers. Anthony Rampton was asked to resign by the Conservative secretary of state for education and science, Mark Carlisle, following criticism by some committee members of his failure to control the committee and take effective decisions. Apparently, the government also had expected a short interim report rather than the 100 pages it got (*Times Educational Supplement*, 22 May 1981). Following the appointment of Lord Swann as chair, the committee turned its attention to broader issues of majority–minority relations.

88 According to the Swann committee, in a democratic pluralist society the ethnic majority 'cannot expect to remain untouched and unchanged by the presence of ethnic minority groups.' Nor can ethnic-minority communities preserve their cultures in their entirety; however, they should be free to maintain those parts of their cultures essential to their sense of ethnic identity without fear of prejudice or persecution by other groups. A truly pluralist society, 'both socially cohesive and culturally diverse,' would offer an 'enrichment of experience of all those within it.' Great Britain, Committee of Inquiry into the Education of Children from Ethnic Minority Groups, *Education for All: Report of the Committee of Inquiry into the Education of Children from Ethnic Minority Groups* (London: Her Majesty's Stationery Office, 1985), 5–6.

89 Ibid., 315; emphasis in the original.

90 Ibid., 317, 322.

91 Great Britain, Secretary of State for Education and Science and Secretary of State for Wales, *Better Schools* (London: Her Majesty's Stationery Office 1985), 61.

92 According to Sally Tomlinson and Maurice Craft, 'The national and local policy objectives which previously embodied a concern for equal opportunities – raising the achievement levels of ethnic minorities, for example – and for a curriculum which offered new knowledge about minorities and redefined the concept of "being British," disappeared abruptly. A broad mainstream drive to raise standards in education and training by introducing market competition between schools, developing a tightly regulated National Curriculum with an associated testing programme and reducing the influence of Local Education Authorities, has been accompanied by a rejection of the rhetoric of equal opportunities' (Sally Tomlinson and Maurice Craft, 'Education for All in the 1990s,' in Sally Tomlinson and Maurice Craft [eds], *Ethnic Relations and Schooling: Policy and Practice in the 1990s* [London: Athlone, 1995], 3–4). Tomlinson and Craft point out that

the first chief executive of the National Curriculum Council (NCC) (Duncan Graham) has documented specific ministerial instructions to remove references to multicultural education from the national curriculum and that the report of a task force set up by the NCC in 1989 to develop proposals for multicultural education in the national curriculum was never published, nor its recommendations implemented (ibid., 5). The list of nineteen eligible foreign languages under the national curriculum included the eight official languages of the European Union plus Arabic, Bengali, Gujerati, Hindi, Japanese, Mandarin or Cantonese Chinese, Modern Hebrew, Punjabi, Russian, Turkish, and Urdu. 'In practice, the languages most widely taught remain French, German and Spanish, and the numbers of pupils taking foreign language examinations in their home language remain relatively insignificant' (Linda Thompson, Michael Fleming, and Michael Byram, 'Languages and Language Policy in Britain,' in Eggington and Wren [eds], *Language Policy*, 118). According to Naz Rassool, 'The debate about second language teaching that had prevailed in mainstream education since the early 1970s came to a grinding halt with the 1988 Education Reform Act and the introduction of the National Curriculum in England and Wales.' Naz Rassool, 'Language, Cultural Pluralism and the Silencing of Minority Discourses in England and Wales,' *Journal of Education Policy* 10 (May–June 1995): 287.

93 In reorganizing the provisions of primary and secondary education in England and Wales, the Education Act of 1944 retained the historical distinction between voluntary schools and state schools. In addition to funding and managing state (now 'county') schools, local education authorities would pay the full costs of controlled voluntary schools and, in return, appoint two-thirds of their managers or governors. The managers of primary aided and special agreement schools and the governors of secondary aided and special agreement schools would continue to be two-thirds foundation members and one-third appointed by the LEAs. As under the 1902 act, LEAs would continue to pay operating costs, and voluntary school managers and governors would be responsible for the capital costs of building and exterior repair of their schools, with an added grant from the Ministry of Education to cover one-half of such costs. In 1959 the Ministry of Education increased its grant towards the capital costs of aided and special agreement schools to 75 per cent, and in 1967 to 80 per cent. Special agreement schools originated in the Education Act of 1936. LEAs were authorized to make grants of 50 to 75 per cent of the cost of building voluntary schools, necessary because of the projected raising of the school-leaving age in 1939. The assistance was given only for accommodation for

senior students and for proposals submitted within three years of the act. The extension of provisions for special agreements was made in the 1944 act as a concession to Roman Catholic schools. On the treatment of religion in planning for educational reconstruction during the Second World War, see P.H.J.H. Gosden, *Education in the Second World War: A Study in Policy and Administration* (London: Methuen, 1976), 271–91, 318–21, 324–6.

94 Great Britain, Schools Council, Religious Education Committee, *A Groundplan for the Study of Religion*, Schools Council Occasional Bulletin from the Subject Committees (London: Schools Council, 1977), 7. According to the 1945 Agreed Syllabus in Surrey, for example, 'The aim of the syllabus is to secure that children attending the schools of the County ... may gain knowledge of the common Christian faith held by their fathers for nearly 2000 years; may seek for themselves in Christianity principles which give a purpose to life and a guide to all its problems, and may find inspiration, power and courage to work for their own welfare, for that of their fellow creatures and for the growth of God's Kingdom.' Quoted in Derek Bastide, *Religious Education 5–12* (London: Falmer Press, 1987), 8.

95 The Central Advisory Council for Education (England), for example, in its 1965 survey of parents, found that 80 per cent approved the existing arrangements for giving religious instruction in school and wanted daily acts of worship to continue (Department of Education and Science, *Children and Their Primary Schools*, 203). None the less, the Plowden committee said, 'We hope that heads of schools and administrators will be sensitive to the needs of minority groups, both for worship and for religious education. The need is especially evident when numbers of immigrant children of other than Christian religion are educated in schools hitherto largely Christian' (ibid., 207).

96 Church of England Commission on Religious Education in Schools, *The Fourth R*; quoted in Bastide, *Religious Education 5–12*, 9.

97 John Hull, 'Introduction: New Directions in Religious Education,' in John Hull (ed.), *New Directions in Religious Education* (Barcombe, Lewes, Sussex: Falmer Press, 1982), xiv.

98 For a helpful discussion of the differences between 'confessional' and 'phenomenological' models of religious education, see Nicola Slee, 'Conflict and Reconciliation between Competing Models of Religious Education: Some Reflections on the British Scene,' *British Journal of Religious Education* 11 (Summer 1989): 127–8.

99 Committee of Inquiry into the Education of Children from Ethnic Minority Groups, *Education for All*, 518–19, 772–3; emphasis in the original.

100 For an account of the issue of religious education during and following the passage of the Education Reform Bill, see Priscilla Chadwick, *Shifting Alliances: Church and State in English Education* (London: Cassell, 1997), 88–102; and also John McLeod, 'Church and State: The Religious Settlement in the 1988 Education Reform Act,' in Robert Morris (ed.), *Central and Local Control of Education after the Education Reform Act 1988* (Harlow, Essex: Longman, 1990), 38–58. In an editorial on the provisions for religious education in the Education Reform Act, John Hull referred to 'the unique British experience of multi-faith dialogue in the classroom' that had developed over the past quarter-century and concluded: 'It is clear, however, that these amendments, which thrust Christianity into a position of embarrassing prominence, are contrary to the British tradition, are not easily compatible with educational principles, are difficult to defend theologically, and seem unlikely to promote a society in which sympathetic acceptance and mutual understanding mark the relations between different religions and communities.' John M. Hull, 'Editorial: Religious Education in the Education Reform Bill,' *British Journal of Religious Education* 11 (Autumn 1988): 2.

101 From 1993 to 1997, around forty new syllabuses were adopted, and an official assessment found that the model agreed syllabuses were having a positive effect on quality and standards of religious education. Great Britain, Office for Standards in Education, *The Impact of New Agreed Syllabuses on the Teaching and Learning of Religious Education: A Report from the Office of Her Majesty's Chief Inspector of Schools* (London: Her Majesty's Stationery Office, 1997), 1–2, 45.

102 See Chadwick, *Shifting Alliances*, 108–11. Following the election of the Labour government, applications for voluntary-aided status were more favourably received by the Department for Education and Training. Between June 1997 and October 2000, approval was granted for one Greek Orthodox, five Jewish, three Muslim, one Seventh Day Adventist, and two Sikh voluntary aided schools.

103 Alex Rodger, 'Religious Education,' in T.G.K. Bryce and W.M. Humes (eds), *Scottish Education* (Edinburgh: University of Edinburgh Press, 1999), 551.

104 Great Britain, Scottish Education Department, *Moral and Religious Education in Scottish Schools*, Report of a Committee Appointed by the Secretary of State for Scotland (Edinburgh: Her Majesty's Stationery Office, 1972), 68–9.

105 Great Britain, Scottish Education Department, Consultative Committee on

the Curriculum, Scottish Central Committee on Religious Education, *Bulletin 1: A Curricular Approach to Religious Education* (Edinburgh: Her Majesty's Stationery Office, 1978), 5.

106 See Great Britain, Scottish Office Education Department, *Curriculum and Assessment in Scotland: National Guidelines: Religious and Moral Education 5–14* (Edinburgh: Scottish Office Education Department, 1992). The 1992 Scottish Office Education Department (SOED) guidelines were rejected by the Scottish Catholic Education Commission (SCEC), but joint SOED/SCEC guidelines were agreed in 1994 and reflected the structure of the guidelines for non-denominational schools with reduced emphasis on other world religions. Nevertheless, the inclusion of the study of other faiths represented a significant development in Catholic primary religious education (James C. Conroy, 'Religious and Moral Education,' in Bryce and Humes [eds], *Scottish Education*, 392). The change in title of the guidelines agreed by the SOED and the SCEC, *Religious Education 5–14: Roman Catholic Schools* (Edinburgh: Scottish Office Education Department, 1994), resulted from the Catholic position that moral life could not be separated from religious beliefs.

107 In its 1944 white paper on educational reconstruction, the government of Northern Ireland proposed that, for maintained (formerly Class II) schools, the local education authority would appoint one-third of their management committees and pay the full cost of their maintenance. Maintenance grants to voluntary (formerly Class III) schools and capital grants to both maintained and voluntary schools would be increased from 50 to 65 per cent of their costs. The white paper also proposed to adopt the English practice of obligatory non-denominational religious instruction and daily religious observances, with conscience clauses for both pupils and teachers, and thus bring the Northern Ireland Education Act into line with the 1920 constitution. In the controversy that followed, the Protestant lobby defended the principle of non-denominationalism while demanding that in practice state schools be Protestant in staffing and curriculum. The Roman Catholic bishops defended the principle of denominational education and attacked the white paper's attempt to entice Catholic schools into accepting maintained status. In the final outcome, the Northern Ireland government insisted on preserving a conscience clause that protected teachers against being required to conduct or attend collective worship or give religious instruction, but dropped its attempt to enforce the constitutional provision for non-denominational religious instruction and observances in state schools.

108 Margaret B. Sutherland, 'Progress and Problems in Education in Northern Ireland,' *British Journal of Educational Studies* 30 (February 1982): 145.

109 Dominic Murray has concluded that the effect of the 1968 amendment to
the Northern Ireland Education Act on primary schools was almost total
polarization based on religion. Protestant children attended county
schools and Roman Catholic children went to maintained schools. Despite
claims that county schools were non-denominational and open to all,
'enough evidence exists to demonstrate that controlled schools are *de facto*
Protestant institutions, in composition at least' and 'reflect the cultural
aspirations of Protestant children.' Maintained primary schools by contrast
were overtly and self-avowedly Roman Catholic. See Dominic Murray,
Worlds Apart: Segregated Schools in Northern Ireland (Belfast: Appletree Press,
1985), 21–3. More recently, Alex McEwen has observed that, despite major
changes resulting from the national curriculum, the denominational
difference endures. 'Curricular differences between the two systems have
now disappeared with the common Northern Ireland Curriculum and the
fact that Catholic primary and non-selective schools now receive 100 per
cent funding for capital and recurrent costs means that they are on equal
financial footing. The significance of the latter lies in the fact that seventy
years on from partition, the voluntary principle, as applied to the Catholic
sector, has been formally and fully incorporated within Northern Ireland's
state funded system of schooling. The main difference now would appear
to be one of ethos: that in the Catholic sector teaching in all subjects is
organised within a comprehensive religious atmosphere and that the state
schools are *de jure* non-denominational but *de facto* Protestant and Unionist
in outlook.' Alex McEwen, *Public Policy in a Divided Society: Schooling, Culture
and Identity in Northern Ireland* (Aldershot: Ashgate, 1999), 121.
110 Seamus Dunn, 'A Historical Context in Education and Church-State Relations in Northern Ireland,' in Robert Osborne, Robert Cormack, and
Anthony Gallagher (eds), *After the Reform: Education and Policy in Northern
Ireland* (Aldershot: Avebury, 1993), 26.
111 In 1998–9 there were twenty-six integrated primary schools (0.3 per cent
of the total) enrolling 4,444 pupils (2.4 per cent of the total) and seventeen secondary schools (7.2 per cent of the total) enrolling 6,164 pupils
(4.1 per cent of the total). The compulsory curriculum specified in the
Education Reform (Northern Ireland) Order 1989 did include two
themes, 'Education for Mutual Understanding' (EMU) and 'Cultural
Heritage,' that aimed to promote acceptance of Northern Ireland as a
pluralist society in county and voluntary schools. As with integrated
schools, implementation of these provisions has been quite limited. Seamus Dean, for example, has argued that the thrust of recent educational reforms in Northern Ireland ('These relate to a more managerial,
measurable and accountable system, including a national curriculum

and attempts to improve efficiency and raise standards') has 'meant that progress in establishing EMU as an integral part of the new statutory curriculum has been hindered by a combination of features – exclusion from formal assessment, integration into existing subjects and optional cross community contact. In addition, some teachers view EMU with suspicion, and those with strong political or religious views perceive it as politically motivated. The result has been that in many schools the subject has limited priority and relatively low status.' Seamus Dean, 'Northern Ireland: Education in a Divided Society,' in David Phillips (ed.), *The Education Systems of the United Kingdom* (Oxford: Symposium Books, 2000), 91–2.

112 English was also the language of instruction in Scotland. In contrast with the close connection between the Welsh language and national identity in Wales, however, Gaelic was not the national language of Scotland after the Middle Ages, and during the nineteenth and twentieth centuries it was steadily reduced as a language of use to the Highlands and Western Isles. The 1918 education act did authorize the use of Gaelic as the language of instruction in Gaelic-speaking areas for the first two (infant) classes of elementary school, and individual teachers continued to use Gaelic as the language of instruction in the Gaelic-speaking regions of the Highlands and Western Isles, although such provision was sporadic and outside the official curriculum (Catherine M. Dunn and A.G. Boyd Robertson, 'Gaelic in Education,' in William Gillies [ed.], *Gaelic and Scotland: Alba Agus a' Ghàidhlig* [Edinburgh: Edinburgh University Press, 1989], 440). With the formation of the Western Isles Regional Council in 1975, a pilot project of bilingual primary schools was initiated with funding by the Scottish Education Department, the first time that a Scottish education authority had used Gaelic officially as a medium for teaching and learning along with English (Boyd Robertson, 'Gaelic Education,' in Bryce and Humes [eds], *Scottish Education*, 245). In 1978 the Highland Regional Council started a similar bilingual project for its primary school on the Isle of Skye, and Gaelic-medium units were also opened in urban primary schools where the programs were more oriented to immersion for pupils whose home language was English, not Gaelic. By 1997–8 there were fifty-five such Gaelic-medium units with 1,736 pupils enrolled. Gaelic instruction was more limited at the secondary level. Bilingual projects were initiated in two Western Isles secondary schools in 1983, and Gaelic-medium units were established in secondary schools in Glasgow, Inverness, and Portree, thus providing continuity for the three largest Gaelic-medium primary units. None the less, at the end of the 1990s there was still no designated Gaelic-medium school anywhere in Scotland, and more than 90 per cent

of secondary pupils had no opportunity to learn Gaelic at their local school (ibid., 248).

113 W.R. Jones, *Bilingualism in Welsh Education* (Cardiff: University of Wales Press, 1966), 60.

114 Great Britain, Department of Education and Science, Central Advisory Council for Education (Wales), *Primary Education in Wales* (London: Her Majesty's Stationery Office, 1967), 213.

115 The Central Advisory Council (Wales) proposed five types of schools: traditional Welsh primary schools (Ysgolion Cynradd) in Welsh-speaking areas, in which Welsh was the language of instruction and English was taught as the second language; bilingual schools (Ysgolion Cymraeg) in English-speaking areas, in which the early years were Welsh immersion with English introduced in later years; English minority-language schools in Welsh-speaking areas, where numbers warranted, in which the basic medium of instruction would be English with provision for instruction in Welsh as a second language; experimental bilingual schools in English-speaking and mixed-language areas, in which the basic medium of instruction was initially English with increasing provision for Welsh as a medium of instruction until there was parity between the two languages; and 'ordinary primary schools,' in which English was the language of instruction and Welsh the second language (ibid., 240–6, 251–2).

116 See Phillip Rawkins, *The Implementation of Language Policy in the Schools of Wales*, Studies in Public Policy Number 40 (Glasgow: University of Strathclyde Centre for the Study of Public Policy, 1979), 75–84; and Colin Baker, *Aspects of Bilingualism in Wales* (Clevedon, Avon: Multilingual Matters, 1985), 54–61.

117 See Great Britain, Welsh Office, *Welsh in the National Curriculum* (Cardiff: Her Majesty's Stationery Office, 1990).

118 See National Assembly for Wales, *Statistics of Education and Training in Wales: Schools 1999* (Cardiff: Government Statistical Service, 1999).

119 A 'procedural republic' is a neutral state, a state of individuals, which has no national collective goals apart from the personal freedom, physical security, and social welfare of its individual citizens. See Michael Sandel, 'The Procedural Republic and the Unencumbered Self,' *Political Theory* 12 (1984): 81–96; and also Michael Walzer, 'Comment,' in Gutmann (ed.), *Multiculturalism and 'The Politics of Recognition,'* 99. The term 'procedural liberalism' is also used by Charles Taylor, 'The Politics of Recognition,' in ibid., 56–61.

120 Only eighteen school districts in these states acted under court order (Reed Sarratt, *The Ordeal of Desegregation: The First Decade* [New York:

Harper and Row, 1966], 350–1). In addition, ten years after *Brown* three school districts in Kentucky had not desegregated, nine in Missouri, and forty-four in Oklahoma. As for the five school boards involved directly in *Brown*, three, including the Board of Education of Topeka, Kansas, desegregated their schools immediately following the decision of the Supreme Court. In the case of the Topeka board, it had voted to end its policy of segregated schools in September 1953, but its plan for desegregation was subject to review and approval by the federal district court. See Mary L. Dudziak, 'The Limits of Good Faith: Desegregation in Topeka, Kansas, 1950–1956,' in Paul Finkelman (ed.), *Race, Law, and American History 1700–1990: The African-American Experience*, vol. 7, *The Struggle for Equal Education* (New York: Garland Publishing, 1992), 351–91.

121 Gary Orfield, *The Reconstruction of Southern Education: The Schools and the 1964 Civil Rights Act* (New York: John Wiley, 1969), 2–3.

122 Ibid., 328–39. The new enforcement strategy was given a helpful push by the U.S. Supreme Court. In May 1968 the court ruled against non-productive 'freedom of choice' plans in *Green* v. *County School Board of New Kent County*. The next year, in *Alexander* v. *Holmes County (Mississippi) Board of Education*, the court decided that 'continued operation of racially segregated schools under the standard of "all deliberate speed" is no longer constitutionally permissible.'

123 In 1968, with 81 per cent of black students attending schools with more than 50 per cent minority enrolment and 78 per cent of them enrolled in schools with more than 90 per cent minority enrolment, the South still had the highest rates of racial segregation in the United States. By 1972, 55 per cent of black students in the South were going to schools with more than 50 per cent minority enrolment and 25 per cent went to schools with more than 90 per cent minority enrolment, in both cases the lowest regional rates of racial segregation. Gary Orfield, *Public School Desegregation in the United States, 1968–1980* (Washington, D.C.: Joint Center for Political Studies, 1983), 4.

124 Gary Orfield, 'Race and the Liberal Agenda: The Loss of the Integrationist Dream, 1965–1974,' in Margaret Weir, Ann Shola Orloff, and Theda Skocpol (eds), *The Politics of Social Policy in the United States* (Princeton: Princeton University Press, 1988), 345.

125 In 1965, for example, HEW officials decided that allegations of violations of the Civil Rights Act were sufficiently serious to withhold federal aid from Chicago schools until an investigation could be completed and a desegregation plan prepared. Following Mayor Richard Daley's protest to President Johnson, the funds were restored after five days, and shortly

thereafter there was a new commissioner in the Office of Education. No other significant enforcement of desegregation requirements of the Civil Rights Act was attempted in any big city outside the South until 1977, when an attempt to enforce desegregation in Kansas City by withholding federal ESEA aid led to an act of Congress outlawing this instrument of enforcement. See Gary Orfield, *Must We Bus? Segregated Schools and National Policy* (Washington, D.C.: Brookings Institution, 1978), 279–318.

126 In this case, the court concluded that the intent of Denver school authorities to create a dual school system was evident in such actions as manipulating school attendance zones and selecting school sites that maximized racial segregation.

127 In this case, the court was presented with a violation of the rights of black children by the Detroit city school district for which the remedy of desegregation required joint action by city and suburban school districts. In a five-to-four decision, the four justices appointed by President Nixon – Chief Justice Warren Burger and Justices Harry Blackmun, Lewis Powell, and William Rehnquist – all voted against ordering suburban school districts to participate in desegregating central city schools. Breaching the boundaries of local governments was permissible only where suburban school districts were accomplices with central city districts in unconstitutional segregation policies or practices.

128 Orfield, *Must We Bus?*, 76, 416–17. Orfield concludes, that 'In practice, the *Milliken* approach institutionalizes a new kind of regional legalized segregation. In the past, because federal courts deferred to state law, a black student who had the misfortune to be born in one of the seventeen states of the southern and border regions had a right to attend only a segregated black school. Today, for different reasons, urban black and Hispanic children in the industrial belt from Connecticut to Illinois must often attend a segregated school, even if a history of de jure segregation has been proved, because they happen to live in a region where the school district lines define segregated residential areas.'

129 Christine H. Rossell, *The Carrot or the Stick for School Desegregation Policy: Magnet Schools or Forced Busing* (Philadelphia: Temple University Press, 1990), 25.

130 Jeffrey A. Raffel, *Historical Dictionary of School Segregation and Desegregation: The American Experience* (Westport, Conn.: Greenwood Press, 1998), 149.

131 After 1981 there were no mandatory reassignment plans implemented in the North and only two in the South (Rossell, *The Carrot or the Stick for School Desegregation Policy*, xiii). By 1981–2 there were 1,019 magnet schools in 138 school districts; a decade later there were 2,433 magnet schools

enrolling 1.2 million students, three times the enrolment in magnet schools a decade earlier (Raffel, *Historical Dictionary of School Segregation and Desegregation*, 150).

132 David J. Armor, *Forced Justice: School Desegregation and the Law* (New York: Oxford University Press, 1995), 168. See also Lauri Steel, Roger E. Levine, Christine H. Rossell, and David J. Armor, *Magnet Schools and Issues of Desegregation, Quality, and Choice* (Palo Alto: American Institute for Research, 1993). Among the school districts in this survey, 13 per cent had a current desegregation plan, 5 per cent had a former plan, and 83 per cent never had a plan. Among very large school districts, however, 60 per cent had a current desegregation plan, 10 per cent had a former plan, and 30 per cent never had a plan.

133 Gary Orfield, 'Turning Back to Segregation,' in Gary Orfield and Susan E. Eaton (eds), *Dismantling Desegregation: The Quiet Reversal of Brown v. Board of Education* (New York: New Press, 1996), 1–2. The three decisions of the United States Supreme Court to which Orfield is referring are *Dowell* v. *Board of Education of Oklahoma City* (1991), *Freeman* v. *Pitts* (1992), and *Missouri* v. *Jenkins* (1995). See also the evidence presented in Gary Orfield and John T. Yun, 'Resegregation in American Schools,' Civil Rights Project, Harvard University, 1999 (*http://www.harvard.edu/civilrights/publications*).

134 Orfield, 'Turning Back to Segregation,' 3; Raffel, *Historical Dictionary of School Segregation and Desegregation*, 24–6; and Armor, *Forced Justice*, 52–3.

135 In the case of *Freeman* v. *Pitts*, the court ruled that 'Where resegregation is a product not of state action but of private choices, it does not have constitutional implications' (quoted in Raffel, *Historical Dictionary of School Segregation and Desegregation*, 110).

136 Gary Orfield, 'Toward an Integrated Future: New Directions for Courts, Educators, Civil Rights Groups, Policymakers, and Scholars,' in Orfield and Eaton (eds), *Dismantling Desegregation*, 331.

137 Historically, the education of Hispanic minorities in the United States was variously marked by inequality, discrimination, and assimilation. On the history of public education for Hispanic minorities in the United States, see Kenneth J. Meier and Joseph Stewart, Jr, *The Politics of Hispanic Education* (Albany: State University of New York Press, 1991), ch. 3.

138 Quoted in ibid., 69.

139 Orfield, *Must We Bus?*, 206.

140 The Bilingual Education Act was introduced by Texas Senator Ralph Yarborough, who saw it as a means to provide equality of educational opportunity for Mexican-American children. Before its final passage, the

bill was expanded to cover all children whose ability to speak English was deficient. See James Crawford, *Hold Your Tongue: Bilingualism and the Politics of 'English Only'* (Reading, Mass.: Addison-Wesley Publishing, 1992), 75–6; and also James Crawford, *Bilingual Education: History, Politics, Theory, and Practice* (Trenton, N.J.: Crane Publishing, 1989), 31–49.

141 The legislative intent of the act was first clarified by a Congressional amendment in 1974 that directed school districts to give instruction in the native language only 'to the extent necessary to allow a child to progress effectively through the educational system' and then made explicit by a further amendment of the act in 1978 that the other language be used in bilingual programs only 'to the extent necessary to allow a child to achieve competence in the English language.' See Crawford, *Bilingual Education*, 37–41; and also Ronald Schmidt, Sr, *Language Policy and Identity Politics in the United States* (Philadelphia: Temple University Press, 2000), 14.

142 The case of *Lau* v. *Nichols* involved Chinese students in San Francisco who could not understand the language of instruction and hence were failing in school. The U.S. Supreme Court held that, under Title VI of the Civil Rights Act, the Chinese-speaking children were entitled to compensatory help in learning English that would enable them to participate equally in the school program. As Thomas Ricento has observed, 'It is important to note that the basis of the court's ruling was not that the children represented in the case had a right to receive education wholly, or in part, in their native language; rather, it was because of the children's deficiency in English that they had been prevented from meaningful participation in the educational programme offered by a school district.' Thomas Ricento, 'Language Policy in the United States,' in Herriman and Burnaby (eds), *Language Policies in English-Dominant Countries*, 138.

143 Shortly after taking office in 1981, President Ronald Reagan asserted that 'it is absolutely wrong and against American concepts to have a bilingual education program that is now openly, admittedly dedicated to preserving their native language and never getting them adequate in English so they can go into the job market and participate' (quoted in Crawford, *Bilingual Education*, 43). The Reagan administration also cut federal spending on bilingual education from $169.5 million in 1980 to $119.6 million in 1986 and $159.7 million in 1988 and aggressively attacked the privileged status of bilingual education as the preferred approach to dealing with English-language deficiencies of minority students.

144 Federal spending for bilingual education was $188.9 million in 1990–1 rising to $198.3 million two years later, fell to $124.8 million in 1993–4, rose to $225 million in 1995–6, was cut to $184.5 million in 1996–7, was

restored to $225 million in 1997–8, and increased to $496.4 million in 1999–2000.
145 Ricento, 'Language Policy in the United States,' 146.
146 Crawford, *Hold Your Tongue*, 190–1.
147 In California, 61 per cent voted in favour of Proposition 227 and 39 per cent against it. For a post mortem on the Proposition 227 campaign, see James Crawford, *At War with Diversity: US Language Policy in an Age of Anxiety* (Clevedon, Avon: Multilingual Matters, 2000), 104–27. In the November 2000 referendum in Arizona, Proposition 203 was approved by a margin of 63 to 37 per cent (*Education Week*, 15 November 2000).
148 Thomas Ricento, 'National Language Policy in the United States,' in Thomas Ricento and Barbara Burnaby (eds), *Language and Politics in the United States and Canada: Myths and Realities* (Mahwah, N.J.: Lawrence Erlbaum Associates, 1998), 98. Ricento cites four 'deep values' that are incompatible with policies of bilingual education: Americans believe (1) in a common national experience that includes speaking English; (2) that the national unity and cultural integrity of the United States would be dangerously threatened by cultural, including linguistic, pluralism; (3) that language and culture belong to the private, not the public, domain, and government should intrude only when the dominant language and culture require protection; and (4) that minority languages and ethnic groups should get no special protection through public policy in order to ensure their continued existence (ibid., 89–91).
149 Orfield and Yun, 'Resegregation in American Schools,' Table 9.
150 In response to a survey made by the National Education Association (NEA) in 1946, only eight state superintendents replied that Bible reading was not permitted in their states, and even this probably underestimated the extent of non-denominational religious observances (Leo Pfeffer, *Church, State, and Freedom* [rev. ed.; Boston: Beacon Press, 1967], 445). For example, New York was listed in the survey as not permitting Bible reading although a by-law of the New York City Board of Education provided that 'the regular assemblies of all schools shall be opened by reading to the pupils a portion of the Bible without comment.' The NEA survey found that twenty-four states had permissive legislation and twelve states had statutory requirements for Bible reading. State laws usually did not specify which version of the Bible was to be used, but almost invariably it was the Protestant King James version.
151 For a summary of these cases, see Donald E. Bales, *The Bible, Religion and the Public Schools* (Ames: Iowa State University Press, 1961).
152 A policy of released time for sectarian instruction was introduced in Gary,

Indiana, in 1913. Faced with a classroom shortage that required rotating instruction, the city superintendent devised a plan to release children for religious classes that would be conducted by the churches on their own premises. Subsequently, the Gary plan was widely adopted. The NEA survey found some type of released-time program operating in thirty-three states in 1946 and forty-three in 1949.

153 Within eight years of the Supreme Court's decision, more than 30 per cent of American students were reported to be participating in some type of released-time program. See Martha McCarthy, *A Delicate Balance: Church, State, and the Schools* (Bloomington, Ind.: Phi Delta Kappa Educational Foundation, 1983), 109.

154 Hence, as E.R. Norman concluded with respect to the court's decision in *Engel* v. *Vitale*, the Supreme Court's interpretation of the First Amendment probably barred 'all comprehensive statements of national religiosity for educational purposes.' *The Conscience of the State in North America* (Cambridge: Cambridge University Press, 1968), 150.

155 Pfeffer, *Church, State, and Freedom*, 478.

156 In the most publicized attempt, on National Prayer Day in May 1982, President Ronald Reagan announced a proposed amendment to allow school prayer that was later introduced in Congress by Senator Strom Thurmond: 'Nothing in this Constitution shall be construed to prohibit individual or group prayer in public schools or other public institutions. No person shall be required by the United States or by any State to participate in prayer.' The amendment was praised by the Moral Majority and the Southern Baptist Convention; it was condemned by the National Council of Churches and the American Jewish Congress. When it came to a vote in the Senate in March 1984, the bill fell eleven votes short of the necessary two-thirds majority. The next year, another presidential amendment, sponsored by Senator Helms, aimed to make 'individual or group silent prayer or reflection' constitutional but was similarly defeated. In November 1995, Representative Ernest Istook of Oklahoma, backed by the influential advocacy of the Christian Coalition, initiated yet another attempt to amend the Constitution to permit prayers in public schools. When the revised version of the Religious Freedom Amendment finally reached the floor of the House of Representatives in June 1998, it was passed by 224 to 203, again failing to meet the two-thirds majority required to proceed. See James W. Fraser, *Between Church and State: Religion and Public Education in a Multicultural America* (New York: St Martin's Press, 1999), 183–4, 208–15.

157 Charles R. Kniker, 'Religious Practices in Public Schools,' in Thomas C.

Hunt and James C. Carper (eds), *Religion and Schooling in Contemporary America: Confronting Our Cultural Pluralism* (New York: Garland Publishing, 1997), 39–40; James John Jurinski, *Religion in the Schools: A Reference Handbook* (Santa Barbara: ABC–CLIO, 1998), 9–11.

158 Just before the Senate hearings on the Helms amendment began in June 1985, the U.S. Supreme Court, by a six-to-three margin in *Wallace* v. *Jaffree*, overturned an Alabama law that provided for a moment of silence in state public schools. A majority of the court indicated that some form of silent moment in public schools was not necessarily unconstitutional, but in this case there was a legislative intent 'to return prayer to the public schools.' In June 1992, thirty years after the *Engel* ruling, the court, by a vote of five to four in *Lee* v. *Weisman*, added that including invocation and benediction prayers as an official part of formal graduation ceremonies also violated the Establishment Clause. In June 2001 the Supreme Court did uphold a 1993 Alabama law allowing prayers initiated by students as long as one religion is not promoted over another and no attempts are made to proselytize. On the issue of school prayers during the presidencies of Ronald Reagan and George Bush, see Robert S. Alley, *School Prayer: The Court, the Congress, and the First Amendment* (Buffalo: Prometheus Books, 1994), 187–219; and for the case of *Lee* v. *Wiseman*, see Robert S. Alley, *Without a Prayer: Religious Expression in Public Schools* (Buffalo: Prometheus Books, 1996), 128–38.

159 In 1875, President Ulysses S. Grant proposed that the Constitution be amended to make free public schools mandatory, to tax church property, and to prohibit the use of any public funds for religiously affiliated schools. The next year, Representative James Blaine of Maine introduced such an amendment in Congress; it passed the House but not the Senate. By the end of the nineteenth century, about forty states had adopted similar measures, which came to be known as 'Blaine Amendments.' See William F. Davis, 'Public Policy, Religion, and Education in the United States,' in Hunt and Carper (eds), *Religion and Schooling in Contemporary America*, 167–8; and also Ward M. McAfee, *Religion, Race, and Reconstruction: The Public School in the Politics of the 1870s* (Albany: State University of New York Press, 1998), 192–220. As late as 1922 the existence of Roman Catholic parochial schools was subject to legislative challenge. In that year, the state of Oregon, claiming that it had the right to ensure that its citizens were adequately educated, passed a law that made attendance at state schools compulsory, with only limited exceptions, for children between ages eight and sixteen. Basing its judgment on the Fourteenth Amendment's protection of liberty and property with due process of law, the U.S.

Supreme Court, in *Pierce* v. *Society of Sisters* (1925), held that the state could not deprive parents unreasonably of their liberty to send their children to any private or religious schools meeting reasonable educational standards set by the state.

160 The Pennsylvania law challenged in *Lemon* v. *Kurtzman* and the Rhode Island law at stake in *Earley* v. *DiCenso* were struck down together in a decision written by Chief Justice Burger on the grounds that they created excessive government entanglement with religion contrary to the First Amendment. Perhaps the most important were two 1973 New York cases in which four kinds of aid were struck down: reimbursement from public funds for tuition paid by parents to send their children to a non-public school, tax deductions from state income tax for costs of sending their children to a non-public school, reimbursement to non-public schools for part of the expenses of maintenance and repair of school facilities and equipment, and partial reimbursement for the costs of record-keeping and testing required by the state. The first three types of aid were struck down in the Supreme Court's decision in *Committee for Public Education* v. *Nyquist*; the fourth was disallowed by the decision in *Levitt* v. *Committee for Public Education*. See R. Freeman Butts, *Public Education in the United States: From Revolution to Reform* (New York: Holt, Rinehart and Winston, 1978), 294.

161 Seven different opinions were written in *Wolman*, and the justices split five different ways on the several legal points at issue. As Butts concluded, 'Jefferson's high and impregnable wall of separation between church and state was becoming more than ever a serpentine affair' (ibid., 295).

162 Quoted in Leo Pfeffer, *Religion, State and the Burger Court* (Buffalo: Prometheus Books, 1984), 43.

163 See Todd Ziebarth, 'Vouchers, Tax Credits, and Tax Deductions,' Education Commission of the States, May 2002 (*http://www.ecs.org/clearinghouse/14/44/1444.htm*).

164 Eligible schools under the Cleveland Scholarship and Tutoring Program included private schools, both religious and non-religious, as well as public schools in districts adjoining Cleveland. No public school districts chose to participate in the program, and thirty-eight of the fifty-two schools initially approved to participate were religious schools (*Education Week*, 17 January 1996).

165 On the role of the courts with regard to the Milwaukee Parental Choice Program, see John F. Witte, *The Market Approach to Education: An Analysis of America's First Voucher Program* (Princeton, N.J.: Princeton University Press, 2000), 177–82.

166 Davis, 'Public Policy, Religion, and Education in the United States,' 177. In November 2000 a voucher plan (Proposition 38) put forward in California that would have given $4,000 per child to allow attendance at a private or religious school was defeated in a state referendum by a margin of 71 to 29 per cent. A plan put forward in Michigan (Proposal 1) proposed to offer vouchers of $3,300 to the parents of children living in school districts that graduated fewer than two-thirds of their students (at the time, seven districts, including Detroit) as well as in any other districts where the voucher plan was adopted by a vote of local residents or the school board. The Michigan plan was defeated by 69 to 31 per cent (*Education Week*, 15 November 2000).
167 Witte, *The Market Approach to Education*, 81–2, 188–9.
168 McCarthy, *A Delicate Balance*, 171.
169 Fraser, *Between Church and State*, 215.
170 By contrast with the use of Welsh and English as official languages of instruction in Wales, the place of Gaelic in Scotland appears to be more analogous to the provision for community or heritage languages in Australia and Canada.

5. Global Capitalism

1 For example, the technical conjunction of microelectronic computers, fibre-optic cable, television, telephones, and satellites has produced a global information network that has compressed both space and time and hence dramatically altered the conditions for human interaction and exchange. See Krishan Kumar, 'New Theories of Industrial Society,' in Phillip Brown and Hugh Lauder (eds), *Education for Economic Survival: From Fordism to Post-Fordism?* (London: Routledge, 1992), 48–51.
2 In public markets, government departments become competitors with other public and private organizations to supply educational services, and citizens become customers who choose their preferred service providers. Typically, public markets are characterized by strong political control, first over supply, by regulating the entry of providers and the terms of their competition for customers, and second over demand, by determining the entitlements of citizens to services and the transfers of public resources that create effective purchasing power. See Jon Pierre, 'The Marketization of the State: Citizens, Consumers, and the Emergence of the Public Market,' in B. Guy Peters and Donald J. Savoie (eds), *Governance in a Changing Environment* (Montreal: McGill-Queen's University Press, 1995), 68–9.

3 Edward Andrew, 'George Grant on Technological Imperatives,' in Richard
  B. Day, Ronald Beiner, and Joseph Masciulli (eds), *Democratic Theory and
  Technological Society* (London: M.E. Sharpe, 1988), 301.
4 The Swedish system of education and training may be cited as a good example of this social-democratic strategy. In upper secondary school, Swedish students choose one of twenty-seven 'lines' or courses of study, which
  are grouped in six divisions: arts and social sciences; care-giving; economics
  and commerce; technology and science; technology and industry; and agriculture, horticulture, and forestry. Through the three-year course of upper
  secondary school, the focus of study progressively narrows from occupational education for a broad industry group to learning the skills for a
  particular job classification. If Sweden represents the social-democratic
  strategy, Japan and Germany are more oriented to the interests of employers. In Japan, vocational secondary education is relatively unimportant.
  Schools aim to give most students in upper secondary school a general
  academic education dominated by language, mathematics, and science;
  and large Japanese business firms then provide virtually all their vocational
  training after new recruits are hired. In Germany the combination of secondary education and apprenticeship training is designed to produce
  workers who have very high technical qualifications but who are also highly
  specialized. Most students are hired by the firms in which they were appren-
  tices, and they cannot move easily to other occupations or employers. See
  Ray Marshall and Marc Tucker, *Learning for a Living: Work, Skills, and the
  Future of the American Economy* (New York: Basic Books, 1992), 51–3, 201–7.
5 Peter Watkins, 'High Technology, Work and Education,' in David Dawkins
  (ed.), *Power and Politics in Education* (London: Falmer Press, 1991), 226.
6 The term 'collective intelligence' is taken from Phillip Brown and Hugh
  Lauder, 'Education, Economy and Society: An Introduction to a New
  Agenda,' in Brown and Lauder (eds), *Education for Economic Survival: From
  Fordism to Post-Fordism?*, 27–34. As they put it, 'Intelligence – the ability to
  think critically about the social and natural worlds, and the ability to apply
  new skills and techniques – is usually seen as an attribute of individuals.
  However, there is a clear sense in which it is determined by forms of production and the social systems they create ... An emphasis on collective
  intelligence would mean that education would no longer be geared to
  selecting the talented few. The implications for education of this change in
  emphasis would be enormous for the related processes of socialisation and
  selection ... It would follow fairly quickly that schools would need to discard
  streaming in favour of mixed ability teaching. In general selection for the
  various routes into industry would be delayed as long as possible in order to

provide the greatest opportunity for students' intelligence and creativity to flourish.'

7 Ibid., 9.

8 Don Smart, 'Reagan Conservatism and Hawke Socialism: Whither the Differences in the Education Policies of the US and Australian Federal Governments?' in William Lowe Boyd and Don Smart (eds), *Education Policy in Australia and America: Comparative Perspectives* (London: Falmer Press, 1987), 22.

9 The minister for education, Senator Susan Ryan, asked the Commonwealth Schools Commission to define new targets for federal funding of schools, and the commission's proposal to establish a 'community standard' based on the resources required to provide schools of high quality was largely accepted by the Hawke government as the basis for future federal funding. See Australia, Commonwealth Schools Commission, *Funding Policies for Australian Schools* (Canberra: Commonwealth Schools Commission, 1984). A new Participation and Equity program (PEP) was announced that would 'make funds available to the States and non-government schools to stimulate broadly-based changes in secondary education' and foster equal educational outcomes by directing assistance to 'schools where students are not gaining the benefits of full participation in education because of the combined effects of cultural and social background and economic factors' (Australia, Commonwealth Schools Commission, *Participation and Equity in Australian Schools* [Canberra: Canberra Printing, 1983], 1–2). Don Smart has described PEP as perhaps 'the one education program which best captured the traditional educational goals and ideals of the ALP' (Don Smart, 'Education,' in Brian W. Head and Allan Patience [eds], *From Fraser to Hawke: Australian Public Policy in the 1980s* [Melbourne: Longman Cheshire, 1989], 312). The Curriculum Development Centre, which had been created by the Whitlam government in 1975 as an independent agency responsible to the Commonwealth minister for education only to be closed by the Fraser government in 1981 as an economy measure, was also reopened by the Hawke government under the aegis of the Commonwealth Schools Commission.

10 Australia, Quality of Education Review Committee, *Quality of Education in Australia: Report of the Review Committee* (Canberra: Australian Government Publishing Service, 1985), 1. According to Don Smart, 'The QERC report appears to have been "forced" on the Minister for Education as a result of intervention by senior bureaucrats in the Departments of Finance and Prime Minister and Cabinet. In their review of the Department of Education's 1984 pre-Budget submission, these bureaucrats asked what evidence

there was to show that the massive increase in federal per pupil school expenditure (of some 50 per cent between 1973 and 1983) had improved the quality of education' (Smart, 'Reagan Conservatism and Hawke Socialism,' 33; see also Smart, 'Education,' 313–14).

11 Under the new funding arrangements, payment of the legislated maximum grants depended on the negotiation of resource agreements between the Commonwealth and government or non-government educational authorities to ensure that increases in federal funds would be directed to national priority areas and that progress in achieving outcomes would be duly accounted. National priority areas were improvement in the general competencies identified by QERC, especially among young children; increased participation of disadvantaged students in years eleven and twelve; gender equality in enrolments and attainments across major subject areas; and aid for teachers to improve the quality of schooling. Administrative responsibility for the two major funding programs for schools, the general recurrent and capital grants programs, was transferred from the Commonwealth Schools Commission to the Department of Education, and negotiation of resource agreements with state and non-government partners was conducted for the Commonwealth government by the department.

12 L.W. Louden and R.K. Browne, 'Developments in Education Policy in the Eighties: Trends in Three Federal Systems, Australia, Canada and the U.S.A.: An Australian Perspective,' paper presented to the annual meeting of the American Educational Research Association, San Francisco, March 1989, 20.

13 According to a statement of principles announced by the Conference of Directors General of state and territorial departments of education in November 1990, 'Subject profiles should provide a framework which can be used by teachers in classrooms to chart the progress of individual learners, by schools to report to their communities, and by systems reporting on student performance as well as being amenable to reporting student achievement at the national level.' See Leo Bartlett, 'National Curriculum in Australia: An Instrument of Corporate Federalism,' *British Journal of Educational Studies* 40 (August 1992): 225.

14 John McCollow and John Graham, 'Not Quite the National Curriculum: Accommodation and Resistance to Curriculum Change,' in Bob Lingard and Paige Porter (eds), *A National Approach to Schooling in Australia? Essays on the Development of National Policies in Schools Education* (Canberra: Australian College of Education, 1997), 66. See also Colin Marsh, 'Putting Profiles to Work: Real Gains and Real Problems,' *Curriculum Perspectives* 15 (September 1995): 54–6. At one end of the continuum of state policy making, the

South Australia Department of Education, Employment and Training (1993) and the Tasmania Department of Education and the Arts (1994) both proceeded to adopt the national statements and profiles as state policy, prepare guidelines and directions for teachers, and plan schedules for putting them into practice in schools (Michael Watt, 'National Curriculum Collaboration: The State of Reform in the States and Territories,' *Curriculum Perspectives* 18 [April 1998]: 28, 29–30). In the Australian Capital Territory (1990), Northern Territory (1992), Victoria (1993), Queensland (1995), and Western Australia (1996), decisions were taken to revise existing curriculum frameworks in order to align them with national statements and profiles (ibid., 26–7, 29, 32; Ross Kimber, 'Using a Curriculum and Standards Framework,' *Curriculum Perspectives* 15 [September 1995]: 72–3; Brian Rout, 'Student Performance Standards,' *Curriculum Perspectives* 15 [September 1995]: 63–4). At the other end of the continuum of state curricular policy development, the most substantial modifications of national statements and profiles occurred in New South Wales, where a major curricular reform was already under way as a result of the Education Reform Act of 1990. In 1993 the minister for education, training and youth affairs asked the Board of Studies to apply the national statements and profiles in its development of state syllabuses, but following the election of a Labor government in March 1995 the new minister suspended this process, pending the report of a review panel chaired by Kenneth Eltis of the University of Sydney. The review panel ultimately endorsed a curriculum framework with syllabuses that specified expected learning outcomes and encouraged continuing involvement in national curriculum collaboration, but it recommended that the national profiles not be incorporated directly in state syllabuses. For an overview of curricular development at the end of the 1990s, see Michael G. Watt, 'The National Education Agenda, 1996–2000: Its Impact on Curriculum Reform in the States and Territories,' *Curriculum Perspectives* 20 (September 2000): 37–47.

15 Kathy McLean and Bruce Wilson, 'The Big Picture,' *Curriculum Perspectives* 15 (September 1995): 56.

16 Janice Dudley and Lesley Vidovich, *The Politics of Education: Commonwealth Schools Policy 1973–1995*, Australian Education Review, no. 36 (Melbourne: Australian Council for Educational Research, 1995), 152. Dudley and Vidovich argue that, as a scheme to establish greater curricular uniformity and thus raise economic productivity and competitiveness, the key competencies were consistent with the national statements and profiles. Both resorted to curricular frameworks that included outcomes-based standards. The key competencies were skills and capacities that should be pursued in

all subject areas, however, and hence were more general than the subject-specific outcomes of the national profiles. Consequently, the key competencies implied some restructuring of the curriculum for years eleven and twelve, but because of their generality, the political challenge to state educational politics and policy making was not so direct and obvious.

17 My summary of the national movement to define key competencies from 1990 to 1996 is based on McCollow and Graham, 'Not Quite the National Curriculum: Accommodation and Resistance to Curriculum Change,' 63–5. For the report of the AEC review committee, which was chaired by Brian Finn, chief executive of IBM, see *Young People's Participation in Post-Compulsory Education and Training: Report of the Australian Education Council Review Committee* (Canberra: Australian Government Publishing Service, 1991). For the report of the AEC advisory committee, which was chaired by Eric Mayer, former managing director of National Mutual, see *Putting Education to Work: Report of the Committee to Advise the Australian Education Council and the Ministers of Vocational Education, Employment and Training on Employment-Related Key Competencies for Post-Compulsory Education and Training* (Canberra: Australian Government Publishing Service, 1992).

18 In 1995 the Ministerial Council for Education, Employment, Training and Youth Affairs, which replaced the Australian Education Council in 1993, agreed that 'cultural understanding' should be added as an eighth competency.

19 Bob Lingard and Paige Porter, 'Australian Schooling: The State of National Developments,' in Lingard and Porter (eds), *A National Approach to Schooling in Australia?*, 19.

20 Australia, Australian National Training Authority (ANTA), *A Bridge to the Future: Australia's National Strategy for Vocational Education and Training 1998–2003* (Brisbane: Australian National Training Authority, 1998), 10, 13; available at the ANTA Web site (*http://www.anta.gov.au*). A decidedly utilitarian-liberal ideology underlies the ANTA vision for a nation in which 'Australian **citizens** place a high value on vocational education and training because of the vital role it plays in the social and economic progress of the nation ... Australian **schools** offer a comprehensive and relevant program of vocational education to all their students and, to do this, establish partnerships with parents, industry and vocational education and training institutions ... [and] Australian **students** freely choose their secondary and post-secondary education and training options based on accurate and balanced career and course information' (ibid., 3; bold in the original).

21 In five of the eight Australian educational jurisdictions, the boards that governed senior secondary studies also had mandates to design and imple-

ment curricular plans for compulsory education from pre-school to year ten. Accreditation, assessment, and certification of senior secondary students in the 1990s were the functions of the Board of Senior Secondary Studies in the Australian Capital Territory, the Senior Secondary Assessment Board of South Australia (SSABSA), and the Schools Board in Tasmania. Jean Russell, 'Postcompulsory Curriculum and Certificates in the 1990s,' *Curriculum Perspectives* 15 (June 1995): 2–21; see also Watt, 'National Curriculum Collaboration: The State of Reform in the States and Territories,' 22–31.

22 W.F. Connell, *Reshaping Australian Education 1960–1985* (Hawthorn, Victoria: Australian Council for Educational Research, 1993), 312–14.

23 In addition to credits totalling 100 points (1 semester unit = 66 hours = 6 points), to get the Year 12 Certificate, students in the Australian Capital Territory were required to complete an educational program approved by their college as having provided a 'coherent pattern of study.' With the implementation of the Western Australian Certificate of Education in 1997, students had to complete at least ten full-year (or equivalent) courses (1 course = 110 hours), obtaining an average grade of C or better in at least eight courses, with at least four courses at the level of Year 12.

24 For a summary of the convergence of academic and vocational studies across the states, see Barry McGaw, *Their Future: Options for Reform of the Higher School Certificate* (Sydney: New South Wales Department of Training and Education Co-ordination, 1996), 33–5. In response to McGaw's strong recommendations for convergence of academic and vocational studies, the New South Wales government's white paper affirmed as core principles to 'ensure the integrity of vocational studies within the Higher School Certificate' that vocational education and training courses should 'be potentially appropriate for all students in the Higher School Certificate and should be accessible to all, including those who move from secondary to higher education; be offered in sufficient variety to satisfy different student needs; contribute to the broad education of students; be recognised by both secondary and vocational education accreditation authorities; be offered in response to demand established from industry needs, using the State Training Profile; offer training relevant to the industries in the State Training Profile rather than merely to narrowly focused occupations or the specific needs of single enterprises; result, on successful completion, in the award of a vocational qualification under the Australian Qualifications Framework or in clearly established credit towards such a qualification; have clear links to post-school destinations, particularly further vocational education and training and employment; be developed in collaboration between the

secondary education and vocational education and training sectors and industry; and have a component of structured workplace training to allow for competencies to be developed and assessed in the workplace to the extent deemed appropriate by, and available in, industry.' New South Wales, *Securing Their Future: The New South Wales Government's Reforms for the Higher School Certificate*, 1997, 16 (*http://www.det.nsw.gov.au/reviews/index.htm*).

25 See Russell, 'Postcompulsory Curriculum and Certificates in the 1990s,' 6, 19. In addition, there were two pathways for postcompulsory students in New South Wales through courses delivered by institutions of technical and further education, one leading to the Higher School Certificate that combined general education and vocational studies, and the other limited to vocational education and training. In Western Australia, pathways were developed in agriculture/natural resources management; art and design; health, social, and community services; performing arts; applied sciences; business systems; hospitality/food/tourism; and technology and design. Western Australia, Ministry of Education, *Annual Report 1991–1992* (Perth: Government Printer, 1992), 13.

26 Peter Aucoin, *The New Public Management: Canada in Comparative Perspective* (Montreal: Institute for Research on Public Policy, 1995), 124–5. The number of departments was reduced from twenty-eight to eighteen, each department was represented in cabinet by a senior minister, and junior ministers assigned to a portfolio were subordinate to their portfolio minister.

27 *DEET News*, no. 1 (26 August 1987); quoted in Ian Birch and Don Smart, 'Economic Rationalism and the Politics of Education in Australia,' in Douglas E. Mitchell and Margaret E. Goertz (eds), *Education Politics for the New Century*, The Twentieth Anniversary Yearbook of the Politics of Education Association (London: Falmer Press, 1990), 138.

28 Simon Marginson's assessment of the Commonwealth Schools Commission also covered the Commonwealth Tertiary Education Commission. With regard to these two agencies, he argued, 'The CTEC and CSC had operated at "arm's length" from the government, with a separate legal identity and the responsibility to report to Parliament; and were closer to the institutions and authorities in education than a department could have been. They were governed by Government policy while interpreting it more or less as they saw fit; and they had developed distinctive policy discourses that at times were very influential' (Simon Marginson, *Educating Australia: Government, Economy and Citizen* [Cambridge: Cambridge University Press, 1997], 163–4). The advisory functions of the Commonwealth Schools Commission were transferred to the new National Board of Employment,

Education and Training, which had four separate councils for schools,
higher education, employment and skills formation, and research. Following the election of the Liberal–National coalition government led by John
Howard in 1996, the National Board and its subsidiary, the Schools Council, were abolished.

29 John Knight and Bob Lingard, 'Ministerialisation and Politicisation: Changing Structures and Practices of Educational Policy Production,' in Lingard
and Porter (eds), *A National Approach to Schooling in Australia?*, 33–4.

30 Simon Marginson, *Markets in Education* (St Leonards, N.S.W.: Allen and
Unwin, 1997), 192.

31 Following the re-election of the Liberal party government in Victoria in
1979, for example, the new minister for education, Alan Hunt, initiated a
series of reviews of the department, including one by a firm of management consultants, that proposed to shift control over educational policy
from the department to the minister (symbolized by renaming the office of
director general as chief executive officer) and to reorganize the divisional
structure of the department from schools (primary, secondary, technical)
to functions (operations, administration) (Don Smart, 'Reversing Patterns
of Control in Australia: Can Schools Be Self-Governing?' *Education Research
and Perspectives* 15 [December 1988]: 19). When the Labor party won power
in 1983, the title of director general was restored, but in the reorganization
that followed the Liberal–National victory in October 1992, the title of the
senior administrative position was changed again to secretary of education.
In Western Australia, based on the work of the Functional Review Committee, which was examining government departments to improve efficiency
in the public sector, a report issued by the Education Department in 1987
recommended that the renamed Ministry of Education be reorganized into
three basic divisions of schools, policy, and technical and further education;
the director general would become chief executive officer, and the number
of positions in head office would be reduced from 1,200 to 600. See Western Australia, Ministry of Education, *Better Schools in Western Australia: A
Programme for Improvement* (Perth: Government Printer, 1987). When technical and further education was amalgamated in the Department of Employment, Vocational Education and Training, the Ministry of Education
operated as four major divisions dealing with schools operations, corporate
development, resources and services, and human resources, each headed
by an executive director under the chief executive officer. Brian Scott's
management review of the New South Wales department, following the
election of the Liberal–National coalition government led by Nick Greiner
in 1987, proposed the establishment of the Central Policy Committee as the

senior policy-making body in the new Department of School Education, comprising the director general, two deputy directors general (one for regions and schools, the other for educational programs and planning), two assistant directors general in head office (one for human resources, the other for administration and finance), and ten regional assistant directors general. The Queensland Department of Education adopted a corporate management plan in 1989 under which the basic divisions based on directorates of pre-school, primary, secondary, special, and technical and further education, as well as various educational and administrative services, were reorganized between two large divisions, studies and corporate services, each headed by a deputy director general, and the regional directors were formally recognized as part of the department's executive management group. When the department was reorganized in 1994 for purposes of implementing the report of the Wiltshire committee, *Shaping the Future*, the division of studies was renamed 'curriculum' and a third deputy director general (schooling) was appointed to head the Shaping the Future Implementation Unit.

32 The Northern Territory also preserved its organization of a northern region or directorate administered from Darwin and a southern region administered from Alice Springs. In contrast with the state departments of education, the Northern Territory department had substantially decentralized school operations between the two regions since the 1970s, when the South Australia Department of Education ceased to have administrative responsibility for territorial education.

33 The dual concern of Labor governments for efficiency and democracy was well stated in the Victorian Labor government's fourth ministerial paper issued in 1984: 'The Government is confident that School Councils, principals and teachers will see this change as providing an historic opportunity for enhanced professional effectiveness; providing shorter lines of communication; real local responsibility and accountability; and greater educational effectiveness through parent and community support, both psychological and material, for agreed policies.' Under the Education Act of 1984, school councils were given greater powers not only to decide curriculum objectives and develop improvement plans but also to appoint school principals. When the Liberal–National coalition government of Jeffrey Kennett gained office, however, its Education (Amendment) Act of 1993 provided for principals to be selected by panels on which half the members would represent the school and the other half were nominees of the central Directorate of School Education, the minister was empowered to issue directions or guidelines to school councils, and school charters that

set performance and accountability requirements were subject to review
and approval by the director (Gerry Tickell, 'Learning the Lessons of
Decentralization,' in Roy Martin, John McCollow, Lesley McFarlane, Grant
McMurdo, John Graham, and Robin Hall (eds), *Devolution, Decentralisation
and Recentralisation: The Structure of Australian Schooling* [South Melbourne,
Victoria: Australian Education Union, 1994], 40–1). In the debate over the
role of school councils in South Australia in 1992–3, the Labor minister of
education, Susan Lenehan, said that her department would be aiming for
'shared responsibility' (Jenni Mulraney, 'South Australia: Devolution to
Shared Responsibility to ... What's in a Name,' in ibid., 27), but following
the arrival into office of a Liberal government in December 1993, the
burden of local management and accountability was clearly put on school
principals. Similarly, in Tasmania, when the minority Labor government
initiated a scheme for school councils in 1991, its rationale included the
need for parents and community to be involved in policy making for their
schools, but the lines of accountability for both school councils and principals ran through the district superintendents and the secretary for education to the minister. Following the election of a Liberal government in
February 1992, a new policy document, *Local Leadership and Management*
(1993), instructed principals to keep their school community informed but
also to produce outcomes commensurate with central goals and priorities.
R.J.S. Macpherson, 'Educative Accountability Policies for Tasmania's
Locally Managed Schools: Interim Policy Research Findings,' *International
Journal of Educational Reform* 5 (January 1996): 36–7.

34 For an excellent account of the reforms in Victoria by the Liberal–National
coalition following its election in 1992, see Brian J. Caldwell and Donald K.
Hayward, *The Future of Schools: Lessons from the Reform of Public Education*
(London: Falmer Press, 1998), 14–15, 38–80. Hayward was the minister of
education in the coalition government.

35 For a discussion of these reports, see Ronald Manzer, *Public Schools and
Political Ideas: Canadian Educational Policy in Historical Perspective* (Toronto:
University of Toronto Press, 1994), 212–37; and also Ronald Manzer,
'Political Ideas in Policy Analysis: Educational Reform and Canadian
Democracy in the 1990s,' in Martin W. Westmacott and Hugh P. Mellon
(eds), *Public Administration and Policy: Governing in Challenging Times*
(Scarborough, Ont.: Prentice-Hall Allyn and Bacon Canada, 1999), 159–61.

36 These percentages are calculated on the basis of grades ten to twelve for
Alberta, Nova Scotia, and Prince Edward Island, Secondary IV and V for
Quebec, grades eleven and twelve in British Columbia, and grades nine to
twelve in Ontario. In Ontario, where there were no compulsory courses in

grade thirteen, the required credits over grades nine to thirteen comprised 27.3 per cent. The curriculum and graduation requirements for the Yukon Territory are based on those for British Columbia; those for the Northwest Territories are based on the requirements of Alberta. The sources for these calculations for the early 1980s and subsequent comparisons with the early and middle 1990s include Council of Ministers of Education, Canada, *Secondary Education in Canada: A Student Transfer Guide 1983* (4th ed.; Toronto: Council of Ministers of Education, Canada, 1983), 3–28; Council of Ministers of Education, Canada, *Secondary Education in Canada: A Student Transfer Guide 1991* (5th ed.; Toronto: Council of Ministers of Education, Canada, 1991), 3–44; Margaret Gayfer, *Education in Canada: An Overview* (4th ed.; Toronto: Canadian Education Association, 1991), 12–15; and Paula Dunning, *Education in Canada: An Overview* (5th ed.; Toronto: Canadian Education Association, 1997), 28–31.

37 Credits in physical education and health were also required in British Columbia and Alberta.

38 Saskatchewan did not require credits in physical education and health. New Brunswick, which was the only province still specifying credits in terms of different programs of study, did not require science in the business education and practical programs, and social studies was replaced in the practical program by 'social education.' In Manitoba, 57.1 per cent of total credits were specified by required subjects, 58.3 per cent in Newfoundland, and 52.4 per cent in Saskatchewan. In New Brunswick, 66.7 per cent of total credits were specified as required subjects in the college program, 53.3 per cent in the industrial, home economics, and practical programs, and 46.6 per cent for business education.

39 In general there were no options during Secondary I and II, one option in Secondary III and IV, and three in Secondary V. Phillippe Dupuis et al., *Le système d'éducation au Québec* (Boucherville: Gaëtan morin éditeur, 1991), 113, 116.

40 In Ontario, requirements had been gradually tightened, beginning in 1974–5 with four English courses and two Canadian studies courses, expanded in 1977–8 to include three compulsory credits in mathematics and science, and expanded again in 1979–80 to include four credits in the arts and physical and health education. Based on a major review of secondary education in 1980–1, the new curriculum removed the distinction between the former Secondary School Graduation Diploma (twenty-seven credits), and the Secondary School Higher Graduation Diploma (thirty-three credits) which was granted after any six honour credits in grade thirteen. Out of thirty credits, the new Ontario Secondary School Diploma required

five English (or français) with at least two at the senior level, two mathematics, two science, one French (or anglais), one Canadian geography, one Canadian history, one senior social science, one physical and health education, one arts, and one business or technological studies.

41 The graduation requirements also specified that at least five of the eighteen credits had to be grade-twelve courses. The graduation requirements for students with at least eight credits in vocational subjects were slightly different: three courses in language arts, including a first-language course at the grade-twelve level; two mathematics courses; and either two sciences and one social studies or one science and two social studies.

42 In addition to these major changes in previously less restrictive provinces, the number of credits to graduate for Saskatchewan students entering grade ten in September 1988 was raised from twenty-one to twenty-four, and fifteen credits (62.5 per cent) were specified as compulsory core subjects. The changes in requirements in Saskatchewan resulted from a major review of curriculum and instruction for kindergarten to grade twelve that was initiated in 1981. The report of the Curriculum and Instruction Review Committee in 1984 recommended the development of a core curriculum, and the Department of Education unveiled the new standards in its March 1987 policy statement, *Policy Directions for a Core Curriculum*. According to the department's *Annual Report 1986–87*, 'The purpose of a core curriculum is to provide all Saskatchewan students with a uniform education that will serve them well regardless of their career choices upon completing school. It would reinforce the teaching of basic skills and also introduce new, contemporary fields of study.'

43 In Saskatchewan, provincial examinations were required only for admission to university for students whose teachers were not accredited by the Department of Education. As in Newfoundland and Quebec, the results of the provincial examinations and teachers' assessments were each weighted 50 per cent in determining final marks. Alberta also offered provincial examinations, which were not mandatory, to students who wished to take them in order to improve their graduation marks. See Margaret Gayfer, *An Overview of Canadian Education* (2nd ed.; Toronto: Canadian Education Association, 1978), 18.

44 Provincial examinations were administered in mathematics in 1991 and 1992, biology and physics in 1993, chemistry in 1994, and social studies in 1995. See John Bishop, 'High School Diploma Examinations: Do Students Learn More? Why?' *Policy Options* 19 (July–August 1998): 9.

45 The subjects with provincial examinations for francophone students were grade-twelve français; grade-eleven history, mathematics, and chemistry;

and grade-ten geography and physics. A provincial examination in English as a second language was added later. The provincial examinations in English and mathematics for anglophone students counted for 30 per cent of their final marks.

46 Christopher J. Bruce and Arthur M. Schwartz, 'Education: Meeting the Challenge,' in Christopher J. Bruce, Ronald D. Kneebone, and Kenneth J. McKenzie (eds), *A Government Reinvented: A Study of Alberta's Deficit Elimination Program* (Toronto: Oxford University Press, 1997), 392.

47 The reduction in the Ontario testing program was recommended by the Education Quality and Accountability Office in order to reduce costs and avoid test overload. R.D. Gidney, *From Hope to Harris: The Reshaping of Ontario's Schools* (Toronto: University of Toronto Press, 1999), 237.

48 Proponents of national testing under SAIP emphasized the need to focus on educational outcomes – the acquisition of basic knowledge and skills – judged against established national standards. According to the president of the Business Council on National Issues, for example, the business community in Canada strongly supported standardized testing because it would improve the quality of high school graduates: 'A considerable number of students arriving in the work force are unable to read, write and do their numbers. Standardized tests are one way to introduce excellence into our education systems. The tests set goals for people to shoot at.' Opponents of the national tests, which included provincial teachers' unions and the Canadian Teachers' Federation, objected that the proposed national tests were not based on provincial curricula and argued that assessment of even basic knowledge and skills should be based on what is taught in schools, how it is taught, and who the learners are (Manzer, *Public Schools and Political Ideas*, 244–5).

49 See ibid., 230–2.

50 Canadian School Boards Association, *Who's Running Our Schools? Education Governance in the 90's: Provincial/Territorial Summaries* (Ottawa: Canadian School Boards Association, 1995), 3.

51 R.D. Gidney, assessing the educational reforms of the Conservative government from 1995 to 1998, has observed that 'given the level of decentralization that held sway from the late 1960s onward, greater central control over the curriculum and more uniformity in what was taught across the province might seem like a new departure. But it was hardly more than a return to traditional ways of doing things in Ontario, at least between the late nineteenth century and the mid-1960s' (Gidney, *From Hope to Harris: The Reshaping of Ontario's Schools*, 276).

52 In both New Brunswick and Prince Edward Island there was formal provi-

sion in the school act for optional local levies, but school boards found
these procedures extremely cumbersome and voters unwilling to give
approval. See Gerald Hopkirk, 'Public Education in Prince Edward Island:
Focus on School Boards,' in Edward H. Humphreys, Stephen B. Lawton,
Richard G. Townsend, Victoria E. Grabb, and Daina M. Watson, *Alternative
Approaches to Determining Distribution of School Board Trustee Representation*, vol.
1, *Trustee Representation: Theory and Practice in Canada* (Toronto: Queen's
Printer for Ontario, 1986), 171; Robin J. Enns and Valerie M. O'Hara,
'School Trustee Election Bases: The Case of New Brunswick,' in ibid., 209.
53 The Nova Scotia government contributed 81 per cent directly through
provincial grants and 12 per cent by a mandatory tax on local property.
Optional levies in Nova Scotia were subject to approval by the local governments of the municipalities that overlapped school districts and amounted
to about 4 per cent of school board revenues. In Quebec, school boards
were prohibited from levying a tax greater than 6 per cent of their funded
expenditures, or 2.5 mills, whichever was lower, unless the levy was approved in a local referendum. In 1990 the Liberal government raised the
ceiling on local taxation to 3.5 mills, and the percentage ceiling became
based on weighted student population. As a result of these changes, the
contribution of provincial grants to the revenues of school commissions fell
to 82 per cent by 1996–7, local taxes rose to 12 per cent, and other sources
also increased to 6 per cent. William J. Smith and Helen M. Donahue, *The
Historical Roots of Québec Education* (Montreal: Office of Research on Educational Policy, McGill University, 1999), 88; William J. Smith, William F.
Foster, and Helen M. Donahue, *The Contemporary Education Scene in Québec:
A Handbook for Policy Makers, Administrators and Educators* (Montreal: Office
of Research on Educational Policy, McGill University, 1999), 265, 274–85.
54 In Alberta, school boards were allowed to seek approval through a local
referendum for special levies to finance one-time expenditures up to a
maximum of 3 per cent of their approved budget allocation; in Ontario,
optional levies were prohibited. In both Alberta and Ontario the centralization of property taxation was challenged in the courts on the grounds that
it infringed the right of separate school boards to tax the property of their
supporters guaranteed since Confederation under section 93 of the BNA
Act and therefore, by extension based on a 'mirror equality' argument, the
same authority enjoyed by public school boards. In both cases, provincial
courts of appeal, which were subsequently upheld by the Supreme Court of
Canada, ruled that neither public nor separate school boards had any
constitutionally protected taxing authority. Rather, direct taxation is merely
one particular method of funding denominational education, which is the

true object of constitutional protection. J. Paul R. Howard, 'Of Storms, School Boards and the Supreme Court,' *Education Canada* 40 (Fall 2000): 38; Susan Luft, 'Case Note: Supreme Court Upholds Constitutionality of Alberta School Funding Scheme,' *Education and Law Journal* 11 (2001–2): 275–8.

55 For a summary of current Canadian laws governing labour relations in elementary and secondary education in Canada, see Stephen B. Lawton, George Bedard, Duncan MacLellan, and Xiaobin Li, *Teachers' Unions in Canada* (Calgary: Detselig Enterprises, 1999), 53–60.

56 Lawton, Bedard, MacLellan, and Li conclude that the B.C. Public Education Labour Relations Act 'must be viewed as a failure. In both rounds of bargaining to date, the province has undercut the employers' negotiating body by taking over bargaining and reaching a settlement' (ibid., 98).

57 On the restructuring of education in Alberta, see Bruce and Schwartz, 'Education: Meeting the Challenge,' 383–416; Stephen B. Lawton, 'Comment on Chapter 11,' in Bruce, Kneebone, and McKenzie (eds), *A Government Reinvented: A Study of Alberta's Deficit Elimination Program*, 417–20; Trevor W. Harrison and Jerrold L. Kachur (eds), *Contested Classrooms: Education, Globalization, and Democracy in Alberta* (Edmonton: University of Alberta Press and Parkland Institute, 1999); and Alison Taylor, *The Politics of Educational Reform in Alberta* (Toronto: University of Toronto Press, 2001), 73–96.

58 The issue of restructuring local educational governance in Newfoundland and Quebec was dominated by proposals to terminate its denominational basis, but the amalgamation of 27 denominational school boards into 10 integrated boards in Newfoundland and 158 confessional boards to 71 linguistic boards in Quebec was in each case driven primarily by considerations of efficiency. In Saskatchewan the voluntary amalgamation of 20 school districts into 8 in 1997 and the consolidation of 9 francophone school boards to form 1 provincial francophone board in 1998 resulted in a relatively modest decrease from 114 to 99, the largest number of districts in a province where elementary and secondary school enrolment exceeded only those of the Atlantic provinces.

59 Teachers were excluded from membership on Manitoba's Advisory Councils for School Leadership, and there were no community members on the School Parent Committees in New Brunswick or the school councils of Prince Edward Island. The school law in British Columbia, Nova Scotia, Ontario, and Quebec provided for representation of support staff as well as teachers. In Quebec, teachers and parents were equally represented on the governing boards of elementary schools; the principal and two community

representatives did not have votes. In secondary schools, some student representatives were permitted to sit on governing boards as voting members in place of parents.

60 *CEA Newsletter,* No. 480 (January 1998): 1; see also William J. Smith, William J. Foster, and Helen M. Donahue, 'The Transformation of Educational Governance in Québec: A Reform Whose Time Has *Finally* Come,' *McGill Journal of Education* 34 (Fall 1999): 215–19. School councils in Quebec ('orientation committees') were first introduced by law in 1971, and then strengthened in 1988. The 1988 act (Bill 107) also provided for the establishment of 'school committees' comprising parents to promote participation in the educational activities of their school and advise the orientation committee and the school commission. On the functional role of these committees, Yvonne Martin concluded, 'Although orientation and school committees in Quebec also have a requisite advisory role, they are not primarily advisory bodies. The primary functions of an orientation committee are to determine aims and objectives, adopt rules of conduct, and approve the principal's choice of extra-curricular activities, among other things. School committees also have a functional role. They see to the implementation of the plans adopted by the orientation committee and the school board has a duty to consult them on a number of specified decisions.' Yvonne M. Martin, 'A Comparative Legislative Analysis of Parental Participation Policy in British Columbia, Alberta and Quebec,' *Education and Law Journal* 4 (1992–3): 76.

61 For an overview of recent public campaigns and political lobbying by Canadian teachers' unions, see Lawton, Bedard, MacLellan, and Li, *Teachers' Unions in Canada,* 75–85.

62 See Education Amendment Act (No. 2) 1987.

63 According to the New Zealand Qualifications Authority (NZQA) plan, units would be developed at eight levels of achievement, beginning at the end of fifth form and leading to three nationally recognized qualification titles: the National Certificate for work over levels one to four, the National Diploma for work over levels five to seven, and the Degree, first granted for work completed at level seven with graduate degrees and higher diplomas granted for work completed successfully at level eight. NZQA proposed to phase out both the Sixth Form Certificate and the Higher School Certificate, issued to all students who were successful in passing seventh-form subjects, as work on units leading to the National Certificate was introduced in sixth and seventh forms.

64 New Zealand, New Zealand Qualifications Authority, *Designing the Framework: A Discussion Document* (Wellington: New Zealand Qualifications Au-

thority, 1991), 32; emphasis in the original. As Roger Peddie has observed, 'The Authority wanted to shift the thinking of teachers and students from process to outcome, from norms to standards, and from passing and failing to competence and mastery ... The original belief was that standards would be set by the appropriate bodies, would be monitored and occasionally changed by these bodies and, after being written into the unit standards, would thus be transparent to students, teachers and employers.' See Roger Peddie, 'Plus ça change ...? Assessment, Curriculum and the New Zealand Qualifications Authority,' *Proceedings of the Biennial Conference of the New Zealand Educational Administration Society* ('Ten Years On: Reforming New Zealand Education'), Wellington, 11–14 January 1998, vol. 1, 465. See also Peter Roberts, 'A Critique of the NZQA Policy Reforms,' in Mark Olssen and Kay Morris Matthews (eds), *Education Policy in New Zealand: The 1990s and Beyond* (Palmerston North: Dunmore Press, 1997), 162–89, and David McKenzie, 'The Cult of Efficiency and Miseducation: Issues of Assessment in New Zealand Schools,' in ibid., 56–62.

65 The *National Qualifications Framework: Green Paper* and the white paper were both issued under the auspices of the coalition government led by the National party. Following the 1999 election, the new coalition government led by the Labour party eventually retreated from making revisions to the NZQA plan in order to avoid turning the National Certificate of Educational Achievement into an electoral issue in 2002 (which the education critic for the National party threatened his party would do), but implementation of the first stage was delayed from 2001 to 2002.

66 The commission included representatives of both the New Zealand Treasury and the State Services Commission who were very influential in shaping the final report (Peter D.K. Ramsay, 'Picot – Vision and Reality in New Zealand's Schools: An Insider's View,' in Bob Lingard, John Knight, and Paige Porter [eds], *Schooling Reform in Hard Times* [London: Falmer Press, 1993], 263–4). In its brief to the Labour government, which was re-elected in 1987, the Treasury already had constructed what 'amounted to a draft charter for the radical reconstruction of the education system' (Gerald Grace, 'Labour and Education: The Crisis and Settlements of Education Policy,' in Martin Holland and Jonathan Boston [eds], *The Fourth Labour Government: Politics and Policy in New Zealand* (2nd ed.; Auckland: Oxford University Press, 1990), 171). In its brief, the Treasury used an array of empirical evidence to demonstrate the failure of public education in New Zealand and advanced a powerful argument to replace the bureaucratic administration of public schools with a combination of public and private markets. For the Treasury's recommendation on reducing the costs and

increasing the benefits of state intervention in education, for example, see
New Zealand, Treasury, *Government Management: Brief to the Incoming Government: Volume II Education Issues* (Wellington: Government Printer, 1987),
293.

67 New Zealand, Taskforce to Review Education Administration, *Administering
for Excellence: Effective Administration in Education* (Wellington: Government
Printer, 1988), 22, 35–6.

68 See New Zealand, Office of the Minister of Education, *Twenty Thousand: A
Summary of Responses to the Report of the Taskforce to Review Education Administration* (Wellington: Government Printer, 1988) and *Tomorrow's Schools: The
Reform of Education Administration in New Zealand* (Wellington: Government
Printer, 1988). Implementation of the Picot task force's report proceeded
in the context of comprehensive restructuring under the State Sector Act
of 1988 and the Public Finance Act of 1989, under which the 'chief executives' of operational departments were delegated managerial authority over
their organizations with the level of departmental resources, outputs
delivered, and criteria for evaluation specified in formal agreements
between ministers and chief executives.

69 Taskforce to Review Education Administration, *Administering for Excellence*, xi.

70 Fourteen independent education service centres were formed from the ten
former education boards and three regional offices of the Department of
Education to manage school services such as transportation, payrolls,
property, and supplies on a contractual basis.

71 One student enrolled full-time in a class above third form (year nine) may
also be elected as a student representative, and boards of integrated schools
may include members appointed by their proprietors. Boards may co-opt
additional members – for example, to ensure that there is gender balance
on the board or that the board represents the ethnic and socio-economic
composition of the student body. Under the Education Amendment Act
1991, boards of trustees are also allowed to co-opt additional members to
secure expertise in management, and persons other than parents may be
elected as members of boards of trustees.

72 As conceived by the Picot task force, the charter was a contract that would
involve school boards, central authority, and local community. During
implementation of the task force's report, the charter was redefined as an
agreement between the minister and the school. Following a review by the
State Services Commission from December 1989 to April 1990, boards of
trustees were made responsible to the minister, and the minister's commitment to provide funds on the basis of objectives agreed in the school's
charter was weakened. 'The effect of this series of changes was to devolve

responsibility for day-to-day school administration to the boards of trustees and to leave control in the hands of the Minister, who also had the power to dismiss the boards.' Roger Dale, 'The State and Education,' in Andrew Sharp (ed.), *Leap into the Dark: The Changing Role of the State in New Zealand since 1984* (Auckland: Auckland University Press, 1994), 78.

73 The Taskforce to Review Education Administration proposed that bulk grants to schools have two components: a teaching salaries grant calculated on the basis of a notional staff roll for each school, including prescribed limits on the number of senior-scale staff, and an operational activities grant to cover administration, ancillary support, maintenance, and non-salary aspects of teaching (*Administering for Excellence*, 49). Implementation of the task force's proposal for bulk funding of teachers' salaries was postponed, in part because of problems with devising the formula, in part because of opposition from teachers' unions. In February 1992 the Ministry of Education began a three-year trial, involving sixty-nine volunteer boards of trustees, under which the cost of teachers' salaries was included in their bulk funding. The 'fully funded' option, which was extended to other schools on a voluntary basis in 1996, continued to be controversial. Despite encouragement from the ministry, boards generally resisted having the salaries of classroom teachers included in their block grants, and by September 1998, only 14 per cent of schools had agreed to be fully funded (*New Zealand Herald*, 1 September 1998). Starting in 1993 a grant to cover the salaries of principals and other senior teachers in designated management positions was made directly to all boards of trustees. In addition to the costs of teachers' salaries and school transport, the Ministry of Education pays directly for the costs of major capital works, maintenance that recurs on a cycle longer than ten years, and for teachers' removal expenses.

74 Taskforce to Review Education Administration, *Administering for Excellence*, 42. Peter Ramsay, a member of the task force, has said that, in the form envisaged by the Picot task force, the school charter would be a contract between, on the one hand, the school and its community and, on the other hand, the school and the government. The intention was that teachers and the board of trustees would develop a charter in collaboration with their school's community. Once that was done, the charter would go to the minister for approval (Ramsay, 'Picot – Vision and Reality in New Zealand's Schools: An Insider's View,' 265–6).

75 Ken Rae, a senior policy analyst in the Ministry of Education, has pointed to 'the extensive and prescriptive nature of the mandatory component' of school charters, a feature that is very different from the recommendation of the Taskforce to Review Education Administration: 'The major Educa-

tion Act, when introduced, redefined the charter away from the three way *contract* between school professionals, community and central government envisaged by Picot, so that it became an *undertaking* offered by the board to the Minister of Education concerning its control of the school' (Ken Rae, 'Whakaritorito Te Tupu O Te Harakeke – Growing the Flax Shoots: Dilemmas of Devolution in New Zealand Schools,' *Proceedings of the Biennial Conference of the New Zealand Educational Administration Society*, 509; emphasis in the original).

76 Under the National Administration Guidelines, boards are required to 'develop and implement personnel and industrial policies ... which promote high levels of staff performance, use education resources effectively and recognise the needs of students'; be good employers as defined in the State Sector Act 1988; and comply with the conditions contained in employment contracts. They are required to allocate funds in accordance with their school's priorities, to monitor and control school spending, and to ensure that annual accounts are prepared and audited. With regard to property management, they have to comply with the negotiated conditions of any current asset management agreement and implement a proper maintenance program for their school.

77 From 1989 to 1998 the Ministry of Education appointed forty-six commissioners to replace boards of trustees (*New Zealand Herald*, 1 September 1998). The educational effectiveness of primary and secondary schools is evaluated every three years by the Education Review Office (ERO), based on students' attainments; reviewers also judge the management of each school against ministry guidelines. Negative ERO reviews of school curricular management commonly have cited failure to deliver a balanced curriculum, poor planning and evaluation procedures, and inadequate monitoring of students' performance. Poor management practices have included failure to implement proper administrative frameworks, adequate systems of performance management, and ongoing processes of self-review, as well as failure to manage problems that result from high staff turnover, conflict between board and principal or board and community, or falling enrolments. Where a review discloses poor performance, the result for about 12 per cent of the schools reviewed annually, the ERO will conduct another review within eighteen months. For a critical assessment of the work of the Education Review Office in its dealings with schools in areas of socio-economic disadvantage, see Martin Thrupp, 'Shaping a Crisis: The Education Review Office and South Auckland Schools,' in Olssen and Matthews (eds), *Education Policy in New Zealand: The 1990s and Beyond*, 145–61.

78 Representatives of the Ministry of Education as well as the New Zealand

School Trustees Association continued to be a party to the negotiations on the government side. From 1 July 1997, the State Services Commissioner delegated responsibility for conducting negotiations as 'employer party' to the Ministry of Education.

79 Gerald Grace, 'Welfare Labourism Versus the New Right: The Struggle in New Zealand's Education Policy,' *Proceedings of the Biennial Conference of the New Zealand Educational Administration Society*, 100.

80 This observation on the DES interpretation of the LEA reports in reply to Circular 14/77 was made by a former HMI, Pauline Perry; quoted in Stephen Ball, *Politics and Policy Making in Education: Explorations in Policy Sociology* (London: Routledge, 1990), 151. Pauline Perry elaborated: 'The British education system had no curriculum, and there was no curriculum philosophy, no curriculum theory, the LEAs didn't even know what curriculum was going on in their schools.'

81 Great Britain, Secretary of State for Education and Science and Secretary of State for Wales, *Better Schools* (London: Her Majesty's Stationery Office, 1985).

82 Ball, *Politics and Policy Making in Education*, 146. See also the analysis of the period from Prime Minister Callaghan's Ruskin College speech to the introduction of the Education Reform Bill, during which the Department of Education and Science worked to undermine the existing educational subgovernment and assert its domination of national policy making, in John Fletcher, 'Policy-making in DES/DfE via Consensus and Contention,' *Oxford Review of Education* 21 (June 1995): 139–42.

83 In its 'consultation document,' issued in July, the government observed that there was now substantial agreement on the aims of compulsory schooling, as well as much agreement about subjects and content, and that many local education authorities had made important advances in their five-to-fifteen curriculum. 'But progress has been variable, uncertain, and often slow. Improvements have been made, some standards of attainment have risen. But some improvement is not enough. We must raise standards consistently, and at least as quickly as they are rising in competitive countries. The Government now wishes to move ahead at a faster pace to ensure that this happens and to secure for all pupils in maintained schools a curriculum which equips them with the knowledge, skills and understanding that they need for adult life.' Great Britain, Department of Education and Science and Welsh Office, *The National Curriculum 5–16: A Consultation Document* (London: Department of Education and Science, 1987), 2–3.

84 Attainment targets (ATs) were subsequently defined by the National Curriculum Council as 'objectives for each foundation subject setting out the

knowledge, skills and understanding which pupils of different abilities and maturities are expected to develop in each subject'; programs of study were the 'matters, skills and processes which must be taught to pupils during each key stage in order to meet the objectives set in the ATs.' Great Britain, National Curriculum Council, *Starting Out with the National Curriculum: An Introduction to the National Curriculum and Religious Education* (York: National Curriculum Council, 1992), 20–1.

85 Implementation of the national curriculum was also affected by suspicion on the part of the Conservative government, including Prime Minister Thatcher, that there was too much reliance on teachers' judgments and too little on national standardized testing. See the statement of Prime Minister Thatcher's views on the report of the Task Group on Assessment and Testing in a letter from her private secretary to the private secretary of the secretary of state for education and science printed in *The Independent*, 10 March 1988; quoted in Clyde Chitty, *The Education System Transformed: A Guide to the School Reforms* (Manchester: Baseline Books, 1992), 55–6.

86 See Ron Dearing, *The National Curriculum and Its Assessment: Final Report* (London: Schools Curriculum and Assessment Authority, 1993). Following the election of the Labour government in May 1997, primary schools were given even more flexibility in what to teach outside the core subjects of mathematics, English, information technology, and science. Other subjects in the ten-subject national curriculum for Key Stages 1 and 2 – history, geography, art, music, design and technology, and physical education – remained part of the curriculum; but in order to make more time for the higher priorities of literacy and numeracy, teachers were freed from the statutory obligation to teach full programs of study in all subjects, and OFSTED inspections of primary schools would be modified accordingly. Jim Docking, 'The Revised National Curriculum,' in Jim Docking (ed.), *New Labour's Policies for Schools: Raising the Standard?* (London: David Fulton Publishers, 2000), 77–8.

87 In April 1978 the Schools Council recommended that a wider group of subjects should replace the traditional three A-level subjects in sixth form, but in June 1979 the secretary of state for education and science informed the chair of the Schools Council that this proposal was not acceptable to the Conservative government. Again, in June 1988 a committee to review A levels, chaired by G.R. Higgison, reported in favour of 'leaner, tougher syllabuses, and programmes of study which involve five subjects as a norm for full-time students rather than three' (Great Britain, Department of Education and Science and Welsh Office, *Advancing A Levels: Report of a Committee Appointed by the Secretary of State for Education and Science and the*

Secretary of State for Wales [London: Her Majesty's Stationery Office, 1988], 13). In addition, one-fifth of the A-level assessment should be based on course work rather than the final examination. The Conservative government immediately rejected these recommendations.

88 According to Dearing, 'The proposed national framework for awards makes plain that academic, applied and vocational qualifications at the same level are of equal value' (Ron Dearing *Review of Qualifications for 16–19 Year Olds: Summary Report* [London: Schools Curriculum and Assessment Authority, 1996], 7). The National Council for Vocational Qualifications was established in 1986 as an accrediting body for vocational qualifications awarded by about six hundred examining bodies in England, Northern Ireland, and Wales. Approved qualifications were designated as either National Vocational Qualifications (NVQ), which were taken mainly by people in employment or youth training for specific occupations, or General National Vocational Qualifications (GNVQ), which were offered in broad vocational areas such as art and design, business, health and social care, leisure and tourism, and manufacturing for full-time students aged sixteen to eighteen. 'By the mid-1990s most schools with sixth forms and all further education colleges were providing a good range of GNVQ courses at Intermediate and Advanced levels. In the public mind, however, GNVQ courses are a poor second best to Advanced levels and it is still the case that few students with the academic ability to succeed at Advanced level take GNVQ courses, although most institutions organise the curriculum in such a way that students can take one A-level and one GNVQ Advanced course.' John Dunford, 'Towards Rationalisation? The 14–19 Curriculum,' in Clyde Chitty and John Dunford (eds), *State Schools: New Labour and the Conservative Legacy* (London: Woburn Press, 1999), 57.

89 Compared with its definite agenda for compulsory education (ages five to sixteen) the new Labour government's approach to post-compulsory education and training has been described as 'much more cautious, voluntarist, and experimental' (Ann Hodgson and Ken Spours, *New Labour's Educational Agenda: Issues and Policies for Education and Training from 14+* [London: Kogan Page, 1999], 129). Based on its election manifesto followed by a white paper in July 1999 (*Qualifying for Success: Post-16 Curriculum Reform*), the Labour government did create a new national qualification to assess achievement at three levels in the 'Key Skills' of communication, application of number, and information technology, as well as encouraging courses in the more general key skills of improving own learning and performance, problem solving, and working with others. In October 1997 the School Curriculum and Assessment Authority and the National Council

for Vocational Qualifications were merged to form the Qualifications and Curriculum Authority, which, with its counterparts in Wales (Qualifications, Curriculum and Assessment Authority for Wales) and Northern Ireland (Council for the Curriculum, Examinations, and Assessment), became responsible not only for the national curriculum and its assessment but also for the development of a national qualifications framework and occupational standards. The Learning and Skills Act, given Royal Assent in July 2000, established the Learning and Skills Council in England and the National Council for Education and Training for Wales (ELWa), which were assigned jurisdiction over funding and planning all post-compulsory education and training outside the universities. When the Learning and Skills Council began operation in April 2001, the secretary of state for education and training (David Blunkett) stated that 'We want to give pupils the option of taking predominantly vocational courses from the age of 14 and support them if they choose an apprenticeship at 16. There will be two clear routes. These can be combined, allowing students to take vocational GCSEs and A-levels alongside their academic equivalents' (*Times Educational Supplement*, 23 March 2001). In August 2001, ELWa released a green paper that envisaged breaking down the barriers between academic and vocational pathways, permitting students to mix academic and vocational qualifications and work-based options, and thus creating parity of esteem for academic, technical, and vocational learning pathways. See Great Britain, National Assembly for Wales, *The Learning Country: A Paving Document: A Comprehensive Education and Lifelong Learning Programme to 2010 in Wales*, 32; available at the ELWa Web site (*http://www.learningwales.gov.uk*). Along similar lines, a green paper issued by the Department for Education and Skills in February 2002 proposed more vocational qualifications and new hybrid qualifications that would combine traditional general subjects with their vocational counterparts, make no distinction in labelling between existing GCSEs and the new vocational GCSE subjects, and consider dropping the separate labelling of traditional and vocational A-level subjects. The green paper also proposed a 'Matriculation Diploma' as a new overarching award at age nineteen that 'would offer a means of recognising that genuine learning can take place in a variety of ways – including general and academic programmes, mixed vocational and general study, vocational study at school and college, and achievements in Modern Apprenticeships in a work-based programme' and hence promote 'parity of esteem between vocational and academic programmes of study.' See Great Britain, Department for Education and Skills, *14–19: Extending Opportunities, Raising Standards Consultation Document* (London: Her Majesty's Stationery Office,

2002), 30, 35, 41; available at the DfES Web site (*http://www.dfes.gov.uk/14-19greenpaper*).

90 'Unlike the English National Curriculum, the Scottish programme does not have the force of law: for this to happen would require major change, since the statutory powers of the Secretary of State for Scotland are confined to the issuing of "guidance" on the curriculum. In practical terms, however, observance of the guidelines is mandatory: they constitute an important part of the framework which the inspectorate uses to judge the work of a school, and no school can today afford to risk an adverse judgement.' John Darling, 'Scottish Primary Education: Philosophy and Practice,' in T.G.K. Bryce and W.M. Humes (eds), *Scottish Education* (Edinburgh: Edinburgh University Press, 1999), 34.

91 After 1965 the key curricular document for primary schools was *Primary Education in Scotland*, a memorandum prepared by a committee of teachers, college lecturers, and Her Majesty's Inspectors that described the best practices and proffered advice on methods, facilities, and organization in the classroom and school from an essentially child-centred educational perspective (Margaret M. Clark, 'Developments in Primary Education in Scotland,' in Margaret M. Clark and Pamela Munn [eds], *Education in Scotland: Policy and Practice from Pre-School to Secondary* [London: Routledge, 1997], 37). The curriculum for the compulsory years in Scottish secondary schools derived from two 1977 reports that led to the introduction of Standard Grade courses and examinations: the Consultative Committee on the Curriculum, chaired by James Munn, and a committee on assessment led by Joseph Dunning. See Great Britain, Scottish Education Department, Consultative Committee on the Curriculum, *The Structure of the Curriculum in the Third and Fourth Years of the Scottish Secondary School* (Edinburgh: Her Majesty's Stationery Office, 1977); and Great Britain, Scottish Education Department, Committee to Review Assessment in the Third and Fourth Years of Secondary Education in Scotland, *Assessment for All: Report of the Committee to Review Assessment in the Third and Fourth Years of Secondary Education in Scotland* (Edinburgh: Her Majesty's Stationery Office, 1977). The Munn committee recommended a two-tier core of seven subjects plus options for the third and fourth years of Scottish secondary education that would be taught at different levels (those offered to the whole age group would have three levels). The Dunning committee endorsed the proposal for syllabuses at three levels of ability and recommended that certificates be awarded at three corresponding levels (credit, general, and foundation) based on a combination of internal assessment and external examination. Initially rejected by the Labour secretary of state for Scotland, Bruce Millan,

SCE Standard Grade courses replaced SCE Ordinary Grades in 1984, and
the first examinations were taken in 1986. Students in the third and fourth
years of Scottish secondary schools take seven or eight Standard Grade
courses. They must take English, mathematics, a social subject (history,
geography, modern studies), a modern language, at least one science, a
creative and aesthetic subject (art, drama, music), and a technology subject
(computing, technological studies, home economics). 'Thus the "core"
takes up some 90 per cent of the pupil's week, and while there is choice
within some of these core areas, once religious and moral education, PE
and social education are added, there is little time for further choice.'
Brian Boyd, 'The Statutory Years of Secondary Education: Change and
Progress,' in Clark and Munn (eds), *Education in Scotland: Policy and Practice
from Pre-School to Secondary*, 60.

92 Great Britain, Secretary of State for Scotland, *Curriculum and Assessment in
Scotland: A Policy for the '90s* (Edinburgh: Scottish Office Education Depart-
ment, 1987), 9; see also Frank R. Adams, '5–14: Origins, Development and
Implementation,' in Bryce and Humes (eds), *Scottish Education*, 352.

93 Because of the curricular reforms resulting from the work of the Munn and
Dunning committees that were initiated in 1984–5 for the third and fourth
years of secondary education, the Scottish curricular and testing reforms
beginning in 1987 were limited to the years five to fourteen, rather than
five to sixteen as in England and Wales. An overview of the national guidelines for Scotland can be found in Great Britain, Scottish Office Education
Department, *Structure and Balance of the Curriculum 5–14* (Edinburgh: Her
Majesty's Stationery Office, 1993). Working groups of professional educators, including teachers, head teachers, subject specialists, and special
needs advisers, began work in 1989, national guidelines were published
between 1991 and 1993, and implementation was completed by 1999–2000.

94 Great Britain, Scottish Office Education Department, *Upper Secondary
Education in Scotland: Report of the Committee to Review Curriculum and Examinations in the Fifth and Sixth Years of Secondary Education in Scotland* (Edinburgh: Her Majesty's Stationery Office, 1992), 46–7. The curriculum for
the Scottish certificate would put the emphasis on core skills, utilizing a
modular structure that would be integrated with secondary vocational
qualification and prepare students for employment, further training, or
more advanced education. The curriculum for the Scottish baccalaureate
would be based on seven core subjects – English, a modern language,
mathematics, science, and a social studies subject in all three years; information technology in year one; and music or history of art in years two and
three – plus two options chosen from a range of subjects. The weighting of
subjects and choice of options would vary between alternative 'lines of

study,' one in arts and the other in science, with the potential to combine academic and vocational education (ibid., 75–6).

95 Great Britain, Scottish Office, *Higher Still: Opportunity for All* (Edinburgh: Her Majesty's Stationery Office, 1994), 7.

96 National Certificates for students who completed accredited courses in secondary schools or colleges of further education were awarded by the Scottish Vocational Education Council (SCOTVEC), which was established in 1984 to replace existing vocational qualifications examining bodies. SCOTVEC also accredited and awarded Scottish Vocational Qualifications and General Scottish Vocational Qualifications equivalent to the National Vocational Qualifications and General National Vocational Qualifications in other countries of the United Kingdom. Under the white paper's proposal, courses would vary in length, but each course would be classified at one of five levels, depending on its difficulty – Foundation, General, Credit, Higher, or Advanced Higher. As a result, it was argued, 'Students should always have available a course at the appropriate level in their chosen subjects. The range of courses on offer should allow them to progress at the fastest pace of which they are capable' (ibid., 9). To administer this unified system, the 1996 Education (Scotland) Act created the Scottish Qualifications Authority (SQA), which took over the functions of SCOTVEC and the Scottish Examination Board in April 1997.

97 David Raffe, Cathy Howieson, and Teresa Tinklin, 'The Scottish Educational Crisis of 2000: An Analysis of the Policy Process of Unification,' *Journal of Education Policy* 17 (March–April 2002): 177. Raffe, Howieson, and Tinklin conclude, 'Given that the process of introducing a flexible unified system is inherently conflict-prone, the remarkable thing is not that Higher Still has attracted controversy, but that support for the reform has remained so strong. This may be a testimony to the strength of the initial consensus' (ibid., 184). Among other results of the political crisis, the chief executive of the SQA resigned in August 2000, two committees of the Scottish Parliament held inquiries, a new education minister announced that Her Majesty's Inspectorate would become an executive agency and lose its policy-making powers, and a National Qualifications Steering Group was established to give various interests in the policy community a voice with regard to the future implementation of Higher Still.

98 In 1996, parents earning under about £10,000 received full fee remission, while those with incomes up to £30,000 received partial remission. In 1995–6, 293 independent schools in England offered assisted places. See Geoff Whitty, Sally Power, and Tony Edwards, 'The Assisted Places Scheme: Its Impact and Its Role in Privatization and Marketization,' *Journal of Education Policy* 13 (March–April 1998): 238.

99 In particular, although LEAs would continue to be formal employers of teachers in county schools and the chief education officer had to be consulted in the case of appointments of head and deputy head teachers, school governors decided who and how many would be employed as teaching and non-teaching staff in their school.

100 The Thatcher government's purpose in creating grant-maintained schools as a new type of educational provider was to 'add a new and powerful dimension to the ability of parents to exercise choice within the publicly provided sector of education. The greater diversity of provision which will result should enhance the prospects of improving educational standards in all schools. Parents and local communities would have new opportunities to secure the development of their schools in ways appropriate to the needs of their children and in accordance with their wishes, within the legal framework of the national curriculum' (Great Britain, Department of Education and Science, *Grant Maintained Schools: Consultation Paper* (London: Department of Education and Science, 1987), paragraph 20). The decision to apply for grant-maintained status depended on a majority vote of the governors or a petition of parents representing at least 20 per cent of the registered pupils followed by approval of a majority of the parents voting in a secret postal referendum. Assuming that the secretary of state approved the conversion to the status of grant-maintained school, the governing body became owner of the school's premises and employers of its teachers, and the school got its funding directly from the central authority based on what the LEA would have spent on the school, including the cost of providing central services and benefits to the school, all of which was deducted from the LEA's grant. The Education Act of 1993 created the Funding Authority for Schools and the Funding Council for Wales as quasi-independent bodies, appointed respectively by the secretaries of state for education and science and for Wales, responsible for funding grant-maintained schools.

101 According to the Citizen's Charter issued by Prime Minister John Major in 1991, 'If an Inspectorate is too close to the profession it is supervising there is a risk that it will lose touch with the interests of people who use the service. It may be captured by fashionable theories and lose the independence and objectivity that the public needs. Professional inspectorates can easily become part of a closed professional world' (quoted in John Dunford, 'Inspection: From HMI to Ofsted,' in Chitty and Dunford [eds], *State Schools: New Labour and the Conservative Legacy*, 118). This point in the Citizen's Charter referred to professional inspectorates in general, but Dunford observes that HMI was the principal target.

102 The Conservative government's last education act, passed in 1997, extended the jurisdiction of OFSTED with the help of the Audit Commission to inspect local education authorities, and the secretary of state for education and employment was given substantial powers to intervene, including centralization or privatization of educational services, where an OFSTED report established an LEA's failure adequately to support its schools. In addition to OFSTED, the Education (Schools) Act, 1992, created the Office of Her Majesty's Chief Inspector in Wales, which was independent of OFSTED. For a helpful comparison of policies for school inspection in England and Wales, see Gerran Thomas and David Egan, 'Policies on Schools' Inspection in Wales and England,' in Richard Daugherty, Robert Phillips, and Gareth Rees (eds), *Education Policy-Making in Wales: Explorations in Devolved Governance* (Cardiff: University of Wales Press, 2000), 149–68.

103 Tom Nolan, 'The Future of Education Post the Education Reform (NI) Order, 1989: An Education and Library Board Administrator's Account,' in Robert Osborne, Robert Cormack, and Anthony Gallagher (eds), *After the Reform: Education and Policy in Northern Ireland* (Aldershot: Avebury, 1993), 63. As in England and Wales, county schools were empowered to opt out entirely from the jurisdiction of education and library boards, but to become grant-maintained schools they had to become integrated schools enrolling both Protestant and Roman Catholic students.

104 Alex McEwen, *Public Policy in a Divided Society: Schooling, Culture and Identity in Northern Ireland* (Aldershot: Ashgate, 1999), xiii. As one chief education officer put it, 'the fact that I get my funding 100 per cent from central government means that I'm accountable through the permanent secretary in the DENI to the Public Accounts Committee. I know exactly where I stand as chief executive' (ibid., 123).

105 Great Britain, Scottish Education Department, *Assisted Places Scheme: A Brief Guide for Parents* (3rd ed.; Edinburgh: Scottish Education Department, 1985); quoted in Geoffrey Walford, 'The Scottish Assisted Places Scheme: A Comparative Study of the Origins, Nature and Practice of the APSs in Scotland, England and Wales,' *Journal of Education Policy* 3 (April–June, 1988): 147.

106 Under the Education (Scotland) Act, 1981, parents could be denied their choice of schools if it would require the employment of additional staff or alterations to school buildings or would be seriously detrimental to good order and discipline in the chosen school. In contrast with the case of England and Wales, parents in Scotland did not have to give the local authority any reason for their choice of school, and they had a right of

appeal if their choice were refused. Provisions for parental freedom to choose their children's school similar to those in Scotland were extended to England and Wales in the 1988 Education Reform Act.

107 Devolved school management was introduced in Scotland in 1993, with full implementation achieved over the next five years, but budgetary authority was devolved directly to head teachers rather than school boards. In general, Scottish school boards proved to be reluctant to become involved in school decision making, and head teachers were not seriously challenged about the way in which they managed their schools. Pamela Munn, 'Devolved Management of Schools,' in Munn and Clark (eds), *Education in Scotland: Policy and Practice from Pre-School to Secondary*, 131–4.

108 As John Dunford has observed, 'It was surprising that it had not been abolished in the early 1970s when Margaret Thatcher was Secretary of State, because the Schools Council represented all that she detested about the world of education.' John Dunford, 'Towards Rationalisation? The 14–19 Curriculum,' in Chitty and Dunford (eds), *State Schools: New Labour and the Conservative Legacy*, 48.

109 Under the Education Act of 1993, the National Curriculum Council and the School Examinations and Assessment Council were merged to form the School Curriculum and Assessment Authority.

110 In 1991 the School Teachers' Review Body (STRB), its members appointed by the government, was established to make recommendations to the secretary of state for education and science about teachers' salaries and conditions of employment. This change in institutions from the Burnham Main Committee to the STRB was accompanied by a change in the criterion for determining teachers' salaries and working conditions. The main criterion for collective bargaining through the Burnham Main Committee during the 1970s was 'comparability.' During the 1980s, Margaret Thatcher and Keith Joseph rejected comparability in favour of 'affordability.' Mike Ironside and Roger Seifert, *Industrial Relations in Schools* (London: Routledge, 1995), 13, 22–3.

111 The teachers' pay dispute in Scotland is briefly described in Malcolm Green, 'The Local Governance of Education: A Political Perspective,' in Bryce and Humes (eds), *Scottish Education*, 149–50; and Willis Pickard, 'The History of Scottish Education, 1980 to the Present Day,' in ibid., 228–9.

112 Approximately 33,000 students, 7 per cent of enrolments in independent schools, held places under the Assisted Places Scheme. Donald Mackinnon and June Statham, *Education in the United Kingdom: Facts and Figures* (3rd ed.; London: Hodder and Stoughton, 1999), 186.

113 Great Britain, Department for Education and Employment, *Excellence in Schools* (London: Her Majesty's Stationery Office, 1997), 72.

114 The 1992 white paper argued that, in addition to choice among county
    schools, voluntary schools, and (thanks to the Assisted Places Scheme)
    independent schools, as well as among grammar schools, comprehensive
    schools, grant-maintained schools, bilateral schools (operating selective
    and non-selective streams of entry), and city technical colleges within the
    public sector, some comprehensive schools had developed specializations
    in particular subjects such as music or technology. All maintained schools
    would continue to be required to teach the national curriculum to the
    highest standards, but that would not prevent schools from choosing to
    develop an expertise in a particular subject. The government would be
    seeking to achieve greater diversity by encouraging the formation of
    different types of schools and schools specializing in particular subjects
    (Great Britain, Secretary of State for Education and Secretary of State
    for Wales, *Choice and Diversity: A New Framework for Schools* [London: Her
    Majesty's Stationery Office, 1992], 1, 43). In the 1996 white paper, the
    Conservative government's policy for 'parents to be able to choose from a
    range of good schools of different types, matching what they want for their
    child with what a school offers' again referred to the existence of inde-
    pendent schools, church schools, grammar schools, city technology
    colleges, and grant-maintained schools as options to comprehensive sec-
    ondary schools, and remarked that the government 'had also encouraged
    schools to specialise in particular subjects such as technology and lan-
    guages.' Great Britain, Secretary of State for Education and Employment
    and Secretary of State for Wales, *Self-Government in Schools* (London: Her
    Majesty's Stationery Office, 1996), 2–3.
115 In its manifesto for the 1997 general election, the Labour party explicitly
    rejected any return to the eleven-plus examination but recognized the
    legitimacy of internal selection: 'We favour all-in schooling which identi-
    fies the distinct abilities of individual pupils and organises them in classes
    to maximise their progress in individual subjects ... There should be no
    return to the 11–plus. It divides children into successes and failures at far
    too early an age. We must modernise comprehensive schools. Children
    are not all of the same ability, nor do they learn at the same speed. That
    means "setting" children in classes to maximise progress, for the benefit of
    high-fliers and slower learners alike' (Labour Party Manifesto, 1997, 3–4,
    7; quoted in David Gillborn, 'Race, Nation and Education: New Labour
    and the New Racism,' in Jack Demaine [ed.], *Education Policy and Contem-
    porary Politics* [London: Macmillan, 1999], 92–3). This view was repeated in
    the white paper published in July 1997: 'Setting, particularly in science,
    maths and languages, is proving effective in many schools. We do not
    believe that any single model of grouping pupils should be imposed on

secondary schools, but unless a school can demonstrate that it is getting
better than expected results through a different approach, we do make
the presumption that setting should be the norm in secondary schools. In
some cases, it is worth considering in primary schools. Schools should
make clear in reports to parents the use they are making of different
grouping approaches. OFSTED inspections will also report on this' (Department for Education and Employment, *Excellence in Schools*, 38). On
specialization versus selection in Labour policy, see also Tony Edwards,
Geoff Whitty, and Sally Power, 'Moving Back from Comprehensive Education,' in Demaine (ed.), *Education Policy and Contemporary Politics*,
32–6.

116 Ron Letch, 'The Role of Local Education Authorities,' in Docking (ed.),
New Labour's Policies for Schools: Raising the Standards?, 174.

117 Peter Downes, 'Changing Pressures in the Secondary School,' in Chitty
and Dunford (eds), *State Schools: New Labour and the Conservative Legacy*, 42.
Downes adds, 'Whether this will happen in practice is one of the unanswered questions for the future. It could be that the tension between "Old
Labour" in the LEAs and "New Labour" in Westminster will be the political battleground of the new era' (ibid.).

118 Arthur Midwinter, Michael Keating, and James Mitchell, *Politics and Public
Policy in Scotland* (London: Macmillan, 1991), 61.

119 In July 1997 the Labour government presented to Parliament white papers
that proposed to create a Scottish parliament and a Welsh national assembly. On 10 April 1998, multiparty negotiations ended with an agreement
on devolution to a Northern Ireland assembly ('The Agreement Reached
in Multiparty Negotiations,' which is generally called the 'Belfast Agreement' or the 'Good Friday Agreement'). The Government of Wales Act
1998 was given Royal Assent in July 1998 and the Scotland Act 1998 and
the Northern Ireland Act 1998 in November. With the exception of
certain enumerated areas, the Scottish Parliament and the Northern
Ireland Assembly have been given general powers to adopt primary
legislation that includes the area of education and training. The National
Assembly for Wales was granted powers to enact subordinate legislation
(such as orders, rules, and regulations issued under authority conferred by
an Act of Parliament); primary legislation for Wales, including that for
education and training, continues to be made in Westminster, with the
National Assembly for Wales serving as an advisory body to Parliament.
See Noreen Burrows, *Devolution* (London: Sweet and Maxwell, 2000),
55–91; and Vernon Bogdanor, *Devolution in the United Kingdom* (Oxford:
Oxford University Press, 1999), 201–86. In contrast with Scotland and

Wales, in Northern Ireland the future of devolution continues to be uncertain. On 14 October 2002, following a breakdown of power-sharing in the Northern Ireland government, the secretary of state for Northern Ireland suspended the Northern Ireland Assembly and the Executive and, with the Northern Ireland Office ministers of state, assumed responsibility for direction and control of Northern Ireland departments, including DENI.

120 The members of the National Commission on Excellence in Education included three university presidents, a community college president, two professors, two principals, a teacher, two business executives, a former governor, and five education officials.

121 United States, National Commission on Excellence in Education, *A Nation at Risk: The Imperative for Educational Reform* (Washington, D.C.: United States Department of Education, 1983), 5.

122 Ibid., 18.

123 As Thomas B. Timar and David L. Kirp have observed, in the early to middle 1980s there were more rules and regulations generated by state boards, superintendents, departments, and legislatures about all aspects of public education than over the previous twenty years. Moreover, the new state regulatory regimes were remarkably similar in purpose and content. 'Across the nation, educational standards have been ratcheted upwards. Academic requirements have increased: students must spend more time in school, take more credits for graduation, and enroll in more "solid" courses such as science, math, and foreign languages; in many schools new courses in the use of computers have been added. To meet higher academic expectations, more dedicated and more highly qualified teachers are needed. That is why states have tried both to make it harder to become a teacher and more attractive to remain one. In order to provide necessary leadership to the schools, principals must acquire new skills consistent with their new roles as instructional leaders, as opposed to their traditional roles as managers.' Thomas B. Timar and David L. Kirp, *Managing Educational Excellence* (New York: Falmer Press, 1988), 112–13.

124 See United States, Department of Education, Center for Statistics, *Digest of Education Statistics 1985–86* (Washington, D.C.: United States Government Printing Office, 1986), 102–4; and United States, Department of Education, National Center for Educational Statistics, *Digest of Education Statistics 1997* (Washington, D.C.: United States Government Printing Office, 1997), 149–54.

125 In addition, four English courses were required for the college-preparatory certificate in Missouri and the Regents' diploma in New York. Four

states required three courses in social studies for their élite academic programs: Arkansas, Indiana, Missouri, and North Carolina. Texas began to require four courses in social studies starting in 2000.

126 Vermont required all students to complete a total of five courses in mathematics and science. In addition, five states required at least three courses in mathematics for their élite academic programs, and three states required at least three courses in science for their élite academic programs.

127 The national goals, in turn, closely resembled those developed for the year 2000 by the Southern Regional Education Board in 1988. See Richard W. Riley, 'The Goals 2000: Educate America Act. Providing a World-Class Education for Every Child,' in John F. Jennings (ed.), *National Issues in Education: Goals 2000 and School to Work* (Bloomington, Ind., and Washington, D.C.: Phi Delta Kappa International and the Institute for Educational Leadership, 1995), 11–12.

128 See John F. Jennings, 'Introduction,' in Jennings (ed.), *National Issues in Education*, ix-x. On the politics in Congress with regard to Goals 2000, see Dale E. Kildee, 'Enacting Goals 2000: Educate America Act,' in ibid., 27–45; and also John A. Boehner, 'The Unmaking of School Reform,' in ibid., 47–58.

129 The Clinton administration's Goals 2000: Educate America Act incorporated the six national goals agreed at the Charlottesville summit and added foreign languages and the arts to the list of 'demonstrated competency in challenging subject matter.' Amendments in Congress added civics and government and economics to the national goal of student achievement and citizenship as well as two additional goals concerning teacher education and professional development (by the year 2000 teachers would have access to programs for the continued improvement of their professional skills and the opportunity to acquire the knowledge and skills needed to prepare students for the next century) and parental participation (every school would promote partnerships that would increase parental involvement and participation in promoting the social, emotional, and academic growth of children).

130 As the former governor observed, 'The first obstacle we faced was that South Carolina had never developed standards that would explicitly state what we want our kids to know and be able to do – not just for now, but for the new century in which these kids will live and work.' Carroll A. Campbell, Jr, 'The Governors and the National Education Goals,' in Jennings (ed.), *National Issues in Education*, 90.

131 The six goals and seventy-five valued outcomes resulted from the work of

the Council on School Performance Standards, appointed by the governor to advise on what students should know and be able to do (James G. Hougland, Jr, Mark C. Berger, and Edward Kifer, 'Public Reactions to Education Reform: A Study of Attitudes during the First Four Years of the Kentucky Education Reform Act,' *International Journal of Educational Reform* 3 [January 1994]: 53). See also Diane Massell, 'Achieving Consensus: Setting the Agenda for State Curriculum Reform,' in Richard F. Elmore and Susan H. Fuhrman (eds), *The Governance of Curriculum*, 1994 Yearbook of the Association for Supervision and Curriculum Development (Alexandria, Va: Association for Supervision and Curriculum Development, 1994), 96–8; and Jennifer O'Day, 'Systemic Reform and Goals 2000,' in Jennings (ed.), *National Issues in Education*, 99–115.

132 Beverley B. Geltner, 'Juggling the Reinvention of Michigan's Schools,' *International Journal of Educational Reform* 3 (October 1994): 403.

133 Idaho was developing state educational standards in 1998–9. Arizona, Nevada, Rhode Island, and South Carolina had adopted standards in three core academic subjects; Montana, Pennsylvania, and Wyoming in two; and North Dakota in one. See the special issue of *Education Week*, 11 January 1999, 114. By fall 2001, forty-eight states had adopted standards in four core subjects, Rhode Island had set standards in three subjects, and Iowa still had no state-sanctioned standards (*Education Week*, 19 January 2002).

134 In fall 2001, forty-three states got passing grades for clear and specific standards for mathematics at all three levels of elementary, middle, and high school, and thirty-nine states had passing grades for science. Twenty-four states received passing evaluations at all three levels for their English/language arts standards, and seven were judged to have clear and specific standards for social studies/history.

135 The highest frequency of student assessments occurred in grade eight, where forty-four states had multiple-choice tests and/or performance assessments, followed by grade four, in which forty states administered multiple-choice tests and or performance assessments. At the level of high school, state provisions for measuring student performance were divided between grade ten (thirty states) and grade eleven (twenty-seven states). For details on the types of measures and subjects assessed, see *Education Week*, 11 January 1999. By fall 2001, all states except for Idaho and Nebraska were using multiple-choice tests to measure student performance at all three levels of elementary, middle, and high school, and twenty-five states had short-answer tests at all three levels. Thirty-nine states had extended-response assessments at all three levels in English, but only thirteen used extended-response assessments for other subjects. Kentucky and

Vermont were the only states to use portfolios as ways to measure student or school performance (*Education Week*, 10 January 2002).

136 The three states above the national averages for students scoring at least proficient on all eight tests were Connecticut, Massachusetts, and Minnesota. The states consistently below average were the southern states of Alabama, Arkansas, Georgia, Louisiana, Mississippi, South Carolina, and Tennessee; Arizona, California, and New Mexico in the West/Southwest; and Hawaii. Not all states participated in each national test, and South Dakota did not participate in any of the eight tests. See *Education Week*, 11 January 1999; and ibid., 10 January 2002.

137 During the decade following the change in Illinois (1973) and South Dakota (1974) from popular election of the state superintendent of education to gubernatorial appointment of the state board of education, which in turn appointed the state superintendent, the only permanent change in the constitution of educational governance at the state level was the restoration of an elective superintendent of public instruction in Indiana in 1982. Changes were also made in Kansas, Massachusetts, and Tennessee, but these were later reversed.

138 The four models below follow the typology used by Donald W. Burns, Robert M. Palaich, Aims McGuinness, and Patricia Flakus-Mosqueda, *State Governance of Education: 1983* (Denver: Education Commission of the States, 1983); Martha McCarthy, Carol Langdon, and Jeannette Olson, *State Education Governance Structures* (Denver: Education Commission of the States, 1993); and Kristin Cracium and Todd Ziebarth, 'Models of State Education Governance,' Education Commission of the States, March 2002 (*http://www.ecs.org/clearinghouse/13/31/1331.doc*). In classifying the states by model, I have relied on their work, but I have reclassified all but one (New York) of the states that they have described as 'unique' according to their closest fit among the four models.

139 In Arizona, Florida, Georgia, Idaho, Indiana, Montana, North Carolina, South Carolina, and Wyoming, the election was a partisan contest; in California, North Dakota, Oklahoma, Washington, and Wisconsin, the election was non-partisan. The Florida state board of education, which was the last surviving ex officio board of elected cabinet members, comprised the governor, secretary of state, attorney general, comptroller, treasurer, commissioner of agriculture, and commissioner of education; but, effective January 2003, the Florida state board of education became appointed by the governor and the commissioner of education appointed by the board. Sixteen members of the South Carolina state board of education were elected by state legislative delegations, and one member was ap-

pointed by the governor. In Washington, local school boards elected nine members of the state board of education, one was elected by the governing boards of state-approved private schools (and voted only on matters pertaining to private schools), and one was the superintendent of public instruction. Wisconsin did not have a state board of education.

140 The eleven states were Arkansas, Connecticut, Illinois, Kentucky, Maryland, Massachusetts, Missouri, New Hampshire, Rhode Island, Vermont, and West Virginia. In Massachusetts the governor also appointed the secretary of education, who was a cabinet member. As an approximation of this model, after the reform of 1984 the governor appointed five members of the Mississippi state board of education, the lieutenant-governor and the speaker of the House each appointed two members, and the board appointed the superintendent. In Alaska the secretary of education was nominated by the state board of education and appointed by the governor.

141 In four of these nine states (Alabama, Colorado, Kansas, and Michigan), the elections for state board of education were partisan; in five (Hawaii, Nebraska, Nevada, Ohio, and Utah), elections were non-partisan. New Mexico also adhered essentially to this model, as ten members of its state board of education continued to be chosen in partisan elections but, under a 1986 constitutional amendment, five members were appointed by the governor. Louisiana, where since 1968 the state board of education comprised eight members chosen through partisan elections and three appointed by the governor, also could be classified under this model, beginning in 1985 when the state assembly passed legislation empowering the state board to appoint the superintendent of education. In Ohio, as a result of legislation passed in July 2000, eleven members of the state board of education continued to be elected, and eight were appointed by the governor with the advice and consent of the state Senate.

142 This model was operative in eight states in the late 1930s and early 1940s, but there were only four (New Jersey, Pennsylvania, Tennessee, and Virginia) in 1972 when it was restored in Maine as part of a general reorganization to enhance the authority of the governor. During the first wave of educational reform following the publication of A Nation at Risk, the governor acquired authority to appoint the director of education in Iowa and the commissioner of education in Minnesota. In South Dakota the office of the state superintendent, who was appointed by the state board, was abolished in 1991 by an executive reorganization order that consolidated its functions with those of the secretary of education and cultural affairs, appointed by the governor. Similarly, a reform of state educational

governance in Delaware that took effect on 1 July 1999 transferred authority to appoint the secretary of education from the state board of education
to the governor. As a result of the major reform of Texas education in
1990, the commissioner of education became appointed by the governor
rather than being popularly elected. The Texas state board of education
continued to be popularly elected, however, although its regulatory and
policy-making authority was reduced. In Minnesota the governor appointed both the commissioner and the state board of education until the
board was abolished as part of educational reform legislation passed in
April 1998. In Pennsylvania, seventeen members of the state board of
education are appointed by the governor; the other members are the
majority and minority chairs (or their proxies) of the education committees of the state House of Representatives and the Senate.

143 In Georgia in the early 1980s, county board members were usually appointed by a grand jury but might be elected (and in one case the board
was self-perpetuating), while members of 'independent' school boards
were usually appointed by city councils but in some cases were popularly
elected. A decade later, the situation had been reversed: most county and
independent boards were elected but some were still appointed. Effective
1 January 1994, all Georgia school boards became elected. Similarly, in
Tennessee the school law provided for county school boards to be appointed by county governing bodies, but special legislation permitted
election in nearly half the counties, while city boards were variously
appointed by city councils, appointed by the mayor, popularly elected, or
comprised of city officials serving ex officio. In 1992 a change in the law
required that all county boards be elected.

144 See United States, Bureau of the Census, *1992 Census of Governments*, vol.
1, *Government Organization* (Washington, D.C.: United States Government
Printing Office, 1994); and *1997 Census of Governments*, vol. 1, *Government
Organization* (*http://www.census.gov/prod/gc97/gc971-1.pdf*).

145 Several cities were exceptions to the prevailing model in their state. In
three cases, the school boards were fiscally independent but their members were appointed by the mayor with the approval of city council
(Chicago), by the mayor from a slate of nominees chosen by a local
nominating panel (Cleveland), or six by the mayor and one by the governor (Detroit). In the state of New York, five large city school boards were
all fiscally dependent on their city governments, their members elected in
the case of Buffalo, Rochester, and Syracuse, appointed by the mayor in
the case of Yonkers, and appointed by the mayor and borough presidents
in the case of New York city.

146 In New Jersey, 552 'type 2' school boards were elected and fiscally independent, but the ('type 1') school boards of eighteen cities or towns and
four townships were appointed by the mayor or other chief executive
officer of the municipality and were fiscally dependent on the local municipal authority. The Boston School Committee was appointed by the
mayor, and the members of the School Reform Commission in Philadelphia were appointed jointly by the mayor (two) and the governor (three).

147 The Baltimore board of school commissioners was appointed by the city
council, and the twenty-three county boards of education were formerly
all appointed by the governor of Maryland. Following the adoption of a
'home rule' charter in 1948, Montgomery County became the first county
to elect its board of education. Seven more counties voted for popular
election of their board of education during the 1970s and two during the
1980s. In the case of Prince George's County, however, in order to end a
bitter struggle between the board and the superintendent over control of
county schools, the Maryland state assembly in April 2002 replaced the
elected board of education with one appointed jointly by the state governor and the county executive (*Education Week*, 13 February 2002; 17 April
2002). Until 1992, when the General Assembly gave local school districts
the option to elect their school boards, the members of Virginia's forty-
one city and two town school boards were appointed by their city or town
council, and the ninety-four county school boards were appointed by a
school board selection commission appointed by the circuit court or
(given voter approval) the county governing body. By November 2001,
105 of the 134 Virginia school districts had opted to elect the members of
their local board.

148 The classification of basic support programs is based on judgments made
by the authors of descriptions of state programs of educational finance as
interpreted and summarized by Catherine C. Sielke and C. Thomas
Holmes, 'Overview of Approaches to State School Funding,' in United
States, Department of Education, National Center for Education Statistics,
Catherine C. Sielke, John Dayton, C. Thomas Holmes, and Anne L. Jefferson (eds), *Public School Finance Programs of the United States and Canada:
1998–99*, NCES 2001–309 (Washington, D.C.: National Center for Education Statistics, 2001). Their overview, which is chapter 1 of the report, has
been posted at the World Wide Web site of the American Education Finance Association (*http://www.ed.sc.ed/aefa/reports/nces_rpt.html*), and individual state reports can be found at the Web site of the National Center
for Education Statistics (*http://www.nces.ed.gov*). See also Stephen D. Gold,
David M. Smith, and Stephen B. Lawton (eds), *Public School Finance Pro-*

grams of the United States and Canada 1993–94, vol. 1 (Albany: American Education Finance Association and Center for the Study of the States, Nelson A. Rockefeller Institute of Government, State University of New York, 1995), 24. Indiana and Wisconsin have guaranteed tax-yield programs, and New York uses a foundation-type percentage equalizing grant. The long-standing flat grant in Delaware is accompanied by a separate equalization component. Vermont used a percentage equalizing grant from 1969 to 1987, when a foundation formula was put in place. In February 1997, in response to a suit brought by parents who were frustrated by low levels of state funding for public education, the Supreme Court of Vermont decided that this funding system was unconstitutional. A new educational finance law, passed in June 1997, provided for a first tier of state aid in the form of a block grant (initially $5,010) per student and a second tier based on a guaranteed tax yield.

149 In contrast with the positive role taken by federal courts in combating racially segregated schools, based on the 1954 decision of the U.S. Supreme Court in *Brown* v. *Board of Education of Topeka, Kansas*, that segregated schools violated the principle of equal protection, federal courts were effectively closed to litigation over disparities in school funding by the Supreme Court's decision in *San Antonio Independent School District* v. *Rodriguez* (1973). In this challenge to interdistrict funding disparities in Texas, based on the equal protection clause of the U.S. Constitution, which in turn had national implications because of the similarity between the Texas foundation program and those of other states (twenty-eight state attorneys general filed briefs defending its constitutionality), the Supreme Court in a five-to-four decision concluded that public education 'is not among the rights afforded explicit protection under the Federal Constitution.' An excellent overview of the courts and school finance from the 1970s to the 1990s is provided by K. Forbis Jordan and Teresa S. Lyons, *Financing Public Education in an Era of Change* (Bloomington, Ind.: Phi Delta Kappa Educational Foundation, 1992), 54–81. A helpful summary of important cases can be found in the textbook by Vern Brimley, Jr, and Rulon R. Garfield, *Financing Education in a Climate of Change* (8th ed.; Boston: Allyn and Bacon, 2002), 218–37.

150 According to Jordan and Lyons, 'The *Robinson* cases present a striking example of legislation from the bench. Throughout the seven cases, there was considerable debate about whether a court has the power to order the reallocation of money appropriated by the legislature. Under the doctrine of separation of powers, appropriation is clearly the prerogative of the legislative branch. But in the New Jersey Supreme Court's view, when the

legislature continued to act in an unconstitutional fashion in its educational appropriations, the court had an obligation to provide a remedy by enjoining the expenditure of appropriated funds. *Robinson* illustrates the potential reach of judicial power and serves to explain why state courts have continued to be used as mechanisms for seeking changes in state school funding systems' (*Financing Public Education in an Era of Change*, 73). In a similar case, the Supreme Court of Washington State in 1978 held that the state constitution placed a duty on the state to make 'ample' provision for public education, thus forcing a revision of the system of educational finance that resulted in full state funding.

151 See the summary of the disposition of court cases in Brimley, Jr, and Garfield, *Financing Education in a Climate of Change*, 235–6; and also Paul A. Minorini and Stephen D. Sugarman, 'School Finance Litigation in the Name of Educational Equity: Its Evolution, Impact, and Future,' in Helen F. Ladd, Rosemary Chalk, and Janet S. Hansen (eds), *Equity and Adequacy in Education Finance: Issues and Perspectives* (Washington, D.C.: National Academy Press, 1999), 42–5.

152 Ibid., 47.

153 *Rose* v. *Council for Better Education, Inc.*, 790 S.W. 2d 186 (Ky 1989); *Helena Elementary School District No. 1* v. *State*, 769 P. 2d 684 (Mont. 1989); *Edgewood Independent School District* v. *Kirby*, 777 S.W. 2d 391 (Tex. 1989).

154 Paul A. Minorini and Stephen D. Sugarman, 'Educational Adequacy and the Courts: The Promise and Problems of Moving to a New Paradigm,' in Ladd, Chalk, and Hansen (eds), *Equity and Adequacy in Education Finance: Issues and Perspectives*, 196–9. In Vermont the state court of appeal relied on fiscal inequity rather than educational inadequacy in judging the state's educational finance program to be unconstitutional, while courts in Wyoming (1995) and Ohio (1997) relied on a combination of equity and adequacy arguments.

155 See Brimley, Jr, and Garfield, *Financing Education in a Climate of Change*, 235–6. Pending cases are excluded from my tabulation. Jordan and Lyons conclude that 'Using the courts to achieve equity in state school finance systems can be characterized as a continuing but unattainable quest ... Given the decentralized nature of America's schools, state funding systems are not sufficiently refined to ensure sufficient funds for every child in every classroom. The resulting diversity may be both the greatest strength and greatest weakness of our public schools. And the unfairness of that diversity will be a continuing subject of litigation. The quest for equity likely will continue as long as the nation's schools are administered through 15,000 local school districts, which operate 80,000 individual

schools, and as long as these districts have some discretionary spending and operational authority over such items as teacher salaries, course offerings, and instructional materials and equipment' (Jordan and Lyons, *Financing Public Education in an Era of Change*, 80).

156 Louann Bierlein and Mark Bateman, 'Charter Schools v. the Status Quo: Which Will Succeed?' *International Journal of Educational Reform* 5 (April 1996): 160.

157 From 1991 to 2000, legislation authorizing the establishment of charter schools was passed in Minnesota (1991); California (1992); Colorado, Georgia, Massachusetts, Michigan, New Mexico, and Wisconsin (1993); Arizona, Hawaii, and Illinois (1994); Alaska, Arkansas, Delaware, Kansas, Louisiana, New Hampshire, Rhode Island, Texas, and Wyoming (1995); Connecticut, Florida, New Jersey, North Carolina, and South Carolina (1996); Mississippi, Nevada, Ohio, and Pennsylvania (1997); Idaho, Missouri, New York, Utah, and Virginia (1998); and Oklahoma and Oregon (1999) (Chester E. Finn, Jr, Bruno V. Manno, and Gregg Vanourek, *Charter Schools in Action: Renewing Public Education* [Princeton: Princeton University Press, 2000], 24; and *Education Week*, 11 January 2001). The U.S. Congress also approved a charter school law for the District of Columbia in 1996. The expansion of charter schools in the second half of the 1990s was facilitated by federal aid. When the Elementary and Secondary Education Act was reauthorized in 1994, $15 million was authorized for starting charter schools. The initial appropriation of $6 million for 1994–5 increased annually to $80 million for the 1998 fiscal year, and the Charter School Expansion Act passed in 1998 increased federal spending to $100 million for the 1999 fiscal year. On the federal government's role in the charter school movement, see David L. Leal, 'Congress and Charter Schools,' in Robert Maranto, Scott Milliman, Frederick Hess, and April Gresham (eds), *School Choice in the Real World: Lessons from Arizona Charter Schools* (Boulder, Colo. Westview Press, 1999), 58–67.

158 See Bierlein and Bateman, 'Charter Schools v. the Status Quo: Which Will Succeed?' 160, 164, and also Bryan C. Hassel, 'Charter Schools: A National Innovation, An Arizona Revolution,' in Maranto, Milliman, Hess, and Gresham (eds), *School Choice in the Real World: Lessons from Arizona Charter Schools*, 80–4. Hassel's tables, for example, show strong charter laws in Arizona, District of Columbia, Minnesota, North Carolina, and Texas that all make legal independence of charter schools possible, give broad and automatic waivers of state laws and regulations, do not allow local boards a veto over the establishment of charter schools, do not limit the number of schools or unduly restrict the range of individuals and organizations who

can start a charter school, and ensure that full per-student state operating funding follows children from regular public schools to charter schools. The weak charter laws in Alaska, Arkansas, Georgia, Mississippi, and Wisconsin had none of these provisions.

159 Ratings of charter school laws are made by the Center for Education Reform, 'Charter School Legislation: State Rankings,' October 1998, as reported in *Education Week*, 11 January 1999.

160 As Bierlein and Bateman observe, 'Reforms must fit within the current power structure of education: local school boards, state boards of education, state departments, legislators, the federal government, and unions. The current power structure seeks to mold legislation to meet its needs, not necessarily the needs of students, and it is difficult to break down the ingrained system of power' (Bierlein and Bateman, 'Charter Schools v. the Status Quo: Which Will Succeed?,' 167).

161 The coefficient of variation ($V = s/\overline{X}$, where s is standard deviation and $\overline{X}$ is the mean) for student-teacher ratios is 0.05 for the mid-1970s, 0.13 for the mid-1990s, and 0.15 for the turn of the century.

162 This model of direct administrative agency was also introduced in New Brunswick in 1994, when the Liberal government of Premier Frank McKenna abolished school boards as administrative agents of the provincial ministry, substituting an arrangement for school councils and parental advisory committees, but the scheme was subsequently abandoned in 2000, following the election of a Conservative government.

163 Hence the standards for disadvantaged children, who are the target group of the ESEA, would be the standards for all children. John F. Jennings, *Why National Standards and Tests? Politics and the Quest for Better Schools* (Thousand Oaks, Calif.: Sage Publications, 1998), 149.

164 Frederick M. Wirt and Michael W. Kirst, *The Political Dynamics of American Education* (Berkeley, Calif.: McCutchan Publishing, 1997), 287.

Conclusion: Educational Regimes and Comparative Ideas of Democracy

1 The distinction between 'single' and 'multiple' publics in stratified and egalitarian societies is analysed by Nancy Fraser, 'Rethinking the Public Sphere: A Contribution to the Critique of Actually Existing Democracy,' in Craig Calhoun (ed.), *Habermas and the Public Sphere* (Cambridge, Mass.: MIT Press, 1992), 109–42. By egalitarian societies Fraser means 'non-stratified societies, societies whose basic framework does not generate unequal social groups in structural relations of dominance and subordination. Egalitarian societies, therefore, are societies without classes and

without gender or racial divisions of labor. However, they need not be culturally homogeneous. On the contrary, provided such societies permit free expression and association, they are likely to be inhabited by social groups with diverse values, identities, and cultural styles, and hence to be multicultural' (ibid., 125).

2 Perhaps the exceptions to the stratification of social blocs in regimes of public instruction were the educational regimes of Quebec and Newfoundland. In Quebec, equality between minority Protestant and majority Roman Catholic blocs, as well as equality between minority English and majority French blocs, were operative principles; indeed, because of the generally higher property valuations in their school districts, Protestant schools were generally better provided than either French or English Roman Catholic schools. In Newfoundland, all the denominational schools, with the exception of the élite grammar schools in St John's, endured severe poverty and hence offered universally inadequate educational provision.

3 One obvious exception to this correspondence between the prevailing idea of democratic community and the form of political accountability for central educational policy and administration occurred in Ontario, where there was both a dual educational regime, implying a concept of a multiform public, and individual ministerial responsibility. In this case, the contradiction derives from an acute tension and uneasy compromise between the constitutional protection of separate schools and the political dominance of liberal ideas about political accountability for public policy. Two other exceptions occurred in the states of Connecticut and Massachusetts, where the prevailing idea of community was evidently a uniform public but the governor's appointment of the state board of education as a select group of civic notables who would in turn appoint the state superintendent as their policy adviser and chief executive officer seemed to be closer to the practices of educational jurisdictions operating under the assumptions of a multiform public. In contrast with central boards in the British colonies, however, where the priority in appointing central boards was representation of social blocs in educational decision making, the appointment of state boards in Connecticut and Massachusetts appears to have been motivated by a distrust of mass democracy and a consequent desire to separate educational policy and administration from the vagaries of partisan politics.

4 On party strategies and policy change, see Francis G. Castles, 'The Dynamics of Public Policy Transformation,' in Malcolm Alexander and Brian Gallagher (eds), *Comparative Political Studies: Australia and Canada* (Melbourne: Pitman, 1992), 115–16.

5 Michael Walzer, 'Comment,' in Amy Gutmann (ed.), *Multiculturalism and 'The Politics of Recognition': An Essay by Charles Taylor* (Princeton: Princeton University Press, 1992), 99. The theory of utilitarian liberalism being summarized here is similar to contemporary models of 'procedural liberalism' as described by Michael Sandel, 'The Procedural Republic and the Unencumbered Self,' *Political Theory* 12 (1984): 81–96. The term 'procedural liberalism' is also used by Charles Taylor, 'The Politics of Recognition,' in Gutmann (ed.), *Multiculturalism and 'The Politics of Recognition,'* 56–61. The utilitarian-liberal educational regime corresponds to 'the state of individuals' in Amy Gutmann's typology of educational regimes in her *Democratic Education* (Princeton: Princeton University Press, 1987), 33–41.

6 What I have called 'ethical' liberalism might be considered to be a communitarian version of liberalism. See, for example, John Gray, *Endgames: Questions in Late Modern Political Thought* (Cambridge: Polity Press, 1997), 11–50.

7 From the viewpoint of communitarian conservatives, state education in a communal confederation will be organized for communal socialization and assimilation, but the cultural community into which young people are socialized will depend on which cultural communities dominate particular provinces of the federal state. Hence, communal confederations do not differ in principle from communitarian-conservative nationalism. They simply assume that provinces are the true nations and that a federal state can be constructed as a strategic alliance through which communal identities are protected and developed in the constituent provinces. In a conservative communal consociation, by contrast, collective cultural rights in education are recognized throughout the state. Both majority and minority schools are established in all parts of the state rather than simply in those territories defined as majority or minority cultural homelands.

8 Taylor, 'The Politics of Recognition,' 59.

9 In Ontario, for example, a key recommendation of the Royal Commission on Learning, subsequently adopted by the Conservative government, was a distinction between Ontario Academic Courses, which would 'be offered on an academic basis' and required for university entrance and Ontario Applied Courses, which would be given 'with an emphasis on application' and linked to the entrance requirement for community college. Courses in such areas as Family Studies, Physical Education, Life Skills, Drama, and Business would be 'common courses, blending academic and applied approaches, with no special designation.' Similarly, in New South Wales there were two officially recognized pathways through senior secondary school to the Higher School Certificate, one focused on academic and

general education and another that combined general education with vocational education and training. In Scotland the Howie Committee's proposal for two tracks, one leading to the general and vocational Scottish certificate and the other, for those bound for university, to the Scottish baccalaureate, was rejected in favour of retaining the traditional academic Highers examination, introducing an Advanced Highers examination, and integrating existing vocational courses and certificates into a unified qualifications framework. Despite resistance to reforming the School Certificate, Sixth Form Certificate, and University Entrance, Bursaries, and Scholarship Examination, the New Zealand Qualifications Authority eventually succeeded with its scheme to establish a unified national qualifications framework. Only in England, Northern Ireland, and Wales did Sir Ron Dearing's proposal for pathways from compulsory schooling to postsecondary careers continue explicitly to differentiate academic through GCSEs to A levels, applied through General National Vocational Qualification intermediate and advanced levels, and vocational through job-related National Vocational Qualifications.

10 On the experiment with charter schools in Alberta, initiated in 1994, see Lynn Bosetti, 'Alberta Charter Schools: Paradox and Promise,' *Alberta Journal of Educational Research* 66 (Summer 2000): 179–90.

Index of Names

Index of Subjects

Alabama: collective bargaining 484n144; educational finance 292, 482n139; local governance 66, 290, 410n108, 449–50n122, 481–2n136; national testing 558n136; racial segregation of schools 417n132; religion in schools 520n158; state governance 67, 68, 480n131, 559n141

Alaska: charter schools 564n157, 564–5n158; local governance 177, 290; state governance 176, 480n130, 559n140

Alberta: collective bargaining 153, 266; Department of Education 263, 267, 426n29; educational finance 212, 265, 427–8n34, 463n53; language of instruction 206, 210, 494n32; local governance 43, 207, 265, 267, 496n39; *Mahé* v. *Alberta* 207, 495–6n38, 496n39; provincial governance 43, 46, 265, 309, 426n29, 427n33; public examinations and testing 94, 262, 263, 534n43; religion in schools 40, 43, 131, 244, 306, 308; school organization and curri-

culum 93, 131, 148, 151, 260–1, 335; state aid for private schools 212

Alberta School Trustees' Association 429n38

Alberta Teachers' Alliance 428n36, 428–9n37, 429n38

All Children Together (Northern Ireland) 228

American Federation of Labor, Committee on Industrial Education 117

American Federation of Teachers 179, 288, 301, 484n145

American Jewish Congress 519n156

Anglican church 31, 33, 34, 41, 47, 51, 394–5n29, 496n42; *see also* Church of England

Arizona: bilingual education 235, 242; charter schools 564n157; collective bargaining 484n144; educational finance 292, 483n141, 483n142; national testing 558n136; school organization and curriculum 557n133; state aid for private schools 239; state governance 67, 479n128, 558–9n139

Studies in Comparative Political Economy and Public Policy